AI-Powered Cognitive Tutors and the New Frontier of Personalized Learning

Samra Maqbool
https://orcid.org/0000-0001-5958-3800
Beijing Normal University, China

Hafiz Muhammad Ihsan Zafeer
https://orcid.org/0000-0002-8757-9478
Henan University, China

Ayesha Tariq
https://orcid.org/0009-0001-9222-9544
The Islamia University of Bahawalpur, Pakistan

IGI Global
Scientific Publishing
Publishing Tomorrow's Research Today

Vice President of Editorial Melissa Wagner
Director of Acquisitions Mikaela Felty
Director of Book Development Jocelynn Hessler
Production Manager Mike Brehm
Cover Design Jose Rosado

Published in the United States of America by
IGI Global Scientific Publishing
701 East Chocolate Avenue
Hershey, PA, 17033, USA
Tel: 717-533-8845 | Fax: 717-533-7115
Website: https://www.igi-global.com E-mail: cust@igi-global.com

Library of Congress Cataloging-in-Publication Data

LCCN: 2025029836 (CIP Data Pending)
ISBN13: 979-8-3373-4217-7
Isbn13Softcover: 979-8-3373-4218-4
EISBN13: 979-8-3373-4219-1

British Cataloguing in Publication Data
A Cataloguing in Publication record for this book is available from the British Library.

Table of Contents

Detailed Table of Contents

This chapter explores the transformative role of Natural Language Processing (NLP) in skill-based education and training, emphasizing personalized, adaptive, and competency-focused learning. It examines emerging trends such as multimodal NLP, AI-powered coaching, and adaptive microlearning, which enhance engagement, provide real-time feedback, and support scalable learning environments. The chapter highlights opportunities for data-driven assessment, interactive practice, and tailored instruction while addressing challenges related to language diversity, contextual understanding, ethical design, and data privacy. Recommendations for educators and developers emphasize the responsible and effective use of NLP's educational impact.

This systematic review examines the integration of Artificial Intelligence (AI) into leadership practices, focusing on its impact on decision-making, employee engagement, and organizational change. AI technologies, including machine learning, natural language processing, and data analytics, have transformed traditional leadership practices by enabling data-driven decision-making, improving operational efficiencies, and fostering innovation. The review synthesizes findings from 10 studies that explore AI's role in enhancing leadership strategies, including its influence on resource allocation, talent management, and team collaboration.

appreciate context-specific linguistic variations, labeling non-standard expressions or culturally differentiated arguments as "poor grammar" or "unclear thinking." Content suggestions in learning platforms also appeared to support Western-centric narratives. Several participants reported that AI-generated predictions regarding their academic performance did not match their actual learning efforts. This chapter had several practical implications.

This chapter provides a thematic and bibliometric review of the use of artificial intelligence (AI) in education to promote green learning environments and sustainability. We used VOSviewer to map research trends and collaborative clusters in accordance with SDG 4.7 under the Four-in-Balance model: Vision, Infrastructure, Digital Content, and Competencies. The literature showed rapid expansion in learning analytics and e-learning; sustainability and the SDGs; higher education's institutional reform and digital adoption; and emerging technologies, including big data, generative AI, and Industry 4.0. The results show uneven progress: Vision and Competencies lag, leading to fragmented, reactive adoption, while Infrastructure and Digital Content have improved, including intelligent tutoring, IoT-enabled classrooms, and adaptable resources. Few institutions incorporate environmental goals into strategy, and persistent gaps in AI literacy and sustainability skills limit responsible use.

This study explores the impact of Generative AI and digital learning tools on student engagement and academic achievement in middle school classrooms. With the rapid integration of AI technologies like ChatGPT and educational tools such as learning management systems and gamified apps, the research aims to understand how these innovations affect student motivation, participation, and academic outcomes. A mixed methods approach was employed, involving surveys of 200 middle school students, academic performance records, and classroom observations. The results reveal strong positive correlations between the use of AI tools, student engagement, and academic performance. The study highlights how personalized, interactive learning experiences facilitated by AI enhance cognitive, emotional, and behavioural engagement, leading to improved academic outcomes. Findings emphasize the potential of digital tools to support differentiated instruction and foster student-centered learning, offering actionable insights for educators and policymakers in integrating technology to optimize educational practices in middle school settings.

Artificial intelligence (AI) is transforming psychotherapeutic practice by enhancing accessibility, personalization, and early intervention in mental health care. This chapter explored diverse AI applications, including chatbots delivering cognitive behavioral therapy (CBT), virtual reality (VR) exposure therapy, digital phenotyping, and clinical decision support systems. Tools like Woebot and Tess demonstrate promise in reducing depressive symptoms and engaging users, while AI-augmented VR enables real-time adaptation of therapeutic environments. Digital phenotyping offers continuous monitoring for early detection of crises, and natural language processing facilitates objective assessment of therapeutic alliance and empathy. However, challenges such as ethical risks, algorithmic bias, data privacy, and clinician acceptance must be addressed. The concept of "Artificial Wisdom" is proposed to integrate empathy, cultural sensitivity, and ethical reasoning into AI systems. The chapter advocated for collaborative human AI models that preserve the relational depth of therapy while leveraging AI's scalability and analytical capabilities for improved mental health outcomes.

Decolonial theory offers a framework for comprehending and contesting the impacts of colonialism on the creation and distribution of knowledge. The review focused on the critical thinking and AI integration in higher education, the study employed a quick systematic review of the previous publications, especially those that were published and accessible on google scholars and Scopus from 2019-2025. The reviews focus on decolonising scholarly writings, how ai can promote critical thinking, ai ethical usage in Higher education and action to be taken. After the searches on google scholar and Scopus and screening all the documents, 35 publications were finally used in the systematic review in line with the research questions. AI presents a unique and timely opportunity to decolonise scholarly writing and knowledge production by disrupting entrenched hierarchies, enhancing access to marginalised knowledge, and empowering scholars to write from culturally grounded positions. There are a lot of moral and practical problems with using AI in decolonial academics. Natural language processing (NLP) models tailored to local languages such as Swahili, Luo, Gikuyu, and Luganda can make content more accessible and Inclusive. Ai tools could be developed to assist in translating critical texts into indigenous languages or analysing works.

Conversational AI tutors, powered by Natural Language Processing (NLP) and Large Language Models (LLMs), are reshaping education by offering personalized, adaptive, and interactive learning experiences. Unlike static digital tools, these systems simulate human-like dialogue, support inquiry-based learning, and provide real-time feedback tailored to individual needs. This chapter explores the evolution of conversational AI in education, core technological components, real-world applications, and ethical considerations. Through case studies such as Duolingo Max and Carnegie Learning's Mika, it highlights the transformative potential of AI tutors across K–12, higher education, and professional training. It also addresses future research directions including emotional intelligence, multimodal interaction, and teacher-AI collaboration, emphasizing the need for pedagogical grounding and responsible deployment. Conversational AI tutors are poised to become vital partners in next-generation learning ecosystems.

This chapter critically examines the systemic challenges and limitations of implementing artificial intelligence (AI)—particularly cognitive tutors and adaptive

Preface

In an era defined by rapid technological transformation, education stands at the threshold of a profound evolution—one that reimagines the very essence of teaching, learning, and human development. *AI-Powered Cognitive Tutors and the New Frontier of Personalized Learning* emerges from this pivotal moment. As editors, we recognize that the rise of artificial intelligence in education is not merely a matter of technological innovation—it represents a deeper, systemic shift in how we understand learners, how we design instruction, and how we cultivate the skills and mindsets needed for the 21st century and beyond.

AI-powered cognitive tutors embody one of the most promising frontiers in this transformation. These intelligent systems extend the dream of personalized learning by simulating the adaptive guidance of a human tutor—diagnosing misconceptions, adjusting instruction in real time, and providing feedback that aligns with each learner's unique cognitive profile. Yet, as this book emphasizes, the power of AI in education lies not only in automation but in amplification: amplifying human insight, pedagogical creativity, and learner agency.

This edited volume brings together leading researchers, educators, technologists, and policymakers to examine how intelligent tutoring systems (ITS) are redefining the learning experience across diverse contexts—from early childhood education to higher education and professional development. The chapters within this collection investigate the theoretical foundations, practical applications, and ethical dimensions of AI-powered cognitive tutoring. Contributors explore how these systems can enhance engagement, support equitable access, and foster deeper, more reflective learning.

We have sought to ensure that this book is not only an academic inquiry but also a pragmatic resource. For educational researchers, it offers theoretical grounding and empirical analysis; for teachers and curriculum designers, practical insights into implementation and classroom integration; for developers, guidance on ethical and human-centered AI design; and for policymakers, a critical lens through which to view the broader social implications of AI in education.

Importantly, this book also confronts the challenges and tensions inherent in this new educational frontier—issues of data privacy, algorithmic bias, transparency, and the irreplaceable role of human judgment and empathy in learning. We believe that meaningful progress in this domain requires balance: between innovation and ethics, automation and agency, data and humanity.

Ultimately, *AI-Powered Cognitive Tutors and the New Frontier of Personalized Learning* is both a roadmap and an invitation. It charts the landscape of AI-driven personalized learning while inviting readers to engage critically with its possibilities and limitations. We envision a future in which cognitive tutors do not replace teachers, but empower them; do not standardize learning, but personalize it; and do not diminish human intellect, but deepen it.

We hope this volume serves as a catalyst for dialogue, collaboration, and responsible innovation—guiding educators, researchers, and technologists toward a shared goal: building smarter classrooms that nurture smarter, more thoughtful minds.

ORGANIZATION OF THE BOOK

Chapter 1: Leveraging Natural Language Processing in Practical Skills Education and Training

The opening chapter introduces readers to the transformative role of Natural Language Processing (NLP) in skills-based education and professional training. It explores how AI-driven language models and multimodal systems are advancing adaptive microlearning, real-time feedback, and competency-based instruction. By examining developments in AI-powered coaching and data-driven assessment, the chapter demonstrates how NLP enables scalable and personalized learning environments. The authors also foreground critical considerations—language diversity, contextual nuance, ethical design, and data privacy—reminding readers that the responsible implementation of NLP is essential to ensuring equity and efficacy in education.

Chapter 2: Transforming Leadership Practices through Artificial Intelligence: A Systematic Review

This chapter systematically reviews how AI technologies are reshaping leadership across sectors. Synthesizing insights from ten empirical studies, it highlights the ways machine learning, data analytics, and natural language processing tools enhance decision-making, resource allocation, and team collaboration. The authors show that AI can foster innovation and strengthen organizational culture through improved communication and engagement tools such as chatbots and virtual assistants. Yet, the review also cautions against ethical risks, biases, and overreliance on automation, calling for leadership models that balance data-driven insight with human judgment.

Chapter 3: Challenges and Limitations of Implementing AI in Schools: Barriers to Equitable and Effective Integration in K–12 Education

In this chapter, the authors critically examine the systemic barriers that impede equitable AI integration in K–12 education. Focusing on five dimensions—infrastructure, pedagogy, teacher readiness, ethics, and policy—they illuminate issues of digital inequity, inadequate teacher training, and weak ethical frameworks. Drawing from international case studies, the chapter argues for comprehensive professional development, stronger data governance, and visionary policymaking to ensure that AI serves as a tool for inclusion rather than division. It reminds readers that while AI can reshape learning, education remains a fundamentally human endeavor.

Chapter 4: AI in Mental Health: From Digital Companions to Clinical Decision-Making and Training for Tomorrow

This chapter investigates how AI technologies are redefining the landscape of mental health care. From digital companions and diagnostic tools to clinical decision-making systems and therapist training programs, AI is shown to augment accessibility, precision, and efficiency in psychological practice. The authors discuss ethical imperatives surrounding privacy, consent, and empathy in machine-mediated care, underscoring the need for responsible design and human–AI collaboration. The chapter concludes by advocating for a balanced integration of technological innovation with the deeply human dimensions of mental health work.

Chapter 5: Exploring the Barriers and Opportunities of ICT Integration in Virtual Campuses: A Case Study of Higher Education in Pakistan

Through a qualitative case study of two major Pakistani universities, this chapter explores how Information and Communication Technologies (ICT) are transforming virtual campuses in developing contexts. The analysis reveals both the promise and the pitfalls of digital education—enhanced access and flexibility on one hand, and persistent challenges such as inadequate infrastructure, limited digital literacy, and cultural resistance on the other. By foregrounding participants' lived experiences, the authors shed light on the global digital divide and the need for context-sensitive strategies to realize ICT's transformative potential in higher education.

Chapter 6: Redesigning AI for Inclusion: University Students' Experiences with Cultural Exclusion in AI Learning Systems

This chapter offers a compelling exploration of how AI learning systems can inadvertently marginalize students from diverse linguistic and cultural backgrounds. Drawing on phenomenological interviews with university students, the authors reveal how algorithmic biases manifest in feedback mechanisms and predictive analytics, often privileging Western-centric norms. The study calls for inclusive AI design principles that respect linguistic variation and cultural context, emphasizing that personalization must go hand in hand with equity. Practical recommendations are offered for reimagining AI as a vehicle for inclusion rather than exclusion.

Chapter 7: A Bibliometric Review of AI-Driven Green Education Using the Four-in-Balance Framework for Sustainable Learning Environments

In this chapter, the authors provide a bibliometric and thematic review of research connecting AI with sustainability education. Using the Four-in-Balance model—Vision, Infrastructure, Digital Content, and Competencies—they map global trends in AI-enabled sustainable learning aligned with the UN's SDG 4.7. The findings reveal robust development in infrastructure and digital content but lagging progress in vision and competencies. The authors argue for stronger institutional strategies that integrate environmental consciousness and AI literacy, advancing the twin goals of technological and ecological sustainability.

Chapter 8: Impact of Generative AI and Digital Learning Tools on Student Engagement and Academic Achievement in Middle School Classrooms

This empirical study explores the impact of generative AI technologies and digital tools on student engagement and achievement. Drawing from mixed-methods data collected in middle school classrooms, the authors demonstrate that AI-enhanced learning environments—such as those powered by ChatGPT or gamified applications—boost motivation, participation, and academic outcomes. The chapter situates these findings within the broader discourse on personalized learning, showing how interactive AI tools foster cognitive, emotional, and behavioral engagement that deepens learning and supports academic growth.

Chapter 9: Digital Healing: AI's Emerging Role in Psychotherapeutic Practice

Building upon the intersection of mental health and technology, this chapter examines how AI innovations—from chatbots like Woebot and Tess to virtual reality and digital phenotyping—are transforming psychotherapeutic practice. The authors trace emerging forms of "digital healing," highlighting the promise of early intervention, continuous monitoring, and enhanced therapeutic engagement. However, they also warn of ethical and epistemic challenges that accompany AI's growing role in care. The chapter introduces the concept of "Artificial Wisdom" as an aspirational ideal, blending empathy, ethics, and cultural sensitivity into AI-driven therapy.

Chapter 10: Decolonizing Minds with Machine: AI as a Partner in Reimagining Critical Thinking Pedagogy for East Africa's Academic Renaissance

This chapter situates AI within the decolonial turn in higher education, arguing that AI can serve as both a tool and a partner in reimagining critical thinking pedagogy across East Africa. Through a systematic review of recent scholarship, the authors reveal how AI can challenge Eurocentric knowledge hierarchies, democratize access to scholarship, and amplify marginalized voices. Yet they also caution against uncritical adoption, emphasizing the moral and practical tensions of using AI in decolonial academia. The chapter calls for contextually grounded, ethically informed AI use that supports epistemic justice and intellectual sovereignty.

Chapter 11: Natural Language Processing in Conversational AI Tutors: Toward Human-Like Learning Companions

This chapter delves into the growing sophistication of conversational AI tutors powered by Natural Language Processing and Large Language Models. Through examples such as Duolingo Max and Carnegie Learning's Mika, the authors illustrate how AI tutors simulate human-like dialogue, support inquiry-based learning, and offer personalized feedback in real time. The chapter balances optimism with caution, addressing the need for emotional intelligence, multimodal interaction, and human–AI collaboration. Ultimately, it envisions a future where conversational AI tutors act not as replacements for educators but as empathetic, adaptive learning companions.

Chapter 12: Challenges and Limitations of Implementing AI in Schools

Complementing earlier discussions, this chapter revisits the complexities of AI integration in primary and secondary education. It critically analyzes technological inequality, algorithmic bias, teacher displacement, and policy inertia as structural barriers to equitable innovation. The authors argue that realizing AI's transformative potential requires systemic reform grounded in ethical responsibility and pedagogical soundness. Through a comparative international lens, the chapter reaffirms the principle that equity and human centrality must remain at the heart of any AI-driven educational transformation.

Chapter 13: Integration of AI with Emerging Educational Technologies

This chapter surveys the convergence of AI with emerging educational technologies such as intelligent tutoring systems, predictive analytics, and adaptive learning platforms. It highlights how systems like Knewton and Squirrel AI are revolutionizing instruction by providing continuous, personalized support that extends beyond the classroom. The authors also address administrative and operational efficiencies enabled by AI, from automated grading to dynamic scheduling. Despite these advances, they emphasize the need for critical engagement with issues of dependency, teacher roles, and the long-term pedagogical implications of intelligent automation.

Chapter 14: Use of Natural Language Processing in Cognitive Tutoring

Focusing specifically on cognitive tutoring, this chapter examines how Natural Language Processing enhances interactivity and personalization in educational systems. By enabling tutors to interpret, respond to, and generate human-like language, NLP allows for more natural, dialogic learning experiences that mirror authentic cognitive engagement. The authors outline the theoretical underpinnings of cognitive tutoring and explore the tangible benefits of NLP integration—richer feedback, adaptive pacing, and improved learner motivation—while acknowledging the technical and ethical challenges that accompany such innovation.

Chapter 15: STEM for All: An Equity-Oriented AI Personalization Framework for Inclusive Cognitive Tutoring

The concluding chapter presents the Equity-Oriented AI Personalization Framework (EAPF), a visionary model for embedding inclusion and justice within AI-powered STEM education. Drawing upon frameworks such as Universal Design for Learning and Culturally Relevant Pedagogy, the EAPF emphasizes Access, Representation, Adaptivity, and Agency as key pillars of equitable personalization. The authors provide actionable strategies for educators and developers to mitigate bias and promote culturally responsive learning. This chapter closes the volume with a powerful call to reimagine AI not merely as a technical tool but as an ethical and humanistic force for inclusion in education.

CONCLUSION

As editors, we conclude this volume with both a sense of accomplishment and anticipation. *AI-Powered Cognitive Tutors and the New Frontier of Personalized Learning* represents more than a compilation of research—it is a collaborative inquiry into the evolving relationship between intelligence, technology, and human learning. Across the chapters, contributors have illuminated the multifaceted ways in which artificial intelligence, and particularly AI-powered cognitive tutoring systems, are transforming education's core processes: how we teach, how we learn, and how we understand knowledge itself.

The research and reflections gathered here make one truth unmistakably clear: AI is not a distant horizon but an immediate presence shaping educational ecosystems around the world. From natural language processing in tutoring systems to AI applications in mental health, from inclusive design in virtual learning spaces to the ethical imperatives of data governance, the chapters collectively chart a rich terrain of possibility and responsibility. Together, they remind us that the future of education will not be defined by technology alone, but by the wisdom, ethics, and intentionality with which we choose to employ it.

What emerges from this collective work is a vision of AI as an amplifier of human potential rather than its substitute. Cognitive tutors and adaptive learning systems can expand access to quality education, enhance engagement, and close persistent equity gaps—but only if they are guided by inclusive design, pedagogical insight, and human oversight. The same algorithms that can personalize learning experiences also demand vigilant attention to bias, transparency, and fairness. As such, the call to action that threads through this volume is both technological and moral: to design with empathy, implement with integrity, and evaluate with humility.

In reflecting on these themes, we are reminded that education is not simply about content mastery or skill acquisition—it is about cultivating agency, curiosity, and critical thought. The promise of AI-powered cognitive tutors lies not in their ability to replicate teaching, but in their potential to extend the reach of mentorship, to foster self-directed learning, and to create responsive environments where every learner is seen and supported.

As this book illustrates, the path forward requires collaboration among educators, technologists, researchers, and policymakers. It requires cross-disciplinary dialogue that bridges cognitive science, data ethics, and educational practice. And it requires sustained commitment to ensuring that AI serves the goals of equity, inclusion, and lifelong learning for all.

We envision a future where smarter classrooms nurture not only smarter minds but also more compassionate, creative, and critically aware individuals—learners who can navigate a complex world with both technological fluency and human understanding. In that spirit, we offer this volume as both a reflection of progress made and an invitation to continue the conversation: to question, to innovate, and to shape a future where intelligent systems truly empower human intelligence.

Chapter 1
Leveraging Natural Language Processing in Practical Skills Education and Training

Barno Matchanova
Urgench State Pedagogical Institute, Uzbekistan

Zilolakhon Ruzmetova
Mamun University, Uzbekistan

Rayhon Sapaeva
Urgench State University, Uzbekistan

Munir Ahmad
https://orcid.org/0000-0003-4836-6151
Survey of Pakistan, Pakistan

ABSTRACT

This chapter explores the transformative role of Natural Language Processing (NLP) in skill-based education and training, emphasizing personalized, adaptive, and competency-focused learning. It examines emerging trends such as multimodal NLP, AI-powered coaching, and adaptive microlearning, which enhance engagement, provide real-time feedback, and support scalable learning environments. The chapter highlights opportunities for data-driven assessment, interactive practice, and tailored instruction while addressing challenges related to language diversity,

DOI: 10.4018/979-8-3373-4217-7.ch001

contextual understanding, ethical design, and data privacy. Recommendations for educators and developers emphasize the responsible and effective use of NLP's educational impact.

INTRODUCTION

The concept of skill-based education and training has taken center stage in contemporary learning paradigms, whereby having a practical competence that is crucial to professional and personal growth is not only taught through theoretical knowledge (Barbee & Martin, 2013; Selim, 2020). In contrast to the traditional models of education, which tend to focus on elements of rote learning and standardized scoring, the skill-based models focus on experience, critical thinking, and the capacity to utilize the knowledge in practice. This transformation is associated with the growing need of industries and workplaces to hire workers who are able to complete their duties and tasks, keep up with changes in various challenges, and demonstrate a certain level of skills.

Simultaneously, the idea of individualized learning has become prominent, as teachers have realized that learners possess different abilities, previous knowledge, and learning preferences. The use of competency-based approaches, where the determination of progress is based on the mastery of the skills displayed over time as opposed to time spent in a classroom, also indicates that there is a necessity to have educational approaches that are flexible enough to potentially adapt to the needs of individual learners. In this regard, technology-based solutions are vital in providing scalable, flexible, and custom leadership experiences that facilitate not only the acquisition of skills but also sustained enhancement (Divayana et al., 2021; Hadžiomerović et al., 2023; Prasittichok et al., 2024; Romli et al., 2022).

Artificial intelligence in the form of Natural Language Processing (NLP), which is concerned with processing, interpreting, and producing human language, has a massive potential in improving practical skills learning. Through NLP, learning devices can determine learner feedback, give real-time feedback, and offer adaptive content that matches the individual's progress. They are applied in automated writing and language testing as well as smart tutoring platforms and chatbots simulating the environment of a workplace or a professional interaction. Platforms powered by NLP not only promote the building of cognitive skills but also good communication, critical thinking, and problem-solving skills, bridging the disconnect between theoretical learning and practical competence (Alqahtani et al., 2023; Jose Gonzalez-Gomez et al., 2024; Shaik et al., 2022).

This chapter addresses the transformative nature of NLP in skills-based education and training, the applications, advantages, and challenges of NLP in these areas. It analyses the scope of the NLP-based tools that support individual learning, competency assessment, and engagement of the learners in various fields. In addition, the chapter raises essential issues like the diversity of languages, the understanding of the context, and the aspects of ethics, offering a broad view on how NLP may be successfully implemented into the modern educational and training practice.

FUNDAMENTALS OF NLP IN EDUCATION

NLP is the core of a vast line of intelligent educational technologies because it allows machines to comprehend human language, interpret, and produce it meaningfully. In its simplest form, NLP is a combination of linguistics, computer science, and artificial intelligence that is used to convert textual and verbal information into actionable information. NLP can be used in educational settings not only to analyze the reactions of the learners, but also to improve individual instruction, adaptive feedback, and interactive sphere development. Learning the basics of NLP is important to grasp how transformative NLP can be applied in the context of skills-based learning and training.

Key NLP Concepts and Techniques

NLP involves numerous ideas and methods that are integrated to process and comprehend the human language. There are several important methods applicable in education, and these are given as:

These methods allow systems to derive meaning, uncover major concepts, and process text created by learners at an advanced semantic level. NLU enables NLP systems to extend beyond some simple grammar checking to the structure, reasoning, and flow of the answers. As an illustration, automated essay scoring systems can be used to assess the structure of arguments, flow of ideas, and readability, which gives subtle information on the quality of writing. NLU can use reports, emails, or proposals as a means of professional skill development, analyzing reports to clarify and make them concise, and maintain domain-specific conventions, allowing the learner to improve the content and style of these reports (Egger & Gokce, 2022; Karanikolas et al., 2023; Vayadande et al., 2024).

Sentiment analysis can be used by educators and AI systems to measure the engagement of the learner, their motivation, and their confidence by determining the emotional tone of written or verbal answers. Positive sentiment can be a sign of understanding and interest, whereas negative sentiment (frustration, confusion, disengagement) can prompt immediate response, follow-up, or helpful feedback. An example is a sentiment-analyzed reflective journal that could identify trends of learner uncertainty and then motivate exercises accordingly, or trigger a motivational prompt, or peer recommendations about support, all of which promote more effective learning and positive emotionality (Jim et al., 2024; Raghunathan & Saravanakumar, 2023; Wankhade et al., 2022).

Speech recognition platforms can transcribe spoken inputs of learners into text, making them useful in the assessment of pronunciation and fluency, as well as linguistic correctness in language instruction or oral tests. NLG augments this by producing coherent, contextually relevant feedback, explanation, or practice exercises that are based on the performance of the learner. As an illustration, when presenting an NLG-based system with a spoken response of a learner, immediate feedback regarding the grammatical errors, a better way of stating the idea, or even follow-up practice questions may be offered. These technologies can all be used to facilitate interactive learning, skill training, and one-on-one instruction in such areas as language learning, oratory, and communication training (Thakur et al., 2023; Thomas et al., 2022; Usmaan & Singh, 2025).

AI-based conversational agents use dialogue systems to simulate realistic conversations, allowing learners to learn to communicate, negotiate, and act to solve problems in realistic contexts. Such systems are able to respond dynamically to the level of proficiency, the situation, and prior contacts of the learner so as to produce a personalized and interactive learning experience. As an example, a chatbot can simulate a customer call to conduct a sales training game, role-play a job interview to conduct a professional development exercise, or walk learners through cooperative problem-solving exercises (Attigeri et al., 2024; Janjua et al., 2024). Conversational AI promotes confidence, critical thinking, and practical competence through the provision of instant feedback and the ability to repeat the process without a human supervisor in educational and professional settings. To synthesize the diverse NLP techniques covered in this section, Table 1 provides a structured overview of their functions, educational relevance, and illustrative examples.

Table 1. Key NLP concepts, educational applications, and examples

NLP Technique	Core Function	Educational Application	Example Use Case
Text Analysis & Natural Language Understanding (NLU)	Extracts meaning, identifies key concepts, and interprets deep semantics in learner-generated text	Evaluates essays, reports, and professional documents for coherence, clarity, and domain-specific accuracy	Automated essay grading, assessing argument structure and progression
Sentiment Analysis	Detects emotional tone in written or spoken responses	Monitors learner engagement, motivation, and confidence to trigger timely interventions	Analyzing reflective journals to detect frustration or uncertainty and provide adaptive exercises
Speech Recognition & Natural Language Generation (NLG)	Converts speech to text and generates coherent, tailored responses	Evaluates pronunciation, fluency, and grammar in oral tasks; generates feedback and practice exercises	Language learning system providing instant correction on spoken responses
Conversational AI & Chatbots	Simulates realistic, adaptive dialogue for practice and problem-solving	Supports interactive skill development in communication, negotiation, or teamwork	AI-driven job interview simulation with real-time adaptive feedback

How NLP Processes Learner Inputs

NLP can only become effective in education when it can correctly process and interpret the inputs of the learners. This generally entails several steps:

Student communication, be it in the form of written, verbal, and coded text, or in multimodal interactions, is obtained via digital mediums, online educational programs, or audio/video interfaces. This step guarantees that any pertinent learner activity is captured to be analyzed, such as submissions made in classrooms, exercises over the Internet, oral responses through microphones, or interactive conversations with conversational agents. Good quality of input acquisition is paramount to precise downstream processing, since noisy inputs, incomplete inputs, and inconsistent inputs may undermine the credibility of NLP-based evaluation and feedback.

The raw input is sanitized, normalized, and formatted to be fed into computational analysis. In the case of text data, it involves tokenization (dividing text into words, sentences, or phrases), stemming or lemmatization (reducing words to their base or root forms), and dropping stop words and punctuation or other irrelevant symbols. In the case of spoken response, preprocessing can be a speech-to-text conversion, noise reduction, dividing an audio into phonemes or sentences, and normalization of speech patterns. Effective preprocessing means that NLP algorithms concentrate on linguistic features that matter, that it decreases the complexity of the computation, and that it enhances the precision of other stages of analysis.

In the current step, preprocessed text or speech is converted into numerical representations or representations that algorithms can process. Word embeddings (e.g., Word2Vec, GloVe), and the use of text vectors, as well as the contextual representation based on a state-of-the-art language model like BERT or GPT, are common. Speech data can be mapped into acoustic feature vectors that reflect the pitch, intonation, and rhythm. These models enable NLP applications to identify semantic meaning, syntactic structures, sentiment, and stylistic patterns, the basis of which correct interpretation and performance evaluation are established.

NLP algorithms compare the input of the learner to the pre-specified criteria, which can involve grammar and syntax, domain-specific, or learning goals. Methods employed in this phase are classification, grouping, pattern identification, semantic similarity evaluation, and predictive modelling. As an example, during a coding exercise, the system can detect logical errors, efficiency problems, or any compliance with coding standards. Grammar, coherence, tone, and context-appropriateness are examined in a language learning situation. The findings that are produced at this level are the foundation of individual guidance and competence assessment.

Dependent on the analysis, the system gives real-time personalized feedback, recommendations, or extra learning materials. Adaptive learning systems are capable of adjusting the content, the challenge, or the flow of instructions based on the ability, engagement, or gaps within the skill of the learner. As an example, a writing tutor can propose the use of different wordings, point out frequent grammatical errors, or prescribe specific activities, whereas a conversational agent can simulate more complicated conversations to test the communicational abilities of a learner. Through the incorporation of a continuous feedback loop, NLP-powered systems strengthen learning, facilitate self-guided practice, and help promote mastery via iterative interaction.

General NLP Applications vs. Skill-Focused NLP in Education

Although NLP is a technique that can be used in many areas of industry, such as customer service, health, and finance, its implementation in skill-based education needs to be given particular attention. General NLP systems, frequently given the task of information retrieval, sentiment detection, or language translation, do not always factor in pedagogical goals. On the contrary, skill-oriented NLP systems will aim at improving the learning outcomes by:

- The modern NLP applications in skill-based education do not just determine whether some spelling or grammar mistakes happen but evaluate more profound facets of learner performance, including clarity, coherence, logic, and persuasiveness. As an illustration, with professional writing, such systems can help assess the ability of a report to deliver the intended message, the logical organization of the arguments, and the ability of language decisions to increase the readability and interest. Equally applicable, in technical or scientific writing, NLP is capable of checking conventional compliance, accuracy of terminology, and the effectiveness of communication in general, allowing learners to have a more holistic approach to the acquisition of professional skills instead of learning them at the superficial level of correctness.

- Complementing NLP applications such as conversational AI tools and interactive applications gives learners access to practice and context-specific skills that have genuine representation in the real world. As an example, job interview candidates can engage with artificial intelligence-powered agents simulating the interviewer, question order, and situational feedback, and train articulation, tone, and problem-solving in a safe setting. During client meetings or group work, NLP-biased simulations can simulate a negotiation process, teamwork struggles, or conflict resolution, providing learners with repeated exposure to various scenarios, and allowing them to progressively enhance the process with few problems related to logistics and reliance on human trainers.
- Skiing NLP personalized training and feedback to the learner with respect to individual performance, so learning trajectories are made at a level of mastery of particular skills. Through the consistent monitoring of responses, errors, and engagement patterns, NLP systems can highlight areas in which the learner needs more assistance, prescribe exercises, and dynamically change difficulty. As an illustration, a coding tutor could identify common logical mistakes and offer additional problems based on the learner, and a language learning system could provide advanced vocabulary practice to learners who show the ability to learn simple grammar and sentence structure. This individualization assists in getting the most out of learning, learner confidence, and mastery-based development.
- In contrast to the conventional NLP application, which can work in the non-realtime or batch mode, the skill-oriented educational NLP is constantly tracking the inputs made by learners and giving real-time feedback. This self-evaluation is in real time, where learners can correct their errors immediately, reinforce good practice, and reflect on the learning process during process. As an example, the system is able to indicate unclear wording, recommend other word choices, or indicate the wrong step in negotiation strategy as the conversation progresses in a live role-play with a conversational agent. In the same way, during professional writing exercises, learners can be instantly corrected in terms of tone, structure, or the clarity of their arguments during

the drafting process, allowing them to achieve continuous formative assessment, which can be easily incorporated into the learning process.

These systems help close the technology-versus-pedagogy divide by integrating innovative NLP with pedagogical approaches, producing learning bodies that are highly sensitive, personalized, and competency-based.

NLP-DRIVEN TOOLS FOR SKILL DEVELOPMENT

NLP in skill-based learning resulted in the design of the new advanced tools that serve not only to measure the performance of the learners but also facilitate the process of practical skills acquisition. The tools utilize language analysis, machine learning, and context to develop dynamic, interactive, and personalized learning spaces. Automation of repetitive activities and real-time insights made available by NLP-based tools increase the efficiency of instructions and learner engagement.

Automated Feedback Systems

NLP-driven Automated feedback systems are potent tools that allow direct responses to learner submissions, be they as written texts, verbal replies, or coding tasks. These systems help identify errors, recommend areas of improvement, and areas of strength by using methods like syntax analysis, semantics assessment, error identification, and pattern recognition to continually improve their skills. Unlike other conventional forms of feedback, where manual assessment usually causes a delay in feedback, automated assessment goes real-time time thus making the learning more iterative and responsive (Botelho et al., 2023; Liang, 2025).

Automated feedback platforms can be used in language learning to check grammar, spelling, use of words, sentence structure, and overall coherence, and give learners specific recommendations on how to learn how to be clearer and more stylistic. Mature systems even examine tone, register, and idiomatic expressions, thereby aiding learners to gain subtle writing and speaking abilities. As an illustration, a student writing an essay in English may get suggestions on more accurate vocabulary, sentence structure, and to correct his or her syntactical mistakes, whereas a student giving an oral answer may be checked on pronunciation, fluency, and intonation. Such immediate and detailed feedback allows learners to correct early on, to strengthen the correct patterns, and to feel good about themselves (Bauer et al., 2023; Hashir et al., 2024).

Automated feedback systems in the area of professional skills training offer their services not only in the sphere of language learning but also in a great variety of workplace skills. Reports, presentations, email drafts, and other professional communications may be assessed on clarity and tone, as well as compliance with organizational or industry guidelines. Likewise, in coding instruction, automated feedback systems can verify submitted code for syntax errors, logic, and efficiency, and offer step-by-step recommendations on how to fix errors and to streamline solutions. These focused measures promote the development of skills faster and decrease the necessity of constant instructions from the instructor.

Moreover, automated feedback systems increase engagement, increase skill acquisition rate, and scale of education and employment by delivering timely, regular, and data-driven instructions (Ranalli, 2021). Combined with other NLP-inspired applications, including intelligent tutoring systems and conversational agents, automated feedback now plays a role in a system of learning, constantly aiding learners in developing mastery and functional competence in a wide variety of fields.

Smart Tutoring Systems

Intelligent Tutoring Systems (ITS) apply NLP to provide individual, adaptive learning in accordance with the abilities, progress, and learning preferences of a learner. Through constant tracking and evaluation of the interaction between learners, the ITS can dynamically adjust the difficulty of content, offer context-based clues, propose remedial materials, and steer learners in mastering certain skills. In comparison to the conventional type of instruction, which usually occurs in a one-size-fits-all manner, ITS changes dynamically, producing a highly personalized learning experience that matches the pace of the learner, the level of his or her knowledge, and strengths and weaknesses.

An example is in the teaching of computer programming, where an ITS can learn to examine the submitted computer code of a student and identify the conceptual mistakes, syntax, or inefficient logic, and step-by-step advice to rectify the mistake can be given to the student. The system can propose exercises that focus on particular concepts of programming, track performance over time, and increase difficulty as one becomes more competent. In the same way as business communication training, an ITS might analyze written emails, reports, or proposals in terms of tone, clarity, structure, and professional suitability, with corrective suggestions and alternative wording depending on contextual clues. The system can simulate a personalized tutor to provide prompt feedback and direct instructions to learners that help to reinforce the learning goals (Nozima et al., 2026; Sumana et al., 2022).

In addition to providing reactive support, ITS platforms may also include predictive analytics to predict the challenges learners will experience and prescribe proactive interventions to them. As an example, the system could be used to detect the same misunderstandings in problem-solving exercises, and hence, additional training could be introduced before the learner lags. In professional development applications, ITS may simulate complex situational difficulties, including negotiating with a client or handling a project, assessing more than one dimension of performance, such as decision-making, critical thought, and communication, and giving customized feedback to boost overall competence (Troussas et al., 2023; Yang, 2025).

Further, ITS combines programs of structured instruction and dynamic feedback to facilitate competency-based learning. Instead of following predetermined schedules, learners are allowed to move across modules or skillsets once they prove that they have been able to master skills, and thus, knowledge acquisition is comprehensive and practical. ITS also allows learners to learn with deep content interaction, faster learning skills, and bring mastery of skills in various educational and professional environments.

Conversational Agents and Chatbots

Chatbots and other conversational agents powered by AI are becoming an influential tool in improving skill-based learning as they start to offer an interactive, realistic, and personalized learning environment. Using state-of-the-art NLP methods to produce dialogue, analyze sentiment, and use context, these systems can simulate a broad range of real-world situations, allowing learners to learn communication, negotiation, critical thinking, and problem-solving skills in a safe and contained environment. Conversational agents offer two-way feedback, engaging dynamic interaction that is responsive and varies with the learner's input, difficulty, and the goals of the learning, compared to the traditional classroom exercises or uninvolving e-learning modules (Joseph & Eapen, 2023; Ouaddi et al., 2024; Shrivastava et al., 2025).

Chatbots in professional training may simulate a complex interaction in the work setting, including client meetings, job interviews, teamwork, or negotiation. As an example, a learner who was expecting to participate in a sales negotiation could be interacting with a chatbot that is designed to resemble a demanding client, encouraging them to reply tactically, stay professional, and change tone and language as their conversational context evolves. Likewise, in the case of corporate onboarding, chatbots may train an incoming worker in scenario-based exercises, where the strategy of problem-solving, understanding policy, or conflict management may be evaluated in real time. Conversational agents in language learning are used to give a learner an experience of an immersive dialogue during which the learner can train pronunciation, fluency, idiomatic expressions, and culturally appropriate responses. Chatbots also enable learners to rectify their mistakes early by giving real-time feedback on tone, mistakes, and context, and gain confidence in their communication.

Individual conversational agents are not the only ones whose adaptability is limited. Numerous systems record user performance across several sessions and determine trends in answers, strengths, and weaknesses. Personalized learning paths can, in turn, be informed by this data, which can recommend specific exercises or more challenging situations to challenge the users and increase skill retention. Also, chatbots allow repeated exposure to varied situations, allowing learners to practice unpopular or stressful situations - e.g., dealing with angry customers, making important business decisions, participating in high-pressure negotiations, or situations that could be hard to simulate in typical training environments.

Conversational agents also enhance the scalability and availability of training programs by decreasing the use of human instructors to repeat the practice or provide practice that is time-consuming. Continuous practice is more practical than with other learning formats since learners can access interactive simulations on any basis, no matter their physical location, in both remote and distributed learning. These systems also promote learner agency by promoting experimentation, contemplation, and cyclic refinement, by enabling a person to experiment with various strategies and obtain constructive feedback without being afraid of criticism.

Assessment Platforms

Assessment systems based on NLP are transforming the way applied skills are assessed by automating the process of grading, benchmarking, and competency analysis to allow more effective, consistent, and data-driven methods of assessing learners. Such platforms utilise innovative NLP, like text and speech analysis, semantic comprehension, and pattern recognition to understand learner inputs, ranging from essays and verbal responses to coding tasks and scenario-based learning. Assessment platforms offer objective and standardized assessments for submissions by systematically comparing submissions to predetermined rubrics or learning objectives, thereby minimizing the variability and possible bias of manual assessment methods (Ariely et al., 2023; Hutson & Plate, 2023; Rodriguez-Ruiz et al., 2021).

Automated scoring systems used in learning languages measure various elements of the performance of the learners, such as pronunciation, intonation, fluency, vocabulary use, grammar, and coherence. As an example, students who submit oral tasks can be assessed in real-time on pronunciation and rhythm, whereas written tasks can be evaluated based on sentence structure and logical coherence, as well as clarity of style. Likewise, in professional skills training, the assessment platforms are used to evaluate problem-solving strategies, decision-making styles, quality of technical reports, and compliance with organizational norms or protocols. Scenario-based exercises enable the learners to engage with the realistic scenarios, and NLP algorithms can use responses to evaluate both content accuracy and applied logic to offer more insight into the mastery of skills compared to traditional multiple-choice assessments.

In addition to scoring, NLP-based assessment systems produce detailed reports that can give educators, trainers, and learners practical recommendations. Such reports frequently have been presented in the form of visual dashboards, in-depth feedback on areas of strength and weakness, competency heatmaps, and recommendations on specific interventions or additional resources. These platforms allow educators to individualize the learning process due to the possibility of performing granular analysis of the learner performance and thus being able to fill in the knowledge gaps of individual learners in the most effective manner.

The other strong point of NLP-based assessment systems is scalability. Large groups can be compared in one go and under uniform criteria, saving teachers the burden of grades and assessment that is labor-intensive. The described scalability would be especially useful when it comes to online learning, corporate training, and large university courses, where ensuring the same quality of assessment across the populations of various learners may prove quite problematic. Also, automated platforms help to create fairness and equity by reducing human bias and by holding all learners to the same standards, irrespective of backgrounds, language, or bias of the instructor.

Lastly, such platforms present the possibility of longitudinal skill tracking and competency benchmarking by cohort, institution, or organization. They also enable administrators to pinpoint recurring deficiencies in learning over a period of time, improve curriculum development, and undertake evidence-based intervention in training programs. When it is used together with other NLP-driven applications, including intelligent tutoring systems and conversational agents, assessment platforms deliver a feedback loop, so that learners can practice, get guidance, and re-assess their progress in real-time, eventually promoting continuous improvement and the learning of practical skills. To consolidate the discussion of the four categories of NLP-driven tools, Table 2 provides a comparative overview. It highlights each tool's core function, educational and professional applications, and representative examples. This structured summary helps illustrate how these tools collectively transform skill development, bridging theoretical knowledge with applied practice in scalable and personalized ways.

Table 2. NLP-driven tools for skill development — functions, applications, and examples

Tool Category	Core Function	Educational/Professional Application	Example Use Case
Automated Feedback Systems	Deliver real-time, detailed feedback on learner submissions (text, speech, or code) using syntax, semantics, and error detection	Improve writing clarity, refine spoken fluency, enhance coding accuracy, and support independent practice	Essay grading with grammar/style suggestions; code debugging with logic optimization
Intelligent Tutoring Systems (ITS)	Provide adaptive, personalized instruction by analyzing learner progress and tailoring content dynamically	Support programming education, professional writing, and scenario-based training through step-by-step guidance	ITS analyzing coding errors, suggesting remedial exercises, and escalating complexity as proficiency improves
Conversational Agents & Chatbots	Simulate realistic, adaptive dialogues for practice in communication, negotiation, and problem-solving	Facilitate language learning, professional training, and workplace scenario simulations	AI chatbot role-playing job interviews or simulating client negotiations with instant feedback
Assessment Platforms	Automate grading, benchmarking, and competency analysis using NLP-based semantic and structural evaluation	Standardize evaluation across large cohorts, track learner progress, and provide actionable insights	Automated scoring of spoken language tasks; dashboards reporting learner strengths/weaknesses

APPLICATIONS ACROSS DOMAINS

NLP technologies are also altering the nature of skill-based education more and more by providing context-aware, adaptive, and personalized learning experiences. In a variety of fields, including language learning, as well as professional growth and workplace training, NLP instruments help learners to acquire practical skills, train their skills in real-life situations, and get real-time, data-driven feedback.

Language Learning

One of the most popular and significant areas of NLP applications remains language learning. The NLP-based tools help the learners form the necessary language skills- pronunciation, grammar, vocabulary, writing, and speaking, among others, with the help of continuous and adaptive feedback. An example is that a sophisticated speech recognition and phonetic analysis technology can identify minor pronunciation inaccuracies, intonational rules, and fluency problems and provide instant corrections and specific practice. This enables learners to repeat without necessarily having to wait to be told by the instructor some information, which is especially helpful in large classrooms or in remote learning.

The grammar, syntax, use of vocabulary, the coherence of the sentences, and the general structure of the text are assessed through automated writing evaluation systems. In addition to detecting errors, such systems will offer quite specific improvement recommendations, including suggested changes in wording, style suggestions, or additions of domain-specific terminology. Chatbots based on conversational AI also facilitate language learning by simulating conversations in a wide variety of situations, both in informal situations, such as ordering food or providing directions, and in formal situations, such as negotiating a contract or delivering a presentation. These chatbots can tailor their answers to the level of the learner and give more complicated interactions that involve comprehension and expression. Through the combination of multimodal feedback such as text, speech, and contextual cues, NLP tools assist learners in gaining confidence, decreasing anxiety, and advancing at their own pace the end making the process of language acquisition more interactive, more efficient, and more effective.

Professional Skills Development

In career competency, NLP is considered indispensable in the development of communication, technical competency, and human skills that are most important in career growth. Presentation coaching systems, as an example, can look at clarity of speech, pacing, volume, tone, and nonverbal information to give positive feedback on delivery, articulation, and connection with the audience. The learners can repeat the presentation delivery process several times, whereby they are given some actionable feedback that enables them to improve their presentation style and suit different professional situations.

Platforms of negotiation and business communication use NLP-based simulations as an opportunity to train learners in the art of persuasive communication, conflict resolution, and business correspondence. As an example, learners can simulate negotiation with the client in the system in which their tone, word choice, argument structure, and responsiveness are tested, and feedback on their effectiveness and alignment to business goals is given by the system. Support tools of technical writing equally evaluate reports, documentation of coding, manuals, and professional communication to determine whether they are clear, coherent, and accurate so that learners are able to meet industry standards.

Workplace Training

NLP has gained more significance in training in the workplace, where scenario-based learning as well as interactive simulations are relevant in developing practical competencies. Training platforms may emulate a real-life work scenario, like customer interactions, compliance processes, teamwork, or problem-solving activities, and allow employees to rehearse and perfect their responses in a safe and regulated setting. As an example, customer service simulations may evaluate conversations based on empathy, effectiveness, responsiveness to conversation conflict, and general effectiveness, and compliance training platforms may evaluate written or oral responses to policy scenarios or regulation scenarios.

Assessment systems driven by NLP monitor performance and learning patterns, and detect knowledge or skills gaps, creating individual learning pathways to achieve ongoing enhancement. These platforms enable adaptive training plans, recommend specific resources, and give feedback on how a manager or educator can maximize workforce preparedness. NM's ability to train large groups of people, minimize onboarding time, and keep a high level of competence at any time and at any moment is achieved through the scalability of NLP solutions. Also, interactive simulations, real-time feedback, and data-driven insight provide employees with the opportunity to acquire job-ready skills effectively and organizations with the increased efficiency of operations and a ready-to-workforce population.

By means of these applications within the domain, NLP proves its adaptability to the development of practical skills education and training. Be it the facilitation of language acquisition, professional competence, or workplace preparedness, NLP-based systems provide individual, responsive, and interactive learning processes that are compatible with personal needs, objectives, and situations of learners. These tools combine automated feedback, scenario-based simulations, and competency tracking to bridge the gap between theory taught and application of skills in challenging, dynamic environments as learners become prepared to succeed. Table 3 summarizes the applications of NLP in language learning, professional skills development, and workplace training. It highlights the focus areas, representative tools/techniques, and key outcomes that illustrate how NLP supports personalized, adaptive, and scalable skill development across diverse contexts.

Table 3. Applications of NLP across educational and professional domains

Domain	Focus Areas	Representative Tools & Techniques	Key Outcomes
Language Learning	Pronunciation, grammar, vocabulary, writing, and conversational fluency	Speech recognition, phonetic analysis, automated writing evaluation, conversational chatbots	Improved accuracy, confidence, and fluency; adaptive practice; reduced learner anxiety
Professional Skills Development	Communication, presentation, negotiation, and technical writing	Presentation coaching systems, negotiation simulations, business communication platforms, and technical writing support tools	Enhanced clarity, persuasion, professionalism, and technical precision; readiness for career advancement
Workplace Training	Customer service, compliance, team collaboration, job-specific skills	Scenario-based simulations, compliance training platforms, and NLP-driven assessment systems	Scalable and consistent training, real-time performance feedback, personalized learning paths, improved workforce readiness

CHALLENGES AND CONSIDERATIONS

NLP has much potential in improving education and training based on skills; however, when it is applied, there are numerous challenges and issues that should be considered. These cut across linguistic, technical, ethical, and contextual areas and have to be well covered in order to guarantee effective, fair, and accountable application. These challenges are critical to educators, developers, and policymakers who want to use NLP to enhance learning outcomes and reduce possible risks.

Language Diversity

Among the greatest obstacles to using NLP in education is the fact that languages, dialects, and even terminologies specific to a particular domain vary strikingly among learners introduced into the educational setting (Ranta & Goutte, 2021). Most NLP models are trained on broadly spoken or standard languages and may not interpret well inputs of those who speak regional dialects, colloquialisms, or code-mixed phrases or languages with less representation. As an example, a learner may present a technical report in English and use industry terms, abbreviations, or mixed words, such as English mixed with local words. When the NLP system fails to identify these words, it can give incorrect feedback, misunderstand content, or fail to assess proficiency, which can impact the learning process to be impacted.

In the classroom of a multi-lingual setting, learners tend to alternate languages according to situations or the requirements of the task. A learner might answer in his or her mother tongue with English terms of technical terms, or professional terms. NLP systems should thus be in a position to identify and adjust to mixed use of language, such as transliterations, code switching, and sentence mixes. Lack of consideration of this linguistic difference may result in unfair evaluation, decrease the self-esteem of learners, and the access to educational assistance may be impaired.

To overcome such issues, developers and educators need to invest in multilingual and culturally sensitive NLP models, which are trained on a variety of information that reflects various dialects and sociolects, as well as professional fields. Domain-specific embeddings, contextual transfer learning, and adaptive language models can be incorporated to enhance the ability of the system to identify specialized vocabulary and emerging terminologies and the changing linguistic trends. It is also necessary to update NLP models regularly to keep abreast of the changing language, especially the use of new jargon, acronyms, and practices within a profession or technical terminology that are rapidly on the rise.

Moreover, fairness and inclusivity can be improved by incorporating the language adaptation strategies. As an example, NLP systems can incorporate dynamic language detection to alternate between two or more language processing pipelines or utilize context-driven embeddings in order to more effectively process mixed-language input. Teachers may also augment automated systems with human supervision of complex or uncertain cases, so that learners are provided with correct feedback and evaluation. With NLP-based educational tools taking a more active approach to linguistic diversity, it becomes possible to deliver more precise, culturally sensitive, and equal learning experiences, which will in turn facilitate the acquisition of skills by the learners with different linguistic and professional profiles.

Contextual Understanding

Proper contextualization is one of the key needs of NLP-based educational tools to provide valuable, applicable, and actionable feedback (Janjua et al., 2024; Sangeetha et al., 2023). Learner responses are not only affected by their language proficiency; they are also affected by the larger context in which they are produced, such as prior knowledge, intended purpose, task type, and the particular learning scenario. As an example, a phrase that is tolerable and even imaginative in a literature or creative writing assignment can be deemed too casual, unclear, or unsuitable in a technical report or professional documentation assignment. Likewise, a student may use a legitimate yet nonstandard method of solving one of the coding exercises or business simulations that is not accepted by a traditional NLP system, and therefore, the system may give the wrong feedback or poor performance classification.

To overcome these complexities, NLP systems have to include mechanisms beyond literal text and semantic parsing to determine intent, appropriately judge appropriateness, and coordinate evaluation with domain-specific conventions. This usually entails a combination of sophisticated semantic analysis methods, context-dependent rules, ontologies, and structured bodies of knowledge to offer context-sensitive interpretations. As an instance, on a professional communication training platform, the system can check an email with regard to grammar, but also to tone, clarity, audience appropriateness, and compliance with organizational communication standards. NLP in a workplace simulation may be used to evaluate the logical effect of steps to solving a problem and the relevance of those steps to the context, even though they do not conform to common templates.

The other critical part of contextual understanding is iterative feedback loops. Based on the educator input, corrections, and annotations, systems can learn to improve their interpretation of what learners have submitted over time. This enables the NLP system to identify a variety of legitimate strategies, new ways of doing things, and hidden elements of a situation, and therefore they can help to give very correct, precise and adaptive, and fair advice. In the absence of strong contextual knowledge, NLP devices face the risk of giving false or generic feedback, punishing unconventional but correct answers, or missing creative problem-solving, and, when such occurs, erodes the confidence, involvement, and mastery of learners.

With the incorporation of context-sensitive analytics, adaptive interpretation systems, and constantly updating learning abilities, NLP-based educational tools may be better adapted to fill the gap between the machine evaluation and the subtleties demanded in the practical application of skills. This is to provide learners with a direction that is not only technically accurate but also contextually appropriate, which will aid in the development of meaningful skills across a wide range of domains and contexts of learning.

Ethical and Privacy Concerns

Responsible NLP system design and implementation in education requires consideration of ethical and privacy issues (Vaccino-Salvadore, 2023). Online assessment and feedback systems should be fair and should not have biases that may disfavour a learner due to gender, cultural backgrounds, socioeconomic status, learning style, or language differences. Without proper data representation (skewed training data) or without diversity in their design, automated systems can lead to biased evaluations, a wrong interpretation of a learner's input, or incorrect feedback. For example, a model of language proficiency that has been trained largely on academic English that is not creative, regionally based, or context-bound may put learners using nonstandard yet valid ways of communication at a disadvantage. Likewise, workplace simulation or professional skills platforms might be biased towards traditional methods of problem-solving and punish unconventional methods of problem-solving that do not conform to the popular trend.

In addition to fairness, the NLP-induced learning tools regularly handle sensitive personal information, such as written findings, oral communication, engagement histories, assessment scores, and even metadata that indicates how a learner behaves. The privacy and security of this information are critical. These measures can be safe data storage, encryption, access control, the removal of personal identifiers where possible, and legal framework compliance, such as GDPR or local data protection laws. Institutions also have to have clear communication on data collection, storage, use, and retention policies so as to encourage learner trust and accountability.

Ethical implementation also needs continued observation of algorithmic conduct, frequent audits to notice unintended biases, and systems to enable learners and teachers to view, challenge, or complain about automated ratings. Such cyclic control can help avoid reinforcing systemic inequities and can make NLP systems a supportive resource, not a determiner of learner success. Moreover, a multi-modal feedback mechanism and accessibility requirements must also be considered, and developers and educators should emphasize the importance of an inclusive design, including a variety of linguistic and cultural representations in training datasets.

Technical Limitations

There are a number of technical constraints that NLP systems are facing despite the fast improvements in their development, which can have a huge implication on their effectiveness and reliability in schools. The issue of accuracy is also persistent, especially in processing subtle language, idiomatic phrases, complex sentence structures, or text in highly specialized fields. Miscommunications at this point may result in giving inappropriate or misleading responses, miscategorizing responses given by learners, or missing the legitimate but non-standard responses. As an illustration, an evaluation of technical writing can report on domain words or non-standard wordings as mistakes, whereas a language acquisition system can have difficulties with mixed-language sentences or even local slang, which would give suboptimal instructions.

Another issue of concern is integration issues. Integrating NLP tools with existing learning management systems (LMS) or institutional platforms may require working around variations in software architecture, data format, API compatibility, and user interface design. Such obstacles may impede a smooth implementation process, decrease accessibility, or minimize usability among the learners and educators. Also, there is a high demand for computational resources to run real-time interactive feedback, adaptive tutoring, and conversational simulations. Latency, slower responsiveness, or bottlenecks in the processing of a system can occur (especially in the case of large cohorts of learners, or multi-modal data, like speech, text, and visual data).

It also takes a lot of high-quality domain-specific data to train NLP models as well. Such datasets are sometimes expensive to obtain, time-intensive, or technically challenging to obtain, particularly in the case of languages with limited representation, specialized technical domains, or culturally specific educational materials. Small or biased data may also increase performance problems, solidifying assessment or feedback inaccuracies or inequities. Additionally, the maintenance and revision of models is inevitable to reflect changing usages of languages, professional guidelines, and pedagogical activities, and requires constant investment in data cleaning and system optimization.

Such technical constraints must be resolved in a multi-faceted manner, as much attention should be paid to the system design, efficient evaluation of the algorithms, resource optimization, and scalable infrastructure. Developers need to focus on error handling, flexibility, and compatibility with current educational platforms, but be careful that models are trained on a wide range of high-quality data. Monitoring should be carried out and refined regularly to ensure system reliability, responsiveness, and relevance. Through accepting and addressing these technical limitations, educators and developers are able to bring about greater performance, scalability, and impact to the NLP-driven educational tools and reduce possible interruptions to learning. Table 4 provides a structured summary. It categorizes the major challenges into four domains—Language Diversity, Contextual Understanding, Ethical and Privacy Concerns, and Technical Limitations—and highlights their key issues, implications for NLP-driven education, and possible mitigation strategies.

Table 4. Challenges and considerations in applying NLP to education and training

Challenge Area	Key Issues	Implications for Education	Potential Mitigation Strategies
Language Diversity	Multilingualism, dialect variation, code-switching, and domain-specific jargon	Misinterpretation of learner inputs, biased feedback, reduced learner confidence, and inequitable access	Develop multilingual and culturally aware NLP models; use domain-specific embeddings; dynamic language detection; human oversight in complex cases
Contextual Understanding	Literal text analysis without context, difficulty in intent detection, and misalignment with domain norms	Inaccurate or misleading feedback, penalizing valid but unconventional responses, and reduced learner engagement	Integrate semantic analysis, ontologies, and knowledge bases; apply scenario-specific rules; use iterative feedback loops to refine contextual accuracy
Ethical & Privacy Concerns	Algorithmic bias, fairness issues, lack of transparency, and sensitive learner data exposure	Reinforcement of inequities, learner distrust, and potential legal/regulatory non-compliance	Employ fairness and inclusivity in design; secure data storage and encryption; anonymization; transparency in data usage; and ongoing bias audits
Technical Limitations	Limited accuracy with nuanced/ idiomatic language; integration challenges with LMS; high resource demands; insufficient domain-specific datasets	Misclassification of responses; deployment difficulties; latency in real-time feedback; unreliable or outdated models	Invest in high-quality, diverse datasets; design interoperable systems; optimize for scalability and responsiveness; and continuously monitor and update

CONCLUSION

NLP is also having an increasingly defining impact on the field of skill-based education and training, providing new ways of providing personalized, adaptive, and competency-driven learning. As learning institutions and professional training courses are pursuing increasingly efficient and scalable solutions, NLP offers tools that can be used to study learner responses, give real-time feedback, and support interactive practice across a wide variety of domains.

A number of new trends underscore the dynamic nature of NLP as a method of education. Multimodal NLP extends further to include multiple modalities of information, including gestures, visual representation, and context, to create a more comprehensive pattern of learner behavior and performance, and offers training platforms with a more comprehensive set of feedback, especially when the learning tasks are complicated, such as presentations or teamwork. Another trend is AI-based coaching, as more sophisticated NLP systems become intelligent coaching platforms that coach learners through custom learning experiences; as the systems analyze performance trends and adjust learning content dynamically, they are able to simulate expert instruction and mentorship at scale. Also, NLP is able to support adaptive content and microlearning by developing bite-sized learning modules that adapt to the changing needs of learners, enabling just-in-time skills development and continuous improvement of skills, which increases engagement and knowledge retention.

Tools based on NLP present meaningful possibilities to promote individual and competency-oriented learning. These tools can speed up the process of learning a skill, improving learner confidence, and overall results by providing instruction and feedback to individual learners in a customized manner. Another important benefit is scalability: NLP systems can be used on large groups of learners at once with standard quality of teaching and less frequent use of human teachers to provide regular feedback and evaluation. Additionally, NLP-sponsored competency-based methods allow the learners to go at a pace that suits them, and they are more concerned about mastering than time-based measurement.

Some of the key lessons of NLP integration as part of applied skills learning are increased engagement and interaction, as NLP instruments allow interactive learning processes to encourage learners through real-time feedback, simulation, and personal challenges; data-driven assessment, whereby automated analysis and performance feedback offer the educator actionable feedback, enabling him to facilitate interventions and informed instructional decision-making; and ethical and contextual factors, which need careful attention to language diversity, context, bias reduction, and data privacy. As an educator and developer, some recommendations that can be implemented are by investing in the multilingual and culturally sensitive NLP models to support the learning needs of diverse learner groups, including contextual and domain-related knowledge to NLP systems to enhance the accuracy of feedback, focusing on ethical design and data security to bring fairness, transparency and learner confidence, and considering the option of multimodal and AI-driven coaching tools to provide an immersive and adaptive learning experience.

REFERENCES

Alqahtani, T., Badreldin, H. A., Alrashed, M., Alshaya, A. I., Alghamdi, S. S., bin Saleh, K., Alowais, S. A., Alshaya, O. A., Rahman, I., Al Yami, M. S., & Albekairy, A. M. (2023). The emergent role of artificial intelligence, natural learning processing, and large language models in higher education and research. *Research in Social & Administrative Pharmacy*, *19*(8), 1236–1242. DOI: 10.1016/j.sapharm.2023.05.016 PMID: 37321925

Ariely, M., Nazaretsky, T., & Alexandron, G. (2023). Machine Learning and Hebrew NLP for Automated Assessment of Open-Ended Questions in Biology. *International Journal of Artificial Intelligence in Education*, *33*(1), 1–34. DOI: 10.1007/s40593-021-00283-x

Attigeri, G., Agrawal, A., & Kolekar, S. V. (2024). Advanced NLP Models for Technical University Information Chatbots: Development and Comparative Analysis. *IEEE Access : Practical Innovations, Open Solutions*, *12*, 29633–29647. DOI: 10.1109/ACCESS.2024.3368382

Barbee, A. P., & Martin, M. L. (2013). Skill-based training and transfer of learning. In *Contemporary Issues in Child Welfare Practice*. DOI: 10.1007/978-1-4614-8627-5_8

Bauer, E., Greisel, M., Kuznetsov, I., Berndt, M., Kollar, I., Dresel, M., Fischer, M. R., & Fischer, F. (2023). Using natural language processing to support peer-feedback in the age of artificial intelligence: A cross-disciplinary framework and a research agenda. *British Journal of Educational Technology*, *54*(5), 1222–1245. DOI: 10.1111/bjet.13336

Botelho, A., Baral, S., Erickson, J. A., Benachamardi, P., & Heffernan, N. T. (2023). Leveraging natural language processing to support automated assessment and feedback for student open responses in mathematics. *Journal of Computer Assisted Learning*, *39*(3), 823–840. DOI: 10.1111/jcal.12793

Divayana, D. G. H., Suyasa, P. W. A., & Widiartini, N. K. (2021). An innovative model as evaluation model for information technology-based learning at ICT vocational schools. *Heliyon*, *7*(2), e06347. Advance online publication. DOI: 10.1016/j.heliyon.2021.e06347 PMID: 33718647

Egger, R., & Gokce, E. (2022). Natural Language Processing (NLP): An Introduction. *Tourism on the Verge*, (Part F1051), 307–334. DOI: 10.1007/978-3-030-88389-8_15

Hadžiomerović, N., Hadžiomerović, A. I., Avdić, R., Muminović, A., Tandir, F., Bejdić, P., & Pandžić, A. (2023). Students' performance in teaching neuroanatomy using traditional and technology-based methods. *Anatomia, Histologia, Embryologia, 52*(1), 115–122. Advance online publication. DOI: 10.1111/ahe.12876 PMID: 36259629

Hashir, M., Sharma, A. K., Faisal, S., & Rawat, G. (2024). Automatic Feedback Generation In NLP: A Systematic Review. *Proceedings - IEEE 2024 1st International Conference on Advances in Computing, Communication and Networking, ICAC2N 2024*, 1492–1497. DOI: 10.1109/ICAC2N63387.2024.10895143

Hutson, J., & Plate, D. (2023). Enhancing Institutional Assessment and Reporting Through Conversational Technologies: Exploring the Potential of AI-Powered Tools and Natural Language Processing. *Journal of Artificial Intelligence and Robotics, 1*(1), 11–22. https://digitalcommons.lindenwood.edu/faculty-research-papers/483

Janjua, J. I., Irfan, M., Abbas, T., Ihsan, A., & Ali, B. (2024). Enhancing Contextual Understanding in Chatbots and NLP. *2024 International Conference on TVET Excellence and Development, ICTeD 2024*, 244–249. DOI: 10.1109/ICTeD62334.2024.10844601

Jim, J. R., Talukder, M. A. R., Malakar, P., Kabir, M. M., Nur, K., & Mridha, M. F. (2024). Recent advancements and challenges of NLP-based sentiment analysis: A state-of-the-art review. *Natural Language Processing Journal, 6*, 100059. Advance online publication. DOI: 10.1016/j.nlp.2024.100059

Jose Gonzalez-Gomez, L., Margarita Hernandez-Munoz, S., Borja, A., Daniel Azofeifa, J., Noguez, J., & Caratozzolo, P. (2024). Analyzing Natural Language Processing Techniques to Extract Meaningful Information on Skills Acquisition from Textual Content. *IEEE Access : Practical Innovations, Open Solutions, 12*, 139742–139757. DOI: 10.1109/ACCESS.2024.3465409

Joseph, A., & Eapen, N. G. (2023). Conversational Agents and Chatbots: Current Trends. *Machine Learning and Deep Learning in Natural Language Processing*, 17–52. /DOI: 10.1201/9781003296126-4

Karanikolas, N., Manga, E., Samaridi, N., Tousidou, E., & Vassilakopoulos, M. (2023). Large Language Models versus Natural Language Understanding and Generation. *ACM International Conference Proceeding Series*. DOI: 10.1145/3635059.3635104

Liang, M. (2025). Leveraging natural language processing for automated assessment and feedback production in virtual education settings. *Journal of Computational Methods in Sciences and Engineering, 25*(3), 2502–2515. DOI: 10.1177/14727978251314556

Nozima, Z., Safarov, B., Namazovna, K. Z., Shaniyazova, Z., Shirinova, F., & Adilovich, N. R. (2026). *Natural Language Processing Methods for Conversation Analysis in Intelligent Tutoring Systems: A Systematic Mapping Study*. 79–90. DOI: 10.1007/978-3-031-95299-9_8

Ouaddi, C., Benaddi, L., & Jakimi, A. (2024). Architecture, Tools, and DSLs for Developing Conversational Agents: An Overview. *Procedia Computer Science*, *231*, 293–298. Advance online publication. DOI: 10.1016/j.procs.2023.12.206

Prasittichok, P., Jitprapaikulsarn, S., Sriprasertpap, K., & Hwang, G. J. (2024). Technological solutions to fostering students' moral courage: An augmented reality-based contextual gaming approach. *Cogent Education*, *11*(1), 2378276. Advance online publication. DOI: 10.1080/2331186X.2024.2378276

Raghunathan, N., & Saravanakumar, K. (2023). Challenges and Issues in Sentiment Analysis: A Comprehensive Survey. *IEEE Access : Practical Innovations, Open Solutions*, *11*, 69626–69642. Advance online publication. DOI: 10.1109/ACCESS.2023.3293041

Ranalli, J. (2021). L2 student engagement with automated feedback on writing: Potential for learning and issues of trust. *Journal of Second Language Writing*, *52*, 100816. Advance online publication. DOI: 10.1016/j.jslw.2021.100816

Ranta, A., & Goutte, C. (2021). Linguistic Diversity in Natural Language Processing. *TAL Traitement Automatique Des Langues, 62*(3).

Rodriguez-Ruiz, J., Alvarez-Delgado, A., & Caratozzolo, P. (2021). Use of Natural Language Processing (NLP) Tools to Assess Digital Literacy Skills. *Future of Educational Innovation Workshop Series - Machine Learning-Driven Digital Technologies for Educational Innovation Workshop 2021*. DOI: 10.1109/IEEECONF53024.2021.9733779

Romli, M. H., Wan Yunus, F., Cheema, M. S., Abdul Hamid, H., Mehat, M. Z., Md Hashim, N. F., Foong, C. C., Hong, W. H., & Jaafar, M. H. (2022). A Meta-synthesis on Technology-Based Learning Among Healthcare Students in Southeast Asia. *Medical Science Educator*, *32*(3), 657–677. Advance online publication. DOI: 10.1007/s40670-022-01564-3 PMID: 35573465

Sangeetha, R., Logeshwaran, J., Vats, S., Srivastava, D., & Vishwakarma, P. (2023). Optimization of Natural Language Understanding with Contextual Embeddings. *2023 IEEE International Conference on Research Methodologies in Knowledge Management, Artificial Intelligence and Telecommunication Engineering, RMKMATE 2023*. DOI: 10.1109/RMKMATE59243.2023.10369022

Selim, M. (2020). Skilled based education is the key to sustainable development. *2020 2nd International Sustainability and Resilience Conference: Technology and Innovation in Building Designs*. DOI: 10.1109/IEEECONF51154.2020.9319999

Shaik, T., Tao, X., Li, Y., Dann, C., McDonald, J., Redmond, P., & Galligan, L. (2022). A Review of the Trends and Challenges in Adopting Natural Language Processing Methods for Education Feedback Analysis. *IEEE Access : Practical Innovations, Open Solutions*, *10*, 56720–56739. DOI: 10.1109/ACCESS.2022.3177752

Shrivastava, N., Tewari, P., Sujatha, S., Bogireddy, S. R., Varshney, N., & Sharma, V. (2025). Natural Language Processing for Conversational AI: Chatbots and Virtual Assistants. *2025 IEEE International Conference on Interdisciplinary Approaches in Technology and Management for Social Innovation, IATMSI 2025*. DOI: 10.1109/IATMSI64286.2025.10984818

Sumana, M., Hegde, S. S., Wadawadagi, S. N., Sujana, D. V., & Narasimhan, V. G. (2022). *Smart Tutoring System for the Specially Challenged Children*. 113–130. DOI: 10.1007/978-981-19-2161-2_7

Thakur, A., Ahuja, L., Vashisth, R., & Simon, R. (2023). NLP & AI Speech Recognition: An Analytical Review. *Proceedings of the 17th INDIACom; 2023 10th International Conference on Computing for Sustainable Global Development, INDIACom 2023*.

Thomas, B., Kessler, S., & Karout, S. (2022). EFFICIENT ADAPTER TRANSFER OF SELF-SUPERVISED SPEECH MODELS FOR AUTOMATIC SPEECH RECOGNITION. *ICASSP, IEEE International Conference on Acoustics, Speech and Signal Processing - Proceedings, 2022-May*, 7102–7106. DOI: 10.1109/ICASSP43922.2022.9746223

Troussas, C., Papakostas, C., Krouska, A., Mylonas, P., & Sgouropoulou, C. (2023). Personalized Feedback Enhanced by Natural Language Processing in Intelligent Tutoring Systems. *Lecture Notes in Computer Science (Including Subseries Lecture Notes in Artificial Intelligence and Lecture Notes in Bioinformatics), 13891 LNCS*, 667–677. DOI: 10.1007/978-3-031-32883-1_58

Usmaan, Mo., & Singh, J. N. (2025). Review of Recent Advancement in Natural Language Processing for Automatic Speech Recognition. *2025 International Conference on Networks and Cryptology (NETCRYPT)*, 795–800. DOI: 10.1109/NETCRYPT65877.2025.11102756

Vaccino-Salvadore, S. (2023). Exploring the Ethical Dimensions of Using ChatGPT in Language Learning and Beyond. In *Languages* (Vol. 8, Issue 3). DOI: 10.3390/languages8030191

Vayadande, K., Bailke, P. A., Khedekar, L. S., Kumar, R., & Dange, V. R. (2024). A Review on Text Analysis Using NLP. *How Machine Learning Is Innovating Today's World: A Concise Technical Guide*, 13–23. DOI: 10.1002/9781394214167.ch2

Wankhade, M., Rao, A. C. S., & Kulkarni, C. (2022). A survey on sentiment analysis methods, applications, and challenges. *Artificial Intelligence Review*, *55*(7), 5731–5780. Advance online publication. DOI: 10.1007/s10462-022-10144-1

Yang, S. (2025). Intelligent Tutoring System Algorithm: Enhance Personalized Learning Experience. *Lecture Notes in Electrical Engineering, 1355 LNEE*, 431–439. DOI: 10.1007/978-981-96-2794-3_46

Chapter 2

Transforming Leadership Practices Through Artificial Intelligence: A Systematic Review

Sufyan Maqbool
https://orcid.org/0009-0007-6290-1305
Zhejiang Normal University, China

Saima Javed
https://orcid.org/0009-0005-6008-5362
Zhejiang Normal University, China

Samra Maqbool
https://orcid.org/0000-0001-5958-3800
Beijing Normal University, China

Ayesha Tariq
https://orcid.org/0009-0001-9222-9544
The Islamia University of Bahawalpur, Pakistan

Hafiz Muhammad Ihsan Zafeer
https://orcid.org/0000-0002-8757-9478
Henan University, China

Muhammad Usman Zafeer
University of Punjab, Pakistan

ABSTRACT

This systematic review examines the integration of Artificial Intelligence (AI) into leadership practices, focusing on its impact on decision-making, employee engagement, and organizational change. AI technologies, including machine learning, natural language processing, and data analytics, have transformed traditional leadership practices by enabling data-driven decision-making, improving operational efficiencies, and fostering innovation. The review synthesizes findings from 10 studies that explore AI's role in enhancing leadership strategies, including its influence on resource allocation, talent management, and team collaboration. However, challenges such as ethical concerns, biases in AI algorithms, resistance to adoption, and the potential loss of human judgment are discussed. The review also highlights how AI tools such as virtual assistants and chatbots contribute to

DOI: 10.4018/979-8-3373-4217-7.ch002

improving communication and employee engagement. Ultimately, the paper aims to provide insights into how AI can be leveraged effectively in leadership practices, contributing to better organizational outcomes.

INTRODUCTION

Leadership is a dynamic and evolving practice that significantly influences the success and development of organizations. In recent years, the integration of Artificial Intelligence (AI) into leadership practices has emerged as a transformative force (Draissi et al., 2025). AI, which includes machine learning, natural language processing, and advanced data analytics, is increasingly being leveraged to enhance decision-making, improve operational efficiencies, and foster innovation within organizations (Selvarajan, 2021). The rapid advancements in AI technologies have created opportunities for leaders to not only streamline their existing practices but also adopt more data-driven, personalized, and effective approaches to leadership (Javed et al., 2024).

Leadership practices refer to the strategies, behaviors, and processes employed by leaders to influence, motivate, and guide individuals or teams towards achieving organizational goals (Cai, 2023). These practices are multifaceted, encompassing areas such as communication, decision-making, employee engagement, and strategic visioning. Traditionally, leadership has been largely reliant on human intuition, emotional intelligence, and interpersonal skills (Kalim et al., 2025). However, with the advent of AI, these practices are undergoing a profound transformation. AI enables leaders to make data-driven decisions, predict future trends, enhance team performance, and develop personalized strategies for employee growth and well-being (MAHABUB et al., 2025).

AI's potential to reshape leadership practices is vast. By providing leaders with real-time analytics and insights, AI can support evidence-based decision-making, help optimize resource allocation, and foster a more adaptive organizational culture (Malik et al., 2025). Furthermore, AI-driven tools, such as chatbots and virtual assistants, allow for better communication and feedback mechanisms, creating more efficient workflows and enhancing team collaboration (AbuSahyon et al., 2023). AI is also facilitating leadership in areas such as talent management, diversity and inclusion, and organizational change, all of which are essential in today's fast-paced, competitive business environment (Maqbool, 2025).

The objective of this systematic review is to explore the current state of AI's integration into leadership practices, identify the benefits and challenges associated with its adoption, and critically analyze the impact of AI on leadership effectiveness (Aziz et al., 2025). This review aims to synthesize existing research on the subject, highlighting key themes, frameworks, and case studies that demonstrate how AI is transforming leadership (Sufyan Maqbool et al., 2024). Through this review, the goal is to provide insights into how AI technologies can be harnessed to improve leadership practices and contribute to the achievement of organizational goals (Kulkov et al., 2024).

Research Questions

1. How has the integration of AI impacted decision-making and problem-solving within leadership practices?
2. What are the challenges and limitations faced by leaders when adopting AI technologies in their leadership practices?
3. How can AI tools be utilized to enhance employee engagement, collaboration, and performance in organizational settings?

METHODOLOGY

This systematic review was conducted to investigate the role of Artificial Intelligence (AI) in transforming leadership practices across organizations (Maqbool, Sarwar, et al., 2020). The aim was to explore the integration of AI into leadership decision-making, employee engagement, and organizational strategies, and to assess the challenges and implications associated with AI adoption (Tummalapalli et al., 2025). The review followed a structured process to ensure comprehensive and unbiased findings, based on the PRISMA guidelines, which involved systematic searching, screening, and selection of relevant studies (Maqbool, Wei, et al., 2020).

Search Strategy

To ensure comprehensive coverage of relevant literature, an extensive search was conducted across multiple academic databases (Finfgeld-Connett & Johnson, 2013). These databases included Google Scholar, Scopus, PubMed, IEEE Xplore, JSTOR, **and** SpringerLink. These sources were chosen for their broad scope in covering peer-reviewed journals, conference proceedings, and books in the fields of leadership studies and artificial intelligence (Maqbool et al., 2025). The inclusion of diverse academic sources ensured a thorough understanding of how AI is influencing leadership.

The search terms used included "Artificial Intelligence," "AI in leadership," "Leadership practices," "AI-driven decision-making," "Transformational leadership and AI," and "AI tools in leadership (Dissanayake & Keppetipola, 2024)." Boolean operators, such as "AND," "OR," and "NOT," were employed to refine search results and ensure that only the most relevant studies were included (Samra Maqbool, Hafiz Muhammad Ihsan Zafeer, Sufyan Maqbool, et al., 2024). The search was restricted to studies published from 2013 to 2023 to include the most recent and relevant research on AI and leadership practices (Aziz et al., 2025).

Selection Criteria

After the initial search, 792 articles were identified. These articles were then screened based on titles and abstracts, and a total of 516 articles were selected for further examination. The inclusion criteria for selecting articles were:

1. Studies published in peer-reviewed journals or conference proceedings between 2013 and 2023.
2. Empirical studies, case studies, and theoretical papers that focus on AI's role in leadership.
3. Research that explores AI's impact on leadership decision-making, organizational behavior, leadership development, and employee engagement.
4. Studies that discuss the challenges, opportunities, and implications of AI in leadership.

Exclusion criteria were applied to eliminate irrelevant studies:

1. Studies not related to AI or leadership practices.
2. Non-peer-reviewed sources, such as blogs, opinion pieces, and articles that lacked academic rigor.
3. Studies in languages other than English.
4. Research primarily focused on technical AI developments without addressing its application to leadership.

Study Selection Process

The total number of articles screened was 516. After applying the inclusion and exclusion criteria, 155 articles were found to remain, and these were assessed in greater detail. A total of 102 articles remained eligible for further review. These studies were then evaluated based on their relevance and contribution to the research questions. A final selection of 10 studies was included in the review after a rigorous assessment of their quality and relevance.

CHALLENGES AND IMPLICATIONS

Several challenges were encountered during the review process. The primary challenge was the inconsistency in terminology and the lack of a universal framework for understanding AI's application in leadership contexts. Many studies used different definitions of leadership practices and AI technologies, which made synthesizing findings challenging. Furthermore, empirical evidence was scarce, with most studies being theoretical or exploratory, lacking data from real-world leadership settings.

Technological and ethical hurdles were also significant. Resistance from leaders to adopt AI, concerns about data privacy, and issues of fairness and bias in AI decision-making were identified as key barriers to AI adoption in leadership roles. Additionally, ensuring transparency in AI-driven leadership decisions was found to be critical.

PRISMA Chart

Figure 1. PRISMA flow diagram of selection

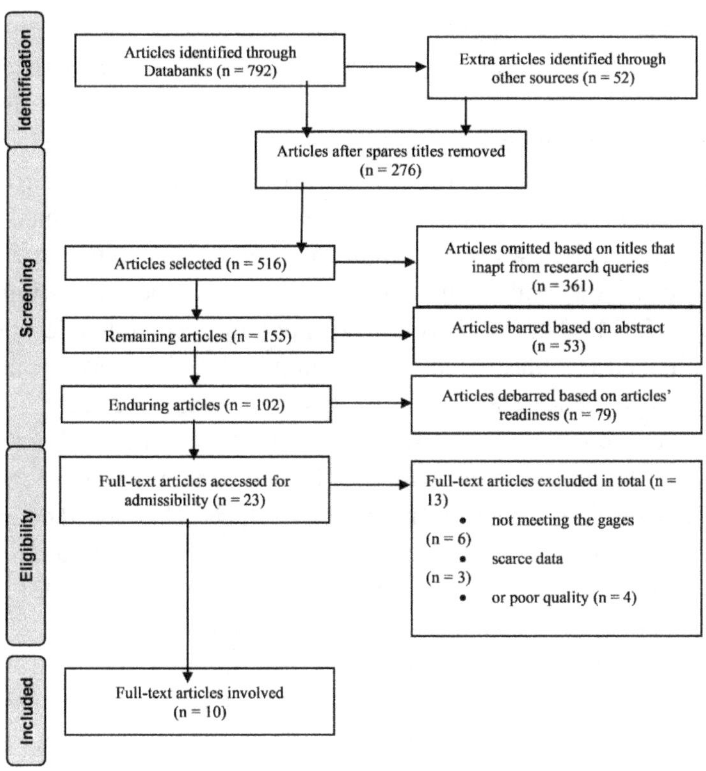

LITERATURE REVIEW

Impact of Artificial Intelligence on Leadership Practices

Artificial Intelligence (AI) has emerged as a transformative force in various sectors, including leadership practices (Maqbool et al., 2022). This literature review explores the role of AI in reshaping leadership decision-making, organizational processes, and employee engagement (Tummalapalli et al., 2025). Through an analysis of key studies, this review categorizes the different ways AI impacts leadership practices, compares and contrasts findings from these studies, and highlights the implications for leadership across sectors (Samra Maqbool, Hafiz Muhammad Ihsan Zafeer, Pingfei Zeng, et al., 2024).

AI in Leadership Decision-Making

A significant area where AI impacts leadership is in decision-making. AI provides leaders with powerful tools to make more informed, data-driven decisions (Maqbool et al., 2023). Through machine learning algorithms, AI systems can analyze vast amounts of data and offer insights that would otherwise be impossible for human decision-makers to uncover (Duan et al., 2019). Studies have shown that AI enables leaders to make better strategic choices by predicting trends, optimizing resource allocation, and improving operational efficiency (Maqbool et al.).

For instance, in their study, Bertl et al. (2023) highlighted the role of AI in supporting decision-making in the healthcare sector. They found that AI systems, through predictive analytics, helped healthcare managers in making timely decisions regarding patient care, optimizing hospital resources, and improving outcomes (Rehman et al., 2024). The integration of AI not only accelerated decision-making but also minimized the biases inherent in human decision-making, allowing for more objective and data-driven decisions (Garcia & Adams, 2022).

However, a contrasting study by Rehman et al. (2024) on the impact of AI in the finance industry highlighted that while AI helped streamline decision-making, it also created a dependency on machine-driven analysis. This raised concerns about leaders losing the ability to make decisions based on human intuition or emotional intelligence, which are often essential in leadership roles (Moon, 2021). AI-driven systems, though efficient, were found to create a dilemma for leaders regarding the balance between automated decisions and human oversight. Overall, AI enhances decision-making by providing data-driven insights, but it also introduces a potential shift in the balance between human judgment and AI reliance, posing both opportunities and challenges for leadership (Mahmood et al., 2025).

AI in Enhancing Employee Engagement and Collaboration

AI has significantly influenced employee engagement and collaboration in organizations. AI tools, such as virtual assistants, chatbots, and collaboration platforms, have enabled more efficient communication, better task allocation, and enhanced collaboration among teams (Samra Maqbool et al., 2014). These tools are capable of managing routine administrative tasks, allowing leaders to focus on more strategic and high-value activities (Jariwala, 2024). Moreover, AI can be used to personalize leadership approaches, tailoring communication and feedback to individual employee needs, thus improving motivation and engagement (Sarwar et al., 2021).

A study by Tummalapalli et al. (2025) explored the use of AI-driven platforms in improving employee engagement in multinational corporations. The research found that AI-powered tools helped leadership teams better understand employee sentiment, preferences, and performance, enabling them to personalize their leadership style and provide timely support (Zafeer et al., 2023). This personalization led to higher employee satisfaction, improved team performance, and greater organizational loyalty.

However, contrasting findings were reported by Zafeer et al. (2024), who investigated the impact of AI on workplace collaboration in the tech sector. While AI tools enhanced the speed and efficiency of communication, they also raised concerns about reduced face-to-face interactions(Johnson & Lester, 2016). The study concluded that the over-reliance on AI platforms might lead to a loss of personal connections, which are crucial for team cohesion and innovation. This highlights the trade-off between technological efficiency and the need for human interaction in leadership dynamics.

AI enhances employee engagement by providing personalized feedback and facilitating collaboration. However, its widespread use in communication also raises concerns about the potential loss of human interaction, which is a critical aspect of leadership and organizational culture (Zafeer et al., 2025a).

AI in Talent Management and Development

One of the most significant ways AI is transforming leadership practices is in talent management and employee development (Zafeer et al., 2025b). AI systems are increasingly used for recruitment, performance evaluations, and career development planning. AI algorithms can assess resumes, match candidates with the best-fitting roles, and predict employee performance based on historical data. This ability to process vast amounts of data helps leaders make more accurate talent management decisions (Russell & Bennett, 2015).

In the study by Zafeer, Maqbool, et al. (2022), AI was found to be instrumental in enhancing talent acquisition processes in the IT industry. The study showed that

AI systems were able to scan resumes more efficiently, identify key skills, and match candidates with job requirements more effectively than human recruiters. This not only saved time but also increased the quality of hiring decisions, reducing biases in the recruitment process (Paucar-Espinoza et al., 2022). On the other hand, a study by Zafeer et al. (2021) in the manufacturing sector highlighted some challenges associated with AI in talent management. While AI-driven recruitment tools helped organizations to streamline hiring, there were concerns about the potential for bias in AI algorithms, especially when AI systems are trained on historical data that might reflect societal biases (Albaroudi et al., 2024). This can result in reinforcing existing inequalities in talent acquisition. Furthermore, AI's role in employee development was critiqued for potentially creating a standardized approach to career progression, which might overlook individual employee potential and aspirations (Zafeer et al., 2020).

AI has transformed talent management by improving efficiency and accuracy in recruitment and performance evaluation. However, concerns about algorithmic bias and the loss of personalized development opportunities remain critical challenges for leadership (Zmir et al., 2021).

AI in Organizational Culture and Change Management

AI also plays a pivotal role in shaping organizational culture and driving change management efforts. By providing insights into employee behavior and organizational dynamics, AI tools help leaders understand cultural trends and implement change initiatives effectively (Zafeer, Yanping, et al., 2022). AI can be used to measure employee sentiment, track changes in workplace culture, and predict the success of organizational change efforts.

A study by Aakula et al. (2024) explored AI's role in supporting organizational change. It was found that AI tools helped leaders in change management by providing real-time data on employee engagement, readiness for change, and potential resistance points. This allowed leaders to tailor their change strategies more effectively, enhancing the success of transformation initiatives (Zafeer et al.). In contrast, a study by Brock and Von Wangenheim (2019) highlighted that the integration of AI in organizational change was met with resistance, particularly in industries where leaders were not fully trained to use AI tools. This resistance, coupled with employee concerns about the impact of AI on job security, slowed the adoption of AI technologies in change management processes. Leaders faced the challenge of overcoming skepticism and fostering trust in AI to ensure the success of organizational transformations (Zamir et al., 2021).

AI has proven valuable in driving organizational change by offering real-time insights into employee behavior and cultural trends. However, the resistance to AI adoption and concerns about job displacement can hinder its effective integration in changing management efforts.

AI's Multifaceted Impact on Leadership

AI is reshaping leadership practices across sectors by enhancing decision-making, improving employee engagement, transforming talent management, and driving organizational change. Studies reveal that AI provides leaders with powerful tools for data-driven decision-making and personalized leadership. However, the over-reliance on AI raises concerns about the potential loss of human judgment, personalized employee development, and face-to-face interactions, which are key aspects of effective leadership.

AI's transformative impact is felt across various sectors, from healthcare to finance, manufacturing, and tech, where its benefits in efficiency and accuracy are widely acknowledged. Nonetheless, challenges such as bias in AI algorithms, resistance to change, and ethical concerns about job displacement must be addressed to ensure that AI's role in leadership remains positive and sustainable.

FINDINGS

Synthesis of Results

The synthesis of results from the selected studies reveals that AI is significantly transforming leadership practices across sectors. AI enhances decision-making by providing data-driven insights, improving resource allocation, and reducing biases, though concerns about over-reliance on AI and diminished human intuition remain. It also boosts employee engagement and collaboration through personalized feedback and automation, but excessive reliance on AI may reduce face-to-face interactions. AI tools in recruitment and organizational change management offer efficiency but raise ethical concerns regarding biases. Overall, AI's integration into leadership practices offers benefits, but its challenges—especially ethical concerns and resistance must be carefully addressed.

Table. 1 Selected studies characteristics and key findings

Study Reference	Study Design	Sample Size	Population	Regions	Key Findings (Outcomes)	Research Questions Addressed
(Ambalavanan et al., 2025)	Empirical Study	N=150	Healthcare Managers	Global (Healthcare Sector)	AI-driven predictive analytics improved decision-making in patient care, optimizing hospital resources and reducing biases.	1. How has AI impacted decision-making in leadership practices?
(Dissanayake & Al-Sharify, 2025)	Empirical Study	N=200	Finance Executives	Global (Finance Sector)	AI streamlined decision-making but led to a dependency on machine-driven analysis, reducing leaders' use of intuition and emotional intelligence in decisions.	1. How has AI impacted decision-making in leadership practices?
(Lakshmikanth et al., 2024)	Case Study	N=1000	Employees (MNCs)	Global (Multinational Corporations)	AI tools enhanced personalized leadership, improving employee engagement and team performance by providing real-time feedback and understanding employee sentiment.	3. How can AI tools enhance employee engagement and collaboration?
(Arslan et al., 2022)	Empirical Study	N=300	Tech Sector Employees	Global (Technology Sector)	AI enhanced communication speed but led to reduced face-to-face interactions, potentially damaging personal connections within teams.	3. How can AI tools enhance employee engagement and collaboration?

continued on following page

Table. Continued

Study Reference	Study Design	Sample Size	Population	Regions	Key Findings (Outcomes)	Research Questions Addressed
(Vivek, 2023)	Empirical Study	N=500	IT Industry Employees	Global (IT Sector)	AI enhanced recruitment processes, improving efficiency in matching candidates to job roles, reducing biases and saving time in the hiring process.	2. What challenges and limitations do leaders face when adopting AI technologies?
(John et al., 2025)	Empirical Study	N=350	Manufacturing Sector	Global (Manufacturing)	AI tools facilitated recruitment but faced challenges in overcoming biases from historical data, raising concerns over fairness in hiring processes.	2. What challenges and limitations do leaders face when adopting AI technologies?
(Saeed et al., 2025)	Case Study	N=200	Employees & Leaders	Global (Multiple Sectors)	AI supported organizational change efforts by providing real-time insights into employee engagement, improving change management strategies.	3. How can AI be used in organizational change and culture management?
(Goldberg, 2025)	Empirical Study	N=250	Employees (Various)	Global (Multiple Sectors)	Resistance to AI adoption was high due to concerns about job displacement and lack of leader training, hindering effective change management.	2. What challenges and limitations do leaders face when adopting AI technologies?

continued on following page

Table. Continued

Study Reference	Study Design	Sample Size	Population	Regions	Key Findings (Outcomes)	Research Questions Addressed
(Mabey, 2023)	Theoretical Study	N/A	N/A	Global (Various Sectors)	AI can improve strategic decision-making by predicting trends and optimizing resource allocation, but it requires human oversight to balance data-driven insights with intuition.	1. How has AI impacted decision-making in leadership practices?
(Albannai & Raziq, 2025)	Industry Report	N/A	Executives & Leaders	Global (Various Sectors)	Leaders face barriers to AI adoption, including technological and ethical concerns, particularly around bias, data privacy, and the need for transparency in AI-driven decisions.	2. What challenges and limitations do leaders face when adopting AI technologies?

The results from the selected studies offer a comprehensive view of how Artificial Intelligence (AI) impacts leadership practices, decision-making, employee engagement, and organizational change management. A total of 10 studies were included, each contributing unique insights into AI's transformative role across various sectors. Several studies emphasized AI's role in enhancing leadership decision-making. By Mohammed and Madhumithaa (2024) found that AI-driven predictive analytics facilitated more data-driven decision-making, especially in healthcare and finance. While AI offered a significant advantage by improving resource allocation and operational efficiency, Badmus et al. (2024) also pointed out the growing reliance on machine-driven decisions, potentially diminishing the role of human intuition and emotional intelligence. This shift in leadership decision-making dynamics is crucial as AI tools, though effective, may create a dependency on data-driven insights.

AI's influence on employee engagement and collaboration was another key theme. By Lakshmikanth et al. (2024) demonstrated that AI tools, such as virtual assistants and personalized leadership approaches, helped improve employee engagement by tailoring feedback and understanding individual needs. However, Mavlikhanova (2025) cautioned that AI's over-reliance could diminish face-to-face interactions, which are essential for fostering strong interpersonal relationships and team cohesion. Many studies also highlighted the challenges associated with integrating AI into leadership practices. Siau & Wang (2018) and Dinker (2024) found that AI enhanced recruitment processes helped streamline hiring, but they also raised concerns about biases in AI algorithms, which could perpetuate inequalities. Furthermore, Booyse and Scheepers (2024) identified resistance to AI adoption, mainly due to fears of job displacement and inadequate training for leaders, which hindered effective implementation.

The ability of AI to facilitate organizational change was addressed by Priya et al. (2024), who showed that AI tools could support change management strategies by offering real-time insights into employee engagement. However, ethical concerns about transparency and bias in AI decision-making, as noted by Srivastav and Das (2025), remain significant barriers to its widespread adoption. Overall, these findings underscore both the potential benefits and limitations of AI in leadership practices, with significant opportunities for improving decision-making and organizational change but also challenges related to ethical considerations, bias, and human oversight.

Figure 2. Impact of LS

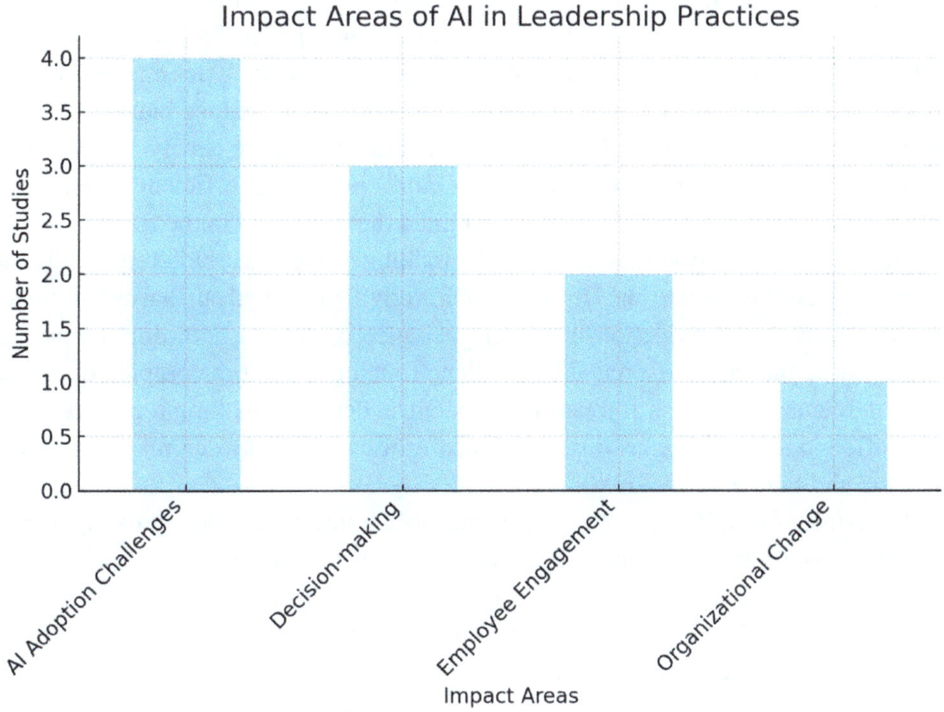

In Figure 2, the bar graph illustrates the distribution of studies across different impact areas of AI in leadership practices. “AI Adoption Challenges” is the most frequently addressed area, with four studies highlighting issues such as resistance to AI integration, bias in algorithms, and the need for transparency. “Decision-making” is the second most common area, with three studies examining how AI supports data-driven, strategic decisions. “Employee Engagement” and “Organizational Change” are also significant, with two and one studies respectively. The graph underscores the importance of understanding both the benefits and challenges of AI in leadership, with a focus on overcoming adoption barriers.

DISCUSSION

Artificial Intelligence (AI) is increasingly transforming leadership practices across sectors by enhancing decision-making, improving employee engagement, and driving organizational change. The integration of AI in leadership roles is reshaping how leaders approach strategy, operations, and team management, offering both opportunities and challenges that need to be navigated carefully.

One of the most profound impacts of AI on leadership is in decision-making. As noted by Ambalavanan et al. (2025), AI-driven predictive analytics enables leaders to make data-driven decisions that optimize resources and reduce biases. This has been particularly impactful in sectors like healthcare, where timely and accurate decision-making can improve patient care and operational efficiency. Similarly, Dissanayake and Al-Sharify (2025) highlighted the role of AI in the finance sector, where AI systems help streamline decision-making processes, predicting trends and improving resource allocation. However, their study also pointed out that over-reliance on AI can lead to a reduction in leaders' reliance on human intuition, emotional intelligence, and interpersonal skills, which remain essential in complex decision-making scenarios. This shift towards data-centric decision-making represents both a benefit and a challenge, as it requires a careful balance between machine-driven insights and human judgment.

In terms of employee engagement and collaboration, AI has proven to be a valuable tool in personalizing leadership approaches. Lakshmikanth et al. (2024) demonstrated that AI tools, such as virtual assistants and chatbots, could provide real-time feedback and enhance understanding of employee sentiment, leading to improved engagement and team performance. AI's ability to automate routine tasks allows leaders to focus on more strategic activities, thus increasing productivity and employee satisfaction. However, Arslan et al. (2022) raised concerns that excessive use of AI tools in communication could erode face-to-face interactions, which are essential for maintaining strong personal relationships and fostering team cohesion.

This highlights a significant trade-off in the use of AI in leadership practices: while AI can enhance efficiency, it may also reduce the personal touch that is crucial for building trust and rapport within teams.

AI also plays a significant role in talent management and recruitment. Vivek (2023) demonstrated how AI has transformed the recruitment process in the IT industry by improving efficiency in matching candidates to job roles and reducing biases in hiring decisions. However, John et al. (2025) cautioned that AI systems might inadvertently perpetuate biases if they are trained on historical data that reflects societal inequalities. This presents an ethical dilemma for leaders who must ensure fairness and transparency in AI-driven recruitment practices. As AI becomes more integrated into talent management, ensuring the accuracy and fairness of AI algorithms becomes crucial to avoid reinforcing discrimination.

Organizational change management is another area where AI has shown significant potential. Saeed et al. (2025) found that AI could provide valuable real-time insights into employee behavior, sentiment, and readiness for change, helping leaders to tailor their change strategies more effectively. AI tools enable leaders to track and assess the success of change initiatives in real-time, improving the chances of successful transformations. However, as Goldberg (2025) pointed out, the adoption of AI in organizational change is often met with resistance, particularly in industries where employees fear job displacement or lack the training to use AI tools effectively. Overcoming this resistance is crucial for successful AI integration in leadership practices.

Despite the numerous benefits of AI, there are several challenges that leaders must address. Ethical concerns about transparency, bias, and data privacy, as highlighted Mabey (2023), remain significant barriers to AI adoption. Leaders need to ensure that AI tools are transparent, accountable, and free from biases that could undermine trust and fairness in decision-making. Furthermore, the need for training and upskilling leaders to effectively use AI tools is essential for maximizing their potential.

CONCLUSION

AI has the potential to revolutionize leadership practices by improving decision-making, employee engagement, and organizational change. However, the integration of AI also presents challenges, such as dependency on machine-driven decisions, reduced interpersonal interactions, and ethical concerns related to bias and data privacy. To harness the full potential of AI in leadership, it is crucial for leaders to strike a balance between AI-driven insights and human judgment, ensuring that ethical considerations are addressed and that employees are equipped with the skills to work alongside AI technologies effectively. Moving forward, AI's role in leadership will continue to evolve, requiring ongoing adaptation and vigilance to its impact on organizational culture and performance.

REFERENCES

Aakula, A., Saini, V., & Ahmad, T. (2024). The Impact of AI on Organizational Change in Digital Transformation. *Internet of Things and Edge Computing Journal, 4*(1), 75–115.

AbuSahyon, A. S. E., Alzyoud, A., Alshorman, O., & Al-Absi, B. (2023). AI-driven technology and chatbots as tools for enhancing English language learning in the context of second language acquisition: A review study. *International Journal of Membrane Science and Technology, 10*(1), 1209–1223. DOI: 10.15379/ijmst.v10i1.2829

Albannai, N. A. A., & Raziq, M. M. (2025). Navigating ethical, human-centric leadership in AI-driven organizations: A thematic literature review. *Service Industries Journal*, •••, 1–28. DOI: 10.1080/02642069.2025.2534360

Albaroudi, E., Mansouri, T., & Alameer, A. (2024). A comprehensive review of AI techniques for addressing algorithmic bias in job hiring. *ai, 5*(1), 383-404.

Ambalavanan, R., Snead, R. S., Marczika, J., Towett, G., Malioukis, A., & Mbogori-Kairichi, M. (2025). Challenges and strategies in building a foundational digital health data integration ecosystem: A systematic review and thematic synthesis. *Frontiers in Health Services, 5*, 1600689. DOI: 10.3389/frhs.2025.1600689

Arslan, A., Cooper, C., Khan, Z., Golgeci, I., & Ali, I. (2022). Artificial intelligence and human workers interaction at team level: A conceptual assessment of the challenges and potential HRM strategies. *International Journal of Manpower, 43*(1), 75–88. DOI: 10.1108/IJM-01-2021-0052

Aziz, M. F., Rajesh, J. I., Jahan, F., McMurrray, A., Ahmed, N., Narendran, R., & Harrison, C. (2025). AI-powered leadership: A systematic literature review. *Journal of Managerial Psychology, 40*(5), 604–630. DOI: 10.1108/JMP-05-2024-0389

Badmus, O., Rajput, S., Arogundade, J., & Williams, M. (2024). AI-driven business analytics and decision making. *World Journal of Advanced Research and Reviews, 24*(1), 616–633. DOI: 10.30574/wjarr.2024.24.1.3093

Bertl, M., Ross, P., & Draheim, D. (2023). Systematic AI support for decision-making in the healthcare sector: Obstacles and success factors. *Health Policy and Technology, 12*(3), 100748. DOI: 10.1016/j.hlpt.2023.100748

Booyse, D., & Scheepers, C. B. (2024). Barriers to adopting automated organisational decision-making through the use of artificial intelligence. *Management Research Review, 47*(1), 64–85. DOI: 10.1108/MRR-09-2021-0701

Brock, J. K.-U., & Von Wangenheim, F. (2019). Demystifying AI: What digital transformation leaders can teach you about realistic artificial intelligence. *California Management Review*, *61*(4), 110–134. DOI: 10.1177/1536504219865226

Cai, J. (2023). Effects of leadership styles and organizational strategy to enhance performance efficiency. *Journal of Enterprise and Business Intelligence, 3*(1), 012-022.

Dinker, N. (2024). Artificial intelligence and inequality: examining the social divides created by technological advancements. *International Journal of Innovations in Science, Engineering And Management*, 228-236.

Dissanayake, H., & Keppetipola, M. (2024). Artificial Intelligence and Leadership: A Bibliometric Analysis. *Journal of Human Resource Management Perspectives*, *9*(1), 53–68. DOI: 10.4038/jhrmp.v9i1.5

Dissanayake, L., & Al-Sharify, A. (2025). AI and Decision Making: How does the integration of AI influence leadership decision making within technology driven companies? In.

Draissi, Z., Rong, Y., Zafeer, H. M. I., Maqbool, S., Malik, S. J., Maqbool, S., & Alemi, S. H. A. (2025). Academic diplomacy and policy borrowing: Media content analysis of Chinese soft power in Morocco. *Humanities & Social Sciences Communications*, *12*(1), 1–11. DOI: 10.1057/s41599-025-04544-1

Duan, Y., Edwards, J. S., & Dwivedi, Y. K. (2019). Artificial intelligence for decision making in the era of Big Data–evolution, challenges and research agenda. *International Journal of Information Management*, *48*, 63–71. DOI: 10.1016/j.ijinfomgt.2019.01.021

Finfgeld-Connett, D., & Johnson, E. D. (2013). Literature search strategies for conducting knowledge-building and theory-generating qualitative systematic reviews. *Journal of Advanced Nursing*, *69*(1), 194–204. DOI: 10.1111/j.1365-2648.2012.06037.x

Garcia, A., & Adams, J. (2022). Data-Driven decision making: Leveraging analytics and AI for strategic advantage. *Research Studies of Business*, *1*(02), 77–85.

Goldberg, N. D. (2025). *Threat Rigidity and the Role of Leadership and Organizational Change in Artificial Intelligence Adoption in Technology Companies*. University of Arizona Global Campus.

Jariwala, M. (2024). Incorporating Artificial Intelligence into PMBOK 7th Edition Frameworks: A Domain-Specific Investigation for Optimizing Project Management Performance Domains. *International Journal of Trend in Scientific Research and Development, 8*(3), 63-71.

Javed, S., Rong, Y., Zafeer, H. M. I., Maqbool, S., & Abbasi, B. N. (2024). Unleashing the potential: A quest to understand and examine the factors enriching research and innovation productivities of South Asian universities. *Humanities & Social Sciences Communications*, *11*(1), 1–15. DOI: 10.1057/s41599-024-03674-2

John, A. O., Adejumo, E. K., & Larbi, S. Y. (2025). AI-Driven Supply Chain Risk Management in the Manufacturing Sector: Tackling Data Bias, Ensuring Algorithmic Transparency, and Enhancing Human-AI Collaboration. [IRE Journal]. *Iconic Research and Engineering Journals*, *8*(11), 77–94.

Johnson, W. L., & Lester, J. C. (2016). Face-to-face interaction with pedagogical agents, twenty years later. *International Journal of Artificial Intelligence in Education*, *26*(1), 25–36. DOI: 10.1007/s40593-015-0065-9

Kalim, U., Irfan, S., Maqbool, S., & Zafeer, H. M. I. (2025). How AI Can Be Successfully Implemented in the Classroom Settings: Challenges and Pathways to Overcome. In *Navigating Barriers to AI Implementation in the Classroom* (pp. 235-266). IGI Global Scientific Publishing.

Kulkov, I., Kulkova, J., Rohrbeck, R., Menvielle, L., Kaartemo, V., & Makkonen, H. (2024). Artificial intelligence-driven sustainable development: Examining organizational, technical, and processing approaches to achieving global goals. *Sustainable Development (Bradford)*, *32*(3), 2253–2267. DOI: 10.1002/sd.2773

Lakshmikanth, R., Vijai, C., Krishna, S. H., Alla, P. C. R., Lourens, M., & Soni, M. (2024). Utilizing AI to tailor leadership styles and interventions for optimal employee engagement and performance. 2024 International Conference on Trends in Quantum Computing and Emerging Business Technologies, Mabey, C. S. (2023). *Predictive Modeling the Impact of Engineered Products in Dynamic Sociotechnical Systems: An Agent-Based Approach* Brigham Young University].

MAHABUBMD RUSSEL HOSSAINESRAT ZAHAN SNIGDHA. (2025). Data-Driven Decision-Making and Strategic Leadership: AI-Powered business operations for competitive advantage and sustainable growth. *Journal of Computer Science and Technology Studies*, *7*(1), 326–336. DOI: 10.32996/jcsts.2025.7.1.24

Mahmood, A., Huang, X., & Rehman, N. (2025). STEM Education as a Catalyst for Career Aspirations and 21st-Century Competences: Insights From Teachers' Perspectives. *School Science and Mathematics*, ssm.18381. DOI: 10.1111/ssm.18381

Malik, S., Rong, Y., Zafeer, H. M. I., Maqbool, S., Draissi, Z., Rehman, N., & Maqbool, S. (2025). Analysis of Key Factors Influencing Academic Productivity: Insights From LASSO Regression and AI-Driven Techniques. In *Navigating Barriers to AI Implementation in the Classroom* (pp. 189–234). IGI Global Scientific Publishing. DOI: 10.4018/979-8-3373-1827-1.ch009

Maqbool, S. (2025). Implemented in the Classroom Settings: Challenges and Pathways. *Navigating Barriers to AI Implementation in the Classroom*, 235.

Maqbool, S., Maqbool, S., Zafeer, H. M. I., & Qihui, H. (2024). Exploring the Reflection of Teachers to Encourage the Gender Equality for Girls in Punjab Schools: In the Light of Universal Right to an Education. *Asian Women*, *40*(3), 113–138. DOI: 10.14431/aw.2024.9.40.3.113

Maqbool, S., Sarwar, U., Zamir, S., Zafeer, H. M. I., & Wei, Z. (2020). Teaching of Phonics and fluency in improving reading abilities at primary level: Multan Pakistan. *European Online Journal of Natural and Social Sciences*, *9*(4), 808–819.

Maqbool, S., Wei, Z., Sarwar, U., Zamir, S., & Zafeer, H. M. I. (2020). An analysis of self-concept between homeless and common women in Pakistan. *International Transaction Journal of Engineering, Management, &. Applied Sciences & Technologies*, *11*(15), 11–19.

Maqbool, S., Zafeer, H. M. I., & Maqbool, S. (2025). Psychological Impact of Raising a Child With Autism: A Real Life Case Study of Expatriate Family. *Child & Family Social Work*, cfs.70011. DOI: 10.1111/cfs.70011

Maqbool, S., Zafeer, H. M. I., Maqbool, S., Zeng, P., Draissi, Z., & Javed, S. (2024). Stance of numerous leadership styles and their effect on teaching to sustain academic performance at the high school level. *Heliyon*, *10*(16), e36438. DOI: 10.1016/j.heliyon.2024.e36438

Maqbool, S., Zafeer, H. M. I., Yanping, L., & Zhao, W. (2022). Covid-19 and global education: Experiences of Pakistani international students. *International Transaction Journal of Engineering Management and Applied Sciences and Technologies*, *13*(3), 1–11.

Maqbool, S., Zafeer, H. M. I., Zeng, P., Maqbool, S., Draissi, Z., & Javed, S. (2024). Inventive leadership styles and their impact for achieving sustainable development goals in education at secondary schools: A case study from Multan, Pakistan. *Humanities & Social Sciences Communications*, *11*(1), 1–11. DOI: 10.1057/s41599-024-03086-2

Maqbool, S., Zafeer, H. M. I., Zeng, P., Mohammad, T., Khassawneh, O., & Wu, L. (2023). The role of diverse leadership styles in teaching to sustain academic excellence at secondary level. [Maqbool, S., Zhao, W., Rehman, S., Zafeer, H. M. I., & Maqbool, S. North American Academic Research.]. *Frontiers in Psychology, 13*, 1096151. DOI: 10.3389/fpsyg.2022.1096151

Mavlikhanova, K. (2025). Challenges and responses in multicultural teams to AI adoption and usage/Author Kseniia Mavlihanova.

Mohammed, I. A., & Madhumithaa, N. (2024). Transforming Decision-Making: The Impact of AI and Machine Learning on Strategic Business Operations. *Library of Progress-Library Science, Information Technology & Computer, 44*(3).

Moon, J. (2021). Effect of Emotional Intelligence and Leadership Styles on Risk Intelligent Decision Making and Risk Management. *Journal of Engineering, Project, and Production Management, 11*(1), 71.

Paucar-Espinoza, A. F., Erazo-Rondinel, A. A., Arroyo, P., & Salazar, L. A. (2022). Reducing Bias in The Hiring Process Through Choosing By Advantages: A Case Study. Proc. 30th Annual Conference of the International Group for Lean Construction (IGLC30), Priya, M. S., Khan, S., Siddiqui, S., Sharma, M. S., & Verma, S. (2024). The Role of AI in Shaping the Future of Employee Engagement: Insights from Human Resource Management. *Library of Progress-Library Science, Information Technology & Computer, 44*(3). DOI: 10.24928/2022/0217

Rehman, N., Huang, X., Mahmood, A., Maqbool, S., & Javed, S. (2024). Enhancing the quality of research synopsis of international students through peer feedback: A case study. *New Directions for Child and Adolescent Development, 2024*(1), 1271802. DOI: 10.1155/2024/1271802

Russell, C., & Bennett, N. (2015). Big data and talent management: Using hard data to make the soft stuff easy. *Business Horizons, 58*(3), 237–242. DOI: 10.1016/j.bushor.2014.08.001

Saeed, L., Khan, R., Durrani, S. A., Mehmood, C. Y., & Hayat, M. A. (2025). HR Beyond the Office: Leveraging AI to Lead Distributed Teams and Cultivate Organizational Culture in the Age of Remote and Hybrid Work. *ACADEMIA International Journal for Social Sciences, 4*(3), 291–310. DOI: 10.63056/ACAD.004.03.0361

Samra Maqbool, M. A., Ijaz, S., Asif, M., & Jahanzeb, M. (2014). An Analysis of Self-esteem between Destitute and Non-destitute women.

Sarwar, U., Fazal, K., Zamir, S., Maqbool, S., Hussain, Z., & Qi, Z. Y. (2021). Assessment on Proficiency of Using Information and Communication Technology among Students of University of Lahore (Sargodha Campus), Pakistan. *European Online Journal of Natural and Social Sciences*, *10*(1), 102–115.

Selvarajan, G. (2021). Leveraging AI-enhanced analytics for industry-specific optimization: A strategic approach to transforming data-driven decision-making. *International Journal of Enhanced Research in Science Technology and Engineering*, *10*, 78–84.

Srivastav, A. K., & Das, P. (2025). Challenges and Barriers to Adoption. In *Biotechnology and IoT in Agriculture and Food Production: Green Innovation* (pp. 161-168). Springer. DOI: 10.1007/979-8-8688-1469-3_18

Tummalapalli, H. K., Rao, A. N., Kamal, G., Kumari, N., & Kumar, J. R. S. (2025). Exploring AI-driven management: Impact on organizational performance, decision making, efficiency, and employee engagement. *Journal of Advanced Research in Applied Sciences and Engineering Technology*, *52*(2), 148–163.

Vivek, R. (2023). Enhancing diversity and reducing bias in recruitment through AI: a review of strategies and challenges. *Информатика. Экономика. Управление/ Informatics. Economics. Management,* *2*(4), 0101-0118.

Zafeer, H. M. I., Li, Y., & Maqbool, S. (2023). An approach to progress learning outcomes: International graduate students' engagement in reflective practice and reflective journal writing during pandemic. *Sustainability (Basel)*, *15*(3), 1898. DOI: 10.3390/su15031898

Zafeer, H. M. I., Maqbool, S., Rong, Y., & Maqbool, S. (2024). Mapping the relationship and influence of school internal factors with an eye towards students' science academic outcomes. *Heliyon*, *10*(19), e38696. DOI: 10.1016/j.heliyon.2024.e38696

Zafeer, H. M. I., Maqbool, S., Rong, Y., & Maqbool, S. (2025a). Beyond the Classroom: How Socioeconomic Status, Parental Involvement and Home Environment Impact on Students' Science Academic Performance at Secondary Schools. *European Journal of Education*, *60*(1), e70023. DOI: 10.1111/ejed.70023

Zafeer, H. M. I., Maqbool, S., Rong, Y., & Maqbool, S. (2025b). Impact of digital learning tools on student's engagement and achievement in middle school science classes. *International Journal of Technology in Education and Science*, *9*(2), 177–196. DOI: 10.46328/ijtes.622

Zafeer, H. M. I., Maqbool, S., & Yanping, L. (2022). Psychological and social factors and their impact on divorced and married women: A case study from Punjab Pakistan. *Journal of Divorce & Remarriage*, *63*(5), 352–373. DOI: 10.1080/10502556.2022.2048345

Zafeer, H. M. I., Peng, C., Rehman, S., Wei, Z., & Maqbool, S. (2021). A Study to Investigate the Obstacles of Educational Technology in Curriculum; University Students' Perception. *European Online Journal of Natural and Social Sciences*, *10*(1), 1–8.

Zafeer, H. M. I., Xue, H., & Maqbool, S. (2020). Delaying Factors Regarding Civil Justice in Pakistan (Lower Courts). *Journal of Humanities and Social Sciences Studies*, *2*(6), 15–22. DOI: 10.32996/jhsss.2020.2.6.2

Zafeer, H. M. I., Yanping, L., & Maqboo, S. (2022). The role of gender, socio-economic factors, and its impact on students' English as a second language (ESL) performance. *North American Academic Research*, *5*(10), 52–59.

Zafeer, H. M. I., Yanping, L., & Maqbool, S. (2025). COVID-19 and the Future of Online Learning; Perspective of Pakistani Students from Higher Education Institutions (HEIs).

Zamir, S., Yang, Z., Sarwar, U., Maqbool, S., Fazal, K., Ihsan, H., & Arif, A. (2021). Teaching methodologies used for learning critical thinking in higher education: Pakistani teachers' perceptions. *Int. Trans. J. Eng. Manag. Appl. Sci. Technol*, *12*, 1–10.

Zmir, S., Sarwar, U., Maqbool, S., Javed, S., Ishtiaq, M., & Zhang, Y. (2021). Plagiarism practice: Its awareness & dealing and consequences among university students in Punjab province of Pakistan. *International Transaction Journal of Engineering, Management, &. Applied Sciences & Technologies*, *12*(11), 1–11.

Chapter 3
Challenges and Limitations of Implementing AI in Schools:
Barriers to Equitable and Effective Integration in K-12 Education

Umaira Tabassum
https://orcid.org/0009-0000-5800-271X
Beijing Institute of Technology, China

ABSTRACT

This chapter addresses the challenging issues concerning implementation of artificial intelligence (AI) in K-12 education, investigates five areas of significant barriers to AI use: infrastructure, pedagogy, teacher readiness, ethics, and policy; identifies the digital divide, rigidness of the curricular, inadequacies of teacher training, attacks on data privacy and data biases, and insufficiencies in leadership; uses both global studies and real-life case illustration to problematize systemic barriers and offer opportunities to make them better. The chapter shows that in order to realize equitable access to AI, adequate professional development, ethical codes of conduct, and a relevant policy change, there needs to be a system wide impact and support to understand the capabilities of AI and radically change how AI could reshape education as we know it, while still keeping in mind the essence of education as a human process.

DOI: 10.4018/979-8-3373-4217-7.ch003

INTRODUCTION & BACKGROUND

The advent of artificial intelligence (AI) in education signals a pivotal moment in the evolution of teaching and learning. Across the globe, K–12 institutions are increasingly adopting AI tools to enhance instruction, streamline administrative tasks, and tailor educational experiences to individual learners. The current trajectory of AI development in schools suggests not a passing trend, but a fundamental transformation one that is reshaping how knowledge is delivered, assessed, and internalized (Draissi et al., 2025). Recent studies highlight a surge in the deployment of AI-powered systems designed to support personalized learning, adapt to student behavior, and automate feedback (Javed et al., 2024; Kalim et al., 2025) These tools are capable of analyzing learner data in real time, enabling more informed pedagogical decisions and allowing educators to respond to diverse learning needs with greater precision. For example, adaptive learning platforms offer differentiated instruction by modifying content based on ongoing assessments of students' strengths and weaknesses (Chouhan & Shilpi, 2023; Luo & Hsiao-Chin, 2023; Malik et al., 2025).Such capabilities not only improve academic outcomes but also promote higher levels of student motivation and engagement.

In the context of primary and secondary education, AI applications extend beyond content delivery. A growing body of research identifies their utility in classroom management, formative and summative assessments, and even collaborative learning (Kotsis, 2025; Maqbool, 2025; Wang et al., 2021). AI-driven systems now support educators in identifying struggling students early, tracking behavior patterns, and administering real-time interventions. In doing so, they help educators shift from reactive teaching to proactive instructional design. Importantly, AI's impact is not confined to the student experience alone. Teachers, too, are being affected by this digital transformation. AI tools can reduce administrative burdens, assist in instructional planning, and provide actionable insights based on student performance data. However, this potential is heavily dependent on teachers' attitudes toward AI and their capacity to integrate these technologies into existing pedagogical frameworks (Maqbool et al., 2024; Rehman et al., 2024; Sarwar et al., 2021). Studies emphasize that when teachers are equipped with AI literacy and feel confident in the use of AI tools, the adoption process becomes significantly smoother and more impactful (Black et al., 2024; Woodruff et al., 2023; Zafeer et al., 2023). Despite these advances, the implementation of AI in schools remains uneven and fraught with challenges. While some institutions are pioneering the use of AI to foster collaborative, inclusive, and data-informed learning environments, others are hindered by structural, technical, and pedagogical constraints. These disparities reflect a larger issue: the readiness and capacity of educational systems to support the responsible integration of AI (Zmir et al., 2021).

The promise of AI in education is compelling, but its realization is contingent upon navigating a complex landscape of limitations. Schools face numerous hurdles from infrastructural inadequacies and professional development gaps to curriculum misalignment and ethical dilemmas. These challenges are often magnified in under-resourced settings, where disparities in internet access, digital device availability, and institutional support create additional barriers to equitable implementation (Zafeer et al., 2023). As such, this chapter critically examines the multifaceted challenges of implementing AI in schools. Drawing on a broad range of research and practice-based insights, it explores the infrastructural, pedagogical, human, ethical, and administrative dimensions of AI integration (Zamir et al., 2021). Through this analysis, we aim to provide a clear and comprehensive understanding of the limitations currently constraining AI's transformative potential in K–12 education.

In this chapter, we describe Shulman's knowledge base (and the way complexity can be investigated using TPACK) by examining pedagogy and curriculum (the interplay between technology, pedagogy, and content) and Diffusion of Innovations to explain asymmetrical adoption (relative advantage, compatibility, complexity, trialability, and observability). It was used as a lens for classroom examples of how SAMR could be a light rubric for depth of change (substituting to redefinition). We draw attention to this lens at the beginning of each new section for continuity throughout the chapter. While SAMR, TPACK, and Rogers' diffusion theory each offer valuable insights, they should not be treated in isolation. UNESCO's competency frameworks for teachers and students emphasise a human-centred mindset, ethics, technical knowledge, and system design. State guidance, such as the Massachusetts AI roadmap, also recommends aligning AI use with curriculum standards, professional development, and legal compliance. By synthesizing SAMR's continuum of transformation with TPACK's balanced knowledge domains, diffusion theory's adoption stages, and these competency frameworks, educators can plan AI implementation as a gradual progression, moving from substitution to redefinition, while ensuring ethical, pedagogical, and curricular alignment at each step (Maqbool et al., 2022; Rehman, Huang, Mahmood, et al., 2024; Zafeer et al., 2021) The discussion begins with a closer look at the foundational layer of AI readiness: the technical and infrastructural challenges that shape what is possible and what remains aspirational in school-based AI implementation.

THEORETICAL FRAMEWORKS FOR AI INTEGRATION

To make sense of the disparate examples and challenges discussed in this chapter, it is helpful to anchor our analysis in established models of educational technology adoption. One widely used model is the SAMR framework, which describes a continuum from Substitution (where AI tools merely replace existing practices, such as automated grading) through Augmentation and Modification to Redefinition, where new technologies enable learning experiences that would be impossible otherwise. Most school-based AI initiatives currently operate at the substitution or augmentation level, indicating that truly transformative uses are still emergent, (Zafeer et al., 2025). A second model is Technological Pedagogical Content Knowledge (TPACK), which emphasizes that effective technology integration requires a balance between teachers' subject expertise (content knowledge), instructional methods (pedagogical knowledge) and understanding of technology's affordances (Rehman, Huang, Sarwar, et al., 2024). AI tools can be powerful only when teachers understand how to align them with curriculum goals and pedagogical strategies, rather than treating them as stand-alone solutions.

Finally, Rogers's Diffusion of Innovations theory explains why some schools adopt AI faster than others. Innovations spread gradually through social systems, influenced by factors such as relative advantage, compatibility with existing values and the presence of "change agents." This perspective highlights the importance of leadership and school culture in moving from early experimentation to widespread adoption (Maqbool, Sarwar, et al., 2020). Across all three frameworks, equitable and transparent implementation is paramount federal guidance warns that AI adoption must "root out bias in the design and use of new technologies" and ensure that students' rights and dignity remain at the centre of innovation.

TECHNICAL AND INFRASTRUCTURE CHALLENGES

While the vision of AI-powered classrooms is gaining global traction, the foundational infrastructure necessary to support such innovation remains inconsistently available particularly across public K–12 schools. The integration of AI technologies into school systems relies not only on access to the latest tools but also on a robust digital ecosystem that can support continuous connectivity, real-time data processing, and equitable access (Zafeer et al., 2025c). Unfortunately, many schools are grappling with infrastructural limitations that hinder the scalability and sustainability of AI adoption.

INFRASTRUCTURE GAPS AND DIGITAL DIVIDES

A recurring obstacle in the implementation of AI in schools is the lack of basic technological infrastructure. In many educational institutions, especially in rural or underfunded regions, internet connectivity is unreliable, bandwidth is insufficient, and devices such as computers and tablets are either outdated or unavailable (Aderibigbe et al., 2023; Saidakhror, 2024). Without these foundational elements, even the most promising AI tools remain inaccessible. These limitations are not just technical they are deeply structural. Research shows that the digital divide disproportionately affects students from low-income backgrounds, further entrenching educational inequity (Barsha & Munshi, 2024; Zhang & Tahir, 2023). While affluent schools may experiment with intelligent tutoring systems or predictive analytics, their less-resourced counterparts often struggle to maintain a functioning Wi-Fi connection, let alone engage in AI-enhanced pedagogy.

Furthermore, many AI solutions require cloud-based access or continuous data synchronization, making consistent internet access a non-negotiable requirement. This presents a serious challenge in communities where broadband infrastructure is weak or prohibitively expensive. Without government intervention and targeted investments, these inequities risk widening the achievement gap, making AI a tool for the privileged rather than a universal asset.

ACCESS TO DIGITAL DEVICES AND RESOURCES

Beyond connectivity, access to digital devices is another limiting factor. In many school districts, the availability of tablets, laptops, or desktops is insufficient to support classroom-wide engagement with AI-powered platforms. Even where devices are available, they are often shared among multiple students or outdated to the point of incompatibility with modern AI software (Polak et al., 2022; Singh et al., 2024). This shortage of hardware not only restricts the practical implementation of AI tools but also affects students' digital literacy. Those without regular access to devices at home or school are less likely to develop the technological fluency needed to benefit from AI-enhanced learning. Consequently, any long-term strategy for AI integration must prioritize equitable device access and consistent maintenance and upgrade cycles. Efforts to provide one-to-one device programs where each student receives a personal laptop or tablet have proven effective in improving AI readiness. However, without parallel investments in cybersecurity, cloud services, and maintenance, these initiatives risk becoming short-lived interventions rather than systemic solutions.

READINESS OF SCHOOL INFRASTRUCTURE FOR AI DEPLOYMENT

Technology readiness encompasses more than devices and connectivity it includes institutional capacity to support and manage AI systems. Many schools are not equipped with the backend infrastructure needed to store and process large volumes of student data securely. Servers, learning management systems, and data analytics tools often operate in isolation, lacking the interoperability required for seamless AI integration (Arvin et al., 2023; Zhang & Tur, 2024). Moreover, AI implementation requires technical personnel with the expertise to maintain complex systems and troubleshoot issues in real time. However, most schools particularly those outside major urban centers lack dedicated IT staff trained in AI-related technologies. This leads to overburdened teachers and administrators who are expected to manage technical problems alongside their core responsibilities.

Research also points to a lack of institutional frameworks that can support experimentation and innovation with AI. In many cases, schools are hesitant to adopt AI tools due to concerns about sustainability, vendor dependence, or the absence of clear long-term strategies. This reflects not only a resource problem but a planning and governance gap that needs to be addressed at both the institutional and policy levels (Casal-Otero et al., 2023; Van Brummelen et al., 2021).

BRIDGING THE GAP: TOWARD EQUITABLE INFRASTRUCTURE

Addressing infrastructure challenges is foundational to any meaningful discussion of AI in education. Without stable access to technology, digital resources, and skilled personnel, AI tools cannot fulfill their potential in enhancing teaching and learning. Equitable infrastructure development targeting the most underserved regions must therefore be a top priority for policymakers, school administrators, and funding agencies (Zafeer et al., 2022). Investments should extend beyond devices and connectivity to include professional IT support, secure data systems, and ongoing evaluation of digital capacity. Public-private partnerships may also play a critical role in accelerating access to AI-ready infrastructure, particularly in developing regions or under-resourced school districts.

As schools lay the groundwork for AI integration, these infrastructural improvements will form the bedrock on which more complex pedagogical, ethical, and administrative challenges must be addressed. In the next section, we turn our attention to one of the most pressing areas of tension: the impact of AI on teaching practices and curriculum design and the limitations that emerge when new technologies are introduced into legacy systems of instruction.

PEDAGOGICAL AND CURRICULUM CHALLENGES

While infrastructure provides the necessary foundation for AI integration, it is the pedagogy the art and science of teaching that determines its actual impact on learning. As AI tools begin to permeate classrooms, questions arise about how they align with existing teaching methodologies, curricular goals, and instructional philosophies (Zafeer et al., 2020). Despite their potential to enhance educational delivery, AI technologies often encounter systemic friction when introduced into traditional classroom practices, exposing a range of pedagogical and curricular challenges.

Shifting Teaching Methodologies in the AI Era

The integration of AI technologies in K–12 education is prompting a gradual shift from traditional, teacher-centered instruction to more personalized, student-driven learning. AI-powered systems can now deliver differentiated instruction, adjust content in real-time, and offer immediate feedback tailored to individual learners (Casal-Otero et al., 2023; Maqbool et al., 2024). This shift holds the promise of transforming how students engage with content, allowing for deeper learning and increased motivation. However, this pedagogical transformation is not without complications. Many teachers find themselves caught between longstanding instructional norms and the demands of AI-enhanced practices. The introduction of AI often challenges conventional teaching strategies by requiring a reconfiguration of lesson planning, assessment design, and classroom management approaches (Rathore et al., 2023; Zafeer, Maqbool, et al., 2022). Educators are asked not only to teach but also to curate content, analyze data, and co-facilitate learning with intelligent systems roles for which many are not adequately prepared.

Moreover, the risk of over-reliance on AI in teaching raises concerns about diminished teacher-student interaction. AI tools may efficiently handle content delivery and assessment, but they cannot replicate the empathy, intuition, and cultural sensitivity that human educators bring to the learning process (Karan & Angadi, 2023). As such, pedagogical models must strike a balance between leveraging AI's strengths and preserving the essential human elements of teaching.

CURRICULUM LIMITATIONS AND INFLEXIBILITY

Despite the growing momentum behind AI in education, most K–12 curricula remain slow to adapt. In many educational systems, curriculum frameworks are rigid, standardized, and slow-moving designed more for administrative accountability than for technological agility (Warr & Heath, 2025). This inflexibility makes it difficult to meaningfully integrate AI into existing content areas or to introduce new AI-related subjects. One significant limitation is the lack of structured curriculum content dedicated to AI itself (Zafeer et al., 2025). While students may interact with AI-driven tools, they are rarely taught the underlying principles, ethical considerations, or societal implications of the technology. The absence of AI education as a formal curricular component represents a missed opportunity to prepare learners for a digital future in which AI will be ubiquitous (Karataş et al., 2025; Pucchio et al., 2022).

Besides, existing subjects often lack the modularity required to incorporate AI applications. Teachers may find it challenging to integrate AI-supported projects into rigid lesson plans that are dictated by national standards or high-stakes testing requirements. Without curricular flexibility and institutional support, educators may be discouraged from experimenting with AI tools, even when they recognize their potential.

Misalignment with National and Local Education Standards

Another major barrier to AI integration lies in the misalignment between available technologies and formal educational standards. Many AI tools are developed in isolation from the academic benchmarks that govern school curricula. As a result, there is often a disconnect between what AI systems offer adaptive quizzes, predictive analytics, gamified learning and what teachers are mandated to teach and assess according to national or local guidelines (Alenezi, 2024; Maqbool et al., 2023; Schleiss et al., 2023). Frameworks like TPACK (Technological Pedagogical Content Knowledge) offer guidance for integrating technology in ways that respect pedagogical goals. Yet, in practice, these frameworks are rarely translated into actionable policy or professional practice at the school level. Teachers are left without clear direction on how to align AI tool usage with assessment criteria, curriculum pacing, or subject-specific learning outcomes (Ng et al., 2023). Without systemic alignment, even the most advanced AI applications risk being underutilized or misapplied. To address this, policymakers must collaborate with educators and technology developers to create guidelines that ensure AI tools enhance not disrupt curriculum coherence and instructional quality.

Toward a Pedagogically Grounded Use of AI

To overcome these curricular and instructional challenges, schools must adopt a pedagogically grounded approach to AI integration. This begins with rethinking curriculum design to include space for AI literacy, ethical exploration, and interdisciplinary learning. Curricula should not only accommodate AI-enhanced instruction but also prepare students to be critical, informed users and creators of AI technologies (Maqbool, Wei, et al., 2020). Simultaneously, professional development must empower teachers to use AI tools as extensions of their pedagogical expertise, rather than as replacements. Instructional innovation should be supported by flexible curricula, clear guidelines, and sufficient time for experimentation and adaptation. As schools adapt to the realities of AI-enhanced learning, the human element remains paramount. AI can support instruction, but it cannot define pedagogy. Teachers must remain at the center of the educational process facilitators, mentors, and mediators of meaning in an increasingly digital classroom.

With pedagogical and curricular challenges now outlined, we turn in the next section to a closely related domain: the role of teachers themselves, and the specific barriers they face in engaging with AI technologies in practice.

Curriculum Alignment and AI Literacy

Effective AI integration requires aligning AI use with existing curriculum standards and digital-literacy frameworks. The Massachusetts Department of Elementary and Secondary Education recommends that districts "align classroom AI use with core content curriculum frameworks and Digital Literacy and Computer Science standards" and identify subject areas where AI enhances inquiry, creativity, and analysis (Massachusetts Department of & Secondary, 2024). Schools should therefore assess where AI helps students meet content standards, embed AI-related experiences within courses, and ensure equitable access to age-appropriate tools. UNESCO's AI competency framework for students outlines twelve competencies across four dimensions human-centered mindset, ethics of AI, AI techniques & applications, and AI system design organized into the progression levels Understand, Apply, and Create (Miao & Shiohira, 2024; Zafeer et al., 2024). These competencies emphasize critical judgement, citizenship responsibilities, and inclusive design.

Table 1. UNESCO AI competency dimensions and progression levels

Dimension	Understand	Apply	Create
Human-centered mindset	Recognize AI's human impact and agency	Reflect on AI's benefits and risks; show empathy	Advocate for inclusive design
Ethics of AI	Identify fairness and privacy concerns	Practice data protection and bias mitigation	Design ethically responsible AI solutions
AI techniques & applications	Explain basic AI concepts	Use AI tools responsibly in projects	Build simple AI applications and evaluate outcomes
AI system design	Describe how AI systems are built	Modify existing AI workflows to solve problems	Plan and prototype new AI systems

Teachers' Attitudes Toward AI in Classrooms

Teachers' willingness to engage with AI tools is heavily influenced by their beliefs about the relevance, reliability, and ethical implications of these technologies. While many educators recognize the potential of AI to support personalized learning and improve instructional efficiency, others remain cautious if not skeptical about its impact on pedagogy and student development (Maqbool et al., 2024). Studies show that concerns over job displacement, dehumanization of learning, and erosion of the teacher-student relationship continue to shape teachers' perceptions of AI (Zormanová, 2024). Some fear that AI systems may eventually undermine the role of educators, reducing them to overseers of algorithm-driven instruction rather than facilitators of meaningful engagement.

These attitudes are further compounded by apprehensions surrounding data privacy, algorithmic bias, and the opaque decision-making processes behind many AI systems. When teachers do not fully understand how AI works or how its decisions are made they are less likely to trust its outputs, particularly in high-stakes contexts like grading or academic placement (Maqbool et al., 2025). Building positive attitudes toward AI, therefore, requires more than technical demonstrations; it requires transparent communication, evidence of pedagogical alignment, and reassurance that AI is a tool for enhancement not replacement.

Gaps in Teacher Training and Professional Development

Perhaps the most significant barrier to effective AI adoption is the widespread lack of teacher training. Most educators especially those trained before the digital era have not received formal instruction in AI literacy, ethical data use, or technology integration. As a result, they may feel unprepared to use AI tools meaningfully or to guide students in understanding their implications. Professional development offerings, where they exist, often focus on general digital tools rather than AI-specific competencies. Teachers are rarely provided with opportunities to engage in hands-on learning with AI systems, explore real-world classroom applications, or discuss the ethical and social ramifications of these technologies.

Moreover, professional development is frequently treated as a one-time event rather than an ongoing process. Yet, given the rapid pace of technological advancement, teachers require continuous training and support to stay abreast of emerging tools and pedagogical approaches (Maqbool et al.).As of fall 2024, roughly half of U.S. school districts reported providing some form of generative-AI training, with high-poverty districts lagging behind, and more than 70 percent of teachers said they had received no AI-related professional development (Diliberti et al., 2025; Schwartz, 2024). Without this, even well-intentioned teachers may revert to traditional methods, underutilizing or misapplying the AI systems available to them.

To bridge this gap, schools and districts must invest in sustained, practice-oriented professional development programs that empower teachers to become informed decision-makers and innovators in their own classrooms.

PRACTICAL AND INSTITUTIONAL BARRIERS

Beyond mindset and training, teachers also face structural obstacles that inhibit AI adoption. Time constraints are a major factor educators already operate under intense workloads, and learning to use new AI tools requires time for exploration, experimentation, and integration into existing lesson plans (Kitcharoen et al., 2024). Additionally, institutional support for AI integration is often lacking. Teachers may not receive the technical assistance, administrative backing, or curricular flexibility needed to pilot new tools effectively. Without a collaborative, school-wide culture that encourages innovation, even the most capable teachers may feel isolated or unsupported in their efforts to use AI (Ng et al., 2023).

Furthermore, disparities in access to infrastructure across schools mean that some teachers are better positioned to adopt AI than others. Those working in underfunded or rural districts may lack the basic resources devices, internet access, software licenses needed to implement AI tools at all, let alone evaluate their pedagogical value. Lastly, ethical ambiguities and a lack of clear policy guidelines leave many educators unsure of how to navigate AI responsibly. Questions about data collection, student consent, and algorithmic decision-making are often left unanswered, placing an additional burden on teachers to make ethical judgments without institutional guidance (Dr. Khaled, 2024).

EMPOWERING TEACHERS AS AI NAVIGATORS

Despite these challenges, teachers remain the single most important factor in determining the success of AI in education. AI systems may be sophisticated, but they cannot replace the judgment, empathy, and contextual understanding that educators bring to the learning process. To harness the potential of AI meaningfully, schools must invest in the professional agency of teachers equipping them not just with tools, but with knowledge, time, and voice. This includes embedding AI literacy into teacher education programs, fostering interdisciplinary collaboration, and creating safe spaces for professional experimentation. In short, AI should serve teachers not the other way around. And until educators are fully supported in this transition, the promise of AI in education will remain partially fulfilled.

With the human element of teaching explored, the next section addresses a set of critical questions that underpin much of the hesitation around AI adoption: issues of ethics, data privacy, and equity, particularly in how AI technologies affect vulnerable or marginalized student populations.

STUDENT AND COMMUNITY PERSPECTIVES ON AI

Recent surveys show that students are already engaging heavily with generative-AI tools. In a 2024 Common Sense Media/APA study, seven in ten U.S. teenagers reported using AI for homework and research, and about half did so with their teacher's permission (Madden et al., 2024). Many of these students described feeling both excited and anxious: they appreciated AI's ability to suggest ideas, yet they checked outputs against other sources and worried about misinformation and job prospects. European surveys indicate that 74 percent of students believe AI will be critical to their future careers, yet fewer than half feel adequately prepared and nearly half worry that AI could deepen inequalities (Felton, 2023). Parents share these mixed feelings. A 2024 survey found that 93 percent of parents were concerned about AI in schools, with 51 percent worried about inappropriate content, 50 percent worried about biased or incorrect AI outputs, and 46 percent worried about data privacy (Gen Digital, 2024). Despite these concerns, 69 percent of parents supported AI for research and 49 percent approved of AI-assisted schoolwork. These findings underscore the need for transparent communication, culturally responsive design, and digital citizenship education. They also highlight that Black students are disproportionately flagged by AI-detectors (Madden et al., 2024), emphasising the importance of fairness and inclusivity in AI deployment.

ETHICAL USE OF AI IN TEACHING AND LEARNING

One of the foundational ethical challenges in AI-based education is the lack of transparency in how AI systems function. Many AI tools operate as "black boxes," making decisions about student performance, learning pathways, or assessments without clearly explaining how those decisions were reached (Chan & Zary, 2019). This lack of explain ability raises serious concerns about accountability and fairness. Furthermore, AI systems are typically trained on large datasets, and if these datasets reflect social biases, the systems can perpetuate or even amplify inequality. For instance, students from marginalized backgrounds may be unfairly labeled as "low performing" due to biased data or poorly contextualized algorithms (George & Wooden, 2023). Without rigorous oversight, AI may reinforce stereotypes, influence teacher expectations, and shape student experiences in harmful ways.

Teachers and school leaders are also navigating a shifting professional landscape, where AI systems may recommend instructional content, assessments, or interventions that override or even conflict with their professional judgment (Maqbool et al., 2014). This poses ethical questions about teacher autonomy and the integrity of pedagogical decisions. To navigate these tensions, schools need clear ethical frameworks that define the appropriate boundaries of AI use in instruction. Educators should be empowered not only to use AI but also to question and critique it, ensuring that decisions remain grounded in educational values and human-centered reasoning. Explainable AI (XAI) helps teachers and students understand how AI systems generate recommendations, making transparency critical for accountability and trust. Practical XAI features include traceable feedback, instructor override, and institutional audit trails, all of which allow educators to challenge or refine AI outputs when necessary.

Schools should adopt data-governance policies aligned with key privacy laws, emphasising data minimization, strong security measures, careful vendor vetting, and clear procedures for parental consent. These safeguards protect student rights while maintaining public confidence in AI use. Culturally responsive AI requires training models on diverse datasets and accommodating local languages. Research shows that some student groups are disproportionately flagged by AI detectors, and underrepresented communities often lack access to tailored content. Ethical frameworks should therefore include regular bias audits, community input, and mechanisms for students and parents to opt out of AI systems. Embedding ethical reflection and transparency in everyday classroom routines helps students critically engage with AI, turning technology from an opaque tool into a subject of inquiry and dialogue.

STUDENT DATA PRIVACY AND SECURITY

AI systems depend heavily on data to function often collecting detailed information about students' academic behavior, cognitive patterns, emotional states, and even biometric responses. This level of surveillance raises urgent concerns about data privacy, student consent, and potential misuse. In many school systems, data protection laws have not kept pace with the capabilities of modern AI. Students and parents are frequently unaware of how much data is being collected, who has access to it, or how long it is stored (Sabharwal et al., 2023; Shtayyat et al., 2025). The use of commercial AI products in classrooms some of which may use data for marketing or third-party analysis exacerbates these risks.

Breaches of student data not only compromise safety but also undermine trust. Once compromised, personal educational data can have long-term consequences for students' reputations, educational opportunities, or mental well-being. Moreover, because children are a legally protected population, the ethical obligation to safeguard their data is even greater. To protect student privacy, schools must implement transparent data governance policies that define what data is collected, how it is secured, and who is accountable for its use. These policies must comply with legal frameworks like FERPA or GDPR, but they must also go further ensuring that privacy is treated not as a technical requirement but as an ethical imperative.

EQUITY AND INCLUSION IN AI ACCESS

AI is often framed as a democratizing force in education capable of closing achievement gaps and providing personalized support for every learner. However, the reality is more complicated. In practice, AI implementation often reflects and reproduces existing inequities, particularly when it comes to access and representation. Students from underprivileged communities frequently lack the devices, internet connectivity, and digital skills required to benefit from AI technologies (Danial et al., 2022; Trang & Thu, 2024). Without targeted interventions, the very tools designed to support learning can end up deepening educational divides giving more advantages to those who already have them, while leaving others further behind.

In addition, the design of many AI tools fails to reflect the diversity of student populations. AI systems trained on non-representative data may ignore cultural contexts, learning styles, and linguistic diversity, thereby marginalizing students whose backgrounds differ from the assumed norm (Al-Jarf, 2021; Ikevuje et al., 2023). Inclusive AI design must begin with diverse data and include input from educators, students, and communities who understand the nuances of their local educational needs. Financial constraints further complicate access. Schools in economically disadvantaged areas are often unable to invest in AI technologies or the infrastructure required to support them. Without sustained public funding and strategic partnerships, these communities risk being excluded from the AI-driven transformation of education (Fatmawati et al., 2025). Ultimately, AI should not be viewed as a one-size-fits-all solution. It must be implemented thoughtfully, with attention to the cultural, linguistic, socio-economic, and cognitive diversity of student populations. This means designing for equity from the start not retrofitting inclusivity as an afterthought.

THE IMPERATIVE FOR RESPONSIBLE AI IN EDUCATION

As AI becomes a more permanent fixture in K–12 education, the stakes grow higher. The decisions we make today about data privacy, algorithmic transparency, ethical boundaries, and equitable access will shape how education systems serve (or fail) future generations. The responsible use of AI requires more than policy compliance. It demands a values-based approach that prioritizes student dignity, educational justice, and institutional accountability. Teachers and school leaders must be empowered to ask hard questions, challenge unjust systems, and advocate for learners who may be left behind in the rush toward digital innovation. In the next section, we explore another critical dimension of AI implementation: the role of policy and school leadership in either enabling or impeding systemic integration of AI technologies in education.

POLICY AND ADMINISTRATIVE LIMITATIONS

While technical readiness, pedagogical alignment, and ethical awareness are crucial to AI integration in schools, the role of policy and administrative leadership is equally foundational. The deployment of AI at scale requires more than isolated pilot programs or enthusiastic teachers it demands coherent strategies, supportive regulations, and institutional leadership capable of bridging the gap between innovation and implementation. Unfortunately, educational systems often fall short in these areas. Across regions, AI integration is constrained by fragmented policy environments, vague regulatory frameworks, and school leadership that lacks the training, authority, or resources to drive systemic change.

Inadequate Educational Policy Frameworks

One of the most critical barriers to AI adoption in K–12 education is the absence of robust, forward-looking policy frameworks. Most national and regional education policies are not designed to accommodate the complex requirements of AI implementation. They may include general guidelines on digital literacy or ICT use but rarely address AI-specific issues such as algorithmic accountability, ethical deployment, or data governance (Lotfi & Laajan, 2025; Obioha Val, 2024). This policy vacuum creates uncertainty for schools attempting to adopt AI. Without clear mandates or legal backing, administrators are left to make high-stakes decisions about technology procurement, data use, and curriculum design with little institutional support. Moreover, the lack of standardization across districts and countries leads to wide disparities in how AI is understood, deployed, and evaluated.

Research shows that in the absence of coherent national policies, schools often adopt reactive or fragmented approaches implementing AI tools without long-term planning, pedagogical coherence, or evaluation metrics (Roshan et al., 2024). This piecemeal approach undermines the sustainability and scalability of AI initiatives, relegating them to short-term experiments rather than systemic reforms.

SCHOOL LEADERSHIP AND ADMINISTRATIVE CHALLENGES

The successful integration of AI depends not only on what policies say but on how school leaders interpret, implement, and support those policies. Yet many administrators face substantial challenges when attempting to bring AI into their institutions. First, few school leaders have received training in AI literacy or strategic technology leadership. As a result, they may struggle to evaluate AI tools, manage vendor relationships, or ensure ethical implementation (Kim & Wargo, 2025). The technical complexity of AI can intimidate even experienced administrators, leading to hesitation or over-reliance on external consultants with limited understanding of educational contexts. Second, resistance from staff rooted in concerns about job displacement, increased workload, or ethical implications often falls to administrators to address. School leaders must play a critical role in fostering buy-in, promoting professional development, and building a culture that embraces innovation without fear. However, doing so requires time, resources, and institutional autonomy that many leaders simply do not have (Kim & Wargo, 2025; Purba et al., 2025).

Finally, administrators are caught between competing demands: meeting short-term academic targets, complying with outdated accountability systems, and navigating evolving expectations for digital transformation. Without systemic support, many find themselves forced to prioritize immediate operational concerns over long-term strategic planning leaving AI adoption underdeveloped or abandoned.

REGULATORY AND GOVERNANCE CONSTRAINTS

Beyond school walls, the broader regulatory environment presents further complications. Most legal systems lag behind the technological advances unfolding in schools, offering little clarity on AI-related responsibilities, rights, or liabilities (Jeongwan, 2023).

Key areas of concern include:

- **Data protection**: Existing laws like FERPA (in the U.S.) or GDPR (in Europe) offer some guidance on student privacy but may not account for the scale and sensitivity of data collected by AI systems.
- **Procurement and compliance**: Schools face unclear or restrictive rules when selecting AI vendors, raising concerns about cost, accountability, and the long-term sustainability of commercial products.
- **Algorithmic fairness**: There are few legal precedents or regulatory safeguards addressing bias, discrimination, or opacity in AI-driven educational decisions.
- **Interoperability**: Without standards for data exchange, schools often struggle to integrate AI tools into existing digital ecosystems hindering efficiency and raising risks of data fragmentation.

In the absence of comprehensive regulation, schools operate in a legal gray area vulnerable to privacy breaches, inequitable practices, and public backlash. To address these concerns, governments and education authorities must develop AI-specific regulatory frameworks that ensure transparency, accountability, and alignment with democratic values.

BUILDING INSTITUTIONAL READINESS THROUGH POLICY AND LEADERSHIP

Policy and leadership are not merely administrative functions they are levers for transformation. To overcome systemic barriers, educational leaders at all levels must shift from passive compliance to proactive vision-setting. This includes:

1. Developing national AI strategies for education that clarify goals, responsibilities, and ethical boundaries.
2. Supporting school leaders with AI-specific training, funding, and decision-making autonomy.
3. Encouraging cross-sector collaboration between educators, technologists, and policymakers to align AI development with real-world educational needs.
4. Creating feedback loops that allow schools to inform policy through lived experience, ensuring that regulations evolve alongside practice.

AI's transformative potential will not be realized through isolated efforts or ad hoc initiatives. It requires coordinated leadership grounded in ethics, equity, and educational purpose to shape systems where AI enhances rather than disrupts the human mission of education. In the next section, we move from abstract challenges to practical insights by examining real-world case studies and documented failures, which reveal how these limitations play out on the ground and what lessons they offer for the future of AI in schools.

CASE STUDIES AND REAL-WORLD FAILURES

The promises of artificial intelligence in education often come tempered by the realities of practice. While many schools and districts have experimented with AI implementation through pilot programs and technological interventions, numerous case studies reveal that the path to effective adoption is fraught with setbacks, missteps, and unintended consequences. These documented failures offer critical insights not only into the limitations of AI technologies themselves but also into the structural, pedagogical, and cultural challenges that schools must address to realize AI's potential.

One recurring theme in these case studies is the misalignment between the design of AI tools and the educational realities they are meant to serve. In a study by (Tyson & Sauers, 2021), school leaders implementing the ALEKS platform encountered significant challenges in teacher buy-in and system integration. Although the tool was intended to personalize instruction, educators expressed concerns about the accuracy of the system's assessments and the relevance of its feedback. These concerns were exacerbated by a lack of comprehensive training and limited alignment with classroom objectives, leading to underuse and skepticism toward the technology. Similarly, (Aldous & Ismail, 2025) explored the application of AI for school health and safety monitoring. Despite its technical sophistication, the AI system's effectiveness was hampered by infrastructural limitations and an institutional culture unprepared for automation. Teachers felt untrained in using the system and were hesitant to rely on AI for safety-critical decisions, highlighting a broader tension between technological ambition and human trust. The case reinforces the lesson that successful AI deployment must be accompanied by robust support structures and confidence-building measures among staff. (, 2025) Guo examination of AI in music education revealed another form of disconnect this time between curricular rigidity and the adaptive possibilities of AI. While the technology demonstrated potential for individualizing instruction, teachers struggled to reconcile its use with existing curriculum constraints and performance standards. The tool, though well-designed, could not overcome the structural limitations imposed by assessment-driven systems, leading to minimal pedagogical innovation despite substantial investment.

Other cases underscore the dangers of insufficient ethical foresight. (Kim, 2024) reported that the use of learning analytics in STEM education raised concerns about student consent, data misuse, and algorithmic opacity. Teachers questioned the validity of AI-generated insights and expressed discomfort with making instructional decisions based on black-box systems. The lack of transparency not only undermined trust but also provoked resistance from both educators and parents, revealing the critical need for explain ability and ethical governance in AI applications. Even efforts that showed initial success were often derailed by financial and logistical obstacles. In the case described by (Purba et al., 2025), schools that adopted AI to support primary education encountered sustainability issues once pilot funding ended. Without a long-term financial plan, schools could not afford to maintain the tools or provide ongoing training, leading to the eventual collapse of the initiative. The authors emphasized that effective AI integration requires not only short-term enthusiasm but sustained institutional commitment and resourcing.

Meanwhile, efforts to implement AI for emergency preparedness, as detailed by (Aldous & Ismail, 2025), revealed the difficulties of integrating AI tools with pre-existing school safety protocols. Teachers expressed anxiety about using unfamiliar systems in high-pressure situations, and the lack of consistent training across staff led to uneven adoption. The result was a fragmented deployment that fell short of its original promise, emphasizing the importance of coordinated planning and capacity-building. Cultural and perceptual barriers also emerged as significant hindrances. In the study conducted by (Roberts & Richardson, 2025), school leaders noted that stakeholder disagreement over the role of AI often stalled implementation. Concerns from teachers about professional autonomy, along with parental fears about data privacy, created a climate of caution that slowed institutional buy-in. This case illustrates how resistance, even in technologically equipped environments, can stem from deep-rooted values and legitimate concerns, not just technical deficiencies.

From a curricular standpoint, the analysis presented in "Designing AI-driven Curriculum and Assessment" (2024) confirmed that curriculum inflexibility remains a major bottleneck in AI integration. Educators involved in the study noted that while AI tools could enhance student learning through personalization and real-time feedback, their use was often constrained by rigid pacing guides and standardized testing schedules. The disconnect between dynamic AI systems and static curricula led to frustration among teachers and reduced the transformative potential of the technology. In a case focused on the development of a smart analytics framework, (Abisoye, 2024) found that despite the promise of AI in STEM education, issues related to inclusivity and access persisted. Schools serving marginalized communities faced infrastructural gaps that made it difficult to use AI tools effectively, even when pedagogical support was available. Moreover, students from underrepresented backgrounds often did not see themselves reflected in the AI content, highlighting the importance of culturally responsive design. Even promising strategies faltered when stakeholders lacked clarity on ethical boundaries. The AI My Data curriculum, introduced by (Sanusi et al., 2024), integrated machine learning with ethical education for middle school students. Although the initiative successfully engaged learners in critical reflection, it also revealed inconsistencies in teacher preparedness to handle discussions on data ethics, bias, and algorithmic decision-making. This underlines the need for dual emphasis on both technological fluency and ethical literacy in teacher training.

Ultimately, the case studies reviewed across these various contexts paint a common picture: AI in education is not a turnkey solution. Its success depends on thoughtful design, sustained investment, institutional readiness, ethical safeguards, and above all, active human involvement. The documented failures do not suggest that AI has no place in education; rather, they underscore that meaningful adoption must be deeply contextualized, inclusive, and anchored in the lived realities of teaching and learning.

These real-world insights provide a crucial foundation for moving forward. For example, the adaptive learning platform Siyavula in South Africa leverages AI to personalise mathematics practice for under-resourced learners. By 2024 the platform had reached 1.5 million students and helped students in rural areas achieve parity with their urban peers. In Singapore, the Ministry of Education's Student Learning Space uses predictive analytics to flag at-risk learners, contributing to a 10% drop in failure rates. Mexico's VirtuLab uses immersive AI simulations in science classes and reported a 40% increase in student engagement. India's Modern School adopted AI-driven essay-scoring systems that reduced teacher workload and provided real-time feedback. Nigeria's Smart Class and Kenya's M-Shule adapt content to local languages and individual learning profiles, demonstrating the importance of cultural relevance and data privacy. These examples illustrate that AI can succeed when designed for local contexts, aligned with curricula and accompanied by teacher training and ethical safeguards. In the final section of this chapter, we turn to forward-looking strategies that can guide schools, educators, and policymakers in overcoming these challenges and unlocking the transformative potential of AI in education.

DOCUMENTED FAILURES AND LIMITATIONS IN AI-POWERED SCHOOL INITIATIVES

While artificial intelligence continues to be championed as a transformative force in education, many documented initiatives in school settings have not achieved their intended outcomes. Across various pilot programs and implementation efforts, persistent limitations both technical and systemic have emerged. These setbacks not only illustrate the complexity of integrating AI into school systems but also underscore the critical need for ethical foresight, institutional readiness, and teacher involvement from the earliest stages of planning. One of the most recurring limitations involves the disconnect between the design of AI tools and the pedagogical realities of classrooms. As (Nazaretsky et al., 2021) point out, teachers often distrust AI-generated recommendations when they conflict with their professional judgment and understanding of students' needs. In cases where AI tools suggest interventions based on rigid or opaque criteria, educators are left unsure about the logic behind those decisions. This misalignment can result in skepticism, inconsistent usage, or outright rejection of the technology.

Ethical concerns have also been at the center of several AI implementation failures. (Babu & Jeneliya, 2025) emphasizes the importance of developing generative AI systems that align with ethical instructional design. However, in practice, many schools have deployed AI tools without sufficient attention to ethical considerations such as bias, fairness, and data governance. The absence of transparency in how student data is collected, analyzed, and used often leads to stakeholder resistance. In some instances, as observed by (Woodruff et al., 2023), teachers express discomfort with automated assessments that do not account for the socio-emotional aspects of learning, which cannot be captured through algorithms alone. Resource constraints represent another widespread limitation. (da Silva et al., 2024) highlight how insufficient funding and infrastructure have impeded the continuity of AI projects. Schools that initially adopt AI systems under external funding often struggle to sustain them after pilot phases conclude. Without consistent investment in technical support, hardware upgrades, and teacher training, even successful AI programs are vulnerable to collapse. This scenario played out in several cases where promising AI initiatives were abandoned due to lack of long-term financial planning (Purba et al., 2025).

Teacher training is another critical area where implementation frequently falters. (Velmurugan et al., 2025) argue that many teachers lack access to professional development focused on AI, resulting in low confidence and competence in using these tools. In several documented cases, educators received limited or one-time training sessions that did not prepare them for real-time decision-making with AI-powered platforms. The lack of ongoing support, combined with the complexity of the technologies, created barriers to effective adoption. In addition to training gaps, misalignment with curriculum frameworks presents a significant limitation. Zhunussov (Жунусов, 2024) notes that AI tools often struggle to integrate with traditional curricula that prioritize standardized content and assessment. Teachers in his study reported that while AI platforms offered adaptive content and real-time feedback, they had little flexibility to act on these insights due to fixed pacing guides and testing schedules. This constraint diminishes the pedagogical value of AI and reinforces the perception that it is an add-on rather than an integrated part of instruction.

Another notable issue is that many AI systems fail to accommodate diverse learning needs. (Woodruff et al., 2023) found that students with special educational needs or language barriers are often underserved by generic AI models. This limitation is exacerbated when teachers have no means of modifying the AI's parameters or interpreting its logic. As a result, the technology inadvertently reinforces inequities, leading teachers to disengage from platforms they view as insufficiently inclusive. At the leadership level, administrative challenges are often responsible for undermining AI efforts. (Roberts & Richardson, 2025) point out that inconsistent leadership, poor communication with stakeholders, and lack of ethical governance have all contributed to failed implementations. School administrators are frequently caught between the desire to innovate and the pressure to conform to policy frameworks that have not yet evolved to accommodate AI. This tension results in cautious, fragmented adoption strategies that lack coherence and long-term vision.

Some initiatives also suffer from cultural resistance, particularly in communities where digital literacy is limited or where AI is viewed as a threat to traditional teaching values. (Borasi et al., 2024) detail how fear of dehumanization and loss of pedagogical autonomy caused significant pushback among teachers, leading to disengagement and, in some cases, active resistance to AI tools. These sentiments are not unfounded, as overreliance on AI can marginalize teacher input and obscure the relational dimensions of education that are essential to student development. Feedback mechanisms are another area where limitations are evident. (Velmurugan et al., 2025) emphasize the importance of teacher feedback in the successful deployment of AI, yet many programs fail to implement responsive, iterative design processes. Once deployed, AI systems are rarely adjusted based on classroom realities or teacher concerns. This rigidity undermines the dynamic potential of AI and prevents the co-construction of solutions that truly serve educational goals.

Furthermore, the limitations of AI tools in addressing cross-disciplinary or non-STEM subjects continue to emerge. As noted by (Jantanukul, 2024), while AI has shown promise in enhancing STEM education, its adaptation to humanities or creative fields remains underdeveloped. Teachers in these areas often report that AI tools do not align with the nature of their content or the skills they aim to cultivate, such as interpretation, emotional expression, and critical reflection. These documented failures and limitations point to a common conclusion: AI cannot be introduced into schools as a self-contained solution. Successful integration demands comprehensive planning that addresses not only technological compatibility but also pedagogical alignment, teacher empowerment, cultural readiness, and ethical safeguards. Without these supporting conditions, even the most promising tools are likely to falter in practice.

These cases offer more than a critique they serve as valuable learning opportunities. The limitations described here have informed more refined implementation strategies, emphasizing stakeholder engagement, iterative design, and ethical integration. In the next section, we turn our attention to pilot programs that have learned from these early missteps and developed more sustainable, inclusive, and effective models for AI use in education.

CONCLUSION

The integration of artificial intelligence into K–12 education has emerged as a defining issue of contemporary educational reform. AI's promise lies not only in its ability to automate routine instructional processes but also in its potential to personalize learning, support differentiated instruction, and reshape pedagogical relationships. Yet this potential remains tempered by significant technical, ethical, curricular, and institutional challenges that must be addressed with nuance, foresight, and equity in mind. A critical insight from this review is that the implementation of AI in schools is far from a purely technical endeavour it is a deeply human one. The path forward therefore requires vigilance, vision, and above all, partnership. Policymakers, educators, developers, and communities must work together to ensure that AI technologies are implemented in ways that are ethical, inclusive, and pedagogically meaningful. If these conditions are met, AI has the potential not only to transform classrooms but also to help reimagine education as more personalized, just, and responsive to the diverse needs of twenty-first-century learners.

RECOMMENDATIONS AND FUTURE DIRECTIONS

To realise AI's promise while addressing its challenges, schools should adopt a phased, evidence-based approach. First, create AI "sandboxes" or pilot programmes that allow educators to experiment with AI tools in controlled settings and evaluate impacts on learning and equity before scaling. Second, use readiness checklists and maturity models such as those developed by CoSN and the Council of the Great City Schools to assess infrastructure, policy, and literacy preparedness across schools (CoSn, 2024). Third, co-design curricula with teachers, students, and communities, aligning AI use with academic standards and digital-literacy frameworks, and ensuring age-appropriate access. Finally, develop sustainable funding models by combining public resources with philanthropic and private partnerships and by planning for maintenance and evaluation rather than one-off pilots. Together, these recommendations provide a roadmap for equitable, ethical and effective AI integration in K–12 education.

REFERENCES

Жунусов, Е. (2024). РОЛЬ ИСКУССТВЕННОГО ИНТЕЛЛЕКТА В СОВРЕМЕННОМ ОБРАЗОВАНИИ: ПРЕИМУЩЕСТВА, ВЫЗОВЫ И ПУТИ К УСПЕХУ. *Вестник Северо-Казахстанского Университета им. М. Козыбаева*, (2 (62)), 180–188.

Abisoye, A. (2024). Creating a Conceptual Framework for AI-Powered STEM Education Analytics to Enhance Student Learning Outcomes. *International Journal of Research and Innovation in Social Science*.

Aderibigbe, A. O., Ohenhen, P. E., Nwaobia, N. K., Gidiagba, J. O., & Ani, E. C.Adebayo Olusegun AderibigbePeter Efosa OhenhenNwabueze Kelvin Nwaobia-Joachim Osheyor GidiagbaEmmanuel Chigozie Ani. (2023). Artificial intelligence in developing countries: Bridging the gap between potential and implementation. *Computer Science & IT Research Journal*, *4*(3), 185–199. DOI: 10.51594/csitrj.v4i3.629

Al-Jarf, R. (2021). Investigating digital equity in distance education in Saudi Arabia during the COVID-19 pandemic. Conference proceedings of» eLearning and Software for Education «(eLSE), Aldous, S. M., & Ismail, G. A. (2025). AI for Sustainable Emergency Preparedness and Response in Schools. In *Convergence of AI, Education, and Business for Sustainability* (pp. 51-74). IGI Global Scientific Publishing.

Alenezi, A. (2024). *Obstacles to the Use of AI Applications in Blackboard for Faculty Members at Northern Border University*. MIER Journal of Educational Studies Trends and Practices. DOI: 10.52634/mier/2024/v14/i2/2581

Arvin, N., Hoseinabady, M., Bayat, B., & Zahmatkesh, E. (2023). Teacher experiences with ai-based educational tools. *AI and Tech in Behavioral and Social Sciences*, *1*(2), 26–32. DOI: 10.61838/kman.aitech.1.2.5

Babu, C. S., & Jeneliya, J. S. (2025). Ethical Uses of Generative Artificial Intelligence in Instructional Design: Case Strategies for Responsible Implementation. In *Transformative AI Practices for Personalized Learning Strategies* (pp. 219-268). IGI Global Scientific Publishing.

Barsha, S., & Munshi, S. A. (2024). Implementing artificial intelligence in library services: A review of current prospects and challenges of developing countries. *Library Hi Tech News*, *41*(1), 7–10. DOI: 10.1108/LHTN-07-2023-0126

Black, N. B., George, S., Eguchi, A., Dempsey, J. C., Langran, E., Fraga, L., Brunvand, S., & Howard, N. (2024). A framework for approaching AI education in educator preparation programs. Proceedings of the AAAI Conference on Artificial Intelligence, Borasi, R., Miller, D. E., Vaughan-Brogan, P., DeAngelis, K., Han, Y. J., & Mason, S. (2024). An AI wishlist from school leaders. *Phi Delta Kappan*, *105*(8), 48–51.

Casal-Otero, L., Catala, A., Fernández-Morante, C., Taboada, M., Cebreiro, B., & Barro, S. (2023). AI literacy in K-12: A systematic literature review. *International Journal of STEM Education*, *10*(1), 29. DOI: 10.1186/s40594-023-00418-7

Chan, K. S., & Zary, N. (2019). Applications and challenges of implementing artificial intelligence in medical education: Integrative review. *JMIR Medical Education*, *5*(1), e13930. DOI: 10.2196/13930 PMID: 31199295

Chouhan, D., & Shilpi, S.Dr.Neha ChouhanDr. Sonam Shilpi. (2023). A study on artificial intelligence in education. *International Journal of Engineering Technology and Management Sciences*, *7*(1), 449–456. DOI: 10.46647/ijetms.2023.v07i01.063

CoSn. (2024, 2024-04-09). *CoSN Unveils Groundbreaking CoSN/CGCS K-12 Gen AI Maturity Tool*. Consortium for School Networking (CoSN). https://www.cosn.org/cosn-news/cosn-unveils-groundbreaking-cosn-cgcs-k-12-gen-ai-maturity-tool/

da Silva, M. C. F., Saraiva, A. C. G. T., Malta, D. P. L. N., da Silva, J. E. C., da Silva, R. L., & dos Santos, S. A. (2024). A INTEGRAÇÃO DE INTELIGÊNCIA ARTIFICIAL NA PERSONALIZAÇÃO DO ENSINO: UM NOVO PARADIGMA PARA A EDUCAÇÃO BÁSICA. *ARACÊ*, *6*(3), 5956–5972. DOI: 10.56238/arev6n3-100

Danial, A., Rafiq, A. H., & Izzuddin, F. (2022). Bridging the Digital Divide: Ensuring Access to Technology in Education for All Children. Proceeding of The International Conference of Inovation, Science, Technology, Education, Children, and Health, Diliberti, M. K., Lake, R. J., & Weiner, S. R. (2025). More Districts Are Training Teachers on Artificial Intelligence: Findings from the American School District Panel.

Dr. Khaled, A. (2024). A Proposed Model For Improving The Quality Of Life Of Persons With Disabilities And Rehabilitating Them Professionally Using Artificial Intelligence Applications. *Educational Administration: Theory and Practice*, *30*(6), 553–558. DOI: 10.53555/kuey.v30i6.5244

Draissi, Z., Rong, Y., Zafeer, H. M. I., Maqbool, S., Malik, S. J., Maqbool, S., & Alemi, S. H. A. (2025). Academic diplomacy and policy borrowing: Media content analysis of Chinese soft power in Morocco. *Humanities & Social Sciences Communications*, *12*(1), 1–11. DOI: 10.1057/s41599-025-04544-1

Fatmawati, F., Fadillah, N., Faizi, A., & Kurnia, H. (2025). Kebijakan Pemerintah Untuk Meningkatkan Akses Pendidikan Bagi Masyarakat Kurang Mampu. *Innovations in Multidisciplinary Education Journal, 2*(1), 1–7. DOI: 10.61476/q1dfs358

Felton, L. (2023). *AI in European schools: A European report comparing seven countries.* https://skillsuploadjr.eu/docs/contents/AI_in_European_schools.pdf

Gen Digital, I. (2024). *Parents Cautiously Optimistic on AI in Schools: Content Safety and Data Privacy Among Top Worries.* https://www.prnewswire.com/news-releases/parents-cautiously-optimistic-on-ai-in-schools-content-safety-and-data-privacy-302227077.html

George, B., & Wooden, O. (2023). Managing the strategic transformation of higher education through artificial intelligence. *Administrative Sciences*, *13*(9), 196. DOI: 10.3390/admsci13090196

Ikevuje, A. H., Kwakye, J. M., Ekechukwu, D. E., & Benjamin, O. (2023). Energy justice: Ensuring equitable access to clean energy in underprivileged communities. *J. Sustainable Energy*, *45*(4), 298–314.

Jantanukul, W. (2024). AI and Human Synergy: Utilizing AI to Enhance Teaching and Learning. *Journal of Education and Learning Reviews*, *1*(4), 1–12. DOI: 10.60027/jelr.2024.749

Javed, S., Rong, Y., Zafeer, H. M. I., Maqbool, S., & Abbasi, B. N. (2024). Unleashing the potential: A quest to understand and examine the factors enriching research and innovation productivities of South Asian universities. *Humanities & Social Sciences Communications*, *11*(1), 1–15. DOI: 10.1057/s41599-024-03674-2

Jeongwan. (2023). A Review of the Legislative Issues of Artificial Intelligence (AI). *Kyunghee Law School, 58*(4), 117-144.

Kalim, U., Irfan, S., Maqbool, S., & Zafeer, H. M. I. (2025). How AI Can Be Successfully Implemented in the Classroom Settings: Challenges and Pathways to Overcome. In *Navigating Barriers to AI Implementation in the Classroom* (pp. 235-266). IGI Global Scientific Publishing.

Karan, B., & Angadi, G. (2023). Potential risks of artificial intelligence integration into school education: A systematic review. *Bulletin of Science, Technology & Society*, *43*(3-4), 67–85. DOI: 10.1177/02704676231224705

Karataş, F., Eriçok, B., & Tanrikulu, L. (2025). Reshaping curriculum adaptation in the age of artificial intelligence: Mapping teachers' AI-driven curriculum adaptation patterns. *British Educational Research Journal*, *51*(1), 154–180. DOI: 10.1002/berj.4068

Kim, J., & Wargo, E. (2025). Empowering educational leaders for AI integration in rural STEM education: challenges and strategies. Frontiers in Education, Kim, T. K. (2024). Integrating Learning Analytics, AI, and STEM Education: A Comprehensive Review. *International Journal of Research in STEM Education*, *6*(2), 61–72. DOI: 10.33830/ijrse.v6i2.1745

Kitcharoen, P., Howimanporn, S., & Chookaew, S. (2024). Enhancing Teachers' AI Competencies through Artificial Intelligence of Things Professional Development Training. *International Journal of Interactive Mobile Technologies*, *18*(2), 4–15. DOI: 10.3991/ijim.v18i02.46613

Kotsis, K. T. (2025). Integrating Artificial Intelligence into Higher Education Curricula: Challenges and Opportunities for Science-Based Programs.

Lotfi, F. Z., & Laajan, Y. (2025). When AI enters Moroccan primary schools: what uses, challenges, and prospects for tomorrow's education? *EIKI Journal of Effective Teaching Methods, 3*(1).

Luo, Q. Z., & Hsiao-Chin, L. Y. (2023). The influence of AI-powered adaptive learning platforms on student performance in Chinese classrooms. *Journal of Education*, *6*(3), 1–12. DOI: 10.53819/81018102t4181

Madden, M., Calvin, A., Hasse, A., & Lenhart, A. (2024). *The dawn of the AI era: Teens, parents, and the adoption of generative AI at home and school*. Common Sense.

Malik, S., Rong, Y., Zafeer, H. M. I., Maqbool, S., Draissi, Z., Rehman, N., & Maqbool, S. (2025). Analysis of Key Factors Influencing Academic Productivity: Insights From LASSO Regression and AI-Driven Techniques. In *Navigating Barriers to AI Implementation in the Classroom* (pp. 189–234). IGI Global Scientific Publishing. DOI: 10.4018/979-8-3373-1827-1.ch009

Maqbool, S. (2025). Implemented in the Classroom Settings: Challenges and Pathways. *Navigating Barriers to AI Implementation in the Classroom*, 235.

Maqbool, S., Maqbool, S., Zafeer, H. M. I., & Qihui, H. (2024). Exploring the Reflection of Teachers to Encourage the Gender Equality for Girls in Punjab Schools: In the Light of Universal Right to an Education. *Asian Women*, *40*(3), 113–138. DOI: 10.14431/aw.2024.9.40.3.113

Maqbool, S., Sarwar, U., Zamir, S., Zafeer, H. M. I., & Wei, Z. (2020). Teaching of Phonics and fluency in improving reading abilities at primary level: Multan Pakistan. *European Online Journal of Natural and Social Sciences*, *9*(4), 808–819.

Maqbool, S., Wei, Z., Sarwar, U., Zamir, S., & Zafeer, H. M. I. (2020). An analysis of self-concept between homeless and common women in Pakistan. *International Transaction Journal of Engineering, Management, &. Applied Sciences & Technologies*, *11*(15), 11–19.

Maqbool, S., Zafeer, H. M. I., & Maqbool, S. (2025). Psychological Impact of Raising a Child With Autism: A Real Life Case Study of Expatriate Family. *Child & Family Social Work*, cfs.70011. DOI: 10.1111/cfs.70011

Maqbool, S., Zafeer, H. M. I., Maqbool, S., Zeng, P., Draissi, Z., & Javed, S. (2024). Stance of numerous leadership styles and their effect on teaching to sustain academic performance at the high school level. *Heliyon*, *10*(16), e36438. DOI: 10.1016/j.heliyon.2024.e36438 PMID: 39253217

Maqbool, S., Zafeer, H. M. I., Yanping, L., & Zhao, W. (2022). Covid-19 and global education: Experiences of Pakistani international students. *International Transaction Journal of Engineering Management and Applied Sciences and Technologies*, *13*(3), 1–11.

Maqbool, S., Zafeer, H. M. I., Zeng, P., Maqbool, S., Draissi, Z., & Javed, S. (2024). Inventive leadership styles and their impact for achieving sustainable development goals in education at secondary schools: A case study from Multan, Pakistan. *Humanities & Social Sciences Communications*, *11*(1), 1–11. DOI: 10.1057/s41599-024-03086-2

Maqbool, S., Zafeer, H. M. I., Zeng, P., Mohammad, T., Khassawneh, O., & Wu, L. (2023). The role of diverse leadership styles in teaching to sustain academic excellence at secondary level. [Maqbool, S., Zhao, W., Rehman, S., Zafeer, H. M. I., & Maqbool, S. North American Academic Research.]. *Frontiers in Psychology*, *13*, 1096151. DOI: 10.3389/fpsyg.2022.1096151 PMID: 36698584

Massachusetts Department of. E., & Secondary, E. (2024). *Massachusetts Guidance for Artificial Intelligence in K–12 Education*. https://www.doe.mass.edu/edtech/ai/ai-guidance.pdf

Miao, F., & Shiohira, K. (2024). *AI competency framework for students*. UNESCO Publishing.

Nazaretsky, T., Cukurova, M., Ariely, M., & Alexandron, G. (2021). Confirmation bias and trust: Human factors that influence teachers' attitudes towards AI-based educational technology. CEUR Workshop Proceedings, Ng, D. T. K., Leung, J. K. L., Su, J., Ng, R. C. W., & Chu, S. K. W. (2023). Teachers' AI digital competencies and twenty-first century skills in the post-pandemic world. *Educational Technology Research and Development*, *71*(1), 137–161. PMID: 33456286

Obioha Val, O. (2024). The Role of Artificial Intelligence (AI) in Enhancing Cybersecurity for Educational Technologies in US Public Schools. *Asian Journal of Research in Computer Science, 17*(11), 10.9734.

Polak, S., Schiavo, G., & Zancanaro, M. (2022). Teachers' perspective on artificial intelligence education: An initial investigation. CHI conference on human factors in computing systems extended abstracts, Pucchio, A., Rathagirishnan, R., Caton, N., Gariscsak, P. J., Del Papa, J., Nabhen, J. J., Vo, V., Lee, W., & Moraes, F. Y. (2022). Exploration of exposure to artificial intelligence in undergraduate medical education: a Canadian cross-sectional mixed-methods study. *BMC Medical Education, 22*(1), 815. PMID: 36443720

Purba, N., Pujiati, D., Sihombing, P. S. R., Simanjuntak, H., & Sijabat, D. (2025). The Use of AI in Elementary School Learning: A Systematic Literature Review. *QALAMUNA: Jurnal Pendidikan, Sosial, dan Agama, 17*(1), 83-98.

Rathore, A. A., Sultana, N., Zareen, S. J., & Ahmed, A. (2023). Artificial intelligence and curriculum prospects for elementary school. *Pakistan Journal of Humanities and Social Sciences, 11*(4), 4635–4644-4635–4644.

Rehman, N., Huang, X., Mahmood, A., Maqbool, S., & Javed, S. (2024). Enhancing the quality of research synopsis of international students through peer feedback: A case study. *New Directions for Child and Adolescent Development, 2024*(1), 1271802. DOI: 10.1155/2024/1271802

Rehman, N., Huang, X., Sarwar, U., Fatima, H., & Maqbool, S. (2024). Exploring the impact of family, school and society on the perception and reputation of vocational training in Pakistan: A statistical analysis. *Education + Training*.

Roberts, A. B., & Richardson, J. W. (2025). The role of artificial intelligence in schools: A case of policy formation. *Journal of Cases in Educational Leadership, 28*(1), 136–146. DOI: 10.1177/15554589241299320

Roshan, S., Iqbal, S. Z., & Qing, Z. (2024). Teacher training and professional development for implementing AI-based educational tools. *Journal of Asian Development Studies, 13*(2), 1972–1987. DOI: 10.62345/jads.2024.13.2.154

Sabharwal, D., Kabha, R., & Srivastava, K. (2023). Artificial intelligence (ai)-powered virtual assistants and their effect on human productivity and laziness: Study on students of delhi-ncr (india) & fujairah (uae). *Journal of Content. Community and Communication, 17*(9), 162–174. DOI: 10.31620/JCCC.06.23/12

Saidakhror, G. (2024). The impact of artificial intelligence on higher education and the economics of information technology. *International Journal of Law and Policy, 2*(3), 1–6. DOI: 10.59022/ijlp.125

Sanusi, I. T., Martin, F., Ma, R., Gonzales, J. E., Mahipal, V., Oyelere, S. S., Suhonen, J., & Tukiainen, M. (2024). AI MyData: Fostering middle school students' engagement with machine learning through an ethics-infused AI curriculum. *ACM Transactions on Computing Education, 24*(4), 1–37. DOI: 10.1145/3702242

Sarwar, U., Fazal, K., Zamir, S., Maqbool, S., Hussain, Z., & Qi, Z. Y. (2021). Assessment on Proficiency of Using Information and Communication Technology among Students of University of Lahore (Sargodha Campus), Pakistan. *European Online Journal of Natural and Social Sciences, 10*(1), 102–115.

Schleiss, J., Laupichler, M. C., Raupach, T., & Stober, S. (2023). AI course design planning framework: Developing domain-specific AI education courses. *Education Sciences, 13*(9), 954. DOI: 10.3390/educsci13090954

Schwartz, S. (2024). Teachers desperately need AI training. How many are getting it? *Education Week.* https://www.edweek.org/technology/teachers-desperately-need-ai-training/2024/03

Shtayyat, A., Gawanmeh, A., & Mashaleh, A. (2025). Risk Analysis of AI Integration in Educational Systems: Toward Ethical and Equitable Innovation. In *Examining Cybersecurity Risks Produced by Generative AI* (pp. 401-428). IGI Global Scientific Publishing.

Singh, V. V., Kumar, N., Singh, S., Kaul, M., Gupta, A. K., & Kapur, P. (2024). Assessment of artificial intelligence-based digital learning systems in higher education amid the pandemic using analytic hierarchy. *International Journal of System Assurance Engineering and Management, 15*(8), 4069–4084. DOI: 10.1007/s13198-024-02411-x

Trang, N. T. Q., & Thu, P. T. (2024). The role of AI in improving student learning outcomes: Evidence in vietnam. *International Journal of Multidisciplinary Research and Analysis, 7*(06), 2806–2810. DOI: 10.47191/ijmra/v7-i06-48

Tyson, M. M., & Sauers, N. J. (2021). School leaders' adoption and implementation of artificial intelligence. *Journal of Educational Administration, 59*(3), 271–285. DOI: 10.1108/JEA-10-2020-0221

Van Brummelen, J., Heng, T., & Tabunshchyk, V. (2021). Teaching tech to talk: K-12 conversational artificial intelligence literacy curriculum and development tools. Proceedings of the AAAI conference on artificial intelligence, Velmurugan, P. R., Swadhi, R., Varshney, K. R., Regins, J. C., & Gayathri, K. (2025). Creating Engaging and Personalized Learning Experiences in Distance Education: AI and Learning Analytics. In *AI and Learning Analytics in Distance Learning* (pp. 103-126). IGI Global Scientific Publishing.

Wang, R., Li, J., Shi, W., & Li, X. (2021). Application of artificial intelligence techniques in operating mode of professors' academic governance in american research universities. *Wireless Communications and Mobile Computing*, *2021*(1), 3415125. DOI: 10.1155/2021/3415125

Warr, M., & Heath, M. K. (2025). Uncovering the Hidden Curriculum in Generative AI: A Reflective Technology Audit for Teacher Educators. *Journal of Teacher Education*, *76*(3), 245–261. DOI: 10.1177/00224871251325073

Woodruff, K., Hutson, J., & Arnone, K. (2023). Perceptions and barriers to adopting artificial intelligence in K-12 education: A survey of educators in fifty states.

Zafeer, H. M. I., Li, Y., & Maqbool, S. (2023). An approach to progress learning outcomes: International graduate students' engagement in reflective practice and reflective journal writing during pandemic. *Sustainability (Basel)*, *15*(3), 1898. DOI: 10.3390/su15031898

Zafeer, H. M. I., Maqbool, S., Rong, Y., & Maqbool, S. (2024). Mapping the relationship and influence of school internal factors with an eye towards students' science academic outcomes. *Heliyon*, *10*(19), e38696. DOI: 10.1016/j.heliyon.2024.e38696 PMID: 39397972

Zafeer, H. M. I., Maqbool, S., Rong, Y., & Maqbool, S. (2025a). Beyond the Classroom: How Socioeconomic Status, Parental Involvement and Home Environment Impact on Students' Science Academic Performance at Secondary Schools. *European Journal of Education*, *60*(1), e70023. DOI: 10.1111/ejed.70023

Zafeer, H. M. I., Maqbool, S., Rong, Y., & Maqbool, S. (2025b). Culturally Sustaining Cognitive and Behavioral Interventions for Reducing Anxiety in Autistic School-Aged Students: A Systematic Review. *Psychology in the Schools*, pits.70077. DOI: 10.1002/pits.70077

Zafeer, H. M. I., Maqbool, S., Rong, Y., & Maqbool, S. (2025c). Impact of digital learning tools on student's engagement and achievement in middle school science classes. *International Journal of Technology in Education and Science*, *9*(2), 177–196. DOI: 10.46328/ijtes.622

Zafeer, H. M. I., Maqbool, S., & Yanping, L. (2022). Psychological and social factors and their impact on divorced and married women: A case study from Punjab Pakistan. *Journal of Divorce & Remarriage*, *63*(5), 352–373. DOI: 10.1080/10502556.2022.2048345

Zafeer, H. M. I., Peng, C., Rehman, S., Wei, Z., & Maqbool, S. (2021). A Study to Investigate the Obstacles of Educational Technology in Curriculum; University Students' Perception. *European Online Journal of Natural and Social Sciences*, *10*(1), 1–8.

Zafeer, H. M. I., Xue, H., & Maqbool, S. (2020). Delaying Factors Regarding Civil Justice in Pakistan (Lower Courts). *Journal of Humanities and Social Sciences Studies*, *2*(6), 15–22. DOI: 10.32996/jhsss.2020.2.6.2

Zafeer, H. M. I., Yanping, L., & Maqboo, S. (2022). The role of gender, socio-economic factors, and its impact on students' English as a second language (ESL) performance. *North American Academic Research*, *5*(10), 52–59.

Zamir, S., Yang, Z., Sarwar, U., Maqbool, S., Fazal, K., Ihsan, H., & Arif, A. (2021). Teaching methodologies used for learning critical thinking in higher education: Pakistani teachers' perceptions. *Int. Trans. J. Eng. Manag. Appl. Sci. Technol*, *12*, 1–10.

Zhang, P., & Tur, G. (2024). A systematic review of ChatGPT use in K-12 education. *European Journal of Education*, *59*(2), e12599. DOI: 10.1111/ejed.12599

Zhang, X., & Tahir, S. (2023). LEVERAGING TECHNOLOGY TO ENHANCE ACCESS TO QUALITY LEGAL EDUCATION IN MALAYSIA. *International Journal of Social Science and Business Management*, *1*(02). Advance online publication. DOI: 10.59021/ijssbm.v1i02.46

Zmir, S., Sarwar, U., Maqbool, S., Javed, S., Ishtiaq, M., & Zhang, Y. (2021). Plagiarism practice: Its awareness & dealing and consequences among university students in Punjab province of Pakistan. *International Transaction Journal of Engineering, Management, &. Applied Sciences & Technologies*, *12*(11), 1–11.

Zormanová, L. (2024). Attitudes of Czech Teachers Towards the Use of Artificial Intelligence in Schools. *Horyzonty Wychowania*, *23*(65), 31–41. DOI: 10.35765/hw.2024.2365.05

Chapter 4
AI in Mental Health:
From Digital Companions to Clinical Decision-Making and Training for Tomorrow

Aiman Batool
https://orcid.org/0009-0001-6539-3461
University of the Punjab, Pakistan

Hafiz Tayyab Mustafa
https://orcid.org/0000-0003-3992-4457
Zhejiang Normal University, China

Nadia Rehman
https://orcid.org/0000-0002-4172-625X
Zhejiang Normal University, China

Hamza Mustafa
https://orcid.org/0000-0003-3610-2888
University of Cassino and Southern Lazio, Cassino, Italy

Amir Mehmood
https://orcid.org/0000-0002-0215-0278
Zhejiang Normal University, China

ABSTRACT

This chapter explores the significant impact of Artificial Intelligence (AI) on mental health, highlighting the use of digital companions, AI-enhanced diagnostics, and the incorporation of AI into clinical training. This analysis explores the ways in which chatbots and virtual therapists offer accessible mental health support, the functionalities and ethical considerations surrounding AI-powered diagnostic tools,

DOI: 10.4018/979-8-3373-4217-7.ch004

and the changing educational requirements for mental health professionals in a world increasingly influenced by AI. This chapter provides a thoughtful examination of the potential benefits and obstacles associated with incorporating AI into psychological practice, drawing from a blend of interdisciplinary research and practical examples from the real world. The importance of establishing ethical frameworks, fostering human-AI collaboration, and promoting inclusive policies is highlighted to guarantee the responsible implementation of AI in mental healthcare.

INTRODUCTION

The integration of Artificial Intelligence (AI) into mental health care represents a significant evolution in how psychological support is conceptualized, delivered, and sustained. While traditional services remain indispensable, structural challenges of accessibility, scalability, and cost continue to limit their reach. Against this backdrop, AI is emerging as a complementary approach capable of providing more personalized, adaptive, and context-sensitive care that extends beyond conventional clinical settings.

The trajectory of AI in mental health can be traced back to early natural language processing experiments such as *ELIZA* (Weizenbaum, 1966). Although rudimentary, ELIZA demonstrated the potential for machines to simulate aspects of therapeutic dialogue. In contrast, contemporary AI systems draw upon advanced machine learning, natural language understanding, and large-scale data modeling to deliver interventions that are increasingly nuanced, responsive, and scalable. Several global developments have accelerated this shift: the availability of behavioral and biometric data through smartphones and wearables enabling early detection of distress (Torous & Roberts, 2017); the COVID-19 pandemic, which intensified demand for remote and scalable mental health solutions (World Health Organization, 2022); and advances in large language models (LLMs), such as GPT-4, which have given conversational agents the ability to engage in context-aware, personalized dialogue (Gilbert et al., 2023). In line with the broader scope of this volume, this chapter extends the paradigm of personalization into the domain of mental health. Just as AI tutors adapt to learners' cognitive needs, AI-enabled mental health tools respond to individuals' emotional and psychological needs, underscoring that cognitive growth and emotional well-being are deeply interconnected.

While these innovations are technologically significant, their broader impact can only be understood through a socio-technical perspective. This chapter adopts the Socio-Technical Ecosystem Framework (STEF) (Liu & Zhang, 2024) as its guiding lens. The framework emphasizes that the success of AI in mental health depends on the interaction of multiple interconnected layers. The technological layer comprises

AI algorithms, data infrastructures, and digital platforms. The interpersonal layer captures the lived experiences of patients, caregivers, and clinicians, whose trust and engagement determine system effectiveness. The community layer reflects healthcare institutions, clinical workflows, and professional practices that shape integration into everyday care. Finally, the societal layer embodies cultural values, ethical norms, and policy environments that govern the acceptance and responsible use of AI. This layered perspective positions AI-enabled mental health not merely as a technical innovation but as part of a broader socio-technical ecosystem in which technology, people, institutions, and society co-evolve. Within the socio-technical ecosystem framework this chapter is structured around three interrelated themes:

1. **AI-Driven Digital Companions and Chatbots** software agents that deliver scalable emotional support, therapeutic dialogue, and adaptive interventions.
2. **AI Clinical and Decision-Support Systems** technologies that synthesize multimodal patient data to support diagnostic accuracy and personalized treatment planning.
3. **AI Literacy and Training for Mental Health Professionals** initiatives designed to equip practitioners with the competencies needed to collaborate effectively with AI systems while safeguarding ethics and trust.

By integrating these themes within the socio-technical ecosystem framework, the chapter demonstrates how AI is contributing to the emergence of a personalized, learner-centered mental health ecosystem. As they explicitly defines the chapter aims. As Firstly, it examines how emerging AI applications are reshaping mental health care through digital companions, clinical decision-support systems, and professional training. Secondly, it analyzes these developments through the lens of the **Socio-Technical Ecosystem Framework**, emphasizing the interdependence of technological, interpersonal, community, and societal dynamics. Finally, it considers the implications of these shifts for researchers, practitioners, and policymakers who are seeking to integrate AI responsibly into both clinical and educational contexts.

AI-DRIVEN DIGITAL COMPANIONS AND CHATBOTS

AI driven digital companions and chatbots are software-based agents that utilize AI, NLP, and ML to simulate human-like interactions. These tools have emerged as pivotal technologies in mental health care, offering scalable, accessible, and personalized support for emotional well-being, behavioral interventions, and psychoeducation. At their core, digital companions are designed to understand user inputs text, voice, or behavioral patterns and respond with tailored prompts, reflections, and suggestions, mimicking the dynamics of a therapeutic conversation (Inkster et al., 2018). Within the socio-technical ecosystem framework, these companions are best understood through the interpersonal layer, where the interaction between users and AI agents shapes trust, acceptance, and therapeutic value.

Historical Development and Theoretical Context

The concept of AI-based digital companions finds its roots in early NLP and the nascent efforts of computer-aided psychotherapy. The pivotal moment in this endeavor came in the 1960s with the advent of ELIZA, designed to simulate a psychotherapeutic conversation by responding to user inputs with pre-programmed, reflective questions (Weizenbaum, 1966). Though primitive by contemporary standards, ELIZA demonstrated, for the first time, the potential for a computer program to mimic elements of a therapeutic interaction. Its behavior, inspired by the principles of Rogerian therapy, offered a glimpse of how technology might facilitate a human–machine dialogue that felt both authentic and supportive.

From the 1980s onward, researchers began exploring the possibility of embedding psychotherapeutic techniques especially those rooted in cognitive behavioral therapy (CBT) within digital interfaces.(Provoost et al., 2017). CBT's structured, goal-oriented approach was not jusat particularly suited to algorithmic implementation, but also Western epistemologies of mental health, privileging cognitive restructuring and individual agency over collective, relational, or spiritual modes of healing. Such design choices risk reinforcing a narrow cultural lens while marginalizing alternative traditions of care.

Throughout the 1990s and early 2000s, advances in NLP and the emergence of statistical ML laid the groundwork for a new generation of digital companions that could adapt to user input through probabilistic modeling rather than fixed decision trees. This period coincided with the proliferation of mobile technologies and increased connectivity, which together accelerated the accessibility and reach of digital companions. The smartphone revolution of the late 2000s, combined with advances in deep learning and neural language modeling, paved the way for sophisticated AI driven chatbots that could operate in real time across a range of platforms. By the late 2010s, platforms such as Woebot and Wysa emerged as exemplars of this new generation of digital companions. These tools combined CBT, dialectical behavior therapy (DBT), and mindfulness-based interventions within mobile applications, making evidence-based mental health support available to individuals across the globe (Fulmer et al., 2018). Importantly, these platforms leveraged advances in NLP to recognize linguistic markers of emotional distress, providing timely, personalized interventions that responded to the user's specific needs. The development of AI-based digital companions in mental health can be understood as a gradual progression from early rule-based systems to today's large-scale, data-driven chatbots (Figure 1).

Figure 1. Evolution of AI-based digital companions in mental health

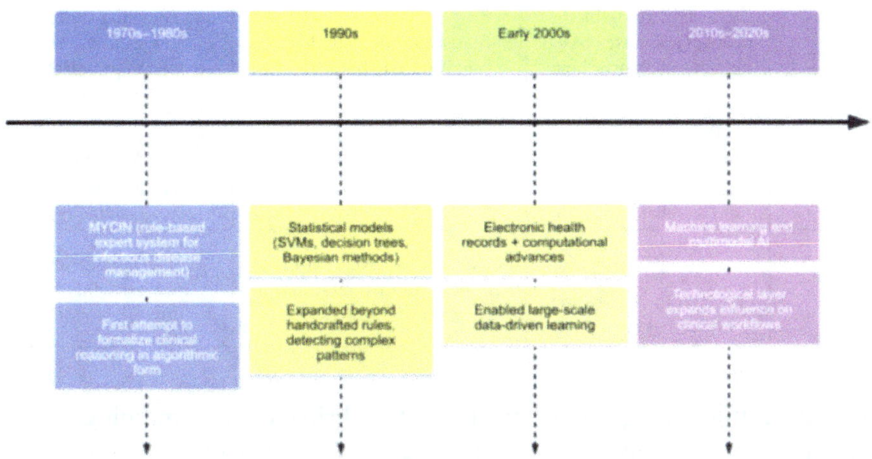

Functionality and Typologies

Digital companions in mental health are interactive AI systems designed to engage users in conversation and provide emotional support, guidance, or therapy like interventions. These range from simple rule-based scripts to sophisticated agents powered by large language models. In terms of functionality, chatbots can track mood and symptom logs; deliver cognitive behavioral therapy (CBT) exercises and coping strategies; answer questions about mental health; facilitate mindfulness sessions; and encourage help-seeking behavior (Feng et al., 2025). Chatbots also vary in **typology** as described in Table 1 They can be broadly categorized as (1) rule-based bots (2) MLdriven bots and (3) large language model-based systems that generate open-ended dialogue. (Gaffney et al., 2019).

Table 1. Typology and functionality of mental health chatbots

Typology	Description	Key Technology	Primary Functions
Rule-Based	Pre-programmed scripts and decision trees, Predictable and guided responses	Pattern matching, keyword recognition (Early ELIZA, many structured screening bots)	Mood tracking, delivering pre-set CBT exercises, answering FAQs, crisis resource referral
ML-Driven	Machine learning models to adapt responses based on patterns in user input and data.	Statistical NLP, sentiment analysis(Woebot, Wysa)	Personalized coping strategies, basic emotional support, adaptive psychoeducation
LLM-Based	Powered by large language models capable of generating novel, open-ended dialogue.	Transformer-based models (e.g., GPT)	Open-ended companionship, complex conversation, creative exercises, simulating empathy
Voice/Avatar-Based	Spoken dialogue or through a virtual character to convey non-verbal cues.	Speech-to-Text, Text-to-Speech, Animation(Amazon Alexa skills, X2AI's Tess)	For users preferring speech, increased engagement through embodiment

In practice, these categories often blur, with hybrid models combining rule-based safeguards with ML-driven personalization or LLM-based dialogue flexibility. This hybridity illustrates both the innovation and complexity of classifying chatbot technologies.

Limitations and Risks

Despite the promising role of AI in expanding access to mental health support, the use of digital companions comes with several critical limitations and risks that merit close attention. One of the most significant concerns is the potential for over-reliance on these tools Individuals may substitute chatbot interaction for genuine human contact, which can exacerbate isolation and delay professional help-seeking (Hoermann et al., 2017). Importantly, users often adapt these tools creatively, treating them as journaling partners, "venting spaces," or supplemental coping aids rather than full substitutes. Clinicians, too, develop strategies for integrating chatbots safely, framing them as adjunctive resources within stepped-care models rather than stand-alone therapies.

Another serious limitation is the potential for misinformation and clincal safety. Large language models may generate plausible but inaccurate responses ("hallucinations"), potentially offering misleading or unsafe guidance (Hatem et al., 2023). Although some platforms include crisis-detection protocols, these safeguards remain uneven and unregulated.

Third, there are cultural and linguistic limitations. The dominance of Western-developed CBT frameworks often clashes with collectivist or spiritual traditions of healing, producing cultural mismatches (Mesko, 2018). Likewise, most systems are designed in English and exclude non-dominant languages, reinforcing global inequities. In low and middle-income countries (LMICs), access is further constrained by digital literacy gaps, infrastructure barriers, and uneven smartphone penetration (World Health Organization, 2022).

Finally, questions of trust and accountability remain unresolved. Chatbots often lack transparency about data use, raise privacy concerns, and risk widening disparities if designed without inclusivity at the core. Within the socio-technical ecosystem, each of these risks corresponds to potential coping mechanisms at the technological, interpersonal, community, or societal layer. Table 2 summarizes these risks alongside mitigation strategies.

Table 2. Ethical risks in AI-enabled digital companions and corresponding mitigation strategies.

Ethical Risk	Description	Mitigation Strategy
Algorithmic Bias	Skewed outcomes due to underrepresented data	Inclusive datasets, bias audits, diverse teams
Privacy & Confidentiality	Patient data misuse or breaches	Encryption, consent protocols, data minimization
Overdiagnosis	Excessive labeling of normal behavior	Human oversight, context-sensitive algorithms
Accountability	Unclear responsibility for AI errors	Shared governance, regulatory frameworks

Future Directions and Best Practices

The future of AI-driven companions will likely center on greater personalization, leveraging multimodal data such as voice tone, typing speed, or facial expressions to infer emotional states more accurately (Gaffney et al., 2019). Rigorous evaluation protocols including randomized controlled trials and transparent reporting of outcomes are needed to move beyond anecdotal success. Importantly, evaluation should include not only symptom reduction but also engagement, retention, cultural resonance, and potential harm.

Equity and inclusivity must also be prioritized. Next-generation systems should incorporate diverse cultural idioms of distress, expand language availability, and be tested in LMIC contexts to avoid perpetuating global inequities. Ethical safeguards including privacy by design, explicit user consent, and crisis escalation protocols must be embedded from the start (Floridi et al., 2018). Developers should regularly stress-test systems under adversarial conditions to ensure resilience against bias and harmful outputs.

In sum, while digital companions hold great potential as accessible and scalable tools, their effectiveness depends on addressing cultural, ethical, and technical limitations through careful design, regulation, and continuous evaluation.

AI CLINICAL AND DECISION SUPPORT SYSTEMS

AI diagnostic and decision-support tools in mental health are software systems that leverage machine learning (ML) and related algorithms to assist clinicians in patient assessment and management (Kleine, 2024). These tools ingest large-scale data clinical notes, survey responses, sensor signals, or even speech and images and generate patient-specific insights (Perumal et al., 2025). Within the socio-technical ecosystem framework, these systems primarily represent the technological layer, where algorithms, infrastructures, and platforms generate outputs that then filter into interpersonal and community-level decision-making.

Historical Development

The roots of AI diagnostic and decision support can be traced back to the early expert systems developed in the 1970s and 1980s, a period when researchers first began exploring ways to encode medical knowledge and clinical reasoning within computational frameworks. At the forefront of this endeavor was MYCIN, a pioneering expert system developed at Stanford University, which utilized rule-based inference to support clinical decision-making in the context of infectious disease management (Shortliffe, 1976). Though MYCIN was designed to aid in selecting appropriate antimicrobial treatments, its architectural design inspired a generation of researchers to consider the application of AI across a range of clinical disciplines. Its rule-based structure, built upon a formalization of clinical expertise, laid the groundwork for the idea that medical knowledge could be translated into a machine-readable, algorithmic form, making complex clinical reasoning accessible to computational platforms.

Throughout the 1990s and early 2000s, advances in statistical modeling and the growing availability of digital health records catalyzed a shift from purely rule-based expert systems toward statistical learning approaches. Researchers began to utilize a range of methods including support vector machines (SVM), decision trees, and Bayesian modeling to detect intricate patterns in clinical data that exceeded the analytical scope of traditional statistical techniques (Shatte et al., 2019; Kleine et al., 2024). The proliferation of electronic medical records, combined with advances in computational processing, enabled AI researchers to move beyond handcrafted rules and toward data-driven approaches that learned patterns directly from patient information as shown in figure 2 (Perumal et al., 2025). This shift illustrates how the technological layer of the socio-technical ecosystem gradually expanded its influence on clinical workflows and decision-making practices.

Figure 2. Historical progression of AI clinical and decision-support systems

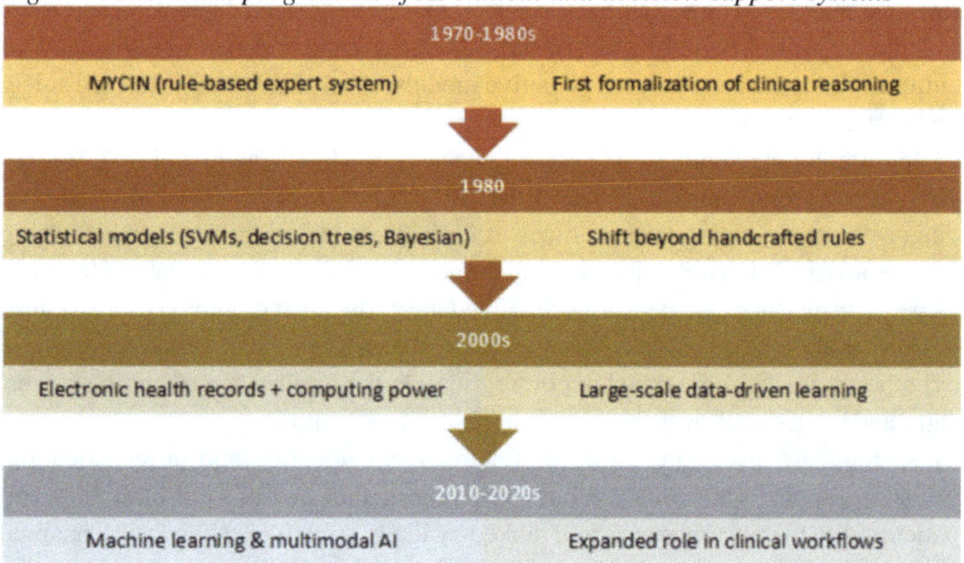

Clinical Applications and Capabilities

These tools can be categorized into several functional types: diagnostic or predictive AI, which identifies conditions or forecasts risks; treatment selection AI, which recommends therapy options; and self-help AI, which offers psychoeducation or symptom monitoring for users outside of clinical settings. At each phase of mental health care from symptom screening to treatment planning. AI can augment clinical judgment by synthesizing data and generating actionable insights (Kleine et al., 2024).

AI has already demonstrated utility in screening and triage. In the United Kingdom, the AI chatbot Limbic Access screened over 210,000 patients for common mental health conditions such as depression, anxiety, and PTSD, reportedly achieving 93% diagnostic accuracy. By integrating into NHS workflows, this tool has contributed to a 45% reduction in diagnostic revisions by helping clinicians prioritize cases based on severity. However, claims of diagnostic accuracy often lack methodological scrutiny; reported percentages are frequently drawn from internal evaluations without independent replication, raising questions about generalizability and bias.

Similarly, the U.S.-based company Kintsugi developed a voice-analysis AI that detects biomarkers of depression and anxiety using brief speech samples, deployed during customer service calls or app usage. These AI screening tools address a longstanding limitation of primary care, underdiagnosis of depression, which occurs in nearly half of cases (Mitchell, 2009). Comparable tools are also being piloted in low- and middle-income countries, such as smartphone-based depression screeners in India and WHO-led initiatives in sub-Saharan Africa, underscoring the need for culturally adapted and resource-sensitive models rather than systems trained solely on Western datasets.

In differential diagnosis, AI systems such as large language models (LLMs) are also gaining prominence. In a study using GPT-3, the AI correctly included the right diagnosis among its top three choices in 88% of clinical vignettes, outperforming laypersons (54%) but not quite reaching the accuracy of physicians (96%). However, its performance in triage decisions remained lower than that of human professionals (Gilson et al., 2023). These findings suggest that while AI can generate plausible hypotheses, it lacks contextual depth, reinforcing the importance of clinician oversight and the risks of overconfidence in "black box" outputs.

AI tools are also being explored for treatment selection and prognostication. Decision-support platforms are being developed that can present clinicians and patients with therapy options, often ranked by likely effectiveness and accompanied by simplified explanations. Predictive AI models trained on electronic health records or mobile phone data are being tested to forecast suicide risk, relapse probability, or treatment response. Some platforms analyze "voice biomarkers" from user diaries to detect shifts in mood or relapse patterns in depression. Although many of these approaches are experimental, they represent an evolution in personalized mental health care moving from reactive to proactive support (Kleine, 2024; Perumal et al., 2025).

Underlying Technologies and Modalities

Technologically, these systems rely on a range of AI techniques. ML, especially deep learning (DL), dominates the space, with algorithms trained to identify complex patterns in structured and unstructured data. For instance, convolutional neural networks have been used to classify neuroimaging scans for depressive disorders or dementia subtypes (Di Stefano, 2024; Yamaguchi et al., 2024). Natural language processing (NLP) techniques allow systems to parse clinical narratives or patient dialogue, making sense of free-text responses or verbal cues. Tools like Woebot and Tess leverage NLP to conduct brief psychological interventions or screen for distress (Fitzpatrick et al., 2017). More sophisticated multimodal models can integrate audio, visual, and text inputs to better assess mental health status (Kleine, 2024).

Voice and speech analysis, in particular, has become a specialized subfield. By examining prosody, pitch, and language content, algorithms can predict depressive states or emotional distress with considerable sensitivity. For example, Kintsugi's models are trained on over 250,000 voice recordings, demonstrating how rich speech data can be leveraged for passive mental health screening. Similarly, neuroimaging data, including fMRI and EEG, have been analyzed using supervised learning methods to predict outcomes in conditions such as schizophrenia or bipolar disorder (Di Stefano, 2024; Yamaguchi et al., 2024).

Accuracy, Validation, and Performance

When compared directly to human clinicians, AI tools show varying degrees of effectiveness. Controlled studies indicate that AI achieves near-human performance in certain narrow diagnostic tasks but struggles with broader clinical reasoning. Gilson et al. (2023) found that GPT-3 lagged behind physicians in triage accuracy, highlighting the need for cautious deployment. Moreover, many published models rely on small or non-representative samples, lack external validation, and are rarely tested across different populations, limiting their robustness and raising risks of algorithmic harm.

Ethical and Social Considerations

Ethical concerns are central to the conversation around AI in psychiatry. One major issue is transparency. Many DL systems function as "black boxes," offering limited insight into how conclusions are reached. Without explainability, clinicians may be reluctant to trust or act upon AI recommendations. Bias is another major concern: algorithms trained on non-representative datasets risk amplifying existing disparities in care. In addition, overdiagnosis can occur when models prioritize sensitivity over specificity, possibly leading to unnecessary treatment or anxiety. Accountability remains a grey area if an AI system errors, it is often unclear whether responsibility lies with the clinician, developer, or institution. Global inequities also deserve attention: most datasets disproportionately represent English-speaking, high-income contexts, while populations in LMICs remain underrepresented. Language exclusions further marginalize users, restricting AI's relevance to global mental health needs. Real-world harms have already surfaced for example, predictive algorithms misclassifying suicide risk or producing biased outcomes for racial minorities illustrating that ethical challenges are not hypothetical but immediate and pressing (O'Neil, 2016).

These issues are compounded by differences in AI vendors. Publicly funded systems, such as those integrated into the NHS, often emphasize transparency and accountability, whereas private corporate tools may rely on proprietary datasets and opaque methods, limiting clinician oversight. The divergence between public and private approaches has implications for trust, data access, and equity. Table 2 contrasts these dynamics to illustrate how vendor type shapes the socio-technical ecosystem in which AI tools for mental health are developed and deployed."

Table 3. Public vs. private AI vendors in mental health

Dimension	Public / Academic Initiatives	Private / Commercial Vendors
Transparency	Higher transparency; open methods and peer-reviewed publications (e.g., university-led projects).	Often proprietary "black-box" models with limited disclosure of algorithms or datasets.
Data Access	Use of open datasets or research collaborations; limited by funding and ethical constraints.	Large-scale, exclusive datasets collected via apps, wearables, or commercial partnerships.
Bias Mitigation	Explicit focus on fairness and inclusivity in academic research; emphasis on ethical guidelines.	Bias often addressed post-deployment; varies widely by company policy and market pressure.
Validation	Peer-reviewed studies, smaller sample sizes, rigorous but slow.	Large user bases allow rapid iteration; validation may be unpublished or industry-driven.
Regulatory Oversight	Aligned with institutional ethics boards, public funding bodies, and academic standards.	Influenced by investors, market competition, and evolving regulatory compliance.
Accessibility	Tools often free, open-source, or available through health systems (e.g., NHS pilots).	Subscription-based, preemium models; risk of widening digital health inequities.

As the socio-technical ecosystem framework reminds us, these vendor-level distinctions operate not only at the technological layer (through algorithms and datasets) but also ripple across community and societal layers, influencing institutional adoption, public trust, and policy regulation.

Integration into Clinical Workflows

Integration into real-world clinical workflows poses both technical and organizational challenges. AI systems must connect seamlessly with electronic health records and existing telehealth platforms. Early pilot studies suggest that efficiency gains are possible for example, using the Limbic chatbot reportedly saved clinicians an average of 40 minutes per intake. However, clinicians must be adequately trained to interpret and incorporate AI outputs into their practice. Without proper onboarding and process redesign, these tools may disrupt rather than enhance care delivery (Kleine, 2024).

TRAINING MENTAL HEALTH PROFESSIONALS

AI has emerged as one of the most significant technological innovations in reshaping mental health care. Its application ranges from clinical decision support and diagnostic systems to digital therapy platforms and chatbots that can detect early warning signs of psychiatric conditions (Dwyer et al., 2018). Yet, despite its revolutionary potential, AI also brings forth unprecedented ethical, clinical, and systemic challenges. As AI increasingly becomes a part of clinical practice, the imperative for training mental health professionals to integrate AI effectively and ethically has become a pressing priority. Within the socio-technical ecosystem framework, professional training is situated at the community and societal layers, where institutions, curricula, and policy environments shape how clinicians engage with new technologies.

Several factors underscore the urgency of AI training for mental health professionals.

Bridging the Gap Between Humans and Machines.

AI can aid in diagnosis and prediction, but it operates as a statistical tool that lacks the relational depth, clinical context, and moral reasoning possessed by trained human practitioners. Without adequate training, clinicians may risk over-relying upon AI recommendations, potentially leading to dehumanization and compromising patient care. As one expert in digital health has asserted, AI should augment, not replace, the human elements of clinical care (Larsen, 2024). Similarly, Miner, 2021 emphasizes that AI can be a valuable adjunct to psychotherapy when used to support clinical judgement, but its role must be clearly understood by trained clinicians. Researchers have also warned that, unless mental health professionals can critically assess AI outputs, there is a risk that these tools will undermine trust and the therapeutic alliance (Milasan & Scott-Purdy, 2025).

Ethical Training and Building Trust in AI

The ethical dilemmas posed by AI in mental health are profound and multifaceted. These range from privacy concerns and data security to questions about patient consent and algorithmic discrimination (Vaidyam et al., 2019). The American

Psychiatric Association has underscored that patient privacy and confidentiality must remain a central priority when integrating AI technologies into psychiatric practice. At the global level, the World Health Organization has emphasized that AI can introduce "false, inaccurate, and biased" outcomes if trained on unrepresentative data, underscoring the urgent need for clinicians to understand both the benefits and limitations of these tools. Tilala et al. (2024) further highlights the risk of algorithmic discrimination and privacy breaches, arguing that mental health professionals must be trained to implement AI within a robust ethical framework that prioritizes patient safety and accountability. Training should move beyond abstract ethical principles and include case-based exercises, such as scenarios involving privacy dilemmas, consent processes, and algorithmic bias detection, to build applied competence

Trust is central to the successful adoption of AI in clinical settings. Patients and clinicians alike must understand AI's role, benefits, limitations, and assumptions for its recommendations to be embraced (Gaffney et al., 2019). Yet evidence suggests that both patients and providers remain cautious. In a review conducted for the UK House of Commons, 2025, researchers observed that one in six patients and one in ten clinicians expressed skepticism about AI-driven mental health interventions, citing concerns about privacy and data security. The review further emphasized that trust can only be fostered when clinicians are trained to understand AI tools, allowing them to assess the reliability and safety of AI-derived recommendations and communicate these insights openly to patients . Similarly, Larsen,2024 argues that trust emerges from transparency and dialogue between AI developers and clinicians, making AI literacy an essential component of clinical training. Implementation should therefore include communication skills training, teaching clinicians how to explain AI recommendations to patients clearly and responsibly.

Future-Proofing Clinical Practice.

As AI becomes an increasingly common feature of clinical environments, training in AI literacy has evolved from an option to an urgent necessity. The WHO has called upon health institutions to integrate AI literacy within medical and nursing education, citing its role in facilitating patient safety, clinical quality, and workforce resilience. In the United Kingdom, the NHS has implemented the Topol Digital Fellowship to support clinicians in acquiring digital literacy and AI competencies. Similar recommendations have been offered by the American Psychiatric Association, which advocates for the incorporation of AI literacy into psychiatry training and ongoing continuing medical education.

Tilala et al. (2024) further highlight that training in AI ethics and transparency can enable mental health professionals to critically assess AI-derived recommendations, fostering error detection and safeguarding patient trust. The WHO likewise emphasizes the critical role of AI literacy in promoting patient centered care and guiding clinicians to adapt effectively within an evolving digital landscape. Training formats should include blended delivery (online and in-person workshops), short certificate courses, and integration into psychiatry residency curricula, ensuring accessibility for diverse professionals at different stages of their careers.

Core Competencies for AI Literacy in Mental Health Care

As AI tools become increasingly embedded within clinical practice, it is imperative that psychologists and other mental health professionals are trained to utilize these tools effectively, ethically, and in ways that augment patient care. This pressing need has been underscored by scholars and clinical leaders across disciplines. Bloch-Atefi 2025, for example, argues that future therapists require more than technical proficiency: "they must also cultivate critical thinking and adhere to robust ethical guidelines" to ensure that AI "enhance rather than undermines the core human elements of therapeutic practice" Similar concerns have been echoed in a recent National Academies panel, which warned that if educators fail to integrate AI literacy across health professions, "there is a risk of creating a workforce ill-prepared for the future demands of AI-enabled clinical care" (Lomis et al., 2021).

Following table explains the foundational components of an effective AI training framework for psychologists and other mental health practitioners.

Table 4. Core competencies for AI literacy in mental health care

Competency Area	Foundational	Intermediate	Advanced
AI Knowledge	Basic concepts (ML, NLP, data limits).	Interpret outputs, detect errors/bias.	Contribute to tool design and validation.
Ethics & Privacy	Awareness of consent, confidentiality.	Apply ethics in practice.	Lead governance and policy development.
Clinical Integration	Use AI as adjunct to care.	Incorporate into treatment planning.	Design workflows and train peers.
Collaboration	Recognize role of other disciplines.	Engage in cross-disciplinary projects.	Lead interdisciplinary and regulatory initiatives.
Policy & Lifelong Learning	Know key guidelines (APA, WHO, NHS).	Maintain certification and CME.	Shape curricula and mentor colleagues.

Interdisciplinary Collaboration

AI integration also demands a collaborative approach across disciplines. The NHS has emphasized that AI tools in clinical practice "must be developed in a regulated way, and as a collaboration between clinicians, software engineers, data scientists, and product designers" . Charow et al. (2021) similarly stress the necessity for multidisciplinary teamwork in shaping AI training for mental health professionals, urging that such training be co-designed by psychologists, psychiatrists, technologists, and patients In this context, Marketa Wills, the American Psychiatric Association's CEO, has asserted that mental health professionals must adopt a "leadership role in the AI development process" to ensure that clinical priorities and patient well-being remain central as these technologies evolve.

Continuing Education and Lifelong Learning

The rapid evolution of AI technologies demands a model of training that promotes ongoing learning. As Paranjape, 2020 and Shatte et al. 2019, both emphasize, AI literacy must evolve from a one-off endeavor to a continuous, career-spanning process that adapts to new advances in AI tools and their clinical implications. The WHO Academy has advocated for incorporating AI literacy into continuing medical education, stating that mental health professionals must "engage in lifelong learning and collaborative skill-building" to maintain AI proficiency and adhere to best practices Similar recommendations have been put forth by the American Psychiatric Association which has introduced continuing education offerings and certification opportunities for psychologists and psychiatrists to keep pace with AI advances.

Implementation Frameworks and Policy Context

Training must also embed an understanding of relevant legal, clinical, and institutional frameworks that govern AI use. At the global level, the WHO has articulated guiding principles for AI deployment in health, highlighting the vital role of accountability, patient safety, and data protection within AI-enhanced clinical practice. The United Nations has likewise called for AI ethics and governance frameworks grounded in equity, fairness, and transparency. At the national level, NHS England has issued guidance for AI adoption in clinical practice, making it clear that staff must be trained to "evaluate AI tools critically, understand their limitations, and adhere to national data protection policies" Embedding these policy contexts into training ensures that AI literacy is aligned with not just technological progress but also legal and societal responsibilities

Future Directions and Regulatory Frameworks

As AI continues its rapid integration into mental health care, its future rests upon a delicate balance between innovation and ethical stewardship. The promise of AI to enable precision psychiatry, facilitate early intervention, and support collaborative patient-clinician relationships is profound. Yet, these advances also call for a robust and forward-thinking regulatory infrastructure that ensures AI operates within well defined clinical, ethical, and legal boundaries. From the perspective of the socio-technical ecosystem, this requires coordination across technological design, clinician training, institutional workflow integration, and societal governance to create a balanced and trustworthy system.

CONCLUSION

The integration of AI into mental health care is reshaping clinical practice, research, and the delivery of psychological support. This chapter has examined three interrelated domains: the rise of AI-powered digital companions, the emergence of clinical diagnostic and decision-support systems, and the training of mental health professionals to engage with these technologies. Taken together, these developments demonstrate how AI can expand access to care, enhance diagnostic accuracy, and create new opportunities for personalized intervention.

Digital companions such as mental health chatbots and mobile applications—already extend therapeutic reach beyond the clinic, offering evidence-based exercises in CBT, mindfulness, and crisis support. Clinical decision-support systems leverage multimodal data, from speech biomarkers to electronic health records, to inform more precise diagnosis and treatment planning. At the same time, training initiatives underscore the critical role of clinicians, ensuring that these technologies are applied ethically, responsibly, and in ways that preserve trust and therapeutic alliance.

Yet, these innovations must be approached with caution. Over-reliance on AI tools, gaps in cultural and linguistic inclusivity, and persistent global inequities in access present significant risks. AI is not a substitute for the human connection at the core of mental health care; rather, it is a tool that must augment the empathy, contextual judgment, and ethical sensitivity of trained professionals. Without adequate training, clinicians may misuse or mistrust these tools, undermining their potential.

For this reason, AI literacy should be embedded as a core professional competency across psychology, psychiatry, social work, and allied disciplines. Curricula must extend beyond technical familiarity to encompass applied ethics, interdisciplinary collaboration, and policy awareness. International frameworks, such as those advanced by WHO and UNESCO, provide essential guidance by emphasizing transparency, fairness, data protection, and respect for patient autonomy.

Looking forward, the socio-technical ecosystem framework(figure 3) reminds us that the success of AI in mental health depends on alignment across multiple layers: technological innovation, clinician patient interactions, institutional training and workflows, and societal governance. Actionable priorities include: (1) integrating AI literacy into professional training programs; (2) expanding inclusivity through culturally adaptive, multilingual AI tools; (3) strengthening regulatory mechanisms to ensure accountability and transparency; and (4) fostering global research collaborations to validate AI applications across diverse populations.

Figure 3. Socio-technical ecosystem framework

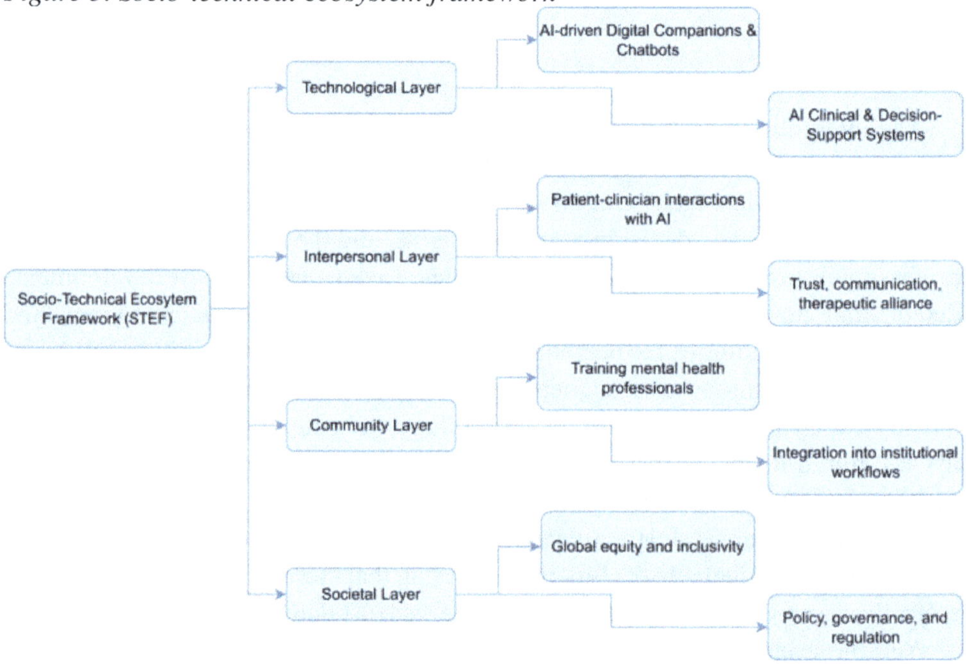

In this light, AI is best understood not as an end in itself, but as a means of advancing more equitable, responsive, and human-centered care. By actively shaping how these tools are developed, implemented, and governed, mental health professionals can ensure that technology serves as a partner in healing rather than a replacement for it. The future of mental health care will depend not only on technological progress but also on the collective commitment of clinicians, researchers, and policymakers to embed AI within systems that are intelligent, ethical, and compassionate.

REFERENCES

American Psychiatric Association. (2024). *Privacy and patient security in AI-enhanced psychiatric care*. Retrieved from https://www.psychiatry.org

Bloch-Atefi, A. (2025). Balancing ethics and opportunities: The role of AI in psychotherapy and counselling. *Psychotherapy and Counselling Journal of Australia, 8*(2), 15–27. DOI: 10.59158/001c.129884

Charow, R., Jeyakumar, T., Younus, S., Dolatabadi, E., Salhia, M., Al-Mouaswas, D., Anderson, M., Balakumar, S., Clare, M., Dhalla, A., Gillan, C., Haghzare, S., Jackson, E., Lalani, N., Mattson, J., Peteanu, W., Tripp, T., Waldorf, J., Williams, S., & Wiljer, D. (2021). Artificial intelligence education programs for health care professionals: A scoping review. *JMIR Medical Education, 7*(4), e31043. DOI: 10.2196/31043 PMID: 34898458

Di Stefano, V., D'Angelo, M., Monaco, F., Vignapiano, A., Martiadis, V., Barone, E., Fornaro, M., Steardo, L., Solmi, M., Manchia, M., & Steardo, L.Jr. (2024). Decoding Schizophrenia: How AI-Enhanced fMRI Unlocks New Pathways for Precision Psychiatry. *Brain Sciences, 14*(12), 1196. DOI: 10.3390/brainsci14121196 PMID: 39766395

Dwyer, D. B., Falkai, P., & Koutsouleris, N. (2018). Machine learning approaches for clinical psychology and psychiatry. *Annual Review of Clinical Psychology, 14*(1), 91–118. DOI: 10.1146/annurev-clinpsy-032816-045037 PMID: 29401044

Feng, Y., Hang, Y., Wu, W., Song, X., Xiao, X., Dong, F., & Qiao, Z. (2025). Effectiveness of AI-Driven Conversational Agents in Improving Mental Health Among Young People: Systematic Review and Meta-Analysis. *Journal of Medical Internet Research, 27*, e69639. DOI: 10.2196/69639 PMID: 40367506

Fitzpatrick, K. K., Darcy, A., & Vierhile, M. (2017). Delivering cognitive behavior therapy to young adults with symptoms of depression and anxiety using a fully automated conversational agent (Woebot): A randomized controlled trial. *JMIR Mental Health, 4*(2), e19. DOI: 10.2196/mental.7785 PMID: 28588005

Floridi, L., Cowls, J., Beltrametti, M., Chatila, R., Chazerand, P., Dignum, V., Luetge, C., Madelin, R., Pagallo, U., Rossi, F., Schafer, B., Valcke, P., & Vayena, E. (2018). AI4People—An ethical framework for a good AI society: Opportunities, risks, principles, and recommendations. *Minds and Machines, 28*(4), 689–707. DOI: 10.1007/s11023-018-9482-5 PMID: 30930541

Fulmer, R., Joerin, A., Gentile, B., Lakerink, L., & Rauws, M. (2018). Using psychological artificial intelligence (Tess) to relieve symptoms of depression and anxiety: Randomized controlled trial. *JMIR Mental Health*, *5*(4), e64. DOI: 10.2196/mental.9782 PMID: 30545815

Gaffney, H., Mansell, W., & Tai, S. (2019). Conversational agents in the treatment of mental health problems: Mixed-method systematic review. *JMIR Mental Health*, *6*(10), e14166. DOI: 10.2196/14166 PMID: 31628789

Gilbert, H., Sandborn, M., Schmidt, D. C., Spencer-Smith, J., & White, J. (2023, November). Semantic compression with large language models. In *2023 Tenth International Conference on Social Networks Analysis, Management and Security (SNAMS)* (pp. 1-8). IEEE.

Gilson, A., Safranek, C. W., Huang, T., Socrates, V., Chi, L., Taylor, R. A., & Chartash, D. (2023). How does ChatGPT perform on the United States Medical Licensing Examination? The implications of large language models for medical education and knowledge assessment. *JMIR Medical Education*, *9*, e45312. DOI: 10.2196/45312 PMID: 36753318

Hatem, R., Simmons, B., & Thornton, J. E. (2023). A Call to Address AI "Hallucinations" and How Healthcare Professionals Can Mitigate Their Risks. *Cureus*, *15*(9), e44720. DOI: 10.7759/cureus.44720 PMID: 37809168

Hoermann, S., McCabe, K. L., Milne, D. N., & Calvo, R. A. (2017). Application of synchronous text-based dialogue systems in mental health interventions: Systematic review. *Journal of Medical Internet Research*, *19*(8), e267. DOI: 10.2196/jmir.7023 PMID: 28784594

House of Commons. (2025). AI and mental healthcare: Opportunities and delivery considerations. *House of Commons Library POSTnote, 737*, 1–21. https://researchbriefings.files.parliament.uk/documents/POST-PN-737/POST-PN-737.pdf

Inkster, B., Sarda, S., & Subramanian, V. (2018). An empathy-driven, conversational artificial intelligence agent (Wysa) for digital mental well-being: Real-world data evaluation. *JMIR mHealth and uHealth*, *6*(11), e12106. DOI: 10.2196/12106 PMID: 30470676

Kleine, A. K.. (2024). AI-enabled clinical decision support tools for mental healthcare. *Journal of Medical Systems*. Advance online publication. DOI: 10.1016/j.artmed.2024.103052 PMID: 39662140

Larsen, L. (2024). Revolutionizing mental healthcare through AI-enhanced provider–patient relationships. *Patient Safety & Quality Healthcare*. Retrieved from https://www.psqh.com/

Liu, J., & Zhang, Y. (2024). Understanding and Facilitating Mental Health Help-Seeking of Young Adults: A Socio-technical Ecosystem Framework. *arXiv preprint arXiv:2401.08994*.

Lomis, K., Jeffries, P., Palatta, A., Sage, M., Sheikh, J., Sheperis, C., & Whelan, A. (2021). A call to action: Integrating AI in health professions education. *Journal of Health Professions Education, 12*(3), 127–130. DOI: 10.31478/202109a PMID: 34901780

Mesko, Bertalan. (2018). Future Directions of Digital Health. http://dx.doi.org/DOI: 10.1007/978-3-319-61446-5_22

Milasan, L. H., & Scott-Purdy, D. (2025). The future of artificial intelligence in mental health nursing practice: An integrative review. *International Journal of Mental Health Nursing, 34*(1), e70003. Advance online publication. DOI: 10.1111/inm.70003 PMID: 39844734

Miner, A. (2021). Augmenting psychotherapy with artificial intelligence. *Stanford HAI News*. Retrieved from https://hai.stanford.edu

Mitchell, A. J., Vaze, A., & Rao, S. (2009). Clinical diagnosis of depression in primary care: A meta-analysis. *Lancet, 374*(9690), 609–619. DOI: 10.1016/S0140-6736(09)60879-5 PMID: 19640579

O'Neil, C. (2016). *Weapons of math destruction: How big data increases inequality and threatens democracy*. Crown Publishing., DOI: 10.5860/crl.78.3.403

Paranjape, K., Schinkel, M., Nannan Panday, R. A., Car, J., & Nanayakkara, P. (2020). Introducing artificial intelligence training in medical education. *JMIR Medical Education, 6*(1), e16048. DOI: 10.2196/16048 PMID: 31793895

Perumal, M. K. K.. (2025). *Artificial intelligence-driven clinical decision support systems in healthcare: Opportunities and challenges*. PMC., DOI: 10.3389/froh.2025.1592428

Provoost, S., Lau, H. M., Ruwaard, J., & Riper, H. (2017). Embodied conversational agents in clinical psychology: A scoping review. *Journal of Medical Internet Research, 19*(5), e151. DOI: 10.2196/jmir.6553 PMID: 28487267

Shatte, A. B. R., Hutchinson, D. M., & Teague, S. J. (2019). Machine learning in mental health: A scoping review of methods and applications. *Psychological Medicine*, *49*(9), 1426–1448. DOI: 10.1017/S0033291719000151 PMID: 30744717

Shortliffe, E. H. (1976). *Computer-Based Medical Consultations: MYCIN*. American Elsevier., DOI: 10.1097/00004669-197610000-00011

South Eastern European Journal of Public Health. (2024). Ethical considerations in the era of artificial intelligence: Implications for mental health, well-being, and digital health. https://doi.org/DOI: 10.70135/seejph.vi.2893

Tilala, M. H., Chenchala, P. K., Choppadandi, A., Kaur, J., Naguri, S., Saoji, R., & Devaguptapu, B. (2024). Ethical considerations in the use of artificial intelligence and machine learning in healthcare. *Health Care*, *11*(3), 588–595. DOI: 10.3390/healthcare11030588

Torous, J., & Roberts, L. W. (2017). The ethical use of mobile health technology in clinical psychiatry. *The Journal of Nervous and Mental Disease*, *205*(1), 4–8. DOI: 10.1097/NMD.0000000000000596 PMID: 28005647

UNESCO. (2021). *Recommendation on the ethics of artificial intelligence*. United Nations Educational, Scientific and Cultural Organization.

Vaidyam, A. N., Wisniewski, H., Halamka, J. D., Kashavan, M. S., & Torous, J. B. (2019). Chatbots and conversational agents in mental health: A review of the psychiatric landscape. *Canadian Journal of Psychiatry*, *64*(7), 456–464. DOI: 10.1177/0706743719828977 PMID: 30897957

Weizenbaum, J. (1966). ELIZA — A computer program for the study of natural language communication between man and machine. *Communications of the ACM*, *9*(1), 36–45. DOI: 10.1145/365153.365168

Wills, M. (2024). New APA CEO on uses of artificial intelligence in mental health, the future of psychiatry and more. *AMA Update*. https://www.ama-assn.org/doctor-news/

World Health Organization. (2022). *Global strategy on digital health 2020–2025*. WHO.

World Health Organization. (2024). WHO releases AI ethics and governance guidance for large multi-modal models. Geneva, Switzerland. Retrieved from https://www.who.int/news/

Yamaguchi, H., Sugihara, G., Shimizu, M., & Yamashita, Y. (2024). Generative artificial intelligence model for simulating structural brain changes in schizophrenia. *Frontiers in Psychiatry*, *15*, 1437075. Advance online publication. DOI: 10.3389/fpsyt.2024.1437075 PMID: 39429522

Chapter 5
Exploring the Barriers and Opportunities of ICT Integration in Virtual Campuses:
A Case Study of Higher Education in Pakistan

Samra Maqbool
https://orcid.org/0000-0001-5958-3800
Beijing Normal University, China

Hafiz Muhammad Ihsan Zafeer
https://orcid.org/0000-0002-8757-9478
Henan University, China

Sufyan Maqbool
https://orcid.org/0009-0007-6290-1305
Zhejiang Normal University, China

Ayesha Tariq
https://orcid.org/0009-0001-9222-9544
The Islamia University of Bahawalpur, Pakistan

Al-Masaeid Mohammad
Flinders University, Australia

Abida Rasool
https://orcid.org/0000-0002-0830-9948
Beijing Normal University, China

ABSTRACT

This study explored the role of Information and Communication Technologies (ICT) in revolutionizing virtual campuses and e-learning at two major Pakistani universities: Virtual University and Allama Iqbal Open University. With the rapid shift towards digital education, this research aims to understand the effectiveness, challenges, and opportunities of ICT integration in higher education. A qualitative approach was used, involving 41 participants from diverse academic backgrounds, including students, faculty, and administrators. Data was collected through face-to-face and

DOI: 10.4018/979-8-3373-4217-7.ch005

WhatsApp online interviews, with thematic analysis applied to identify key themes such as the effectiveness of ICT in enhancing learning, technological infrastructure challenges, and the need for digital literacy training, student engagement, and socio cultural barriers. The findings revealed that while ICT has the potential to significantly improve access and flexibility in education, challenges such as unreliable internet connectivity, lack of digital skills, and cultural resistance remain prevalent.

INTRODUCTION, PROBLEM, PURPOSE AND IMPORTANCE

The rapid advancement of Information and Communication Technologies (ICT) has dramatically transformed the landscape of education globally (Ukpe, 2023). The proliferation of digital tools, the internet, and e-learning platforms has not only enhanced access to education but also changed how teaching and learning occur (Bagde et al., 2021). In Pakistan, higher education institutions are increasingly adopting ICT tools to deliver educational content through virtual campuses and e-learning platforms (Asad et al., 2021; Qazi et al., 2024). However, despite the growing implementation of these technologies, there remains a significant gap in understanding how ICT is truly revolutionizing education in Pakistani universities. While ICT has immense potential to improve educational quality, access, and equity, its adoption and impact within the context of Pakistan still face several challenges (Akram et al., 2021; Zmir et al., 2021). This study seeks to explore the role of ICT in revolutionizing virtual campuses and e-learning in Pakistan, examining its benefits, challenges, and the potential future of digital education in the country.

In Pakistan, the higher education sector is undergoing significant transformation due to the integration of ICT in academic environments. The COVID-19 pandemic accelerated the shift toward online learning, compelling universities to adopt virtual learning environments quickly (Webb et al., 2021; Zamir et al., 2021). According to a report by the Higher Education Commission (HEC) of Pakistan, there was a notable increase in the use of Learning Management Systems (LMS) and online classes during the pandemic (Alturki & Aldraiweesh, 2021; Zafeer et al.).

However, despite these efforts, several systemic issues continue to hinder the full realization of the benefits of ICT in education. Firstly, infrastructure limitations pose a significant barrier to the effective use of ICT in education. Many students, especially those from rural areas, lack access to stable internet connections and modern computing devices. According to the Pakistan Telecommunication Authority (PTA), internet penetration in rural areas is lower compared to urban centers, further exacerbating the digital divide (Lateef et al., 2025; Zafeer, Yanping, et al., 2022). Secondly, there is a lack of digital literacy among both students and faculty members, which hampers the effective utilization of e-learning platforms. A study by Akram et al. (2021) highlighted that many university faculty members in Pakistan were not adequately trained to use e-learning technologies, leading to ineffective teaching methods in virtual classrooms (Zafeer et al., 2020).

Moreover, there are concerns regarding the quality and accessibility of online education. While virtual campuses have provided a way for students to continue their education during the pandemic, the quality of online education varies significantly across universities. Some institutions struggle to maintain the same level of academic rigor in virtual environments as they do in traditional classrooms (Zafeer et al., 2025a; Zafeer et al., 2021). Furthermore, there is limited research on how e-learning platforms in Pakistan impact student engagement, academic performance, and overall learning outcomes. These challenges indicate that while ICT has the potential to transform education, its successful implementation in Pakistan requires addressing multiple barriers (Zafeer, Maqbool, et al., 2022).

The purposed of this study is to examine how Information and Communication Technologies are revolutionizing virtual campuses and e-learning in Pakistani universities. By investigating the perspectives of both students and faculty, the study aims to provide a comprehensive understanding of the challenges, opportunities, and outcomes associated with the integration of ICT in higher education. This study also explored how virtual campuses are reshaping the educational experience in Pakistan, focusing on the impact on student engagement, academic performance, and learning outcomes.

The study is crucial for several reasons. First, it will contribute to the ongoing discourse on digital education in Pakistan by offering insights into the effectiveness of virtual learning environments and identifying key factors that influence their success. Second, the findings helped policymakers, university administrators, and faculty members understand the current state of ICT integration in Pakistani higher education and provide recommendations for enhancing the adoption of ICT in teaching and learning. Finally, the study offered a deeper understanding of the barriers to digital education in Pakistan, such as infrastructure limitations, digital literacy, and socio-cultural factors, which can guide future policy interventions and investments in education technology (Zafeer et al., 2025c).

In addition to addressing the practical challenges of ICT adoption, this study also contributed to the academic literature on e-learning and virtual campuses in developing countries. By focusing on the specific context of Pakistan, the homework provided valuable insights into the unique challenges faced by universities in the Global South, where educational technology adoption is often hindered by factors such as resource constraints, limited access to technology, and socio-economic inequalities.

This study is important because it provided an evidence based assessment of how ICT is reshaping the educational landscape in Pakistan. By focusing on both the challenges and opportunities presented by digital transformation, the research highlighted the potential of ICT to improve access to education, especially in underserved regions of the country. Additionally, understanding the impact of ICT on student engagement and academic performance is crucial for ensuring that virtual campuses and e-learning platforms can achieve their intended goals. The findings not only benefit Pakistani universities but also contributed to the global conversation on the future of education in the digital age.

THEORETICAL PERSPECTIVE AND LITERATURE REVIEW

The role of Information and Communication Technologies (ICT) in reshaping educational practices is grounded in several theoretical frameworks. One of the central theories in understanding the integration of ICT in education is the Technology Acceptance Model (TAM), proposed by Granić and Marangunić (2019), which suggested that perceived ease of use and perceived usefulness determine an individual's intention to use a technology. In the context of e-learning in Pakistan, this model can help explain how students and faculty adopt and adapt to virtual campuses (Kanwal & Rehman, 2017; Zafeer et al., 2024). According to TAM, the greater the ease of use and perceived usefulness of e-learning platforms, the more likely they are to be accepted by students and educators. However, it is important to note that in the Pakistani context, factors such as digital literacy, infrastructure, and socio-cultural attitudes may influence the effectiveness of this model (Jin et al., 2024; Zafeer et al., 2023).

Another relevant theory is Constructivism, as articulated by Coupal (2004) and Mattar (2018), which emphasized the importance of active, social, and contextual learning. In the context of ICT in education, constructivist theories supported the use of digital tools to foster interactive and student centered learning. E-learning platforms can enable this type of learning by providing opportunities for collaborative work, interactive content, and real-time feedback, helping students construct their knowledge in a more personalized and meaningful way. Thus, constructivist theories argue that ICT, when used effectively, can enhance the educational experience by promoting deeper engagement and critical thinking (Lunenburg, 2011; Sarwar et al., 2021).

A third theoretical perspective is Diffusion of Innovations by Mbatha (2024) and Rogers et al. (2014), which explained how new technologies spread within a social system. According to this theory, the adoption of ICT in higher education is influenced by factors such as the perceived advantages of the technology, its compatibility with existing systems, the complexity of use, and the potential for trial ability. In Pakistan, the diffusion of ICT is influenced by a combination of government initiatives, university policies, and the willingness of faculty and students to embrace technological change (Ahmad et al., 2023; Samra Maqbool et al., 2014). This theory helps to explored why certain universities or individuals may be more inclined to adopt e-learning tools than others, considering the systemic barriers to ICT integration.

The role of ICT in transforming education, particularly in the form of virtual campuses and e-learning, has been widely studied across different contexts, with various studies examining both the opportunities and challenges associated with this digital shift. In this section, we review the existing literature on ICT in education, focusing on studies that specifically address the adoption of e-learning and virtual campuses in developing countries, with a particular emphasis on Pakistan (Rehman, Huang, Sarwar, et al., 2024).

ICT IN EDUCATION: GLOBAL AND REGIONAL TRENDS

Globally, the integration of ICT in education has been shown to enhance access, engagement, and learning outcomes. According to UNESCO (2013), ICT has the potential to improve education systems by making learning more accessible, efficient, and inclusive (Meskhi et al., 2019; Rehman, Huang, Mahmood, et al., 2024). In developed countries, the widespread availability of high-speed internet, advanced learning management systems (LMS), and digital content has enabled the expansion of virtual campuses. For instance, studies in the United States and European Union highlighted how ICT has been used to create blended learning environments, combining face-to-face teaching with online resources (Rehman, Huang, Mahmood, et al., 2024; Zagouras et al., 2022).

In contrast, in developing countries like Pakistan, the picture is more complex. Several studies have documented the significant potential of ICT to improve education in these regions, but challenges related to infrastructure, digital literacy, and policy support remain pervasive. A study by Afzal et al. (2023) highlighted that in developing countries, the success of ICT integration depends largely on bridging the digital divide and ensuring that all students, regardless of their socio-economic status, have access to the necessary technological tools. This is particularly relevant to Pakistan, where rural-urban disparities in access to ICT infrastructure persist (Maqbool et al.; Xu & Rangra, 2024).

E-LEARNING AND VIRTUAL CAMPUSES IN PAKISTAN

The integration of ICT in Pakistan's higher education system has gained momentum in recent years, particularly with the rise of virtual campuses and e-learning platforms (Asad et al., 2021). According to HEC (2020), during the COVID-19 pandemic, Pakistani universities rapidly adopted online learning platforms to ensure continuity in education. However, the quality and effectiveness of e-learning in Pakistan remain a subject of debate (Farid et al., 2015; Maqbool et al., 2023). Studies have shown that while e-learning platforms like Moodle and Blackboard were introduced in many universities, their impact on student engagement and academic performance has been mixed (Samra Maqbool, Hafiz Muhammad Ihsan Zafeer, Pingfei Zeng, et al., 2024; Poondej & Lerdpornkulrat, 2020).

A study by Iqbal et al. (2022) examined the adoption of e-learning in Pakistani universities and found that while students appreciated the convenience and flexibility of online learning, challenges such as limited access to reliable internet, inadequate technological infrastructure, and the lack of digital literacy hindered the effective use of these platforms. In rural areas, these challenges are even more pronounced, as students often lack the necessary devices and stable internet connections to participate in online learning fully (Das et al., 2021; Maqbool et al., 2022). Furthermore, a study by Zalat et al. (2021) explored faculty perspectives on the use of ICT in teaching and found that many faculty members faced difficulties in adapting to online teaching methods due to insufficient training in the use of e-learning tools. This finding echoes a broader concern about the need for faculty development programs to enhance digital literacy and pedagogical skills for teaching in virtual environments (Aithal & Aithal, 2023; Samra Maqbool, Hafiz Muhammad Ihsan Zafeer, Sufyan Maqbool, et al., 2024).

STUDENT ENGAGEMENT AND LEARNING OUTCOMES IN VIRTUAL CAMPUSES

The effectiveness of ICT in enhancing student engagement and academic outcomes is a key concern for researchers studying virtual campuses and e-learning. A study by Rajabalee and Santally (2021) found that students who participated in online learning environments reported higher levels of engagement and satisfaction when the courses were designed to incorporate interactive elements, such as discussion forums, quizzes, and multimedia content. This finding is supported by research from the World Bank (2014), which emphasized that the success of e-learning programs depends on the quality of instructional design, the use of interactive tools, and the alignment of online courses with students' needs (Debattista, 2018; Maqbool et al., 2025).

In Pakistan, however, the challenge of fostering engagement in virtual learning environments remains significant. A study by Iqbal et al. (2022) found that while students enrolled in e-learning courses in Pakistan were generally satisfied with the flexibility of online learning, they struggled with issues such as the lack of real-time interaction with instructors and peers, which negatively impacted their engagement and learning outcomes. These findings underscored the importance of incorporating synchronous elements into e-learning platforms, such as live lectures and virtual group discussions, to enhance student interaction and engagement (Adeshola & Agoyi, 2023; Mansour, 2024).

BARRIERS TO ICT ADOPTION IN HIGHER EDUCATION

Several studies have identified key barriers to the adoption of ICT in higher education sector. As mentioned earlier, infrastructure limitations, including unreliable internet access, especially in rural areas, are significant barriers (Qazi et al., 2024). Another study major barrier found that the lack of digital literacy among both students and faculty, which impedes the effective use of e-learning platforms (Qashou, 2022). A study by Rafeeq and Ali (2021) highlighted that faculty members in Pakistani universities were often hesitant to adopt ICT in their teaching due to insufficient training and a lack of technical support (Maqbool, Wei, et al., 2020).

In addition to infrastructure and digital literacy, socio-cultural factors also played a role in the adoption of ICT in education. A study by Ali et al. (2021) examined the cultural perceptions of e-learning in Pakistan and found that traditional views of education, which prioritize face-to-face interaction and teacher-centered pedagogy, sometimes hinder the acceptance of online learning. This highlighted the need for a cultural shift towards more technology-friendly educational practices in Pakistan (Maqbool, Sarwar, et al., 2020).

METHOD AND PROCEDURE OF DATA COLLECTION

This study adopted a qualitative research approach to explore the perspectives of students, faculty, and administrators regarding the role of ICT in virtual campuses and e-learning in Pakistan. The data was gathered from a sample of 41 participants from Virtual University and Allama Iqbal Open University. The participants were selected to represent a diverse group, including male and female students, faculty members, and administrators, with varying educational backgrounds such as MS, diplomas, and short courses. These participants were engaged in both online and offline classes, providing a comprehensive understanding of how ICT is perceived across different groups in the educational environment.

To gather in-depth insights, the researcher conducted semi-structured interviews with the participants. These interviews were carried out in two formats: face-to-face and WhatsApp online interviews. Face-to-face interviews were held with those participants who were available for in person interaction, while the WhatsApp interviews were conducted for participants who were more comfortable or only available through online means. Each interview lasted approximately 65 minutes, offering ample time for participants to express their views in detail.

An interview guide was employed to direct the interview process, with flexibility built into the questions to allow for follow-up and probing for deeper insights. This guided structure provided the researcher with the ability to explore specific issues in detail, monitor changes in tone, and observe body language during face-to-face interviews, which helped to enrich the data. To ensure that participants were comfortable and could express themselves more easily, the interviews were conducted in both English and Urdu, depending on the participant's preference. This language flexibility helped ensure that the participants fully understood the questions and could share their opinions without any barriers to communication.

Thematic analysis was used to analyze the data, following the six steps outlined by Zafeer et al. (2023) for qualitative data analysis. These steps included data preparation (transcribing the interviews), organizing data (sorting the transcripts), coding the data (identifying key words or phrases), categorizing the codes into themes, interpreting the findings, and verifying the accuracy of the analysis. After transcribing all 41 interviews, the researcher meticulously coded the data, grouping related codes into categories. These categories were then analyzed to develop five main themes, which provided a comprehensive understanding of the role of ICT in virtual campuses and the challenges and opportunities it presents figure1. The researcher revisited these themes several times to ensure they addressed the research questions thoroughly.

Figure 1. Research Question with Themes details

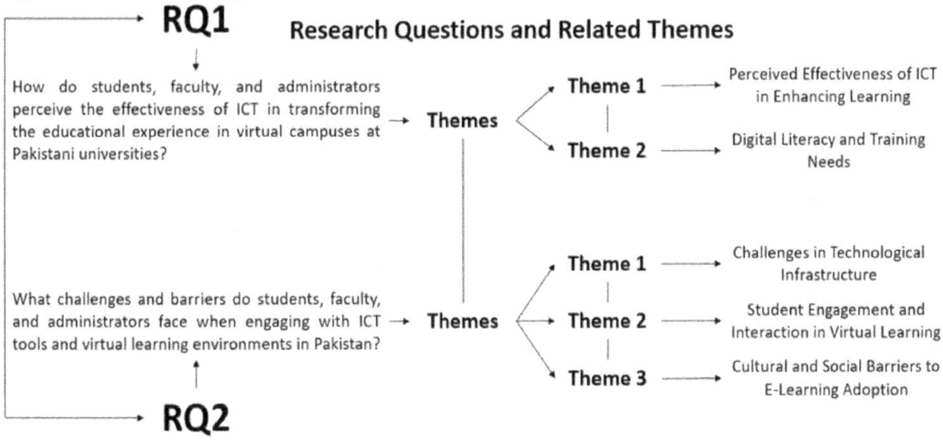

Data Analysis

The thematic analysis of the data led to the identification of five key themes, which provided a framework for understanding the role of ICT in virtual campuses and e-learning. These themes were as follows:

Perceived Effectiveness of ICT in Enhancing Learning: This theme focused on how participants perceived the effectiveness of ICT in improving the quality of education, increasing accessibility, and facilitating the learning process in virtual campuses. The theme explored how students, faculty, and administrators viewed the integration of digital tools such as Learning Management Systems (LMS), online lectures, and digital content in transforming traditional education methods.

Challenges in Technological Infrastructure: This theme addressed the infrastructural challenges participants faced when engaging with ICT tools. It highlighted issues such as unreliable internet connections, limited access to computing devices, and the lack of technical support at both student and institutional levels. This theme provided insights into how these challenges affected the adoption and effective use of virtual learning platforms.

Digital Literacy and Training Needs: This theme explored the level of digital literacy among students, faculty, and administrators. It examined how the lack of adequate digital skills and training hindered effective use of e-learning tools and impacted overall engagement with virtual campuses. The theme also looked at the need for faculty development programs to improve digital competency.

Student Engagement and Interaction in Virtual Learning: The theme focused on the engagement of students in virtual learning environments. It explored how ICT tools contributed to or hindered student interaction with instructors and peers, the perceived quality of online interactions, and how students maintained motivation in an online setting. It also examined how virtual campuses could enhance or detract from students' academic performance and overall satisfaction.

Cultural and Social Barriers to E-Learning Adoption: This theme investigated the cultural and social challenges to the widespread adoption of ICT in education. It addressed factors such as traditional views on education, resistance to change, and the preference for face-to-face interaction in Pakistani society. The theme aimed to understand how these cultural attitudes influenced the acceptance of virtual learning environments.

Ethical Considerations

Ethical consent was obtained from all participants prior to the interviews. Each participant was fully informed about the purpose of the study, the voluntary nature of their participation, and their right to withdraw at any point without consequences. Consent was obtained for both face-to-face and online interviews, and participants were assured that their responses would remain confidential and anonymous. The researcher ensured that no identifying information would be shared in the study's results, and all recordings were stored securely. For participants who opted for online interviews, written consent was obtained via WhatsApp before beginning the data collection. By adhering to ethical principles, the researcher ensured that participants' rights were respected throughout the study.

Challenges Faced During Data Collection

Several challenges emerged during the data collection process. One major challenge was scheduling interviews, as participants had busy academic and professional schedules. This required flexibility on the part of the researcher, who had to adjust timings to accommodate the participants' availability. Additionally, technical difficulties with internet connections during online interviews were frequent, particularly with participants from rural areas who had unstable internet access. These issues occasionally interrupted the flow of interviews and required re-scheduling. Furthermore, while the use of both English and Urdu helped alleviate language barriers, some participants still struggled to express their thoughts in English, leading to occasional misunderstandings during the interviews. To address this, the researcher offered clarification and translated when necessary to ensure accurate communication. Despite these challenges, the data collection process was successfully completed over five months, allowing the researcher to gather rich insights into the use of ICT in Pakistani higher education.

In conclusion, this study's qualitative approach, utilizing thematic analysis and semi-structured interviews, provided a detailed understanding of how ICT is transforming education in Pakistan's virtual campuses.

FINDINGS OF EACH THEME AND PARTICIPANT RESPONSES

The following findings were derived from the thematic analysis of the interviews conducted with the 41 participants from Virtual University and Allama Iqbal Open University. Each theme presents the key findings and responses from the participants, grouped by the five identified themes.

1. Perceived Effectiveness of ICT in Enhancing Learning

Participants largely acknowledged the effectiveness of ICT tools in making education more accessible, flexible, and efficient. Both students and faculty saw the potential of virtual campuses to enhance the learning experience by offering the convenience of online lectures, digital resources, and interactive tools. However, some participants expressed concerns about the lack of personal interaction in online environments, which they felt might impact the quality of learning.

Participants' Responses

Student 1 (Virtual University): *"I find online lectures helpful, especially when I can watch them at my own pace. But sometimes I feel that face-to-face interaction is missing, which makes it harder to understand some topics."* Faculty 3 (Allama Iqbal Open University): "*ICT has made it easier for me to share course materials and track students' progress. It also allows me to engage with students beyond the classroom, though it's not the same as face-to-face teaching.*" Administrator 2 (Virtual University): "*The virtual campus is very effective for students who need flexibility. The use of tools like LMS has been a game-changer for us in terms of delivering quality education."*

2. Challenges in Technological Infrastructure

Technological infrastructure emerged as a major barrier to the effective use of ICT in education. Several students from rural areas reported issues with internet connectivity, while faculty mentioned the lack of proper hardware and technical support at the institutional level. Many participants noted that these infrastructural challenges hindered their ability to fully participate in or deliver virtual learning.

Participants' Responses

Student 5 (Virtual University): *"I live in a rural area, and sometimes the internet disconnects during my classes. It's very frustrating because I miss out on important lectures."* Faculty 7 (Allama Iqbal Open University): "*While I have the technology to teach, not all students do. Some of them don't have a stable internet connection, and that creates a gap in their learning.*" Administrator 4 (Virtual University): "*We've been trying to upgrade our infrastructure, but it's a challenge. We have limited resources, and the quality of internet services is not uniform across the country.*"

3. Digital Literacy and Training Needs

Both faculty and students emphasized the need for enhanced digital literacy to maximize the benefits of ICT tools. While students with basic digital skills adapted quickly, faculty members struggled with using the e-learning platforms effectively due to a lack of adequate training. Many respondents highlighted that the absence of formal training programs for teachers and students was a significant hurdle.

Participants' Responses

Student 8 (Virtual University): *"I am comfortable with using digital tools, but some of my classmates struggle with the LMS. They aren't familiar with how to use it efficiently."* Faculty 10 (Allama Iqbal Open University): "*Although I have experience using computers, I wasn't trained to use the LMS for teaching. I had to learn by trial and error, which wasn't ideal.*" Administrator 1 (Virtual University): "*Digital literacy is a critical issue. We need more workshops and training programs for both students and faculty to improve their technological skills.*"

4. Student Engagement and Interaction in Virtual Learning

Student engagement in virtual learning was a mixed experience. While some students enjoyed the flexibility of online classes, others reported feeling disconnected from the learning process due to limited interaction with instructors and peers. Faculty members noted that maintaining engagement through online platforms was more challenging compared to traditional face-to-face teaching.

Participants' Responses

Student 12 (Allama Iqbal Open University): "*I prefer online classes because I can manage my schedule. But sometimes, I feel like I'm just listening to a lecture without interacting much. I miss the discussions we used to have in class.*" Faculty 5 (Virtual University): *"Engaging students online requires a different approach. I try to use discussion forums and quizzes, but it's hard to replicate the interaction we had in the classroom. Some students don't participate at all."* Administrator 6 (Allama Iqbal Open University): "*We've seen a drop in student participation in virtual classes. We're exploring ways to increase engagement, such as introducing more interactive features like live sessions.*"

5. Cultural and Social Barriers to E-Learning Adoption

Cultural attitudes toward traditional education and resistance to change were significant barriers to the widespread adoption of ICT in education. Many participants mentioned that students and faculty members who preferred face-to-face interaction were initially reluctant to embrace online learning. Social factors, such as gender roles and access to technology, also influenced the adoption of e-learning tools, particularly in rural and conservative areas.

Participants' Responses

Student 15 (Virtual University): "*Some of my relatives think online learning isn't as valuable as traditional classroom learning. They still believe that face-to-face classes are more legitimate.*" Faculty 9 (Allama Iqbal Open University): "*There's a cultural resistance to online learning among some of my colleagues. They're used to the old ways of teaching and believe that the quality of learning is compromised in virtual settings.*" Administrator 3 (Virtual University): "*In rural areas, there's a significant gap in terms of access to technology, especially for female students. The social barriers limit their ability to participate in online education.*"

The findings from this study underscored both the potential and challenges of ICT in revolutionizing education in Pakistan's virtual campuses. While there is a clear recognition of the benefits of online learning, including increased flexibility and access to resources, the barriers such as infrastructural limitations, lack of digital literacy, and cultural resistance pose significant challenges to effective implementation. These findings provided valuable insights into the factors that need to be addressed in order to enhance the effectiveness of ICT tools and e-learning environments in Pakistani higher education.

DISCUSSION AND CONCLUSION

The findings of this study on the use of Information and Communication Technologies (ICT) in virtual campuses and e-learning environments at Virtual University and Allama Iqbal Open University align with and contributed to the broader discourse on ICT adoption in higher education, particularly in developing countries. While the integration of ICT holds significant promise for transforming education, the challenges identified in this study reflect common issues faced by many institutions worldwide, especially in countries with limited infrastructure and resources. The discussion is organized according to the themes identified in the findings: Perceived Effectiveness of ICT in Enhancing Learning, Challenges in Technological Infrastructure, Digital Literacy and Training Needs, Student Engagement and Interaction, and Cultural and Social Barriers to E-Learning Adoption. The result of this study indicated that most participants both students and faculty recognized the potential of ICT in enhancing the learning experience (Sufyan Maqbool et al., 2024). Students valued the flexibility that e-learning offered, particularly in terms of access to recorded lectures and resources, while faculty acknowledged the ability to deliver content and track student progress efficiently (Maqbool, 2025). However, the lack of face-to-face interaction was a common concern. This finding resonated with previous research, which has also highlighted the mixed perceptions regarding the effectiveness of online education. El-Sabagh (2021) and Lasekan et al. (2024) emphasized the flexibility of ICT tools, but also pointed out that the absence of direct interaction in virtual learning environments could affect student engagement and the depth of learning (Malik et al., 2025).

Similarly, a study by Gul et al. (2023) found that while students in Pakistan appreciated the convenience of online learning, many felt that the lack of personal interaction detracted from the quality of their education (Javed et al., 2024; Kalim et al., 2025). Furthermore, this study supported the notion put forward by Al-Gerafi et al. (2024) that e-learning platforms can be effective if designed thoughtfully to include interactive elements. Despite the positives, our findings indicated that the full potential of ICT is yet to be realized in Pakistan due to underlying infrastructural and engagement-related challenges (Draissi et al., 2025).

The technological infrastructure limitations identified in this study specifically unreliable internet connectivity and limited access to devices mirror challenges reported in other developing countries. According to Anderson (2023) the digital divide remains a major barrier to the effective implementation of ICT in education, particularly in rural areas. This study discovered by Sartika et al. (2021) found that students in rural areas faced significant challenges in participating in online education due to poor internet access, a finding that is consistent with research by Kazi et al. (2021), who pointed out the stark contrast in internet access between urban and rural regions of Pakistan. These findings also align with the concerns raised by the World Bank (2014), which argued that despite the growing adoption of ICT tools, the infrastructure gap often prevents students from fully benefiting from digital education (Rehman et al., 2025; Timotheou et al., 2023). This highlighted the urgent need for investment in digital infrastructure and equitable access to technology in Pakistan, particularly in remote areas, to ensure that no student is left behind in the digital education revolution.

The lack of digital literacy among both students and faculty emerged as another significant barrier in this study. This finding is consistent with previous studies that have shown the importance of digital literacy in the successful adoption of ICT in education. The study by Shahzad and Khan (2024) indicated that faculty members in Pakistan were often not adequately trained to use e-learning platforms, which limited their ability to deliver effective online teaching. Similarly, Wade et al. (2024) reported that many students struggled to navigate Learning Management Systems (LMS) due to insufficient training and support. The current study also revealed that both students and faculty expressed the need for more training programs to improve their digital skills, supporting the argument made by Vyortkina and Elsawy (2024) that faculty development is critical for the successful integration of ICT in teaching. While some students were able to adapt to online learning, others faced challenges in using digital tools effectively, pointing to the need for targeted training programs that can equip both students and faculty with the necessary skills to fully engage with e-learning platforms.

Student engagement in online learning environments is a critical issue, as highlighted by several studies. Our findings revealed that while some students appreciated the flexibility of online learning, others reported feeling disengaged due to the lack of interaction with instructors and peers. This aligns with the findings of Mansour (2024), who found that students reported higher engagement when online courses included interactive elements, such as discussion forums and real-time feedback. Additionally, the World Bank (2014) emphasized that the effectiveness of online education depends not only on the technology itself but also on how it is implemented to foster engagement and collaboration (Menberu, 2024; Zafeer et al., 2025b). The current study highlighted the importance of synchronous elements, such as live sessions and real-time discussions, to keep students engaged in virtual learning (Tu et al., 2025). This finding mirrors the work of Han (2024), who suggested that blended learning models, which combine both synchronous and asynchronous components, can lead to greater engagement and better learning outcomes. The faculty members in this study acknowledged the challenges of maintaining student engagement and expressed the need for more interactive features to create a more dynamic learning experience.

The cultural and social barriers identified in this study particularly resistance to online learning and the gender divide echo findings from other research on ICT adoption in education. In Pakistan, as noted by Ferrero and Álvarez Sainz (2024), cultural attitudes toward traditional face-to-face learning often lead to reluctance in adopting e-learning tools. The study found that some students and faculty members preferred the traditional classroom setting, believing that it offered better learning outcomes. This aligns with a broader body of literature suggested that cultural resistance to ICT is common in many parts of the world, particularly in regions where education has traditionally been face-to-face and teacher-centered (Abuali & Ahmed, 2025). Furthermore, the issue of gender and access to technology was a significant concern, particularly for female students in rural areas. The study revealed that female students in conservative regions faced additional challenges in accessing ICT resources, reinforcing the findings of Barra et al. (2024), who identified gender as a key barrier to the adoption of ICT in education in developing countries. This emphasized the need for policies that promote gender equality and ensure equitable access to technology, especially for marginalized groups.

This study's findings contributed to the growing body of literature on ICT integration in education, particularly in the context of developing countries like Pakistan. While there is considerable potential for ICT to revolutionize education, significant challenges remain, including technological infrastructure, digital literacy, student engagement, and cultural resistance. Addressing these barriers will require comprehensive strategies that include investment in infrastructure, targeted training programs for both students and faculty, and efforts to foster a culture of digital learning. The findings of this study are aligned with existing research and highlighted the urgent need for a more equitable and inclusive approach to ICT adoption in Pakistan's higher education system.

RECOMMENDATIONS AND FUTURE RESEARCH

To address the challenges identified in this study, it is recommended that Pakistani universities invest in improving technological infrastructure, particularly in rural areas where access to reliable internet and digital devices is limited. Universities should collaborate with governmental and non-governmental organizations to ensure equitable access to technology for all students, regardless of their geographic location or socio-economic background. Additionally, faculty development programs should be implemented to enhance digital literacy and equip educators with the necessary skills to effectively use e-learning tools. This would enable faculty members to create more engaging and interactive online learning experiences, thereby improving student engagement and academic outcomes. Finally, universities should consider integrating both synchronous and asynchronous learning methods to increase student interaction and foster a sense of community within virtual campuses.

Future research should focus on evaluating the long-term impact of ICT adoption on student performance and engagement in virtual learning environments in Pakistan. Studies could explore the effectiveness of blended learning models and the role of interactive elements, such as live discussions and group projects, in enhancing student engagement. Additionally, research could investigate the cultural and social factors that influence the acceptance of e-learning, particularly in rural and conservative areas, and how these factors can be addressed to promote more widespread adoption. This would provide valuable insights into how ICT can be leveraged to improve education in developing countries and contribute to the development of more inclusive and equitable educational systems.

REFERENCES

Abuali, T., & Ahmed, A. A. (2025). Challenges and Opportunities in Implementing E-Learning in Developing Countries. *The Open European Journal of Social Science and Education (OEJSSE)*, 1-12.

Adeshola, I., & Agoyi, M. (2023). Examining factors influencing e-learning engagement among university students during covid-19 pandemic: A mediating role of "learning persistence". *Interactive Learning Environments*, *31*(10), 6195–6222. https://doi.org/https://doi.org/10.1080/10494820.2022.2029493. DOI: 10.1080/10494820.2022.2029493

Afzal, A., Khan, S., Daud, S., Ahmad, Z., & Butt, A. (2023). Addressing the digital divide: Access and use of technology in education. *Journal of Social Sciences Review*, *3*(2), 883–895. https://doi.org/https://doi.org/10.54183/jssr.v3i2.326. DOI: 10.54183/jssr.v3i2.326

Ahmad, S., Mohd Noor, A. S., Alwan, A. A., Gulzar, Y., Khan, W. Z., & Reegu, F. A. (2023). eLearning acceptance and adoption challenges in higher education. *Sustainability (Basel)*, *15*(7), 6190. DOI: 10.3390/su15076190

Aithal, P., & Aithal, S. (2023). How to empower educators through digital pedagogies and faculty development strategies. [IJAEML]. *International Journal of Applied Engineering and Management Letters*, *7*(4), 139–183. https://doi.org/http://dx.doi.org/10.2139/ssrn.4674876. DOI: 10.47992/IJAEML.2581.7000.0198

Akram, H., Aslam, S., Saleem, A., & Parveen, K. (2021). The challenges of online teaching in COVID-19 pandemic: A case study of public universities in Karachi, Pakistan. *Journal of Information Technology Education*, *20*, 263–282. https://doi.org/https://doi.org/10.28945/4784. DOI: 10.28945/4784

Al-Gerafi, M. A., Goswami, S. S., Khan, M. A., Naveed, Q. N., Lasisi, A., AlMohimeed, A., & Elaraby, A. (2024). Designing of an effective e-learning website using inter-valued fuzzy hybrid MCDM concept: A pedagogical approach. *Alexandria Engineering Journal*, *97*, 61–87. https://doi.org/https://doi.org/10.1016/j.aej.2024.04.012. DOI: 10.1016/j.aej.2024.04.012

Ali, S., Gulliver, S. R., Uppal, M. A., & Basir, M. (2021). Research investigating individual device preference and e-learning quality perception: Can a one-solution-fits-all e-learning solution work? *Heliyon*, *7*(6), e07343. Advance online publication. DOI: 10.1016/j.heliyon.2021.e07343 PMID: 34195441

Alturki, U., & Aldraiweesh, A. (2021). Application of learning management system (Lms) during the covid-19 pandemic: A sustainable acceptance model of the expansion technology approach. *Sustainability (Basel), 13*(19), 10991. https://doi.org/https://doi.org/10.3390/su131910991. DOI: 10.3390/su131910991

Anderson, S. (2023). The Digital Divide and Changing Education in Pandemic Times: A Case Study of Teacher Experiences in a Rural Town.

Asad, M. M., Hussain, N., Wadho, M., Khand, Z. H., & Churi, P. P. (2021). Integration of e-learning technologies for interactive teaching and learning process: An empirical study on higher education institutes of Pakistan. *Journal of Applied Research in Higher Education, 13*(3), 649–663. https://doi.org/https://doi.org/10.1108/JARHE-04-2020-0103. DOI: 10.1108/JARHE-04-2020-0103

Bagde, P., Bobde, A., & Bagde, L. P. (2021). Information and Communication Technology (ICT) enabled Higher Education: Current Trends and Challenges. *Ilkogretim Online, 20*(1). Advance online publication. DOI: 10.17051/ilkonline.2021.01.286

Barra, C., Grimaldi, M., Muazzam, A., Troisi, O., & Visvizi, A. (2024). Digital divide, gender gap, and entrepreneurial orientation: How to foster technology adoption among Pakistani higher education students? *Socio-Economic Planning Sciences, 93*, 101904. https://doi.org/https://doi.org/10.1016/j.seps.2024.101904. DOI: 10.1016/j.seps.2024.101904

Coupal, L. V. (2004). Constructivist learning theory and human capital theory: Shifting political and educational frameworks for teachers' ICT professional development. *British Journal of Educational Technology, 35*(5), 587–596. https://doi.org/https://doi.org/10.1111/j.0007-1013.2004.00415.x. DOI: 10.1111/j.0007-1013.2004.00415.x

Das, N. K., Sahoo, S., & Pati, L. (2021). Online learning: Challenges for education in rural and remote areas. *suicide, 8*(7). https://doi.org/DOI: 10.17148/IARJSET.2021.8712

Debattista, M. (2018). A comprehensive rubric for instructional design in e-learning. *The International Journal of Information and Learning Technology, 35*(2), 93–104. https://doi.org/https://doi.org/10.1108/IJILT-09-2017-0092. DOI: 10.1108/IJILT-09-2017-0092

Draissi, Z., Rong, Y., Zafeer, H. M. I., Maqbool, S., Malik, S. J., Maqbool, S., & Alemi, S. H. A. (2025). Academic diplomacy and policy borrowing: Media content analysis of Chinese soft power in Morocco. *Humanities & Social Sciences Communications, 12*(1), 1–11. DOI: 10.1057/s41599-025-04544-1

El-Sabagh, H. A. (2021). Adaptive e-learning environment based on learning styles and its impact on development students' engagement. *International Journal of Educational Technology in Higher Education*, *18*(1), 53. https://doi.org/https://doi.org/10.1186/s41239-021-00289-4. DOI: 10.1186/s41239-021-00289-4

Farid, S., Ahmad, R., Niaz, I. A., Arif, M., Shamshirband, S., & Khattak, M. D. (2015). Identification and prioritization of critical issues for the promotion of e-learning in Pakistan. *Computers in Human Behavior*, *51*, 161–171. https://doi.org/https://doi.org/10.1016/j.chb.2015.04.037. DOI: 10.1016/j.chb.2015.04.037

Ferrero, A. M., & Álvarez Sainz, M. (2024). Attitudes of university students towards traditional face-to-face learning systems and learning with ICT. *E-Learning and Digital Media*, *21*(2), 180–200. https://doi.org/https://doi.org/10.1177/20427530231156185. DOI: 10.1177/20427530231156185

Granić, A., & Marangunić, N. (2019). Technology acceptance model in educational context: A systematic literature review. *British Journal of Educational Technology*, *50*(5), 2572–2593. https://doi.org/https://doi.org/10.1111/bjet.12864. DOI: 10.1111/bjet.12864

Gul, R., Tahir, T., & Ishfaq, U. (2023). Perspectives of the teachers on challenges and possibilities to online system of education amid COVID-19 outbreak in Balochistan, Pakistan. *SAGE Open*, *13*(1), 21582440231155063. https://doi.org/https://doi.org/10.1177/21582440231155063. DOI: 10.1177/21582440231155063 PMID: 36843652

Han, X. (2024). Associations between effectiveness of blended learning, student engagement, student learning outcomes, and student academic motivation in higher education. *Education and Information Technologies*, •••, 1–31. https://doi.org/https://doi.org/10.1007/s10639-024-13246-1

Iqbal, S. A., Ashiq, M., Rehman, S. U., Rashid, S., & Tayyab, N. (2022). Students' perceptions and experiences of online education in Pakistani universities and higher education institutes during COVID-19. *Education Sciences*, *12*(3), 166. https://doi.org/https://doi.org/10.3390/educsci12030166. DOI: 10.3390/educsci12030166

Javed, S., Rong, Y., Zafeer, H. M. I., Maqbool, S., & Abbasi, B. N. (2024). Unleashing the potential: A quest to understand and examine the factors enriching research and innovation productivities of South Asian universities. *Humanities & Social Sciences Communications*, *11*(1), 1–15. DOI: 10.1057/s41599-024-03674-2

Jin, P., Yu, L., Ahmad, K., Shafique, H. M., & Ahmad, A. (2024). Evaluating the factors influencing the adoption of digital culture among university students in developing areas of South Punjab. *Information Development, 02666669241270909,* 02666669241270909. https://doi.org/https://doi.org/10.1177/02666669241270909. DOI: 10.1177/02666669241270909

Kalim, U., Irfan, S., Maqbool, S., & Zafeer, H. M. I. (2025). How AI Can Be Successfully Implemented in the Classroom Settings: Challenges and Pathways to Overcome. In *Navigating Barriers to AI Implementation in the Classroom* (pp. 235-266). IGI Global Scientific Publishing.

Kanwal, F., & Rehman, M. (2017). Factors affecting e-learning adoption in developing countries–empirical evidence from Pakistan's higher education sector. *IEEE Access : Practical Innovations, Open Solutions, 5,* 10968–10978. DOI: 10.1109/ACCESS.2017.2714379

Kazi, A. M., Ahsan, N., Jamal, S., Khan, A., Mughis, W., Allana, R., Kazi, A. N., Kalimuddin, H., Ali, S. A., McKellin, W., & Collet, J.-P. (2021). Characteristics of mobile phone access and usage among caregivers in Pakistan–A mHealth survey of urban and rural population. *International Journal of Medical Informatics, 156,* 104600. https://doi.org/https://doi.org/10.1016/j.ijmedinf.2021.104600. DOI: 10.1016/j.ijmedinf.2021.104600 PMID: 34638012

Lasekan, O. A., Pachava, V., Godoy Pena, M. T., Golla, S. K., & Raje, M. S. (2024). Investigating factors influencing students' engagement in sustainable online education. *Sustainability (Basel), 16*(2), 689. https://doi.org/https://doi.org/10.3390/su16020689. DOI: 10.3390/su16020689

Lateef, A., Noor, K., & Yousaf, S. (2025). Digital Divide in Education: Barriers to Equitable Access in Punjab, Pakistan. *Journal of Social Signs Review, 3*(2), 434–456.

Lunenburg, F. C. (2011). Critical thinking and constructivism techniques for improving student achievement. National Forum of Teacher Education Journal, Malik, S., Rong, Y., Zafeer, H. M. I., Maqbool, S., Draissi, Z., Rehman, N., & Maqbool, S. (2025). Analysis of Key Factors Influencing Academic Productivity: Insights From LASSO Regression and AI-Driven Techniques. In *Navigating Barriers to AI Implementation in the Classroom* (pp. 189-234). IGI Global Scientific Publishing.

Mansour, N. (2024). Students' and facilitators' experiences with synchronous and asynchronous online dialogic discussions and e-facilitation in understanding the Nature of Science. *Education and Information Technologies, 29*(12), 15965–15997. https://doi.org/https://doi.org/10.1007/s10639-024-12473-w. DOI: 10.1007/s10639-024-12473-w

Maqbool, S. (2025). Implemented in the Classroom Settings: Challenges and Pathways. *Navigating Barriers to AI Implementation in the Classroom*, 235.

Maqbool, S., Maqbool, S., Zafeer, H. M. I., & Qihui, H. (2024). Exploring the Reflection of Teachers to Encourage the Gender Equality for Girls in Punjab Schools: In the Light of Universal Right to an Education. *Asian Women, 40*(3), 113–138. DOI: 10.14431/aw.2024.9.40.3.113

Maqbool, S., Sarwar, U., Zamir, S., Zafeer, H. M. I., & Wei, Z. (2020). Teaching of Phonics and fluency in improving reading abilities at primary level: Multan Pakistan. *European Online Journal of Natural and Social Sciences*, *9*(4), 808–819.

Maqbool, S., Wei, Z., Sarwar, U., Zamir, S., & Zafeer, H. M. I. (2020). An analysis of self-concept between homeless and common women in Pakistan. *International Transaction Journal of Engineering, Management, &. Applied Sciences & Technologies*, *11*(15), 11–19.

Maqbool, S., Zafeer, H. M. I., & Maqbool, S. (2025). Psychological Impact of Raising a Child With Autism: A Real Life Case Study of Expatriate Family. *Child & Family Social Work*, cfs.70011. DOI: 10.1111/cfs.70011

Maqbool, S., Zafeer, H. M. I., Maqbool, S., Zeng, P., Draissi, Z., & Javed, S. (2024). Stance of numerous leadership styles and their effect on teaching to sustain academic performance at the high school level. *Heliyon*, *10*(16), e36438. DOI: 10.1016/j.heliyon.2024.e36438 PMID: 39253217

Maqbool, S., Zafeer, H. M. I., Yanping, L., & Zhao, W. (2022). Covid-19 and global education: Experiences of Pakistani international students. *International Transaction Journal of Engineering Management and Applied Sciences and Technologies*, *13*(3), 1–11.

Maqbool, S., Zafeer, H. M. I., Zeng, P., Maqbool, S., Draissi, Z., & Javed, S. (2024). Inventive leadership styles and their impact for achieving sustainable development goals in education at secondary schools: A case study from Multan, Pakistan. *Humanities & Social Sciences Communications*, *11*(1), 1–11. DOI: 10.1057/s41599-024-03086-2

Maqbool, S., Zafeer, H. M. I., Zeng, P., Mohammad, T., Khassawneh, O., & Wu, L. (2023). The role of diverse leadership styles in teaching to sustain academic excellence at secondary level. [Maqbool, S., Zhao, W., Rehman, S., Zafeer, H. M. I., & Maqbool, S. North American Academic Research.]. *Frontiers in Psychology*, *13*, 1096151. DOI: 10.3389/fpsyg.2022.1096151 PMID: 36698584

Mattar, J. (2018). Constructivism and connectivism in education technology: Active, situated, authentic, experiential, and anchored learning. *RIED-Revista Iberoamericana de Educación a Distancia, 21*(2). https://doi.org/doi.org/10.5944/ried.21.2.20055

Mbatha, B. (2024). Diffusion of innovations: How adoption of new technology spreads in society. In *Information, Knowledge, and Technology for Teaching and Research in Africa: Human Machine Interaction and User Interfaces* (pp. 1-18). Springer. https://doi.org/https://doi.org/10.1007/978-3-031-60267-2_1

Menberu, A. W. (2024). Technology-mediated financial education in developing countries: A systematic literature review. *Cogent Business & Management, 11*(1), 2294879. DOI: 10.1080/23311975.2023.2294879

Meskhi, B., Ponomareva, S., & Ugnich, E. (2019). E-learning in higher inclusive education: Needs, opportunities and limitations. *International Journal of Educational Management, 33*(3), 424–437. https://doi.org/https://doi.org/10.1108/IJEM-09-2018-0282. DOI: 10.1108/IJEM-09-2018-0282

Poondej, C., & Lerdpornkulrat, T. (2020). Gamification in e-learning: A Moodle implementation and its effect on student engagement and performance. *Interactive Technology and Smart Education, 17*(1), 56–66. https://doi.org/https://doi.org/10.1108/ITSE-06-2019-0030. DOI: 10.1108/ITSE-06-2019-0030

Qashou, A. (2022). Obstacles to effective use of e-learning in higher education from the viewpoint of faculty members. *Turkish Online Journal of Distance Education, 23*(1), 144–177.

Qazi, M. A., Sharif, M. A., & Akhlaq, A. (2024). Barriers and facilitators to adoption of e-learning in higher education institutions of Pakistan during COVID-19: Perspectives from an emerging economy. *Journal of Science and Technology Policy Management, 15*(1), 31–52. https://doi.org/https://doi.org/10.1108/JSTPM-01-2022-0002. DOI: 10.1108/JSTPM-01-2022-0002

Rafeeq, K., & Ali, M. Q. (2021). OPPORTUNITIES AND CHALLENGES IN THE USE OF ICT AT TERTIARY LEVEL: TEACHERS'PERCEPTIONS. [BBE]. *Bulletin of Business and Economics, 10*(4), 28–37.

Rajabalee, Y. B., & Santally, M. I. (2021). Learner satisfaction, engagement and performances in an online module: Implications for institutional e-learning policy. *Education and Information Technologies, 26*(3), 2623–2656. https://doi.org/https://doi.org/10.1007/s10639-020-10375-1. DOI: 10.1007/s10639-020-10375-1 PMID: 33199971

Rehman, N., Huang, X., Mahmood, A., Maqbool, S., & Javed, S. (2024). Enhancing the quality of research synopsis of international students through peer feedback: A case study. *New Directions for Child and Adolescent Development, 2024*(1), 1271802. DOI: 10.1155/2024/1271802

Rehman, N., Huang, X., Mahmood, A., Zafeer, H. M. I., & Mohammad, N. K. (2025). Emerging trends and effective strategies in STEM teacher professional development: A systematic review. *Humanities & Social Sciences Communications*, *12*(1), 1–23. DOI: 10.1057/s41599-024-04272-y

Rehman, N., Huang, X., Sarwar, U., Fatima, H., & Maqbool, S. (2024). Exploring the impact of family, school and society on the perception and reputation of vocational training in Pakistan: A statistical analysis. *Education + Training*.

Rogers, E. M., Singhal, A., & Quinlan, M. M. (2014). Diffusion of innovations. In *An integrated approach to communication theory and research* (pp. 432–448). Routledge.

Samra Maqbool, M. A., Ijaz, S., Asif, M., & Jahanzeb, M. (2014). An Analysis of Self-esteem between Destitute and Non-destitute women.

Sartika, F., Ritonga, M., Lahmi, A., Rasyid, A., & Febriani, S. R. (2021). Online learning in the low Internet area, planning, strategies and problems faced by students during the Covid-19 period. *Artificial intelligence for COVID-19*, 413-421. https://doi.org/https://doi.org/10.1007/978-3-030-69744-0_23

Sarwar, U., Fazal, K., Zamir, S., Maqbool, S., Hussain, Z., & Qi, Z. Y. (2021). Assessment on Proficiency of Using Information and Communication Technology among Students of University of Lahore (Sargodha Campus), Pakistan. *European Online Journal of Natural and Social Sciences*, *10*(1), 102–115.

Shahzad, K., & Khan, S. A. (2024). Role of e-learning for the continuing professional development of university librarians of Pakistan to deliver value-added services: an explanatory study. *Global Knowledge, Memory and Communication*. https://doi.org/https://doi.org/10.1108/GKMC-11-2023-0453

Timotheou, S., Miliou, O., Dimitriadis, Y., Sobrino, S. V., Giannoutsou, N., Cachia, R., Monés, A. M., & Ioannou, A. (2023). Impacts of digital technologies on education and factors influencing schools' digital capacity and transformation: A literature review. *Education and Information Technologies*, *28*(6), 6695–6726. https://doi.org/https://doi.org/10.1007/s10639-022-11431-8. DOI: 10.1007/s10639-022-11431-8 PMID: 36465416

Tu, Y., Wang, Q., & Huang, C. (2025). Facilitating students' emotional engagement in synchronous online learning: A systematic literature review. *International Review of Research in Open and Distance Learning, 26*(1), 261–282. https://doi.org/https://doi.org/10.19173/irrodl.v26i1.7732. DOI: 10.19173/irrodl.v26i1.7732

Ukpe, E. (2023). Information and communication technologies (ICTS) for E-Learning in tertiary education. *Open Journal of Social Sciences, 11*(12), 666–680. DOI: 10.4236/jss.2023.1112044

Vyortkina, D., & Elsawy, A. (2024). A Systematic Professional Development Framework for Enhancing ICT Skills in the Teacher Education Faculty. EDULEARN24 Proceedings, Wade, B., Dianati, S., Searle, B., & Sankey, M. (2024). Navigating an LMS Review process: Harnessing Next-Generation Digital Learning through evidence-based decision-making. *Journal of University Teaching & Learning Practice, 24*(7), 63–89.

Webb, A., McQuaid, R. W., & Webster, C. W. R. (2021). Moving learning online and the COVID-19 pandemic: A university response. *World Journal of Science. Technology and Sustainable Development, 18*(1), 1–19.

Xu, H., & Rangra, N. (2024). Bridging the Digital Divide: The Impact of Public Investment on Urban-Rural Disparities in Pakistan. *Library of Progress-Library Science, Information Technology & Computer, 44*(3).

Zafeer, H. M. I., Li, Y., & Maqbool, S. (2023). An approach to progress learning outcomes: International graduate students' engagement in reflective practice and reflective journal writing during pandemic. *Sustainability (Basel), 15*(3), 1898. https://doi.org/https://doi.org/10.3390/su15031898. DOI: 10.3390/su15031898

Zafeer, H. M. I., Maqbool, S., Rong, Y., & Maqbool, S. (2024). Mapping the relationship and influence of school internal factors with an eye towards students' science academic outcomes. *Heliyon, 10*(19), e38696. DOI: 10.1016/j.heliyon.2024.e38696 PMID: 39397972

Zafeer, H. M. I., Maqbool, S., Rong, Y., & Maqbool, S. (2025a). Beyond the Classroom: How Socioeconomic Status, Parental Involvement and Home Environment Impact on Students' Science Academic Performance at Secondary Schools. *European Journal of Education, 60*(1), e70023. DOI: 10.1111/ejed.70023

Zafeer, H. M. I., Maqbool, S., Rong, Y., & Maqbool, S. (2025b). Culturally Sustaining Cognitive and Behavioral Interventions for Reducing Anxiety in Autistic School-Aged Students: A Systematic Review. *Psychology in the Schools*, pits.70077. DOI: 10.1002/pits.70077

Zafeer, H. M. I., Maqbool, S., Rong, Y., & Maqbool, S. (2025c). Impact of digital learning tools on student's engagement and achievement in middle school science classes. *International Journal of Technology in Education and Science*, *9*(2), 177–196. DOI: 10.46328/ijtes.622

Zafeer, H. M. I., Maqbool, S., & Yanping, L. (2022). Psychological and social factors and their impact on divorced and married women: A case study from Punjab Pakistan. *Journal of Divorce & Remarriage*, *63*(5), 352–373. DOI: 10.1080/10502556.2022.2048345

Zafeer, H. M. I., Peng, C., Rehman, S., Wei, Z., & Maqbool, S. (2021). A Study to Investigate the Obstacles of Educational Technology in Curriculum; University Students' Perception. *European Online Journal of Natural and Social Sciences*, *10*(1), 1–8.

Zafeer, H. M. I., Xue, H., & Maqbool, S. (2020). Delaying Factors Regarding Civil Justice in Pakistan (Lower Courts). *Journal of Humanities and Social Sciences Studies*, *2*(6), 15–22. DOI: 10.32996/jhsss.2020.2.6.2

Zafeer, H. M. I., Yanping, L., & Maqboo, S. (2022). The role of gender, socio-economic factors, and its impact on students' English as a second language (ESL) performance. *North American Academic Research*, *5*(10), 52–59.

Zafeer, H. M. I., Yanping, L., & Maqbool, S. COVID-19 and the Future of Online Learning; Perspective of Pakistani Students from Higher Education Institutions (HEIs).

Zagouras, C., Egarchou, D., Skiniotis, P., & Fountana, M. (2022). Face to face or blended learning? A case study: Teacher training in the pedagogical use of ICT. *Education and Information Technologies*, *27*(9), 12939–12967. https://doi.org/https://doi.org/10.1007/s10639-022-11144-y. DOI: 10.1007/s10639-022-11144-y PMID: 35729873

Zalat, M. M., Hamed, M. S., & Bolbol, S. A. (2021). The experiences, challenges, and acceptance of e-learning as a tool for teaching during the COVID-19 pandemic among university medical staff. *PLoS One*, *16*(3), e0248758. https://doi.org/https://doi.org/10.1371/journal.pone.0248758. DOI: 10.1371/journal.pone.0248758 PMID: 33770079

Zamir, S., Yang, Z., Sarwar, U., Maqbool, S., Fazal, K., Ihsan, H., & Arif, A. (2021). Teaching methodologies used for learning critical thinking in higher education: Pakistani teachers' perceptions. *Int. Trans. J. Eng. Manag. Appl. Sci. Technol*, *12*, 1–10.

Zmir, S., Sarwar, U., Maqbool, S., Javed, S., Ishtiaq, M., & Zhang, Y. (2021). Plagiarism practice: Its awareness & dealing and consequences among university students in Punjab province of Pakistan. *International Transaction Journal of Engineering, Management, &. Applied Sciences & Technologies*, *12*(11), 1–11.

Chapter 6
Redesigning AI for Inclusion:
University Students' Experiences With Cultural Exclusion in AI Learning Systems

Amjad Islam Amjad
https://orcid.org/0000-0002-4250-7526
Department of Education, The University of Lahore, Pakistan

ABSTRACT

The current study examined how AI systems marginalize students from diverse cultural and linguistic backgrounds and proposed strategies to enhance inclusivity in AI-driven educational environments. Using a phenomenological design, in-depth semi-structured interviews were conducted with 11 university students. The data were analyzed using a thematic data analysis technique. The findings showed that students liked how AI systems made learning more personalized. However, most of them reported cultural biases in how the AI systems gave feedback and predicted their performance. The students reported that automated feedback often failed to appreciate context-specific linguistic variations, labeling non-standard expressions or culturally differentiated arguments as "poor grammar" or "unclear thinking." Content suggestions in learning platforms also appeared to support Western-centric narratives. Several participants reported that AI-generated predictions regarding their academic performance did not match their actual learning efforts. This chapter had several practical implications.

DOI: 10.4018/979-8-3373-4217-7.ch006

INTRODUCTION

The integration of Artificial Intelligence (AI) into higher education (HE) has transformed traditional pedagogical practices by providing new platforms for personalised learning, student support, and administrative decision-making (Anierobi et al., 2025). AI-driven learning platforms that track students' behaviour, evaluate their performance patterns, and generate predictions to inform timely educational interventions (Amjad et al., 2024). AI systems can foster educational outcomes by providing data-driven insights that support academic rigor (Lin & Albahli, 2025). AI tools have become increasingly popular in higher education within the current tech-driven era (Malik & Amjad, 2025). Higher education students now heavily rely on applications like ChatGPT and other generative AI platforms for academic support (Nguyen, 2025). These tools assist them in their academic tasks, such as writing, summarizing texts, answering content-related queries, and providing explanations in multiple languages (AlShaikh et al., 2024). Typically, university students utilize these AI tools for academic tasks, such as providing feedback and clarifying concepts, and occasionally for academic writing assistance (Khalifa & Albadawy, 2024).

Although these AI platforms have several advantages. However, some serious concerns exist regarding how culturally and linguistically diverse students experience these AI systems (Olmos-Gómez et al., 2022). These AI tools are trained on large datasets that reflect dominant Western values and context, language structures, and cultural preferences (Lewis et al., 2025; Tao et al., 2024). So, students from non-Western or multilingual backgrounds find that these tools do not understand their ways of reasoning, expression, or writing. For example, students receive feedback that their grammar is incorrect or that their arguments are unclear, even based on valid cultural communication styles. These experiences highlight concerns regarding fairness, inclusion, and cultural sensitivity in AI use (Cachat-Rosset & Klarsfeld, 2023).

In this regard, the opinions of university students are often overlooked when discussing AI in education. In the past, researchers have focused on the technological aspects or output of AI tools (Mikalef et al., 2023; Olan et al., 2022). There is limited insight into how culturally and linguistically sensitive students perceive communication with these AI-enabled systems. Students from rural regions or lower socio-economic backgrounds may not only face linguistic exclusion but also lack digital capital, resulting in compounded marginalization (Kukulska-Hulme et al., 2023). Similarly, gendered language norms or expectations may not be accounted for in feedback algorithms, further deepening the misalignment between AI systems and student realities(S. Jiang et al., 2024). Research suggests that these intersecting identities shape students' access, recognition, and inclusion in algorithmic environments (Alam & Imran, 2015; Mohamed, 2024). In this respect, student experiences can matter in assessing how these tools work out in real, context-based learning in varied settings (Ma, 2021). Students may lose confidence in their academic performance and sense of belonging when deprived of AI suggestions and/or feedback, as they feel misrepresented, misunderstood, or excluded (Olmos-Gomez et al., 2022). This issue is particularly relevant in multicultural societies, such as Pakistan, where the language spoken by various students in the classroom reflects diverse linguistic and cultural backgrounds.

In the present research, this gap is filled. This researcher examined the perceptions and experiences of cultural and linguistic bias that university students in Pakistan reported regarding the use of AI apps, including ChatGPT and related tools. The study focused on uncovering and investigating how these tools may unintentionally marginalize students from diverse backgrounds. The current study also proposes ways to make AI platforms more inclusive in higher education. It is a significant study because it centers student perspectives and highlights how bias in digital tools can contribute to broader educational inequalities. Focusing on the voices and experiences of university students, it provides insights to help teachers, AI developers, and institutions critically reflect on how AI tools are designed and used in linguistically and culturally sensitive learning environments. The objective of the current study was to explore the lived experiences and perceptions of Pakistani higher education students regarding cultural and linguistic bias in AI-powered learning platforms, and to identify implications for inclusive and equitable digital learning environments.

Research Questions

The following research questions guided the current study.

1. How do university students from diverse cultural and linguistic backgrounds perceive and experience cultural bias in AI-powered learning platforms?
2. How do these experiences affect university students' engagement, sense of inclusion, and academic representation in AI-driven learning environments?

LITERATURE REVIEW

AI tools, such as ChatGPT and similar operators, are transforming various aspects of higher education, including assessment, reflection, academic writing, and feedback (Malik et al., 2024). University students can utilize these AI platforms to seek writing assistance, detailed summaries of their work, explanations of complex terms and concepts, and even code generation (Khalifa & Albadawy, 2024; Wong et al., 2023). The literature supports the notion that these tools enhance learning opportunities for students by offering self-paced learning and individualized support. Although a significant number of university teachers, both locally and internationally, are utilizing these AI tools and acknowledge their potential in academic tasks such as assignment writing, text paraphrasing, and exam preparation (Imran & Almusharraf, 2023). However, the functionality of these tools is lacking in several aspects, such as critical attention is required to examine their cultural and language responsiveness and inclusivity.

It is evident from literature that these AI tools depend on large-scale language models trained on data mostly derived from internet sources, published and unpublished academic work, and social media posts, all of which are shaped by dominant cultural discourses present in the West (Haltaufderheide & Ranisch, 2024; Mishra et al., 2024). As a result, a common concern is the dominance of Euro-American academic norms in AI tools, which often serve as benchmarks for quality, sidelining diverse linguistic and epistemic traditions (Abubakari, 2025). Moreover, the AI outputs feel unfamiliar or inappropriate for students from multilingual or non-Western backgrounds. Research conducted in the past has shown that AI tools often fail to recognise culturally constructive expressions, tone, and structure, indicating improper or low-quality output (Chinta et al., 2025; Franklin et al., 2024; Hristova et al., 2024). This creates a gap between the output of AI tools and the lived experience of language and knowledge in the diverse communities where students reside.

While the literature on AI in education increasingly explores algorithmic accuracy and personalization, it is equally critical to examine the ethical and epistemological dimensions of AI use. One practical framework is epistemic injustice (Vučković & Sikimić, 2025), which refers to the harm done when someone's knowledge or voice is undervalued due to structural or cultural biases. In the context of educational AI, this can occur when students' contributions are misinterpreted or overlooked because they do not align with dominant linguistic or epistemic norms (Amin et al., 2024; Draissi et al., 2025; Javed et al., 2024). This is closely related to the field of decolonial computing, which calls for resisting the reproduction of colonial logics in digital infrastructures (Couldry & Mejias, 2023). Educational platforms, developed mainly in the Global North, often encode assumptions that reflect Western, monolingual, and positivist values. When applied in postcolonial contexts, such as Pakistan, these tools can reinforce exclusion rather than support learning. Additionally, digital inclusion frameworks (Kalim et al., 2025; Zafeer et al., 2025) emphasize the need to extend beyond access to technology and consider whether digital systems effectively support participation, representation, and recognition of diverse learners. These critical perspectives enrich our understanding of how AI systems might marginalize learners, not only technically but also epistemologically.

It is also evident from the previous studies that language bias is one of the most prevalent challenges present in AI-generated feedback (Banihashem et al., 2024). AI tools such as ChatGPT and Google Bard typically require standardized English prompts from students (Ahmed et al., 2024). These Tools typically misinterpret and misunderstand these regionally influenced grammar or mixed-language phrases as misfits or mistakes. Although those responses are valid in the students' local context and language. It appears as a threat to bilingual or multilingual students who write their prompts in their local language and cultural backgrounds (Zimotti et al., 2024). This can raise questions about the credibility of these AI-based platforms, and students may understand that their communication is invalid for these tools. Over time, this impacts their academic identity and discourages authentic expression in their learning.

The literature also critiques that, beyond these language and grammar concerns, AI-powered tools reflect cultural bias in creating texts, interpreting theories, or evaluating students' performance (Mandour, 2025). AI tools like ChatGPT provide specific culture-based (Western) answers when students need examples, explanations, or references in Pakistan's local contexts. These AI tools present data on researchers, historians, case studies, study contexts, or knowledge unfamiliar or irrelevant to local students (Vieriu & Petrea, 2025). Students in Pakistan ask AI tools for culturally relevant content in their local background, but they get responses rooted in European contexts (Dahri et al., 2024). These responses foster non-cooperation and exclusion based on a narrow view of knowledge and academic standards associated with these AI tools.

Another evolving and rising concern is how these AI tools evaluate students' reasoning or argumentation (Gonsalves, 2024). Several students utilize storytelling, community knowledge, and cultural logic to construct arguments for their academic assignments. AI tools trained on Western models of reasoning do not recognize the value of these contexts and approaches (Darwin et al., 2024). On the contrary, they judge them to be vague and unsupported. The bias has the potential to have an adverse effect on the confidence of university students and compromise their willingness to apply their cultural knowledge in academic assignments (Marzuki et al., 2023). It also raises questions about whose knowledge is subscribed to through educational technologies (Gouseti et al., 2024).

The concept of epistemic diversity has gained attention in the discourse on AI and education, particularly about the marginalization of non-Western knowledge systems (Jiang, 2025; Omodan, 2024). Epistemic diversity urges scholars and technologists to recognize multiple ways of knowing, including oral traditions, community-based logic, and context-specific reasoning. In the context of AI-enabled learning, failing to embed pluralistic epistemologies can result in the reproduction of dominant norms and the exclusion of localized knowledge ecologies (Zafeer et al., 2021). In

Pakistan, for instance, educational discourses often intersect with regional, linguistic, and cultural practices that are not easily captured by algorithmic models trained on Western-centric datasets. Thus, the present study contributes to the technical conversation about AI fairness but also to a broader epistemological debate about whose knowledge matters in digital learning environments.

Despite the awareness of these challenges, limited research focuses on students' firsthand experiences with AI tools in the global South (Al-Sofi, 2024). Most existing studies examine algorithm performance, ethical usage, creativity, practice concerns, bias detection in models, or the educational use of AI from a Western perspective (Rodgers et al., 2023; Tavares & Ferrara, 2023). Limited studies include qualitative insights from culturally diverse students who use these tools in their daily academic life (Green et al., 2024). This study is an effort to reduce these knowledge and methodological gaps. Documenting how Pakistani university students understand and respond to linguistic and cultural bias in AI tools like ChatGPT threatens student-centered understanding of digital equity (Bettayeb et al., 2024; Bhullar et al., 2024). The findings may help inform more inclusive design practices and support university teachers in helping all learners in AI-driven environments.

METHODS

The focus of the current study was to gain a deeper understanding of how AI systems pose a threat to students with cultural and linguistic diversity in higher education (HE). Moreover, how can HE be made more inclusive after addressing these challenges? This investigation was a constructivist approach to investigating these challenges. It is worth noting that constructivism facilitates the development of a story by incorporating the views of participants, their lived experiences, and emotions (Burns et al., 2022; Wang et al., 2023), which addresses the challenges associated with AI in the present study. Regarding the implications and utility of constructivism, it proved to be the most suitable paradigm for this study (Sudarsan et al., 2022). When analyzing the views expressed by the participants, it was easy to comprehend the meaning of their emotions and context through the lens of constructivism.

Research Design

The current study adopted a phenomenological research design to investigate culturally and linguistically sensitive issues by immersing itself more deeply in the phenomenon. This helped us understand how AI inadvertently stigmatizes students in language- and culturally sensitive settings by establishing a strong affiliation with individuals when receiving data. As has been established in the literature, when it is planned to establish an effective rapport, get to know each other better, and learn about experiences in detail, then at this point, a phenomenological research design is deemed the most applicable in terms of data collection (Dibley et al., 2020; Jamon et al., 2021). Considering the benefits of employing phenomenological research design, we selected it for our study to conduct interviews with university students.

Participants

In the present study, participants were drawn from universities in different districts of different provinces in Pakistan. The participants were 11 university students from five public sector universities across all provinces of Pakistan (Punjab, Sindh, KPK, Baluchistan, and Gilgit Baltistan). This technique (purposive sampling) involved the selection of students of different cultural backgrounds and different levels of linguistic aptitude, ensuring a diverse and well-informed sample that can become a source of valuable information, but regarding the purpose of the study. A selection criterion was created and designed among the participants. For example, the selection included only students who were currently enrolled in a graduate university program, had already used or were using learning analytics or tools powered by AI in their academic work, and were classified as members of a minority cultural or linguistic group based on their affiliation in the classroom or university. Additionally, students who failed to meet the selection criteria were eliminated. It was also ensured that the respondents had a relevant connection to the tools in question and could provide their opinions from a cultural perspective.

Measure

Data collection was based on a multi-step process that employed the development of a semi-structured interview guide. As an example, during the initial step, the researcher used an extended literature review to reflect AI in education, learning analytics, reflecting language and cultural disparities in algorithmic treatments to form a series of interview questions regarding the study of the research objective and questions (Abedi et al., 2023; Alkhamees, 2024; Bettayeb et al., 2024; Cai et al., 2023; Lewis et al., 2025; Nawaz, 2024). After that, initial interview questions were prepared, which could be used to gain a deeper understanding of students' experiences and reactions to the use of feedback, content personalization, performance prediction, and a sense of inclusion and exclusion. Following the construction of the interview question, the draft was given to three qualitative research specialists who held a PhD or higher and had a minimum of five years of experience in teaching. They provided their input and suggestions to modify the interview questions, and then the modified questions were piloted with three students who met the inclusion criteria. Based on students' feedback, it was refined again to get clarity and sensitivity of the questions. The final interview guide was structured to promote open dialogue, with follow-up questions to explore deeper meanings. Furthermore, interview times, venues, and the recording medium were also finalized. The data were collected using interview questions, such as "Can you describe your experience using AI-powered learning platforms in your academic tasks?" Have you ever received feedback from an AI system that did not reflect your cultural or linguistic expression? Do you feel that the content and recommendations provided by these platforms are culturally inclusive? How do you think the AI systems understand or misunderstand your academic performance?

Data Collection

After developing the interview guide, the respondents were contacted through their contact numbers. After obtaining their consent, they were interviewed online using Zoom and Google Meet. Data collection took place over a period of five weeks. Each interview lasted between 40 and 55 minutes. Interviews were conducted in English, and, considering cultural sensitivities, they were audio-recorded with permission. The recorded interviews were then transcribed and reviewed repeatedly.

Data Analysis

The interviews were transcribed within the next 12 hours. NVivo software was used for the analysis. The data were analyzed using a thematic analysis technique, guided by the phenomenological tradition of identifying meaningful units and shared essence across the experiences of university students. Analysis was conducted following the six-stage guide by Braun and Clarke (2006). Firstly, the researcher engaged in data familiarization and re-reading transcripts while creating initial codes. Then, the initial codes were generated inductively, highlighting significant statements related to cultural bias, inclusivity, and university students' experiences with AI. These codes were then grouped into potential themes, which were reviewed and refined using comparison across transcripts. Themes were checked for alignment and coherence with raw data and the research questions. Ultimately, the themes were defined, named, and contextualized based on the existing literature on algorithms and digital equity. Throughout the process, reflexivity was maintained through memo-writing and peer debriefing, ensuring the researcher's positionality did not influence interpretation. The themes offer insights into how university students perceive cultural marginalization in the context of AI systems learning and their responses to inclusive educational technology design. The analysis process is explained in Table 1.

Table 1. Thematic coding matrix

Themes	Sub-themes	Codes	Participants	Quotes
Invisibility in feedback	Linguistic non-conformity	Unclear expression, Weak writing, Low coherence.	6/10	AI does not understand how we express ourselves.
	Cultural argument bias	Not analytical, Lacks evidence, Confusing analogy.	7/10	AI tools think it is illogical, but it is logical to us.
Cultural homogeneity	Western-centric content	Euro-American, Foreign systems, No local authors.	7/10	I never see local authors suggested.
	Epistemological exclusion	Formal knowledge only, Framework mismatch, Excluded thinking.	8/10	The AI systems often overlook our traditional methods of learning.
Unfair predictions	Effort not recognized	Worked harder, No improvement, Ignores my efforts.	7/10	I worked hard, but AI still predicted failure.
	Emotional disengagement	Not seen, Discouraged, Do not exist.	6/10	It feels like I am not seen.

Research Ethics

The present study followed ethical standards throughout its design, data collection, and analysis to ensure the protection and dignity of the study's respondents. Before designing the study, ethical approval was obtained from the Initial Review Board of the School Education Department, Government of Punjab, Pakistan. All respondents were informed about the purpose of the study, the voluntary nature of their participation, and their right to withdraw from the study setting at any point without any consequences. Before conducting the interview, informed consent was obtained from the participants. All identifying information was deleted from the transcripts to ensure confidentiality, and pseudonyms were used in all reporting. Audio recordings and transcripts were protected using password-protected access, available only to the researcher. The researcher gave special attention to maintaining cultural and language sensitivity, as the research involved participants from diverse backgrounds. The interview questions were also formulated to avoid discomfort, and participants were not judged for their responses. The data were collected online; thus, no physical harm was involved in the current study. Overall, the ethical framework was guided by the principles of respect for respondents, beneficence, justice, and cultural competence, ensuring that the experiences and voices of university students were treated with care and integrity throughout the study.

RESULTS

After transcribing the interview data, it was analysed using NVivo software. Following the thematic analysis, three major themes and six sub-themes were identified, which offer in-depth insights into how students perceive cultural bias in AI-driven learning analytics platforms. These themes and sub-themes align with the study's research questions and highlight the exclusionary potential of algorithmic systems when cultural diversity is not adequately considered. The details of the themes and sub-themes are presented in Figure 1.

Figure 1. Themes and sub-themes

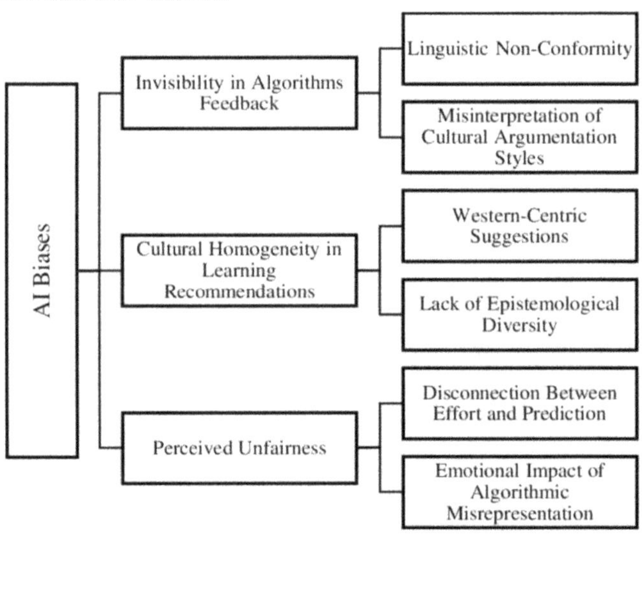

Theme 1: Invisibility in Algorithms: Feedback

The present theme is an effort to address the current study's first research question, which aims to investigate how university students with diverse backgrounds perceive and experience cultural bias in AI-powered learning platforms. It covers codes such as poor grammar, unclear logic, non-standard, and non-critical errors. This theme had two further sub-themes.

Sub-Theme 1.1: Linguistic Non-Conformity

During interviews, university students widely reported that AI-driven feedback often misinterpreted culturally specific linguistic expressions. It was found that automated feedback systems frequently showed non-standard grammatical structures, regional idioms, or alternative styles as errors, even when their meaning were contextually appropriate. For example, in answer to the questions, participants argued,

> *"I got comments like, unclear expression in an essay where I used a proverb common in our culture. That is how we explain things. It is not wrong, but different and awkward." (P2)*
>
> *"Every time I write something in my style, especially using Urdu-English mix or metaphors, the AI flags it as weak writing. It is frustrating." (P6)*
>
> *"My sentence structures are influenced by how we speak in my region, and the system always rates it low in coherence, which does not feel fair." (P9)*

From the above responses of university students, it is evident that AI systems tend to favor standard English, which can marginalize students who use different dialects or writing styles based on their cultural background. This suggests that using non-standard English is a problem rather than valuing how people express themselves. As a result, it overlooks the value of language diversity in the learning process. Moreover, participants reported frustration with tools like Grammarly, which flag culturally embedded phrases as "awkward" or "incorrect." For instance, P6 noted, "It always underlines our proverbs or idioms. It thinks they are mistakes." Tools like ChatGPT and Quillbot also prompted students to use simpler structures or "global" vocabulary, leading to what P9 called "a flattening of my cultural voice."

Sub-Theme 1.2: Misinterpretation of Cultural Argumentation Styles

The analysis revealed that several students found that the AI struggled with arguments rooted in culturally specific logics or community-based reasoning. When their submissions reflected non-Western ways of structuring claims or supporting ideas, the system rated them as less critical or less coherent. For example, in response to different questions, the university students commented,

"In my culture, we explain by building the story slowly. The AI says I am not being analytical enough, but that is just our way of thinking." (P1)

"Our traditions influence how we construct arguments. The AI does not understand that and says I am not showing evidence, even when I am." (P4)

"We use examples that are very local. But the system just sees them as off-topic or confusing." (P10)

From the above responses, it is evident that AI systems operationalize a narrow definition of academic reasoning, often excluding culturally grounded modes of argumentation. This leads to inaccurate assessments and discourages epistemological diversity in students' critical thinking practices.

Theme 2: Cultural Homogeneity in Learning Recommendations

This theme also helps to provide answers to the first research question. It had two further sub-themes.

Sub-Theme 2.1: Western-Centric Suggestions

During the interviews, the researcher found that participants expressed concern that the AI-based recommendation consistently prioritized Euro-American content, perspectives, and case studies. Local examples or regional instances were rarely suggested, making university students feel culturally disconnected from the learning process. In response to interview questions, they responded like,

"I have never seen a Pakistani author in the recommended readings, even in courses where local context matters a lot." (P3)

"Most of the examples are from Western education systems. I do not see how that helps me in our local reality." (P5)

"It is like we are not part of the academic world they designed this tool for." (P8)

The above arguments show that, through dominant Western narratives and content, AI systems can marginalize local knowledge systems. This can result in the reduction of culturally relevant learning materials, limiting students' connection to their educational contexts.

Sub-Theme 2.2: Lack of Epistemological Diversity

Several participants (P1, P2, P5, P6, P8, P9, P10) highlighted how the system prioritized linear, positivist knowledge structures, excluding local ways of knowing. This made university students feel their worldviews were undervalued or invisible in AI-mediated academic spaces. For instance, a few of them argued,

"The AI does not get that some of our knowledge is passed down orally or through experiences, not always from books." (P9)

"It promotes one way of learning, like it is the only way. That is not how we always understand things." (P1)

"The recommendations feel like they expect everyone to think in the same way." (P6)

From the above responses, it is clear that AI-driven platforms represent a monocultural conception of valid knowledge, thereby invalidating alternative epistemologies. This can isolate students from non-Western traditions and reproduce cognitive injustice in digital learning environments.

Theme 3: Perceived Unfairness

This theme attempts to answer the first research question. It has two further sub-themes covering various aspects of the second research question.

Sub-Theme 3.1: Disconnection Between Effort and Prediction

During interviews, most students reported that predictive analytics used by AI systems often fail to consider qualitative factors, such as increased study effort, learning strategies, or contextual challenges, resulting in demotivating or inaccurate performance forecasts. The following arguments further strengthen this narrative.

"I studied more than ever last semester, but the prediction said I would do worse. It made me doubt myself." (P4)

"There is no space in the system to explain why my marks dropped one term. It just predicts I am getting worse." (P8)

"It is like the algorithm only knows numbers, not the story behind them." (P9)

Based on the comment above, it is clear that AI tools are not always capable of correctly recognizing the complexity of the student learning process; they are often incapable of being context-aware and individualized due to the lack of consideration of other factors. This leads to unstable projections, which could negatively affect the student's motivation and self-confidence in applying AI.

Sub-Theme 3.2: Emotional Impact of Algorithmic Misrepresentation

During the analysis, participants noted that being inaccurately categorized by AI systems led to feelings of invisibility and disengagement. Several students described a lack of motivation or confidence when they felt misunderstood by a system that failed to recognize their efforts or cultural context. For example, they answered questions like,

"I feel like the system sees me as a low-performing student even though I work hard." (P3)

"Sometimes it feels like I do not exist in their model. Like I am a stranger that does not matter." (P5)

"It is hard to trust a system that does not even see you properly." (P10)

From the above responses, the researcher found that the psychological impact of being misrepresented by AI systems can be threatening, especially for students from marginalised cultural or linguistic backgrounds. Such experiences may hinder their academic engagement and reinforce feelings of exclusion in digital learning environments. The most repeated words are presented in Figure 2.

Figure 2. Word cloud

DISCUSSION

The first research question was developed to investigate how university students from diverse cultural and linguistic backgrounds perceive and experience cultural bias in AI-powered learning platforms. The analysis of the interview data reveals that students frequently encounter misinterpretations of their cultural expressions, linguistic styles, and reasoning approaches. These results align with previous research indicating that AI systems did not correctly respond to non-standard English or culturally specific discourse (Haltaufderheide & Ranisch, 2024). However, the present study deepens this understanding by immersing itself in the lived experiences of university students in Pakistan. It was found that a non-Western context, where multilingualism and alternative epistemologies are integral to academic identity. In addition to technical studies that focus solely on the flaws of AI systems, this study highlights how university students perceive themselves as personally and academically marginalised.

The sub-theme of linguistic non-conformity suggests that AI systems tend to adhere to dominant norms. Shafqat and Amjad (2024) discussed how automated systems impose rigid standards. Similarly, the current study found that students' expressions influenced by regional dialects or cultural reasoning were flagged as incorrect. In this regard, prior studies have not fully captured the emotional impact of this exclusion(Amjad, Aslam, Abid, et al., 2025; Bettayeb et al., 2024; Bhullar et al., 2024). Students in this study said this inclusivity made them feel invisible, undervalued, and discouraged. These experiences raise serious ethical concerns. They suggest that cultural and linguistic diversity is not recognized or respected in many AI platforms, such as ChatGPT.

The second research question was developed to explore how these biases influence students' engagement and academic performance in academic tasks. The results indicate that students struggled to connect with AI-generated recommendations. Content suggestions often reflected Western responses and examples. Students did not find a link to their own culture or local context. This aligns with the previous studies, which warned of epistemic bias in digital learning (Helm et al., 2024; Ulyshen et al., 2015). However, the current study explores how students interpret this absence as a sign that their identities are not valued. Students' interest and motivation may decline when they feel disconnected from the content.

Another primary concern was predictive analytics. University students argued that performance predictions felt unfair. They mentioned that the AI system ignored their effort, growth, or contextual challenges. Gonsalves (2024) noted similar limitations in predictive models. However, the current qualitative study shows how students felt emotionally impacted. Inaccurate predictions made some students question their abilities. Most students reported feeling a loss of motivation and experiencing feelings of exclusion. This indicates that AI systems can influence students' academic self-perception. Without culturally sensitive design, these systems may deepen educational inequality instead of reducing it.

The findings of this study resonate with global concerns surrounding the ethical deployment of AI in education. Similar issues have been reported in diverse contexts, including South Africa, Brazil, and India (Biju & Gayathri, 2025; Corrêa et al., 2023; Schiff, 2022; Sharma & Sharma, 2025), indicating that the patterns of linguistic marginalization, cultural misrecognition, and algorithmic opacity are not unique to Pakistan. This highlights the urgency for AI designers and educational policymakers to rethink the universalist assumptions embedded in algorithmic systems. The call for epistemic diversity and digital equity is thus not just a local concern but a global imperative, particularly in a world increasingly governed by data-driven decision-making.

The concerns raised by participants in this study echo findings from other post-colonial and multilingual settings. In India, researchers have documented how AI systems in education often fail to accommodate local languages and dialects, reinforcing elite linguistic norms. In South Africa, scholars have explored how predictive analytics can replicate racial and linguistic inequities embedded in apartheid-era systems (Maimela & Mbonde, 2025). Similarly, in Latin America, debates surrounding algorithmic governance and digital colonialism highlight the importance of incorporating indigenous knowledge systems into technological design (Couldry & Mejias, 2023). By connecting our findings to these global contexts, we situate the Pakistani experience into a broader pattern of algorithmic exclusion in postcolonial settings. This highlights the urgent need for culturally responsive AI systems that engage with pluralistic epistemologies and avoid reducing the diversity of student learning to narrow, standardized metrics.

As AI systems continue to shape educational futures, there is a growing global push for ethical regulation and inclusive innovation. Efforts such as the European Union's AI Act and UNESCO's "AI and the Futures of Learning" initiative emphasize transparency, fairness, and cultural responsiveness in the design of AI. For countries in the Global South, including Pakistan, this presents both a challenge and an opportunity. National strategies for AI must move beyond infrastructural concerns to embrace cultural and linguistic equity as a core design principle. Institutions can adopt ethical review boards for AI use, fund local AI research centers, and advocate for international collaborations to promote shared data standards that reflect cultural diversity. These forward-looking strategies can ensure that AI in education becomes a tool for inclusion rather than marginalization.

CONCLUSION

This chapter presents qualitative research that examines the experiences of higher education students regarding the cultural and linguistic biases they encounter in AI-based learning systems. Using a phenomenological design, the researcher gave voice to students from diverse backgrounds in Pakistan. The results showed that several students found the AI systems helpful but also exclusionary. They appreciated the personalization features but felt their language, cultural values, and academic styles were often misunderstood and misinterpreted. The participants reported that feedback systems treated local expressions and alternative reasoning as errors, creating feelings of confusion and frustration among university students. Several university students mentioned that AI did not understand their way of thinking or communicating. The feedback felt impersonal and out of touch with their cultural norms. Content recommendations also favored Western examples, overlooking local knowledge and expertise. This made students feel their culture was not important in the learning process. Moreover, predictive analytics often fail to accurately reflect students' actual efforts. The predictions were based on limited data and did not take into account personal struggles or achievements. Several university students mentioned that this made them feel invisible and discouraged. These experiences show that AI systems are not neutral. They are shaped by the data and values used to build them. If these systems do not include cultural diversity, they may harm rather than help. The present study adds to the on-going debate on the fairness and equity issue in educational technology within the present technological driven era. It brings to the forefront of the experiences of the university students, and they have been ignored in the development of AI. The research results point to the need of more context-aware and inclusive, responsive AI. When it comes to providing inclusive learning to all students with the help of AI, universities must address these implicit biases. Laying these issues aside will only increase the divide that AI asserts to cover.

LIMITATIONS AND FUTURE DIRECTIONS

Despite the numerous significant findings, the present research also had some limitations. For example, the current study was conducted qualitatively, and the data collected from only 11 respondents may raise questions about its generalizability. However, this limitation can be addressed by either increasing the number of respondents or by designing a quantitative study with a larger sample size. Furthermore, the participants were selected exclusively from university settings; therefore, the results may not apply to college or high school students. Thus, a more rigorous sample of school and college students is needed to enhance its significance further.

IMPLICATIONS

The current qualitative study has various implications for AI tool developers, university teachers, and policymakers. Firstly, AI tool developers need to consider issues related to cultural diversity. Developers must embed inclusivity into the core of system design. This includes training models on multilingual, region-specific datasets, supporting non-linear epistemologies, and incorporating culturally diverse content recommendation protocols. Participatory design processes involving students from diverse cultural backgrounds should become standard practice. To fulfil the requirements of diverse students from developing regions, AI developers should focus on localized language patterns, cultural values, and non-Western epistemologies when training the data. This will increase the context-sensitivity and inclusivity of AI programs. Second, universities are recommended to consider the possibilities of cultural fairness on AI platforms before implementation. Teachers should be trained to interpret AI outputs and understand their limitations critically. They must act as mediators between students and the algorithm, providing cultural context where the AI falls short. Educators can also document and report patterns of bias to help refine and localize AI tools for more effective use. Thirdly, these systems ought to be designed and enhanced by the students. They represent the most crucial ones when it comes to feeding back to make AI more ethical and responsive. Finally, digital equity policy frameworks must be defined in a way that prioritizes cultural representation over device ownership or internet access. Institutions that embrace such insights can make sure that AI benefits and does not impede learning for all. Lastly, national and institutional policy frameworks should mandate audits of educational AI systems for cultural and linguistic fairness. Governments in the Global South should invest in culturally grounded AI research and support collaborations between universities and AI labs to build context-aware learning technologies. Ethical review mechanisms for the adoption of AI in education must be institutionalized to ensure continuous oversight.

REFERENCES

Abedi, M., Alshybani, I., Rubayat Bin Shahadat, M., & Murillo, M. S. (2023). *Beyond traditional teaching: the potential of large language models and chatbots in graduate engineering education*. DOI: 10.32388/MD04B0

Abubakari, M. S. (2025). Overviewing Biases in Generative AI-Powered Models in the Arabic Language: AI Fairness for Sustainable Future. *Achieving Sustainability in Multi-Industry Settings With AI*, 361–390. DOI: 10.4018/979-8-3373-2530-9.ch013

Ahmed, W. M., Azhari, A. A., Alfaraj, A., Alhamadani, A., Zhang, M., & Lu, C. T. (2024). The Quality of AI-Generated Dental Caries Multiple Choice Questions: A Comparative Analysis of ChatGPT and Google Bard Language Models. *Heliyon*, *10*(7), e28198. DOI: 10.1016/j.heliyon.2024.e28198 PMID: 38596020

Al-Sofi, B. B. M. A. (2024). Artificial intelligence-powered tools and academic writing: To use or not to use ChatGPT. *Saudi Journal of Language Studies*, *4*(3), 145–161. DOI: 10.1108/SJLS-06-2024-0029

Alam, K., & Imran, S. (2015). The digital divide and social inclusion among refugee migrantsA case in regional Australia. *Information Technology & People*, *28*(2), 344–365. DOI: 10.1108/ITP-04-2014-0083

Alkhamees, A. (2024). Evaluation of Artificial Intelligence as a Search Tool for Patients: Can ChatGPT-4 Provide Accurate Evidence-Based Orthodontic-Related Information? *Cureus*. Advance online publication. DOI: 10.7759/cureus.65820 PMID: 39219978

AlShaikh, R., Al-Malki, N., & Almasre, M. (2024). The implementation of the cognitive theory of multimedia learning in the design and evaluation of an AI educational video assistant utilizing large language models. *Heliyon*, *10*(3), e25361. Advance online publication. DOI: 10.1016/j.heliyon.2024.e25361 PMID: 38352730

Amin, M., Davis, C. J., Amjad, A. I., Parveen, S., Ali, S., & Naqvi, A. (2024). Identifying Acoustic Variability Patterns in Spoken English of Fricative Consonants Among Pakistani Native Punjabi Speakers. *Journal of Asian Development Studies*, *13*(3), 1036–1046. DOI: 10.62345/jads.2024.13.3.84

Amjad, A. I., Aslam, S., Abid, N., Tabassum, U., & Shafqat, F. (2025). Bridging the Gap: Overcoming Teachers' Hurdles in Implementing Gamification for Society 5.0 Education. *SAGE Open*, *15*(2), 21582440251340269. Advance online publication. DOI: 10.1177/21582440251340269

Amjad, A. I., Aslam, S., Tabassum, U., Sial, Z. A., & Shafqat, F. (2024). Digital Equity and Accessibility in Higher Education: Reaching the Unreached. *European Journal of Education*, *12795*(4), e12795. Advance online publication. DOI: 10.1111/ejed.12795

Anierobi, E. I., Amjad, A. I., Agogbua, V. U., Aslam, S., Fakhrou, A., Alanazi, A. A., Nwogbo, V. N., Eleje, L. I., Alshamsi, H., Khan, S., & Javaid, S. (2025). Artificial intelligence utilization: A determinant of academic self-efficacy, engagement, and satisfaction of university students. *Environment and Social Psychology*, *10*(3), 3504. DOI: 10.59429/esp.v10i3.3504

Banihashem, S. K., Kerman, N. T., Noroozi, O., Moon, J., & Drachsler, H. (2024). Feedback sources in essay writing: Peer-generated or AI-generated feedback? *International Journal of Educational Technology in Higher Education*, *21*(1), 1–15. DOI: 10.1186/s41239-024-00455-4

Bettayeb, A. M., Abu Talib, M., Sobhe Altayasinah, A. Z., & Dakalbab, F. (2024). Exploring the impact of ChatGPT: Conversational AI in education. *Frontiers in Education*, *9*, 1379796. DOI: 10.3389/feduc.2024.1379796

Bhullar, P. S., Joshi, M., & Chugh, R. (2024). ChatGPT in higher education - a synthesis of the literature and a future research agenda. *Education and Information Technologies*, *29*(16), 21501–21522. DOI: 10.1007/s10639-024-12723-x

Biju, P. R., & Gayathri, O. (2025). Indic approach to ethical AI in automated decision making system: Implications for social, cultural, and linguistic diversity in native population. *AI & Society*, •••, 1–26. DOI: 10.1007/s00146-025-02381-z

Braun, V., & Clarke, V. (2006). Using thematic analysis in psychology. *Qualitative Research in Psychology*, *3*(2), 77–101. DOI: 10.1191/1478088706qp063oa

Burns, M., Bally, J., Burles, M., Holtslander, L., & Peacock, S. (2022). Constructivist Grounded Theory or Interpretive Phenomenology? Methodological Choices Within Specific Study Contexts. *International Journal of Qualitative Methods*, *21*, 16094069221077758. Advance online publication. DOI: 10.1177/16094069221077758

Cachat-Rosset, G., & Klarsfeld, A. (2023). Diversity, Equity, and Inclusion in Artificial Intelligence: An Evaluation of Guidelines. *Applied Artificial Intelligence*, *37*(1), 2176618. Advance online publication. DOI: 10.1080/08839514.2023.2176618

Cai, Q., Lin, Y., & Yu, Z. (2023). Factors Influencing Learner Attitudes Towards ChatGPT-Assisted Language Learning in Higher Education. *International Journal of Human-Computer Interaction*. Advance online publication. DOI: 10.1080/10447318.2023.2261725

Chinta, S. V., Wang, Z., Palikhe, A., Zhang, X., Kashif, A., Smith, M. A., Liu, J., & Zhang, W. (2025). AI-driven healthcare: Fairness in AI healthcare: A survey. *PLOS Digital Health*, *4*(5), e0000864. DOI: 10.1371/journal.pdig.0000864 PMID: 40392801

Corrêa, N. K., Galvão, C., Santos, J. W., Del Pino, C., Pinto, E. P., Barbosa, C., Massmann, D., Mambrini, R., Galvão, L., Terem, E., & de Oliveira, N. (2023). Worldwide AI ethics: A review of 200 guidelines and recommendations for AI governance. *Patterns (New York, N.Y.)*, *4*(10), 100857. Advance online publication. DOI: 10.1016/j.patter.2023.100857 PMID: 37876898

Couldry, N., & Mejias, U. A. (2023). The decolonial turn in data and technology research: What is at stake and where is it heading? *Information Communication and Society*, *26*(4), 786–802. DOI: 10.1080/1369118X.2021.1986102

Dahri, N. A., Yahaya, N., Al-Rahmi, W. M., Vighio, M. S., Alblehai, F., Soomro, R. B., & Shutaleva, A. (2024). Investigating AI-based academic support acceptance and its impact on students' performance in Malaysian and Pakistani higher education institutions. *Education and Information Technologies*, *29*(14), 18695–18744. Advance online publication. DOI: 10.1007/s10639-024-12599-x

Darwin, R., Rusdin, D., Mukminatien, N., Suryati, N., Laksmi, E. D., & Marzuki, . (2024). Critical thinking in the AI era: An exploration of EFL students' perceptions, benefits, and limitations. *Cogent Education*, *11*(1), 2290342. DOI: 10.1080/2331186X.2023.2290342

Dibley, L., Dickerson, S., Duffy, M., & Vandermause, R. (2020). *Doing Hermeneutic Phenomenological Research: A Practical Guide*. SAGE Publications Ltd., DOI: 10.4135/9781529799583

Draissi, Z., Rong, Y., Zafeer, H. M. I., Maqbool, S., Malik, S. J., Maqbool, S., & Alemi, S. H. A. (2025). Academic diplomacy and policy borrowing: Media content analysis of Chinese soft power in Morocco. *Humanities & Social Sciences Communications*, *12*(1), 1–11. DOI: 10.1057/s41599-025-04544-1

Franklin, G., Stephens, R., Piracha, M., Tiosano, S., Lehouillier, F., Koppel, R., & Elkin, P. L. (2024). The Sociodemographic Biases in Machine Learning Algorithms: A Biomedical Informatics Perspective. *Life (Chicago, Ill.)*, *14*(6), 652. DOI: 10.3390/life14060652 PMID: 38929638

Gonsalves, C. (2024). Generative AI's Impact on Critical Thinking: Revisiting Bloom's Taxonomy. *Journal of Marketing Education*, 02734753241305980. Advance online publication. DOI: 10.1177/02734753241305980

Gouseti, A., James, F., Fallin, L., & Burden, K. (2024). The ethics of using AI in K-12 education: A systematic literature review. *Technology, Pedagogy and Education*, *34*(2), 161–182. DOI: 10.1080/1475939X.2024.2428601

Green, M., Stangl, L., Denz, F., & Cope, S. (2024). A Qualitative Study and Future Research Agenda for Cultivating Critical Thinking in Culturally Diverse Postgraduate Students. *Journal of Marketing Education*, 02734753241295996. Advance online publication. DOI: 10.1177/02734753241295996

Haltaufderheide, J., & Ranisch, R. (2024). The ethics of ChatGPT in medicine and healthcare: A systematic review on Large Language Models (LLMs). *NPJ Digital Medicine*, *7*(1), 1–11. DOI: 10.1038/s41746-024-01157-x PMID: 38977771

Helm, P., Bella, G., Koch, G., & Giunchiglia, F. (2024). Diversity and language technology: How language modeling bias causes epistemic injustice. *Ethics and Information Technology*, *26*(1), 1–15. DOI: 10.1007/s10676-023-09742-6

Hristova, T., Magee, L., & Soldatic, K. (2024). The problem of alignment. *AI & Society*, *40*(3), 1439–1453. DOI: 10.1007/s00146-024-02039-2

Imran, M., & Almusharraf, N. (2023). Analyzing the role of ChatGPT as a writing assistant at higher education level: A systematic review of the literature. *Contemporary Educational Technology*, *15*(4), ep464. DOI: 10.30935/cedtech/13605

Jamon, B. E. V., Boholano, H. B., Cabanes-Jamon, M. G., & Pardillo, M. F. (2021). Teachers lived experiences in the new normal in Philippine public schools: A phenomenology. *International Journal of Research*, *8*(02), 773–782.

Javed, S., Rong, Y., Zafeer, H. M. I., Maqbool, S., & Abbasi, B. N. (2024). Unleashing the potential: A quest to understand and examine the factors enriching research and innovation productivities of South Asian universities. *Humanities & Social Sciences Communications*, *11*(1), 1–15. DOI: 10.1057/s41599-024-03674-2

Jiang, J. (2025). Decolonizing critique through non-Western onto-epistemology: Chinese international students' affective engagement with AI-generated artworks. *Teaching in Higher Education*, *30*(6), 1573–1590. Advance online publication. DOI: 10.1080/13562517.2025.2465999

Jiang, S., McClure, J., Tatar, C., Bickel, F., Rosé, C. P., & Chao, J. (2024). Towards inclusivity in AI: A comparative study of cognitive engagement between marginalized female students and peers. *British Journal of Educational Technology*, *55*(6), 2557–2573. DOI: 10.1111/bjet.13467

Kalim, U., Irfan, S., Maqbool, S., & Zafeer, H. M. I. (2025). How AI Can Be Successfully Implemented in the Classroom Settings: Challenges and Pathways to Overcome. In *Navigating Barriers to AI Implementation in the Classroom* (pp. 235–266). IGI Global Scientific Publishing. DOI: 10.4018/979-8-3373-1827-1.ch010

Khalifa, M., & Albadawy, M. (2024). Using artificial intelligence in academic writing and research: An essential productivity tool. *Computer Methods and Programs in Biomedicine Update*, *5*, 100145. DOI: 10.1016/j.cmpbup.2024.100145

Kukulska-Hulme, A., Giri, R. A., Dawadi, S., Devkota, K. R., & Gaved, M. (2023). Languages and technologies in education at school and outside of school: Perspectives from young people in low-resource countries in Africa and Asia. *Frontiers in Communication*, *8*, 1081155. DOI: 10.3389/fcomm.2023.1081155

Lewis, A. A. Lewis, & Alexus, A. (2025). Unpacking Cultural Bias in AI Language Learning Tools: An Analysis of Impacts and Strategies for Inclusion in Diverse Educational Settings. *International Journal of Research and Innovation in Social Science, 9*(1), 1878–1892. https://EconPapers.repec.org/RePEc:bcp:journl:v:9:y:2025:i:1:p:1878-1892

Lin, H.-C. K., & Albahli, S. (2025). Advancing Sustainable Educational Practices Through AI-Driven Prediction of Academic Outcomes. *Sustainability 2025, Vol. 17, Page 1087, 17*(3), 1087. DOI: 10.3390/su17031087

Ma, L. (2021). An Immersive Context Teaching Method for College English Based on Artificial Intelligence and Machine Learning in Virtual Reality Technology. *Mobile Information Systems*, *2021*(1), 2637439. DOI: 10.1155/2021/2637439

Maimela, C., & Mbonde, P. (2025). Artificial intelligence in South African universities: Curriculum transformation and decolonisation—aid or obstacle? *Frontiers in Sociology*, *10*, 1543471. DOI: 10.3389/fsoc.2025.1543471 PMID: 40697567

Malik, M. A., & Amjad, A. I. (2025). AI vs AI: How effective are Turnitin, ZeroGPT, GPTZero, and Writer AI in detecting text generated by ChatGPT, Perplexity, and Gemini? *Journal of Applied Learning and Teaching*, *8*(1), 91–101. DOI: 10.37074/jalt.2025.8.1.9

Malik, M. A., Amjad, A. I., Aslam, S., & Fakhrou, A. (2024). Global insights: ChatGPT's influence on academic and research writing, creativity, and plagiarism policies. *Frontiers in Research Metrics and Analytics*, *9*, 1486832. DOI: 10.3389/frma.2024.1486832 PMID: 39583913

Mandour, W. S. (2025). AI-Powered Tools for Linguistic and Sentiment Analysis in Language Learning: Applications Using Google Sheets and Large Language Models. In *Using AI Tools in Text Analysis, Simplification, Classification, and Synthesis* (pp. 67–112). IGI Global Scientific Publishing. DOI: 10.4018/979-8-3693-9511-0.ch003

Marzuki, W., Widiati, U., Rusdin, D., Darwin, , & Indrawati, I. (2023). The impact of AI writing tools on the content and organization of students' writing: EFL teachers' perspective. *Cogent Education*, *10*(2), 2236469. Advance online publication. DOI: 10.1080/2331186X.2023.2236469

Mikalef, P., Islam, N., Parida, V., Singh, H., & Altwaijry, N. (2023). Artificial intelligence (AI) competencies for organizational performance: A B2B marketing capabilities perspective. *Journal of Business Research*, *164*, 113998. DOI: 10.1016/j.jbusres.2023.113998

Mishra, T., Sutanto, E., Rossanti, R., Pant, N., Ashraf, A., Raut, A., Uwabareze, G., Oluwatomiwa, A., & Zeeshan, B. (2024). Use of large language models as artificial intelligence tools in academic research and publishing among global clinical researchers. *Scientific Reports*, *14*(1), 1–9. DOI: 10.1038/s41598-024-81370-6 PMID: 39738210

Mohamed, M. S. P. (2024). Exploring Ethical Dimensions of AI-enhanced Language Education: A Literature Perspective. *Technology in Language Teaching and Learning*, *6*(3), 1813. Advance online publication. DOI: 10.29140/tltl.v6n3.1813

Nawaz, M. (2024). AI in STEM Education: Enhancing Problem-Solving and Critical Thinking Skills. *Journal of AI Integration in Education*, *1*(4), 38–48. https://researchcorridor.org/index.php/jaiie/article/view/252

Nguyen, K. V. (2025). The Use of Generative AI Tools in Higher Education: Ethical and Pedagogical Principles. *Journal of Academic Ethics*, *23*(3), 1–21. DOI: 10.1007/s10805-025-09607-1

Olan, F., Ogiemwonyi Arakpogun, E., Suklan, J., Nakpodia, F., Damij, N., & Jayawickrama, U. (2022). Artificial intelligence and knowledge sharing: Contributing factors to organizational performance. *Journal of Business Research*, *145*, 605–615. DOI: 10.1016/j.jbusres.2022.03.008

Olmos-Gómez, C., Luque Suárez, M., Manuel Cuevas Rincón, J., Zobeida Salas-Pilco, S., Xiao, K., & Oshima, J. (2022). Artificial Intelligence and New Technologies in Inclusive Education for Minority Students: A Systematic Review. *Sustainability (Basel), 14*(20), 13572. DOI: 10.3390/su142013572

Omodan, B. I. (2024). The roles of epistemology and decoloniality in addressing power dynamics in university education. *Globalisation, Societies and Education*. Advance online publication. DOI: 10.1080/14767724.2024.2335661;WGROUP:STRING:-PUBLICATION

Rodgers, W., Murray, J. M., Stefanidis, A., Degbey, W. Y., & Tarba, S. Y. (2023). An artificial intelligence algorithmic approach to ethical decision-making in human resource management processes. *Human Resource Management Review*, *33*(1), 100925. DOI: 10.1016/j.hrmr.2022.100925

Schiff, D. (2022). Education for AI, not AI for Education: The Role of Education and Ethics in National AI Policy Strategies. *International Journal of Artificial Intelligence in Education*, *32*(3), 527–563. DOI: 10.1007/s40593-021-00270-2

Shafqat, F., & Amjad, A. I. (2024). Examining Students' Perceptions, Experiences, and Ethical Concerns about Using ChatGPT for Academic Support: A Phenomenological Study. *Pakistan Social Sciences Review*, *8*(2), 443–455. DOI: 10.35484/pssr.2024(8-II)36

Sharma, A. K., & Sharma, R. (2025). Governance in the age of artificial intelligence: A comparative analysis of policy framework in BRICS nations. *AI Magazine*, *46*(2), e70010. DOI: 10.1002/aaai.70010

Sudarsan, I., Hoare, K., Sheridan, N., & Roberts, J. (2022). Giving voice to children in research: The power of child-centered constructivist grounded theory methodology. *Research in Nursing & Health*, *45*(4), 488–497. DOI: 10.1002/nur.22231 PMID: 35478178

Tao, Y., Viberg, O., Baker, R. S., & Kizilcec, R. F. (2024). Cultural bias and cultural alignment of large language models. *PNAS Nexus*, *3*(9), pgae346. Advance online publication. DOI: 10.1093/pnasnexus/pgae346 PMID: 39290441

Tavares, S., & Ferrara, E. (2023). Fairness and Bias in Artificial Intelligence: A Brief Survey of Sources, Impacts, and Mitigation Strategies. *Sci*, *6*(1), 3. DOI: 10.3390/sci6010003

Ulyshen, T. Z., Koehler, M. J., & Gao, F. (2015). Understanding the Connection Between Epistemic Beliefs and Internet Searching. *Journal of Educational Computing Research*, *53*(3), 345–383. DOI: 10.1177/0735633115599604

Vieriu, A. M., & Petrea, G. (2025). The Impact of Artificial Intelligence (AI) on Students' Academic Development. *Education Sciences*, *15*(3), 343. DOI: 10.3390/educsci15030343

Vučković, A., & Sikimić, V. (2025). Global justice and the use of AI in education: Ethical and epistemic aspects. *AI & Society*, *40*(4), 3087–3104. DOI: 10.1007/s00146-024-02076-x

Wang, Y., Zhang, C., & Zhou, Y. (2023). Reconstructing self from the illness: A constructivist grounded theory study of posttraumatic growth in patients with Crohn's disease. *BMC Gastroenterology*, *23*(1), 1–14. DOI: 10.1186/s12876-022-02618-x PMID: 36593456

Wong, M. F., Guo, S., Hang, C. N., Ho, S. W., & Tan, C. W. (2023). Natural Language Generation and Understanding of Big Code for AI-Assisted Programming: A Review. *Entropy 2023, Vol. 25, Page 888, 25*(6), 888. DOI: 10.3390/e25060888

Zafeer, H. M. I., Maqbool, S., Rong, Y., & Maqbool, S. (2025). Impact of Digital Learning Tools on Student's Engagement and Achievement in Middle School Science Classes. *International Journal of Technology in Education and Science*, *9*(2), 177–196. DOI: 10.46328/ijtes.622

Zafeer, H. M. I., Peng, C., Rehman, S., Wei, Z., & Maqbool, S. (2021). A Study to Investigate the Obstacles of Educational Technology in Curriculum; University Students' Perception. *European Online Journal of Natural and Social Sciences*, *10*(1), 1–8. https://european-science.com/eojnss/article/view/6115

Zimotti, G., Frances, C., & Whitaker, L. (2024). The future of language education: Teachers' perceptions about the surge of AI writing tools. *Technology in Language Teaching & Learning*, *6*(2), 1136–1136. DOI: 10.29140/tltl.v6n1.1136

Chapter 7
A Bibliometric Review of AI-Driven Green Education Using the Four-in-Balance Framework for Sustainable Learning Environments

Saima Javed
https://orcid.org/0009-0005-6008-5362
Zhejiang Normal University

Nadia Rehman
https://orcid.org/0000-0002-4172-625X
Zhejiang Normal University, China

Tahira Javed
https://orcid.org/0000-0001-7033-5007
Shandong Xiehe University, China

Sufyan Maqbool
https://orcid.org/0009-0007-6290-1305
Zhejiang Normal University, China

Zineb Draissi
Zhejiang Normal University, China

Uzma Sarwar
Huanggang Normal University, China

ABSTRACT

This chapter provides a thematic and bibliometric review of the use of artificial intelligence (AI) in education to promote green learning environments and sustainability. We used VOSviewer to map research trends and collaborative clusters in accordance with SDG 4.7 under the Four-in-Balance model: Vision, Infrastructure, Digital Content, and Competencies. The literature showed rapid expansion in

DOI: 10.4018/979-8-3373-4217-7.ch007

learning analytics and e-learning; sustainability and the SDGs; higher education's institutional reform and digital adoption; and emerging technologies, including big data, generative AI, and Industry 4.0. The results show uneven progress: Vision and Competencies lag, leading to fragmented, reactive adoption, while Infrastructure and Digital Content have improved, including intelligent tutoring, IoT-enabled classrooms, and adaptable resources. Few institutions incorporate environmental goals into strategy, and persistent gaps in AI literacy and sustainability skills limit responsible use.

INTRODUCTION

21st-century skills are crucial, along with traditional academic knowledge, for preparing children for a competitive future(Rehman, Huang, Mahmood, AlGerafi, et al., 2024). Artificial intelligence (AI) is reshaping education by enabling personalized learning and data-driven decision-making (S. Javed, Y. Rong, & B. N. Abbasi, 2024). At the same time, growing environmental crises underscore the urgency of sustainability education, which seeks to foster knowledge, skills, and values for a more equitable future (Unesco, 2020). While AI is widely recognized as a transformative force, its role in advancing sustainability within education remains underexplored (Kalim et al., 2025; Vinuesa et al., 2020; Zafeer et al., 2021). This chapter positions AI not merely as a technological tool but as a potential catalyst for integrating ecological responsibility into teaching, learning, and institutional practices.

There has never been a more urgent moment to align technological modernization with environmental sustainability. As systems pursue SDG 4.7 inclusive, equitable education that fosters sustainable development, global citizenship, and environmental awareness, recent work shows AI's potential is still underused for ecological goals (Akinsemolu, 2025; Vinuesa et al., 2020; Zafeer, Maqbool, et al., 2022). This chapter argues that AI can redefine environmental education by integrating sustainability into infrastructure, pedagogy, content, and capacity building, transforming not only what we teach but how institutions operate and how learners engage. Realizing this promise requires a policy and evaluation approach that goes beyond isolated pilots (Maqbool, Sarwar, et al., 2020; Zafeer et al., 2020).

In this sense, the Four-in-Balance model originally developed to analyze ICT integration (Sufyan Maqbool et al., 2024), offers a structured lens to evaluate whether AI advances inclusive and sustainable learning environments. Yet few studies examine the AI-environmental literacy intersection through such an evaluative frame; most treat AI integration and green education as separate paradigms, leading to fragmented implementations and policy guidance. By conducting a bibliometric +

thematic synthesis guided by Four-in-Balance, this chapter addresses that gap and provides actionable insights for leaders, educators, and policymakers.

RESEARCH QUESTIONS

RQ1: How is AI being used to advance green education across the Four-in-Balance pillars?
RQ2: What gaps, tensions, and enabling conditions recur across Vision, Infrastructure, Digital Content, and Competencies?
RQ3: What policy levers most strongly predict sustainable outcomes (SDG 4.7)?

This study contributes as (i) the **first policy-evaluation synthesis** of AI for green education mapped to Four-in-Balance; (ii) a **bibliometric map (2010–2025; n = 208)** revealing thematic drivers; and (iii) **actionable levers** (green-AI procurement, localization mandates, competency frameworks, and governance guidelines) to operationalize SDG 4.7.

Figure 1. AI-driven green education pathway with a four-in-balance model and green satisfaction

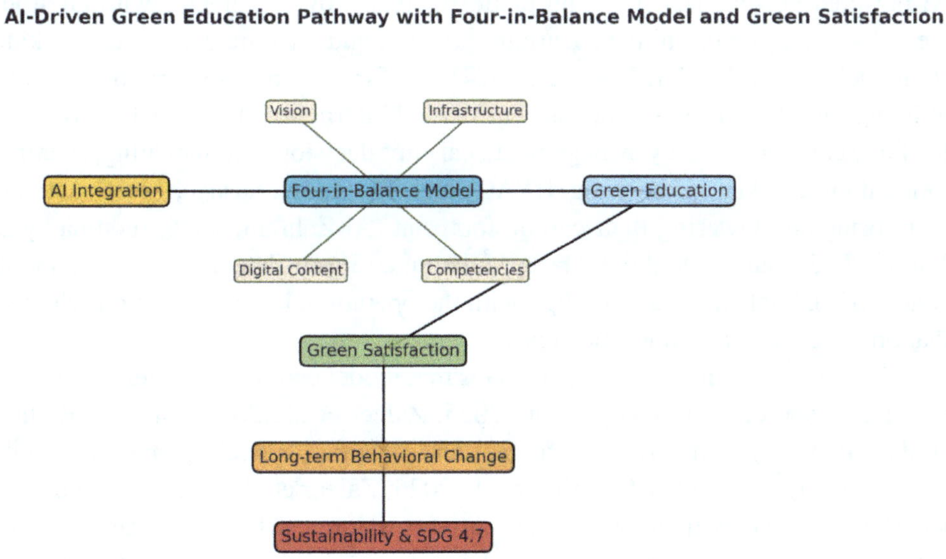

Using the Four-in-Balance paradigm as a guide, Figure 1 depicts how AI integration, through vision, infrastructure, digital content, and competencies, converges to produce green education outcomes (sustainable practices, climate literacy, environmental awareness) and learner green satisfaction.

BACKGROUND

It is crucial to distinguish green education from Education for Sustainable Development (ESD) to contextualize AI's role. Green education emphasizes environmental literacy and eco-practices (e.g., waste reduction, energy conservation, green campus design) (Maqbool, Wei, et al., 2020; Redican et al., 2025). It frequently takes the form of doable projects like recycling programs in schools, environmentally friendly campus layouts, and low-emission classroom operations. By combining environmental, economic, and social factors, sustainability education, Education for Sustainable Development (ESD), adopts a more comprehensive, systems-thinking approach, placing a strong emphasis on critical thinking, global citizenship, intergenerational fairness, and ethical responsibility(AlSagri & Sohail, 2024; Maqbool et al., 2025). As a result, green education is an essential yet more targeted component. This study emphasizes green education as a focused subset of ESD and evaluates AI's contributions across Four-in-Balance.

The use of AI in green education is opening up revolutionary possibilities, (i) AI-powered personalized learning platforms that provide students with environmental science content to their learning profiles, and encourage systems thinking (Indumathy & Mujra, 2025; Kotsis, 2024). (ii) Smart campus operations such as utilizing data-driven environmental controls and Internet-of-things (IoT) sensors, to facilitate intelligent energy management, real-time decisions about lighting, Heating, Ventilation, and Air Conditioning (HVAC), and digital device usage, thereby actively monitoring and lowering their carbon footprint (Al-Zahrani, 2024; Indumathy & Mujra, 2025; Samra Maqbool, Hafiz Muhammad Ihsan Zafeer, Sufyan Maqbool, et al., 2024). Such applications align with the operational goals of "green schools" that practice the very values they teach.

(iii) immersive simulations/virtual labs that model ecological systems with low marginal resource cost (Akinsemolu, 2025; Zafeer et al., 2022; Zawacki-Richter et al., 2019). (iv) dematerialized content and analytics, reducing paper use while delivering targeted feedback (Kalim et al., 2025; Zafeer et al., 2025c) that connect learning objectives with individual or group eco-actions can help encourage students to behave sustainably. Properly governed, these uses align pedagogy and operations with SDG 4.7 (Kalim et al., 2025; Zafeer et al., 2025c).

With the use of technologies like predictive analytics, intelligent tutoring programs, and AI-enhanced learning management systems, green education integrates environmental consciousness, climate literacy, and sustainable habits into instruction.

Environmentally responsible teaching methods can result in Green contentment (Javed, Rong, & Abbasi, 2024; Javed et al., 2020; Kalim et al., 2025; Maqbool et al., 2022) by encouraging both environmental responsibility and personal development, integrating green education that cultivates this kind of fulfillment can help achieve SDG 4.7.

THEORETICAL FRAMEWORK

The Four-in-Balance model created by (FOUDATION, 2015) offers a thorough framework for incorporating digital technologies into educational ecosystems and serves as the foundation for this investigation. To successfully execute educational innovation, the model's four interrelated pillars Vision, Infrastructure, Digital Content, and Competencies align. By Sustainable Development Goal 4.7, which calls for inclusive and high-quality education that fosters sustainable lifestyles and global citizenship, the model provides a structured lens through which to evaluate how artificial intelligence (AI) is being used to enhance sustainability-oriented education. (Rieckmann, 2017; Zafeer et al., 2025b).

The institutional objectives and strategic commitment to integrating AI and sustainability into learning environments are included in the Vision component. Technical and organizational preparedness, such as energy-efficient digital learning platforms and smart campuses, is referred to as infrastructure (Hou et al., 2024; Samra Maqbool, Hafiz Muhammad Ihsan Zafeer, Pingfei Zeng, et al., 2024). Personalized learning environments, AI-powered curriculum tools, and adaptive materials that raise environmental awareness are examples of digital content (Zawacki-Richter et al., 2019). Last but not least, competencies include the digital and sustainability-related abilities required of teachers and students to use AI tools efficiently and sustainably (Luckin & Holmes, 2016; Zafeer et al., 2023).

The study maps the changing research landscape and finds trends, policy orientations, and gaps in the literature by combining bibliometric analysis and thematic synthesis. A data-driven understanding of the relationship between artificial intelligence, education, and sustainability is made possible by VOSviewer's assistance in visualizing keyword co-occurrence, author collaboration, and thematic clusters. Emerging frameworks in sustainability studies and educational technology are consistent with this theoretical approach. For example, (Zawacki-Richter et al., 2019) highlighted the value of systematic mapping to assess AI's impact on education, while (Luckin & Holmes, 2016; Zafeer et al., 2025a) promoted competency development in AI-integrated learning systems. Additionally, (Unesco, 2020) has called attention to the role that AI may play in promoting education for sustainable development and has urged the global education industry to adopt AI tools in ways that are inclusive, ethical, and ecologically responsible (Maqbool et al., 2023; Zamir et al., 2021).

Therefore, the Four-in-Balance model offers a multifaceted framework for examining how AI may propel the shift in educational practices toward more environmentally friendly, adaptable learning environments when paired with bibliometric tools and sustainability objectives.

Figure 2. The four-in-balance model (ALMEIDA & VALENTE, 2016)

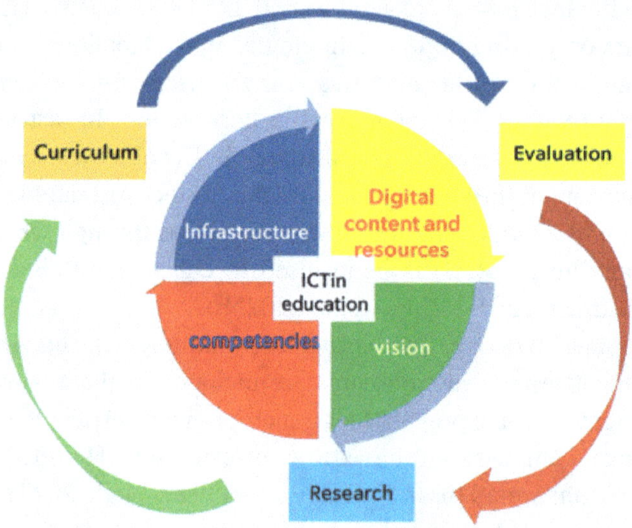

The Four-in-Balance model evaluates digital transformation along four interdependent pillars:

- Vision: institutional objectives and strategic commitment to AI-for-sustainability.
- Infrastructure: technical and organizational readiness (e.g., energy-efficient platforms, smart campuses).
- Digital Content: AI-powered curricula, adaptive materials, and tools that raise environmental awareness.
- Competencies: educator and learner capacities for effective, ethical, and sustainable AI use.

Guided by SDG 4.7, we map the literature onto these pillars and use bibliometrics (VOSviewer) to visualize intellectual structure, collaboration, and thematic clusters.

LITERATURE REVIEW

Artificial Intelligence (AI) in education is increasingly framed as more than a vehicle for personalization; it is emerging as a strategic lever for sustainability. However, existing work remains fragmented, with studies focusing on infrastructure, teacher training, or content design in isolation. Using the Four-in-Balance model [16] as a guide, this review synthesizes evidence across four pillars: Vision, Infrastructure, Digital Content, and Competencies, highlighting patterns, tensions, and gaps in aligning AI adoption with green education and SDG 4.7

VISION

Pattern. Several studies argue that sustainable transformation requires clear institutional strategies linking AI to ecological goals. (Vinuesa et al., 2020) and (AlSagri & Sohail, 2024) emphasize AI's potential for achieving SDGs, while (Strielkowski et al., 2025) and (Henriksen et al., 2024) advocate for embedding sustainability into institutional visions and mindsets. (Maqbool et al., 2024) show how visionary, inclusive leadership styles in Pakistan foster AI readiness and sustainability, echoing calls by (Rieckmann, 2017) and (Unesco, 2020) for education systems to align strategies with SDG 4.7.

Contrasts

Despite strategic potential, many institutions deploy AI reactively for digital efficiency rather than eco-pedagogical change(Badshah et al., 2023; Balážová et al., 2025; Henriksen et al., 2024; Rehman, Huang, Mahmood, AlGerafi, et al., 2024; Sari et al., 2024). Studies like (Allam et al., 2025) and (Draissi et al., 2025). (Chaudhry et al., 2022) highlight policy borrowing and soft power influences, leading to fragmented or externally driven strategies, while (Valente et al., 2017) note lessons from Brazil's ICT policies, where a lack of cohesive vision undermined sustainability impact.

Gaps

Few studies explicitly measure outcomes like green satisfaction (Javed, Rong, & Abbasi, 2024; Javed et al., 2020), or include marginalized learners in policy design. Vision often neglects the lifecycle energy costs of AI systems(Alamäki et al., 2024a; Khlaif et al., 2025).

Implications

Institutions need formal AI-for-sustainability roadmaps that integrate SDG metrics, inclusivity, and ecological targets, supported by dashboards and participatory planning (Balážová et al., 2025; Strielkowski et al., 2025).

INFRASTRUCTURE

Patterns. Infrastructure is both an enabler and a barrier. IoT and AI-powered smart campuses reduce energy and resource use (Akinsemolu, 2025; Aladsani, 2025; Badshah et al., 2023), with (Hou et al., 2024) showing carbon-reduction benefits of digital intelligence in China. GIS-based tools also expand eco-learning opportunities (AlSagri & Sohail, 2024). Research on "Green AI" (Alamäki et al., 2024a; Khlaif et al., 2025; Redican et al., 2025) demonstrates the potential of energy-efficient models, edge computing, and compression to cut energy use by over 50%.

Contrasts

While (Redican et al., 2025) and (Badshah et al., 2023) highlight opportunities in GIS and IoT-based education, (Verdecchia et al., 2023) exposes AI's high energy and water demands, contradicting sustainability goals. Case studies from higher education (Al-Zahrani, 2024) show successful sustainable campus practices, but others highlight digital divides that exclude low-income schools (Badshah et al., 2023; Kalim et al., 2025).

Gaps

Few lifecycle assessments of AI infrastructure exist, and equity in infrastructure distribution remains poorly addressed. Studies rarely consider the repairability or e-waste impacts of devices (Verdecchia et al., 2023; Vinuesa et al., 2020).

Implications

Green-by-design infrastructure requires procurement rules emphasizing low-energy models, renewable-powered data centers, and equitable access. Without this, AI risks worsening rather than reducing ecological footprints.

DIGITAL CONTENT

Patterns

AI-enabled content dominates the literature. Intelligent tutoring systems adapt to environmental science learning (Balážová et al., 2025; Indumathy & Mujra, 2025), while simulations and virtual labs foster systems thinking about climate change (Lee & Kwon, 2024; Redican et al., 2025; Zawacki-Richter et al., 2019).(Salas-Pilco et al., 2022) and (Zafeer et al., 2024, 2025c)show how learning analytics enhances engagement and outcomes in science. Case studies highlight the integration of sustainability into computing curricula(Peters et al., 2023; Verdecchia et al., 2023).

Contrasts

While (Lee & Kwon, 2024) and (Casal-Otero et al., 2023) report positive learning outcomes from AI in K–12, studies like (Peters et al., 2023) caution that many AI tools lack depth and eco-context. (Chaudhry et al., 2022) highlight transparency gaps in AI-generated learning resources. AI's promise for personalization (Lin et al., 2023; Salas-Pilco et al., 2022) is offset by risks of homogenization, bias, and superficial sustainability framing (Chaudhry et al., 2022).

Gaps

Content is often not localized or multilingual (AlSagri & Sohail, 2024), limiting relevance in diverse contexts. Few evaluate transfer to behavioral outcomes like sustainable practices.

Implications. To strengthen green education, AI-driven content must be localized, standards-aligned, fact-checked, and linked to real-world eco-actions. Procurement should require verifiable climate data and student agency in content interaction.

COMPETENCIES

Patterns

Teacher and learner competencies are central. Reviews highlight growing focus on AI literacy + ethics + sustainability (Badshah et al., 2023; Casal-Otero et al., 2023; Fu et al., 2024; Javed, Rong, & Abbasi, 2024; McGovern et al., 2023). (Zawacki-Richter et al., 2019) noted early neglect of educators, a gap partially addressed in recent PD programs [39]. (Rehman, Huang, Mahmood, AlGerafi, et al., 2024; Rehman et al., 2025) show STEM teacher training increasingly integrates sustainability-oriented AI tools. (Alamäki et al., 2024a) and (McGovern et al., 2023) demonstrate experimental programs linking AI literacy to environmental sciences.

Contrasts

While some studies show capacity building improves confidence and eco-awareness (Alamäki et al., 2024b; Fu et al., 2024; McGovern et al., 2023)Others reveal risks: overreliance on AI by students reduces critical thinking [45]; teachers often lack agency in tool use [33]. Research in LMICs (Kalim et al., 2025; Rehman et al., 2025) highlights greater competency and infrastructure gaps compared to high-income contexts.

Gaps

Competency-building often emphasizes tool operation rather than eco-pedagogical integration (Henriksen et al., 2024; Schwartz et al., 2020). Ethical, environmental, and privacy concerns are insufficiently embedded (Chaudhry et al., 2022).

Implications

Effective green AI education requires frameworks that blend technical skills, critical eco-reasoning, and ethical awareness, with ongoing PD for teachers and active student agency.

Across all pillars, systemic integration is lacking. Vision and Competencies lag behind Infrastructure and Content, creating uneven adoption. Studies demonstrate clear benefits from AI-enhanced personalization, smart campuses, and simulations, yet fragmented strategies, inequitable infrastructure, and shallow competencies hinder systemic impact. International collaborations (Javed, Rong, & Abbasi, 2024; Rehman et al., 2025) show promise for bridging gaps, but require policy coherence.

AI's potential for sustainability is real but under-realized. Without cohesive, policy-driven integration across all Four-in-Balance pillars, AI risks reinforcing inequalities and ecological harms instead of catalyzing transformation.

The research indicates that while the incorporation of AI into green education is progressing, it is still dispersed among the Four-in-Balance pillars. In terms of vision, the majority of institutions implement tools reactively for efficiency without long-term eco-pedagogical aims, while just a small percentage link AI with sustainability initiatives. Though large-scale AI models pose energy issues and digital disparities persist, infrastructure studies show that smart campuses, IoT, and GIS are attractive enablers. Lifecycle emissions and e-waste are not given enough attention.

Digital material is the most advanced, with analytics, simulations, and intelligent tutoring systems promoting eco-literacy and personalization. However, content is frequently decontextualized, inadequately localized, and vulnerable to bias and facticity issues. The weakest link is still competencies: while AI literacy among teachers and students is growing, professional development frequently diminishes teacher agency, children run the risk of becoming overly dependent on AI, and eco-pedagogy integration is scarce. Together, these trends show that although AI has great potential to help achieve SDG 4.7, its full potential will only be achieved through systemic, policy-driven integration that takes into account comprehensive competency frameworks, localized and fact-checked content, green-by-design infrastructure, and vision-setting.

DATA AND METHODOLOGY

This study employs a systematic review approach to explore the integration of Artificial Intelligence (AI) in green education, combining bibliometric and thematic analyses to map the research landscape and uncover key trends and gaps. The first phase involves a bibliometric analysis using data extracted from the Clarivate Web of Science Core Collection database, covering the period from 2010 to 2025. Using search terms such as "AI AND Green Education," "Artificial Intelligence AND Sustainable Learning," and "AI for SDG 4.7," the review includes peer-reviewed, English-language studies relevant to education, AI, and sustainability. A total of 208 studies were chosen for the review. VOSviewer was used to conduct publication trend mapping, journal and citation analysis, keyword co-occurrence, co-authorship networks, and country bibliographic coupling to assess scholarly output and influence quantitatively.

In the second phase, a qualitative content analysis was conducted using the Four-in-Balance model, comprising Vision, Infrastructure, Digital Content, and Competencies, as a coding framework. Each selected study was systematically categorized based on how it addressed strategic direction, technical readiness, curriculum content, and skill development related to AI-driven sustainability education. A thematic matrix was created to document these classifications, allowing for a clear visualization of patterns and gaps across the literature. This integrated approach enables a comprehensive understanding of how AI is shaping sustainable education practices while identifying opportunities for future research and policy alignment.

To explore the interplay between artificial intelligence (AI) integration and environmental sustainability in education, a thematic analysis was conducted on 25 peer-reviewed studies published between 2020 and 2025. The analysis was guided by the Four-in-Balance framework, which assesses educational technology implementation through four critical dimensions: Vision, Infrastructure, Digital Content, and Competencies. Each theme represents a strategic domain necessary for understanding how AI facilitates or hinders the advancement of green education. The findings below present key insights and recurring patterns that emerged across the dataset.

BIBLIOMETRIC ANALYSIS

By looking at publishing trends, citation networks, and theme clusters, bibliometric analysis provides a methodical way to map and assess the evolution of research within a particular topic. The intellectual structure, significant writers, networks of collaboration, and new trends that influence scholarly research can all be found using tools like VOSviewer. Bibliometric analysis offers essential insights into how research issues have changed, which countries and academics are driving the discourse, and what areas promise future potential in the context of artificial intelligence (AI) in education and sustainability. Through the integration of visualizations of keyword co-occurrence, co-authorship, co-citation, density, and overlay maps, this approach identifies emerging issues and collaborations that define the theoretical and practical underpinnings of the subject, as well as the prevailing research areas.

Figure 3. Cluster visualization

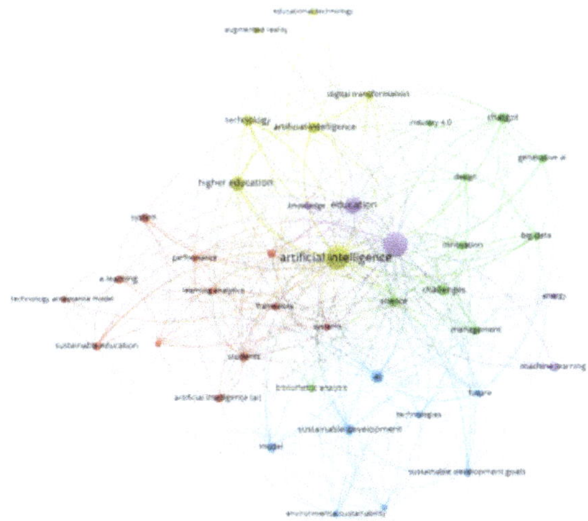

The bibliometric map in Figure 3 shows that the center's primary focus is artificial intelligence, which is strongly related to knowledge systems and education. While the yellow cluster focuses on higher education, educational technology, and digital transformation, the red cluster showcases research on e-learning, learning analytics, performance, and adoption models. The blue cluster links AI research with sustainability and sustainable development goals, while the green cluster showcases cutting-edge developments like ChatGPT, generative AI, big data, and Industry 4.0. When taken as a whole, the map shows how AI in education is being researched from a variety of angles, from adoption frameworks and digital learning to innovative AI applications and more general sustainability goals.

Figure 4. Overlay visualization

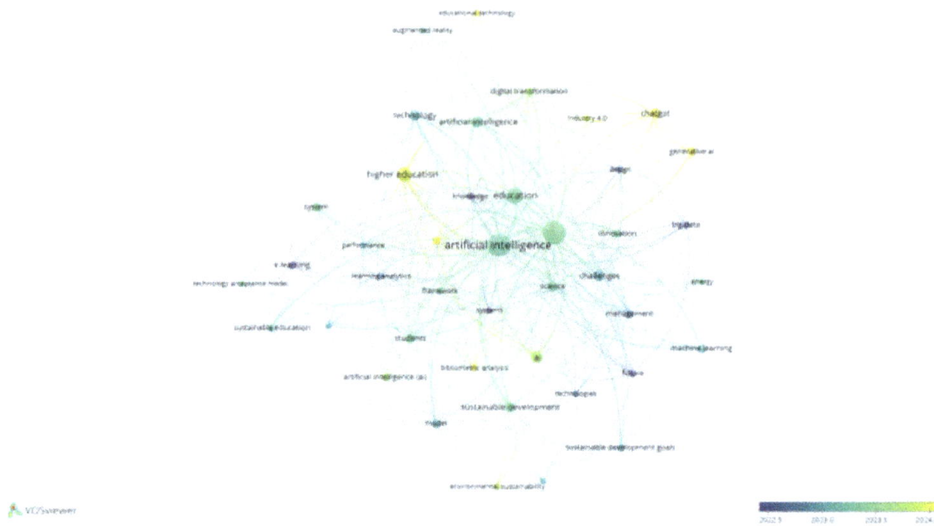

In Figure 4, the map displays an overlay depiction of keyword co-occurrence, with each keyword's average publishing year (ranging from 2022.5 to 2024) represented by a color gradient. Well-known subjects like education, higher education, and artificial intelligence are shown in this map in blue and green, signifying their prior existence in the field. To reflect their increasing relevance in recent literature, emerging topics such as ChatGPT, generative AI, digital transformation, and sustainable education are emphasized in yellow. It shows how things have changed throughout time. While more recent studies (yellow) are moving toward ChatGPT, generative AI, and sustainability, earlier studies focused on artificial intelligence, education, higher education, and e-learning. In practice, this aids in locating new study areas of interest that are influencing existing debates.

Figure 5. Density visualization

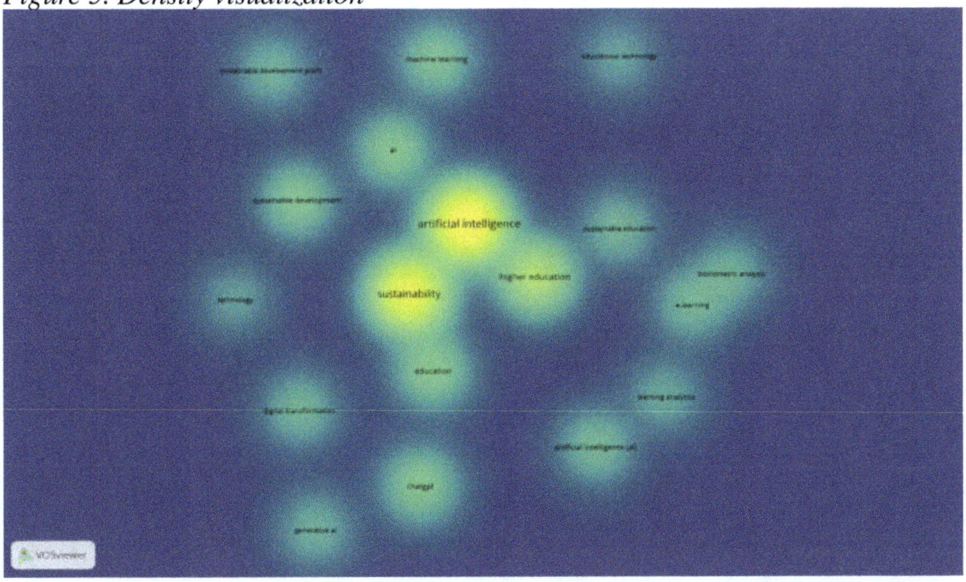

In Figure 5, the density visualization maps shows the terms that co-occur most frequently in the literature and their degree of relationship are displayed in this VOSviewer keyword-density map. "Artificial intelligence" and "sustainability," the two warmest (yellow/green) patches near the center, represent the field's primary focus, which is strongly related to higher education and sustainable education. Associated, sometimes complex concepts like "bibliometric analysis," "e-learning," and "learning analytics" represent well-established educational and methodological threads. More trendy, ancillary phrases like "ChatGPT," "generative AI," "digital transformation," "machine learning," and "educational technology" indicate new or specialized subtopics that feed into the main theme. All things considered, the map shows a research landscape centered on the linkages between AI and sustainability, with generative AI in educational contexts receiving increasing focus.

Figure 6. Overlay visualization of keyword co-occurrence

An overlay visualization of keyword co-occurrence, centered on the relationship between artificial intelligence and sustainability in education research, is shown in Figure 6. Research appears to be primarily focused on key topics such as artificial intelligence, sustainability, higher education, and sustainable development, indicating their fundamental relevance in the subject. However, the fields highlighted in yellow are more recent and emergent, such as ChatGPT, generative AI, digital transformation, and educational technology, which have become more prominent in the most recent literature (2023–2024). The research gains methodological and applied dimensions from related but peripheral subjects, including learning analytics, e-learning, and bibliometric analysis. Overall, this image shows that although sustainability and artificial intelligence (AI) are still key, there has been a noticeable change in recent years toward the use of digital transformation and generative AI tools as forces behind sustainable education.

Figure 7. Co-authorship network visualization

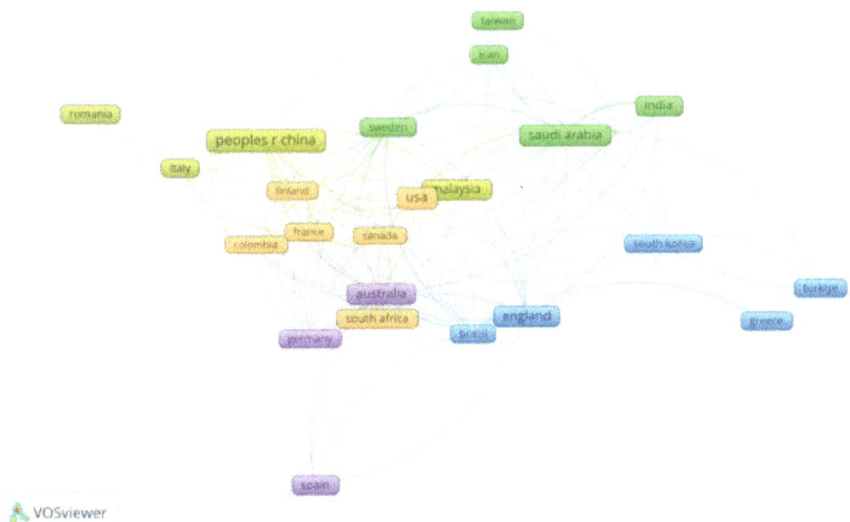

A country co-authorship network visualization created with VOSviewer is shown in Figure 7. Strong regional and interregional research collaborations are demonstrated by the green cluster, which includes countries such as Taiwan, Saudi Arabia, Iran, and India. The yellow-orange cluster, which represents North American and European cooperation, consists of the USA, Malaysia, France, Canada, and Finland. Another network of collaboration is shown by the blue cluster, which includes England, Brazil, South Korea, Greece, and Turkey; the purple cluster links Spain and Germany. China stands out as a significant node, highlighting its robust research output and connections to other clusters, which positions it as a key hub for international cooperation. The map shows how highly internationalized artificial intelligence research is in education, with the United States, China, England, India, and Saudi Arabia serving as essential pillars to support international collaborations.

Figure 8. Co-citation network of authors

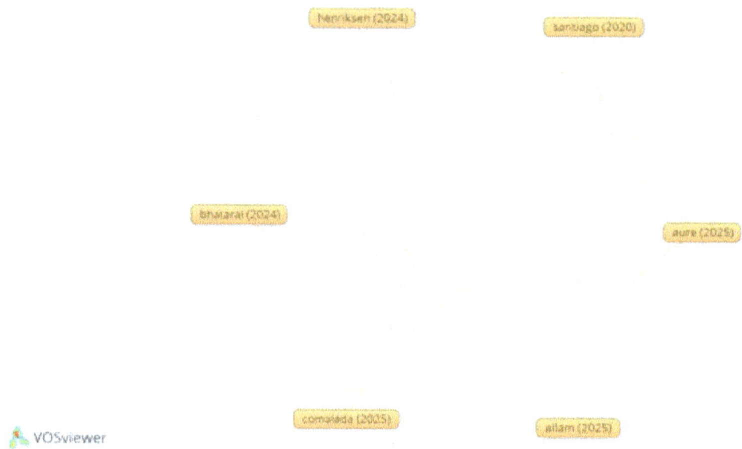

The co-citation network of authors depicted in Figure 8 demonstrates authors like Henriksen (2024), Bhatarai (2024), Comalada (2025), Allam (2025), Aure (2025), and Santiago (2020) create an interconnected citation network, indicating that their works are regularly cited together in research about artificial intelligence and education which shows the increasing scholarly interest and cooperative recognition of new voices in the field, and that their contributions reflect a common philosophical foundation in recent studies, especially in the years 2020–2025.

The bibliometric findings show distinct trends that show strong international partnerships, especially between China, the United States, England, India, and Saudi Arabia, demonstrating that sustainability and artificial intelligence in education are global objectives rather than niche agendas, promoting cross-border initiatives and financial opportunities. Thematic clusters, including e-learning, generative AI, and higher education transformation, reflect the actual use of AI technologies in classrooms, online learning environments, and university systems where pedagogy and assessment are being actively shaped by digital change.

CONTENT ANALYSIS

The content analysis enables researchers to conduct thematic evaluations and draw evidence-based conclusions on how AI tools, platforms, and pedagogies are being leveraged to foster sustainable and inclusive learning environments. For example, studies like (Maqbool et al.; Strielkowski et al., 2025; Zmir et al., 2021) cover all four areas, showcasing a holistic approach to AI implementation, while others like (Verdecchia et al., 2023) focus solely on green infrastructure, such as energy-efficient AI systems. This document serves as a foundation for deeper thematic analysis, policy evaluation, or curriculum development. It can be used to support discussions on how educational institutions are aligning AI applications with global sustainability goals.

Vision

Vision refers to the strategic, institutional, or pedagogical goals guiding the use of AI in education for sustainability. It includes leadership direction, long-term planning, and alignment with Sustainable Development Goals (SDGs).1. The analysis revealed that only a minority of studies presented a well-articulated strategic vision for aligning AI implementation with environmental sustainability. Studies such as (Draissi et al., 2025; Strielkowski et al., 2025) and (Vinuesa et al., 2020) demonstrated a high level of alignment, advocating for a systemic shift in educational policies toward the Sustainable Development Goals (SDGs), particularly SDG 4.7. However, most papers displayed fragmented or reactive approaches, focusing on short-term digital gains rather than long-term eco-pedagogical outcomes. Thematic clustering showed a lack of institutional commitment to integrating sustainability into AI roadmaps, leading to implementation gaps and inconsistent educational impact.

Many studies articulate a clear and forward-thinking vision for integrating AI into green education. (Strielkowski et al., 2025) emphasizes a post-COVID educational reset that incorporates AI not only for personalized learning but for environmental sustainability and resilience. (Vinuesa et al., 2020) and (Allam et al., 2025) advocate for AI to play a transformative role in achieving SDG 4 (quality education) and SDG 13 (climate action) by embedding green values into AI policies. (Henriksen et al., 2024) promote an eco-pedagogical mindset, suggesting that AI systems should align with institutional missions that value sustainability, creativity, and equity. (Balážová et al., 2025) reports institutional efforts to infuse climate awareness into education policy using AI-based planning tools and dashboards. These studies demonstrate that vision-setting is no longer an abstract ideal but an actionable necessity for driving technology alignment in modern green schools.

However, a lack of strategic alignment and sustainability focus is a persistent challenge. Although many institutions adopt AI for general digital transformation, they lack a cohesive vision that aligns AI deployment with environmental sustainability goals. Studies such as (Balážová et al., 2025) and (Zawacki-Richter et al., 2019) highlight that schools often operate without unified frameworks for integrating sustainability, AI, and education, leading to piecemeal implementation with inconsistent outcomes. Research (Henriksen et al., 2024) critiques many institutions for focusing on immediate AI deployment (like chatbot use) without a long-term eco-pedagogical vision. (Lin et al., 2023) and (Casal-Otero et al., 2023) point out that some AI strategies lack inclusiveness, ignoring underrepresented student populations in policy development. Vision remains underdeveloped in many contexts, risking AI adoption that may reinforce digital divides or ignore environmental responsibilities.

Infrastructure

Infrastructure focuses on the physical, digital, and organizational resources necessary for AI-driven green education. This includes hardware (smart boards, sensors), cloud platforms, data networks, and energy-efficient systems. AI-driven infrastructure emerged as both an enabler and a barrier in the transition to green education. Several studies (Balážová et al., 2025; Verdecchia et al., 2023) emphasized the ecological footprint of AI technologies, noting the high energy consumption and limited availability of low-carbon computational resources. In parallel, works by(Badshah et al., 2023; Redican et al., 2025) highlighted promising uses of IoT and AI for energy monitoring in classrooms and data-driven school design. A thematic thread running through the literature was the global digital divide, particularly in rural or under-resourced areas, where infrastructural deficits limit access to AI tools altogether, thereby reinforcing existing educational and environmental inequalities.

Several studies focus explicitly on building eco-resilient infrastructure using AI: (Verdecchia et al., 2023) offers a comprehensive review of "Green AI", focusing on reducing the carbon footprint of AI systems in schools and higher education. (Badshah et al., 2023) emphasize how AI and IoT work together to enable smart classrooms that monitor energy use, classroom occupancy, and digital carbon footprints.(Balážová et al., 2025; Redican et al., 2025)discuss the use of geospatial AI tools to map environmental hazards and engage students in real-world sustainability projects. These contributions highlight that eco-conscious infrastructure is a core enabler, not just a background condition, for AI-enhanced green education.

However, AI implementation often faces technical, environmental, and logistical infrastructure barriers that inhibit sustainable outcomes. Studies like (Maqbool et al., 2014; Verdecchia et al., 2023) expose the enormous energy and water demands of training and running large AI models, contradicting sustainability goals. Study (Badshah et al., 2023) reports significant inequalities in access to electricity, internet, and smart devices in rural or low-income regions, which limit equitable AI use. Institutions often purchase devices or deploy platforms without evaluating lifecycle emissions, noted by (Vinuesa et al., 2020). Infrastructure upgrades are rarely paired with sustainable data governance or repair plans, risking both environmental and data harm. Overall, AI infrastructures are seldom "green by design" and frequently exacerbate rather than mitigate environmental footprints.

Digital Content

Digital Content refers to AI-enabled learning materials and platforms, such as intelligent tutoring systems, digital textbooks, simulations, chatbots, and gamified green curriculum content. Digital content emerged as the most extensively addressed theme. A majority of studies focused on the design and evaluation of AI-powered educational materials that support interactive, personalized, and adaptive learning experiences.(Lin et al., 2023; Zafeer et al.) and (Salas-Pilco et al., 2022), for instance, examined intelligent tutoring systems that tailor environmental science lessons to learner profiles. However, the analysis also highlighted several challenges, including the lack of localized, multilingual content and a tendency toward superficial integration of sustainability themes. Content often lacked depth, contextual nuance, or alignment with climate justice principles. There was a noticeable thematic tension between the promise of intelligent personalization and the perils of content homogenization driven by global algorithms.

Most studies in the review provide innovative examples of AI-driven digital content, such as (Lin et al., 2023), which systematically reviews intelligent tutoring systems that promote STEM and climate literacy by adapting content to individual learner profiles. (Salas-Pilco et al., 2022; Sarwar et al., 2021) and (Zawacki-Richter et al., 2019) explore learning analytics platforms that use AI to monitor student progress and tailor eco-conscious learning resources. (Casal-Otero et al., 2023)designs AI literacy curricula for K–12, embedding environmental ethics and sustainability awareness into digital coding tools. (Lee & Kwon, 2024) focuses on storytelling and simulation tools that introduce sustainability concepts to young learners via AI-enhanced content. (Peters et al., 2023)shows how computing programs incorporate SDG-themed AI modules, linking technology directly to planetary well-being. These studies suggest that digital content is the most developed and widespread application of AI in sustainable education today.

Even though AI-enabled digital content is expanding, several challenges restrict its potential to support green education meaningfully. Studies such as (Allam et al., 2025) and (Redican et al., 2025) argue that much digital content lacks depth, interactivity, or context sensitivity, reducing its value for building climate literacy. (Unesco, 2020) noticed the absence of diverse language content, especially on climate topics tailored to local needs. Research by (Chaudhry et al., 2022) shows that AI-generated educational materials may contain unintended biases, inaccurate climate data, or fail to align with scientific consensus. Most AI tools (e.g., intelligent tutors or LLMs) are not explicitly designed for sustainability curricula, as reported by Sustainability in Computing (Peters et al., 2023). Thus, digital content needs curation, localization, and environmental context to contribute to green education.

Competencies

Competencies refer to the skills, mindsets, and capacities of educators, students, and administrators to effectively use AI for sustainability-related teaching and learning. The development of digital and ecological competencies, particularly among teachers, was another dominant theme. Studies by (Fu et al., 2024; Malik et al., 2025) and (McGovern et al., 2023; Rehman, Huang, Mahmood, Maqbool, et al., 2024) stressed the importance of professional development programs that embed AI literacy alongside environmental ethics. However, competency gaps persist, especially in low and middle-income contexts, where educators are often untrained in the use of AI tools and unaware of their sustainability implications. Moreover, the literature indicated a growing concern regarding student passivity and overreliance on AI-generated responses, as noted in several adaptive learning reviews (2023). Thus, competency-building efforts must balance technical skill acquisition with the cultivation of critical thinking and environmental awareness.

Several studies aim to build human capacity for responsible, impactful AI use (Alamäki et al., 2024b) and (McGovern et al., 2023) emphasize AI literacy and ethics training for educators and students to develop critical digital competencies. (Fu et al., 2024) offers a model for using AI to train pre-service teachers in interpreting sustainability learning data. (Chaudhry et al., 2022; Rehman, Huang, Sarwar, et al., 2024) develops frameworks for evaluating AI tools concerning teacher agency, data privacy, and responsible use. (McGovern et al., 2023) prepares researchers to develop and use AI responsibly in climate education and advocacy.(Balážová et al., 2025) highlights initiatives that equip school leaders with competency dashboards, helping them measure and improve environmental and digital literacy outcomes. Together, these studies reveal that the future of green education lies not just in deploying technology but in creating strategic, human-centered, and sustainability-aligned ecosystems. The Four-in-Balance framework offers a holistic lens through which researchers and policymakers can assess readiness, gaps, and opportunities in AI-enhanced sustainable education.

The human factor, teachers' and students' readiness to use AI for sustainable education, presents some of the most critical and recurring obstacles. Multiple studies (Alamäki et al., 2024b; Lin et al., 2023) highlight that most educators lack AI literacy, let alone how to apply it toward sustainability learning. (Fu et al., 2024) and (Salas-Pilco et al., 2022) note educators about data privacy, algorithmic opacity, and their ability to control AI tools effectively in classrooms. (Sari et al., 2024) reveals concerns that students become dependent on AI-generated answers, reducing critical engagement with environmental topics. Competency-building programs often focus on tool-use rather than eco-pedagogical integration, as criticized by (Henriksen et al., 2024). In short, capacity building remains reactive and fragmented, creating a bottleneck for effective and ethical AI implementation in sustainability-focused learning.

Across all four pillars, the most persistent challenge is the lack of systemic integration; AI is often adopted without cohesive alignment across vision, infrastructure, content, and human capacity. Institutional inertia was frequently cited as a barrier to integrating all four pillars effectively. Many studies have highlighted the need for intersectoral collaboration between educational institutions, environmental agencies, and AI developers. Lastly, there was a recurring call for holistic policy frameworks that move beyond tool adoption to encompass sustainability governance, ethics, and participatory design in AI systems. Thus, thematic analysis underscores the multidimensional nature of implementing AI for green education. While digital content and infrastructure receive considerable attention, vision-setting and competency development often lag. Addressing this imbalance is crucial for leveraging AI not just as a technical solution, but as a transformative catalyst for environmentally conscious learning systems. These challenges suggest the need for proper Green AI procurement guidelines, Sustainability-aligned digital content frameworks, Teacher training focused on environmental pedagogy using AI, and Institutional policy development aligned with SDGs.

RESULTS AND DISCUSSION

The bibliometric (2010–2025; n = 208) and thematic (Four-in-Balance) analyses combined demonstrate that artificial intelligence (AI) has a genuine but inequitable impact on green education: Infrastructure and digital content are more developed than vision and competencies. Four major clusters can be seen in network maps: (i) e-learning/learning analytics and adoption models; (ii) digital transformation in higher education; (iii) sustainability/SDGs; and (iv) emergent generative AI and Industry 4.0. These clusters indicate a field that is growing methodologically while shifting toward generative tools and sustainability goals. Co-authorship networks indicate Saudi Arabia, China, the United States, England, and India as collaborative hubs, suggesting prospects for regional policy harmonization as well as distributed capacity.

Vision: The majority of deployments are reactive and focused on short-term efficiency rather than eco-pedagogy; only a small percentage of studies operationalize AI-for-sustainability plans that are in line with SDG 4.7 and incorporate targets into leadership dashboards. Local strategy may be fragmented by donor-driven logics and policy borrowing. Crucially, measurements for lifecycle energy and green satisfaction are rarely codified as success criteria. Strong technical pilots do not always result in improvements in institutional sustainability, which might be explained by this imbalance. Implication: demand AI roadmaps at the institution level that (1) establish goals linked to the SDGs, (2) allocate funds for computation and energy, and (3) insist that underserved students be included in the design process.

A change in focus from earlier research, which focused on AI, education, and e-learning, to more recent studies (2023–2024) that focus on digital transformation, generative AI, and sustainable learning environments. Highlights that while less well-known subjects like augmented reality and environmental sustainability are starting to emerge as potential areas for future research, artificial intelligence in education and higher education is still the field that has been studied the most. The results show the potential for cross-border collaborations as well as the significance of AI in education on a worldwide scale. China, the United States, England, India, and Saudi Arabia are becoming essential centers of cooperation to promote innovations in education with a sustainability focus.

Infrastructure

Measurable resource usage reductions and enhanced observability of energy behaviors are demonstrated by evidence supporting IoT-enabled smart campuses, GIS, and digital intelligence interventions. However, the energy and water costs of huge models and cloud-heavy pipelines, along with ongoing digital disparities, temper the promise of sustainability. Repairability and low-bandwidth resilience are not well described, and few studies evaluate lifetime or e-waste. Implication: implement equity-first rollout (covering rural/low-income schools) and green-by-design procurement (compressed/edge models when pedagogically possible, renewable-backed compute, gadget repair plans).

Digital Content

This pillar demonstrates the highest level of maturity: immersive simulations and virtual labs, learning analytics, and intelligent tutoring systems all continuously raise engagement and eco-literacy while scaffolding systems thinking about climate processes. Nonetheless, two conflicts still exist: (i) personalization versus context—globalized material frequently flattens local languages and eco-realities; (ii) speed versus veracity—rapid adoption of LLM increases the risks of bias and facticity in climate-related themes. With little proof of transfer to civic action, evaluations place an undue emphasis on involvement proxies. Implication: localized, standards-aligned, low-emission material with fact-checking pipelines and actionable assessments (projects/rubrics linked to SDG 4.7 outcomes) should be required for procurement.

Competencies

The limiting factor is human capacity. Programs for teaching and learning about AI ethics and literacy are growing, but professional development is frequently tool-centric, which limits teacher agency and unintentionally encourages students to rely too much on AI outputs. LMIC evidence is still lacking, and eco-pedagogy, privacy, and civic involvement are not often integrated. Adopting competency frameworks that integrate technological proficiency, eco-ethics, data governance, and project-based green action with controls that maintain instructor oversight and surface model uncertainty is the implication.

The primary mode of failure in the field is asymmetry: fragmented, non-durable influence results from powerful infrastructure and content combined with insufficient vision and competencies. There is more face validity for SDG 4.7 and more potential for green pleasure in projects that explicitly connect strategy (Vision) and capacity (Competencies) with green-by-design infrastructure and locally relevant content.

POLICY IMPLICATIONS AND FUTURE DIRECTIONS

The review's conclusions highlight how, despite AI's widespread adoption in educational settings, its contribution to sustainability and SDG 4.7 is still inconsistent and partial. Policy interventions must shift from ad hoc adoption to systematic, governance-driven integration across the Four-in-Balance pillars in order to fully achieve AI's revolutionary potential.

First, integrating AI-for-sustainability into national and educational policies is necessary to fulfill institutional objectives. The inclusion of clear AI-SDG 4.7 roadmaps in education policies, with quantifiable goals like green satisfaction, decreased carbon footprint, and inclusive access, should be required by ministries and governing bodies. In order to ensure that underrepresented groups are represented in AI design and implementation, vision-setting must also take equity into consideration.

Second, policies pertaining to infrastructure must guarantee that AI deployment is environmentally friendly. This includes procurement guidelines that give preference to low-bandwidth functionality, renewable energy-powered data centers, energy-efficient models, and device repairability. To prevent escalating digital disparities, national financial frameworks should provide incentives for eco-resilient infrastructure, especially in settings with limited resources.

Third, governance of digital content is crucial. AI-enabled information should be localized, bilingual, fact-checked, and in line with national curricula, according to ministries and curriculum authorities. Procurement criteria should include ties to actionable sustainability outcomes, like project-based assessments linked to civic engagement and climate literacy, and demand transparency in the source of material.

Fourth, both teachers and students need to have their competencies consistently developed. Competency dashboards may monitor progress at the school and system levels, and professional development frameworks can incorporate AI literacy, eco-pedagogy, ethics, and data privacy into continuous training. In order to ensure that AI tools enhance rather than replace pedagogical decision-making, policies must safeguard teacher agency.

Lastly, accountability and governance systems are essential. In addition to creating independent monitoring bodies to keep an eye on compliance, national and regional organizations should embrace open standards for Green-AI that address energy reporting, lifecycle emissions, and privacy protections. Platforms for international collaboration can facilitate the exchange of best practices and the alignment of standards in various situations, particularly across systems with high and low resource levels.

In conclusion, policy frameworks need to acknowledge AI as a strategic lever for ecological stewardship rather than just a technical enabler. To convert fragmented adoption into sustainable, SDG 4.7-aligned education ecosystems, it will be crucial to align vision, infrastructure, content, and capabilities through cogent, enforced rules.

Future Directions: Future research should prioritize the development and validation of cross-context evaluation instruments that measure not only learning gains but also operational efficiencies, behavioral change, and green satisfaction as outcomes of AI-enabled sustainability education. Equally important is the creation of open benchmarks for Green-AI in education, including standardized reporting on energy consumption, edge-versus-cloud trade-offs, and lifecycle impacts of digital infrastructure. Building localized, multilingual climate curricula co-designed with teachers, students, and communities—supported by embedded fact-checking, provenance tracking, and contextual relevance—will help ensure both equity and accuracy. In parallel, researchers must test agency-preserving professional development models that strengthen AI literacy, eco-pedagogical practice, and privacy-by-design principles without diminishing teacher autonomy. Finally, comparative implementation studies across high- and low-resource settings are needed to identify minimal viable infrastructure configurations and scalable, equitable pathways for aligning AI integration with SDG 4.7.

REFERENCES

Akinsemolu, A. A. (2025). Green AI in Education: Can Artificial Intelligence Promote Sustainable Learning? *Journal of Theoretical and Empirical Studies in Education*, *10*(2), 596–629.

Al-Zahrani, A. M. (2024). Harnessing AI for sustainable university practices: Toward a greener campus. *International Journal of Sustainability in Higher Education*. Advance online publication. DOI: 10.1108/IJSHE-08-2024-0566

Aladsani, H. K. (2025). Developing postgraduate students' competencies in generative artificial intelligence for ethical integration into academic practices: A participatory action research. *Interactive Learning Environments*, •••, 1–19. DOI: 10.1080/10494820.2025.2487517

Alamäki, A., Nyberg, C., Kimberley, A., & Salonen, A. O. (2024a). Artificial intelligence literacy in sustainable development: A learning experiment in higher education [Original Research]. *Frontiers in Education, Volume 9 - 2024*. https://doi.org/DOI: 10.3389/feduc.2024.1343406

Alamäki, A., Nyberg, C., Kimberley, A., & Salonen, A. O. (2024b). Artificial intelligence literacy in sustainable development: A learning experiment in higher education. Frontiers in Education, Allam, H. M., Gyamfi, B., & AlOmar, B. (2025). Sustainable Innovation: Harnessing AI and Living Intelligence to Transform Higher Education. *Education Sciences*, *15*(4), 398.

ALMEIDA, M. E. B., & VALENTE, J. A. (2016). Políticas de tecnologia na educação brasileira: histórico, lições aprendidas e recomendações. *Centro de Inovação para a educação brasileira*.

AlSagri, H. S., & Sohail, S. S. (2024). Evaluating the role of Artificial Intelligence in sustainable development goals with an emphasis on "quality education". *Discover Sustainability*, *5*(1), 458. DOI: 10.1007/s43621-024-00682-9

Badshah, A., Ghani, A., Daud, A., Jalal, A., Bilal, M., & Crowcroft, J. (2023). Towards Smart Education through Internet of Things: A Survey. *ACM Computing Surveys*, *56*(2), 26. Advance online publication. DOI: 10.1145/3610401

Balážová, K., Galle, Š., Kandlová, A., & Bendl, T. (2025). *AI IN ENVIRONMENTAL EDUCATION: TOOLS, TRENDS, AND FUTURE DIRECTIONS*. https://doi.org/DOI: 10.11118/978-80-7701-025-2-0028

Casal-Otero, L., Catala, A., Fernández-Morante, C., Taboada, M., Cebreiro, B., & Barro, S. (2023). AI literacy in K-12: A systematic literature review. *International Journal of STEM Education, 10*(1), 29. DOI: 10.1186/s40594-023-00418-7

Chaudhry, M. A., Cukurova, M., & Luckin, R. (2022). A Transparency Index Framework for AI in Education. In Rodrigo, M. M., Matsuda, N., Cristea, A. I., & Dimitrova, V. (Eds.), *Artificial Intelligence in Education. Posters and Late Breaking Results, Workshops and Tutorials*. Industry and Innovation Tracks, Practitioners' and Doctoral Consortium. DOI: 10.1007/978-3-031-11647-6_33

Draissi, Z., Rong, Y., Zafeer, H. M. I., Maqbool, S., Malik, S. J., Maqbool, S., & Alemi, S. H. A. (2025). Academic diplomacy and policy borrowing: Media content analysis of Chinese soft power in Morocco. *Humanities & Social Sciences Communications, 12*(1), 1–11. DOI: 10.1057/s41599-025-04544-1

FOUDATION. K. (2015). Four in balance monitor 2015: use and benefits of ICT in education. In: Kennisnet Zoetermeer.

Fu, Y., Weng, Z., & Wang, J. (2024). Examining AI use in educational contexts: A scoping meta-review and bibliometric analysis. *International Journal of Artificial Intelligence in Education*, •••, 1–57.

Henriksen, D., Mishra, P., & Stern, R. (2024). Creative learning for sustainability in a world of AI: Action, mindset, values. *Sustainability (Basel), 16*(11), 4451. DOI: 10.3390/su16114451

Hou, J., Kang, W., Li, Y., Liang, S., & Geng, S. (2024). Does Digital-Intelligence Contribute to Carbon Emission Reduction? New Insights from China. *SAGE Open, 14*(4), 21582440241304462. DOI: 10.1177/21582440241304462

Indumathy, I., & Mujra, P. (2025). *Sustainable Learning. Smart Education and Sustainable Learning Environments in Smart Cities*. IGI Global.

Javed, S., Rong, Y., & Abbasi, B. N. (2024). Convergence analysis of artificial intelligence research capacity: Are the less developed catching up with the developed ones? *Journal of International Development, 36*(4), 2172–2192. DOI: 10.1002/jid.3901

Javed, S., Rong, Y., Zafeer, H. M. I., Maqbool, S., & Abbasi, B. N. (2024). Unleashing the potential: A quest to understand and examine the factors enriching research and innovation productivities of South Asian universities. *Humanities & Social Sciences Communications, 11*(1), 1–15. DOI: 10.1057/s41599-024-03674-2

Javed, T., Mahmoud, A. B., Yang, J., & Zhao, X. (2024). Green branding in fast fashion: Examining the impact of social sustainability claims on Chinese consumer behaviour and brand perception. *Corporate Communications*, *29*(6), 915–934. DOI: 10.1108/CCIJ-12-2023-0169

Javed, T., Yang, J., Gilal, W. G., & Gilal, N. G. (2020). The sustainability claims' impact on the consumer's green perception and behavioral intention: A case study of H&M. *Advances in Management and Applied Economics*, *10*(2), 1–22.

Kalim, U., Irfan, S., Maqbool, S., & Zafeer, H. M. I. (2025). How AI Can Be Successfully Implemented in the Classroom Settings: Challenges and Pathways to Overcome. In *Navigating Barriers to AI Implementation in the Classroom* (pp. 235-266). IGI Global Scientific Publishing. https://doi.org/DOI: 10.4018/979-8-3373-1827-1.ch010

Khlaif, Z. N., Alkouk, W. A., Salama, N., & Abu Eideh, B. (2025). Redesigning assessments for AI-enhanced learning: A framework for educators in the generative AI era. *Education Sciences*, *15*(2), 174. DOI: 10.3390/educsci15020174

Kotsis, K. T. (2024). Integration of artificial intelligence in science teaching in primary education: Applications for teachers. *European Journal of Contemporary Education and E-Learning*, *2*(3), 27–43. DOI: 10.59324/ejceel.2024.2(3).04

Lee, S. J., & Kwon, K. (2024). A systematic review of AI education in K-12 classrooms from 2018 to 2023: Topics, strategies, and learning outcomes. *Computers and Education: Artificial Intelligence*, *6*, 100211. DOI: 10.1016/j.caeai.2024.100211

Lin, C.-C., Huang, A. Y., & Lu, O. H. (2023). Artificial intelligence in intelligent tutoring systems toward sustainable education: a systematic review. *Smart learning environments, 10*(1), 41.

Luckin, R., & Holmes, W. (2016). Intelligence unleashed: An argument for AI in education.

Malik, S., Rong, Y., Zafeer, H. M. I., Maqbool, S., Draissi, Z., Rehman, N., & Maqbool, S. (2025). Analysis of Key Factors Influencing Academic Productivity: Insights From LASSO Regression and AI-Driven Techniques. In *Navigating Barriers to AI Implementation in the Classroom* (pp. 189–234). IGI Global Scientific Publishing., DOI: 10.4018/979-8-3373-1827-1.ch009

Maqbool, S., Maqbool, S., Zafeer, H. M. I., & Qihui, H. (2024). Exploring the Reflection of Teachers to Encourage the Gender Equality for Girls in Punjab Schools: In the Light of Universal Right to an Education. *Asian Women*, *40*(3), 113–138. DOI: 10.14431/aw.2024.9.40.3.113

Maqbool, S., Sarwar, U., Zamir, S., Zafeer, H. M. I., & Wei, Z. (2020). Teaching of Phonics and Fluency in Improving Reading Abilities at Primary Level: Multan Pakistan. *European Online Journal of Natural and Social Sciences*, *9*(4), 808–819.

Maqbool, S., Wei, Z., Sarwar, U., Zamir, S., & Zafeer, H. M. I. (2020). An analysis of self-concept between homeless and common women in Pakistan. *International Transaction Journal of Engineering, Management, & Applied Sciences & Technologies, 11*(15), 11-19. https://doi.org/DOI: 10.14456/ITJEMAST.2020.303

Maqbool, S., Zafeer, H. M. I., & Maqbool, S. (2025). Psychological Impact of Raising a Child With Autism: A Real Life Case Study of Expatriate Family. *Child & Family Social Work*, cfs.70011. Advance online publication. DOI: 10.1111/cfs.70011

Maqbool, S., Zafeer, H. M. I., Maqbool, S., Zeng, P., Draissi, Z., & Javed, S. (2024). Stance of numerous leadership styles and their effect on teaching to sustain academic performance at the high school level. *Heliyon*, *10*(16), e36438. DOI: 10.1016/j.heliyon.2024.e36438 PMID: 39253217

Maqbool, S., Zafeer, H. M. I., Yanping, L., & Zhao, W. (2022). Covid-19 and global education: Experiences of Pakistani international students. *International Transaction Journal of Engineering Management and Applied Sciences and Technologies, 13*(3). https://doi.org/DOI: 10.14456/ITJEMAST.2022.44

Maqbool, S., Zafeer, H. M. I., Zeng, P., Maqbool, S., Draissi, Z., & Javed, S. (2024). Inventive leadership styles and their impact for achieving sustainable development goals in education at secondary schools: A case study from Multan, Pakistan. *Humanities & Social Sciences Communications*, *11*(1), 1–11. DOI: 10.1057/s41599-024-03086-2

Maqbool, S., Zafeer, H. M. I., Zeng, P., Mohammad, T., Khassawneh, O., & Wu, L. (2023). The role of diverse leadership styles in teaching to sustain academic excellence at secondary level. *Frontiers in Psychology*, *13*, 1096151. DOI: 10.3389/fpsyg.2022.1096151 PMID: 36698584

Maqbool, S., Zhao, W., Rehman, S., Zafeer, H. M. I., & Maqbool, S. North American Academic Research.

McGovern, A., Gagne, D. J., Wirz, C. D., Ebert-Uphoff, I., Bostrom, A., Rao, Y., Schumacher, A., Flora, M., Chase, R., Mamalakis, A., McGraw, M., Lagerquist, R., Redmon, R. J., & Peterson, T. (2023). Trustworthy Artificial Intelligence for Environmental Sciences: An Innovative Approach for Summer School. *Bulletin of the American Meteorological Society*, *104*(6), E1222–E1231. https://doi.org/https://doi.org/10.1175/BAMS-D-22-0225.1. DOI: 10.1175/BAMS-D-22-0225.1

Peters, A.-K., Capilla, R., Coroamă, V. C., Heldal, R., Lago, P., Leifler, O., Moreira, A., Fernandes, J. P., Penzenstadler, B., Porras, J., & Venters, C. C. (2023). Sustainability in Computing Education: A Systematic Literature Review. arXiv:2305.10369. Retrieved May 01, 2023, from https://ui.adsabs.harvard.edu/abs/2023arXiv230510369P

Redican, K., Gonzalez, M., & Zizzamia, B. (2025). Assessing ChatGPT for GIS education and assignment creation. *Journal of Geography in Higher Education, 49*(1), 113–129. DOI: 10.1080/03098265.2024.2397332

Rehman, N., Huang, X., Mahmood, A., AlGerafi, M. A., & Javed, S. (2024). Project-based learning as a catalyst for 21st-Century skills and student engagement in the math classroom. *Heliyon, 10*(23), e39988. DOI: 10.1016/j.heliyon.2024.e39988 PMID: 39660178

Rehman, N., Huang, X., Mahmood, A., Maqbool, S., & Javed, S. (2024). Enhancing the quality of research synopsis of international students through peer feedback: A case study. *New Directions for Child and Adolescent Development, 2024*(1), 1271802. DOI: 10.1155/2024/1271802

Rehman, N., Huang, X., Mahmood, A., Zafeer, H. M. I., & Mohammad, N. K. (2025). Emerging trends and effective strategies in STEM teacher professional development: A systematic review. *Humanities & Social Sciences Communications, 12*(1), 1–23. DOI: 10.1057/s41599-024-04272-y

Rehman, N., Huang, X., Sarwar, U., Fatima, H., & Maqbool, S. (2024). Exploring the impact of family, school and society on the perception and reputation of vocational training in Pakistan: A statistical analysis. *Education + Training*.

Rieckmann, M. (2017). *Education for sustainable development goals: Learning objectives*. UNESCO publishing.

Salas-Pilco, S. Z., Xiao, K., & Hu, X. (2022). Artificial intelligence and learning analytics in teacher education: A systematic review. *Education Sciences, 12*(8), 569. DOI: 10.3390/educsci12080569

Samra Maqbool, M. A., Ijaz, S., Asif, M., & Jahanzeb, M. (2014). An Analysis of Self-esteem between Destitute and Non-destitute women.

Sari, H. E., Tumanggor, B., & Efron, D. (2024). Improving educational outcomes through adaptive learning systems using AI. *International Transactions on Artificial Intelligence, 3*(1), 21–31. DOI: 10.33050/italic.v3i1.647

Sarwar, U., Fazal, K., Zamir, S., Maqbool, S., Hussain, Z., & Qi, Z. Y. (2021). Assessment on Proficiency of Using Information and Communication Technology among Students of University of Lahore (Sargodha Campus), Pakistan. *European Online Journal of Natural and Social Sciences*, *10*(1), 102–115.

Schwartz, R., Dodge, J., Smith, N. A., & Etzioni, O. (2020). Green ai. *Communications of the ACM*, *63*(12), 54–63. DOI: 10.1145/3381831

Strielkowski, W., Grebennikova, V., Lisovskiy, A., Rakhimova, G., & Vasileva, T. (2025). AI-driven adaptive learning for sustainable educational transformation. *Sustainable Development (Bradford)*, *33*(2), 1921–1947. DOI: 10.1002/sd.3221

Unesco. (2020). Education for sustainable development: A roadmap. *Transforming Our World: The 2030 Agenda for Sustainable Development A/RES/70/1, available online at.*

Valente, J. A., Almeida, M. E. B. d., & Geraldini, A. F. S. (2017). Metodologias ativas: das concepções às práticas em distintos níveis de ensino. *Revista diálogo educacional, 17*(52), 455-478.

Verdecchia, R., Sallou, J., & Cruz, L. (2023). A systematic review of Green AI. *Wiley Interdisciplinary Reviews. Data Mining and Knowledge Discovery*, *13*(4), e1507. DOI: 10.1002/widm.1507

Vinuesa, R., Azizpour, H., Leite, I., Balaam, M., Dignum, V., Domisch, S., Felländer, A., Langhans, S. D., Tegmark, M., & Fuso Nerini, F. (2020). The role of artificial intelligence in achieving the Sustainable Development Goals. *Nature Communications*, *11*(1), 233. DOI: 10.1038/s41467-019-14108-y PMID: 31932590

Zafeer, H. M. I., Li, Y., & Maqbool, S. (2023). An Approach to Progress Learning Outcomes: International Graduate Students' Engagement in Reflective Practice and Reflective Journal Writing during Pandemic. *Sustainability (Basel)*, *15*(3), 1898. DOI: 10.3390/su15031898

Zafeer, H. M. I., Maqbool, S., Rong, Y., & Maqbool, S. (2024). Mapping the relationship and influence of school internal factors with an eye towards students' science academic outcomes. *Heliyon*, *10*(19), e38696. DOI: 10.1016/j.heliyon.2024.e38696 PMID: 39397972

Zafeer, H. M. I., Maqbool, S., Rong, Y., & Maqbool, S. (2025a). Beyond the Classroom: How Socioeconomic Status, Parental Involvement and Home Environment Impact on Students' Science Academic Performance at Secondary Schools. *European Journal of Education*, *60*(1), e70023. DOI: 10.1111/ejed.70023

Zafeer, H. M. I., Maqbool, S., Rong, Y., & Maqbool, S. (2025b). Culturally Sustaining Cognitive and Behavioral Interventions for Reducing Anxiety in Autistic School-Aged Students: A Systematic Review. *Psychology in the Schools*, pits.70077. Advance online publication. DOI: 10.1002/pits.70077

Zafeer, H. M. I., Maqbool, S., Rong, Y., & Maqbool, S. (2025c). Impact of digital learning tools on student's engagement and achievement in middle school science classes. *International Journal of Technology in Education and Science*, *9*(2), 177–196. DOI: 10.46328/ijtes.622

Zafeer, H. M. I., Maqbool, S., & Yanping, L. (2022). Psychological and social factors and their impact on divorced and married women: A case study from Punjab Pakistan. *Journal of Divorce & Remarriage*, *63*(5), 352–373. DOI: 10.1080/10502556.2022.2048345

Zafeer, H. M. I., Peng, C., Rehman, S., Wei, Z., & Maqbool, S. (2021). A Study to Investigate the Obstacles of Educational Technology in Curriculum; University Students' Perception. *European Online Journal of Natural and Social Sciences*, *10*(1), 1–8.

Zafeer, H. M. I., Xue, H., & Maqbool, S. (2020). Delaying Factors Regarding Civil Justice in Pakistan (Lower Courts). *Journal of Humanities and Social Sciences Studies*, *2*(6), 15–22. DOI: 10.32996/jhsss.2020.2.6.2

Zafeer, H. M. I., Yanping, L., & Maqboo, S. (2022). The role of gender, socio-economic factors, and its impact on students' English as a second language (ESL) performance. *North American Academic Research*, *5*(10), 52–59. DOI: 10.5281/zenodo.7216780

Zafeer, H. M. I., Yanping, L., & Maqbool, S. COVID-19 and the Future of Online Learning; Perspective of Pakistani Students from Higher Education Institutions (HEIs).

Zamir, S., Yang, Z., Sarwar, U., Maqbool, S., Fazal, K., Ihsan, H., & Arif, A. (2021). Teaching methodologies used for learning critical thinking in higher education: Pakistani teachers' perceptions. *Int. Trans. J. Eng. Manag. Appl. Sci. Technol*, *12*, 1–10. DOI: 10.14456/ITJEMAST.2021.90

Zawacki-Richter, O., Marín, V. I., Bond, M., & Gouverneur, F. (2019). Systematic review of research on artificial intelligence applications in higher education–where are the educators? *International Journal of Educational Technology in Higher Education*, *16*(1), 1–27. DOI: 10.1186/s41239-019-0171-0

Zmir, S., Sarwar, U., Maqbool, S., Javed, S., Ishtiaq, M., & Zhang, Y. (2021). Plagiarism practice: Its awareness & dealing and consequences among university students in Punjab province of Pakistan. *International Transaction Journal of Engineering, Management, &. Applied Sciences & Technologies*, *12*(11), 1–11.

Chapter 8

Impact of Generative AI and Digital Learning Tools on Student Engagement and Academic Achievement in Middle School Classrooms

Sufyan Maqbool
https://orcid.org/0009-0007-6290-1305
Zhejiang Normal University, China

Muhammad Usman Zafeer
University of Punjab, Pakistan

Al-Masaeid Mohammad
Flinders University, Australia

ABSTRACT

This study explores the impact of Generative AI and digital learning tools on student engagement and academic achievement in middle school classrooms. With the rapid integration of AI technologies like ChatGPT and educational tools such as learning management systems and gamified apps, the research aims to understand how these innovations affect student motivation, participation, and academic outcomes. A mixed methods approach was employed, involving surveys of 200 middle school

DOI: 10.4018/979-8-3373-4217-7.ch008

students, academic performance records, and classroom observations. The results reveal strong positive correlations between the use of AI tools, student engagement, and academic performance. The study highlights how personalized, interactive learning experiences facilitated by AI enhance cognitive, emotional, and behavioural engagement, leading to improved academic outcomes. Findings emphasize the potential of digital tools to support differentiated instruction and foster student-centered learning, offering actionable insights for educators and policymakers in integrating technology to optimize educational practices in middle school settings.

INTRODUCTION

In recent years, the educational landscape has undergone a transformative shift due to the rapid integration of digital technologies, particularly Generative Artificial Intelligence (AI) (Zmir et al., 2021). As the fourth industrial revolution continues to unfold, educators and policymakers are increasingly interested in how digital innovations influence teaching practices, student learning behaviours, and academic outcomes (Maqbool et al., 2025). Generative AI encompassing tools like ChatGPT, DALL·E, and others represents a new frontier in digital learning, offering personalized content creation, real time feedback, and adaptive learning experiences tailored to individual student needs (Nedungadi et al., 2024; Zamir et al., 2021). These tools can foster increased engagement by transforming passive learners into active participants, thereby enhancing motivation, creativity, and critical thinking (Maqbool et al., 2020).

Digital learning tools, including learning management systems (LMS), educational apps, interactive simulations, and virtual reality environments, have already demonstrated positive effects on student learning across various educational settings (Koh & Kan, 2021). Middle school classrooms, in particular, represent a critical stage in students' academic journey, where cognitive development, learning habits, and motivation can be significantly influenced by educational interventions (Zafeer et al.). The integration of Generative AI into these classrooms has the potential to address diverse learner needs, support differentiated instruction, and bridge gaps in achievement that traditional teaching methods may overlook (Zafeer, Yanping, et al., 2022).

However, despite growing enthusiasm, concerns about the ethical use of AI, data privacy, over reliance on technology, and digital equity remain prevalent (Kumar et al., 2024). Additionally, empirical research that investigates the practical implications of these tools on tangible educational outcomes especially among middle school learners is still emerging (Zafeer et al., 2020). Most studies have either focused on middle education or theoretical frameworks, leaving a gap in understanding their real world application in early adolescent education settings (Maqbool et al., 2020).

Student engagement is a multidimensional construct that includes behavioral, emotional, and cognitive aspects (Ciric & Jovanovic, 2016; Maqbool et al., 2025). It is widely recognized as a critical determinant of academic success (Malik et al., 2025). Integrating generative AI tools in classroom activities could enhance these dimensions by offering students creative, interactive, and real-time learning experiences. Simultaneously, academic achievement typically measured through grades, standardized tests, or formative assessments remains the most commonly used indicator to evaluate the effectiveness of educational strategies (Sufyan Maqbool et al., 2024).

This study seeks to explore how Generative AI and digital learning tools collectively impact student engagement and academic achievement within middle school classrooms (Zafeer et al., 2021). By analyzing the relationship between the use of these technologies and student outcomes, the research aims to provide evidence based insights that can guide educators, school leaders, and policymakers in adopting innovative, student centered teaching approaches (Maqbool, 2025). In an age where digital fluency is as important as literacy and numeracy, understanding these dynamics is not only timely but also essential for shaping the future of education (Zafeer, Maqbool, et al., 2022).

Significance of the Study

This study offers empirical insight into how Generative AI and digital learning tools influence student engagement and academic performance in middle schools, providing educators with data driven guidance to integrate technology meaningfully. The findings will help bridge pedagogical gaps and inform policy development for 21st century education.

Problem Statement

While digital tools and generative AI are rapidly becoming integral to educational settings, limited empirical research examines their specific impact on middle school students' engagement and academic achievement. Most existing studies are concentrated in education or focus solely on technological adoption rather than outcomes. Consequently, educators lack evidence-based guidance for effectively integrating these tools in early adolescent classrooms. Without this understanding, schools risk implementing technologies without realizing their full pedagogical potential or, worse, exacerbating existing educational inequalities. This study addresses this gap by investigating how these innovations influence key learning outcomes in middle school classrooms.

Purpose of the Study

The primary purpose of this study is to examine the influence of Generative AI and digital learning tools on student engagement and academic achievement in middle school classrooms. As technology continues to shape educational environments, it is critical to understand how specific tools impact student learning behaviors and outcomes. This study aims to generate actionable insights for educators, curriculum designers, and policymakers by analyzing both qualitative and quantitative data related to technology use in teaching and learning.

This research is guided by a constructivist framework, emphasizing that learners build knowledge through interaction with their environment, including digital tools and AI interfaces (Alam & Mohanty, 2023; Zafeer et al., 2025b). Generative AI tools such as ChatGPT or AI based content generators enable real time collaboration, automated feedback, and content personalization, potentially transforming passive learning into active knowledge construction. When combined with other digital platforms like Google Classroom, Kahoot, or Minecraft Education Edition, these tools can facilitate diverse learning experiences that promote curiosity, autonomy, and collaboration.

Student engagement, defined as the degree of attention, curiosity, interest, and participation shown by students in the learning process, is an essential predictor of academic success (Rehman et al., 2025; Sengsouliya et al., 2020). Studies have shown that digital learning tools can increase engagement through gamification, multimedia content, and adaptive learning pathways (Sotirov et al., 2024). Similarly, academic achievement often assessed through test scores, course grades, and learning gains is likely to improve when students are actively involved in their learning process.

The study will employ a mixed-methods approach, combining survey data from students and teachers with academic performance records and classroom observations. This methodological design allows for a nuanced understanding of both the measurable academic outcomes and the subjective experiences associated with using Generative AI and digital learning tools.

The research will focus on middle school students (grades 6 to 8), as this age group often transitions from foundational to more complex cognitive tasks and is particularly responsive to learning innovations. The research site will include a representative sample of urban and suburban schools with varying levels of technology access.

Research Questions

1. How does the use of Generative AI and digital learning tools affect student engagement in middle school classrooms?
2. What is the impact of Generative AI and digital learning tools on the academic achievement of middle school students?

Theoretical Perspectives

This study is grounded in the Constructivist Learning Theory, primarily influenced by the work of AlAli and Wardat (2024), and supplemented by Cognitive Load Theory Kong and Yang (2024) and Technology Acceptance Model (TAM). These frameworks provide the conceptual lens through which the integration of Generative AI and digital learning tools in middle school classrooms can be understood.

According to Vygotsky's Social Constructivism, learning occurs through social interaction and the use of cultural tools of which digital technologies are a modern example. In this view, learners actively construct knowledge by engaging with tasks that are scaffolded within their Zone of Proximal Development (ZPD). Generative AI tools like ChatGPT, adaptive tutoring systems, and interactive digital platforms can serve as these scaffolds, enabling students to extend their cognitive capabilities beyond independent performance levels (Brandt et al., 2020).

Cognitive Load Theory (CLT) complements this by emphasizing that learning materials should be designed to avoid cognitive overload, thus enhancing learning efficiency. Generative AI tools can reduce extraneous load by presenting information in personalized, simplified, or visual formats, helping students focus on relevant content (Binhammad et al., 2024). Moreover, AI generated formative feedback can assist in minimizing germane load, optimizing memory retention.

The Technology Acceptance Model (TAM), meanwhile, provides insight into how perceived usefulness and ease of use affect teachers' and students' adoption of these tools. Understanding attitudes toward AI and digital learning tools is critical, as it affects engagement and long-term integration into the learning environment (Fošner, 2024). Together, these theoretical perspectives provide a multifaceted understanding of how digital and AI driven technologies support student engagement and achievement in contemporary educational settings.

LITERATURE REVIEW

Generative AI in Education

Generative Artificial Intelligence (AI) refers to systems capable of producing original content, such as text, images, code, or feedback, in response to prompts (Samra Maqbool, Hafiz Muhammad Ihsan Zafeer, Sufyan Maqbool, et al., 2024). Recent advancements in large language models (LLMs), like GPT 4, have demonstrated their potential in education for real time content generation, personalized tutoring, and automated assessments (Bhatia et al., 2024).

Research by Rong et al. (2025) revealed that middle school students who interacted with AI chatbots for writing assistance showed significant improvements in creativity and engagement (Samra Maqbool, Hafiz Muhammad Ihsan Zafeer, Sufyan Maqbool, et al., 2024). Similarly, AI supported formative feedback has been found to improve writing quality and metacognitive awareness (Guo et al., 2025). However, ethical issues related to bias, dependency, and misinformation necessitate teacher mediation and AI literacy education (Zhang et al., 2025).

Digital Learning Tools and Student Engagement

Digital tools, such as Learning Management Systems (Google Classroom, Moodle), gamified apps (Kahoot, Quizizz), and multimedia tools (Padlet, Edpuzzle), have consistently been associated with high levels of student engagement. Alsawaier (2018) identify engagement as a multidimensional construct behavioral, emotional, and cognitive (Maqbool et al., 2022). Digital tools can promote behavioral engagement through interactive tasks, emotional engagement through gamification, and cognitive engagement through scaffolded content delivery (Zafeer et al., 2025c). Research by Lin et al. (2017) found that digital learning tools increased students' motivation and focus, particularly when features such as instant feedback, multimedia integration, and adaptive difficulty were employed (Zafeer et al., 2025a). In middle school settings, these tools have proven effective in sustaining attention and encouraging self regulated learning both predictors of academic success (Dent & Koenka, 2016).

Impact on Academic Achievement

There is growing evidence supporting the positive impact of technology-enhanced learning on academic achievement. Cheung and Ran et al. (2022) conducted a meta analysis showing that educational software use in K12 schools yielded modest but statistically significant improvements in reading and math scores (Zafeer et al.,

2024). More recent studies by Chen et al. (2025) further confirmed that technology supported instruction can improve conceptual understanding, especially when it aligns with curriculum goals (Kalim et al., 2025).

In the context of Generative AI, experimental findings suggest that AI supported writing tools enhance literacy development and critical thinking (Ali et al., 2024). Moreover, adaptive AI platforms that customize learning paths according to individual progress have shown promise in raising achievement levels among students who are typically underperforming (Zafeer et al., 2023).

However, the effectiveness of these tools depends heavily on implementation. Teachers must be trained in pedagogical strategies for AI integration, and schools must ensure equitable access to prevent exacerbating the digital divide (Ahmed, 2024). Additionally, reliance on AI without fostering foundational skills can hinder long term academic development, raising the need for a balanced approach (Sarwar et al., 2021).

Teacher and Student Attitudes toward Technology

Attitudes and perceptions play a pivotal role in the successful integration of technology (Sarwar et al., 2021). According to the Technology Acceptance Model (Akram et al., 2022), students and teachers are more likely to adopt new technologies if they perceive them as useful and easy to use. In a study conducted by Nazaretsky et al. (2022), teachers who received professional development in AI assisted education reported increased confidence and a willingness to experiment with innovative instructional methods (Pilz, 2025).

For students, positive experiences with AI and digital tools have been shown to enhance self efficacy, digital literacy, and academic confidence all important precursors to sustained academic achievement (Yuan et al., 2024). However, over reliance on digital tools without proper guidance may result in superficial learning or decreased face to face communication skills (Rehman et al., 2024).

METHODOLOGY

Research Design

This study employed a quantitative research design, specifically a descriptive survey method, to investigate the impact of Generative Artificial Intelligence (AI) and digital learning tools on student engagement and academic achievement in middle school classrooms (Rehman et al., 2024). The quantitative approach was chosen to systematically collect numerical data and statistically analyze relationships between technology use, student engagement, and academic outcomes (Bond et al., 2020). A cross sectional survey design was appropriate as it allowed data collection from a large sample within a specific timeframe, providing a snapshot of the current state of technology use in educational settings (Rehman et al., 2024).

Population and Sampling Technique

The target population for this study consisted of middle school students (grades 6–8) enrolled in public and private schools with access to digital learning tools and or AI assisted educational technologies (Maqbool et al., 2023). The sample size comprised 200 students, selected through convenience sampling. This non probability sampling method was used due to its practicality, cost-effectiveness, and ease of access to participants within the school setting (Sarkar et al., 2023).

While convenience sampling does limit generalizability, it was suitable for this exploratory study given time constraints and limited access to randomized school populations (Samra Maqbool, Hafiz Muhammad Ihsan Zafeer, Pingfei Zeng, et al., 2024). The selected students came from multiple schools within a single urban district to ensure exposure to varying degrees of digital tool integration (Draissi et al., 2025). Efforts were made to include students across different grade levels, genders, and socioeconomic backgrounds (Javed et al., 2024; Samra Maqbool et al., 2014).

Instrument of Data Collection

Data were collected using a self-administered structured questionnaire, designed to assess two main constructs: (1) student engagement and (2) academic achievement in relation to their use of generative AI and digital learning tools. The questionnaire included closed-ended questions based on a 5-point Likert scale ranging from "Strongly Disagree" (1) to "Strongly Agree" (5). The student engagement section was adapted from the validated Student Engagement Instrument (Assefa et al., 2025), covering cognitive, behavioral, and emotional dimensions. Sample items included:

- "I feel more interested in school when I use AI tools to learn."
- "Digital platforms help me understand lessons better."

The academic achievement section asked students to self-report their recent academic performance (grades), perceived improvement, and the frequency with which they use AI-supported learning tools (ChatGPT, adaptive quizzes, or gamified learning apps). In addition, demographic items such as age, gender, grade, and school type were included.

Validity and Reliability

To ensure content validity, the questionnaire was reviewed by three experts in educational technology and measurement. Based on their feedback, minor modifications were made to improve clarity and alignment with the study objectives. A pilot test was conducted with 30 middle school students from a non-participating school, and the Cronbach's alpha coefficient for internal consistency was found to be 0.82, indicating high reliability (Baharuddin et al., 2021).

Data Collection Procedure

After obtaining necessary permissions from school administrations and consent from students and their guardians, questionnaires were distributed and completed during regular school hours under the supervision of the researcher and teachers. The process ensured anonymity and confidentiality, encouraging honest responses.

Data Analysis

Collected data were coded and analyzed using Statistical Package for the Social Sciences (SPSS) version 26. Descriptive statistics (mean, standard deviation, frequency) were used to summarize participant demographics and engagement levels. Pearson's correlation coefficient was applied to examine relationships between the use of digital or AI tools and academic achievement. Significance levels were set at $p < 0.05$.

RESULTS

Table 1. Demographic Statistics

Variable	Category	Frequency	Mean	Standard Deviation
Gender	Male Female	98 102	0.51	0.50
Grade	Grade 6 Grade 7 Grade 8	63 69 68	6.98	0.81
School Type	Public Private	102 98	0.49	0.50

This section presents the findings from the quantitative analysis of data collected from 200 middle school students regarding their use of generative AI and digital learning tools, engagement levels, and academic performance. The data were analysed using descriptive statistics and correlation analysis.

Table 2. Descriptive Statistics

Variable	Mean	Standard Deviation	Minimum	Maximum
AI Tool Use	3.5	1.05	2.0	5.0
Engagement Score	3.73	0.69	2.8	4.7
Academic Performance	3.79	0.74	2.7	4.9

Based on the data collected from 200 middle school students, the table presents the descriptive statistics for three key variables: AI Tool Use, Engagement Score, and Academic Performance. The mean score for AI Tool Use is 3.5 (on a 5-point Likert scale), with a standard deviation of 1.05, indicating a moderate to high level of AI integration among students, with some variability in frequency of use. The minimum value of 2.0 and maximum of 5.0 suggest that while some students rarely use AI tools, others use them consistently in their learning activities.

The Engagement Score has a mean of 3.73 and a standard deviation of 0.69, reflecting generally high student engagement when using digital and AI based learning tools. The scores range from 2.8 to 4.7, suggesting that most students report moderate to high engagement levels. Lastly, Academic Performance has a mean of 3.79, with a standard deviation of 0.74, and a range between 2.7 and 4.9. This implies that students who use AI and digital learning tools generally perceive their academic performance to be above average.

Table 3. Correlation Analysis

Variables	AI Tool Use	Engagement Score	Academic Performance
AI Tool Use	1.00	0.91	0.93
Engagement Score	0.91	1.00	0.96
Academic Performance	0.93	0.96	1.00

The table presents the Pearson correlation coefficients among three key variables: AI Tool Use, Engagement Score, and Academic Performance. The values indicate strong positive relationships across all pairs.

The correlation between AI Tool Use and Engagement Score is 0.91, suggesting that students who frequently use AI tools are significantly more engaged in their learning. This aligns with the idea that generative AI and interactive digital platforms promote student involvement, motivation, and interest.

Similarly, the correlation between AI Tool Use and Academic Performance is 0.93, indicating a strong positive association. This suggests that students who use AI tools more often tend to achieve higher academic outcomes, possibly due to better personalized support, instant feedback, and enhanced learning efficiency provided by AI driven platforms. The strongest correlation is between Engagement Score and Academic Performance at 0.96, highlighting that student engagement is a critical factor influencing academic success. Engaged students are likely to participate more actively, retain information better, and perform well in assessments.

DISCUSSION

This study investigated the impact of Generative Artificial Intelligence (AI) and digital learning tools on student engagement and academic performance in middle school classrooms. The findings reveal significant positive correlations between the frequency of AI tool usage, students' engagement levels, and their academic achievements. These results support the hypothesis that technology enhanced learning environments particularly those integrating generative AI can meaningfully enhance both learning experiences and outcomes.

Relationship between AI Tool Use and Student Engagement

The study found a strong positive correlation (**r = 0.91**) between AI tool usage and student engagement, suggesting that students who frequently interact with AI powered platforms tend to be more cognitively and emotionally invested in their learning. This result is consistent with previous studies by Ilyas et al. (2025), who emphasized that student engagement is multidimensional and can be significantly influenced by the learning environment.

Generative AI tools like ChatGPT, interactive simulations, and adaptive quizzes provide students with instant feedback, personalized content, and creative problem solving tasks all of which can increase behavioral, emotional, and cognitive engagement. Selvakumar et al. (2025) noted that AI can function as a "learning companion," enabling personalized scaffolding that keeps students engaged by adjusting content to their level of understanding.

Furthermore, Nsabayezu et al. (2025) demonstrated that middle school students using multimedia learning tools showed high levels of attention, motivation, and persistence, aligning closely with this study's findings. The adaptive and interactive nature of digital tools helps reduce boredom and encourages exploration, which is essential during early adolescent learning stages.

Relationship between AI Tool Use and Academic Performance

The study also found a strong correlation (**r = 0.93**) between AI tool usage and self reported academic performance. This supports the notion that technology-enhanced environments can improve student learning outcomes. According to Kamberovic et al. (2025), students using AI-based writing assistants and personalized feedback systems demonstrated significant improvements in literacy and problem-solving skills.

This result mirrors findings from Valverde-Berrocoso et al. (2022), who conducted a meta analysis showing that educational technology positively affects academic achievement, particularly when tools are aligned with curriculum goals and used consistently. AI-powered platforms allow students to progress at their own pace, review content on demand, and receive personalized remediation, which may contribute to better learning retention and academic outcomes.

Moreover, the strong link between engagement and academic achievement ($r = 0.96$) confirms the established theoretical understanding that engagement is a key predictor of academic success. As noted by Olivier et al. (2020), students who are more engaged tend to achieve high grades and exhibit fewer behavioural problems.

Theoretical Alignment

These findings are well-grounded in Constructivist Learning Theory Iqbal et al. (2025), which posits that learners build knowledge through active engagement with tools and social contexts. In this case, generative AI and digital learning platforms act as mediating tools that support exploration, reflection, and deeper understanding.

Additionally, Cognitive Load Theory Kerres and Kalz is relevant to these findings. Generative AI tools can help reduce extraneous cognitive load by simplifying complex information and offering scaffolded assistance, allowing students to focus on essential learning tasks. The strong academic performance associated with middle school AI usage may partly be explained by this cognitive efficiency.

The Technology Acceptance Model (TAM) Xu (2024) also supports these results, as students are more likely to adopt and benefit from tools they perceive as useful and easy to use. The students in this study appeared to value AI tools for their ability to facilitate learning, reflected in both engagement and academic achievement outcomes.

Comparison with Other Studies

Several recent studies have echoed similar outcomes. For instance, Timotheou et al. (2023) emphasized that digital transformation in schools leads to enhanced conceptual understanding and better academic results, especially when teachers and students are digitally competent. Similarly, Getenet et al. (2024) found that students' positive attitudes toward educational technology were significantly linked to better academic outcomes and improved digital literacy.

A study by Pavone (2025) specifically investigated generative AI use in secondary education and found that AI-supported environments increased motivation, reduced learning anxiety, and allowed students to manage their learning more autonomously. These findings resonate strongly with this study's outcomes, especially in highlighting AI's role in empowering learners through personalization and interaction.

Implications for Educators and Policymakers

The study's results highlight the growing importance of integrating AI tools and digital learning technologies into middle school curricula. Teachers should be encouraged to adopt these tools not as replacements for instruction but as enhancements that support differentiated and student-centered learning. Training programs should focus on pedagogical strategies that combine traditional instruction with AI-driven platforms.

Policymakers should also consider digital equity when implementing such technologies. While this study's sample had access to AI tools, many schools still lack infrastructure or professional development necessary for successful integration. Closing this digital divide is critical to ensuring all students benefit from the advantages of AI and digital learning.

Limitations and Future Research

While the findings are promising, they must be interpreted in light of certain limitations. The study employed convenience sampling, limiting generalizability. Additionally, academic performance was based on self-reported data, which may not perfectly reflect actual academic outcomes.

Future studies should consider longitudinal designs and incorporate objective academic performance data (test scores or grades). Including teacher perspectives and conducting qualitative interviews could also provide richer insights into how AI integration affects classroom dynamics and learning outcomes.

REFERENCES

Ahmed, F. (2024). The digital divide and AI in education: Addressing equity and accessibility. *AI EDIFY Journal*, *1*(2), 12–23.

Akram, H., Abdelrady, A. H., Al-Adwan, A. S., & Ramzan, M. (2022). Teachers' perceptions of technology integration in teaching-learning practices: A systematic review. *Frontiers in Psychology*, *13*, 920317. DOI: 10.3389/fpsyg.2022.920317 PMID: 35734463

AlAli, R., & Wardat, Y. (2024). Opportunities and challenges of integrating generative artificial intelligence in education. *International Journal of Religion*, *5*(7), 784–793. DOI: 10.61707/8y29gv34

Alam, A., & Mohanty, A. (2023). Educational technology: Exploring the convergence of technology and pedagogy through mobility, interactivity, AI, and learning tools. *Cogent Engineering*, *10*(2), 2283282. DOI: 10.1080/23311916.2023.2283282

Ali, M., Siddique, A., Aftab, A., Abid, M. K., & Fuzail, M. (2024). AI-Powered customized learning paths: Transforming data administration for students on digital platforms. *Journal of Computing & Biomedical Informatics*, *6*(02), 195–204.

Alsawaier, R. S. (2018). The effect of gamification on motivation and engagement. *The International Journal of Information and Learning Technology*, *35*(1), 56–79. DOI: 10.1108/IJILT-02-2017-0009

Assefa, Y., Fetene, G. T., & Wolle, G. S. (2025). Adaptation and validation of the University Student Engagement Scale (USES) in the Ethiopian higher education context. *Journal of Applied Research in Higher Education*. Advance online publication. DOI: 10.1108/JARHE-05-2024-0215

Baharuddin, M. F., Masrek, M. N., Shuhidan, S. M., Razali, M., & Rahman, M. S. (2021). Evaluating the content validity of digital literacy instrument for school teachers in Malaysia through expert judgement. *International Journal of Emerging Technology and Advanced Engineering*, *11*(07), 71–78. DOI: 10.46338/ijetae0721_09

Bhatia, A., Bhatia, P., & Sood, D. (2024). Leveraging AI to transform online higher education: Focusing on personalized learning, assessment, and student engagement. *International Journal of Management and Humanities (IJMH) Volume-11 Issue-1*.

Binhammad, M. H. Y., Othman, A., Abuljadayel, L., Al Mheiri, H., Alkaabi, M., & Almarri, M. (2024). Investigating how generative AI can create personalized learning materials tailored to individual student needs. *Creative Education*, *15*(7), 1499–1523. DOI: 10.4236/ce.2024.157091

Bond, M., Buntins, K., Bedenlier, S., Zawacki-Richter, O., & Kerres, M. (2020). Mapping research in student engagement and educational technology in higher education: A systematic evidence map. *International Journal of Educational Technology in Higher Education*, *17*(1), 2. DOI: 10.1186/s41239-019-0176-8

Brandt, N. D., Lechner, C. M., Tetzner, J., & Rammstedt, B. (2020). Personality, cognitive ability, and academic performance: Differential associations across school subjects and school tracks. *Journal of Personality*, *88*(2), 249–265. DOI: 10.1111/jopy.12482 PMID: 31009081

Chen, F., Zhang, Y., & Chen, G. (2025). Exploring the effects of technology-supported collaborative inquiry and students' ICT competency on scientific literacy and subject knowledge in rural science classrooms. *Education and Information Technologies*, *30*(13), 1–28. DOI: 10.1007/s10639-025-13512-w

Ciric, M., & Jovanovic, D. (2016). Student engagement as a multidimensional concept. *Multidimensional Concept. WLC*, 187-194.

Dent, A. L., & Koenka, A. C. (2016). The relation between self-regulated learning and academic achievement across childhood and adolescence: A meta-analysis. *Educational Psychology Review*, *28*(3), 425–474. DOI: 10.1007/s10648-015-9320-8

Draissi, Z., Rong, Y., Zafeer, H. M. I., Maqbool, S., Malik, S. J., Maqbool, S., & Alemi, S. H. A. (2025). Academic diplomacy and policy borrowing: Media content analysis of Chinese soft power in Morocco. *Humanities & Social Sciences Communications*, *12*(1), 1–11. DOI: 10.1057/s41599-025-04544-1

Fošner, A. (2024). University students' attitudes and perceptions towards ai tools: Implications for sustainable educational practices. *Sustainability (Basel)*, *16*(19), 8668. DOI: 10.3390/su16198668

Getenet, S., Cantle, R., Redmond, P., & Albion, P. (2024). Students' digital technology attitude, literacy and self-efficacy and their effect on online learning engagement. *International Journal of Educational Technology in Higher Education*, *21*(1), 3. DOI: 10.1186/s41239-023-00437-y

Guo, K., Zhang, E. D., Li, D., & Yu, S. (2025). Using AI-supported peer review to enhance feedback literacy: An investigation of students' revision of feedback on peers' essays. *British Journal of Educational Technology*, *56*(4), 1612–1639. DOI: 10.1111/bjet.13540

Ilyas, S., Umar, M., Riaz, K., & Tariq, Z. (2025). Emotion Recognition in AI-Powered Classrooms Impacts on Student Engagement and Learning Outcomes. *The Critical Review of Social Sciences Studies*, *3*(3), 86–103. DOI: 10.59075/x1wkpx78

Iqbal, J., Hashmi, Z. F., Asghar, M. Z., & Abid, M. N. (2025). Generative AI tool use enhances academic achievement in sustainable education through shared metacognition and cognitive offloading among preservice teachers. *Scientific Reports*, *15*(1), 16610. DOI: 10.1038/s41598-025-01676-x PMID: 40360573

Javed, S., Rong, Y., Zafeer, H. M. I., Maqbool, S., & Abbasi, B. N. (2024). Unleashing the potential: A quest to understand and examine the factors enriching research and innovation productivities of South Asian universities. *Humanities & Social Sciences Communications*, *11*(1), 1–15. DOI: 10.1057/s41599-024-03674-2

Kalim, U., Irfan, S., Maqbool, S., & Zafeer, H. M. I. (2025). How AI Can Be Successfully Implemented in the Classroom Settings: Challenges and Pathways to Overcome. In *Navigating Barriers to AI Implementation in the Classroom* (pp. 235-266). IGI Global Scientific Publishing.

Kamberovic, M., Delic, A., & Krivic, S. (2025). Investigating AI in Programming Education: Self-Reported AI Usage, Individual Traits, and Learning Outcomes. Adjunct Proceedings of the 33rd ACM Conference on User Modeling, Adaptation and Personalization, Kerres, M., & Kalz, M. Generative AI Chatbots for Self-Regulated Learning while Balancing Cognitive Load: Perceptions, Interaction Patterns, and Instructional Designs in K-12 Learning.

Koh, J. H. L., & Kan, R. Y. P. (2021). Students' use of learning management systems and desired e-learning experiences: Are they ready for next generation digital learning environments? *Higher Education Research & Development*, *40*(5), 995–1010. DOI: 10.1080/07294360.2020.1799949

Kong, S.-C., & Yang, Y. (2024). A human-centered learning and teaching framework using generative artificial intelligence for self-regulated learning development through domain knowledge learning in K–12 settings. *IEEE Transactions on Learning Technologies*, *17*, 1562–1573. DOI: 10.1109/TLT.2024.3392830

Kumar, S., Verma, A. K., & Mirza, A. (2024). Digital revolution, artificial intelligence, and ethical challenges. In *Digital Transformation, Artificial Intelligence and Society: Opportunities and Challenges* (pp. 161-177). Springer. DOI: 10.1007/978-981-97-5656-8_11

Lin, M.-H., Chen, H.-C., & Liu, K.-S. (2017). A study of the effects of digital learning on learning motivation and learning outcome. *Eurasia Journal of Mathematics, Science and Technology Education*, *13*(7), 3553–3564. DOI: 10.12973/eurasia.2017.00744a

Malik, S., Rong, Y., Zafeer, H. M. I., Maqbool, S., Draissi, Z., Rehman, N., & Maqbool, S. (2025). Analysis of Key Factors Influencing Academic Productivity: Insights From LASSO Regression and AI-Driven Techniques. In *Navigating Barriers to AI Implementation in the Classroom* (pp. 189–234). IGI Global Scientific Publishing. DOI: 10.4018/979-8-3373-1827-1.ch009

Maqbool, S. (2025). Implemented in the Classroom Settings: Challenges and Pathways. *Navigating Barriers to AI Implementation in the Classroom*, 235.

Maqbool, S., Maqbool, S., Zafeer, H. M. I., & Qihui, H. (2024). Exploring the Reflection of Teachers to Encourage the Gender Equality for Girls in Punjab Schools: In the Light of Universal Right to an Education. *Asian Women*, *40*(3), 113–138. DOI: 10.14431/aw.2024.9.40.3.113

Maqbool, S., Wei, Z., Sarwar, U., Zamir, S., & Zafeer, H. M. I. (2020). An analysis of self-concept between homeless and common women in Pakistan. *International Transaction Journal of Engineering, Management, &. Applied Sciences & Technologies*, *11*(15), 11–19.

Maqbool, S., Zafeer, H. M. I., & Maqbool, S. (2025). Psychological Impact of Raising a Child With Autism: A Real Life Case Study of Expatriate Family. *Child & Family Social Work*, cfs.70011. DOI: 10.1111/cfs.70011

Maqbool, S., Zafeer, H. M. I., Maqbool, S., Zeng, P., Draissi, Z., & Javed, S. (2024). Stance of numerous leadership styles and their effect on teaching to sustain academic performance at the high school level. *Heliyon*, *10*(16), e36438. DOI: 10.1016/j.heliyon.2024.e36438 PMID: 39253217

Maqbool, S., Zafeer, H. M. I., Yanping, L., & Zhao, W. (2022). Covid-19 and global education: Experiences of Pakistani international students. *International Transaction Journal of Engineering Management and Applied Sciences and Technologies*, *13*(3), 1–11.

Maqbool, S., Zafeer, H. M. I., Zeng, P., Maqbool, S., Draissi, Z., & Javed, S. (2024). Inventive leadership styles and their impact for achieving sustainable development goals in education at secondary schools: A case study from Multan, Pakistan. *Humanities & Social Sciences Communications*, *11*(1), 1–11. DOI: 10.1057/s41599-024-03086-2

Maqbool, S., Zafeer, H. M. I., Zeng, P., Mohammad, T., Khassawneh, O., & Wu, L. (2023). The role of diverse leadership styles in teaching to sustain academic excellence at secondary level. *Frontiers in Psychology*, *13*, 1096151. DOI: 10.3389/fpsyg.2022.1096151 PMID: 36698584

Nazaretsky, T., Ariely, M., Cukurova, M., & Alexandron, G. (2022). Teachers' trust in AI-powered educational technology and a professional development program to improve it. *British Journal of Educational Technology, 53*(4), 914–931. DOI: 10.1111/bjet.13232

Nedungadi, P., Tang, K.-Y., & Raman, R. (2024). The transformative power of generative artificial intelligence for achieving the sustainable development goal of quality education. *Sustainability (Basel), 16*(22), 9779. DOI: 10.3390/su16229779

Nsabayezu, E., Habimana, O., Nzabalirwa, W., & Niyonzima, F. N. (2025). Leveraging multimedia-supported flipped classrooms approach to modernize organic chemistry instruction: Exploring students' engagement and motivation. *Education for Chemical Engineers*. Advance online publication. DOI: 10.1016/j.ece.2025.08.001

Olivier, E., Morin, A. J., Langlois, J., Tardif-Grenier, K., & Archambault, I. (2020). Internalizing and externalizing behavior problems and student engagement in elementary and secondary school students. *Journal of Youth and Adolescence, 49*(11), 2327–2346. DOI: 10.1007/s10964-020-01295-x PMID: 32710241

Pavone, G. (2025). Generative AI in the Learning Process: Threat or Tool? Understanding the Role of Self-Esteem and Academic Anxiety in Shaping Student Motivations. *Journal of Marketing Education*, •••, 02734753251346857. DOI: 10.1177/02734753251346857

Pilz, M. (2025). Guest editorial: Not in high regard: an exploration of low reputation of vocational education in the Global South. *Education + Training, 67*(3), 279–282. DOI: 10.1108/ET-03-2025-569

Ran, H., Kim, N. J., & Secada, W. G. (2022). A meta-analysis on the effects of technology's functions and roles on students' mathematics achievement in K-12 classrooms. *Journal of Computer Assisted Learning, 38*(1), 258–284. DOI: 10.1111/jcal.12611

Rehman, N., Huang, X., Mahmood, A., Maqbool, S., & Javed, S. (2024). Enhancing the quality of research synopsis of international students through peer feedback: A case study. *New Directions for Child and Adolescent Development, 2024*(1), 1271802. DOI: 10.1155/2024/1271802

Rehman, N., Huang, X., Mahmood, A., Zafeer, H. M. I., & Mohammad, N. K. (2025). Emerging trends and effective strategies in STEM teacher professional development: A systematic review. *Humanities & Social Sciences Communications, 12*(1), 1–23. DOI: 10.1057/s41599-024-04272-y

Rong, M., Yao, Y., Li, Q., & Chen, X. (2025). Exploring student engagement with artificial intelligence-guided chatbot feedback in EFL writing: Interactions and revisions. *Computer Assisted Language Learning*, •••, 1–30. DOI: 10.1080/09588221.2025.2539979

Samra Maqbool, M. A., Ijaz, S., Asif, M., & Jahanzeb, M. (2014). An Analysis of Self-esteem between Destitute and Non-destitute women.

Sarkar, B., Islam, N., Das, P., Miraj, A., Dakua, M., Debnath, M., & Roy, R. (2023). Digital learning and the lopsidedness of the education in government and private primary schools during the COVID-19 pandemic in West Bengal, India. *E-Learning and Digital Media*, *20*(5), 473–497. DOI: 10.1177/20427530221117327

Sarwar, U., Fazal, K., Zamir, S., Maqbool, S., Hussain, Z., & Qi, Z. Y. (2021). Assessment on Proficiency of Using Information and Communication Technology among Students of University of Lahore (Sargodha Campus), Pakistan. *European Online Journal of Natural and Social Sciences*, *10*(1), 102–115.

Selvakumar, P., Mishra, B. R., Mohanapriya, T., Shukla, R., & TC, M. (2025). Student Engagement and Motivation in Personalized Learning. In *Integrating Personalized Learning Methods Into STEAM Education* (pp. 123-142). IGI Global Scientific Publishing.

Sengsouliya, S., Soukhavong, S., Silavong, N., Sengsouliya, S., & Littlepage, F. (2020). An investigation on predictors of student academic engagement. *European Journal of Education Studies*.

Sotirov, M., Petrova, V., & Nikolova-Sotirova, D. (2024). Personalized gamified education: Feedback mechanisms and adaptive learning paths. 2024 8th International Symposium on Innovative Approaches in Smart Technologies (ISAS), Timotheou, S., Miliou, O., Dimitriadis, Y., Sobrino, S. V., Giannoutsou, N., Cachia, R., Monés, A. M., & Ioannou, A. (2023). Impacts of digital technologies on education and factors influencing schools' digital capacity and transformation: A literature review. *Education and Information Technologies*, *28*(6), 6695–6726.

Valverde-Berrocoso, J., Acevedo-Borrega, J., & Cerezo-Pizarro, M. (2022). Educational technology and student performance: A systematic review. Frontiers in Education, Xu, Z. (2024). AI in education: Enhancing learning experiences and student outcomes. *Applied and Computational Engineering*, *51*(1), 104–111.

Yuan, X., Rehman, S., Altalbe, A., Rehman, E., & Shahiman, M. A. (2024). Digital literacy as a catalyst for academic confidence: Exploring the interplay between academic self-efficacy and academic procrastination among medical students. *BMC Medical Education*, *24*(1), 1317. DOI: 10.1186/s12909-024-06329-7 PMID: 39548425

Zafeer, H. M. I., Li, Y., & Maqbool, S. (2023). An approach to progress learning outcomes: International graduate students' engagement in reflective practice and reflective journal writing during pandemic. *Sustainability (Basel)*, *15*(3), 1898. DOI: 10.3390/su15031898

Zafeer, H. M. I., Maqbool, S., Rong, Y., & Maqbool, S. (2024). Mapping the relationship and influence of school internal factors with an eye towards students' science academic outcomes. *Heliyon*, *10*(19), e38696. DOI: 10.1016/j.heliyon.2024.e38696 PMID: 39397972

Zafeer, H. M. I., Maqbool, S., Rong, Y., & Maqbool, S. (2025a). Beyond the Classroom: How Socioeconomic Status, Parental Involvement and Home Environment Impact on Students' Science Academic Performance at Secondary Schools. *European Journal of Education*, *60*(1), e70023. DOI: 10.1111/ejed.70023

Zafeer, H. M. I., Maqbool, S., Rong, Y., & Maqbool, S. (2025b). Culturally Sustaining Cognitive and Behavioral Interventions for Reducing Anxiety in Autistic School-Aged Students: A Systematic Review. *Psychology in the Schools*, pits.70077. DOI: 10.1002/pits.70077

Zafeer, H. M. I., Maqbool, S., Rong, Y., & Maqbool, S. (2025c). Impact of digital learning tools on student's engagement and achievement in middle school science classes. *International Journal of Technology in Education and Science*, *9*(2), 177–196. DOI: 10.46328/ijtes.622

Zafeer, H. M. I., Maqbool, S., & Yanping, L. (2022). Psychological and social factors and their impact on divorced and married women: A case study from Punjab Pakistan. *Journal of Divorce & Remarriage*, *63*(5), 352–373. DOI: 10.1080/10502556.2022.2048345

Zafeer, H. M. I., Peng, C., Rehman, S., Wei, Z., & Maqbool, S. (2021). A Study to Investigate the Obstacles of Educational Technology in Curriculum; University Students' Perception. *European Online Journal of Natural and Social Sciences*, *10*(1), 1–8.

Zafeer, H. M. I., Xue, H., & Maqbool, S. (2020). Delaying Factors Regarding Civil Justice in Pakistan (Lower Courts). *Journal of Humanities and Social Sciences Studies*, *2*(6), 15–22. DOI: 10.32996/jhsss.2020.2.6.2

Zafeer, H. M. I., Yanping, L., & Maqboo, S. (2022). The role of gender, socio-economic factors, and its impact on students' English as a second language (ESL) performance. *North American Academic Research*, *5*(10), 52–59.

Zafeer, H. M. I., Yanping, L., & Maqbool, S. COVID-19 and the Future of Online Learning; Perspective of Pakistani Students from Higher Education Institutions (HEIs).

Zamir, S., Yang, Z., Sarwar, U., Maqbool, S., Fazal, K., Ihsan, H., & Arif, A. (2021). Teaching methodologies used for learning critical thinking in higher education: Pakistani teachers' perceptions. *Int. Trans. J. Eng. Manag. Appl. Sci. Technol*, *12*, 1–10.

Zhang, D., Wijaya, T. T., Wang, Y., Su, M., Li, X., & Damayanti, N. W. (2025). Exploring the relationship between AI literacy, AI trust, AI dependency, and 21st century skills in preservice mathematics teachers. *Scientific Reports*, *15*(1), 14281. DOI: 10.1038/s41598-025-99127-0 PMID: 40275054

Zmir, S., Sarwar, U., Maqbool, S., Javed, S., Ishtiaq, M., & Zhang, Y. (2021). Plagiarism practice: Its awareness & dealing and consequences among university students in Punjab province of Pakistan. *International Transaction Journal of Engineering, Management, &. Applied Sciences & Technologies*, *12*(11), 1–11.

Chapter 9
Digital Healing:
AI's Emerging Role in Psychotherapeutic Practice

Summaira Rehman
https://orcid.org/0009-0009-2009-831X
Hazara University, Mansehra, Pakistan

Shagufta Parveen
Hazara University, Mansehra, Pakistan

Nida Munawar
https://orcid.org/0009-0009-8910-1839
Hazara University, Mansehra, Pakistan

Abstract

Artificial intelligence (AI) is transforming psychotherapeutic practice by enhancing accessibility, personalization, and early intervention in mental health care. This chapter explored diverse AI applications, including chatbots delivering cognitive behavioral therapy (CBT), virtual reality (VR) exposure therapy, digital phenotyping, and clinical decision support systems. Tools like Woebot and Tess demonstrate promise in reducing depressive symptoms and engaging users, while AI-augmented VR enables real-time adaptation of therapeutic environments. Digital phenotyping offers continuous monitoring for early detection of crises, and natural language processing facilitates objective assessment of therapeutic alliance and empathy. However, challenges such as ethical risks, algorithmic bias, data privacy, and clinician acceptance must be addressed. The concept of "Artificial Wisdom" is proposed to integrate empathy, cultural sensitivity, and ethical reasoning into AI systems. The

DOI: 10.4018/979-8-3373-4217-7.ch009

chapter advocated for collaborative human AI models that preserve the relational depth of therapy while leveraging AI's scalability and analytical capabilities for improved mental health outcomes.

INTRODUCTION

The integration of artificial intelligence (AI) and mental health care represents one of the most promising yet complex frontiers in contemporary healthcare. As traditional therapeutic models grapple with accessibility challenges, workforce shortages, and increasing demand for mental health services, AI technologies (AI-driven chatbots delivering cognitive behavioral therapy (CBT), virtual reality (VR) exposure therapy enhanced by machine learning, and digital phenotyping) are emerging as potential allies in the quest to democratize and enhance psychotherapeutic practice (Rehman et al., 2025; Zafeer et al., 2022). This chapter explores the multifaceted landscape of AI applications in mental health, examining both the transformative potential and critical challenges that define this rapidly evolving field (Samra Maqbool, Hafiz Muhammad Ihsan Zafeer, Pingfei Zeng, et al., 2024).

The integration of AI into psychotherapy is not merely a technological upgrade to existing practices but represents a fundamental reimagining of how therapeutic interventions can be delivered, monitored, and personalized. From conversational agents that provide round-the clock support to sophisticated algorithms that detect early warning signs of mental health crises, AI is reshaping the therapeutic landscape in ways that were unimaginable just a decade ago (Samra Maqbool, Hafiz Muhammad Ihsan Zafeer, Sufyan Maqbool, et al., 2024) .

THE FOUNDATION: UNDERSTANDING AI'S ROLE IN MENTAL HEALTH

The application of artificial intelligence in mental health encompasses a broad spectrum of technologies and approaches, each addressing different aspects of therapeutic care. Graham et al. (2019) provide a comprehensive framework for understanding these applications, categorizing them into three primary domains: diagnosis and assessment, treatment delivery, and predictive analytics. This tripartite structure offers a useful lens through which to examine the current state and future potential of AI in psychotherapy (Maqbool et al., 2023).

The diagnostic capabilities of AI have shown particular promise in early detection scenarios. Machine learning algorithms can now identify patterns in speech, text, and behavioral data that may indicate the onset of mental health conditions (Zafeer et al., 2025a). These systems excel at processing vast amounts of information that would be impractical for human clinicians to analyze manually, potentially catching subtle warning signs that might otherwise go unnoticed (Javed et al., 2024).

In treatment delivery, AI technologies range from fully automated therapeutic agents to sophisticated tools that augment human therapists' capabilities. This spectrum reflects a critical tension in the field between replacement and enhancement models of AI integration. While some applications seek to provide autonomous therapeutic support, others focus on empowering human clinicians with better tools and insights (Zafeer et al., 2024).

CONVERSATIONAL AGENTS: THE NEW FRONTIER OF ACCESSIBLE THERAPY

Perhaps no application of AI in mental health has garnered more attention than therapeutic chatbots. The landmark study by Maqbool et al. (2025) demonstrated that Woebot, an AI-driven conversational agent delivering cognitive behavioral therapy (CBT), could significantly reduce depressive symptoms in young adults over a 2-3 week period. Participants showed statistically significant improvements on depression measures compared to control groups, with particularly notable engagement levels users initiated conversations daily, suggesting genuine therapeutic value beyond mere novelty (Sufyan Maqbool et al., 2024).

This foundational research established several key principles for therapeutic chatbots. First, the structured approach of CBT translates well to algorithmic implementation, allowing for consistent delivery of evidence-based interventions. Second, the accessibility factor cannot be overstated participants could engage with therapeutic content at any time, removing traditional barriers such as scheduling constraints and geographical limitations (Zafeer et al., 2023).

However, the chatbot landscape is far from monolithic. Miner et al. (2017) distinguished between scripted CBT interventions like Woebot and more dynamic conversational agents like Tess, which attempt to engage in emotionally attuned, open-ended dialogue. This distinction highlights a fundamental challenge in therapeutic AI: balancing structure and flexibility, standardization and personalization (Zafeer et al., 2025c).

The systematic review by Vaidyam et al. (2019) provides a sobering assessment of the therapeutic chatbot landscape, identifying three primary use cases: psychoeducation and self-management, CBT-based symptom tracking and intervention, and crisis support. While these applications demonstrate feasibility in improving accessibility and reducing stigma, the review reveals critical limitations including lack of clinical validation for most tools, privacy concerns with sensitive data, and over-reliance on simplistic algorithms that struggle with complex emotional distress (Maqbool et al., 2022; Rehman et al., 2024a).

BEYOND INDIVIDUAL THERAPY: AI-ENHANCED SOCIAL AND GROUP INTERVENTIONS

The potential of AI extends beyond one-on-one therapeutic interactions to enhance group and peer-based interventions. D'alfonso et al. (2017) explored the innovative integration of AI with online social therapy platforms, demonstrating how machine learning can moderate peer support environments while maintaining safety and therapeutic fidelity. Their approach represents a significant evolution from traditional chatbot models by focusing on augmenting human-to-human connections rather than replacing them (Draissi et al., 2025).

This AI-moderated peer support model addresses several critical challenges in youth mental health services. By using linguistic analysis of peer interactions, AI systems can identify at-risk users, personalize therapeutic content, and maintain supportive environments by detecting harmful content such as self-harm references (Maqbool et al., 2025). The youth-centric design employs familiar social media-style interfaces, potentially reducing the stigma associated with seeking mental health support (Maqbool, Wei, et al., 2020).

The implications of this approach extend far beyond immediate therapeutic benefits. By creating scalable platforms for peer support, AI-enhanced social therapy could address the fundamental mismatch between mental health service demand and availability, particularly for young people who may be more comfortable seeking support through digital platforms (Zafeer et al., 2021; Zamir et al., 2021).

IMMERSIVE TECHNOLOGIES: VIRTUAL REALITY AND AI CONVERGENCE

The integration of AI with virtual reality technologies represents another frontier in therapeutic innovation. Maples-Keller et al. (2017) established VR's foundational efficacy in treating anxiety and psychiatric disorders through exposure therapy, skill-building, and immersive interventions. The technology's ability to create controlled, customizable environments enables clinicians to deliver precise, graded exposure while maintaining patient safety (Zafeer et al., 2020).

Lindner et al. (2017) extended this foundation by exploring how consumer-grade VR hardware could democratize access to advanced exposure therapies, while outlining the potential for AI integration to create truly personalized therapeutic experiences. Their vision of AI-enhanced VR exposure therapy (VRET) includes dynamic adaptation of scenarios based on real-time physiological and behavioral data, creating responsive, patient-tailored therapeutic experiences that adjust automatically to individual needs and progress (Maqbool, Sarwar, et al., 2020; Rehman et al., 2024b).

This convergence of VR and AI technologies addresses several persistent challenges in exposure-based therapies. Traditional exposure therapy requires significant therapist expertise to calibrate difficulty levels and respond to patient reactions. AI-enhanced systems could automate difficulty adjustment, detect subtle anxiety cues, and personalize exposure hierarchies based on continuous monitoring of patient responses (Maqbool, 2025; Zmir et al., 2021).

DIGITAL PHENOTYPING AND PREDICTIVE ANALYTICS: THE PROMISE OF EARLY INTERVENTION

One of the most transformative applications of AI in mental health involves the use of digital phenotyping for early detection and intervention. Torous et al. (2018) reviewed the potential of smartphone sensors, machine learning, and digital phenotyping to enable real-time suicide risk prediction and intervention. By analyzing behavioral markers such as sleep patterns, social activity, and language use, alongside physiological data like heart rate variability, AI models can identify high-risk states with unprecedented immediacy (Zafeer et al.).

This approach represents a paradigm shift from reactive to proactive mental health care. Traditional clinical assessments rely heavily on self-report measures and periodic check-ins, which may miss critical warning signs between sessions. Digital phenotyping offers continuous, passive monitoring that could detect subtle changes in behavior or mood that precede mental health crises (Malik et al., 2025).

The implications for suicide prevention are particularly profound. The ability to identify individuals at high risk in real-time could enable immediate intervention, potentially saving lives through timely outreach and support. However, this capability also raises significant ethical concerns regarding privacy, autonomy, and the potential for false alarms that could unnecessarily alarm individuals or overwhelm mental health systems (Kalim et al., 2025).

ENHANCING HUMAN THERAPY: AI AS CLINICAL DECISION SUPPORT

While much attention focuses on AI as a replacement for human therapists, perhaps more promising applications involve using AI to enhance human-delivered therapy. Several research streams demonstrate how AI can augment clinical practice by providing objective measures of therapeutic processes and outcomes.

(Goldberg et al., 2020) leveraged natural language processing and machine learning to objectively measure therapeutic alliance a key predictor of psychotherapy outcomes. By analyzing session transcripts, their AI model accurately predicted alliance quality as rated by both clients and therapists, demonstrating that computational methods can capture complex relational constructs that are central to effective treatment (Maqbool et al.).

This work represents a significant advancement beyond earlier efforts to evaluate therapeutic techniques. Atkins et al. (2014) pioneered the use of NLP to assess motivational interviewing fidelity, while Xiao et al. (2015) demonstrated how speech and language processing could automatically assess therapist empathy. These applications offer the potential for real-time feedback systems that could help therapists refine their skills and maintain high standards of care (Sarwar et al., 2021).

The development of AI tools for measuring therapeutic alliance and empathy addresses long-standing challenges in psychotherapy research and practice. Traditional methods for assessing these constructs rely on subjective ratings that are time-intensive and potentially biased. AI-based measures could provide objective, scalable alternatives that support both research efforts and clinical supervision (Samra Maqbool et al., 2014).

REAL-WORLD CASE EXAMPLES

Some of real-world case examples and vignettes illustrating the implementation of AI tools in mental health practice:

Cogito: This platform uses real-time AI coaching to analyze voice signals during patient interactions, providing live guidance to care managers. It helps therapists display empathy, build trust, and improve patient engagement, which is critical for successful mental health care. Cogito also monitors behavioral health passively via mobile applications, aiding early detection and intervention of behavioral issues.

Headspace: Utilizing predictive analytics, Headspace identifies individuals at risk of mental health conditions by monitoring behaviors such as increased stress, sleep disturbances, and social withdrawal. When risk patterns are detected, the platform proactively offers support, including connections to mental health coaches.

Through Line: A digital infrastructure platform that connects users with trusted, human-staffed crisis and mental health support services worldwide. Through Line integrates AI principles to match users to the most relevant helplines in a network covering areas such as suicide prevention, abuse, self-harm, and LGBTQ+ support.

Wysa: An AI-driven chatbot providing therapist-assisted cognitive behavioral therapy (CBT) programs for anxiety and other mental health concerns. It features structured modules, psycho-educational videos, and interactive techniques, tracking clinical recovery and integrating with electronic patient records to reduce clinician workload.

Talk space: A mental health platform that employs AI to match users with licensed therapists based on individual needs and preferences. It supports text, audio, and video therapy sessions and allows asynchronous communication for continuous support, improving accessibility and personalization.

Anthropic's Claude AI: Though not a designed therapeutic tool, it provides affective conversations to users seeking emotional support on topics like loneliness, career challenges, and mental health, showing improved user sentiment in many interactions. These examples reflect both the successes in improving accessibility, personalization, and engagement in mental health care and the challenges of maintaining human connection, privacy, and ethical standards in AI deployment.

THE COST-BENEFIT ANALYSIS AND ECONOMIC CONSIDERATIONS OF IMPLEMENTING AI

A synthesis of the cost-benefit analysis and economic considerations of implementing AI in therapy settings:

1. **Cost Savings:** AI-powered mental health tools significantly reduce the cost of therapy. Traditional in-person therapy sessions typically range from $100 to $200 per session, whereas AI-driven platforms and chatbots can provide support for as low as $10 to $20 per session. This reduction in costs arises from eliminating expenses related to human therapists' time, office visits, and geographical barriers.
2. **Accessibility and Scalability:** The affordability and 24/7 availability of AI therapy platforms make mental health care more accessible to populations underserved by traditional services, such as those in rural areas or with limited mental health professional availability. This scalability addresses unmet needs more efficiently.
3. **Insurance and Health Systems Impact:** Insurers are increasingly covering AI-driven therapy services due to their cost-effectiveness. By integrating AI,

health systems can alleviate network adequacy issues, save costs, and provide timely mental health support to more patients.

4. **Economic Burden Reduction:** Considering that the U.S. spends an estimated $225 billion annually on mental health care, wider adoption of cost-effective AI therapy solutions has the potential to substantially reduce this financial burden by enhancing treatment reach and efficiency.
5. **Future Outlook:** While AI therapy bots offer promising economic benefits, ongoing innovations and integration with human therapists are expected to optimize cost-effectiveness without compromising quality of care.

These points reflect the strong financial rationale for adopting AI-assisted psychotherapy, especially to complement existing traditional services and extend the reach of mental health care.

AI therapy costs are generally much lower than traditional psychotherapy expenses. Traditional in-person therapy sessions typically cost depending on the therapist's qualifications and location. In contrast, AI-driven therapy platforms and chatbots can offer services at a fraction of that price, or via subscription models that reduce per-session cost further.

Key factors contributing to the lower cost of AI therapy include the elimination of therapist hourly fees, reduced overhead costs such as office space, and the ability to deliver scalable services to many users simultaneously without increasing costs proportionally. AI therapy also provides 24/7 availability, which is rarely feasible with human therapists.

While AI therapy may not fully replace traditional therapy, especially for complex cases requiring human empathy and judgment, it offers a cost-effective alternative or supplement, improving accessibility and affordability of mental health care.

SUMMARY TABLE COMPARING KEY AI APPLICATIONS IN MENTAL HEALTH

To compare key AI applications in mental health, including their evidence base, benefits, and limitations, relevant sources suggest common categories like AI chatbots, symptom monitoring, predictive analytics, and therapist assistance tools, a summary table.1 can be suitable.

Table 1.

AI Application	Evidence Base	Benefits	Limitations
AI Chatbots (Wysa)	Moderate; clinical trials support CBT efficacy	24/7 availability, scalable, cost-effective, increases engagement	Limited empathy, less effective for complex issues, privacy concerns
Symptom Monitoring Tools (Cogito)	Emerging; user studies ongoing	Real-time behavioral tracking, early detection, aids therapist decisions	Privacy issues, false positives, requires consent
Predictive Analytics (Headspace)	Growing evidence in longitudinal studies	Identifies at-risk users, proactive intervention, personalized support	Data bias, relies on quality of input data
Therapist Assistance AI	Early evidence from pilots	Enhances therapist efficiency, clinical decision support	Integration challenges, risk of overreliance
Crisis Support AI (Through Line)	Operational globally with network data	Rapid connection to human crisis services, improved outcomes	Scope limits without human in loop, cultural adaptation needed

This table helps to understand the applications, evidence, advantages, and challenges associated with AI in psychotherapy, making the review more accessible and engaging.

HUMAN-CENTERED PERSPECTIVES: ENGAGEMENT, TRUST, AND CULTURAL SENSITIVITY

Effective implementation of AI in psychotherapeutic practice hinges on fostering strong patient engagement and trust. AI tools must be transparent about their roles and limitations to build confidence among users, particularly when handling sensitive mental health data. Hybrid models that combine human clinicians with AI support tend to enhance patient trust by preserving human empathy while benefiting from technology's scalability and consistency.

Cultural sensitivity is equally crucial, as AI systems often encounter challenges adapting to diverse populations. Without careful design, AI algorithms risk perpetuating biases, leading to less accurate or irrelevant recommendations for marginalized groups. Addressing these disparities requires inclusive data sets, continuous model refinement, and respect for cultural nuances to ensure equitable mental health care access.

Ultimately, placing the human experience at the center of AI-driven mental health technologies not only improves patient satisfaction and therapeutic outcomes but also supports ethical use and broader acceptance of these innovations in varied cultural contexts.

ETHICAL IMPERATIVES AND REGULATORY FRAMEWORKS

The integration of AI into mental health care raises profound ethical questions that must be addressed to ensure responsible development and deployment. Fiske et al. (2019) identify three core challenges in AI therapy applications: threats to patient autonomy through persuasive design and data-driven nudges, risks of algorithmic bias exacerbating health disparities, and the fundamental empathy gap between human and artificial caregivers.

The autonomy concern is particularly relevant given the vulnerability of individuals seeking mental health support. AI systems designed to be persuasive may inadvertently manipulate users in ways that compromise their ability to make autonomous decisions about their care. This risk is compounded by the potential for AI systems to use personal data to influence behavior in subtle but powerful ways.

Algorithmic bias represents another critical challenge, as highlighted by Lum and Isaac (2016) in their foundational critique of predictive algorithms. The authors demonstrate how historical inequities become encoded in training data, leading to discriminatory outputs that may over-pathologize marginalized groups or misinterpret cultural expressions of distress as pathological symptoms.

Feingold (2020) provides a framework for addressing these ethical challenges, advocating for a collaborative human-AI care model guided by professional standards. This approach emphasizes transparency, accountability, and human oversight while recognizing AI's potential to enhance rather than replace human judgment in therapeutic contexts.

The regulatory landscape is evolving to address these concerns. The FDA's 2023 AI/ML Software as a Medical Device Action Plan outlines critical requirements for adaptive AI systems, bias mitigation, and real-world performance monitoring. These regulatory developments establish validation standards for clinical evidence, ethical guardrails for unique mental health risks, and frameworks that are influencing international policy development.

THE ARTIFICIAL WISDOM PARADIGM

Lee et al. (2021) introduce the concept of "Artificial Wisdom" (AW) as a framework for developing more clinically meaningful and ethically grounded AI tools. This paradigm goes beyond narrow AI applications to emphasize judgment, compassion, and adaptability in therapeutic contexts. Artificial Wisdom systems would integrate emotional regulation, ethical reasoning, and contextual awareness qualities that are essential for effective therapeutic intervention.

This framework addresses a fundamental limitation in current AI applications: the tendency to focus on technical capabilities rather than therapeutic wisdom. While AI systems may excel at pattern recognition or information processing, therapeutic practice requires nuanced understanding of human experience, cultural context, and ethical considerations that current AI systems struggle to navigate.

The Artificial Wisdom paradigm suggests that future AI development should prioritize these higher-order capabilities, creating systems that not only process information effectively but also demonstrate the judgment and sensitivity required for therapeutic work. This approach would require interdisciplinary collaboration involving clinicians, patients, ethicists, and technologists to ensure that AI tools align with therapeutic values and professional standards.

IMPLEMENTATION CHALLENGES AND FUTURE DIRECTIONS

Despite the promising developments in AI applications for mental health, significant challenges remain in translating research findings into clinical practice. Zafeer et al. (2025b) identify key implementation barriers including clinician skepticism, data privacy concerns, workflow integration challenges, and liability issues that are often overlooked in efficacy studies.

Clinician acceptance represents a particularly important factor in successful AI implementation. Mental health professionals may be hesitant to adopt AI tools due to concerns about job displacement, loss of clinical autonomy, or questions about the validity of AI-generated insights. Successful implementation requires addressing these concerns through transparent communication about AI capabilities and limitations, as well as clear frameworks for human-AI collaboration (Zafeer & Yanping, 2022).

Data privacy concerns are especially acute in mental health contexts, where sensitive personal information requires the highest levels of protection. AI systems that collect and analyze behavioral data, speech patterns, or therapeutic communications must implement robust security measures while maintaining transparency about data use and storage practices.

Workflow integration presents practical challenges that must be addressed for successful adoption. AI tools must fit seamlessly into existing clinical practices without creating additional burden for therapists or disrupting established therapeutic relationships. This requires careful attention to user interface design, system interoperability, and integration with electronic health records.

CONCLUSION: TOWARD A COLLABORATIVE FUTURE

The emerging role of AI in psychotherapeutic practice represents both tremendous opportunity and significant responsibility. The research reviewed in this chapter demonstrates that AI technologies can enhance accessibility, provide objective measures of therapeutic processes, enable early intervention, and support clinician decision-making in ways that could fundamentally improve mental health care delivery.

However, realizing this potential requires careful attention to ethical considerations, regulatory requirements, and implementation challenges. The most promising path forward involves collaborative models that leverage AI's strengths while preserving the human elements that are central to effective therapy. This approach recognizes that therapeutic relationships involve complex emotional, cultural, and ethical dimensions that current AI systems cannot fully replicate.

The concept of Artificial Wisdom provides a valuable framework for future development, emphasizing the need for AI systems that integrate technical capabilities with therapeutic wisdom, Transparent AI architectures that clinicians and patients can interrogate and understand, Seamless workflows that combine AI tools with clinician-led therapy, ethical reasoning, and cultural sensitivity. Achieving this vision will require continued interdisciplinary collaboration, rigorous research, and thoughtful consideration of the values and principles that should guide AI development in mental health.

As the field continues to evolve, the ultimate goal should not be the replacement of human therapists with artificial agents, but the creation of hybrid models that combine the accessibility and consistency of AI with the empathy, wisdom, and relational skills of human clinicians. This collaborative approach offers the best hope for addressing the growing mental health crisis while maintaining the therapeutic relationships that are fundamental to healing and recovery.

The journey toward effective AI integration in psychotherapy is still in its early stages, but the foundation established by the research reviewed in this chapter provides a solid base for future development. By maintaining focus on ethical principles, clinical effectiveness, and human values, the field can harness AI's transformative potential while preserving the essential human elements that make therapy a powerful force for healing and growth.

REFERENCES

Atkins, D. C., Steyvers, M., Imel, Z. E., & Smyth, P. (2014). Scaling up the evaluation of psychotherapy: Evaluating motivational interviewing fidelity via statistical text classification. *Implementation Science : IS*, *9*(1), 49. DOI: 10.1186/1748-5908-9-49 PMID: 24758152

D'alfonso, S., Santesteban-Echarri, O., Rice, S., Wadley, G., Lederman, R., Miles, C., Gleeson, J., & Alvarez-Jimenez, M. (2017). Artificial intelligence-assisted online social therapy for youth mental health. *Frontiers in Psychology*, *8*, 796. DOI: 10.3389/fpsyg.2017.00796 PMID: 28626431

Draissi, Z., Rong, Y., Zafeer, H. M. I., Maqbool, S., Malik, S. J., Maqbool, S., & Alemi, S. H. A. (2025). Academic diplomacy and policy borrowing: Media content analysis of Chinese soft power in Morocco. *Humanities & Social Sciences Communications*, *12*(1), 1–11. DOI: 10.1057/s41599-025-04544-1

Feingold, D. (2020). Working with clients who self-medicate using cannabis: Mind the gap in knowledge.

Fiske, A., Henningsen, P., & Buyx, A. (2019). Your robot therapist will see you now: Ethical implications of embodied artificial intelligence in psychiatry, psychology, and psychotherapy. *Journal of Medical Internet Research*, *21*(5), e13216. DOI: 10.2196/13216 PMID: 31094356

Goldberg, S. B., Flemotomos, N., Martinez, V. R., Tanana, M. J., Kuo, P. B., Pace, B. T., Villatte, J. L., Georgiou, P. G., Van Epps, J., Imel, Z. E., Narayanan, S. S., & Atkins, D. C. (2020). Machine learning and natural language processing in psychotherapy research: Alliance as example use case. *Journal of Counseling Psychology*, *67*(4), 438–448. DOI: 10.1037/cou0000382 PMID: 32614225

Graham, S., Depp, C., Lee, E. E., Nebeker, C., Tu, X., Kim, H.-C., & Jeste, D. V. (2019). Artificial intelligence for mental health and mental illnesses: An overview. *Current Psychiatry Reports*, *21*(11), 116. DOI: 10.1007/s11920-019-1094-0 PMID: 31701320

Javed, S., Rong, Y., Zafeer, H. M. I., Maqbool, S., & Abbasi, B. N. (2024). Unleashing the potential: A quest to understand and examine the factors enriching research and innovation productivities of South Asian universities. *Humanities & Social Sciences Communications*, *11*(1), 1–15. DOI: 10.1057/s41599-024-03674-2

Kalim, U., Irfan, S., Maqbool, S., & Zafeer, H. M. I. (2025). How AI Can Be Successfully Implemented in the Classroom Settings: Challenges and Pathways to Overcome. In *Navigating Barriers to AI Implementation in the Classroom* (pp. 235-266). IGI Global Scientific Publishing.

Lee, E. E., Torous, J., De Choudhury, M., Depp, C. A., Graham, S. A., Kim, H.-C., Paulus, M. P., Krystal, J. H., & Jeste, D. V. (2021). Artificial intelligence for mental health care: Clinical applications, barriers, facilitators, and artificial wisdom. *Biological Psychiatry: Cognitive Neuroscience and Neuroimaging*, *6*(9), 856–864. DOI: 10.1016/j.bpsc.2021.02.001 PMID: 33571718

Lindner, P., Miloff, A., Hamilton, W., Reuterskiöld, L., Andersson, G., Powers, M. B., & Carlbring, P. (2017). Creating state of the art, next-generation Virtual Reality exposure therapies for anxiety disorders using consumer hardware platforms: Design considerations and future directions. *Cognitive Behaviour Therapy*, *46*(5), 404–420. DOI: 10.1080/16506073.2017.1280843 PMID: 28270059

Lum, K., & Isaac, W. (2016). To predict and serve? *Significance*, *13*(5), 14–19. DOI: 10.1111/j.1740-9713.2016.00960.x

Malik, S., Rong, Y., Zafeer, H. M. I., Maqbool, S., Draissi, Z., Rehman, N., & Maqbool, S. (2025). Analysis of Key Factors Influencing Academic Productivity: Insights From LASSO Regression and AI-Driven Techniques. In *Navigating Barriers to AI Implementation in the Classroom* (pp. 189–234). IGI Global Scientific Publishing. DOI: 10.4018/979-8-3373-1827-1.ch009

Maples-Keller, J. L., Bunnell, B. E., Kim, S.-J., & Rothbaum, B. O. (2017). The use of virtual reality technology in the treatment of anxiety and other psychiatric disorders. *Harvard Review of Psychiatry*, *25*(3), 103–113. DOI: 10.1097/HRP.0000000000000138 PMID: 28475502

Maqbool, S. (2025). Implemented in the Classroom Settings: Challenges and Pathways. *Navigating Barriers to AI Implementation in the Classroom*, 235.

Maqbool, S., Maqbool, S., Zafeer, H. M. I., & Qihui, H. (2024). Exploring the Reflection of Teachers to Encourage the Gender Equality for Girls in Punjab Schools: In the Light of Universal Right to an Education. *Asian Women*, *40*(3), 113–138. DOI: 10.14431/aw.2024.9.40.3.113

Maqbool, S., Sarwar, U., Zamir, S., Zafeer, H. M. I., & Wei, Z. (2020). Teaching of Phonics and fluency in improving reading abilities at primary level: Multan Pakistan. *European Online Journal of Natural and Social Sciences*, *9*(4), 808–819.

Maqbool, S., Wei, Z., Sarwar, U., Zamir, S., & Zafeer, H. M. I. (2020). An analysis of self-concept between homeless and common women in Pakistan. *International Transaction Journal of Engineering, Management, &. Applied Sciences & Technologies*, *11*(15), 11–19.

Maqbool, S., Zafeer, H. M. I., & Maqbool, S. (2025). Psychological Impact of Raising a Child With Autism: A Real Life Case Study of Expatriate Family. *Child & Family Social Work*, cfs.70011. DOI: 10.1111/cfs.70011

Maqbool, S., Zafeer, H. M. I., Maqbool, S., Zeng, P., Draissi, Z., & Javed, S. (2024). Stance of numerous leadership styles and their effect on teaching to sustain academic performance at the high school level. *Heliyon*, *10*(16), e36438. DOI: 10.1016/j.heliyon.2024.e36438 PMID: 39253217

Maqbool, S., Zafeer, H. M. I., Yanping, L., & Zhao, W. (2022). Covid-19 and global education: Experiences of Pakistani international students. *International Transaction Journal of Engineering Management and Applied Sciences and Technologies*, *13*(3), 1–11.

Maqbool, S., Zafeer, H. M. I., Zeng, P., Maqbool, S., Draissi, Z., & Javed, S. (2024). Inventive leadership styles and their impact for achieving sustainable development goals in education at secondary schools: A case study from Multan, Pakistan. *Humanities & Social Sciences Communications*, *11*(1), 1–11. DOI: 10.1057/s41599-024-03086-2

Maqbool, S., Zafeer, H. M. I., Zeng, P., Mohammad, T., Khassawneh, O., & Wu, L. (2023). The role of diverse leadership styles in teaching to sustain academic excellence at secondary level. [Maqbool, S., Zhao, W., Rehman, S., Zafeer, H. M. I., & Maqbool, S. North American Academic Research.]. *Frontiers in Psychology*, *13*, 1096151. DOI: 10.3389/fpsyg.2022.1096151 PMID: 36698584

Rehman, N., Huang, X., Mahmood, A., Maqbool, S., & Javed, S. (2024a). Enhancing the quality of research synopsis of international students through peer feedback: A case study. *New Directions for Child and Adolescent Development*, *2024*(1), 1271802. DOI: 10.1155/2024/1271802

Rehman, N., Huang, X., Mahmood, A., Maqbool, S., & Javed, S. (2024b). Research Article Enhancing the Quality of Research Synopsis of International Students Through Peer Feedback: A Case Study.

Rehman, N., Huang, X., Sarwar, U., Fatima, H., & Maqbool, S. (2025). Exploring the impact of family, school and society on the perception and reputation of vocational training in Pakistan: A statistical analysis. *Education + Training*, *67*(3), 389–418. DOI: 10.1108/ET-09-2023-0375

Samra Maqbool, M. A., Ijaz, S., Asif, M., & Jahanzeb, M. (2014). An Analysis of Self-esteem between Destitute and Non-destitute women.

Sarwar, U., Fazal, K., Zamir, S., Maqbool, S., Hussain, Z., & Qi, Z. Y. (2021). Assessment on Proficiency of Using Information and Communication Technology among Students of University of Lahore (Sargodha Campus), Pakistan. *European Online Journal of Natural and Social Sciences*, *10*(1), 102–115.

Torous, J., Larsen, M. E., Depp, C., Cosco, T. D., Barnett, I., Nock, M. K., & Firth, J. (2018). Smartphones, sensors, and machine learning to advance real-time prediction and interventions for suicide prevention: A review of current progress and next steps. *Current Psychiatry Reports*, *20*(7), 51. DOI: 10.1007/s11920-018-0914-y PMID: 29956120

Vaidyam, A. N., Wisniewski, H., Halamka, J. D., Kashavan, M. S., & Torous, J. B. (2019). Chatbots and conversational agents in mental health: A review of the psychiatric landscape. *Canadian Journal of Psychiatry*, *64*(7), 456–464. DOI: 10.1177/0706743719828977 PMID: 30897957

Xiao, B., Imel, Z. E., Georgiou, P. G., Atkins, D. C., & Narayanan, S. S. (2015). Rate my therapist": Automated detection of empathy in drug and alcohol counseling via speech and language processing. *PLoS One*, *10*(12), e0143055. DOI: 10.1371/journal.pone.0143055 PMID: 26630392

Zafeer, H. M. I., Li, Y., & Maqbool, S. (2023). An approach to progress learning outcomes: International graduate students' engagement in reflective practice and reflective journal writing during pandemic. *Sustainability (Basel)*, *15*(3), 1898. DOI: 10.3390/su15031898

Zafeer, H. M. I., Maqbool, S., Rong, Y., & Maqbool, S. (2024). Mapping the relationship and influence of school internal factors with an eye towards students' science academic outcomes. *Heliyon*, *10*(19), e38696. DOI: 10.1016/j.heliyon.2024.e38696 PMID: 39397972

Zafeer, H. M. I., Maqbool, S., Rong, Y., & Maqbool, S. (2025a). Beyond the Classroom: How Socioeconomic Status, Parental Involvement and Home Environment Impact on Students' Science Academic Performance at Secondary Schools. *European Journal of Education*, *60*(1), e70023. DOI: 10.1111/ejed.70023

Zafeer, H. M. I., Maqbool, S., Rong, Y., & Maqbool, S. (2025b). Culturally Sustaining Cognitive and Behavioral Interventions for Reducing Anxiety in Autistic School-Aged Students: A Systematic Review. *Psychology in the Schools*, pits.70077. DOI: 10.1002/pits.70077

Zafeer, H. M. I., Maqbool, S., Rong, Y., & Maqbool, S. (2025c). Impact of digital learning tools on student's engagement and achievement in middle school science classes. *International Journal of Technology in Education and Science*, *9*(2), 177–196. DOI: 10.46328/ijtes.622

Zafeer, H. M. I., Maqbool, S., & Yanping, L. (2022). Psychological and social factors and their impact on divorced and married women: A case study from Punjab Pakistan. *Journal of Divorce & Remarriage*, *63*(5), 352–373. DOI: 10.1080/10502556.2022.2048345

Zafeer, H. M. I., Peng, C., Rehman, S., Wei, Z., & Maqbool, S. (2021). A Study to Investigate the Obstacles of Educational Technology in Curriculum; University Students' Perception. *European Online Journal of Natural and Social Sciences*, *10*(1), 1–8.

Zafeer, H. M. I., Xue, H., & Maqbool, S. (2020). Delaying Factors Regarding Civil Justice in Pakistan (Lower Courts). *Journal of Humanities and Social Sciences Studies*, *2*(6), 15–22. DOI: 10.32996/jhsss.2020.2.6.2

Zafeer, H. M. I., & Yanping, L. (2022). The role of gender, socioeconomic factors, and its impact on students' English as a second language (ESL) performance.

Zafeer, H. M. I., Yanping, L., & Maqbool, S. COVID-19 and the Future of Online Learning; Perspective of Pakistani Students from Higher Education Institutions (HEIs).

Zamir, S., Yang, Z., Sarwar, U., Maqbool, S., Fazal, K., Ihsan, H., & Arif, A. (2021). Teaching methodologies used for learning critical thinking in higher education: Pakistani teachers' perceptions. *Int. Trans. J. Eng. Manag. Appl. Sci. Technol*, *12*, 1–10.

Zmir, S., Sarwar, U., Maqbool, S., Javed, S., Ishtiaq, M., & Zhang, Y. (2021). Plagiarism practice: Its awareness & dealing and consequences among university students in Punjab province of Pakistan. *International Transaction Journal of Engineering, Management, &. Applied Sciences & Technologies*, *12*(11), 1–11.

Chapter 10
Decolonizing Minds With Machines:
AI as a Partner in Reimagining Critical Thinking Pedagogy for East Africa's Academic Renaissance

Kidega Charles
https://orcid.org/0009-0004-2646-2219
Zhejiang Normal University, China

Wang Zhanjun
Zhejiang Normal University, China

Ibrahim Mariam Rajabu
Zhejiang Normal University, China

Egbosimba Chinazom Irene
Zhejiang Normal University, China

Amir Mahmood
https://orcid.org/0000-0002-0215-0278
Zhejiang Normal University, China

ABSTRACT

Decolonial theory offers a framework for comprehending and contesting the impacts of colonialism on the creation and distribution of knowledge. The review focused on the critical thinking and AI integration in higher education, the study employed

DOI: 10.4018/979-8-3373-4217-7.ch010

a quick systematic review of the previous publications, especially those that were published and accessible on google scholars and Scopus from 2019-2025. The reviews focus on decolonising scholarly writings, how ai can promote critical thinking, ai ethical usage in Higher education and action to be taken. After the searches on google scholar and Scopus and screening all the documents, 35 publications were finally used in the systematic review in line with the research questions. AI presents a unique and timely opportunity to decolonise scholarly writing and knowledge production by disrupting entrenched hierarchies, enhancing access to marginalised knowledge, and empowering scholars to write from culturally grounded positions. There are a lot of moral and practical problems with using AI in decolonial academics. Natural language processing (NLP) models tailored to local languages such as Swahili, Luo, Gikuyu, and Luganda can make content more accessible and Inclusive. Ai tools could be developed to assist in translating critical texts into indigenous languages or analysing works.

INTRODUCTION

In this chapter, we discuss ways AI can assist in reimagining critical thinking education for intellectual renewal in East Africa. AI can decolonise learning by providing platforms and tools for co-creating knowledge, essential competencies of thinking, and culture-centered learning and pedagogy. With AI in education, we can create learning environments where students can interrogate master narratives, engage with counter narratives, and develop the competencies necessary to succeed in a transforming world (Freire, 1970; Setegn, G. M., & Dejene, 2025; Tuhiwai Smith, 2012). Critical thinking is one of the foundational pillars of decolonial education since it allows students to question and deconstruct the master narrative. For instance, AI-backed simulations enable students to tackle complex environmental and social problems from multiple perspectives and develop a more compassionate understanding of global challenges as interconnected problems (Luckin, 2018; Mignolo, 2011) .

Education systems and every aspect of social life are undergoing drastic changes as a result of the quick development and spread of artificial intelligence (AI) technologies. Recent advancements in educational technologies have transformed artificial intelligence from a mere research subject into an integral element of educational training processes (Wayne et al., 2023);Holmes et al., 2023; Glais, 2023). This transition requires a re-evaluation of curricula, a basic component of education, from an artificial intelligence standpoint . This technological revolution, which influences the future of educational systems, introduces new dimensions to teaching and learning processes and initiates paradigm shifts in curriculum design and implementation, as articulated in the UNESCO (2019) report "Artificial Intelligence in Education.

The greatest challenge remains the massification of higher education, which has overcrowded classes all over the continent (Giacomazzi, M., Fontana, M., & Trujillo, 2022). East African universities are behind the times, discouraging their students' growth of vital competencies, such as critical thinking, creativity, and problem-solving (Mbunge, E., & Batani, 2023). Although it has made education accessible to more individuals, such a high growth rate has placed demands on institutional resources and the provision of individualised learning opportunities required to cultivate critical thinking, making it more challenging (Buckland & Purcell, 2025; Charles et al., 2023). Therefore, students in such an environment do not receive individualised guidance and advice that would enable them to study subject matters more deeply and develop rudimentary analytical skills (D'Agostino, 2023; Xu, 2024). Cites that most university courses prioritize lectures and exams for communicating comprehension above encouraging analytical thought, and alternatively, fostering critical students who question assumptions and develop autonomous thought (Guàrdia, L., Mancini, F., Jacobetty, P., & Maina, 2021). Lacking such abilities, students will be unable to serve the needs of modern-day businesses, in which critical thinking, creativity, and problem-solving skills are given more importance than acquiring knowledge (Vakili, R., Vakili, S., Ajilian Abbasi, M., & Masoudi, 2024). Besides these pedagogical concerns, the digital divide is a strong challenge to fair access to learning materials. Inadequate professional development for educators and restricted student access to artificial intelligence literacy education ensure that there is an argument that the true potential of artificial intelligence remains untapped (Guàrdia, L., Mancini, F., Jacobetty, P., & Maina, 2021). While shifting from conventional teaching modes to artificial intelligence incorporation in learning and teaching is significant, increasing access to technology is needed. Instead of replacing in-depth interaction, universities must add artificial intelligence as an auxiliary (Lee et al., 2025; Rana et al., 2025). Artificial intelligence can bridge the gap between congested classrooms and conventional teaching (Sadman et al., 2021a, 2021b) with the right mindset, encouraging students to interact more meaningfully with course content.

Objectives of the Chapter

The primary objectives of this chapter are to:

1. Discuss how AI can decolonise scholarly writing and knowledge creation.
2. Explain AI as a critical thinking tool.
3. Discuss Ethical issues
4. Suggest implementable actions to be pursued.

Theoretical Review: Decolonial Theory

A combination of decolonial theory and AI ethics, derived from the works of eminent academics in these domains, forms the theoretical basis for incorporating decolonization and AI in scholarly discourse. Decolonial theory offers a framework for comprehending and contesting the impacts of colonialism on the creation and distribution of knowledge, as explained.(Birhane, 2020; Mignolo, 2011). It highlights how crucial it is to acknowledge and value many cultural viewpoints and epistemologies, especially those of historically marginalized groups (McArthur, 2022; Wakunuma et al., 2025). Simultaneously, ethical considerations that tackle bias, justice, and inclusivity as promoted by Safiya Noble and Jackson Longworth guide the incorporation of AI in this setting. These factors emphasize the necessity of designing and implementing AI systems in a way that promotes equity in academia rather than maintaining current disparities (Noble, 2018). The nexus of these two domains provides a distinctive viewpoint on how artificial intelligence (AI) might promote technical innovation and cultivate a more diverse and decolonized academic setting. This theoretical framework lays the groundwork for investigating how AI may support academic writing by non-native English speakers, potentially changing the academic environment to become a more inclusive forum for a range of global viewpoints. The study is further influenced by important ideas like "algorithmic fairness" and "epistemic justice," which build upon the fundamental notions of decoloniality and AI ethics. Barocas, Hardt, and Narayanan (2020) examined the idea of algorithmic fairness, which tackles the difficulties of reducing biases in AI algorithms. This idea is essential to preventing preconceived notions about non-native English speakers from being unintentionally reinforced by AI tools used in academic writing. Furthermore, the concepts of "epistemic justice" as proposed by Fricker (2007) and Omodan (2023) offer a framework for comprehending the significance of granting diverse perspectives in academic debate equal credence. This idea emphasizes how critical it is to identify and address the undervaluation or exclusion of information from marginalized groups. Collectively, these frameworks advance equality and inclusion in the sharing of information by providing a thorough grasp of how AI can be successfully and morally incorporated into academic writing. Together, the theoretical pillars of decoloniality, algorithmic fairness, AI ethics, and epistemic justice pave the way for non-native English speakers to be empowered in academic writing (Veselova, 2021). For non-native English speakers who frequently navigate academic environments dominated by Western paradigms, the decolonial perspective, promoted by (Gautam, 2024; Mignolo, 2011) emphasizes the significance of respecting diverse epistemologies and decentring dominant knowledge systems. In addition, Barocas, Hardt, and Narayanan (2020) advocate algorithmic fairness rules, which guarantee that AI tools used in academic writing are free from biases that could harm non-native speakers.

MATERIALS AND METHODS

The study adopted a systematic literature review on the use of AI to enhance critical thinking and decolonise the minds with machines within the context of East African Higher education not compromising the global demand for decolonisation of knowledge. The systematic review also focused on the potential risk of AI and how it can be solved with support from international bodies.

Identifying Relevant Studies

We searched for relevant studies through Scopus, and Google Scholar, and the study used keywords which were used to search the relevant studies transferred to Excel for analysis and others were analysed from Scopus directly. Both Scopus and Google scholar data were analysed for a systematic review. All the data presented in graphs, charts, and tables were generated from Excel and Scopus. NVivo software version 23 was used to analyse the data, and generated the codes and themes

The search key terms include:

```
Title-abs key (ai and critical and thinking and pedagogy)
and pubyear > 2015 and pubyear < 2025 and (limit-to (language,
"english")) and (limit-to (exactkeyword, "critical thinking")
or limit-to (exact keyword, "artificial intelligence") or
limit-to (exactkeyword, "students") or limit-to (exactkeyword,
"teaching") or limit-to (exactkeyword, "pedagogy")) and (limit-
to (doctype, "ar") or limit-to (doctype, "cp") or limit-to
(doctype, "ch") or limit-to (doctype, "re"))
```

Inclusion Criteria

We developed four inclusion criteria to determine the relevant studies four preliminary search: Studies that focus on AI and Critical thinking, AI integration, Pedagogy and how AI can help to decolonise knowledge and critical thinking among the students and the entire Higher education. Studies published in English and related to the keywords and topic, studies published within the year 2019/2025. It's an holistic review on how AI can revolutionise knowledge and critical thinking in Higher Education around the world but a case is taken into East African Higher

Education. The evaluation of the study involved two senior librarians who have experience in systematic review, one familiar with systematic reviews and the other with education, widely used electronic databases, including Scopus, Springer, and Education Source.

Studies Selecting

Three reviewers who are university professors here at our university completed the title, abstracts, methods, the language, the scope, and the full text reviews through WeChat platform, Google docs. If there was disagreement on the inclusion, exclusion, they discussed it thoroughly and stand point was achieved on the eligible studies. The authors finally completed the entire review of the full text studies for better understanding of the research problem and were able to get an holistic results.

Data Screening and Extraction

A summary of Figure 1, of 1061 abstracts from the publication sources in the database; 850 were removed as duplicates, 500 studies were excluded due to limited access to full texts (only abstracts); 101 were excluded for not being with the scope i.e. AI and critical thinking; 15 studies excluded because they were published in other languages apart from English; 45 were excluded from the study because they are not from education field ; most of the studies were from engineering and medicine and that disqualified them from the study; 15 were excluded for being out of the time scope as the study only focused on the studies conducted between 2019-2025. 37 full text studies met all the requirements and were cross-screened for the second time with direct reference to content and the research direction and recommendation. 2 full text were excluded for being secondary source studies on AI integration in Higher education with focus on critical thinking. Any mismatch between the three reviewers (first two authors) concerning the inclusion or exclusion of an article was then discussed and resolved. The process resulted in 35 publications for independent, detailed evaluation. Data from the included studies were then extracted onto a matrix (on Microsoft Excel), containing ten relevant categories drawn from the research questions, including country, study objectives, disciplines, publication types, the top 15 authors within the same field of AI. Integration, critical thinking area of the study, evaluation(yes/no), and how to evaluate, outcomes, strategies, and suggestions/implications. All data extraction was cross-checked by the second reviewer to enhance reliability

Study Relevance Assessment

35 studies met all the criteria and were used in the analysis

Figure 1. PRISMA Flow diagram

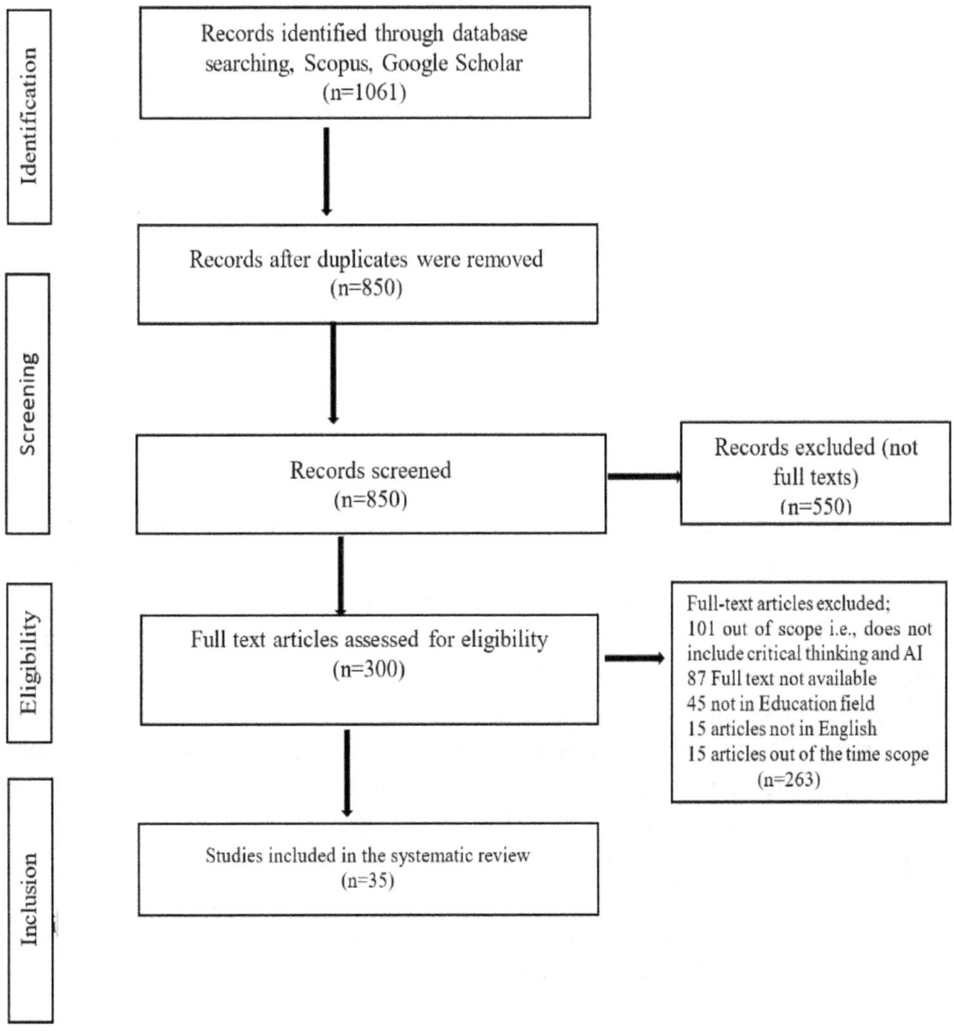

Figure 2. Distribution of documents according to territories

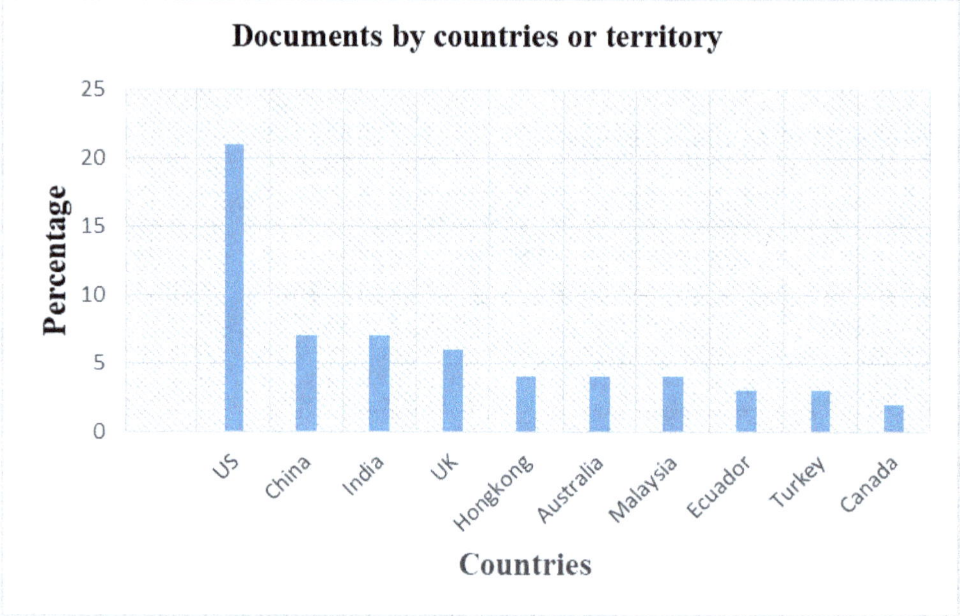

Figure 2 represents the distribution of the documents according to countries around the world. With the rapid technological advancement in the developed world, we have witnessed according to the distribution of publications in the map. The highest distribution of these documents are found in the United states with 21 points, followed by China with 7 points., United Kingdom, 6 points, Australia, 4 points, Turkey, 3 points, Canada, 2 points, and South Africa 1 points. This shows clearly that Africa has continued to face challenges as far as the technological advancement is concerned with more respect to AI integration in Higher Education. The language of instructions in East African Higher Education and the entire African continent is a big threat to the development in Africa more specifically in the education. Most of the schools, tertiary institutions, and universities uses foreign languages and it poses threat to both the teachers and students when it comes to scholarly work. As noted by Strauss (2019) "*This pressure is exacerbated by the tendency of non-native speakers to employ nonstandard forms of English, which may be subject to unfair scrutiny or negative perceptions by native English-speaking reviewers.*" Therefore, there is need to decolonise Education systems and any form of technology to suit our current needs otherwise Africa shall remain the same

Figure 3. Distribution of documents from 2015-2025

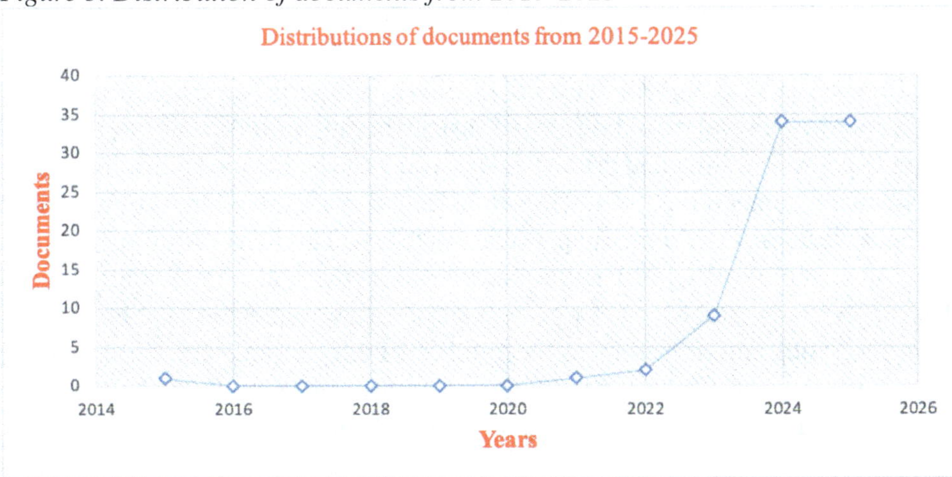

The above graph represents the distribution of documents on AI in regards to our keywords which we used in the data search and analysis according to years. There has been a great improvement in the AI integration in Higher Education since 2015, and with a rise in 2022 with 2 documents, 2023 with 9 documents and it continues to rise up to 34 documents in 2024. This clearly shows that the teachers, students, government agencies and researchers are embracing AI integration in higher education research and scholarly writing but should be decolonise to suits the needs of the local people (Asiedu et al., 2024).

Figure 4. Distribution of document types

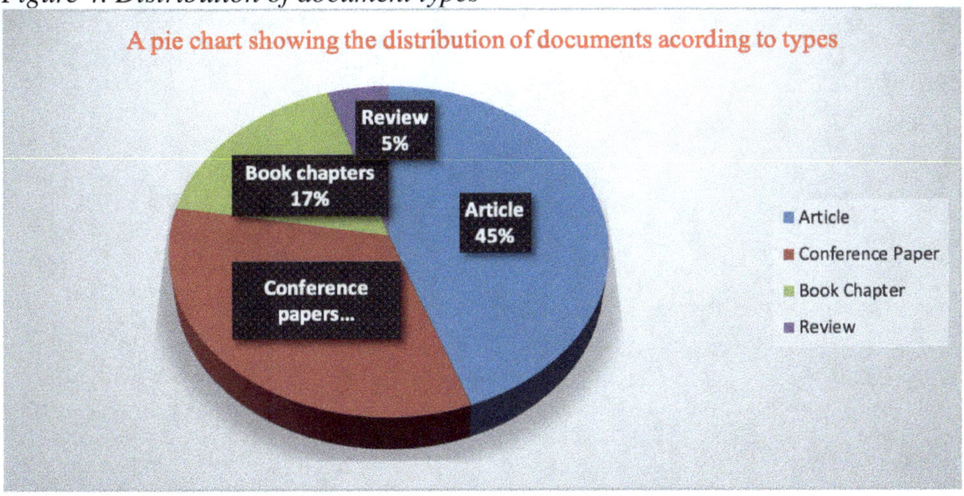

The distribution of academic documents across different publication types, the pie chart is dominated by 45% of articles, 33% of conferences papers, followed by book chapters of 17%, and lastly the review papers of 5%. As far as the integration of AI is concerned in higher education, the review suggests that more focus should be on the research and rapid knowledge sharing because articles has more emphasis on hypothesis testing and critical analysis and maybe the most prevalent which is essential for integrating AI in Higher education, with attention to East African Higher Education. Conference papers reflects the changes in nature of research that focus on technology where AI has become the most prevalent in the conferences and debate. The study established low percentage of reviews and it creates a huge gap in the synthesising and reflecting on the trend of AI integration and critical thinking in Higher education. This calls for more comprehensive analysis and key points to establish solid foundation for future research and AI integration in Higher Education.

Figure 5. A bar graph showing the funding sponsors by documents

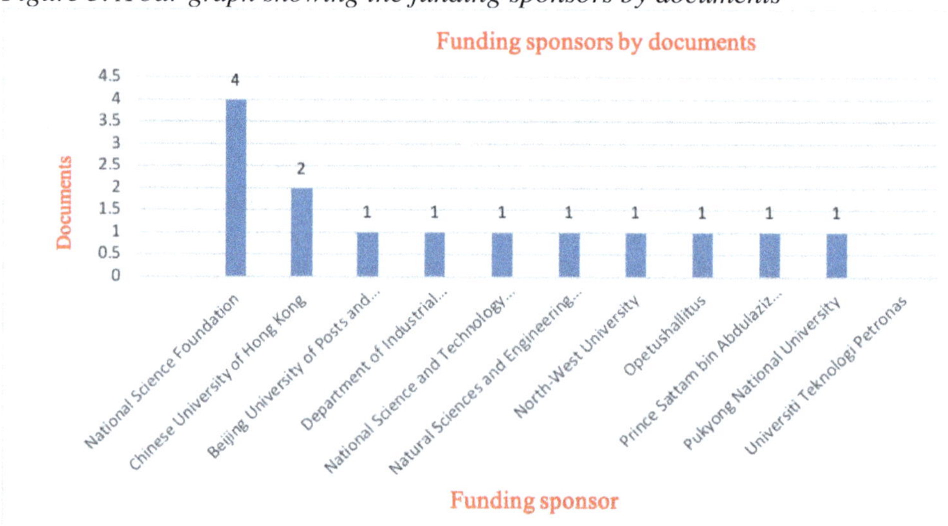

Figure 6. A graph showing the distribution of documents by affiliations

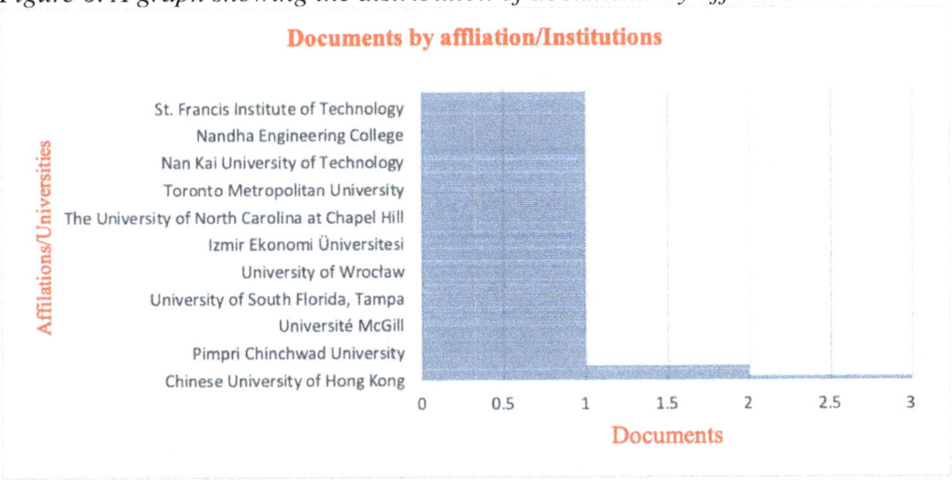

Figure 7. A pie chart showing the distribution of documents according to disciplines

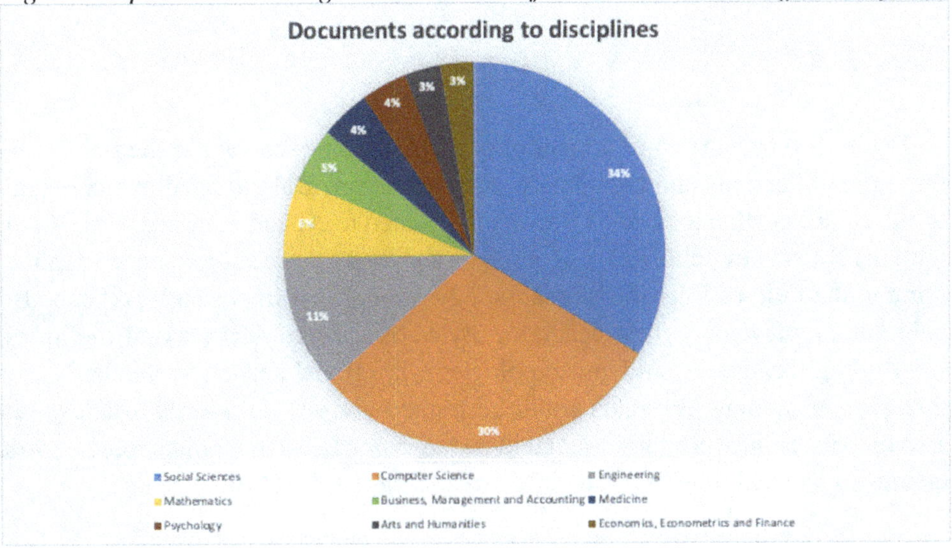

From the above Figure 6, you can understand that ai integration and critical thinking is dominant in social sciences with the greatest percent of 34%, computer science with 30% and other many more disciplines including Engineering, mathematics and Business administration among others. This explains that according to the keywords and the main focus of the study, the Therefore, AI has the potential to be a transformative agent that can help realize a more inclusive and diverse academic world that reflects a variety of perspectives and experiences, rather than only being an operational tool in the academic environment (Balta, 2023)

Figure 8. A bar graph showing the distribution of documents by authors

Figure 8 shows the commitment of academicians or scholars in the field of AI through publications and attending conferences Prof. Dai emerged as the overall of the authors with a total of 55 documents related to AI and keywords. Prof Chan with his colleagues published 7 documents and many more authors hence contributing to the field of Educational technology through AI. Importantly, AI can also help authors develop hybrid academic styles that merge African oral traditions, storytelling techniques, and epistemologies with global academic standards. For instance, AI writing assistants could be trained not just on journal articles,, but also on African proverbs, communal knowledge practices, and philosophical texts, creating a blended model of scholarly articulation(Bird, 2020).

DISCUSS HOW AI CAN DECOLONISE SCHOLARLY WRITING AND KNOWLEDGE CREATION

AI presents a unique and timely opportunity to decolonize scholarly writing and knowledge production by disrupting entrenched hierarchies, enhancing access to marginalized knowledge, and empowering scholars to write from culturally grounded positions (Bertino et al., 2021; Freire, 1970; Tuhiwai Smith, 2012). Recent years have seen a notable uptick in the decolonization movement in academic discourse, which directly challenges the Eurocentric viewpoints that have historically dominated the educational scene (Ndlovu-Gatsheni, 2015). This movement is motivated by the urgent need to acknowledge and take into account a diverse range of cultural viewpoints, with a focus on the experiences and voices of communities and areas that have traditionally been underrepresented in academic settings (Almeida & Kumalo, 2018).

In order to create a more inclusive and really representative global intellectual community, these newly formed spaces aim to elevate and magnify a variety of viewpoints, with an emphasis on those coming from post-colonial origins (Balwant et al., 2019).

More than just including a range of voices, this change aims to redefine knowledge and establish who has the power to define it, radically changing how academia views and interacts with many cultures and viewpoints. Additionally, the use of artificial intelligence (AI) in education is rapidly evolving in tandem with the academic community's decolonization efforts. AI's potential to transform many facets of education is becoming more widely recognized (Eguchi, 2021). AI democratizes scholarly discourse by creating opportunities for a more varied and rich exchange of ideas and guaranteeing that voices from all language origins are heard and comprehended in all of their complexity and depth. In order to level the playing field and enable academics and students from different linguistic backgrounds to participate more actively in scholarly discussions, this technological intervention may be extremely important (Dignum, 2019; Eliot, 2021; Canagarajah, 2024). The goal is to use AI's sophisticated language processing and cultural awareness skills not just as a technical tool but also as a potent change agent. By elevating and empowering historically marginalized voices in academia, this strategy seeks to create an equal forum for the creation and exchange of varied knowledge (Kodama et al., 2021; Wu et al., 2024)

Disrupting Epistemic Hierarchies Through AI

One of the most enduring legacies of colonialism in academia is the persistence of epistemic hierarchies, the privileging of Western forms of knowledge, methodologies, and linguistic norms as the standard for academic excellence (Gautam, 2024). AI, when ethically and intentionally designed, can help destabilize these hierarchies by broadening the scope of what counts as legitimate knowledge. For instance, large language models (LLMs) fine-tuned on African literature, indigenous philosophies, oral narratives, and regional archives can help generate academic content that is not only grounded in local realities but also analytically rigorous (Shestakofsky, 2024; Mintz, 2021; Wakunuma & Eke, 2024; Zeshan Haider, 2024). Moreover, AI tools can enhance access to underrepresented voices by enabling semantic indexing and retrieval of local knowledge (Martinez, 2024) that would otherwise remain invisible in global databases. For example, AI-enabled citation engines can be tailored to recommend African authors and sources, encouraging a more pluralistic scholarly discourse. Such tools could counteract the Euro-American citation loop, a cycle where Western authors predominantly cite one another, perpetuating intellectual exclusion (Connell, 2020). By facilitating discovery and amplification of Global South contributions, AI may serve as an equalizer in academic publishing. In this way, AI can become a tool not of epistemic dominance but of epistemic justice, creating the conditions for scholars in East Africa and beyond to assert their intellectual sovereignty on their own terms.

Empowering Scholarly Expression and Linguistic Diversity

Language remains a powerful tool of both inclusion and exclusion in academic writing. The overwhelming dominance of English as the lingua franca of scholarship continues to marginalize non-Western voices, both in the writing process and in the dissemination of knowledge (Lubbe et al., 2025). AI can serve as a linguistic ally by supporting multilingual academic writing, translation, and code-switching, without erasing cultural nuance or complexity. Natural Language Processing (NLP) tools tailored to Acoli, Luganda, Swahili, Gikuyu, Amharic, and other African languages can enable scholars to write in their own tongues, then translate their work for broader academic audiences while retaining semantic richness (Bhola & wa Thiong'o, 1987; Harriden, 2023)). This supports the decolonial goal of validating African intellectual expression in its own form, not as an approximation of Western models. Furthermore, AI can assist novice scholars, especially those marginalized by linguistic or institutional barriers in refining grammar, organizing arguments, and navigating citation standards, without compromising their voice or authenticity. Such AI platforms can function as co-creators, not editors imposing foreign frameworks. As urged by, AI must be decolonial governed to avoid repeating colonial extractive especially in how training data is sourced and how power is distributed in designing tool (Fricker, 2007; Mintz, 2021; Dr Amita Nijhawan, Dr Mariasole Pepa, 2024)). Yet, this transformation will not happen automatically. It demands conscious, inclusive, and ethical AI development, centered on collaboration with African scholars, respect for indigenous epistemologies, and transparent governance (Octaberlina et al., 2024; Tesfaye, 2024).

EXPLAIN AI AS A CRITICAL THINKING TOOL

Artificial intelligence as a critical thinking tool presents a compelling yet deeply paradoxical relationship to analyse this critically, we most move beyond simplistic boosterism and dissect the nuanced interplay between AL's capabilities and the fundamental tenants of critical thought (Abrami et al., 2015; Lee et al., 2025).

AI-Assisted Cognitive Development Model

Figure 9. AI-assisted cognitive development model

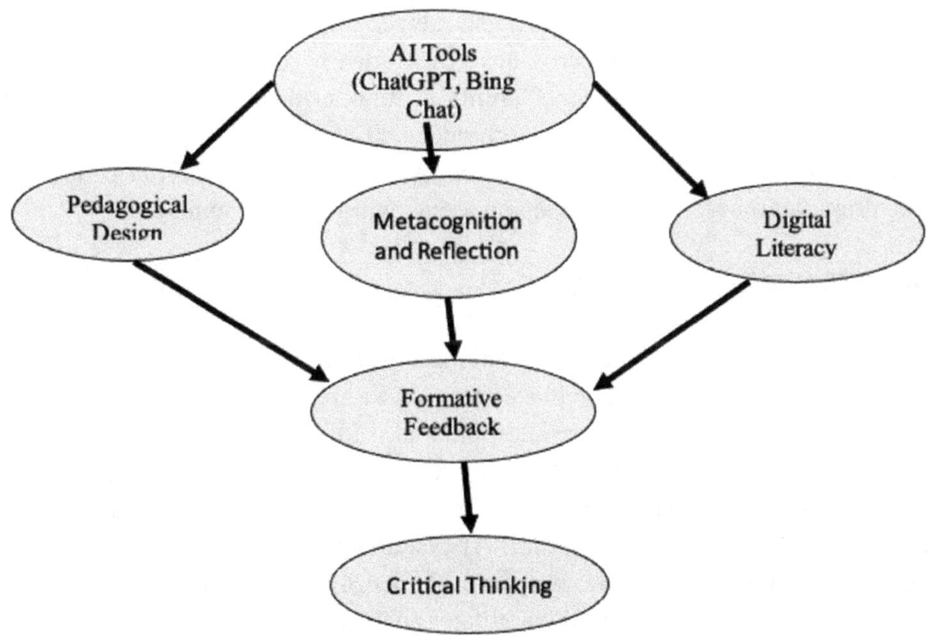

Although arrows show the main paths of influence, the model structure also suggests feedback and reciprocal linkages. Using Flavell's metacognition framework (Flavell, 1979), the model emphasizes the significance of people's awareness and control over their cognitive processes. In line with Flavell's focus on metacognitive development as a catalyst for successful learning and critical analysis, the suggested conceptual model proposes that formative feedback and reflective assignments function as tools to enhance students' metacognitive monitoring and self-regulation. The concept is based on Vygotsky's sociocultural theory (Vygotsky, 1978), which holds that social contact and the application of cultural tools promote higher-order thinking and cognitive growth. As a type of "cognitive scaffolding," the incorporation of AI-powered educational tools promotes guided reflection, cooperative learning, and knowledge co-construction all crucial elements of Vygotsky's paradigm. The paradigm enhances socially and culturally contextualized learning processes by framing AI as a mediator rather than a stand-alone technology component. Modern frameworks for critical thinking and digital literacy are incorporated into the model (UNESCO, 2022; OECD, 2021; Holmes et al., 2021). The frameworks emphasize the value of learning how to assess digital information, practice digital citizenship, and adjust to intricate, technologically driven contexts. According to the paradigm, metacognitive skills and digital competencies play a key role as mediators between the development of advanced critical thinking abilities and technological integration. The logic of the model is informed by theoretical viewpoints, which make clear how formative feedback, digital skills, and metacognitive practices interact in AI-enhanced education. The model provides a theoretically sound explanation of how integrating AI can enhance students' ability to think critically and independently. The model is based on current research and well-established ideas, placing our conceptual framework in the broader scholarly conversation on digital pedagogy, sociocultural learning, and cognitive and metacognitive development.

AI as a Mediator of Thought

"AI as a cognitive mediator" conceptual approach, AI complements thought processes rather than takes their place (Darwin et al., 2024; Luckin, 2018). According to contemporary literature and practical study, generative models such as ChatGPT, Bing Chat, and Co-pilot can serve a variety of purposes depending on the environment and pedagogical design (n.d.; Edwards, 2024; Wakunuma et al., 2025). Sources of heuristic prompting: AI systems produce queries, illustrations, and other viewpoints that inspire students to think critically and solve problems (da Costa et al., 2024; Luckin, 2018). AI facilitates analysis, comparison, interpretation, and debate by acting as a "object to think with" (Glikson, E., & Woolley, 2020; Luckin, 2018; Parra-Valencia & Massey, 2023). Students who lack sufficient digital literacy and critical thinking abilities risk the system becoming a straightforward copying tool that replaces intellectual engagement (Losey, 2024).

Expanding Thinking Horizons

AI as an information synthesis excels at processing vast datasets far beyond human capacity, Identifying correlations, trends, and anomalies invisible to the naked eye (Vaswani, A., Shazeer, N., Parmar, N., Uszkoreit, J., Jones, L., Gomez, A., Kaiser, L., 2017). This can provide the users with richer evidence bases, and reveal hidden systemic factors. AI is a transformative tool that can augment critical thinking by providing unprecedented scale in data processing, pattern recognition, and perspective generation. It excels at revealing hidden patterns that massively enhances human cognition by processing vast amounts of data impossible for human to handle alone. As stated by (Krämer, 2014; Sereno, 2025) AI generates diverse perspectives acting as a tireless brainstorming partner. This means that it can simulate opposing viewpoints and counterarguments, this directly forces exploration of alternative angles, strengthening the thinker's position (Zhumagaliyeva et al., 2025). However, it fundamentally lacks the intentionality, understanding, causal reasoning, and self-reflective capacity that define genuine critical thought. AI can be side to necessitate a higher order of critical vigilance, source skepticism, and human judgment from its users.

Refining and Streamlining Thought

AI acts as a crucial first line of defense against sloppy reasoning. By quickly highlighting potential errors, Al saves the human thinker substantial time and mental effort during the initial review phase. Weston et al. (2015) argued that AI is an efficiency engine for reasoning, significantly boosts critical thinking by acting as a powerful efficiency tool,(Buckland & Purcell, 2025) enhancing both the process and precision of human reasoning It prompts actually the user to pause and critically examine flagged sections: "Are this two statement contradicting this context? This automated streamlining allows the users to focus their deeper potential flaws, rather than starting from scratch to find them(Sereno, 2025).

Freeing Mental Recourses a Cognitive Offloading for Higher-Order Thinking

Critical thinking often gets bogged down by foundational time-intensive tasks. A dramatically accelerate these processes. It can rapidly summarize task. Al dramatically accelerates these processes. According to (Bommasani, et al 2021) it can rapidly summarize complex research papers or lengthy information, by extracting the key point and themes. It liberates significant mental bandwidth. the limited cognitive resources described by theories like cognitive load Theory (Sweller, 1988). Instead of expanding energy on basic comprehension, organization, or drafting, the critical thinker can redirect their full intellectual capacity towards the core, high-value activities of critical analysis. AI doesn't replace critical thinking; it optimizes the process by acting as an automated proof reader for logic and tireless assistant for foundational tasks, (Moluayonge, 2025)it removes friction and frees up the thinker's most valuable asset- their focused attention and judgment for the deep evaluation work that defines true critical thought.

The Potential of AI in Building Critical Thinking

Artificial Intelligence (AI) is rapidly transforming the potential of tertiary education worldwide and the quality of East African university learning is becoming increasingly apparent (Hou et al., 2025). Building critical thinking ability among university students is the most significant area of influence. For a nation whose universities are usually characterised by large student-to-teacher ratios (Popenici, 2023), poor infrastructure, and over-reliance on traditional teaching methods, (Popenici, S., Rudolph, J., Tan, S., & Tan, 2023) AI presents an opportunity to bridge learning gaps and build independent, analytical minds in students. Critical thinking, as the ability to analyses interpret, and evaluate information to make decisions, is the key to academic success, and graduates can solve real-world problems (Rudolph et al., 2024). AI technologies can enhance critical thinking in several practical ways(Reed, 2020). For example, machine learning systems can identify student response patterns, detect misconceptions, and recommend tailored interventions. This ongoing cycle of feedback challenges students from memorization to thinking, reflection, and development in learning over time. These are appropriately located within higher-order thinking activities prescribed under Bloom's Taxonomy in analysis, evaluation, and innovative creation. Teachers also suffer from writing personalized comments on each student, especially in lectures such as those containing enormous amounts of material in conventional colleges. AI fills the gap, providing ongoing, real-time feedback that supports independent learning and autonomous discovery (Rudolph et al., 2024).

AI-Augmented Classroom

Positive examples of AI-augmented learning are already available in East Africa. The AI-augmented platform developed by Learning Equality, called Kolibri, has been deployed in Rwanda, Kenya, and Tanzania to support personalized learning in low-resource environments. While initially released basic education, the same adaptive technology can be adapted for use in a university setting, where students can be assisted by content that is appropriate to their pace of learning and challenges them to think critically about learning (Jamil et al., 2025; Pnevmatikos, 2025(Wachira Kigotho, 2018)(Lu & Mohamed, 2025)). Similarly, applying Natural Language Processing (NLP) features such as AI-graded essay marking and writing assistants can guide students in strengthening argumentation and analytical writing (Gordon, 2024). Moreover, AI can relieve lecturers' administrative burdens by automating grading, timetabling, and plagiarism checking tasks. Notwithstanding the potential of AI, challenges must be overcome to achieve integration in East African universities. Infrastructure remains a key issue; institutions lack reliable internet, power, and suitable hardware to support AI Systems (Valenzuela, 2025). There is also an e-skills shortage in staff and academic staff, to whom massive amounts of training will have to be imparted so that AI can be brought into teaching to maximum benefit (Sylvestri, 2025). Policy leaders and education influencers in East Africa are beginning to realise and act against such challenges. Rwanda's National Strategy for Transformation (NST1) and Kenya's Digital Economy Blueprint highlight the potential role of emerging technologies, including AI, in redesigning education systems (Republic of Rwanda, 2019; Government of Kenya, 2019). Policy reports stress putting money into digital infrastructure (Hanifah & Ismail, 2025; Morrice et al., 2025), developing teacher capacity, and localised tools for AI so that they can become culturally and linguistically appropriate. Implementing AI in East African universities presents a novel opportunity for advancing critical thinking through cross-disciplinary studies. AI can overcome most challenges by facilitating individualised learning, enhancing feedback loops, and empowering teachers and students (Masih et al., 2025; Sarwar et al., 2025). However, to achieve this potential to the maximum, investment in infrastructure, capacity building, and ethical policy-making is required (Wang et al., 2025). With a thoughtful, inclusive strategy, AI has the potential to have a revolutionary influence in creating a generation of autonomous, creative, (Pham, 2025)and critically thinking learners in East Africa.

Lecture-Style of Teaching

Lecture-style teaching is standard and common in East African university classrooms.

The last obstacle to the production of critical thinking is the absence of modern technology and learning materials, which restrict the scope for independent, inquiry-led learning on behalf of the students (Pon & Schendel, 2020). All the universities in East Africa expose lecturers and students to infrastructural limitations such as limited internet availability, dated libraries, and the lack of an adequate number of computers or learning platforms (Yu et al., 2014). This digital divide limits exposure to diverse perspectives and collaborative learning, an interactive component of increasing critical thinking. (Hacker, 2021; Mtebe & Raisamo, 2014) further observe that although there is a drive towards adopting ICT in universities, it is sporadic, limited, and localised to private or urban universities with sufficient funding. Public universities, particularly rural-based universities, continue to be worried about the building blocks of digital inclusion (Zhou et al., 2021). Such containment by technology not only diminishes pedagogical excellence but also disenfranchises learners who do not have personal gadgets or access to the internet in their homes (Stevens-Smith, 2020). Where information technology has the potential to track complex real-world issues, tap massive knowledge bases, and offer worldwide academic networking, East African students have no means, which otherwise would stimulate their critical thinking and problem-solving abilities.

Infrastructural Imbalances

Besides pedagogical and technological constraints, cultural and system environments considerably undermine the establishment of critical thinking ability. East African and other cultures place an extremely high value on respect for age, conformity, and consensus that can suffocate free discussion of ideas in academe. Most East African university graduates have been deprived of community-based projects, interdisciplinary project teams, and internships that compel them to apply what they have learned to new, dynamic settings. Because of limited resources, bureaucratic constraints, and strict academic frameworks, most curricula do not include experiential learning through fieldwork, service-learning, case studies, and entrepreneurial projects. The absence of coordination among universities and outside partners discourages innovation and makes academic programs less relevant to the needs of society (Ramadhani et al., 2025). Such estrangement not only reduces future professions of graduates but also undermines the development of adaptive and critical thinking (Mom et al., 2025). Increased interface between the world of work and higher education by policy incentives, institutional collaboration, and curriculum reform could fundamentally change, which would enforce the cultivation of critical thinking and place higher education more in the realm of influence and change for East African communities (Tupag & Ubayubay, 2025; Karogi & Haule, 2025).

DISCUSS ETHICAL ISSUES

The use of AI writing tools in education presents numerous ethical dilemmas (Glikson, E., & Woolley, 2020; Tulyakul & Meepring, 2020; Yilma, 2025). Given the plethora of updates emerging from AI use, instructors and students must acquire the skills to employ AI properly, steering clear of copyright violations, discriminating language, and improper information (Nakatumba-Nabende, Suuna, & Bainomugisha, 2023; UNESCO, 2023; Farhud, et al, 2021).

Data Privacy

Students and instructors ought to contemplate the privacy ramifications of utilizing AI writing tools. Ensuring that data and tasks are managed meticulously and adhere to privacy standards. (Enkelejda Kasneci et al; 2023) proposed that enhancing awareness among instructors and students, along with implementing advanced technology to thwart unwanted access, could mitigate the risk of data breaches. A study by (Miriam Sullivan, Andrew Kelly, 2025.; Vildan Ozer, et al, 2025; Romele, 2025) on ChatGPT highlighted two primary concerns. Academic integrity and the possibility for improved learning in higher education. Thus, it is apparent that pupils may utilize writing tools for dishonest motives. Consequently, it is essential for faculty to furnish explicit guidance to students concerning the utilization of AI writing tools in their pedagogical practices. Students must recognize that these writing tools are intended solely for enhancement and should not be utilized to produce entire papers for instructors (Dworkin, 2023; Alahmadi, 2025). Excessive use on these technologies may induce complacency in students and impede their writing abilities.

Figure 10. AI Ethical frameworks (Adopted from Nakatumba-Nabende et al., 2023)

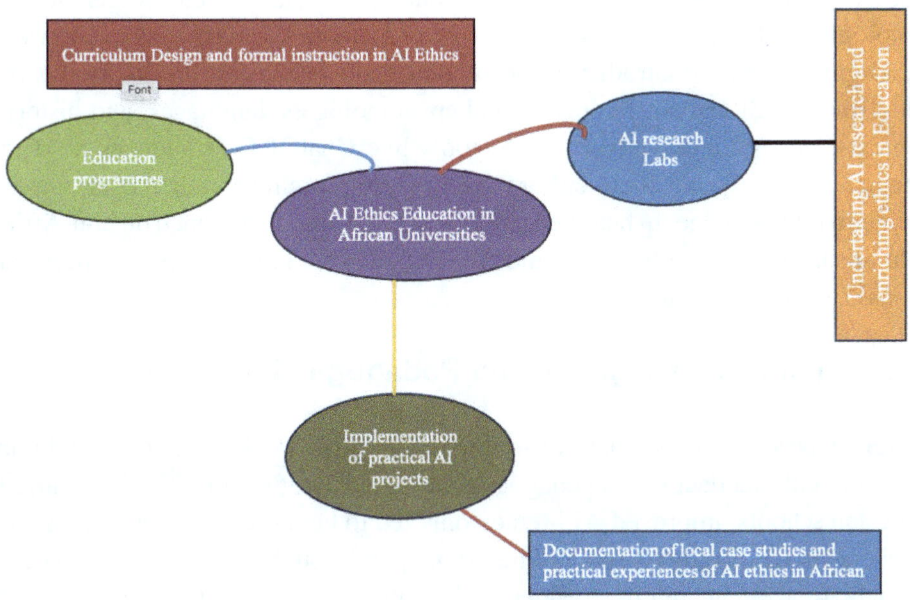

As illustrated in the figure below, AI ethics education in African universities can be approached from two perspectives (*Nakatumba-Nabende et al., 2023;* Inusah, 2025). The first approach is through curriculum design and formal instruction in AI ethics where the focus can also draw heavily on existing AI ethical frameworks, guidelines, and principles (Lombana Diaz, 2025). Secondly, the formal instruction of AI ethics should be approached from AI research labs' perspectives. These are research labs that are undertaking multidisciplinary AI research projects and they provide practical examples of approaches to AI ethics (Raji et al. 2021; Nakakuma et al, 2023; Kim 2019). The research labs present an opportunity to emphasize the documentation of the implementation of practical AI local case studies and practical experiences of AI ethics in the African continent. AI's integration into East African education offers transformative potential for decolonizing pedagogy to shifting from Eurocentric knowledge hierarchies to contextually rooted critical inquiry.

Bias and Digital Neo-Colonialism

Generative AI systems, largely designed in western contexts, tend to embed dominant cultural narratives and language norms, producing outputs steeped in Eurocentric viewpoints that can marginalize indigenous knowledge and languages (Dilmegani, 2025). As the paper Generative AI and Digital Neo-colonialism in Global Education explains, this form of "cultural imperialism" not only alienates learners from non-Western backgrounds, but also sidelines their indigenous epistemologies and practices. AI systems often perpetuate Western-centric knowledge paradigms, directly contradicting decolonial goals (Holdsworth, 2023). Training data from the Global North erases local epistemologies, languages, and historical contexts. For instance, generative AI tools like ChatGPT struggle with African linguistic diversity and socio-cultural nuances, reinforcing stereotypes or omitting indigenous knowledge. In healthcare diagnostics, AI models trained on non-African data misdiagnose conditions common in East Africa e.g. locally prevalent malaria stains) risking lethal outcomes.

Erosion of Human Agency and Pedagogical Integrity

It is imperative to note that over-relying on AI risks weakening critical thinking, the very skill that decolonial pedagogy aims to nurture (Tollon, 2025). In rural Indonesian schools, improved AI literacy only led to better teaching outcomes when teachers also received critical thinking training; without it, according to AI became a crutch, weakening their independent judgment. UNESCO cautions that generative AI might reduce education to transactional exchanges, eroding the teacher–student relationships essential for co-creating contextual knowledge (Steinert & Dennis, 2022). East Africa faces similar challenges in AI-driven "personalized learning" risks that is standardizing curricula in ways that stifle student curiosity and culturally grounded debate. At the 2025 UNESCO–AU International Day of Education, leaders stressed the need to preserve "human intentionality" by ensuring AI supports educators rather than replaces them.

Data Exploitation and Infrastructural Inequity

Artificial intelligence's effectiveness hinges on data, yet East Africa's digital divides exacerbate ethical risks according to on surveillance and ownership mentioned that Nigeria's biometric ID systems and Kenya's World coin ban highlight concerns that foreign AI firms exploit African's data without consent or benefit sharing (Karogi & Haule, 2025; Mom et al., 2025). Student data harvested by ed-tech platforms could deepen neo-colonial dependencies. When it comes to resource disparities stated that only 28% of African schools have reliable internet excluding rural learners. Student data harvested by ed-tech platforms could deepen neo-colonial dependencies. Nigeria's weak AI regulations contrast with its rapid fintech adoption, leaving citizens exposed to algorithmic discrimination in education loans or admissions. UNESCO's Guidance for Generative AI (2023) urges community-led checks and transparent impact assessments. There are a lot of moral and practical problems with using AI in decolonial academics. It is hard to make sure that AI doesn't reinforce biases and unfair situations. AI programs that are trained on biased datasets might support stereotypes and leave out groups that aren't well-represented. Training data biases that favor certain accents or language styles have a big effect on systems that process language. (Tolga Bolukbasi et al.,2016; Greene-Santos, 2024) used word embedding to show that AI can mirror societal biases and make inequality worse. AI tools for school use should be made by people who really understand how they can be used in different situations. said in their work on AI ethics that linguists, ethicists, and cultural leaders need to work together to make AI better.

SUGGEST IMPLEMENTABLE ACTIONS TO BE PURSUED

Teacher Training (Teacher Professional Development)

The transformation of education in East Africa must begin by empowering educators and students as co-creators in the AI learning ecosystem. Rather than simply adopting foreign-built educational apps (Schmied et al., 2024), schools and universities should foster the design of localized AI tools by and for their own communities. Teachers need professional development programs that blend critical pedagogy with AI literacy helping them see AI not as a threat or replacement, but as a dialogic tool to enhance inquiry, creativity, and deep reflection. Workshops and training modules can introduce educators to AI-supported lesson planning, classroom dialogue systems, and local content generation tools, all while maintaining a decolonial lens. Equally important is involving students as active participants in shaping how AI enters their classrooms Ivashenko Amdal & Endresen-Maharaj, 2023;

(Nakatumba-Nabende, Suuna, & Bainomugisha, 2023). Through design-thinking clubs, hackathons, and creative storytelling projects, young people can co-develop AI solutions that reflect their values, cultures, and learning needs. A chatbot that debates the ethics of colonialism, an app that teaches Pan-African history through interactive storytelling, or a game that challenges players to think critically about post-independence governance these are all possibilities when learners are at the centre of design. This participatory approach not only builds digital skills but also restores agency to African learners, allowing them to see themselves as producers of knowledge rather than passive recipients (Tsui et al., 2024).

Building Open Infrastructure and Regional Alliance

To sustain and scale the vision of decolonizing minds with AI, there must be a strong foundation of open infrastructure and regional collaboration (Luckin, 2018; Tapo, A. A., Traoré, A., Danioko, S., & Tembine, 2024). This includes developing open-source datasets derived from African knowledge systems literature, oral histories, community archives, and indigenous science. Public institutions, universities, and libraries should work together to collect and digitize this knowledge ethically, with full community involvement and ownership. AI models trained on these resources can then be used to power culturally relevant educational tools that are both accurate and empowering (Del Sarton & Soler i Lecha, 2024). At a broader level, East African nations should form cross-border alliances to pool resources, talent, and research in AI for education. Regional cooperation can support the creation of shared language models, joint university programs, and standards for ethical AI development in learning environments. Governments, civil society, and the African Union could coordinate efforts to fund and regulate these initiatives, ensuring they align with both educational goals and decolonial principles (Aarts, 1999; Asiedu et al., 2024).

CONCLUSION

Rather than relying on imported content, AI tools can help generate, curate, and adapt educational materials rooted in African history, philosophies, literature, and oral traditions. Natural Language Processing (NLP) models tailored to local languages such as Swahili, Gikuyu, and Luganda can make this content accessible and inclusive. For example, AI tools could be developed to assist in translating critical texts into indigenous languages or analysing works by African intellectuals like Ngũgĩ wa Thiong'o or Julius Nyerere. Speech-based interfaces and discussion platforms in local languages can further democratize access to critical thinking resources. Beyond language, AI can support students and educators in exploring themes of identity, resistance, and postcolonial critique through interactive learning experiences. The responsible and sustainable use of AI in education depends on improving pedagogical participation in the creation of digital learning systems and integrating AI literacy into foundational curriculum.

REFERENCES

Aarts, P. (1999). The Middle East: A region without regionalism or the end of exceptionalism? *Third World Quarterly*, *20*(5), 911–925. DOI: 10.1080/01436599913406

Abrami, , Bernard, R. M., Borokhovski, E., Waddington, D. I., Wade, C. A., & Persson, T. (2015). Strategies for Teaching Students to Think Critically. *Review of Educational Research*, *85*(2), 275–314. DOI: 10.3102/0034654314551063

Alahmadi, D. (2025). AI Ethics Principles for AI Developers in Academia: A Critical Assessment and Analysis. *TEM Journal*, 2514–2529. https://doi.org/DOI: 10.18421/TEM143-55

Almeida, S., & Kumalo, S. H. (2018). (De) coloniality through indigeneity: Deconstructing calls to decolonise in the South African and Canadian university contexts. *Education as Change*, *22*(1), 1–24. DOI: 10.25159/1947-9417/3023

Asiedu, . (2024). The Case for Globalizing Fairness: A Mixed Methods Study on Colonialism, AI, and Health in Africa. *Proceedings of the 4th ACM Conference on Equity and Access in Algorithms, Mechanisms, and Optimization*, 1–24. DOI: 10.1145/3689904.3694708

Balwant, P. T., Birdi, K., Stephan, U., & Topakas, A. (2019). Transformational instructor-leadership and academic performance: A moderated mediation model of student engagement and structural distance. *Journal of Further and Higher Education*, *43*(7), 884–900. DOI: 10.1080/0309877X.2017.1420149

Barocas, S., Hardt, M., & Narayanan, A. (2020). Fairness and machine learning. *Recommender systems handbook, 1*, 453-459.

Bertino, E.. (2021). AI for Security and Security for AI. *Proceedings of the Eleventh ACM Conference on Data and Application Security and Privacy*, 333–334. DOI: 10.1145/3422337.3450357

Bhola, H. S., & wa Thiong'o, N. (1987). Decolonising the Mind: The Politics of Language in African Literature. *African Studies Review*, *30*(2), 102. DOI: 10.2307/524049

Bird, S. (2020). Decolonising Speech and Language Technology. *Proceedings of the 28th International Conference on Computational Linguistics*, 3504–3519. DOI: 10.18653/v1/2020.coling-main.313

Birhane, A. (2020). Algorithmic Colonization of Africa. *Script-ed*, *17*(2), 389–409. DOI: 10.2966/scrip.170220.389

Bommasani, . (2021). On the Opportunities and Risks of Foundation Models. https://doi.org/doi.org/10.48550/arXiv.2108.07258

Buckland, P., & Purcell, R. (2025). Prompt to Podcast: Reimagining Assessment with Generative AI. *Irish Journal of Technology Enhanced Learning*, *9*(1). Advance online publication. DOI: 10.22554/v3h7jn42

Canagarajah, S. (2024). Decolonizing Academic Writing Pedagogies for Multilingual Students. *TESOL Quarterly*, *58*(1), 280–306. DOI: 10.1002/tesq.3231

Charles, K.. (2023). *Exploring Education Access*. Opportunities, and Massification in Higher Education in Uganda.

Connell, R. (2020). *Southern Theory*. Routledge., DOI: 10.4324/9781003117346

D'Agostino, T. (2023). Examination reform for higher order thinking: A case study of assessment-driven reform in Uganda. *International Journal of Educational Development*, *103*, 102918. DOI: 10.1016/j.ijedudev.2023.102918

da Costa, M. de C., Olinda, A. L. S., & dos Santos, A. P. (2024, July). Digital technologies in education: Challenges and opportunities for teaching and learning. *VI Seven International Multidisciplinary Congress*. DOI: 10.56238/sevenVImulti2024-019

Darwin, , Rusdin, D., Mukminatien, N., Suryati, N., Laksmi, E. D., & Marzuki, . (2024). Critical thinking in the AI era: An exploration of EFL students' perceptions, benefits, and limitations. *Cogent Education*, *11*(1), 2290342. DOI: 10.1080/2331186X.2023.2290342

Del Sarto, R. A., & Soler i Lecha, E. (2024). Regionalism and alliances in the Middle East, 2011-2021: From a "flash in the Pan" of regional cooperation to liquid alliances. *Geopolitics*, *29*(4), 1447–1473. DOI: 10.1080/14650045.2023.2268542

Dignum, V. (2019). *Responsible artificial intelligence: How to develop and use AI in a responsible way*. Springer. DOI: 10.1007/978-3-030-30371-6

Dilmegani, C. (2025). *Bias in AI: Examples and 6 Ways to Fix it in 2025*.

Dworkin, W. A. Scott Danzis, Christina Kuhn, Olivia. (2023). Framework for the Future of AI: Senator Cassidy Issues White Paper, Seeks Public Feedback. *Covington Digital Health*. https://www.covingtondigitalhealth.com/2023/09/framework-for-the-future-of-ai-senator-cassidy-issues-white-paper-seeks-public-feedback/

Edwards, B. A. (2024). *Artificial Intelligence in Mediation: What the Future Holds for Mediators*. Edwards Mediation Academy.

Eguchi, A. (2021). *AI-Robotics and AI Literacy*., DOI: 10.1007/978-3-030-77022-8_7

Eliot, L. (2021). Interoperability Of AI-to-AI Multi-Lawyering. SSRN *Electronic Journal*. DOI: 10.2139/ssrn.3990307

Freire, P. (1970). *Pedagogy of the oppressed, translated by Myra Bergman Ramo.*

Fricker, M. (2007). *Epistemic injustice: Power and the ethics of knowing*. Oxford University Press. DOI: 10.1093/acprof:oso/9780198237907.001.0001

Gautam, N. (2024). *Unraveling the Social Impacts of Artificial Intelligence.*

Giacomazzi, M., Fontana, M., & Trujillo, C. C. (2022). Contextualization of critical thinking in sub-Saharan Africa: A systematic integrative review. *Thinking Skills and Creativity*, *43*, 43. DOI: 10.1016/j.tsc.2021.100978

Glais, N. (2023). Challenges of AI in Education: Analysis of UNESCO reports 2019-2021. In *Carnets de Laboratoire RL-2 Bonheurs, 2, 230, ISSN: 2967-3631, 2023.* (Vol. 2, p. 117-129). EDBH. DOI: 10.5281/zenodo.10382844

Glikson, E., & Woolley, A. W. (2020). Human trust in artificial intelligence: Review of empirical research. *The Academy of Management Annals*, *14*(2), 627–660. DOI: 10.5465/annals.2018.0057

Gordon, K. W. (2024). *Replacing the traditional classroom with AI augmented Education. Human?* AI Symbolysis.

Greene-Santos, A. (2024). *Does AI Have a Bias Problem?* Guàrdia, L., Mancini, F., Jacobetty, P., & Maina, M. (2021). Graduates' employability skills in East Africa. *Journal of Teaching and Learning for Graduate Employability*, *12*(2), 169–184.

Hacker, P. (2021). A legal framework for AI training data—From first principles to the Artificial Intelligence Act. *Law, Innovation and Technology*, *13*(2), 257–301. DOI: 10.1080/17579961.2021.1977219

Hanifah, L., & Ismail, N. M. (2025). HUMAN-CENTERED AI IN LANGUAGE CLASSROOMS. *Proceedings of International Conference on Education, 3*(1), 239–246. DOI: 10.32672/pice.v3i1.3481

Harriden, K. (2023). Decolonising your writing. *A Community Blog and Repository of Resources for Improving Research Impact on Complex Real-World Problems.*

Holdsworth, J. (2023). *What is AI bias?* Holmes, W., Bialik, M., & Fadel, C. (2023). *ARTIFICIAL INTELLIGENCE IN EDUCATION.*

Hou, C., Zhu, G., & Sudarshan, V. (2025). The role of critical thinking on undergraduates' reliance behaviours on generative <scp>AI</scp> in problem-solving. *British Journal of Educational Technology*, *56*(5), 1919–1941. DOI: 10.1111/bjet.13613

Inusah, H. (2025). Rethinking AI ethics through an Akan ontology: Advancing an ethics of becoming for sustainable AI. *Canadian Journal of African Studies / Revue Canadienne Des Études Africaines*, 1–18. DOI: 10.1080/00083968.2025.2524342

Jamil, M., Urooj, T., & Muhammad, N. (2025). Fostering Critical Thinking in Teacher Education Programs: Perceptions, Practices, and Challenges of Teacher Educators. *ProScholar Insights*, *4*(3), 13–22. DOI: 10.55737/psi.2025c-43098

Karogi, P. M., & Haule, E. L. (2025). School infrastructure for effective implementation of the Tanzania Education and Training Policy 2014 (2023) Edition in secondary schools: A case study of Mpimbwe District Council. *East African Journal of Education Studies*, *8*(2), 923–938. DOI: 10.37284/eajes.8.2.3223

Kasneci, E., Sessler, K., Küchemann, S., Bannert, M., Dementieva, D., Fischer, F., Gasser, U., Groh, G., Günnemann, S., Hüllermeier, E., Krusche, S., Kutyniok, G., Michaeli, T., Nerdel, C., Pfeffer, J., Poquet, O., Sailer, M., Schmidt, A., Seidel, T., & Kasneci, G.Enkelejda Kasneci a. (2023). ChatGPT for good? On opportunities and challenges of large language models for education. *Learning and Individual Differences*, *103*, 102274. DOI: 10.1016/j.lindif.2023.102274

Kigotho, W. (2018). *Higher education – Caught in a double bind*. University World News. https://www.universityworldnews.com/post.php?story=20180328162530835

Kodama, N., Sugimoto, H., & Minagi, S. (2021). AI in dentistry and clues for starting AI research. [Journal of Okayama Medical Association]. *Okayama Igakkai Zasshi*, *133*(3), 181–183. DOI: 10.4044/joma.133.181

Krämer, W. (2014). Kahneman, D. (2011): Thinking, Fast and Slow. *Statistical Papers (Berlin, Germany)*, *55*(3), 915–915. DOI: 10.1007/s00362-013-0533-y

Lee, . (2025). The Impact of Generative AI on Critical Thinking: Self-Reported Reductions in Cognitive Effort and Confidence Effects from a Survey of Knowledge Workers. *Proceedings of the 2025 CHI Conference on Human Factors in Computing Systems*, 1–22. DOI: 10.1145/3706598.3713778

Lombana Diaz, C. (2025). AI Ethics. *AI and Ethics*, •••, 439–474. DOI: 10.1007/978-3-031-61375-3_5

Losey, R. (2024). *Can AI Replace Human Mediators? Groundbreaking Study Reveals Surprising Results*. Electronic Discovery Reference Model.

Lu, Z., & Mohamed, H. B. (2025). Teaching Critical Thinking in Civic Education: A Qualitative Study of Novice Teachers' Experiences and Challenges. *International Journal of Research and Innovation in Social Science*, *IX*(V), 6433–6445. DOI: 10.47772/IJRISS.2025.905000496

Lubbe, A., Marais, E., & Kruger, D. (2025). Cultivating independent thinkers: The triad of artificial intelligence, Bloom's taxonomy and critical thinking in assessment pedagogy. *Education and Information Technologies*, *30*(12), 17589–17622. DOI: 10.1007/s10639-025-13476-x

Luckin, R. (2018). *Enhancing Learning and Teaching with Technology: What the Research Says*. ERIC.

Martinez, R. (2024). *HOW AI IS SHAPING SOCIAL STRUCTURES: DIVERSITY, EQUITY, INCLUSION AND BELONGING.*

Masih, M., Suleman, S., Khan, M. H., Sahito, D. Z., & Shahid, D. S. (2025). The Future Classroom: Integrating AI and social media for Adaptive Learning. *Inverge Journal of Social Sciences*, *4*(3), 98–111. DOI: 10.63544/ijss.v4i3.150

Mbunge, E., & Batani, J. (2023). *Application of deep learning and machine learning models to improve healthcare in sub-Saharan Africa: Emerging opportunities, trends and implications*. Telematics and Informatics Reports.

McArthur, J. (2022). Critical theory in a decolonial age. *Educational Philosophy and Theory*, *54*(10), 1681–1692. DOI: 10.1080/00131857.2021.1934670

Mignolo, W. (2011). *The darker side of western modernity: Global futures, decolonial options*. Duke University Press.

Mintz, S. (2021). Decolonizing the Academy. *Inside Higher Ed's*.

Moluayonge, G. E. (2025). Cognitive Offload as a Mediator of AI Usage and Critical Thinking Development in Cameroonian Higher Education Learners. *Asian Journal of Education and Social Studies*, *51*(8), 467–476. DOI: 10.9734/ajess/2025/v51i82253

Mom, A. N., Ndamsa, D. T., Abety, P., & Nguena, C.-L. (2025). The Impact of School Infrastructure on Academic Performance in Cameroon: Empirical Evidence from Cameroon. *Innovation Economics Frontiers*, 31–45. DOI: 10.36923/iefrontiers.v28i1.285

Morrice, A., Deering, S., Kemsley, A., & Judge, S. (2025). Making use of AI in the Classics classroom. *Journal of Classics Teaching*, 1–9. DOI: 10.1017/S205863102500008X

Mtebe, J. S., & Raisamo, R. (2014). Investigating perceived barriers to the use of open educational resources in higher education in Tanzania. *International Review of Research in Open and Distance Learning*, *15*(2). Advance online publication. DOI: 10.19173/irrodl.v15i2.1803

Nakatumba-Nabende, J., Suuna, C., & Bainomugisha, E. (2023). *AI Ethics in Higher Education: Research Experiences from Practical Development and Deployment of AI Systems*. Springer International Publishing., DOI: 10.1007/978-3-031-23035-6_4

Nijhawan, D. A., Pepa, D. M., & Adam, D. S. (2024). *Decolonising Academic Writing: Enacting a Self in and Through Writing. Part 1*. Decolonial Dialogues.

Noble, S. U. (2018). *Algorithms of oppression: How search engines reinforce racism* (pp. xv, 229). New York University Press.

Octaberlina, , Muslimin, A. I., Chamidah, D., Surur, M., & Mustikawan, A. (2024). Exploring the impact of AI threats on originality and critical thinking in academic writing. *Edelweiss Applied Science and Technology*, *8*(6), 8805–8814. DOI: 10.55214/25768484.v8i6.3878

Ozer, V., ... (2025). *Performance of GPT-4o in the management of toxicological exposures: A comparative analysis with emergency medicine residents—Ozer—2025—Hong Kong Journal of Emergency Medicine—Wiley Online Library*. https://onlinelibrary.wiley.com/doi/full/10.1002/hkj2.70031

Parra-Valencia, J.-A., & Massey, M.-L. (2023). *Leveraging AI Tools for Enhanced Digital Literacy*. Access to Information, and Personalized Learning., DOI: 10.1007/978-3-031-40635-5_9

Pham, C. H. (2025). *University Students' Sense of Belonging in AI-Mediated EFL Classrooms* (pp. 397–422). DOI: 10.4018/979-8-3373-0969-9.ch011

Pnevmatikos, D. (2025). Creating Critical Thinking Professionals: Challenges for Higher Education. *Higher Education for the Future*, *12*(2), 195–209. DOI: 10.1177/23476311251335374

Pon, C., & Schendel, R. (2020). Exploring processes of teaching and learning in African university contexts: The case of education for critical thinking in Ghana, Kenya and Botswana. *International Journal of African Higher Education*, *7*(1). Advance online publication. DOI: 10.6017/ijahe.v6i2.11355

Popenici, S. (2023). The critique of AI as a foundation for judicious use in higher education. *Journal of Applied Learning & Teaching*, *6*(2). Advance online publication. DOI: 10.37074/jalt.2023.6.2.4

Popenici, S., Rudolph, J., Tan, S., & Tan, S. (2023). A critical perspective on generative AI and learning futures. An interview with Stefan Popenici. *Journal of Applied Learning & Teaching*, *6*(2). Advance online publication. DOI: 10.37074/jalt.2023.6.2.5

Ramadhani, . (2025). Extensiveness of School Committee Involvement in Maintenance of Classroom Infrastructure: A Guarantee to Adequate Learning Facilities in Primary Schools. *International Journal of Innovative Research and Development.* Advance online publication. DOI: 10.24940/ijird/2025/v14/i5/OJSMAY25001

Rana, V., Verhoeven, B., & Sharma, M. (2025). Generative AI in Design Thinking Pedagogy: Enhancing Creativity, Critical Thinking, and Ethical Reasoning in Higher Education. *Journal of University Teaching & Learning Practice*, *22*(4). Advance online publication. DOI: 10.53761/tjse2f36

Reed, S. K. (2020). *Cognitive Skills You Need for the 21st Century.* Oxford University Press., DOI: 10.1093/oso/9780197529003.001.0001

Romele, A. (2025). *|Ethics of AI| as a Floating Signifier; or Towards a Politics of AI Ethics* (pp. 157–168). DOI: 10.1007/978-3-031-85478-1_9

Rudolph, J., Mohamed Ismail, F. M., & Popenici, S. (2024). Higher Education's Generative Artificial Intelligence Paradox: The Meaning of Chatbot Mania. *Journal of University Teaching & Learning Practice*, *21*(06). Advance online publication. DOI: 10.53761/54fs5e77

Sadman, N., Rahman, A., & Gupta, K. D. (2021a). *Promise of AI in Defi, A Literary Analysis.* DOI: 10.20944/preprints202110.0136.v2

Sadman, N., Rahman, A., & Gupta, K. D. (2021b). *Promise of AI in Defi, A Literary Analysis.* DOI: 10.20944/preprints202110.0136.v1

Sarwar, U., et al. (2025). *Navigating Barriers to AI Implementation in the Classroom.* IGI Global. DOI: 10.4018/979-8-3373-1827-1

Schmied, A., Ntonia, I., Ng, M. K. J., Zhu, Y., Gibbs, F., & Zou, H. G. (2024). Co-creating with students to promote science of learning in higher education: An international pioneer collaborative effort for asynchronous teaching. *Trends in Neuroscience and Education*, *35*, 100229. DOI: 10.1016/j.tine.2024.100229 PMID: 38879199

Sereno, S. I. B. (2025). *AI as Academic Partner: Evaluating ChatGPT's Impact on Learning Outcomes and Perceptions Among Business Administration Students.* DOI: 10.6084/m9.figshare.28876175

Setegn, G. M., & Dejene, B. E. (2025). Improving machine learning models through explainable AI for predicting the level of dietary diversity among Ethiopian preschool children. *Italian Journal of Pediatrics*, *5*(1), 91. DOI: 10.1186/s13052-025-01892-1 PMID: 40128875

Shestakofsky, B. (2024). The Social Structures That Shape AI. *The Journal of Applied Behavioral Science,* Nakatumba-Nabende, J., Suuna, C., & Bainomugisha, E. (2023). AI ethics in higher education: Research experiences from practical development and deployment of AI systems. In *AI Ethics in Higher Education: Insights from Africa and Beyond* (pp. 39–55). Springer International Publishing.

Tuhiwai Smith. (2012). *Decolonizing methodologies: Research and indigenous peoples.*

Steinert, S., & Dennis, M. J. (2022). Emotions and Digital Well-Being: On Social Media's Emotional Affordances. *Philosophy & Technology, 35*(2), 36. DOI: 10.1007/s13347-022-00530-6 PMID: 35450167

Stevens-Smith, D. A. (2020). Brain-Based Teaching: Differentiation in Teaching, Learning, and Motor Skills. *Journal of Physical Education, Recreation & Dance, 91*(7), 34–42. DOI: 10.1080/07303084.2020.1781717

Sullivan, M., & Kelly, A. (2025) *ChatGPT in higher education: Considerations for academic integrity and student learning.* https://www.researchgate.net/publication/369378950_

Sweller, J. (n. d.). (1988). *Cognitive Load During Problem Solving: Effects on Learning.*

Sylvestri, B. (2025). *AI in the classroom: What parents need to know.*

Tapo, A. A., Traoré, A., Danioko, S., & Tembine, H. (2024). Machine Intelligence in Africa. *Survey (London, England).*

Tesfaye, A. (2024). Navigating the complexities of decolonizing knowledge production. *A Community Blog and Repository of Resources for Improving Research Impact on Complex Real-World Problems.*

Tollon, F. (2025). Reactive agency and technology. *AI and Ethics, 5*(1), 489–496. DOI: 10.1007/s43681-023-00366-6

Tsui, E., Dragicevic, N., Fan, I., & Cheng, M. (2024). Co-creating curriculum with students, teachers, and practitioners in a technology-enhanced environment. *Educational Technology Research and Development, 72*(2), 869–893. DOI: 10.1007/s11423-023-10301-5

Tulyakul, P., & Meepring, S. (2020). Ethical Issues of Informed Consent: Students as Participants in Faculty Research. *Global Journal of Health Science, 12*(3), 86. DOI: 10.5539/gjhs.v12n3p86

Tupag, R. M., & Ubayubay, R. (2025). Teachers' Practices on Digital Infrastructure towards Schools' Digital Capacity and Transformation. *International Journal on Science and Technology*, *16*(3), 7828. Advance online publication. DOI: 10.71097/IJSAT.v16.i3.7828

Vakili, R., Vakili, S., Ajilian Abbasi, M., & Masoudi, S. (2024). Overcrowded Classrooms: Challenges, Consequences, and Collaborative Solutions for Educators: A Literature Review. *Medical Education Bulletin*, *5*(2), 961–972.

Valenzuela, J. M. (2025). Navigating the Future of Education in Critical Thinking and AI in Digital Citizenship. In *Digital Citizenship and the Future of AI Engagement, Ethics, and Privacy* (pp. 377–404). IGI Global. DOI: 10.4018/979-8-3693-9015-3.ch014

Vaswani, A., Shazeer, N., Parmar, N., Uszkoreit, J., Jones, L., Gomez, A., & Kaiser, L. (2017). *P.* Attention Is All You Need., https://doi.org/doi.org/10.48550/arXiv.1706.03762

Veselova, I. (2021). Postcolonial theory and its Impact upon modern historical-anthropological research of Latin America. *Исторический Журнал: Научные Исследования*, *4*(4), 61–69. DOI: 10.7256/2454-0609.2021.4.36489

Wakunuma, K., & Eke, D. (2024). Africa, ChatGPT, and Generative AI Systems: Ethical Benefits, Concerns, and the Need for Governance. *Philosophies*, *9*(3), 80. DOI: 10.3390/philosophies9030080

Wakunuma, K., Ogoh, G., Akintoye, S., & Eke, D. O. (2025). Decoloniality as an Essential Trustworthy AI Requirement. (Eds), *Trustworthy AI: African Perspectives* (pp. 255–276). Springer Nature Switzerland. DOI: 10.1007/978-3-031-75674-0_12

Wang, X., Gao, Y., Wang, Q., & Zhang, P. (2025). Fostering Engagement in <scp>AI</scp> -Mediate Chinese <scp>EFL</scp> Classrooms: The Role of Classroom Climate, <scp>AI</scp> Literacy, and Resilience. *European Journal of Education*, *60*(1). Advance online publication. DOI: 10.1111/ejed.12874

Wayne, H., Fengchun, M., & UNESCO. (2023). *Guidance for generative AI in education and research*. UNESCO Publishing.

Weston, J., Bordes, A., Chopra, S., Rush, A. M., Van Merriënboer, B., Joulin, A., & Mikolov, T. (2015). Towards ai-complete question answering: A set of prerequisite toy tasks. *arXiv preprint arXiv:1502.05698.*

Wu, Z., Abdul Halim, H., & Mohd Saad, M. R. (2024). Artificial Intelligence (AI) and Gamification in Blended Learning: Enhancing Language and Literacy in Shanxi, China. [MJSSH]. *Malaysian Journal of Social Sciences and Humanities, 9*(12), e003159. DOI: 10.47405/mjssh.v9i12.3159

Xu, J. (2024). Memorisation is not rote learning: Rethinking memorisation as an embodied practice for Chinese students. *Journal of Multilingual and Multicultural Development, 45*(9), 3963–3979. DOI: 10.1080/01434632.2022.2134878

Yilma, K. (2025). Ethics of AI in Africa: Interrogating the role of Ubuntu and AI governance initiatives. *Ethics and Information Technology, 27*(2), 24. DOI: 10.1007/s10676-025-09834-5

Yu, X., Yang, D., Ding, W., & Gan, W. (2014). Preliminary Research and Development on the Problem-Solving Humanoid Machine for K-12 Education. *2014 International Conference of Educational Innovation through Technology*, 99–104. DOI: 10.1109/EITT.2014.25

Zeshan Haider, S. T. (2024). *AI-Driven Pedagogies: Shaping Critical Thinking Skills in a Data-Rich World.* DOI: 10.13140/RG.2.2.23095.12969

Zhou, P., Li, J., Chen, F., Zhou, H., Bao, S., & Li, M. (2021). Design of metacognitive scaffolding for k-12 programming education and its effects on students' problem solving ability and metacognition. *2021 Tenth International Conference of Educational Innovation through Technology (EITT)*, 182–186. DOI: 10.1109/EITT53287.2021.00044

Zhumagaliyeva, G., Tleshova, Z., Amanzhol, M., & Smagulova, M. (2025). THE IMPACT OF AI ON ACADEMIC WRITING: ENHANCING SKILLS OR HINDERING CRITICAL THINKING? *National Center for Higher Education Development, 2*(50). Advance online publication. DOI: 10.59787/2413-5488-2025-50-2-122-134

Chapter 11

Natural Language Processing in Conversational AI Tutors:
Toward Human-Like Learning Companions

Ravikumar R. N.
https://orcid.org/0009-0009-3705-1681
Marwadi University, Rajkot, India

S. Aarthi
https://orcid.org/0009-0006-9064-2091
Marwadi University, Rajkot, India

ABSTRACT

Conversational AI tutors, powered by Natural Language Processing (NLP) and Large Language Models (LLMs), are reshaping education by offering personalized, adaptive, and interactive learning experiences. Unlike static digital tools, these systems simulate human-like dialogue, support inquiry-based learning, and provide real-time feedback tailored to individual needs. This chapter explores the evolution of conversational AI in education, core technological components, real-world applications, and ethical considerations. Through case studies such as Duolingo Max and Carnegie Learning's Mika, it highlights the transformative potential of AI tutors across K–12, higher education, and professional training. It also addresses future research directions including emotional intelligence, multimodal interaction, and teacher-AI collaboration, emphasizing the need for pedagogical grounding and responsible deployment. Conversational AI tutors are poised to become vital partners in next-generation learning ecosystems.

DOI: 10.4018/979-8-3373-4217-7.ch011

INTRODUCTION

Conversational Artificial Intelligence (AI) being transferred into the traditions of education is a groundbreaking occurrence in the patterns of learner-learning exchange and personalisation of learning systems. Conversational AI built on Natural Language Processing (NLP) allows human orientation in interaction between learners and intelligent systems such that learners obtain personalized, adaptive, and interactive learning experiences (Karpagavalli, 2024). Unlike a typical computer-based learning tool, conversational AI tutor may mimic the interactive and versatile qualities of the human tutor and thus can make the educational experience more natural, efficient, and compelling to the learner. Large Language Models (LLMs), such as GPT, Claude and PaLM, allow AI tutors to process, understand, and interpret natural language much more accurately and context-sensitively. These systems can answer questions, clarify things, provide personal-level feedback and take a student through a complex problem-solving process (Borchers et al., 2024). The learner-centric system through this development becomes achievable in the context of the following pedagogical theories: constructivism and inquiry-based learning. As conversational agents become more sophisticated, the opportunities for change in education across the board, K-12, higher education, and professional and graduate fiscal training, are enormous, and conversational agents will close the divide in access, enhance learning, and add to lifelong learning (Bulathwela et al., 2024). The chapter talks about how conversational AI is transforming the field of education and notes the technologies and pedagogies, application techniques and ethics that guide the viability of thinking of such opportunity in modern learning contexts.

PROBLEM STATEMENT

Even with such huge technological changes in the field of education, learners continue to cope with difficulties regarding access to individual, recommendable, as well as adaptive academic assistance. The existing tutoring systems are either resource demanding or simply are not scalable, and most of the digital learning platforms are incapable of providing real-time, contextual, and emotionally intelligent feedback. Self-paced study in many cases can cause difficulties in learning as responses given to individual learners are not responsive to their thinking capabilities and patterns of learning. Furthermore, the current AI-based systems deployed in education usually make people convey the information; they do not facilitate interactive conversation, critical thinking, or inquiry-based learning. Motivation, retention and a thorough level of understanding are held back by the absence of personalized human-like interaction. With schools and educational facilities working towards inclusive, equitable, and high-quality education, the current society expresses interest in AI conversational tutors that may be used to simulate the scaffolding and responsiveness of a human teacher. The creation of such systems also has some technological, pedagogical, and ethical issues to solve, to utilize the potential of AI to the maximum in terms of changing modern education.

RESEARCH GAP

Previous literature has addressed the use of AI in education, mainly under the adaptive learning systems, chatbots, and automated grading. However, there is still a prominent gap in the design of conversational AI tutors that would be capable of supporting complex multi-learner interactions. The existing the majority of the systems are rule-based and not that scalable or those that are generative without enough contextual consistency and explainability. They do not tend to justify Socratic discussions, instantaneous adaptation, and emotional intelligence. In addition, no adequate consideration is given to the matching of these systems to pedagogical theories or inclusiveness of a wide range of learner needs, such as cultural sensitivity and access. Real-world deployments also understudy ethical issues such as bias in an algorithm, data privacy and autonomy in the learner. Specifically, studies do not provide the systems of incorporating NLP innovations into cognitive science and learning design. Therefore, this interdisciplinary gap has to be addressed, and conversational AI systems that are both intelligent and empathetic and ethically and well-educationally founded have to be created and tested.

OBJECTIVES OF THE CHAPTER

This chapter aims to explore the transformative role of Conversational AI tutors in modern education through the lens of NLP and emerging large language models. The objectives are:

- **To trace the evolution of NLP in education**, from early rule-based systems to modern transformer-based language models, highlighting key milestones.
- **To identify the core components** of conversational AI tutoring systems, such as intent recognition, dialogue management, and personalized response generation.
- **To evaluate use cases** across K-12, higher education, and professional training domains, including language learning, STEM support, writing assistance, and test preparation.

- **To discuss technical and pedagogical challenges**, including maintaining instructional accuracy, addressing conversational drift, and aligning AI systems with educational objectives.
- **To address ethical considerations**, including data privacy, bias mitigation, learner autonomy, and inclusivity.
- **To propose future directions** for integrating emotional intelligence, multimodal interaction, and human-centered design in conversational AI for truly personalized digital learning.

These objectives guide a comprehensive analysis of how conversational AI can shape the future of learner-driven education.

BACKGROUND STUDY

The idea of applying AI to the field of education is not novel at all: the beginnings of it can be traced to the rule-based Intelligent Tutoring Systems (ITS) of the 1970s-1980s (SCHOLAR, AutoTutor), which sought to imitate certain features of human tutoring. These systems relied upon compartmentalized scripts and programmed scripts of dialogue, and were highly fixed in character with minimal or no means of adaptation and scaling (Aarthi et al., 2025). The technologies in education began to change to a less rule-based system because with the advent of machine learning, and NLP specifically, increasingly dynamic and conversational technologies of education are becoming viable (Putri et al., 2023). The first chatbots emerged at the very start of 2000s, and those brought a fresh wave of interaction into the education process, but the competence of the latter was also predetermined by the intents and responses.

With the introduction of deep learning and the reformulation of open-ended architectures (BERT, GPT, T5, Claude and PaLM) it has truly broken through. These LLMs facilitated the possibility of attaining unparalleled contextual clarity and coherence and semantic consciousness in dialogue systems (Kang et al., 2023). The technical advances have allowed AI to advance beyond mere presentation vehicles of fixed content, and to also be a sense-making entity capable of reading student output, providing its own answer, and engaging in what can approximate a Socratic dialogue. Achieving factual accuracy, ethical use, and bias despite good intentions of the systems is some of the challenges which these systems must transcend. It has a rich history behind it that leads to emergence of more human-like AI tutors, driven by efforts in NLP, cognitive science, and pedagogical paradigm, as one way to enhance learner engagements, autonomy and performance.

KEY DEFINITIONS

- **Conversational AI Tutor**: An AI-powered system designed to engage learners in natural, interactive dialogues. It simulates human-like tutoring by using NLP to understand and respond to student queries, offering personalized guidance and support.
- **Natural Language Processing (NLP)**: A subfield of AI that focuses on enabling machines to understand, interpret, generate, and respond to human language. In education, NLP powers chatbots, intelligent tutors, and automated feedback systems.
- **Large Language Models (LLMs)**: Advanced neural networks trained on vast textual datasets to understand and generate human-like text. Examples include GPT, Claude, PaLM, and BERT, which are foundational to building responsive AI tutors.
- **Socratic Dialogue**: A form of cooperative argumentative dialogue that stimulates critical thinking and draws out ideas through questioning. AI tutors employ this method to support inquiry-based learning.
- **Intent Recognition**: A component of dialogue systems that identifies the purpose or goal behind a user's input, allowing the AI to respond appropriately in a learning context.
- **Dialogue Management**: The process that controls the flow and structure of conversations between the user and the AI system, ensuring coherence, relevance, and pedagogical alignment.
- **Personalized Learning**: An educational approach where learning experiences are tailored to individual students' needs, preferences, pace, and goals—facilitated by adaptive AI tutors.
- **Conversational Drift**: A phenomenon where AI responses gradually deviate from the original topic, potentially leading to confusion or misalignment with learning objectives.

LITERATURE REVIEW

The cross-section of AI and education has been through an immense change especially with the advent of conversational AI brought about by the developments in NLP (Kumar et al., 2023). The first ITS were mainly rule based and narrow in scope and most were not domain independent offering script-based dialogues that were inflexible contextually. These systems provided the foundation to the (Ni & Cheung, 2023), particularly with the arrival of such models as machine or deep learning, chatbots have become widespread in the educational domain, yet they are still limited by their inability to handle complicated, multi-turn dialogs because of predetermined intents and simple knowledge base (Dowell & Kovanović, 2022). The emergence of transformer-based models and LLMs (GPT, Claude, PaLM) has completely regerminated the scope of Conversational AI, and enabled a more fluid, context-aware, and semantically rich environment between learners and systems.

As per recent studies, such models have the potential to impart not merely the content but they also foster critical thinking, self-reflection, and the ability to problem solve as a result of Socratic questioning and the inquiry-based dialogue (LaGrotta & Shahbazi, 2024). Research has indicated that conversational agents have the potential to improve student engagement, enhance learning results, and offer timely and customized feedback thus resembling the success of the one-to-one human-based tutoring. Along with this, adoption of emotional intelligence, user modeling and adaptive learning pathways in conversational systems has allowed usage of AI tutors to identify the intent of the learner, evaluate their emotional balance and deliver responses that can be individually customized based on the needs and their learning context preferences (Zhang, 2024). Use has been wide-ranging, covering topics as language learning, STEM education, academic writing and test preparation, but it has been highly successful in boosting motivation and retention.

The essential problems are also outlined in literature. Most chatbots are unable to engage in a long conversation and keep themselves consistent, deal with open-ended questions, and be factually accurate(Akgün & Krajcik, 2024). The issue of privacy of information, the bias of algorithms, and transparency of AI decisions remains the subjects of concern in academic contexts. Scientists indicate the necessity of powerful dialogue management modules, which would regulate the back-and-forth and ensure a certain relevance of the discussion as far as the context of open-domain tutoring is regarded (Gobert et al., 2024). Also, high linguistic quality that generative models provide is threatened by conversational drift and hallucination, which may lead to mislearning. These responses have suggested a hybrid of scripted framework and generative elements to attempt to find a middle ground between the control and the creativity. Moreover, they only have universal design and culturally sensitive materials that cannot be included in those systems, and thus are unavailable globally.

Researchers also raise the issue of the lack of cooperation between developers of AI and education practitioners, making their systems potentially excellent in a technical sense and deficient in pedagogical sense(Balta, 2024). With continuing maturity in conversational AI, future research is becoming focused to incorporate a multimodal data feed, including speech, gestures and visual information to develop more immersive and interactive training modules. There is also the potential study of emotional scaffolding, metacognitive reminders, and motivation feedback in order to promote learner autonomy and resilience (Drewery et al., 2022). All said, the literature shows a bright future of conversational AI in education though it demonstrates that technological solutions should be supported by proper instructional design frameworks, ethics and in-depth integration into classrooms practices (Aballa Nkechi et al., 2024). The above insights are the underpinnings towards the creation of intelligently compassionate, and culturally conscious AI tutors that can assist in providing equitable and meaningful learning opportunities across learning environments by learners who are diverse.

MAIN FOCUS OF THE CHAPTER

The major attention of this chapter is devoted to discussing how Conversational AI, facilitated by the recent achievements in NLP and LLMs is transforming the world of education due to the inclusion of intelligent, responsive, and personalized tutoring systems (Tang, 2024). Conversational AI tutors break this barrier since they involve learners in human-like tutoring based on engaging conversation, unlike conventional digital learning tools, that provide stagnant content delivery. In this chapter, attention is paid to the innovative capacity of such systems to provide adaptive feedback, encourage the use of inquiry-based learning and support student autonomy (Karpagavalli, 2024). The chapter allocates a lot of space in discussing the main technological blocks underlying conversational AI such as intent recognition, dialogue management, question answering, and personalized response generation (Müller et al., 2018). These modules help AI tutors to make sense of what students provide, contextualize them, and act in different contexts meaningfully. The chapter also implies several types of deployment, including scripted tutoring systems to the open-domain generative AI agents, and discusses their usage implications to the instructional design and words with the learners. Also, the chapter explores the real-life applications of K-12, higher education and professional training, e.g. AI-based writing aids, STEM problem solvers and language tutors. It points out the benefits of applying conversational AI to facilitate differentiated instruction and the needs of various learners (Avc et al., 2025). Also, of primary importance, the chapter touches upon important issues of privacy on the data used, algorithmic fairness, cultural awareness, and AI utilization ethics in education. The chapter provides an in-depth overview of how conversational AI is likely to become one of the pillars of the next-generation educational ecosystems by bringing together technical, pedagogical, and ethical insights.

PROPOSED METHODOLOGY

The development of a Conversational AI Tutor system using a modular, learner-focused approach rests on the principles of sophisticated NLP applications and Real-Time adaptive feedback systems. This framework begins with Student Interaction Layer where learners interact through use of multimodal inputs which may take a form of text, voice or gestures. These inputs are divided into parts and depending on the tokenization, entities realization, and purpose, the NLP Engine decides what the learner wants to know. Then, the Dialogue Management System is used in controlling a conversation flow, keeping in context and everything in the dialogue, using Socratic questioning to cause critical thinking. The Response Generation module uses domain knowledge base, incorporates emotional intelligence algorithms and makes feedback personal with past performance of a learner. Output Delivery layer also provides understanding on how responses are communicated through proper formats in order to increase accessibility. Lastly, the Learning Analytics & Feedback Loop constantly checks the activities of a learner, monitors academic progress and updates learning path dynamically. Such a data-guided loop guarantees that the system is sensitive, customized, and pedagogically oriented. The methodology focuses on ethical design, inclusion of the cognitive theory and real-time individualization, to aid various learners in K-12, higher education, and workplace learning.

PROPOSED STUDY SCHEMATIC DIAGRAM

The Figure 1 demonstrates the functional stratified architecture of a conversational AI tutor system, how the interaction is scaled by a student to delivery of smart feedback. The Student Interaction Layer is the first layer in which students can interact using a number of the available Input Modalities e.g. voice, gestures or text. The NLP Engine tokenizes, identifies the intent, and extracts the entity of these inputs. That process is then managed by the Dialogue Management System through the process of conversation tracking, flow control and Socratic questioning logic. On these grounds, the Response Generation layer receives knowledge, personalized feedback, and involves emotional intelligence to practice adaptive responses. Output sends the results; text or voice and the Learning Analytics and the Feedback Loop receives data on how, what, and how well and trains the system to do it better every time with a closed feedback loop. The architecture focuses on the active and responsive interpreter-based and student-based nature of AI-based tutoring systems.

Figure 1. Functional Architecture of a Conversational AI Tutor System

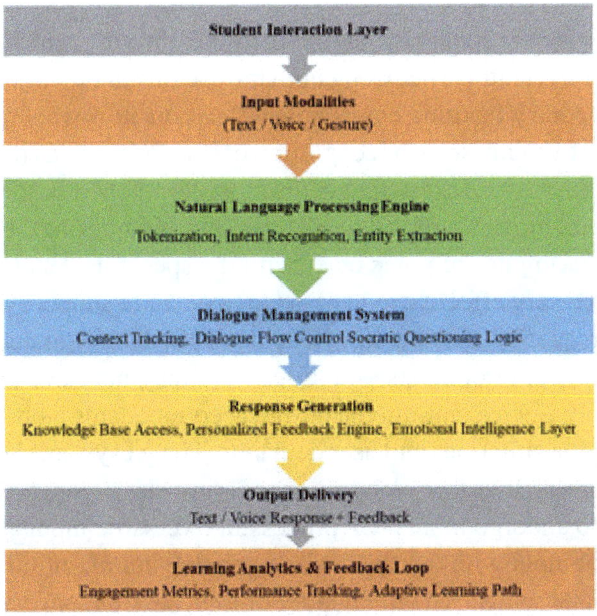

STUDENT INTERACTION LAYER

That is the point where the conversational AI tutor is entered by the learners. It is the interface or platform, such as a chatbot, web application, mobile application, or voice assistant, the students may avail of, to experience the system. This layer gathers the queries, questions or requests by the learners and passes them to the processing components. Depending on the design of a system, the interaction could be synchronous or asynchronous. It also has accessibility by offering intuitive UX/UI features to support the needs of various learners such as users with disabilities. One of the major roles that this layer plays is to launch individualized sessions depending on the profile, past performance and preferences of the student. It monitors the history of interaction, user behavior and session context to provide continuity and flexibility of learning. Initial greetings, directions scaffold or prompts that will direct students are also done in this layer. Stated briefly, the layer of student interactions also acts as the channel of communication between the student and AI tutor and determines the mood of interaction, emotional safety on the border of digital learning environments, and the sense of agency therein.

INPUT MODALITIES (TEXT / VOICE / GESTURE)

Input modalities are identified as the methods through which the student can communicate with AI tutor. The strong human-machine interaction of today implies that in a contemporary learning environment, learners now want more flexible approaches, e.g. text-typing, speech recognition or even gestures as means of inclusive and multimodal learning. Text typing is the most common, it is adopted in chatbots and internet interaction, where one can represent his question and issue clearly. There is an increasing use of voice enter with the speech-to-text technologies, and voice input can be very effective to learn a language or to support visually impaired learners. Less frequently, gesture input may be applied to Augmented Reality (AR) or in virtual world environments where learners may not have access to enough speech or mobility. Such a multimodal design accommodates more people and cater to different learning situations and user demands. The AI system should be provided with the input parsers, interface recognition tools in order to convert these inputs into structured data to undergo more NLP processing. Versatile input allows embracing various modes of input with the system being more natural, intuitive, and closer to a human-like avatar which is a vital quality of a successful conversational tutor AI.

NATURAL LANGUAGE PROCESSING (NLP) ENGINE

The heart of the linguistic analyser of the system is the NLP engine. It converts unstructured human input, typed or spoken, to structured ones that the AI is able to interpret. It comprises of tokenization, where sentences are split into words or subwords. This is then followed by intent recognition where it recognizes a learner goal, that is, a question, a clarification or a feedback request. Subsequently, the entity extraction recognizes important subjects, concepts, or values (i.e. equations, dates, terms) in the input. Such operations make the system not only realize the meaning but also the reality and relevance of the query raised by the student. The newer generations of NLP engines (such as GPT or PaLM) include grammar, syntax, semantics, and even sentiment in their large language models. NLP engine is vital towards facilitated natural, context-sensitive, and dynamic talks. Its capacity to interpret an unclear language, having a proper grammar, and connecting jargon or street language defines how close to a human being and efficient the AI tutor will be to the learners. The engine is the initial key in transforming intention of users into pedagogically appropriate interaction.

DIALOGUE MANAGEMENT SYSTEM

Dialogue Management System (DMS) facilitates how the conversation between AI tutor and the learner occurs. It keeps the interaction continuity, coherence and educationally relevant. Context tracking keeps track of what the learner has already said or been previously doing so that the AI can carry some form of past reference to the queries, answers or performance. The control of the dialogue flow determines the logical order of the communications e.g. it is necessary to give a hint or ask a follow question or change the subject. It either employs the use of decision trees, reinforcement learning or probabilistic model to determine the next action of the system. The logic of Socratic questioning is particularly very important in deep learning where learners are not supposed to offer answers only. It poses thoughtful questions, directs inquiry-based learning and promotes thought. When well designed, DMS adjusts the rate of conversation and the style to suit individual learner behaviour, emotion responses as well as academic objectives. It serves as the educational brain of the AI tutor integrating curriculum logic, adaptive patterns and engagement rules to ensure that interactions remain productive as well as learner-centered.

RESPONSE GENERATION

This element is mandated to create proper, informative and customized responses to the inquiries made by the students. It works on retrieving or creating content of a knowledge base which may encompass textbook, educational resources, and curated learning contents. The automated feedback engine varies the responses according to the current level of knowledge of the student, his history of learning and his learning style. In this context, they might be hints rather than answers, a recommendation of what to do next, or a revision of what has been learned previously. Emotional intelligence level includes the affective side of response- reading frustration, motivation, or confusion in the input of the learner and adjusting message and tone. As an example, in case a student fails on several occasions, the system can provide motivational support or elaborate easier. The result of the new systems is any combination of rule-based templates and generative AI, to generate a diverse, natural, context-sensitive response. The post-processing module keeps the learning loop of input-output between the learner and the AI sensationally supportive, humanlike and pedagogically intentional. In the end, generation of responses will be the deciding factor of how much the AI tutor will actually seem alive and intelligent to the learner.

OUTPUT DELIVERY

Output Delivery is the layer on which the system delivered feedbacks are sent back to the learner in a straightforward, appealing, and inclusive manner. The result may be textual, like it would be best when the user needed to elaborate or use it within academic writing and should be composed in voice, which is particularly helpful with language learning, audibly-delighted learners, or accessibility requirements. It is not only the answers to questions but also the application of some motivational stimulus, aids or follow-up questions to assess deeper comprehension. One major role here is the alignment of future output format to the current mode of input i.e. a user may communicate through voice, and the responses may be in form of speech output via text to speech engines. The delivery system aids in ensuring accuracy of responses as far as grammar, pedagogy and the instructional objective is concerned. It also involves the use of the visual/interactive materials, that is, the charts/diagrams, where necessary. The active functionality of this layer is that it can make complex concepts digestible and more entertaining, therefore, sealing the information interpretation gap between AI and a human system.

LEARNING ANALYTICS & FEEDBACK LOOP

The information created through the interactions of the learner is analyzed and captured by this module to improve the process of tutoring and aid long term academic development. Engagement measures the frequency and level of interaction with the AI as well as the duration, frequency, and response. Performance tracking measures the dynamics of student development- that is, which of the concepts are already mastered, in what areas mistakes are made, and how the performance improves. These analytics facilitate the determination of learning gaps and trend of behavior. The adaptive learning path component can apply such lessons to localizing future material and tutoring advice. The information in this layer provides feedback to the dialogue and response generation systems thus creating a feedback cycle of continuous improvement. In addition, the insights can be used by an educator to report or plan intervention. This layer guarantees that the AI tutor stays alive, sensitive and developing in accordance with the requirement of the learner thus fostering effective, humanitarian and quantifiable outcomes of learning. It closes the circle of smart and data-led educational support.

CASE STUDIES

Education with Conversational AI tutors is changing the interaction between students and content, growth of skills, and individual assistance altogether. Examples of real-life applications, such as Duolingo and Carnegie learnings are important in showing how NLP technology can be used to improve learning performance in various learning settings and environments. Duolingo Max takes advantage of contextual GPT based language models to recreate language conversations in any language, delivering contextual feedback on communication, explanation of grammar, and adaptive conversation experience. This method has led to massive increase in involvement, confidence, and retention levels among learners especially through reducing anxiety in speaking activities (Sengul et al., 2024). But Mika assists the students undergoing algebra problems most of whom are college students by providing step-by-step information, analysis of errors, and inquiry. In use in community colleges, it has aided in an increase in the pass rates and performance that is more academically proficient, particularly regarding resource-poor contexts. These examples show how versatile and powerful conversational AI can be used in informal and formal learning (Tang, 2024). They emphasize the benefits of a such kind of system, such as nurturing personalized, adaptable, and scaled learning, serving a variety of learners via smart, compassionate, and pedagogy-informed conversation.

CASE STUDY 1: DUOLINGO'S AI TUTOR FOR LANGUAGE LEARNING

Duolingo is one of the most popular language training websites in the world and one of its most recent features, called Duolingo Max, is a language learning conversational AI tutor, powered by GPT technologies. The use of this AI tutor integrates the use of the sophisticated NLP and transformer-based models to mirror natural and real-life communication that is multi-lingual in nature (Otermans et al., 2024). Duolingo Max, unlike previous versions of chatbots, is created to support a variety of rich responses and dialog, in-context grammar explanation and remediation, and fluency and progress-based correction. The AI does not only wait to react to input by the learners, but also initiates a dialogue in order to maintain a conversation and encourage language memorization (Thomas et al., 2024). One of the most interesting aspects of the system is the ability to learn the new language through the application of the functionalities called the Explanation of My Answer or the Roleplay mode, through which the user will be able to comprehend their errors and train in a natural conversation in expert scenarios with a highly detailed experience.

Duolingo shared internal research results that showed a 35% difference in speaking confidence among learners who used Duolingo Max compared with those who did not use the AI-powered tool, a 28% difference in vocabulary recall and a 23% increase in the rate of lesson completion in a six-month study (Baumgart & Madany Mamlouk, 2022). Additionally, more than 70% of users testified that the AI tutor made them feel less anxious when it comes to speaking real-time languages, which provides a psychologically safe environment to practice them. The system worked best with beginner and intermediate learners, who did not feel judged and loved experimenting and learning with their mistakes (Meng & Yang, 2025). This makes the success of Duolingo Max an example of how NLP and generative AI can support adjustments and changes, provide empathetic as well as scalable language learning experiences, adapting to the needs of individual learners to ensure high engagement. The case in question is indicative of the possible role of conversational AI tutors in the new education paradigm of informal and app-based studies between the extremes of static content delivery and full-fledged individual tutoring experience (Orucov, 2025). The Figure 2 that shows the quantified effect of Duolingo Max, a conversational AI-programmed language tutor on the significant metrics of learner performance. The four learning outcomes are Speaking Confidence, Vocabulary Recall, Lesson Completion Rate, and Reduced Speaking Anxiety. The % change or favorable response of the learner at each measure is indicated at the y-axis. Duolingo internal research indicate that users in Duolingo Max demonstrated improved speaking confidence with a 35% increase, 28% improvement in vocabulary recall, and 23% increase in lesson completion. Remarkably, 70% of the users stated a drastic decrease in the anxiety of speaking. The findings point to the capability of the system to present scalable, empathetic, and personalized language learning opportunities through NLP and transformer bases models.

Figure 2. Impact of Duolingo Max on Learner Outcomes

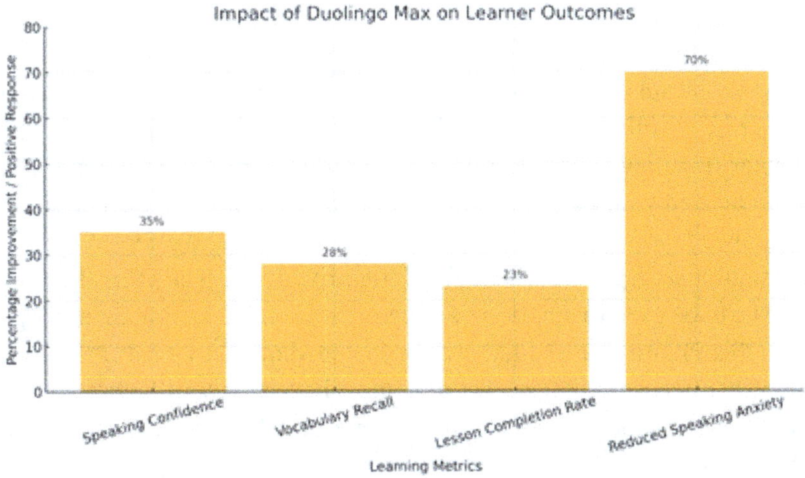

CASE STUDY 2: CARNEGIE LEARNING'S MIKA PLATFORM IN COLLEGE ALGEBRA

Carnegie Learning touts its Mika system as an interesting demonstration of a conversational tutor based on AI in how it can change the results at the higher-ed level in particularly demanding courses such as college-level algebra (Nazaretsky et al., 2024). Mika is an AI based tutoring program that was created to guide community college students, most of whom have limited access to live tutors, through mathematical problems by step. Mika is based on both rule-based logic and NLP technologies. It can detect frequent student mistakes, give explanations in context, and ask probing questions to promote critical thinking, and conceptual learning (Zhai et al., 2021). The AI is dynamic and adjusts to each learner and his/her past performance and pace, creating a mastery-based and personalized learning environment. Institutional checks show that colleges implementing Mika had an average improvement of 22% in student pass rates with some registering up to 25% improvement compared to classrooms without the AI tutor (Popenici & Kerr, 2017). Moreover, there was a 31% increased use of the platform by the students when they were using it at night and over the weekend when the instructor is otherwise not available.

The survey of the learners showed that 68% of the students were more confident when solving problems in algebra which was after applying Mika and 61% had clear understanding of the basic mathematical concepts. This had a particularly strong effect on the first-generation and underrepresented students who have otherwise had greater risks of dropout (Xu, 2024). The real-time, personalized, automated feedback, which was part of the platform offering allowed the company to scale the support to the spheres of both large and diverse pupil and student populations. Mika allowed the colleges to bridge the instructional gaps and enhance the learning outcomes in college consistently and cost-effectively because it minimized the reliance on face-to-face tutoring tools (Németh et al., 2024). This case study has indicated how conversational AI -tutor such as Mika can be effectively used in the academic field that requires high levels of cognitive support and this shows the level at which AI can be used to democratize access to quality learning in under privilege settings. In this Figure 3, the Mika AI tutor system demonstrates its influence on the outcome of learners in college-level algebra. The x-axis will have four indicators of learning performances namely, Improvement in Pass Rates, Increased Usage (Night/Weekend), Confidence in Solving Problems, and Conceptual Understanding. The y-axis indicates improvement in terms of percentage or positive response to learners as reported by institutions and other students who use Mika. The results indicate that the pass rates increased by 25%, the use of the platform outside the presence of the instructor rose by 31% student confidence improved by 68% and conceptual understanding by 61%. These findings show that Mika performs well regarding scalable, customized, and time-based educational assistance particularly in the context of risky students and minority students. This number belongs to the future of conversational AI tutors in terms of closing the instruction gap and helping to improve academic performance in resource-scarce environments.

Figure 3. Impact of Mika AI Tutor on College Algebra Outcomes

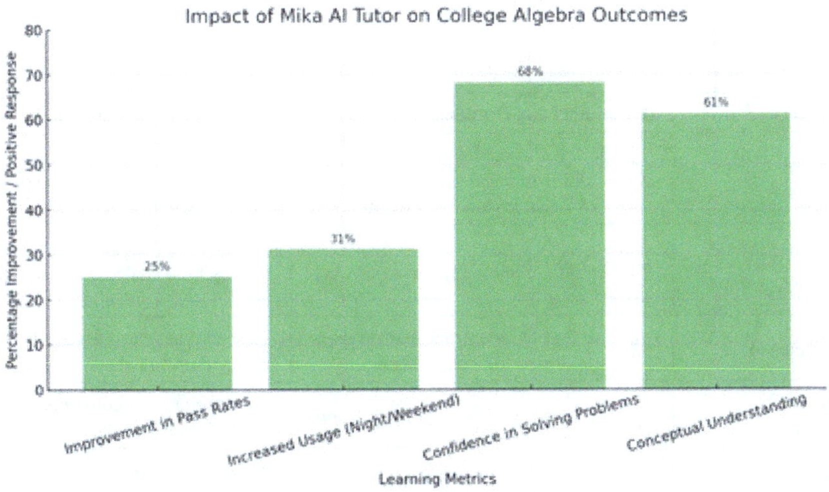

COMPARATIVE CASE STUDY ANALYSIS: DUOLINGO MAX VS. MIKA PLATFORM

The table 1 presents a comparative analysis of two AI-powered tutoring systems Duolingo Max and Mika highlighting their technologies, features, impact, and applicability. It illustrates how conversational AI adapts across domains to enhance personalized learning outcomes.

Table 1 Comparative Analysis of Duolingo Max and Carnegie Learning's Mika Platform

Parameter	Duolingo Max (Language Learning)	Mika (College Algebra)
Target Domain	Language learning (Multilingual)	College-level Algebra
Technology Used	GPT-powered Conversational AI, Transformer-based NLP	Rule-based + NLP-powered AI Tutor
Core Functionalities	Roleplay mode, Explanation of Answers, Real-life language simulations	Step-by-step problem solving, Error analysis, Reflective questioning
Adaptive Features	Fluency-based feedback, Grammar correction, Progress tracking	Personalized pacing, Performance-based content adaptation

continued on following page

Continued

Table 1 Comparative Analysis of Duolingo Max and Carnegie Learning's Mika Platform

Parameter	Duolingo Max (Language Learning)	Mika (College Algebra)
Impact on Performance	35% ↑ in speaking confidence 28% ↑ in vocabulary recall 23% ↑ in lesson completion	22–25% ↑ in pass rates 68% ↑ in confidence 61% ↑ in conceptual understanding
Emotional & Psychological Impact	70% reported reduced speaking anxiety	High impact on first-gen and underserved students' confidence and retention
Usage Behavior	Effective for beginner/intermediate users; app-based informal learning	Increased use during night/weekends; highly useful in absence of instructors
Scalability & Accessibility	High available globally via mobile app	High deployed in community colleges, scalable for large cohorts
Strengths	Empathetic, low-anxiety practice, immersive conversation	Deep cognitive support, mastery-based progression
Challenges Noted	May require strong internet access; limited for advanced fluency learners	Limited to math; potential over-reliance without instructor integration

SOLUTIONS AND RECOMMENDATIONS

It is recommended to consider a variety of strategic solutions and recommendations that will assist mobilizing the opportunities of conversational AI tutors in the educational domain. Firstly, it is essential here that pedagogical alignment which will be the focus of AI systems would be designed, in partnership with the teachers, so that they would be able to affect not only patterns of learning and learning outcomes but also the cognitive development of the young learners, rather than merely delivering the content (Garc\'\ia-Méndez et al., 2024). The thing is that Socratic questioning and feedback loops can be incorporated to facilitate critical thinking and increased comprehension. Second, the design is essential in terms of being ethical. The ways that developers can solve the privacy of data, algorithmic bias and learner autonomy issues include implementing transparent privacy policies of data usage, fairness mechanisms and auditing and personalization as an opt-in feature (Wei, 2024).

Third, the implementation of hybrid systems, which is the integration of knowledge-based tutoring and generative AI, will help to reference accuracy and flexibility, enabling consistency of speech and flexibility. Moreover, conversational AI ought to be culturally aware and accessible to diversity, including accommodating multilingual interface and putting into consideration disability as well as diverse learners. The other area that institutions need to be investing is teacher-AI models of collaboration where the teacher can monitor and offer instructional guidance and reinforce what the AI-based instruction provides. Lastly, it is significant to continuously evaluate and optimize the system based on learner data and feedback to enhance its efficiency over time (Otermans et al., 2024). Those strategies can make conversational AI tutors a game changer in the education sector, with scalable, personalize and equitable education experiences applicable at various academic levels and in various academic courses. The Figure 4 identifies six major strategic areas in which conversational AI tutors can effectively be implemented in order of their importance.

Figure 4. Strategic Solutions for Effective Conversational AI Tutors

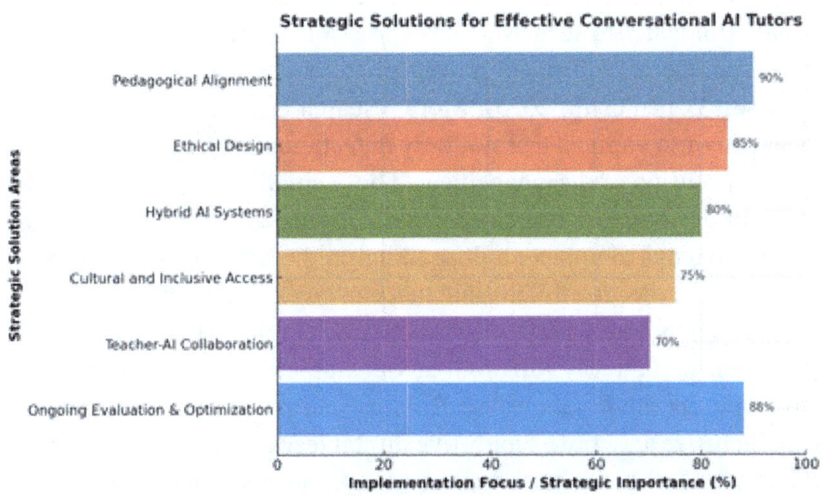

FUTURE RESEARCH DIRECTIONS

Conversational AI is in its implementation stage, and there is certainly need to explore their potential with the assistance of targeted cross-cutting studies since it is rewriting the table in the educational paradigms (Herb & Lloyd, 2024). Whereas the current systems offer a full-fledged, individually-designed, and enjoyable learning experience, several questions must be addressed to ensure that these technologies become tangible in pedagogy, ethics, and technology. The three highest-ranked future research topics, which are (1) Adopting Emotional Intelligence and Empathy in AI Tutors, (2) Creating Multimodal and Multilingual Tutoring Interfaces, and (3) Defining Ethical Frameworks and Fairness in AI-driven Education.

ENHANCING EMOTIONAL INTELLIGENCE AND EMPATHY IN AI TUTORS

The fact that existing conversational AI tutors do not have the capability to have Emotional Intelligence (EI) is one of the largest drawbacks of this kind of tutor. Even though some systems can reproduce empathy by analysing sentiments, or programmed reactions, they are not by far as responsive to emotion as humans (Korhonen et al., 2023). The aspects of integration of affective computing and emotion recognition algorithms in conversation systems should be addressed in the further studies. This includes multimodal data such as facial expression, the tone of the voice, key-stroke patterns, physiological information in order to pinpoint the emotion of the learner more precisely (Chen et al., 2025). More research is necessary to develop flexible emotional response engines that not only detect, but also react in real time to student stress, confusion or disengagement. These emotionally sensitive tutors would be capable of customizing encouragement, varying the speed of teaching or even converting pedagogical approach depending on the mood of the learners (Macina et al., 2023). The other fruitful avenue that can be explored involves examining the role of emotionally intelligent AI on motivation, self-efficacy, and perseverance among students particularly with high-anxiety topics such as mathematics or public speaking. Appropriate emotional scaffolding can minimise the dropout rates and lead to an inclusive and more supportive digital learning space (Wang et al., 2023). The ethical boundary between adaptive support, and emotional manipulation should also be investigated in the future to guarantee a self-respecting and learner-focused interaction with AI.

DEVELOPING MULTIMODAL AND MULTILINGUAL TUTORING INTERFACES

This brings the second era of conversational AI in education the building of multimodal and multilingual interfaces that would make education more available, non-exclusive and fun. Multimodal AI Multi modal AI would be the systems able to both process and respond to some combination of text, speech, images, video, gestures and haptic feedback, and have that better represent the natural human interaction than all the current text-based systems. It has to be found out how the speech recognition, computer vision, and the tactile sensors can be incorporated to serve learners with various needs, like students with disabilities, low-level literacy levels, or early childhood students. As an example, augmented reality visual explanation in combination with verbal instruction may be used to increase understanding in geometry, physics, or anatomy. At the same time, multilingualism is essential in order to disregard the linguistic boundaries and make AI tutoring more democratic. Although LLMs such as GPT-4 have multilingual capabilities, their performance differs greatly across languages, particularly regional and underrepresented language (Goel & Ghanta, 2025). To make it more inclusive, studies may strive to localize models and tailor them with culturally appropriate information, data in local dialect, and the varied phonetics. A multimodal and multilingual design will result in universal tutoring systems that become customized across different cultural, linguistic and cognitive settings. The systems would be instrumental in international education projects due to allowing the conversational AI tutors to become fair and transnationally usable.

ESTABLISHING ETHICAL FRAMEWORKS AND FAIRNESS IN AI-DRIVEN EDUCATION

Due to the ever-increasing integration of conversational AI tutors in the educational setting, the necessity of addressing this aspect in its entirety necessitates a more rapid creation of comprehensive ethical models (Akavova et al., 2023). Such frameworks need to touch upon the question of data privacy, algorithmic bias, transparency, and learner autonomy. To date, the AI-based tutoring platforms are used without clear understanding of the data collection and retention, including the information about ways and the extent to which the learner data is processed which creates a possibility of surveillance, profiling, and possible misuse. In the future, a special focus should be given to the development of privacy-preserving architectures, including federated learning or homomorphic encryption, by means of which AI systems may learn with distributed data without violating the confidentiality of individuals(Molloy et al., 2020). The second domain of importance is the detection and solving of the biases in AI models, be they linguistic, cultural, socioeconomic, or gender. Training data biasness may cause unequal support to the learning process, thus reinforcing inequalities. Also, Explainable AIs (XAI) are required to be studied so that learners, educators, and administrators can trust decisions made by AI tutors and comprehend it(de Carvalho & Zárate, 2020). Studies must also work on a development of AI systems that will not violate the autonomy of the learners, and will allow the option to override or modify AI behaviors. Institutionalization of ethical design should also be done in terms of regulations and policies, teaching standards, and teacher-training programs. These initiatives will assist in ensuring that conversational AI tutors will bring long-term educational justice, integrity, and subjective well-being.

INTEGRATION WITH COGNITIVE SCIENCE AND PEDAGOGICAL THEORY

Lack of adequate combination of cognitive science and educational theory in system designs is also one of the most important research gaps in the design of conversational AI tutors. Most current examples of AI tutors are dense to precisely worded responses and fluency and dialogue in response to them, but fail to form complicated knowledge acquisition pathways based on pedagogical design (Dai et al., 2023). In future studies, researchers ought to examine how the principles of constructivism, behaviourism, and connectivism can be written into the AI algorithms to provide response as well as developmentally appropriate and cognitively consistent instruction. Also, the management of cognitive load needs to be investigated, including the possibility to use AI tutors to scaffold information, pace the problems, and focus the feedback according to the proficiency of the learner (Hattie & Timperley, 2007). Selective injection of metacognitive cues can enhance level of comprehension and foster long-term recalling. The transfer of learning is a second area of focus, which investigates how AI can be used to ensure students successfully transfer concepts to other areas or reality. AI tutors constructed in these same cognitive principles will better mirror more expert human instructors and develop critical thinking, problem-solving, and fineness (Ji et al., 2024). Future systems should be fully trialled in real-life classrooms, as well as interdisciplinary, to ensure the educational validity of systems.

COLLABORATION BETWEEN HUMAN TEACHERS AND AI TUTORS

The prospect of AI education has nothing to do with taking away teaching jobs, but rather helping a teacher to be able to provide high-quality, personalized training. It is imperative that research is carried out into the human-AI collaboration modelling to create a system that would be effective as a co-teacher instead of an independent replacement (Liu et al., 2023). The next area of research needs to center around constructing teacher dashboards with the ability to combine the knowledge produced by AI tutors in their daily instruction planning. Research is needed into how educators can intervene, personalize, and oversight the AI tutor interactions that can and still lack the emotional and pedagogical support that is unique to the teachers. It is also required to conduct a study of the perception and trust of the AI systems of the educators and what training would be required to allow them to become ethical and size confident users of these systems (Morales-Chan et al., 2024). The other direction of research is the identification of the role boundaries, i.e., which teaching functions should be fulfilled by a human or AI. The cooperative AI tutors must be developed to complement the instructor abilities, process regular mental workloads, and permit the instructors to concentrate more on elevated-order coaching, empathizing, and critical intercessions (Pardo et al., 2018). Finally, the prospect that teachers and AI tutors would be able to collaborate harmoniously in the future would mean having classrooms of the future that are highly technological but also highly humanistic where learning outcome of all students can be maximized.

Evaluating Long-term Impact and Learning Outcomes

Although AI-based systems of tutoring prove to be effective instantaneously as per the interaction and learning outcomes, the long-term educational effects are unexplored. One of the future research areas is the longitudinal study aimed at the evaluation of the impact of conversational AI on academic performance, independence, retention, and lifelong learning behavior in the long run (Sugianti & Rosidah, 2024). In that respect, one of the questions that need to be answered is whether using AI tutors excessively might weaken persistence in solving problems or lead to the weakening of the importance of peer collaboration. To manage this, the researchers will have to develop the frameworks, which will capture the quantitative results (scores in the tests, completion rates) and qualitative progress (self-efficacy, motivation, critical thinking). The effects that AI tutors have on the levels of equity in learning is also of interest will AI tutors be truly bridging achievement gaps (M. Panit, 2025). It also requires cross-cultural research in order to determine the difference in the results of learning related to linguistic, cultural and socio-economic background. The development of common assessment procedures and achievement criteria will allow making a comparison among AI tutoring systems as well as situations. Lastly, it should be investigated how conversational AI can inform lifelong learning and in particular how it could be applied in the context of professional and adult learning based on adapting to personal life and career goals, as well as professional transitions. To legitimize the presence of AI tutors as a long-term sustainable growing portion of the learning environment on earth, it is necessary to identify their educational legacy.

CONCLUSION

The introduction of Conversational AI tutors into learning environments will serve as the paradigm shift as it will change the way learners approach the material, acquire cognitive and emotional proficiencies, and access individualized instructions. This chapter has discussed in detail how conversational AI systems, which operate on NLP and LLMs, can evolve, be more capable and respond more intelligently and empathetically to become a learning companion as opposed to a medium of delivering content. Whether it was historical rule-based tutoring systems and transformer-based ones such as GPT, Claude, or PaLM, a recurring pattern is the movement toward an AI agent that can be considered more human-like, adaptive, and context-aware, scaffolding in the way a real tutor can. Key constituents of an effective conversational AI tutor, including intents recognition, dialogue management, response generation, and learning analytics, were addressed in terms of how they allow the creation of personalized inquiry-based, and emotionally sustaining educational activities. Such systems now can be applied to support a real-time, interactive conversation that can support multiple input modalities (text, voice, gesture) and that can respond multimodally, in multiple languages, and be empathetic.

This allows AI tutors to support learners who are of varying age groups, disciplines, and geographical regions, whether it be in the K-12 education or higher education and job training context. Drawing on specific case studies such as Duolingo Max and Mika platform of Carnegie Learning, the chapter revealed the usefulness of AI tutors in improving engaging, retaining, and performance of learners. Examples include Duolingo Max, which raised speech confidence by 35% and lesson completion by 23%, and Mika, which improved the results of under-resourced college algebra students by 22 and 25%. The given examples substantiate that conversational AI in the future can contribute to delivering effective and inclusive scalable and adaptive learning solutions. However, there exist some barriers in the path to high usage of conversational AI tutors. Conversational drift issues, lack of explanatory ability, data privacy, fairness of algorithms, and the low degree of emotional intelligence are valuable questions to explore.

The chapter also placed much focus on the ethical design, regulation, and inclusive development processes that must be involved in order to see that these technologies will benefit all learners in a fair manner. These qualities as multimodal interaction, cultural sensitivity, and alignment with the principles of universal design were also highlighted as prior requirements of developing globally applicable and learner-centric AI systems. The list of suggestions provided, including the idea of incorporating pedagogical theory, collaboration between teachers and AI, and constant improved with the help of learning analytics emphasized the necessity of human in the loop approach. Rather than becoming teachers, AI tutors can be used as co-facilitators to the extent that they can complement the abilities of the latter and allow them to concentrate on the higher-order mentoring process, empathy, and creativity.

Going into the future, further studies should build on refinements in emotional intelligence of the AI, and diversity in multimodal and multilingual functions, as well as an ethical and cognitive foundation. The teamwork across disciplines among AI developers, educators, psychologists and policy makers will be essential in crafting AI tutors that are not only intelligent, but also in the trustworthiness of AI, empathic, and pedagogically responsible as well. Overall, conversational AI tutors will be a paradigm shift in education in that it is the much-needed bridge between the technological improvement and humanity-centered education. When created and used in a responsible way, they will be able to democratize access to quality education, leverage the potential of learners regardless of the environment, and become the key element of teaching and learning in the new era.

REFERENCES

Aarthi, S., Ravikumar, R. N., Khudayberganov, S., Ismailov, A., & Khujaniyozova, O. (2025). Using Intelligent Tutoring Systems to enhance student engagement. In *Advances in Computational Intelligence and Robotics* (pp. 155–188). IGI Global. DOI: 10.4018/979-8-3373-1827-1.ch008

Aballa Nkechi, A., & Ojo, O. A., & A. Eneh, O. (2024). Impact of artificial intelligence in achieving quality education. In *Artificial Intelligence and Education - Shaping the Future of Learning [Working Title]*. IntechOpen.

Akavova, A., Temirkhanova, Z., & Lorsanova, Z. (2023). Adaptive learning and artificial intelligence in the educational space. *E3S Web Conf., 451*, 6011.

Akgün, S., & Krajcik, J. (2024). Artificial intelligence (AI) as the growing actor in education. In *Uses of Artificial Intelligence in STEM Education* (pp. 494–521). Oxford University PressOxford. DOI: 10.1093/oso/9780198882077.003.0022

Avc, G., Owusu-Boateng, O., Vampa, M., & Khalid, A.-M. (2025). Intelligent tutoring systems. In *Deep Science Publishing* (pp. 46–57). Deep Science Publishing. DOI: 10.70593/978-93-49307-53-7_4

Balta, N. (2024). Artificial Intelligence Pedagogical Content Knowledge. *Eur. Educ. Res.*, 1–3.

Baumgart, A., & Madany Mamlouk, A. (2022). A knowledge-model for AI-driven tutoring systems. In *Frontiers in Artificial Intelligence and Applications*. IOS Press.

Borchers, C., Wang, Y., Karumbaiah, S., Ashiq, M., Shaffer, D. W., & Aleven, V. (2024). Revealing networks: Understanding effective teacher practices in AI-supported classrooms using transmodal ordered network analysis. *Proceedings of the 14th Learning Analytics and Knowledge*, 371–381. DOI: 10.1145/3636555.3636892

Bulathwela, S., Pérez-Ortiz, M., Holloway, C., Cukurova, M., & Shawe-Taylor, J. (2024). Artificial Intelligence alone will not democratise education: On educational inequality, techno-solutionism and inclusive tools. *Sustainability (Basel), 16*(2), 781. DOI: 10.3390/su16020781

Chen, X., Xie, H., Qin, S. J., Wang, F. L., & Hou, Y. (2025). Artificial intelligence-supported student engagement research: Text mining and systematic analysis. *European Journal of Education, 60*(1), e70008. DOI: 10.1111/ejed.70008

Dai, W., Lin, J., Jin, H., Li, T., Tsai, Y.-S., Gašević, D., & Chen, G. (2023, July). Can large language models provide feedback to students? A case study on ChatGPT. *2023 IEEE International Conference on Advanced Learning (ICALT)*. DOI: 10.1109/ICALT58122.2023.00100

de Carvalho, W. F., & Zárate, L. E. (2020). A new local causal learning algorithm applied in learning analytics. *Int. J. Inf. Learn. Technol.*, *38*(1), 103–115. DOI: 10.1108/IJILT-04-2020-0046

Dowell, N., & Kovanović, V. (2022). Modeling educational discourse with natural language processing. In *The Handbook of Learning Analytics* (pp. 105–119). SOLAR. DOI: 10.18608/hla22.011

Drewery, D., Woodside, J., & Eppel, K. (2022). Artificial Intelligence and Résumé Critique Experiences. *Cjcd*, *21*(2), 28–39. DOI: 10.53379/cjcd.2022.338

Garc\'\ia-Méndez, S., de Arriba-Pérez, F., & Somoza-López, M. del C. (2024). A review on the use of large language models as virtual tutors. *Sci. & Educ.*

Gobert, J. D., Li, H., Dickler, R., & Lott, C. (2024). Can AI-based scaffolding promote students' robust learning of authentic science practices? In *Uses of Artificial Intelligence in STEM Education* (pp. 250–268). Oxford University PressOxford. DOI: 10.1093/oso/9780198882077.003.0012

Goel, P., & Ghanta, S. (2025). *Assessing large language models for math tutoring effectiveness*. J Emerg Invest. DOI: 10.59720/24-117

Hattie, J., & Timperley, H. (2007). The power of feedback. *Review of Educational Research*, *77*(1), 81–112. DOI: 10.3102/003465430298487

Herb, A., & Lloyd, C. (2024). The future of feedback. *ASCILITE Publications*, 141–142.

Ji, H., Suo, L., & Chen, H. (2024). AI performance assessment in blended learning: Mechanisms and effects on students' continuous learning motivation. *Frontiers in Psychology*, *15*, 1447680. DOI: 10.3389/fpsyg.2024.1447680 PMID: 39737232

Kang, J., Kang, C., Yoon, J., Ji, H., Li, T., Moon, H., Ko, M., & Han, J. (2023). Dancing on the inside: A qualitative study on online dance learning with teacher-AI cooperation. *Education and Information Technologies*, *28*(9), 1–31. DOI: 10.1007/s10639-023-11649-0 PMID: 37361738

Karpagavalli. (2024). ARTIFICIAL INTELLIGENCE BASED TUTOR. In *Futuristic Trends in Information Technology Volume 3 Book 2* (pp. 290–300). Iterative International Publisher, Selfypage Developers Pvt Ltd.

Korhonen, T., Lindqvist, T., Laine, J., & Hakkarainen, K. (2023). Training hard skills in virtual reality: Developing a theoretical framework for AI-based immersive learning. In *AI in Learning: Designing the Future* (pp. 195–213). Springer International Publishing.

Kumar, D., Haque, A., Mishra, K., Islam, F., Kumar Mishra, B., & Ahmad, S. (2023). Exploring the transformative role of artificial intelligence and metaverse in education: A comprehensive review. *Metaverse Basic and Applied Research, 2*, 55. DOI: 10.56294/mr202355

LaGrotta, V., & Shahbazi, Z. (2024, November). Natural Language Processing applications in mechanical engineering education. *Volume 7: Engineering Education.*

Liu, A., Martin, S., Belousov, M., Fung, C. C., Ben-Ari, R., & May, W. (2023). Impact of AI virtual Standardized Patients (AI-VSP) on performance in a clinical skills examination. In *Research Square*. DOI: 10.21203/rs.3.rs-3516363/v1

Macina, J., Daheim, N., Wang, L., Sinha, T., Kapur, M., Gurevych, I., & Sachan, M. (2023). *Opportunities and challenges in neural dialog tutoring.*

Meng, X., & Yang, Y. (2025). Self-evolving generative AI tutors: Reinforcement learning-augmented ITS for personalized, proactive, and context-aware student engagement. In *Research Square*. DOI: 10.21203/rs.3.rs-6107039/v1

Molloy, E., Boud, D., & Henderson, M. (2020). Developing a learning-centred framework for feedback literacy. *Assessment & Evaluation in Higher Education, 45*(4), 527–540. DOI: 10.1080/02602938.2019.1667955

Morales-Chan, M., Amado-Salvatierra, H. R., Medina, J. A., Barchino, R., Hernández-Rizzardini, R., & Teixeira, A. M. (2024). Personalized feedback in Massive Open Online Courses: Harnessing the power of LangChain and OpenAI API. *Electronics (Basel), 13*(10), 1960. DOI: 10.3390/electronics13101960

Müller, S., Bergande, B., & Brune, P. (2018). Robot tutoring. *Proceedings of the 3rd European Conference of Software Education*, 45–49. DOI: 10.1145/3209087.3209093

Nazaretsky, T., Mejia-Domenzain, P., Swamy Vinitra and Frej, J., & Käser, T. (2024). *AI or human? Evaluating student feedback perceptions in higher education.*

Németh, R., Tátrai, A., Szabó, M., & Tamási, Á. (2024). Using a RAG-enhanced large language model in a virtual teaching assistant role: Experiences from a pilot project in statistics education. *Hungarian Statistical Review, 7*(2), 3–27. DOI: 10.35618/hsr2024.02.en003

Ni, A., & Cheung, A. (2023). Understanding secondary students' continuance intention to adopt AI-powered intelligent tutoring system for English learning. *Education and Information Technologies*, *28*(3), 3191–3216. DOI: 10.1007/s10639-022-11305-z PMID: 36119127

Orucov, V. (2025). Didactics of artificial intelligence in physics education: New approache. *Scientific Works*, *92*(3), 122–125. DOI: 10.69682/arti.2025.92(3).122-125

Otermans, P. C. J., Baines, S., Livingstone, C., & Aditya, D. (2024). Talking technology tutors: The perceptions of conversational AI in education through the eyes of parents and teachers worldwide. In *Research Square*. DOI: 10.21203/rs.3.rs-4231361/v1

Panit, M., N. (. (2025). Can critical thinking and AI work together? Observations of science, Mathematics, and language instructors. *Environ. Soc. Psychol.*, *9*(11). Advance online publication. DOI: 10.59429/esp.v9i11.3141

Pardo, A., Bartimote, K., Buckingham Shum, S., Dawson, S., Gao, J., Gašević, D., Leichtweis, S., Liu, D., Martínez-Maldonado, R., Mirriahi, N., Moskal, A. C. M., Schulte, J., Siemens, G., & Vigentini, L. (2018). OnTask: Delivering data-informed, Personalized Learning Support Actions. *Journal of Learning Analytics*, *5*(3), 235–249. DOI: 10.18608/jla.2018.53.15

Popenici, S. A. D., & Kerr, S. (2017). Exploring the impact of artificial intelligence on teaching and learning in higher education. *Research and Practice in Technology Enhanced Learning*, *12*(1), 22. DOI: 10.1186/s41039-017-0062-8 PMID: 30595727

Putri, N. S. F., Widiharso, P., Utama, A. B. P., Shakti, M. C., & Ghosh, U. (2023). Natural Language Processing in higher education. *Bull.Socinf.The.App*, *6*(1), 90–101. DOI: 10.31763/businta.v6i1.593

Sengul, C., Neykova, R., & Destefanis, G. (2024). Software engineering education in the era of conversational AI: Current trends and future directions. *Frontiers in Artificial Intelligence*, *7*, 1436350. DOI: 10.3389/frai.2024.1436350 PMID: 39268193

Sugianti, & Rosidah, I. (2024). The use of Artificial Intelligence (AI) in learning results for scientific Indonesian language courses at PGRI Wiranegara University. *International Journal of Applied Research and Sustainable*, *2*(1), 1–10.

Tang, K. H. D. (2024). Implications of artificial Intelligence for teaching and learning. *Acta Pedagogia Asia*, *3*(2), 65–79. DOI: 10.53623/apga.v3i2.404

Thomas, D. R., Gatz, E., Gupta, S., Lin, J., Tipper, C., & Koedinger, K. (2024). Using generative AI to provide feedback to adult tutors in training and assess real-life performance. In *EdArXiv*. DOI: 10.1007/978-3-031-73427-4_21

Wang, H., Tlili, A., Huang, R., Cai, Z., Li, M., Cheng, Z., Yang, D., Li, M., Zhu, X., & Fei, C. (2023). Examining the applications of intelligent tutoring systems in real educational contexts: A systematic literature review from the social experiment perspective. *Education and Information Technologies*, *28*(7), 1–36. DOI: 10.1007/s10639-022-11555-x PMID: 36643383

Wei, S. (2024). Research on the disruptive transformation and future development of American teaching models in the context of intelligent transformation. *Advances in Economics. Management and Political Sciences*, *72*(1), 201–210.

Xu, Q. (2024). Action research plan: The impact of the use of Artificial Intelligence in education on the cognitive abilities of university students. In *Research Square*. DOI: 10.21203/rs.3.rs-4981281/v1

Zhai, X., Chu, X., Chai, C. S., Jong, M. S. Y., Istenic, A., Spector, M., Liu, J.-B., Yuan, J., & Li, Y. (2021). A review of artificial intelligence (AI) in education from 2010 to 2020. *Complexity*, *2021*(1), 1–18. DOI: 10.1155/2021/8812542

Zhang, Y. (2024). Research on the mechanism of intelligent education enabled by natural language processing technology. In *Advances in Intelligent Systems Research* (pp. 257–267). Atlantis Press International BV.

ADDITIONAL READING

Arafa, M., Dwiastuti, S., Fatmawati, U., & Mahanani, L. (2021). The influence of Novick constructivism learning model on critical thinking skills and motivation in online learning. *Biosfer*, *12*(1), 40–50. DOI: 10.24042/biosfer.v12i1.9613

Cahyani, D., Yunita, F., & Ubaidillah, M. (2022). Application of inquiry collaborative constructivism model in biology learning respiratory system to improve students' critical thinking skills. J. PENDIDIK. [JPS]. *SAINS*, *10*(1), 28.

Doctoral Student Yogyakarta State University Yogyakarta Indonesia candra.2017@student.uny.ac.id, Candra, C., Retnawati, H., & Graduate School Yogyakarta State University Yogyakarta Indonesia heri_retnawati@uny.ac.id. (2020). A meta-analysis of constructivism learning implementation towards the learning outcomes on civic education lesson. Int. J. Instr., 13(2), 835–846.

Doychinova, K. (2023). Teaching methods based on constructivism in environmental education. *Acta Scientifica Naturalis*, *10*(2), 97–108. DOI: 10.2478/asn-2023-0017

Hamaniuk, V. A. (2021). The potential of Large Language Models in language education. *Educ. Dimens.*, *5*, 208–210. DOI: 10.31812/ed.650

Luitse, D., & Denkena, W. (2021). The great Transformer: Examining the role of large language models in the political economy of AI. *Big Data & Society*, *8*(2), 205395172110477. DOI: 10.1177/20539517211047734

Napitupulu, J. F., & Simanjuntak Mariati Purnama and Sinurat, J. (2019). The effect of problem based learning model on students learning results and students' problem solving skills. ISER (Indonesian Science Education Research), 1(1).

Nguyen, T. (2023). Leveraging large language models for educational enhancement: A case study of ChatGPT, BingChat, and Bard. In *Preprints*.

Sugrah, N. U. (2020). Implementasi teori belajar konstruktivisme dalam pembelajaran sains. *Hum*, *19*(2), 121–138. DOI: 10.21831/hum.v19i2.29274

Tanjung, Y. I., Irfandi, I., Sudarma Teguh Febri and Lufri, L., Asrizal, A., & Hardeli, H. (2023). The effect of constructivism learning on student learning outcomes: A meta analysis study. ISER (Indonesian Science Education Research), 5(1).

KEY TERMS AND DEFINITIONS

Conversational AI Tutor: An AI-driven system that engages learners through human-like, interactive dialogue to deliver personalized, adaptive, and responsive instruction.

Natural Language Processing (NLP): A subfield of AI that enables computers to understand, interpret, and generate human language, allowing meaningful interaction in educational systems.

Large Language Models (LLMs): Advanced deep learning models (e.g., GPT, Claude, PaLM) trained on vast datasets to perform tasks like summarization, question answering, and dialogue.

Intent Recognition: The process of identifying the goal or purpose behind a user's input, such as asking a question or requesting feedback.

Dialogue Management System: The component that governs the flow, logic, and structure of the conversation, ensuring coherence and instructional alignment.

Personalized Learning: A learning approach where content, pace, and style are tailored to individual learner needs using adaptive technologies like AI.

Socratic Dialogue: A pedagogical method where understanding is developed through guided questioning and critical thinking, often emulated in AI tutoring systems.

Emotional Intelligence (EI): The AI's ability to detect, interpret, and respond appropriately to the emotional state of the learner to enhance motivation and engagement.

Multimodal Input: The use of multiple types of learner input (e.g., text, speech, gestures) to interact with the AI system, enhancing accessibility and usability.

Conversational Drift: A phenomenon where the AI deviates from the original topic or learning objective during prolonged interactions, potentially confusing the learner.

Chapter 12
Challenges and Limitations of Implementing AI in Schools

S. Ida Evangeline
https://orcid.org/0000-0003-2997-7897
Government College of Engineering, Tirunelveli, India

ABSTRACT

This chapter critically examines the systemic challenges and limitations of implementing artificial intelligence (AI)—particularly cognitive tutors and adaptive learning technologies—in primary and secondary education. While AI is often lauded for its potential to personalize instruction, improve learning outcomes, and bridge educational gaps, its real-world integration remains constrained by technological, pedagogical, ethical, and institutional barriers. Based on international case examples and cross-disciplinary research, the chapter addresses the phenomenon of infrastructural inequality, the prejudice of the algorithm, dislocation of educators, privacy, and policy stagnation. It contends that the transformative possibility of AI in education is only achievable with responsible, context-sensitive implementation approaches that leave equity, transparency and human centrality on a legacy of paradigm-shifting academic innovation.

INTRODUCTION

The integration of artificial intelligence into educational environments—especially in the form of cognitive tutors and adaptive learning systems—represents a sig-

DOI: 10.4018/979-8-3373-4217-7.ch012

nificant technological and pedagogical shift. As AI-powered tools increasingly permeate primary and secondary classrooms worldwide, they bring with them both immense promise and profound challenges. The advocates envisage the possibilities of this Smart Intelligent system where; the systems are able to tailor instruction to the individual needs of the student in real-time, detect student learning problems before they translate into failures and also enable a teacher to apply interventions with previously unknown levels of precision. In theory such innovations may close educational achievement gaps, engage students more and increase inclusivity and equity of learning (Park & Kwon, 2024).

However, in reality, the practical application of AI technologies in schools has not resulted in such a promising picture as the discussed intentions proposed it. Whilst AI applications in education have developed at lightning pace - due to the advancements in machine learning, natural language processing and data analytics - school systems consistently face the problem of integrating them in an accessible, economically viable, and pedagogically valid manner. The classroom is not only a social and an institutional space but it has its constraints beyond technical feasibility. Practically, AI systems will have to exist and work within current infrastructures and curricula, and models of governance with most of them not suited to the dynamic intelligent automation. In addition, the technologies have to overcome historical issues with teacher preparation, diversity among students, and low socioeconomic status (Huang & Qiao, 2024).

The current chapter aims to critically discuss the various impediments that stall the meaningful adoption of AI in K-12 education. Its main point is that although AI technologies can change education technically, their efficacy in the real-life hinges on a complex of mutually interrelated issues such as technological, pedagogical, ethical, or institutional. The chapter will not discuss AI as a single phenomenon but as a continuum of tools and practices the effects of which are dependent on context. There will be special focus on cognitive tutors- AI systems that are developed in such a way as to resemble a human tutor by helping learners improve their understanding through feedback and by scaffolding. Although these systems have demonstrated potential in laboratory settings, their success in the real classroom is limited due to technological-related constraints like lack of proper infrastructure, existence of rigid curriculum, and insufficient teacher acceptance.

Importantly, this chapter does not simply list barriers; it tries to re-frame these barriers as possibilities to do more considerate and responsible design. Contrary to believing that implementation failures can be seen as purely technical deficiencies, the discussion will point out the socio-technical character of AI teaching/learning. In another example, an adaptive learning platform that does not work well in a small town with limited broadband connectivity also has to do with the overall misinvestment and policy disparities in education funding. Likewise, a thinking tutor which excludes non-standard learners due to biased algorithms presents an imminent worry of ethical control and inclusive design.

The analysis is conducted in a number of phases. The chapter will begin by presenting something of the state of the art of current deployments of AI in the K-12 domain, with an emphasis on the burgeoning of cognitive tutors and other adaptive systems. It will subsequently examine the central problems in four thematic areas: technological, pedagogical, ethical-social and institutional. All of these areas will be discussed with regard to both empirical and theoretical critique using international case studies and interdisciplinary research forms. Lastly, the chapter will suggest a list of strategic principles used in the fair and efficient implementation of AI in schools-- that will focus on human-centered design, participatory governance and infrastructural justice.

By putting the empirical difficulty of AI use into the foreground, this chapter also seeks to provide a welcome antidote to the euphoric rhetoric of educational technology. It shouts out a need of recalibration of the expectations- one that keeps alive the idea of transformative power of AI but also demands that the transformation must be pedagogically sound, democratic, and holds equity as a central concern.

CURRENT LANDSCAPE OF AI IN SCHOOLS

The last decade has witnessed a significant acceleration in the development and deployment of artificial intelligence technologies in educational contexts, particularly within primary and secondary (K–12) systems. The push to achieve this is usually brought by the image of changing the conventional classrooms into learning classrooms enriched with data and personalized using intelligent software systems. Of these, cognitive tutors and adaptive learning platforms have received the most attention as highly adaptive to the needs, pace and abilities of each student.

Cognitive tutors-software based upon the principles of cognitive science, imitate human tutoring by analyzing student responses instantaneously and also offering feedback, scaffolding and remediation. The systems built on this premise are based on the design of one-on-one tutoring as an ideal model of learning and are designed to reproduce the advantages of individualised learning by identifying misconceptions through algorithmic means, by tracing learning trajectories, and by responding to each learner in real-time with material of varying difficulty. Initial versions, as those innovated by Carnegie Learning, were in areas of study where the methods of learning can be well defined and modelled, such as in mathematics. Throughout the years, these systems have incorporated more complex AI algorithms such as natural language, probabilistic reasoning and even affective computing to measure student emotions and levels of engagement (Dai et al. 2023).

Adaptive learning platforms have also become another major way of integrating AI into schools besides the use of cognitive tutors. These systems collect data on the interactions of the students to make online real-time adjustments regarding content, pacing and content modality. Unlike conventional software that delivers the same messages to every learner, the adaptive ones attempt to individualize instruction during sustained evaluation of performance and behavioral patterns. Products like DreamBox and Smart Sparrow, and Knewton (acquired by Wiley), have been used in many learning environments, with some teachers getting dashboard views of students to help them derive insights on how students are doing and where they should be focusing their attention.

Regardless of the innovative potential of these technologies, their practical application to the K-12 classrooms is not very homogenous and often scattered. Distribution is skewed towards schools that have greater funding amounts and better digital connectivity and administrative approval of innovation. The usage of AI in a lot of lower-income schools or rural ones is limited due to the weak internet connection, the inability of hardware, and the lack of professional development training of any teachers. In addition, the majority of AI applications are not extensive but instead are in pilot form or even limited to a single subject (Ayanwale et al. 2022).

The situation is made trickier by the business aspect of most AI-based educational tools. A large number are manufactured by commercial entities resulting in proprietary systems of varying quality, interoperability and transparency. Such distinctions leave educators in a difficult situation to discern which tools are the best foundation of evidence and pedagogically sound. Further, the lack of explainability in most AI-based algorithms and data gathers has been of concern to both educators and parents regarding the privacy of students, algorithmic responsibility, and the sale of education data.

The trend of AI in schools is different across the board internationally. In high controlled education environments, such as China and South Korea and their high-speed internet connections, facial recognition accounts have been used to attend school, AI powered homework programs, and AI powered smart classroom analytics. By contrast, education systems in much of sub-Saharan Africa, South Asia, and Latin America have constrained infrastructural and resource capacities that are unlikely to support the adoption of such tools, despite increasingly numerous pilot efforts in urban regions (Díaz & Nussbaum, 2024).

Although these are the, undoubtedly, significant disparities, there is an emerging consensus, a consensus among policymakers, a consensus among technologists, a consensus among educators that the future of education is going to feature an increasing central role played by AI. It is, therefore, important to find out what the stage of AI adaptation in schools is not only to determine the level of technological maturity but also to pinpoint preconditions (social, institutional, and ethical) that an effective use of AI may require. These systems hold a lot of promise as means of promoting personalized education, but until we understand the multitude of influences that make them succeed/fail, research them/understand them, and pursue them/for those who should have access to them, they cannot possibly achieve their potential.

TECHNOLOGICAL CHALLENGES

While AI-powered systems such as cognitive tutors and adaptive learning platforms promise to revolutionize personalized education, their implementation in schools is often obstructed by fundamental technological challenges. Such concerns are not just the subject of software optimization or algorithmic improvements but structural firmly situated within infrastructures and operations of school systems. Hereinafter, this section will decode the key technological impediments; that is, scalability, system reliability, systematic limitations of integration and the DD, which hinder the large-scale and equitable implementation of AI in the K-12 school system.

Scalability is one of the most nagging of them all. Numerous AI-based tools can be successful in small-scale trials or tight experiments, but they do not consistently yield the results that may be expected when the same tool is scaled up to all of a given school district or a nationwide system. The scalability issue is both due to the computing intensity of AI solutions and the heterogeneity of the school context. Whereas an intelligent tutor can adopt readily to the educational setup of batch of students in a well-equipped urban school with its high-bandwidth of internet connection, digital connectedness and other infrastructure, the same sophistication would flounder in a remote location where bandwidth is low, equipment obsolete, and other technical assistance near nil. Advanced AI systems have high performance demands, including speed, low-latency, real-time analyses, and high-resolution input readings which may overload legacy systems that many schools still use, causing crashes, slowdowns, or a total inability to operate (Kuleto et al. 2021).

Granted in near perfect partnership with scalability is the concern over reliability and robustness of the system. Reliability is a requirement in educational situations. When an AI system temporarily locks mid-way through a high-stakes assessment, provides inaccurate feedback, or logs out halfway through a session, it can potentially cause disruptions in learning, as well as negative perceptions towards an educational institution by teachers, students and parents. In contrast to consumer software, which can be dropped at any time by the user, educational tools become integrated within classroom practice and learning progressions. Any unreliability thus has reinforced effects In addition, unlike within the tech industries, updates and bug fixes can be slow or ineffective in the education sector, as no teacher will have time to constantly update, and many will lack expertise to fix any bugs or change with very frequent updates.

The other insurmountable barrier is integration with legacy systems and other existing technologies of teaching. Most schools have already implemented different platforms-learning management systems (LMS), student information systems (SIS) assessment platforms, as well as digital content repositories. AI functionalities that do not have direct interoperability with each other create unnecessary administrative overhead, instead of alleviating it. By forcing teachers to log into one system after another, or export data by hand, or reconcile performance reports that contradict each other, the efficiency and the popularity of the AI integration can be compromised. Moreover, the absence of standardization among platforms means that there are no unified learning analytics or that there exists no possibility of transferring the information about different students without risking information leakage or data loss (Dimitriadou & Lanitis, 2023).

By far, the most widespread technological issue, however, is the digital divide. This gap is reflected in both usability and quality: Some students have stable connections, personal devices and tech-savvy parents and guardians, others might have to share and outdated devices or depend on unreliable in-school connectivity. Such poor access drastically restricts the individualization that AI systems are supposed to offer. As an example, suppose an adaptive learning tool is intended to improve over time by requiring near-daily use to adjust its algorithm; in a bandwidth-limited area, students will end up being re-set to an initial state indefinitely, thus never experiencing the advertised personalization. Furthermore, the design of AI is often based on assumptions that do not reflect the conditions and diversity of real classrooms, e.g., assumptions that include always-on connectivity, all datainputs to be based on touchscreens, and that the language to be used is English.

All these obstacles are added to the fact that most AI systems applied in education are biased in nature, with more focus on business than teaching purposes. The culture of time-to-market, proprietary construction and data monetization could therefore create a system that is very technically advanced but poorly adapted to the realities of education. Even the best AI tools cannot be used or become relevant in practice without thorough field testing in different school settings (Celik et al. 2022).

In short, technological problems of AI application in schools cannot be resolved as mere bugs that can be fixed - they are simply the expression of more systemic problems between the rate of development with AI and the ability of educational systems to keep pace with these changes. These difficulties will only be solved by the beginning of stronger technology along with a continued investment in infrastructure, teacher education, and cross-system interoperability. Despite its wonderful technology, however, great technology alone is not sufficient to be successful and as will be shown in later sections, it must fit in with the pedagogical, ethical and institutional ecologies into which it is injected.

PEDAGOGICAL MISALIGNMENTS

While much of the discourse surrounding AI in education emphasizes its technological sophistication and data-driven potential, the pedagogical implications often receive less attention. This oversight is critical, as even the most advanced AI systems must ultimately function within the complex ecosystem of teaching and learning. In this context, pedagogical misalignment refers to the disconnect between the instructional logic embedded within AI tools and the broader goals, values, and methods of effective education. In this section we look at how AI systems, specifically cognitive tutors and adaptive platforms, can end up being directly opposite to fundamental pedagogical principles, especially those grounded in constructivist, student centred and socio-cultural views of learning (Currie, 2021).

The central tension inherent at the center of this is the parceling out of behaviorist and data-centric approaches in AI-driven learning software. To work, most cognitive tutors record finer-grained data on what the student entered, e.g. clicks and responses or time spent on task and use statistical models or machine learning algorithms that predict what the student knows. Such inferences are used to prompt automated feedback and the subsequent ordering of content. Although this is an efficient, scaleable process, in many cases, it reduces learning to a combination of observable behaviours and discrete competencies. Because of this, it prioritizes memorizing and retention of problems over more in-depth approaches to investigation, thinking, and reflection. Possibly, students can become competent in exploring the system and not comprehending the underlying principles and not developing the critical way of thinking.

This reductionist-oriented background is specifically antagonistic to constructivist pedagogies, which focus on active, contextualized and learnings whereby students develop knowledge through experience, discussion and social interaction. The constructivist approach to teaching promotes open-ended questions, exploration by collective effort and shared meaning, from which constructivist tutors are unable to completely proficiently structure tutoring. Cognitive tutors look to the structured route, even archaic, in the classrooms that aim to develop creativity, agency, and interdisciplinary thinking. In addition, AI systems usually follow a linear path of learning content but in real life learning is not linear rather nonlinear, iterative and highly dependent on culture, emotion and background knowledge (Tedre et al. 2021).

Of interest also is the loss of teacher agency and pedagogical autonomy. To the extent that AI tools are able to become more prescriptive, and thus, recommend automated lesson plans, learning objectives, and student recommendations, they risk placing teachers in the role of facilitating algorithmic choices at the expense of designing quality learning experiences. This is, in particular, damaging in an environment where educators are assessed by their statuses according to student evaluation measures developed by AI tools. Because of this, teachers may be tempted to teach to the algorithm instead, i.e. they may align their teaching with what is rewarded in the system instead of teaching what they know to be sound pedagogically. This dynamic, in the long run, can undermine professional judgment, as well as change the role of a teacher, who becomes a content controller, instead of a mentor, a guide, or a co-learner.

Moreover, assumptions implemented in AI systems can promote limited ideas of learning success, which is often connected to the standardised assessment and predetermined learning outcomes. To maximize objective returns in performance improvements, AI tutors can overlook more subjective, less measurable outcomes of education- curiosity, the ability to persevere, tolerance, and the ability to reason about ethical issues. The excessive focus on data-driven personalization may even result in so-called personalization traps when learners are compelled to constantly encounter information that they had performed well in the past and thus are unaware of fresh concepts or difficult material. Rather than widening intellectual horizons, these systems have instead the danger of reinforcing current behavioral patterns of success or failure (Karataş et al. 2025).

There exists as well a major cultural and linguistic incompatibility with the AI tools and the diverse student body that they serve. Cognitive tutors are constructed within and may reflect the larger cultural assumptions of a particular cultural group (in most cases, Western, English-speaking societies) and may implicitly include biases in the use of language, the explication of problems, or the approach to interactions. By having these biases, they can leave some students who do not fit the expectation of the system alienated. Such as, a collectivist-culture learner might enjoy the collaborative environment but fail to succeed in the individual-focused AI programs that fail to support peer to peer learning.

Lastly, pedagogical misalignments are also of concern when AI systems start being used in classrooms with no apparent instructional purpose or integration strategy. Although applied in isolation, AI tutors have the risk of introducing disruption to the customary pedagogical rhythm, potentially resulting in a disjointed training session or confusion among learners as to the role the technology plays in relation to their overall aims. Without a well-orchestrated curriculum and the overall responsiveness of the teachers, adopting AI can be simply more of a distraction than an opportunity (Zou et al. 2025).

Finally, technology is not everything, and its comfortable usage in educational institutions is the result of adequate integration of AI. It must be profoundly conformed to pedagogical ideologies that respect the multi-dimensionality of human learning. Without this congruence, even the most advanced AI technology has the potential to diminish education--turning inherently dialogic, transformative, and collaborative educational processes into data exchange and feedback events. The following segment will elaborate on this criticism by looking at the additional complication of ethical and social issues in schools (e.g., privacy, bias, and transparency).

ETHICAL AND SOCIAL RISKS

As AI technologies increasingly shape the contours of contemporary education, concerns over their ethical and social implications have intensified. Unlike traditional educational tools, AI systems operate through opaque algorithms, collect vast amounts of personal data, and make autonomous decisions that can directly influence learning outcomes and student futures. These risks are especially threatening when such systems are introduced into K12 classrooms, as they expose the already vulnerable child to risks of experiencing and knowing about these procedures without consent and without understanding by either the students or by their guardians. This section reviews the major risks (ethical as well as social) that accompany the use of AI in schools: invasion of privacy, algorithmic discrimination, lack of transparency/occurrence of distrust and erosion of democratic values (Akgun & Greenhow, 2022).

Data privacy and surveillance is the most obvious and imminent risk. Solely, I systems demand big data operations-monitoring not only academic excellence but also behavioral trends, emote reactions and even biometric data. In a number of classrooms, classrooms now see students being subject to a near constant level of data capture with digital learning platforms, webcams, keystroke monitors, and location tracking. Though this data can help to make personalization even more profitable, it also leads to the possibility of intrusive, and potentially threatening, surveillance. All this is worsened by the use of third-party software whose terms of use are often unclear, and information may be stored in other anonymous servers with unknown terms of service. Information gathered to be used in education has in some instances been diverted either in marketing or profiling purposes, which is of great concern to both the autonomy and consent of students.

Adding spice to the issue of privacy is the fact that in many educational systems there are no effective data governance structures. Schools are usually inadequately equipped with a team of experts to evaluate security practices of AI vendors or even enforce compliance of the current legislation e.g. family educational rights and privacy act (FERPA) in the USA or the general data protection regulation (GDPR) in Europe. In addition, policies often follow technology, and until it catches up, students would be exposed to breaches and misuse or may be tracked over the long run. There are an especially high set of ethical stakes involved when it comes to marginalized groups as communities who may already feel a high level of suspicion regarding institutional surveillance due to their ongoing historical miscarriage of justice or possibly institutional racism or similar failings (du Boulay, 2023).

In close relation to the concerns with privacy, there is talk of algorithmic discrimination and bias. Any AI system is merely as objective as the data itself on which it is trained- educational data is far not impartial. Historical inequalities, test scores, teacher evaluations, and disciplinary data tend to lay bare the different social and racial prejudices. These datasets when applied to train predictive models reproduce or even exacerbate the inequities present in them. An example of this is when an AI platform suggests an academic path or a learning-track based off performance, disadvantaged students will often be systematically guided towards low-level material, so they are effectively locked into the opportunity gap instead of pulled out of it. This trend (sometimes called the automation of inequality) constitutes a fundamental risk to the concept of equality of educational opportunity.

Although they may perform as designed, when algorithms are considered because of the absence of transparency and explainability (the so-called black box of issues), also arise ethical questions. Students and teachers do not always know how decisions are reached, what information is being utilized and how results are arrived at. Users are not able to dispute or interpret the foundation of recommendations, feedback, and of assessments, without transparent explanations. Such opacity makes accountability suffer as well as reduces educational value of the technology. Learning is not only about results- it is also an understanding process. By providing advice where it is not possible to understand their line of thought, AI systems break this fundamental dynamic, and they may undermine the skills of critical thinking (Dieterle et al. 2024).

All these ethical risks create a risk of losing trust not only in technology, but also in education institutions themselves. When students sense that they are being watched and when their unknown identities in data practices elicit feelings of being misunderstood, when parental involvement is left out in the dark and when teachers are rendered pawns by unknown algorithms, the social fabric of their schoolings starts to unweave. Trust is a pillar of learning environment, and AI systems should be developed and implemented in a manner that will add to, but not erode, trust.

Lastly, there is the more general democratic issue of how AI technologies can dangerously affect the values and norms that inform education. Schools are not only places of transmission of knowledge, but they are also a place where civic identities are constructed. By prioritizing efficiency, standardization, and control over deliberation, inclusiveness, and critical engagement, AI tools may simply not be compatible with democratic ideals, and they are likely to re-shape education accordingly. As an illustration, predictive analytics that show a student as at risk can also lead to unintended stigmatization or lowered potential by conditioning both the self-concept and the expectations of teachers. Such progress demands extreme caution with regard to what kinds of citizens are being fashioned by our educational technologies.

The bottom line is that ethical and social risks of AI in education are not minor and peripheral but central instead. To solve them, it will take more than a technological solution; it will take participatory governance, transparent algorithms, regulatory oversight and accountability to respect the rights and dignity of every learner. In the following section, we discuss institutional and policy-level barriers to the implementation of AI that need to be addressed in concert with technical and ethical concerns.

INSTITUTIONAL AND POLICY BARRIERS

Beyond the technological, pedagogical, and ethical challenges previously outlined, the implementation of AI in schools is deeply shaped by institutional dynamics and policy ecosystems. Schools are not neutral or uniform sites of innovation; they are embedded within complex bureaucratic, cultural, and regulatory frameworks that often hinder the adoption of new technologies—especially those as transformative and disruptive as AI. This part examines how institutional inertia, policy ambiguity, teacher training inadequacies, and systemic inequalities are the cliffs on which meaningful and equity-based integration of AI in K-12 teaching are doomed (Tutsoy, 2021).

One of the institutional problems that are central to the issue concerns the inferior readiness of educational workers and principals to interact with AI on a meaningful level. Little or no coursework on AI literacy, ethical data use, and algorithmic accountability, is included in the teacher training programs. This has caused teachers to be pressured into implementing some of these advanced AI tools without understanding how to rate their design, the meaning of their output, or how to use them pedagogically. Training by vendors in most cases is on how to use the platform most times and not really on critically engaging it on the limitations, etc. As a result of this skills mismatch, there is not only under use, misuse or shallow adoption of AI as a cosmetic addition but not a transformative pedagogical tool.

Also, when the integration of AI happens without truly collaborative engagement with teachers, their professional identity and autonomy can become threatened. They can create adversity, apathy and even resistance in those tasked with implementing AI tools when the top-down implementation models are used where decision-makers procure AI-related tools without the respective input of frontline educators. When a teacher is perceived as a mere implementer as opposed to a co-designer, the chances of effective integration are reduced to a great extent. On the contrary, collaborative forms of procedure, including teacher input on the choice, personalization, and assessment of AI-based tools, have been identified to stimulate the adoption success rate as well as learning results. However, such models need time, funding and institutional flexibility, which is something that is limited in systems of public education (Schiff, 2022).

On the policy level, a significant inhibitor is the lack of precise regulatory tools and norms on how to use AI in the education sector. Several countries have outlined ambitious digitalization initiatives or AI plans, but there are few specific policies to deal with the special issues of AI in education. Critical concerns like data governance, algorithmic accountability, procurement transparency, and fair access are often left entirely to the decision of the various individual school districts or even individual schools. This regulatory gap enables the comparatively variable practice, exposes students to the risks of breaches of privacy and bias, and hinders the assessment of the effect of AI interventions in different settings.

Implementation is delayed further by policy inertia and bureaucracy. Educational systems and especially those of the public sector change reluctantly over long periods of time. Curriculum, evaluation, and technology integration choices are made by following a chain of command and at times must support a regime of standardized tests, budget constraints, and political interest. In that kind of atmosphere, rates of AI innovation may be too fast as system is not able to change as fast. This process can take months to get a new tool approved, trained on, and utilized and by that time more than likely it is outdated or misaligned with current pedagogical practices. The time lag is not only resource- wasting but also it induces the scepticism of the value of using AI in education (McDonald et al. 2025).

Combined with issues we already face are systemic inequities that impact where resources go and who has power in and across schools. Well-funded schools in wealthy areas have a better chance to possess the infrastructure, leadership support and digital literacy that may allow them to experiment with AI tools, whereas underfunded schools have to struggle just to meet the basic technological requirements. Unless specific policies are in place to enhance fair access to them, AI promises to be one more way in which educational inequality may be perpetuated.

Also, there is a lack of proper accountability and evaluation systems of AI in schools. There is rock-solid agreement on how to measure AI system effectiveness, fairness or pedagogical soundness. Current assessment scales focus on the short-term academic achievements (e.g. test scores) and overlook longer-term educational impacts such as well-being, inclusion, or awareness of ethics. Such limited perspective may incentivize the adoption of the AI systems that maximize the measured outcome to the detriment of overall learning (Park & Kwon, 2024).

In short, institutional and policy obstacles can be described as a crucial series of levels of difficulty involving the use of AI at school. Even the most ethical and pedagogically thoughtful AI tool will simply fail when put to use in a situation where teachers are ill-trained and under-prepared, where research is policy-agnostic, and where system access disparities are not closed. Wrapping up these barriers involves something beyond local interventions- it involves the need to overhaul and design institutional platforms, teacher growth and policy models to accommodate the realities and promise of AI-enhanced education.

CASE STUDIES AND REAL-WORLD EXAMPLES

To move from theoretical critique to empirical grounding, this section examines real-world attempts to implement AI—particularly cognitive tutors and adaptive learning platforms—in primary and secondary education systems. Based on the analysis of pilot programs and mass implementations in both the developed and developing worlds, one can get a better idea of how some of the challenges and limitations reviewed in previous sections take place in practice. The case studies are evidence of the variety of outcomes in implementing AI, at the same time, pointing at the importance of local context, policy frameworks, and institutional capacity in making AI implementation successful or not.

Case 1: Carnegie Learning in the United States

Carnegie Learning's MATHia, one of the earliest and most researched cognitive tutor systems, has been implemented across several U.S. school districts with mixed results. The platform, which combines cognitive modeling and adaptive learning, was designed to provide real-time, personalized feedback in secondary mathematics instruction. Controlled studies have reported modest increases in student achievement over that achieved in traditional instruction, but large-scale implementation has provoked opposition because of the deficit of teacher training and harmonization with local curricula.

In other districts, teachers felt hindered by the software as far as its sequencing and feedback mechanisms were inconsistent with their own pace and approach to teaching. Technical glitches, as well as poor motivation among the students, were other factors that were stated as barriers by others. At lower-income schools, facility issues with stable access and adequate supply of devices precluded equitable use, thereby contributing to disparate engagement and a growing disparity between schools with over- and under-resource levels. These results support the determination of infrastructural preparedness and pedagogical alignment (Kim & Wu, 2024).

Case 2: Squirrel AI in China

Squirrel AI represents one of the most ambitious applications of AI-powered adaptive learning globally, with thousands of learning centers across China. Based on deep learning algorithms and a knowledge space theory, our system micro-personalizes teaching in areas such as math and English. The sophistication of its analytics and scalability has received global attention and very large investments.

The high rate of data surveillance, such as facial recognition and emotions monitoring, however, raises ethical issues that trouble the program. The Privacy campaigners have criticized the possibility of minor persons giving an informed consent to such surveillance and have alleged that^^ emotional AI is tantamount to behavioral manipulation. Beyond that, some educators have also stated that the game-based system that the platform employs, the test-based model, promotes rote learning and discourages critical thinking. Although Squirrel AI helps to show what can be done with technology, it also brings to light that ethical limitations must be formed with care, particularly, when the system is working at scale and without sufficient external control (Li et al. 2025).

Case 3: Kolibri in Sub-Saharan Africa

In regions with limited internet connectivity, open-source platforms like Kolibri have attempted to bridge the digital divide through offline, low-cost adaptive learning systems. Kolibri, developed by Learning Equality, allows schools in underserved areas to access curated educational content and basic adaptive features without real-time data streaming. In Kenya, Tanzania and Rwanda, pilots have demonstrated potential in increasing student engagement and access to quality resources.

Yet the relatively weak AI endowment of these systems is part and parcel of a bigger compromise between universality and technological advancement. Without constant input of data and personalization, the learning process loses its dynamism as more comprehensive artificial intelligence platforms do. Besides, teacher facilitation continues to play an essential role, but most educators have little training, which can reduce the perceived effect of the system. The case highlights the fact that AI systems required should be both high-tech and context and resource-aware (Agbeyangi & Suleman, 2024).

Case 4: EdTech Pilot Framework in the United Kingdom

In the UK, the Department for Education has supported a structured framework for piloting EdTech tools, including AI-driven platforms, in public schools. One such initiative involved adaptive literacy platforms used in primary schools across several regions. This initiative stands out because of the formality of evaluation procedures with the pedagogical criteria, the criteria on inclusion, class data protection, and survey of teachers.

Although the initial results were not outstanding in terms of academic improvements, the pilot focused on transparency and the participation of stakeholders. Teachers were important in the adaption of how the tools can be utilized and there has been a strict adherence in data privacy. This model reflects the role that institutional support, evaluation infrastructure, and participatory governance can play in reducing many of the risks posed by AI adoption in schools, despite technological performance falling short of transformative on its own (Bhutoria, 2022).

Table 1. Comparative evaluation of real-world AI implementations in K–12 education

Case Study	Tech Robustness	Pedagogical Fit	Ethical Safeguards	Institutional Adaptability	Summary
Carnegie Learning	Medium	Low	Medium	Medium	High potential, but limited by training and curriculum fit
Squirrel AI	High	Low	Low	High	Scalable but ethically problematic and rigidly test-driven
Kolibri	Low	Medium	High	Medium	Contextually adapted, but low in AI sophistication
UK EdTech Pilot	Medium	Medium	High	High	Strong governance and participatory alignment

Table 1 presents the comparative evaluation of real-world AI implementations in K–12 education. These examples reveal that technological advancement alone does not predict successful implementation. Squirrel AI excels in scalability but falters ethically. Kolibri, despite its technical limitations, demonstrates the importance of contextual alignment and equity focus. The UK's structured pilot approach—though less flashy—emerges as a promising model of participatory, ethically aligned implementation. This comparative lens emphasizes the need for a balanced framework, where innovation is matched by governance, pedagogy, and infrastructure.

STRATEGIC PRINCIPLES FOR RESPONSIBLE AI IMPLEMENTATION

Given the multifaceted challenges explored in earlier sections—technological limitations, pedagogical misalignments, ethical risks, and institutional constraints—

the path forward for AI in education must be guided by deliberate and principled strategies. Those strategies must not seek short term solutions and shallow integration but must focus on a long-term cross-sector vision-one grounded on education equity, transparency, and a human-centered design. The following section describes four strategic principles to applying responsible AI in the school setting, referencing empirical data and the cross-disciplinary best-practices.

Participatory Design and Localized Adaptation

One of the most consistent findings across successful AI integration efforts is the importance of involving educators, students, and communities in the design and deployment process. Participatory design ensures that AI systems are not imposed upon classrooms but co-evolve with them. Such an approach acknowledges that the teacher is not an uninvolved subject to technology but a participant who has pedagogical and localised knowledge.

Educational establishments should not impose ready-made products of AI, but flexible systems that can be customized to match the local requirements; whether language, cultural context, in-line with the curriculum, or other infrastructural limitations. Co-design processes, pilot feedback cycles, and prototyping can be some of the helpful methods of tethering AI innovation to a real educational context. Not only does this enhance usability and uptake but encourages trust and shared ownership (Dodick, 2024).

Teacher-AI Collaboration Models

A responsible approach to AI in schools must reject zero-sum narratives that position AI as a replacement for human teachers. Instead, emphasis should be placed on hybrid models where AI augments teacher capacities—handling routine tasks, analyzing student data, and offering personalized feedback—while educators retain the central role of instructional designers, mentors, and ethical guides.

Such collaboration will require strong professional development for the teachers that goes beyond operational training to AI literacy and critical evaluation of ethical use. Organizations ought to invest in AI fluency initiatives that enable teachers to understand the suggestions made by the algorithm, challenge computer-based judgments, and inform the direction and form of AI implementation into teaching techniques. The purpose is to upgrade the teachers and not marginalize them (Kim, 2024).

Robust Data Governance and Algorithmic Transparency

Responsible AI integration requires rigorous attention to data ethics and governance. This includes establishing clear protocols for data collection, storage, access, and use—guided by legal regulations (e.g., GDPR, FERPA) and ethical norms. Consent should be informed and where possible opt-in and data minimization should be practiced.

No less significant is the question of algorithmic transparency Schoolchildren, parents, and teachers need to have a right to accessible explanations about how AI systems work, with which data they work, and how their decisions are made. Where possible, tools must also include explainable AI (XAI) interfaces and the provision of feedback, contestation or override. Vague next generation AI without transparency and accountability can bring serious consequences even to the best intentions and bring distrust and degrade educational integrity (Filgueiras, 2024).

Equitable Infrastructure and Support Systems

Equity must be a cornerstone of AI deployment in education. Policymakers and school leaders must ensure that technological advancements do not deepen existing disparities. This involves proactive initiatives to assist underfunded schools with specific funding, public/private partnerships, and infostructure investments especially in broad band connectivity, device usage and repairs.

In addition, AI activation needs to be coupled with wrap around supports, such as, tech support units, training centers, and digital equity assessments. Designs of tools must be considered not only as effective but also as inclusive to make sure that it can meet the needs of learners with disability or language non-uniformity, non-standard learning paths, etc. Devoid of equity lens, the positive impacts of AI will continue to accrue in privileged settings (Bulathwela et al. 2024).

The combination of these principles is a guide into departing with the hit or miss integration process and instead working towards a responsibly integrated AI. They challenge technologists, educators, and policymakers to jointly not only develop superior tools, but also redesign the institutional environments that allow it to take full advantage of those tools. The last section of this chapter will summarize the main lessons learned and reinstill the need to view AI in education with optimistic caution and critical resolve.

Toward an Integrated Framework for AI Implementation in Schools

The previous sections have highlighted AI-related challenges in education across technological, pedagogical, ethical, and institutional domains. However, these are not standalone issues—they are deeply interconnected. For instance, *pedagogical misalignments* often emerge because *policy frameworks* fail to mandate inclusive teacher training, and *ethical risks* like algorithmic bias intensify when *technological design* overlooks local cultural or socioeconomic contexts. To move beyond a checklist of obstacles, this chapter proposes a socio-technical ecosystem model, where effective AI integration is seen as contingent on four interdependent pillars: (1) human-centered pedagogy, (2) ethical AI governance, (3) inclusive infrastructure, and (4) participatory policy-making. These pillars must not be addressed in isolation but co-developed through iterative, locally responsive, and interdisciplinary strategies.

This framework serves not only as a diagnostic lens but as a strategic roadmap. It encourages school systems to assess readiness not just by technological availability, but by their capacity to align AI use with democratic pedagogical values, equitable access, and transparent oversight mechanisms. In the next section, we conclude by outlining how these elements might be mobilized into long-term, actionable strategies.

CONCLUSION

The integration of AI in K–12 education stands at a critical crossroads. While its promise lies in advancing personalized learning, augmenting teacher capacities, and fostering equity, the real-world outcomes remain fragmented and contingent on structural, pedagogical, and ethical preparedness. As this chapter demonstrates, the success of AI in schools is not merely a technical matter—it is a sociotechnical challenge that requires alignment across systems, stakeholders, and values.

To move forward, we must shift from tool-centric enthusiasm to systems-level thinking. This involves rethinking how AI is introduced and supported: expanding teacher training beyond operational use to include AI ethics and critical evaluation; redefining success metrics to go beyond standardized test performance; and embedding governance frameworks that prioritize transparency, algorithmic accountability, and student data protection.

AI must also be context-aware and designed for inclusivity—whether implemented in broadband-rich urban schools or resource-constrained rural classrooms. It should not standardize learning, but adapt to diverse educational needs, cultural backgrounds, and pedagogical values. This necessitates co-created design processes, robust teacher-AI collaboration models, and equitable funding strategies.

To this end, concrete recommendations emerge:

- For policy-makers: develop AI ethics regulations tailored to education; mandate AI literacy in teacher training; fund public infrastructure for underserved schools; and require participatory pilot programs with educator involvement.
- For educators and school leaders: critically assess the pedagogical assumptions of AI tools; ensure classroom-level inclusivity and student transparency; advocate for explainable AI use; and build peer learning communities around responsible AI use.

Future research should prioritize long-term, interdisciplinary studies that examine not only effectiveness but also equity, ethics, and empowerment. Only by harmonizing AI's technical potential with democratic educational goals—like student agency, collaboration, and justice—can we realize truly transformative, equitable, and human-centered educational futures.

REFERENCES

Agbeyangi, A., & Suleman, H. (2024, November). Advances and challenges in low-resource-environment software systems: A Survey. [). MDPI.]. *Informatics (MDPI)*, *11*(4), 90. DOI: 10.3390/informatics11040090

Akgun, S., & Greenhow, C. (2022). Artificial intelligence in education: Addressing ethical challenges in K-12 settings. *AI and Ethics*, *2*(3), 431–440. DOI: 10.1007/s43681-021-00096-7 PMID: 34790956

Ayanwale, M. A., Sanusi, I. T., Adelana, O. P., Aruleba, K. D., & Oyelere, S. S. (2022). Teachers' readiness and intention to teach artificial intelligence in schools. *Computers and Education: Artificial Intelligence*, *3*, 100099. DOI: 10.1016/j.caeai.2022.100099

Bhutoria, A. (2022). Personalized education and artificial intelligence in the United States, China, and India: A systematic review using a human-in-the-loop model. *Computers and Education: Artificial Intelligence*, *3*, 100068. DOI: 10.1016/j.caeai.2022.100068

Bulathwela, S., Pérez-Ortiz, M., Holloway, C., Cukurova, M., & Shawe-Taylor, J. (2024). Artificial intelligence alone will not democratise education: On educational inequality, techno-solutionism and inclusive tools. *Sustainability (Basel)*, *16*(2), 781. DOI: 10.3390/su16020781

Celik, I., Dindar, M., Muukkonen, H., & Järvelä, S. (2022). The promises and challenges of artificial intelligence for teachers: A systematic review of research. *TechTrends*, *66*(4), 616–630. DOI: 10.1007/s11528-022-00715-y

Currie, A. (2021). Misaligned education. *Journal of the Philosophy of Sport*, *48*(3), 332–343. DOI: 10.1080/00948705.2021.1951612

Dai, Y., Liu, A., Qin, J., Guo, Y., Jong, M. S. Y., Chai, C. S., & Lin, Z. (2023). Collaborative construction of artificial intelligence curriculum in primary schools. *Journal of Engineering Education*, *112*(1), 23–42. DOI: 10.1002/jee.20503

Díaz, B., & Nussbaum, M. (2024). Artificial intelligence for teaching and learning in schools: The need for pedagogical intelligence. *Computers & Education*, *217*, 105071. DOI: 10.1016/j.compedu.2024.105071

Dieterle, E., Dede, C., & Walker, M. (2024). The cyclical ethical effects of using artificial intelligence in education. *AI & Society*, *39*(2), 633–643. DOI: 10.1007/s00146-022-01497-w PMID: 36185064

Dimitriadou, E., & Lanitis, A. (2023). A critical evaluation, challenges, and future perspectives of using artificial intelligence and emerging technologies in smart classrooms. *Smart Learning Environments*, *10*(1), 12. DOI: 10.1186/s40561-023-00231-3 PMID: 40478141

Dodick, D. (2024). Localizing AIED: Moving beyond North–South narratives to serve contextual needs. *AI & Society*, •••, 1–11.

du Boulay, B. (2023). Artificial intelligence in education and ethics. In *Handbook of open, distance and digital education* (pp. 93–108). Springer Nature Singapore. DOI: 10.1007/978-981-19-2080-6_6

Filgueiras, F. (2024). Artificial intelligence and education governance. *Education, Citizenship and Social Justice*, *19*(3), 349–361. DOI: 10.1177/17461979231160674

Huang, X., & Qiao, C. (2024). Enhancing computational thinking skills through artificial intelligence education at a STEAM high school. *Science & Education*, *33*(2), 383–403. DOI: 10.1007/s11191-022-00392-6

Karataş, F., Eriçok, B., & Tanrikulu, L. (2025). Reshaping curriculum adaptation in the age of artificial intelligence: Mapping teachers' AI-driven curriculum adaptation patterns. *British Educational Research Journal*, *51*(1), 154–180. DOI: 10.1002/berj.4068

Kim, D., & Wu, J. (2024, October). Artificial intelligence in higher education: Examining the AI policy landscape at US institutions. In *Proceedings of the 25th Annual Conference on Information Technology Education* (pp. 68-73). DOI: 10.1145/3686852.3687076

Kim, J. (2024). Leading teachers' perspective on teacher-AI collaboration in education. *Education and Information Technologies*, *29*(7), 8693–8724. DOI: 10.1007/s10639-023-12109-5

Kuleto, V., Ilić, M., Dumangiu, M., Ranković, M., Martins, O. M., Păun, D., & Mihoreanu, L. (2021). Exploring opportunities and challenges of artificial intelligence and machine learning in higher education institutions. *Sustainability (Basel)*, *13*(18), 10424. DOI: 10.3390/su131810424

Li, H., Fan, X., & Liang, J. (2025). The squirrel AI adaptive learning system accompanying millions of children in their growth. In *Digital transformation of regional education in China* (pp. 51–53). Springer Nature Singapore. DOI: 10.1007/978-981-97-8144-7_7

McDonald, N., Johri, A., Ali, A., & Collier, A. H. (2025). Generative artificial intelligence in higher education: Evidence from an analysis of institutional policies and guidelines. *Computers in Human Behavior: Artificial Humans*, *3*, 100121. DOI: 10.1016/j.chbah.2025.100121

Park, W., & Kwon, H. (2024). Implementing artificial intelligence education for middle school technology education in Republic of Korea. *International Journal of Technology and Design Education*, *34*(1), 109–135. DOI: 10.1007/s10798-023-09812-2 PMID: 36844448

Schiff, D. (2022). Education for AI, not AI for education: The role of education and ethics in national AI policy strategies. *International Journal of Artificial Intelligence in Education*, *32*(3), 527–563. DOI: 10.1007/s40593-021-00270-2

Tedre, M., Toivonen, T., Kahila, J., Vartiainen, H., Valtonen, T., Jormanainen, I., & Pears, A. (2021). Teaching machine learning in K–12 classroom: Pedagogical and technological trajectories for artificial intelligence education. *IEEE Access : Practical Innovations, Open Solutions*, *9*, 110558–110572. DOI: 10.1109/ACCESS.2021.3097962

Tutsoy, O. (2021). COVID-19 epidemic and opening of the schools: Artificial intelligence-based long-term adaptive policy making to control the pandemic diseases. *IEEE Access : Practical Innovations, Open Solutions*, *9*, 68461–68471. DOI: 10.1109/ACCESS.2021.3078080

Zou, D., Xie, H., & Kohnke, L. (2025). Navigating the Future: Establishing a Framework for Educators' Pedagogic Artificial Intelligence Competence. *European Journal of Education*, *60*(2), e70117. DOI: 10.1111/ejed.70117

KEY TERMS AND DEFINITIONS

Artificial Intelligence (AI): A field of computer science focused on creating systems capable of performing tasks that typically require human intelligence, such as decision-making, pattern recognition, and language understanding. In education, AI powers tools like adaptive learning platforms and cognitive tutors.

Cognitive Tutor: A type of AI-powered educational software that simulates human tutoring by providing personalized, step-by-step feedback based on cognitive models of how students learn. These systems adapt in real time to student inputs and performance.

Personalized Learning: An instructional approach that tailors learning experiences to individual student needs, preferences, and progress. AI enables personalized learning by continuously analyzing student data and adjusting content delivery.

Adaptive Learning System: A software platform that modifies the presentation of material based on student performance, engagement, and learning patterns. These systems use algorithms to recommend content or adjust difficulty levels dynamically.

Digital Divide: The gap between individuals or communities with adequate access to digital technologies and those without. In education, it refers to disparities in internet connectivity, devices, and digital literacy that affect equitable access to AI tools.

Algorithmic Bias: Systematic errors in AI decision-making that result from biased data or model assumptions. In education, this can lead to unfair treatment or outcomes for certain student groups based on race, gender, socio-economic status, or language background.

Data Privacy: The protection of personal and sensitive information collected by digital systems. In educational settings, data privacy involves safeguarding student records, performance data, and behavioral information from unauthorized access or misuse.

Teacher-AI Collaboration: A model of technology integration where AI tools support rather than replace teachers—enhancing instruction, providing real-time analytics, and allowing educators to focus on more complex, human-centered tasks.

Pedagogical Misalignment: A mismatch between the instructional methods embedded in educational technologies and the teaching philosophies or learning needs of a classroom. For example, AI tools may emphasize rote learning in environments that prioritize critical thinking and collaboration.

Institutional Inertia: Resistance to change within educational systems, often due to entrenched policies, bureaucratic processes, or cultural norms. It can delay or hinder the adoption of innovative tools like AI, even when evidence supports their efficacy.

Explainable AI (XAI): An area of AI research focused on making algorithmic processes transparent and understandable to human users. In education, XAI helps teachers and students interpret how learning recommendations or assessments are generated.

Chapter 13
Integration of AI With Emerging Educational Technologies

V. Rajeswari
Karpagam College of Engineering, India

P. Selvakumar
https://orcid.org/0000-0002-3650-4548
Department of Science and Humanities, Nehru Institute of Technology, Coimbatore, India

Jaya Saxena
https://orcid.org/0000-0001-5365-046X
Indira University, Pune, India

Swati Raturi
https://orcid.org/0000-0001-7293-6113
The ICFAI University, Dehradun, India

Biswo Ranjan Mishra
https://orcid.org/0009-0006-5394-9609
Utkal University, Bhubaneswar, India

Shabina Fred Rishma F.
Vel Tech Rangarajan Dr. Sagunthala R&D Institute of Science and Technology, India

ABSTRACT

Modern education, revolutionizing how students learn, how teachers instruct, and how educational institutions operate. The integration of intelligent tutoring systems and predictive analytics—has significantly impacted both traditional and digital learning environments. This transformation is fueled by the global demand for, accessible, and effective educational experiences. While potential, it also raises complex.Moreover, AI contributes to These such as Knewton or Squirrel AI, can provide immediate assistance, answer questions, and offer explanations 24/7, without the limitations of human availability. qualified teachers or where classroom sizes are too large for individualized attention. These technologies not only supplement teacher instruction but also enable continuous learning outside the classroom,

DOI: 10.4018/979-8-3373-4217-7.ch013

supporting the development of lifelong learning habits. In terms of administrative efficiency, AI applications streamline various Tools automate grading, manage scheduling, track attendance, and even learners.

THE RISE OF AI IN EDUCATION: OPPORTUNITIES AND CHALLENGES

Modern education, revolutionizing how students learn, how teachers instruct, and how educational institutions operate. The integration of intelligent tutoring systems and predictive analytics—has significantly impacted both traditional and digital learning environments. This transformation is fueled by the global demand for, accessible, and effective educational experiences. While potential, it also raises complex. Moreover, AI contributes to These such as Knewton or Squirrel AI, can provide immediate assistance, answer questions, and offer explanations 24/7, without the limitations of human availability. (Athavale et al., 2025) qualified teachers or where classroom sizes are too large for individualized attention. These technologies not only supplement teacher instruction but also enable continuous learning outside the classroom, supporting the development of lifelong learning habits. In terms of administrative efficiency, AI applications streamline various Tools automate grading, manage scheduling, track attendance, and even learners. Learning management systems integrated with AI can generate insights into course effectiveness and student engagement, helping educators refine their teaching strategies. Universities are increasingly using AI to predict student outcomes, enabling academically emotionally. Another significant advantage is the enhancement of accessibility and inclusion. AI-driven and Google's Read Along app help learners with dyslexia and reading challenges by reading aloud, highlighting text, and providing visual cues. Similarly, AI-powered translation tools can support multilingual education, allowing non-native speakers to engage more effectively with educational content. The global reach of AI-enabled education also holds transformative potential for developing nations. AI-powered mobile learning platforms can deliver quality education to remote and underserved areas, addressing teacher shortages and lack of infrastructure. For instance, apps like M-Shule in Kenya via SMS students areas with limited internet connectivity. This democratization of learning helps bridge the educational divide and promotes inclusive growth, making quality education a reality for more people worldwide. Without stringent regulations and safeguards, sensitive student information can be exploited or misused. transparent data policies, ethical AI frameworks, and stronger oversight respects student rights and maintains public trust. amplify these biases. For example, predictive analytics used in college admissions or scholarship recommendations may unintentionally disadvantage certain groups if historical data reflects systemic inequalities and inclusivity continuous diverse datasets, involvement from ethicists, educators, and marginalized communities.

While can handle many instructional and administrative tasks, it cannot replicate the emotional intelligence, mentorship, and nuanced understanding of human teachers. that reduce education transactional process, undermining the relational and social aspects that are crucial to student development. (Athavale et al., 2025) Instead of replacing teachers to augment their capabilities, allowing them to focus on high-impact, creative, and empathetic teaching. Furthermore, there exists a digital divide that may exacerbate inequalities in access to AI-driven education. Students in low-income households or rural areas may lack the necessary devices, internet access, or digital literacy to benefit from AI tools. This divide could widen existing achievement gaps unless addressed through targeted policies, infrastructure investment, and community support. Governments and educational institutions must ensure that the deployment AI technologies efforts promote digital inclusion equity. The regulation and standardization of AI in education is another critical area requiring attention. Currently, there is a lack of consistent policies governing schools and universities. As AI becomes more embedded in educational systems, stakeholders responsible use, accountability, transparency. This includes determining who is responsible when AI systems fail, setting quality benchmarks. Rise landscape rich with promise and complexity. It offers unprecedented opportunities to personalize learning, enhance accessibility, improve efficiency, and expand educational reach. At the same time, it raises serious educators. To navigate evolving terrain, a collaborative approach is essential—one

THE POTENTIAL OF AI: ENHANCING EMERGING EDUCATIONAL TECHNOLOGIES

Driven by rapid evolution emerging technologies. As traditional teaching models face growing pressure to adapt to the needs of a digital-native generation and an increasingly globalized world, educational institutions are embracing new tools that promise to enhance learning effectiveness, accessibility, (Baker et al., 2025) and engagement. These learning analytics—are reshaping the way knowledge is delivered, assessed, and retained. Together, they signal that is more personalized, flexible, interactive, and student-centered than ever before. this space is the integration of Artificial Intelligence (AI) into various aspects of education. AI-powered tools such as adaptive learning platforms, intelligent tutoring systems, and predictive analytics are revolutionizing both teaching and learning. These systems pacing, and preferences. Moreover, educators scheduling, and progress tracking, thereby allowing them to focus more on student interaction mentorship. Applications like

Google Expeditions and zSpace offer such experiential learning opportunities that deepen understanding and retention by engaging multiple senses. abstract concepts can be difficult to grasp through traditional methods alone. Another transformative trend is the rise of gamification and game-based learning. By incorporating elements like point scoring, competition, and rewards into educational content, gamified platforms such as Kahoot! Classcraft, and Duolingo make learning more engaging and motivating.

Game-based learning fosters active participation and encourages can be particularly effective in early education, language learning, and subjects requiring repetition and memorization. Gamification also taps into intrinsic motivation by making learning fun and goal-oriented student outcomes. (Baker R. et al. 2025) Predictive models can even anticipate student dropouts or learning gaps before they occur, enabling timely interventions. In higher education, institutions like Purdue University and Georgia State University have used such tools to improve retention rates and academic success. Blackboard allow for seamless integration of multimedia resources, assessments, forums, and tracking tools. These platforms support hybrid and fully online learning models, providing flexibility and continuity in learning regardless of location or time constraints. Cloud-based tools enable collaborative learning through shared documents, video conferencing, and group projects, creating dynamic virtual classrooms that mirror or even enhance physical ones. Especially cloud technology proved indispensable in maintaining educational continuity across the globe. Mobile learning (m-learning) is another critical aspect of modern education, driven by the widespread availability of smartphones and tablets. Mobile apps provide on-the-go access to learning materials, microlearning modules, and interactive content. Platforms like Coursera, edX, and Khan Academy offer mobile-compatible content, this shift toward mobility supports lifelong learning and accommodates the increasingly busy and flexible schedules of students, professionals, and adult learners alike. Additionally, mobile learning extends the reach of education to remote and underserved communities, helping bridge the digital divide.

AI-POWERED VIRTUAL AND AUGMENTED REALITY: IMMERSIVE LEARNING EXPERIENCES

In education, particularly in its ability to enhance and expand the capabilities of emerging educational technologies. As schools, universities, and edtech companies integrate AI into their systems, adaptive, (Baker R. et al. 2025) efficient, and inclusive ecosystem. AI's potential lies not only in automating traditional educational tasks but in amplifying the effectiveness of technologies such as virtual and augmented reality (VR/AR), learning analytics, gamification, mobile learning, and blockchain.

When strategically implemented, AI transforms these tools into intelligent, dynamic systems capable of revolutionizing how learners engage with content, how educators deliver instruction, and how institutions manage educational processes. A key area where AI significantly enhances educational technologies is personalized and adaptive learning. Traditional educational models often fail to address individual learning differences, but the learner's interactions. When coupled with mobile or online platforms, this AI-enhanced adaptivity ensures that learners receive support tailored not just to their academic level but also to their learning style and pace, thus maximizing engagement and retention. AI and learning analytics also work hand in hand to enable data-informed decision-making for educators and administrators. Through AI-enhanced analytics, massive volumes of data—ranging from click patterns in online courses to speech in classroom discussions enabling proactive interventions. Tools like IBM Watson Education and BrightBytes provide dashboards powered by AI that visualize learner progress and recommend instructional strategies. This insight allows institutions to continuously refine teaching methodologies, curricula, and student support systems based on real evidence rather than assumption or retrospective analysis.

Gamification, which involves applying game design elements to educational environments, is another field significantly bolstered by AI. While gamified learning platforms already boost motivation through points, leaderboards, and rewards, the integration of AI adds a new layer of responsiveness and adaptivity. AI can analyze how a student responds to various game mechanics and adjusts the difficulty (Baker et al. 2025), pacing, or feedback style to maintain engagement and foster mastery. It can also help design more nuanced learning games that adapt narratives, challenges, or strategies based on real-time learner behavior. Platforms like Classcraft and Quizizz are beginning to explore these potentials, where AI-driven personalization enhances the gamified experience, making it not only more enjoyable but also more effective. The combination holds particular promise in creating immersive, intelligent learning environments. While VR/AR technologies already such as conducting virtual science experiments or exploring ancient cities—AI enhances this by making these environments context-aware and responsive. For instance, an AI-enhanced VR tutor could adjust its explanations based on a learner's gaze patterns or questions, effectively acting as a real-time guide inside the virtual space. AI can also dynamically generate scenarios in AR environments that suit a learner's progress, ensuring experiences are neither too easy nor too overwhelming. Educational apps integrating AI with AR, such as Google Lens or Curiscope's Virtuali-Tee, offer interactive and evolving experiences that adjust based on user interaction, significantly boosting engagement and comprehension. Mobile learning—a major pillar of educational access and convenience—is also being redefined through AI integration. Mobile apps supported by AI offer features like voice recognition, natural language processing, and conversational interfaces, enabling more interactive and user-friendly experiences. optimize question sequences, predict errors, and personalize lesson plans. Similarly, AI chatbots embedded in mobile platforms provide on-demand tutoring, answer frequently asked questions, and support time management. These AI-driven mobile experiences ensure that learners are continuously supported, regardless of location or time constraints, making education truly accessible and flexible.

AI-DRIVEN GAMIFICATION: ENHANCING ENGAGEMENT AND MOTIVATION

Combining the sensory-rich environments of VR/AR with the cognitive capabilities of AI, educators and developers are creating powerful tools that engage learners more deeply, adapt. This intersection is not merely a technological upgrade—it represents a pedagogical shift that places students (Chen & Liu, 2025a) supported by intelligent dynamically behaviors, choices, and progress. Virtual and augmented reality alone have demonstrated remarkable potential to immerse learners in simulated or enhanced environments. VR enables full immersion into computer-generated worlds, train in technical, environments with interactive content. Both technologies have been applied in diverse educational fields—from medical and engineering training to language learning and history education—with evidence showing increased motivation, engagement, and knowledge retention. However, when AI is integrated into these immersive technologies, the result is not just interaction but intelligent interaction—one where the system understands, interprets, and adapts to the learner's actions. One of the most powerful enhancements AI brings to VR/AR learning environments is real-time personalization. AI algorithms can monitor a learner's progress within a virtual environment, analyzing actions, decision-making speed, errors, and behavioral patterns to adapt the learning experience in real time. For instance, in a VR simulation designed to teach chemistry lab safety, AI can detect if a student is consistently overlooking a critical step and immediately adjust the scenario to offer hints, reintroduce key concepts, or slow down the simulation. This adaptability ensures that each learner receives a tailored experience, reducing frustration and improving understanding. In AR, AI might analyze how a user scans or interacts with digital overlays and provide contextually relevant prompts or additional layers of information based on that analysis. Such intelligent personalization is critical in meeting diverse learner needs and optimizing educational outcomes.

Virtual assistants or avatars can serve as guides or tutors within VR/AR environments, capable of holding natural conversations, answering questions, and offering encouragement. These AI agents can recognize (Chen & Liu, 2025b) voice commands, facial expressions, and gestures, allowing for more intuitive and human-like interactions. For example, in a language learning VR program, an AI-driven avatar might engage the learner in real-time conversations, assess pronunciation using NLP, and adjust its responses based on the learner's fluency level. In AR educational apps, AI can enable real-time object recognition—such as identifying a plant or anatomical model—and offer immediate, tailored explanations. AI also plays a crucial role in dynamic content generation within immersive environments. Rather than relying on static scenarios or pre-scripted lessons, AI can generate new learning experiences on the fly, adjusting difficulty levels, narrative paths, and problem sets based on learner input. In VR-based coding or engineering platforms, for example, AI might design increasingly complex simulations as a learner demonstrates proficiency, or introduce challenges based on prior mistakes. This dynamic approach prevents stagnation and ensures continual progression. In AR applications used in field education—such as environmental science or archaeology—AI can update overlays with real-time data, suggest exploratory paths, or adapt content based on geographical location and learner behavior. This level of content flexibility turns immersive learning into a living experience that evolves with the learner. Another area where AI enhances VR/AR education is through. Traditionally, immersive learning environments have struggled with evaluating learner performance beyond basic interaction metrics. AI changes this by providing deeper analytics on how students learn, think, and solve problems within a virtual or augmented space. Using machine learning models, AI can assess complex behaviors—such as how a medical student performs a simulated surgery in VR or how a construction trainee interacts with virtual machinery—and provide detailed, formative feedback. This feedback can include not just a final score but analysis of decision-making, efficiency, attention to detail, and even emotional engagement, using biometric and behavioral cues. These insights help both learners and educators understand strengths and areas for improvement in a way that static tests cannot.

AI-POWERED LEARNING ANALYTICS: INSIGHTS FOR PERSONALIZED LEARNING

Experience into one that is interactive, goal-oriented, and rewarding. However, the next major evolution in gamified learning is being driven by Artificial Intelligence (AI), which enhances gamification by personalizing experiences, adapting challenges in real time, and providing data-driven insights into learner behaviour, (Agrela Rodrigues et al. 2024). At heart AI-driven gamification personalization. Traditional gamified systems often apply a uniform structure across all learners, offering the same challenges and rewards regardless of individual ability, preference, or learning style. AI transforms this model by enabling dynamic personalization, where the system continuously analyzes learner performance, behavior, and preferences to adjust game elements accordingly. For instance, reduce the difficulty level, offer contextual hints, or change the type of challenge to match the learner's style—be it visual, auditory, or kinesthetic. Conversely, for advanced learners, the system can introduce higher-level challenges, alternative missions, or optional "boss levels" to maintain interest and prevent stagnation. This responsive design ensures that each learner remains within their optimal zone of development, balancing challenge and skill to maximize engagement—a principle closely aligned with Vygotsky's Zone of Proximal Development. Another way AI elevates gamification is through real-time feedback and adaptive progression. Traditional educational games provide fixed feedback based on predefined outcomes, but AI enables more nuanced and timely feedback mechanisms. By analyzing learners' interactions and decisions predict future performance, deliver tailored feedback that is immediate, relevant, and constructive. For example, if a learner repeatedly makes errors in a math game, the AI can infer misconceptions and introduce targeted micro-lessons or practice drills before allowing the learner to progress reflection, reinforcement improves learning outcomes but also sustains motivation by acknowledging effort, guiding improvement, and celebrating incremental successes.

Figure 1. AI-integrated with emerging technologies for Metaverse applications

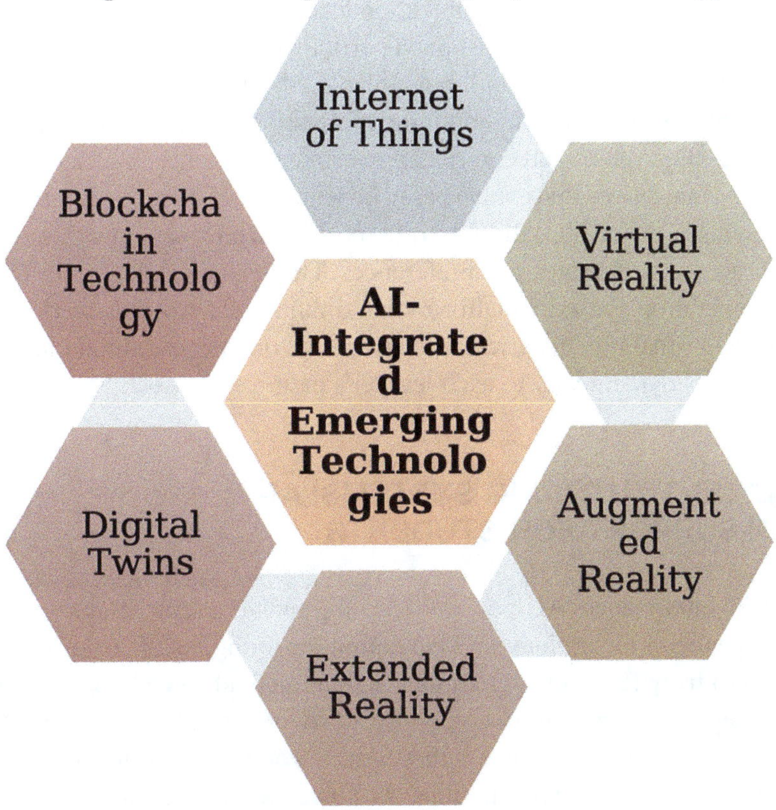

Motivation theory plays a key role in understanding how AI-driven gamification impacts learners. Drawing on frameworks like AI can design gamified experiences that fulfill these psychological drivers. AI systems support autonomy by offering learners choices in how they navigate content—selecting missions, customizing avatars, or choosing learning paths. They enhance competence by ensuring tasks are neither too easy nor too difficult, promoting a sense of accomplishment and growth. (Anderson et al. 2020) AI can also foster relatedness through collaborative or competitive features that connect learners with peers, enabling cooperative missions, social recognition, or team-based challenges. These elements are dynamically adjusted based on user engagement, ensuring that learners stay emotionally connected to the experience most innovative aspects gamification to employ to inform and refine the gamified experience. response times, error rates, game strategies, and emotional indicators (such as hesitation or rapid guessing)—to build detailed learner profiles. These profiles help the system predict which types of gamified elements are most effective for each user, allowing for highly responds best to narrative-driven challenges and collaborative play, and thus restructure future lessons to emphasize those elements. This level of customization leads to more meaningful engagement and increases the likelihood of sustained participation and achievement. AI-driven storytelling and narrative generation are also powerful tools in gamified learning. Storylines are often central to maintaining motivation in educational games, as they provide context, purpose, and emotional investment. AI can enhance this by generating adaptive narratives that evolve based on learner decisions and progress. Rather than following a linear plot, the AI crafts personalized story arcs that respond to learner choices, success rates, and preferences. This technique, known as procedural narrative generation, is used in platforms that simulate real-world scenarios—such as ethical decision-making, historical re-enactments, or business simulations—where the story adapts dynamically to each learner's path.

INTELLIGENT TUTORING SYSTEMS: AI-DRIVEN SUPPORT FOR STUDENTS

Artificial Intelligence (AI)-powered learning analytics represents a groundbreaking convergence of technology and education, enabling a shift from standardized instruction to truly leveraging quantities educational advanced, learning analytics provides deep, These insights not only inform educators but also empower learners by shaping individualized pathways that adapt As education systems strive to serve increasingly diverse student populations, AI-powered learning analytics has emerged critical optimizing instruction promoting academic on a large scale (Filiz et al. 2025) modeling, making it possible to interpret complex datasets with speed and precision. Unlike traditional analytics tools that focus primarily on assessment scores or attendance, AI-powered systems consider a much broader range of indicators—such as time spent on tasks, clickstream data, emotional responses, forum participation, eye-tracking, and even biometric inputs. These multifaceted data streams provide a holistic picture of how students learn, where they struggle, and what motivates them. system may automatically assign foundational review materials, interactive practice modules, or recommend one-on-one tutoring. Conversely, a high-performing student might be fast-tracked through introductory content and presented with enrichment challenges. This adaptability ensures that every learner receives instruction that is neither too easy nor too difficult, supporting mastery and sustained engagement. AI-driven personalization also extends to learning path recommendations. Based on a learner's prior knowledge, goals, and performance history, the system can suggest the most relevant modules, resources, or activities. These recommendations they evolve learning journey to remain flexible and responsive. In platforms like Knewton, DreamBox Learning, and Squirrel AI, students are guided through non-linear learning paths that are continually optimized for their growth.

In addition to guiding students, supporting educators and instructional designers. Through intuitive dashboards and visualizations, teachers can monitor class-wide and individual performance in real time, (Filiz et al. 2025). They can identify students who are falling behind, spot misconceptions, and assess the effectiveness of specific instructional strategies. These insights allow for timely and targeted interventions—such as offering feedback, modifying teaching approaches, or initiating parent-teacher communication. Furthermore, AI can highlight trends across multiple classes or semesters, aiding curriculum development and long-term planning. capabilities in this domain. By identifying patterns and correlations in AI can such as course completion, test performance, or risk of dropout power institutions often before students themselves are aware of their risk. For example, if a university's analytics platform detects that a student's engagement and grades are declining, it can alert advisors or instructors to provide support—whether through counseling, tutoring, or workload adjustments. Predictive modeling can also inform admissions, placement, and resource allocation decisions at the institutional level, optimizing educational systems for better outcomes. AI-powered learning analytics is also instrumental in formative assessment and feedback. Instead of term, AI systems continuously assess learners through their interactions with digital content. These systems can evaluate not only whether an answer is correct but how it was reached—considering timing, process, and effort. Feedback is then tailored to guide improvement rather than simply reporting errors. For instance, in language learning platforms like Duolingo or Lingvist, AI assesses pronunciation accuracy and grammatical choices in real time, providing corrective prompts and alternative phrasing based on the user's linguistic patterns. This form of real-time, low-stakes assessment helps learners understand their mistakes and build confidence.

AUTOMATED GRADING AND FEEDBACK: AI-POWERED ASSESSMENT

offering tailored, real-time instructional support to students. Designed to simulate the guidance and adaptivity monitor learner performance, diagnose misunderstandings, and provide instant feedback and personalized instruction one-on-one tutoring and traditional classroom instruction, offering scalable, responsive, and highly individualized support. As education continues to transition toward digital and hybrid environments, ITS are becoming increasingly integral in creating effective, equitable, and engaging learning experiences for a wide range of learners, (Fischer & Lutz, 2020). At their core, Intelligent Tutoring Systems are built upon a combination of four key components the how instruction should be delivered; and the user interface, which facilitates interaction. AI enhances each of these components by allowing the system to adapt dynamically to each learner's unique needs. For instance, a mathematics ITS might adjust problem difficulty in real time, provide hints when a learner struggles, and recommend review topics based on prior errors. This responsiveness mirrors the personalized attention of a human tutor but with the scalability of digital technology. A central strength of ITS lies in their ability to provide real-time formative assessment. By analyzing every learner interaction—keystrokes, problem-solving steps, time spent on questions—AI can identify not just what a student got wrong, but why. This allows the system to differentiate between conceptual misunderstandings, procedural errors, and careless mistakes, tailoring feedback accordingly. For example, in an ITS like Carnegie Learning's MATHia, when a student repeatedly misapplies a formula, the system might trigger a targeted explanation of the underlying concept, while for a simple computational error, it might encourage retrying the step. This granular feedback helps correct misconceptions early and supports deeper understanding.

Moreover, ITS can adapt their instructional strategies to align with a learner's profile and behavior. By continuously updating the student model based on new data, the AI adjusts its teaching methods—whether it's offering more practice, switching to a different type of explanation, or introducing gamified elements to maintain engagement. varying prior knowledge, learning speeds, and motivational drivers. In systems like ALEKS or ASSISTments, AI personalizes learning paths so that students are neither bored by content they've already mastered nor overwhelmed by material they're not ready for, optimizing their learning trajectory, (Fischer & Lutz, 2020). One of the most innovative capabilities of modern ITS facilitate conversational interaction. AI-powered tutors like AutoTutor or Jill Watson engage learners through dialogue, posing questions, interpreting responses, and guiding students through Socratic questioning. These systems simulate the experience of a tutoring conversation, explain reasoning, in natural language. This conversational approach not only improves comprehension but also promotes metacognition—helping learners reflect on their thought processes and develop self-regulation skills essential for lifelong learning. Additionally, ITS contribute to self-paced and mastery-based learning, where students advance only after demonstrating proficiency. Unlike traditional models constrained by fixed schedules. This flexibility supports a more equitable learning experience, as it accommodates different learning speeds without penalizing students who need more time to grasp certain concepts. In systems like DreamBox or Knewton, students receive individualized learning journeys that emphasize mastery over rote progression, building strong conceptual foundations and confidence.

landscape by offering scalable, consistent, and immediate evaluation of student work. Traditionally, assessment has been a time-intensive task for educators, especially in large classrooms or online learning environments where individualized feedback is critical but often unattainable due to time constraints, (Fischer & Lutz, 2020). AI-powered assessment tools are addressing these challenges by automating the grading process for various coding tasks even spoken responses—while simultaneously providing targeted, formative feedback. enhances quality and timeliness feedback students receive, fostering more effective learning. These tasks, while straightforward, become significantly more efficient when handled by AI, especially in massive open online courses (MOOCs) and large-scale standardized testing. AI can rapidly scan thousands of submissions with near-perfect accuracy and consistency, eliminating human error or bias that may arise from fatigue or subjectivity. However, the true potential of AI-powered assessment lies beyond simple grading—its capacity to analyze complex, open-ended responses and offer constructive feedback is what distinguishes it as a transformative educational tool written work. Tools like ETS's e-rater, Grammarly, and Turnitin's Revision Assistant analyze syntax, vocabulary usage, argument strength, and even stylistic elements such as tone or clarity. These platforms provide students with suggestions to improve their writing—such as rephrasing awkward sentences, eliminating redundancy, or enhancing thesis statements—before or after submission. AI systems are increasingly capable of identifying nuanced issues, including logical fallacies, insufficient evidence, or off-topic responses, thereby helping students refine critical thinking and academic writing skills.

Grading that may take days or weeks, AI can deliver real-time feedback moments after assignment submission. This immediacy enhances learning by closing the feedback loop quickly—students can identify and address their mistakes while the material is still fresh. For example, in a language learning platform, (Fischer & Lutz, 2020). AI may analyze pronunciation in spoken responses and suggest phonetic corrections, while in a coding environment, it might highlight syntax errors and suggest debugging strategies. This continuous, low-stakes feedback encourages iterative learning and reduces the fear of failure by normalizing revision and experimentation. Scalability and efficiency are key advantages of AI-powered grading, particularly in online education or large enrollment courses. Instructors can assign more open-ended and higher-order thinking tasks without worrying about grading overload. For instance, a computer science instructor using an AI-assisted code evaluation platform like Mimir or Gradescope can assign real-world coding problems and receive not only automated scores but also detailed analytics on common errors, logic patterns, and runtime efficiency. Similarly, language instructors using AI-supported tools can monitor students' grammar and vocabulary development across thousands of essays, gaining insights that would be impossible to gather manually. reducing grading bias and improving consistency Human graders are subject to unconscious biases related to student identity, handwriting, tone, or even mood during assessment. AI, when properly trained and tested for fairness, can provide uniform evaluations across all student submissions. For example, early automated essay scoring systems were criticized for favoring longer essays or those with complex vocabulary—even when such traits didn't equate to stronger arguments. Today, more sophisticated models are

FUTURE TRENDS IN AI AND EMERGING EDUCATIONAL TECHNOLOGIES

AI systems monitor wide range of data points—time on task, quiz scores, click patterns, mistakes, engagement levels, and even emotional cues where available. This data is synthesized to build and update a comprehensive learner profile, which represents not just what the student knows, but how they learn best. Based on this profile, the AI makes intelligent decisions about what content to present next, when to review material, and how to scaffold upcoming lessons, ensuring the student remains challenged but not overwhelmed. quickly masters introductory algebraic concepts, the system may skip redundant lessons and present more advanced material, accelerating progress. Conversely, if the same student struggles with word problems, (Fisher T. et al. 2021) the AI may offer additional practice, alternative explanations, or visual supports tailored to the learner's preferences. This just-in-time adaptation is fundamental to maintaining motivation and preventing both boredom and frustration. Platforms like DreamBox Learning (for math), Duolingo (for language), and Coursera (for higher education) use these adaptive systems to guide learners through nonlinear, personalized pathways. Goal alignment and learner agency are central to AI-driven personalization. These systems often allow students to set short- and long-term goals—such as mastering a skill, passing an exam, or preparing for a career path—and then tailor content accordingly. AI acts as a learning concierge, recommending modules, resources, or activities that align with the learner's aspirations and prior achievements. For instance, in a career-focused platform, a student interested in data science might be guided through an optimized mix of statistics, Python programming, and machine learning modules, with the path adjusting based

on strengths and areas of difficulty. This level of customization gives learners a sense of control and relevance, increasing both engagement and persistence.

Furthermore, AI-driven personalized learning paths can account for learning styles and preferences, adjusting delivery methods to suit individual needs. While the concept of learning styles remains debated in pedagogical theory, personalization through AI can adapt instruction modes to include multimedia, simulations, interactive problem-solving, textual explanations, or collaborative projects—based on what engages the learner most effectively. A student who learns best through visuals might be guided toward infographic-based lessons and interactive diagrams, while another who thrives on auditory input might receive voice explanations and podcasts. The system tracks which formats lead to higher comprehension and retention and adjusts future recommendations accordingly. Formative feedback and scaffolding are essential features embedded in AI-driven paths. As students move through content, the AI not only monitors performance but offers real-time, targeted feedback to reinforce correct approaches and correct errors. This feedback is often scaffolded to support learner independence: initial errors may prompt hints or additional context, while repeated mistakes could trigger more in-depth remediation or suggest a review of foundational concepts, (Fisher et al. 2021). This dynamic support ensures that learners are neither left behind nor overly dependent, fostering deeper understanding and resilience. The feedback loop also feeds back into the AI system itself, helping it refines its recommendations through continuous learning. In conclusion, uniform instruction toward a flexible, learner-centric model. By analyzing real-time data and adapting content to fit each learner's unique journey, AI empowers students to learn more effectively, efficiently, and confidently. These systems support equity, foster independence, and allow educators to focus on higher-order teaching. As long as implementation is guided by ethical considerations, inclusivity, and sound pedagogy, personalized AI learning paths will continue to be a cornerstone of future-ready education systems.

TEACHER TRAINING AND SUPPORT: PREPARING EDUCATORS FOR AI-DRIVEN EDUCATION

Disparities in digital literacy and the ability to use advanced technological tools. In many parts of the world, platforms increasingly become the norm in classrooms, students without access to these resources are at a disadvantage. Without internet access or devices, students cannot participate in AI-driven learning environments, and their educational opportunities are significantly diminished. In addition to access to technology, there is also the issue of digital literacy, (Rizzo et al. 2020). Even when skills necessary to navigate AI-based educational platforms effectively. AI-driven tools often require a certain level of digital fluency, including the ability to use platforms, interpret AI-generated feedback, and interact with adaptive learning systems. In regions where digital literacy is not widespread, students may struggle to use these tools productively, leading to disparities in educational outcomes. This disparity is compounded in communities where teachers themselves needed classrooms. Moreover, non-representative datasets, they may unintentionally favor certain student groups over others. For example, AI systems designed to grade essays may be biased against students who use dialects or non-standard English, leading to unfair evaluations. Similarly, AI-driven learning platforms may unintentionally favor students from certain cultural or linguistic backgrounds, while leaving others behind. These biases can undermine the promise of personalized education, reinforcing existing inequalities rather than addressing them is unclear how decisions are being made or why certain recommendations are being given. For instance, an AI system may recommend specific learning resources or courses to a student, but without transparency, students and educators may not understand why these particular suggestions were made. In situations where AI systems are used for grading or providing feedback, this lack of transparency can be especially problematic. If students feel that AI is unfairly assessing their work, without an understanding of how or why decisions were made, it can lead to frustration and distrust. Furthermore, without accountability mechanisms, AI systems may continue to perpetuate biases, and there may be little recourse for those affected by unjust decisions.

Moreover, there is concern about the potential leading to the reduction of human interaction in the classroom. While AI tools can help personalize learning, they can never education, support, mentorship, the ability to foster creativity and critical thinking. AI-based education, if over-relied upon, (Rizzo et al. 2020) may inadvertently lead to a depersonalization of learning, particularly in underfunded or overcrowded educational settings. In regions where resources are already scarce, the push toward AI-driven education could result in a greater focus on efficiency at the expense of personal engagement and holistic development. It is vital that AI in education complements, rather than replaces, human teaching and mentorship, and that educators continue in ways that foster meaningful student-teacher relationships funding infrastructure to support AI technologies. Even in wealthier areas, disparities exist between schools and districts in terms of access to cutting-edge AI tools. As a result, there is a risk that AI-driven education could deepen existing inequalities, benefiting well-resourced schools while leaving underserved communities further behind. To address this challenge, governments, private companies, and educational institutions provide technologies, ensuring that the most marginalized students are not excluded also poses challenges to equity. While certain countries and educational systems are quick to integrate AI technologies, others lag behind due to a variety of factors, including financial constraints, political instability, and lack of infrastructure. Students in regions without robust technological infrastructure may miss out on the opportunities that AI-powered education provides. To address this, there must be concerted efforts from global organizations, governments, and tech companies that resources are allocated to the region's most in need.

IMPLEMENTING AI-POWERED EDUCATIONAL TECHNOLOGIES: STRATEGIES AND CONSIDERATIONS

One of the primary challenges educators faces when familiarity with the technology. Many teachers have not received formal training in AI, which can create feelings of uncertainty or reluctance when it comes to using AI tools in their classrooms. effectively use technologies, crucial teachers to confidently navigate AI-driven education. Just as digital literacy became an essential skill for educators, AI literacy is now necessary for educators to thrive in the AI-enhanced learning environment, (Saldaña et al. 2023). Training programs aimed at improving AI literacy should include a mix of theoretical knowledge and data analytics, as well as how these concepts apply to educational technology. Additionally, teachers should learn how AI can be used to support their teaching goals, such as tailoring content its integration. While AI literacy is important, it is equally essential that teacher training programs emphasize the pedagogical aspects of AI. never replace the core teaching practices that foster critical thinking, creativity, and social-emotional development; rather, they should complement and support these practices. Training programs should emphasize pedagogical frameworks that align with AI integration, ensuring that teachers are equipped to use AI in ways that promote effective learning. For instance, teachers should be trained to use AI for differentiation, allowing, while also ensuring teacher-student interaction remain central to the learning process. Programs should also focus on how their peers in ways that would not be possible in traditional, one-size-fits-all classrooms' data privacy, security, and fairness. Training should include discussions about algorithmic transparency and how AI can impact student agency, ensuring that teachers are not only equipped to use AI effectively but also in ways that are ethical and inclusive.

AI is not a static technology; it evolves rapidly, with new tools and updates emerging constantly, (Saldaña et al. 2023). As such, teacher training must Teachers require continuous professional development (PD) to stay current with the latest AI advancements and learn how to developments. School districts organizations should invest in continuous PD programs focused on AI. These programs should not only provide teachers with access to the latest AI tools but also offer opportunities for collaborative learning and peer support. their experiences using AI, exchange best practices, and troubleshoot challenges together. This collaborative approach ensures that teachers are not isolated in their efforts to integrate AI, but rather have a network of support from colleagues, tech experts, and instructional leaders. In addition to formal PD programs, teachers can benefit from personalized coaching and mentoring. Coaches who are familiar with AI technologies can work with teachers individually or in small groups to provide tailored guidance contexts. This personalized support ensures that teachers feel empowered to experiment with AI tools and receive targeted feedback that helps them refine their practice over time. For AI tools to truly meet the needs of educators, there must be ongoing collaboration between teachers and EdTech developers. While many AI tools functionality may not always align with the realities of the classroom. Teachers are often the best source of feedback on the practical usability of AI tools, as they understand firsthand what works and what doesn't in terms of student engagement, assessment, and support.

EVALUATING EFFECTIVENESS: ASSESSING THE IMPACT OF AI-DRIVEN EDUCATION

The successful implementation of AI-powered educational technologies requires a robust technological infrastructure. AI technologies demand significant computing power, reliable internet connectivity, and up-to-date hardware and software systems. Educational and the overall technical capacity of the institution. In many cases, schools and universities may need to make substantial investments in upgrading their infrastructure to accommodate AI-powered tools, (Singh et al. 2025). For example, crucial in safeguarding student privacy and maintaining the trust of all stakeholders' educators to use AI in ways that enhance the learning experience, promote student engagement, and support differentiated instruction. Professional development programs should be designed to help teachers understand how these technologies can be used to support various learning styles and needs. Teachers should also be trained to interpret AI-generated instruction. In addition to technical training, teachers must be supported in developing pedagogical strategies that maximize the effectiveness of AI tools. This requires ongoing, hands-on professional development and access to support networks, such as peer learning communities and mentoring from AI experts that these systems are ethical and free from bias. AI tools are built on algorithms that algorithms can sometimes be biased or unrepresentative. a dataset that historical or unequal access educational resources, the system. This can perpetuate existing inequalities and create new challenges in achieving equity in education. To address these concerns, educational institutions must implement strong oversight and accountability mechanisms for fairness, transparency accuracy to ensure they are not reinforcing biases or discriminatory practices. Moreover, AI when training their algorithms to reduce the risk of bias. Additionally, institutions should foster in education, designed to be with diverse needs. Additionally, AI systems should be educational to ensure a population.

Governments, private sector companies, and educational institutions must work together -powered educational (Singh et al. 2025) technologies. This could cost or subsidized devices and internet access for low-income students, as well as supporting used in low-resource environments. powered educational technology's function, privacy and security are key considerations in their implementation about kept secure and that respected at all times is encrypted, anonymized, and stored securely. Additionally, clear policies should be established regarding risks involved. Institutions should also implement procedures for monitoring and responding to potential data breaches to minimize the risk of exposure. For AI-powered educational technologies to have a lasting impact, they must be scalable and sustainable. This means that educational institutions should consider how to expand AI initiatives over time and ensure that they can continue to evolve with technological advancements. Implementing AI in education is not a one-time event but a long-term investment that requires ongoing support, updates, and improvements. Scalability also involves ensuring adapted educational contexts institutions. What works well in one setting may not necessarily work in another, so AI technologies should be flexible enough diverse environments. Additionally, should plan for the costs of technology, training, and maintenance are manageable and can be sustained over time.

ENSURING DATA PRIVACY AND SECURITY: AI-DRIVEN EDUCATION AND DATA PROTECTION

Goal integrating into enhance by providing students with tailored, data-driven instruction and helping teachers streamline administrative tasks and improve their teaching methods. However, comes with a need for careful assessment. Evaluating the effectiveness of AI-driven education is critical for several reasons. Understanding Impact on Student Learning The central concern (Smith et al. 2021) of Effective evaluation helps determine whether AI tools are genuinely improving learning outcomes such as knowledge retention performance. Ensuring Equity and Inclusivity reduce educational that cater to diverse student needs. However, they also have identify whether tools are benefiting all students equitably or inadvertently reinforcing existing biases. Improving Teaching Practices AI can help Evaluating AI systems helps determine whether these tools are effectively supporting teachers in delivering high-quality instruction and creating more engaging learning environments. Informed Decision-Making: a worthwhile investment, educational institutions need data that clearly demonstrates the benefits and challenges associated with their use. Evaluation provides actionable insights that can inform decisions about scaling, modifying, or discontinuing AI tools, as well as guide future investments in AI technologies. In short, evaluation is vital for measuring and ensuring that benefits this powerful technology are fully realized while minimizing potential drawbacks. One of the most critical areas to evaluate when assessing AI-driven education is These outcomes include academic performance critical thinking, collaboration. Evaluating learning outcomes helps determine whether AI tools are enhancing student achievement and providing

To evaluate this, researchers and educators can compare student performance before and introduction tools, track improvements in student engagement and retention, and assess how well students are mastering learning objectives. Additionally, comparing AI-driven education with traditional teaching methods. technologies are designed to increase student engagement by personalizing the learning (Smith et al. 2021) experience. For instance, individual pace, helping them stay motivated and avoid frustration. Similarly, gamified AI tools can increase intrinsic motivation by making learning more interactive and enjoyable. Measuring student engagement involves evaluating not only academic performance but also students' attitudes toward learning, their participation in classroom activities, and their emotional connection to the material. Surveys, interviews, and usage analytics from AI platforms can provide whether those tools lead to higher levels of interest and motivation. AI technologies also aim to support offering insights into instructional strategies effectiveness of supporting teachers evaluate how well they assist in enhancing teaching practices. This includes examining whether teachers are able to provide more personalized instruction, adjust their teaching strategies based on AI feedback, and spend more time on meaningful student interactions. Teacher satisfaction is another important metric to assess. If AI tools are not user-friendly or do not significantly reduce workload, teachers may be reluctant to use them effectively. Evaluating teacher feedback, professional development, and changes in instructional practices can help determine whether AI tools are genuinely enhancing teacher effectiveness.

UNLOCKING THE POTENTIAL: AI AND THE FUTURE OF EDUCATION

importance ensuring privacy security in education cannot be overstated. As educational institutions and technology providers integrate AI tools, they must recognize that the data they collect can reveal intimate details about students' lives, behaviors, learning styles, could not only privacy violations but also contribute to broader issues of inequality, exploitation, and discrimination. prevent data breaches and misuse while fostering trust and safeguarding students' rights. In this context, understanding the (Tatar et al. 2022) fundamental aspects of data privacy powered educational technologies, and the strategy for mitigating these risks is of utmost importance. AI-powered educational technologies work by analyzing large datasets to make personalized recommendations, adjust learning management systems (LMS) and about a student's learning progress, preferences, interactions performance. This data enables AI systems to offer tailored content, suggest resources that align with a predict most effective next steps for their learning journey. Moreover, AI systems often employ machine learning algorithms that their predictive capabilities and enhance their decision-making. For instance, AI algorithms can track students' interactions with content, assess their responses to various learning activities, and use this data to continuously adjust lesson plans and activities. As such, the data collected by AI-powered systems is invaluable not only in supporting individualized learning but also in optimizing the functionality and effectiveness of educational technologies. However, this extensive use raises serious. For AI to provide truly personalized learning experiences, it needs detailed information about students' behaviors, attitudes, and performance. If handled improperly, this sensitive exposed, even exploited. Consequently, developers that the data is protected through effective.

Data-driven nature -powered educational technologies makes them prone to a range of privacy and security risks. These risks can institutions if not adequately addressed. Some of the key risks include AI-driven educational systems student data, making them attractive cybercriminals. Data breaches cyberattack can expose even behavioral data. Such loss of academic reputation. Additionally, the misuse of student data can have lifelong consequences for individuals, especially if that data is used for malicious purposes or to create harmful profiles of students. (Tatar et al. 2022). Many AI systems collect data without explicitly. Lack of transparency can undermine trust in AI-powered education. Students and their families and they may control how their data is used. ethical poses significant risks individual privacy rights. AI systems that use large datasets to make decisions are vulnerable to bias them incomplete. In education, biased systems can reinforce existing inequalities, disproportionately affecting students from marginalized groups. For instance, AI systems may unintentionally penalize students from different cultural backgrounds, those with disabilities, or students who speak non-standard dialects Another key concern in AI-driven education is data retention—the length of time for which student data is stored. Data retention policies must be carefully managed to ensure that personal information is not kept longer than necessary for educational purposes. Extended data retention periods can increase and leaks of sensitive student. Additionally, purpose creep refers to the situation in which the data collected for one purpose (e.g., personalized learning) is later used for another purpose (e.g., marketing or profiling). Without clear limits on how student data is used, AI-driven systems could contribute to privacy violations and exploitation of students' personal information.

CONCLUSION

Over last decade, advancements in AI have prompted a rethinking of how education systems operate, how learning is delivered, and how educational outcomes are achieved. The potential of AI is vast, offering presenting certain to be navigated carefully. they are increasingly poised to redefine how educators teach, how students learn, and how educational systems operate at scale. powered tools that enhance personalized learning, improve teacher effectiveness, support learners with diverse needs, and foster global collaboration. By leveraging AI's capabilities, education systems can unlock new avenues for better learning outcomes, equity, and inclusion, all while fostering a more efficient, responsive, and scalable educational environment. ways is poised transform through. Traditionally, education systems have struggled preferences within a single classroom. AI addresses this challenge by enabling personalized learning pathways for interests. powered tools such as curriculum to fit their specific needs gather quizzes, assignments, and even classroom interactions, to create tailored learning experiences. This means that students who may need extra time to grasp a concept can receive additional support, while those who are ready to move ahead can progress faster. By adapting to the individual pace of each learner, AI can help close learning gaps, keep students engaged, and prevent boredom or frustration. Moreover, AI can support a more proactive approach to learning by identifying early signs of struggle or disengagement, enabling, providing teachers with insights that can help them adjust instruction and offer timely support. While AI is often seen through the lens of student learning, its educators is equally transformative educational experience, but they are often assisting teachers time-consuming, allowing them their core mission. powered tools automate grading for assignments, delivered more quickly, allowing students to adjust their learning strategies as needed. Furthermore, help the class as a whole may need additional support or where an individual student may be excelling. Beyond administrative support, AI can also enhance teacher training and professional development. virtual assistants teachers, helping them refine powered simulations can also allow teachers to practice and improve their skills in realistic classroom scenarios, fostering continuous improvement and professional growth. Potential support diverse learners, technologies offer tailored to physical, cognitive, or emotional disabilities, helping them achieve greater educational outcomes. provide customized interventions tools, interactive lessons, tools that help with focus and concentration. AI can also enable ways that were previously inaccessible, through technologies such as voice-activated assistants and adaptive devices. In addition, AI can help create content that is visually and auditorily appealing to students with various sensory needs, enhancing accessibility and environment. supporting teachers by providing data-driven insights about students' specific challenges and progress. This can allow for more targeted and effective interventions and accommodations a timely manner. can help educators and institutions design personalized support plans that thrive academically socially, reducing barriers to their success.

REFERENCES

Agrela Rodrigues, F. de A., Moreira da Silveira, F., Moreira de Lima, M. R., & Pinto Uchôa, K. S. (2024). Identificando a Inteligência em Crianças: Traços Físicos e Comportamentais. Ciencia Y Reflexión, 3(2), 21–51.

Anderson, T., & Dron, J. (2020). Emerging technologies in education: An overview. *Educational Technology Research and Development*, *68*(2), 463–475.

Athavale, V. A., Selvakumar, P., Poorani, S., Anand, T., & Rathore, D. S. (2025). Designing Chatbots for Educational Leadership. In Musundire, A. (Ed.), *Chatbots in Educational Leadership and Management* (pp. 181–204). IGI Global Scientific Publishing., DOI: 10.4018/979-8-3693-8734-4.ch008

Baker, R., & Chen, M. (2025). AI-driven adaptive learning systems: The future of student-centered education. *Journal of Artificial Intelligence in Education*, *31*(1), 1–20.

Baker, T., & Xia, W. (2025). AI-driven curriculum design: Enhancing educational accessibility and inclusivity. *Educational Policy Review*, *19*(3), 78–95.

Chavarría Hidalgo, C. (2024). Calculation of productive capacity: From theory to practice. Ciencia Y Reflexión, 3(2), 194–214.

Chen, Y., & Liu, H. (2025a). AI-driven adaptive learning systems: Enhancing personalized education. *Journal of Educational Technology & Society*, *28*(1), 45–62.

Chen, Y., & Liu, H. (2025b). AI-enhanced literacy development: The role of predictive models in student learning. *Journal of Educational Psychology*, *39*(4), 215–232.

Chiu, C., & Baker, T. (2025). AI-driven curriculum design: Enhancing educational accessibility and inclusivity. *Educational Policy Review*, *19*(3), 78–95.

Chiu, C., & Baker, T. (2025). AI-enhanced literacy development: The role of predictive models in student learning. *Journal of Educational Psychology*, *39*(4), 215–232.

Da Silva Santos, F., & López Vargas, R. (2020). Efecto del Estrés en la Función Inmune en Pacientes con Enfermedades Autoinmunes: una Revisión de Estudios Latinoamericanos. Revista Científica De Salud Y Desarrollo Humano, 1(1), 46–59.

Dai, X. (2025). AI-driven assessment tools: Improving learning outcomes through automation. *Assessment & Evaluation in Higher Education*, *50*(1), 33–49.

Davis, L., & Karmakar, S. (2022). AI in education: Opportunities and challenges for teaching and learning. *Computers & Education*, *179*, 104446.

Davis, L., & Karmakar, S. (2022). AI in education: Opportunities and challenges for teaching and learning. *Computers & Education, 179*, 104446.

Dörner, R., Klimmt, C., & Hille, A. (2020). The effects of virtual reality on player engagement: A systematic review. *Computers in Human Behavior, 104*, 106157.

Fernández, A. (2023). The Social Impact of Independent Audiovisual Production in the Age of social media: A Case Study in Zamora, Ecuador. *Revista Veritas De Difusão Científica, 4*(1), 161–180. DOI: 10.61616/rvdc.v4i1.42

Filiz, O., Kaya, M. H., & Adiguzel, T. (2025). Teachers and AI: Understanding the factors influencing AI integration in K-12 education. *Education and Information Technologies, 30*(13), 17931–17967. DOI: 10.1007/s10639-025-13463-2

Fischer, M., & Lutz, M. (2020). Virtual reality in education: A review of current applications. *International Journal of Educational Technology in Higher Education, 17*(1), 1–18.

Gao, L., & Liu, Y. (2023). Blockchain technology in education: A systematic review. *Journal of Educational Computing Research, 61*(4), 745–766.

Gao, L., & Liu, Y. (2023). Blockchain technology in education: A systematic review. *Journal of Educational Computing Research, 61*(4), 745–766.

Huang, Y. M., & Liaw, S. S. (2022). The effects of mobile technology on student learning outcomes: A meta-analysis. *Computers & Education, 176*, 104325.

Kenchakkanavar, A. Y., Rathod, A., & Kamble, A. A. (2024). *Artificial Intelligence in Indian Education: Transforming Teaching and Learning for the Digital Age.* International Research Journal of Innovations in Engineering & Technology.

Kim, J., & Lee, H. (2020). The role of gamification in education: A systematic review. *Educational Technology Research and Development, 68*(2), 555–576.

Kumar, S., & Sharma, P. (2025). AI-powered assessment models: Revolutionizing grading and feedback in education. *Assessment & Learning Technologies, 14*(2), 33–49.

Leiton Leiton, D. R., Engracia Carvallo, D. E., Tamayo León, J. A., Ramírez González, S. Y., & Ramírez González, E. G. (2024). Estrategia metodológica para el mejoramiento del rendimiento académico en la asignatura de ciencias naturales en los estudiantes de educación básica. Estudios Y Perspectivas Revista Científica Y Académica, 4(2), 273–291.

Lemoine, P., & Mott, B. W. (2021). Adaptive learning technologies: Trends and future directions. *Journal of Educational Technology & Society, 24*(4), 1–14.

Lim, C. P., & Chai, C. S. (2021). Technology in education: Past, present, and future. *Journal of Computer Assisted Learning*, *37*(5), 1–12.

Liu, M., & Chang, C. (2023). Digital equity in education: The role of technology in bridging gaps. *Journal of Educational Technology Systems*, *51*(1), 25–45.

Madani, F., & Esfandiari, R. (2022). The influence of social media on student engagement in higher education. *Computers in Human Behavior*, *127*, 107043.

Magaña Lara, M. J., Zavala Pérez, I. C., Olea Gutiérrez, C. V., & Valle Solís, M. O. (2024). Programa de Educación para la Salud: Cartografías sociales sobre Lactancia Materna en estudiantes de Enfermería Universidad de Nayarit, México. Emergentes -. *Revista Científica (Maracaibo)*, *4*(1), 142–157.

Martínez, O., Aranda, R., Barreto, E., Fanego, J., Fernández, A., López, J., Medina, J., Meza, M., Muñoz, D., & Urbieta, J. (2024). Los tipos de discriminación laboral en las ciudades de Capiatá y San Lorenzo. [Recuperado a partir de.]. *Arandu UTIC*, *11*(1), 77–95.

McCarthy, J., & Wolf, K. (2023). The impact of online learning platforms on student performance: A review. *Education and Information Technologies*, *28*(2), 2331–2345.

Mehta, A. K., Yashoda, L., Selvakumar, P., Mishra, B. R., Das, A., & C. T. C., M. (2025). Teaching Methods: Techniques for Disadvantaged Learners. In S. Hai-Jew (Ed.), Mitigating Learner Disadvantages in Teaching and Learning (pp. 181-206). IGI Global Scientific Publishing

Mikropoulos, T. A., & Natsis, A. (2020). Educational virtual environments: A systematic review. *Computers & Education*, *154*, 103891.

Miller, A. (2020). The impact of augmented reality on the gaming industry. *Games and Culture*, *15*(3), 288–303.

Mishra, P., & Koehler, M. J. (2020). Technology integration for meaningful learning. *Educational Technology Research and Development*, *68*(4), 931–946.

Naidu, S., & O'Leary, M. (2022). Designing for learning: The role of learning analytics. *International Journal of Educational Technology in Higher Education*, *19*(1), 1–17. PMID: 35013716

Niemi, H. (2025). AI in education: Transforming communication, lifestyle, and learning environments. *Educational Review*, *47*(2), 112–130.

Ouyang, J., & Yu, L. (2025). AI-powered intelligent tutoring systems: A new era in education. *Computers & Education*, *190*, 104563.

Owusu-Acheaw, M., & Larson, A. (2020). The role of e-learning in higher education: A review. *International Journal of Educational Management, 34*(6), 1119–1136.

Poushneh, A., & Vasquez-Parraga, A. Z. (2020). Augmented reality in retail: A systematic review of the literature. *Journal of Retailing and Consumer Services, 53*, 102100.

Pradeep, E., Mukherjee, S. K., Selvakumar, P., Koppaka, A. K., Chandel, P. S., & Vats, C. (2025). Empowering Social Media Users With Ethical AI. In Chakraborty, S. (Ed.), *Ethical AI Solutions for Addressing Social Media Influence and Hate Speech* (pp. 91–118). IGI Global Scientific Publishing., DOI: 10.4018/979-8-3693-9904-0.ch005

Reina-Parrado, M., Román-Graván, P., & Hervás-Gómez, C. (2025). Integration of artificial intelligence and machine learning in education: A systematic review. *International Journal of Educational Methodology, 11*(2), 203–216. DOI: 10.12973/ijem.11.2.203

Rizzo, A. S., Koenig, S. T., & Daugherty, M. (2020). Virtual reality and immersive technologies in the treatment of anxiety disorders. *Journal of Anxiety Disorders, 73*, 102227.

Saldaña, M., & Martínez, R. (2023). The future of technology in education: Trends and predictions. *Journal of Educational Technology, 34*(1), 47–58.

Singh, R., & Patel, M. (2025). AI-driven personalized learning: Enhancing student engagement through adaptive systems. *Journal of Educational Technology Research, 15*(2), 78–95.

Smith, R. D., & Jones, T. M. (2021). AI and personalized learning: An exploratory study. *Journal of Computer Assisted Learning, 37*(3), 777–790.

Tama Sánchez, F. A., Vasquez Falconí, J. A., Aguilar Mejía, R. M., Rodríguez Pérez, J. C. A., López Solórzano, A. A., & Paredes Jeréz, K. D. (2024). Xeroderma Pigmentoso Reporte De Caso Y Revisión De La Literatura. Revista Científica De Salud Y Desarrollo Humano, 5(2), 44–55.

Tatar, E., & Akçay, H. (2022). Digital storytelling in education: Enhancing student engagement. *Educational Media International, 59*(2), 95–111.

Treve, M. (2024). Integrating Artificial Intelligence in Education: Impacts on Student Learning and Innovation. *International Journal of Vocational Education and Training Research, 10*(2), 203–216. DOI: 10.11648/j.ijvetr.20241002.14

Treve, M., & Adiguzel, T. (2025). AI-enhanced classroom dynamics: The impact of intelligent tutoring systems. *Journal of Educational Computing Research*, *42*(4), 89–105.

Vega Alvarez, E., & Huang Chang, Y. (2024). Blended Learning, and Its Impact on English Speaking Skills in Pronunciation in Group 11-4 of Liceo de Santo Domingo, I Quarter 2024. Ciencia Y Reflexi6n, 3(2), 159–173.

Vongkhamthath, K., & Chiu, S. (2021). The impact of technology on learning outcomes: A longitudinal study. *Journal of Educational Computing Research*, *59*(4), 800–824.

Wang, F., & Hannafin, M. J. (2020). Design-based implementation research: An emerging approach to improve educational practices. *Educational Technology Research and Development*, *68*(4), 1059–1075.

Wang, Y., Wu, M., & Zhang, X. (2023). The role of augmented reality in surgical training: A systematic review. *Surgical Innovation*, *30*(1), 20–30. PMID: 35582732

Wu, D., & Zhang, J. (2025). Generative artificial intelligence in secondary education: Applications and effects on students' innovation skills and digital literacy. *PLoS One*, *20*(5), e0323349. DOI: 10.1371/journal.pone.0323349 PMID: 40344078

Wu, P., & Yu, Z. (2025). AI-powered chatbots in education: Enhancing student engagement and support. *Computers in Human Behavior*, *134*, 107345.

Xia, L., & Zhang, Y. (2025). AI and creativity in education: Fostering critical thinking through adaptive learning systems. *Educational Technology Research and Development*, *73*(2), 98–115.

Chapter 14

Use of Natural Language Processing in Cognitive Tutoring

Lakshmi Ganesan
https://orcid.org/0000-0001-6789-3147
SRM Institute of Science and Technology, India

Dhivya Devi S.
https://orcid.org/0000-0002-2837-9011
SRM Institute of Science and Technology, India

ABSTRACT

Natural Language Processing (NLP) has revolutionized many fields, and its application in cognitive tutoring systems is proving to be a game-changer in personalized education. The chapter titled "Use of Natural Language Processing in Cognitive Tutoring" explores how NLP can enhance cognitive tutoring systems by enabling more natural, interactive, and effective learning experiences. Cognitive tutoring aims to model human thinking and provide individualized feedback, helping students understand complex subjects at their own pace. By incorporating NLP, these systems can become more responsive to students' needs, leading to improved engagement, learning outcomes, and overall educational effectiveness. The chapter begins by providing an overview of cognitive tutoring systems, which aim to provide personalized support to students based on their individual learning patterns and progress.

DOI: 10.4018/979-8-3373-4217-7.ch014

INTRODUCTION TO NATURAL LANGUAGE PROCESSING IN EDUCATION

Natural Language Processing (NLP) is a branch of artificial intelligence dedicated to enabling machines to understand, interpret, generate, and respond to human language in ways that are both meaningful and contextually appropriate. Drawing from linguistics, computer science, and cognitive psychology, NLP bridges the gap between human communication and computational understanding. It encompasses a wide range of techniques, from basic text analysis to advanced machine learning models capable of semantic reasoning and interactive dialogue generation.

Within the domain of cognitive tutoring, NLP plays a pivotal role in transforming how learners engage with educational technologies. Traditional computer-based tutoring systems were often constrained by rigid, predefined inputs and responses, limiting their ability to handle the complexity of human expression. By contrast, NLP allows cognitive tutors to process free-form natural language, making it possible to address one of the most persistent challenges in education: the ambiguity and variability in student responses. Whether a learner provides an incomplete answer, uses unconventional phrasing, or expresses uncertainty, NLP enables the system to interpret meaning and respond with clarity, thereby reducing misunderstandings and fostering deeper learning.

Equally important, NLP supports adaptability by enabling systems to make real-time instructional adjustments based not only on the content of student responses but also on emotional cues embedded in their language. For instance, variations in tone, hesitations, or repeated errors can signal frustration or disengagement. NLP-driven analysis helps tutors detect such cues and adapt feedback or difficulty levels accordingly, creating a more supportive and empathetic learning environment.

Beyond these functions, NLP enhances personalization by constructing detailed learner profiles over time. By analyzing patterns in vocabulary, sentence structures, and response styles, cognitive tutors can infer cognitive states, learning preferences, and engagement levels. This allows the system to tailor communication strategies, instructional pacing, and even motivational feedback to each learner's unique needs.

Moreover, NLP contributes to scalability by automating tasks such as essay evaluation, question answering, and conversational tutoring, thereby extending individualized support to a larger population of learners without overburdening human instructors.

In this way, NLP serves as a cornerstone in the evolution of cognitive tutors from rule-based systems to intelligent, adaptive, and empathetic learning companions. By resolving challenges such as ambiguity in student inputs and fostering emotional awareness, NLP empowers educational technologies to deliver richer, more human-like interactions that enhance comprehension, motivation, and overall academic performance.

Historical Evolution of NLP in Educational Technologies

The integration of Natural Language Processing (NLP) into educational technologies has evolved over several decades, driven by advances in computational linguistics, artificial intelligence, and the growing demand for personalized learning experiences. The journey of NLP in education began in the 1960s and 1970s with rule-based systems that attempted to simulate language understanding through hand-coded grammars and scripts. Early efforts, such as the ELIZA program, demonstrated that even basic NLP could engage users in simple dialogue, although these interactions were limited in scope and intelligence.

By the 1980s and 1990s, the field saw the emergence of Intelligent Tutoring Systems (ITS) that began to incorporate NLP for understanding student inputs. Systems like SOPHIE and WHY were among the first to attempt deeper semantic analysis, aiming to infer student misconceptions and provide corrective feedback. However, these systems relied heavily on symbolic AI approaches, which struggled with the variability and ambiguity of natural language.

The early 2000s marked a significant shift with the rise of statistical NLP. The availability of large educational datasets and improvements in machine learning enabled more accurate text classification, information retrieval, and language modeling. This era saw the development of systems such as AutoTutor, which engaged students in natural language dialogue and used latent semantic analysis (LSA) to assess the content of student responses and deliver adaptive feedback.

From 2010 onward, the emergence of deep learning revolutionized NLP capabilities. Tools such as word embeddings, recurrent neural networks (RNNs), and transformers significantly improved the system's ability to process and generate human-like language. Educational platforms began to adopt NLP for automated grading, real-time speech recognition, and intelligent conversational agents. Notably, cognitive tutors like Carnegie Learning's MATHia and virtual teaching assistants began leveraging NLP to personalize content and simulate human-like tutoring experiences (Kovanović et al., 2015).

The current era, marked by the advent of large language models (LLMs) such as BERT, GPT, and T5, has enabled unprecedented advancements in NLP-driven educational tools. These models offer contextual understanding, content generation, and dialogue management with near-human fluency. They have paved the way for cognitive tutors that can hold meaningful conversations, understand complex learner inputs, and provide individualized instruction at scale.

The historical evolution of NLP in educational technologies reflects a trajectory from simple rule-based systems to sophisticated AI-powered platforms. This progress has transformed how students interact with learning systems, enabling more natural, responsive, and personalized educational experiences.

Relevance to Cognitive Tutoring Systems:

Natural Language Processing (NLP) plays a pivotal role in enhancing the intelligence, adaptability, and interactivity of cognitive tutoring systems. These systems aim to simulate human tutoring by providing personalized guidance, feedback, and instruction tailored to each learner's needs. NLP serves as a critical enabler in achieving this goal by allowing tutors to understand, interpret, and respond to learners' natural language inputs—whether spoken or written. Xu, Chen, & Chen, 2020.

The relevance of NLP to cognitive tutoring lies primarily in its ability to facilitate meaningful dialogue between the system and the learner. Unlike traditional rule-based systems that depend on fixed responses, NLP-powered cognitive tutors can analyze free-text responses, detect grammatical or conceptual errors, and provide nuanced feedback. This capability allows the tutor to engage in Socratic questioning, encourage critical thinking, and support deeper learning. (Liu, Okonkwo, & Xu, 2022)

Moreover, NLP contributes significantly to the learner modeling, which is essential for personalization. By analyzing students' language use—vocabulary, syntax, sentiment, and frequency—cognitive tutors can infer learner knowledge levels, misconceptions, emotional states, and learning preferences. This information is used to adjust the difficulty, pacing, and style of instruction in real time, ensuring an adapti Learner modeling and profiling through NLPve learning experience. Nye, Graesser, & Hu, 2014.

In addition, NLP supports a range of auxiliary functions such as automated essay scoring, question generation, summarization of content, and speech-to-text transcription. These functions not only improve system efficiency but also enhance the overall learning experience by providing immediate, context-aware support.

Thus NLP transforms cognitive tutoring systems from static, pre-programmed tools into dynamic, conversational learning companions. It enables these systems to interact with students in a human-like manner, fostering engagement, motivation, and improved academic outcomes.

CORE NLP TECHNIQUES FOR COGNITIVE TUTORS

Text Classification and Clustering

Text classification and clustering are foundational Natural Language Processing (NLP) techniques that enable cognitive tutoring systems to understand, organize, and respond to learner inputs effectively. These methods help in managing large volumes of unstructured text data generated by students through written responses, queries, discussions, and assignments. By leveraging these techniques, cognitive tutors can deliver personalized support, provide relevant feedback, and identify patterns in student learning behavior.

Text classification involves assigning predefined categories or labels to textual data. In the context of cognitive tutoring, it is used to categorize student responses based on correctness, relevance, sentiment, or topic. For instance, when a student answers an open-ended question, the system can classify the response as correct, partially correct, or incorrect using machine learning models trained on annotated datasets. Similarly, sentiment classification helps tutors understand learners' emotional states—whether they are confused, frustrated, or confident—enabling affect-sensitive interventions.

Applications of text classification in cognitive tutoring include:

- Automated grading of short answers and essays
- Identification of misconception patterns
- Filtering inappropriate or off-topic inputs
- Tailoring feedback based on detected intent and accuracy

Text clustering, on the other hand, is an unsupervised learning technique that groups similar pieces of text together without predefined labels. This method is useful for discovering hidden structures in data and is often employed when student inputs are too diverse to be classified manually. In cognitive tutoring systems, clustering can be used to:

- Group similar questions asked by learners to provide unified answers
- Identify common themes or learning difficulties across a class or cohort
- Inform curriculum updates based on emerging trends in learner queries

For example, if multiple students submit varied responses to a critical thinking prompt, clustering can help the system recognize central ideas and provide feedback that addresses commonalities and outliers.

Text classification and clustering enhance a cognitive tutor's ability to understand and manage learner interactions at scale. They support real-time analysis, improve instructional efficiency, and drive informed, adaptive pedagogical strategies. As cognitive tutoring systems continue to evolve, these NLP techniques will remain central to delivering responsive, data-driven, and learner-centric education.

Named Entity Recognition (NER)

Named Entity Recognition (NER) is a Natural Language Processing (NLP) technique that involves identifying and classifying key elements—referred to as "entities"—in a text into predefined categories such as names of people, organizations, locations, dates, quantities, and specific domain-related terms. In the context of cognitive tutoring systems, NER plays a crucial role in understanding the content and context of student inputs, enabling more intelligent, relevant, and personalized interactions.

The primary value of NER in educational settings lies in its ability to extract meaningful information from learner-generated text. When students write responses, ask questions, or interact with digital learning platforms, they often reference subject-specific concepts, historical figures, scientific units, or mathematical expressions. NER helps the cognitive tutor recognize these elements, map them to relevant instructional content, and respond appropriately.

In STEM subjects, NER can be used to identify technical terms, chemical compounds, mathematical functions, and scientific phenomena. This capability enhances the tutor's ability to provide targeted feedback and reinforce concept comprehension.

NER also contributes to adaptive learning by helping to track which entities a student has mastered and which require further reinforcement. This can inform real-time decision-making by the system and allow for a customized learning trajectory.

NER enhances the semantic understanding capabilities of cognitive tutors, allowing for richer and more accurate interpretation of student language. By enabling the system to recognize what learners are referencing, NER improves both instructional relevance and the learner's overall engagement with the content.

Sentiment and Emotion Analysis

Sentiment and emotion analysis are powerful Natural Language Processing (NLP) techniques that enable cognitive tutoring systems to go beyond understanding the content of student responses to also interpreting their emotional tone and psychological state. By analyzing the sentiment (positive, negative, or neutral) and specific emotions (e.g., frustration, confusion, joy, confidence) expressed in learners' language, cognitive tutors can offer more empathetic, responsive, and adaptive support (Zhang & Chen, 2023)

In traditional learning environments, human instructors often rely on visual and verbal cues to gauge a student's emotional state and adjust their teaching accordingly. In digital learning contexts, where such cues are limited or absent, sentiment and emotion analysis serve as critical tools for enabling emotionally intelligent interactions. These tools process text inputs—such as written answers, chat messages, or forum posts—to identify affective signals embedded in language.

Applications of sentiment and emotion analysis in cognitive tutoring systems include:

- Affective feedback: Delivering responses that acknowledge and respond to the student's emotional state.
- Dropout prevention: Identifying signs of disengagement or frustration that may indicate risk of dropout.
- Adaptive pacing: Slowing down or speeding up instruction based on learner confidence and emotional readiness.
- Empathy-driven dialogue: Enhancing conversations with emotionally appropriate responses that mimic human empathy.

Emotion-aware tutors are particularly impactful in self-paced and remote learning environments, where students often lack immediate support. By recognizing and responding to emotional cues, these systems can maintain learner motivation, reduce anxiety, and foster a more supportive learning atmosphere.

Overall, sentiment and emotion analysis enrich the cognitive tutor's understanding of the learner as a whole person—cognitively and emotionally. This holistic approach is essential for creating truly personalized and human-centered educational experiences in the age of AI-powered learning technologies.

Syntax and Semantic Analysis

Syntax and semantic analysis are central components of Natural Language Processing (NLP) that enable cognitive tutoring systems to accurately interpret and respond to learner inputs. These two levels of linguistic analysis work together to extract both structural and meaningful insights from language, empowering tutors to provide intelligent, context-aware, and pedagogically sound support.

Syntax analysis, also known as parsing, focuses on the grammatical structure of sentences. It identifies the relationships between words, such as subject, verb, and object, and builds a syntactic tree that represents the hierarchical structure of the sentence. This analysis is essential for detecting sentence correctness, grammar usage, and linguistic complexity in student-generated text.

In cognitive tutoring, syntactic analysis helps:

- Evaluate sentence structure and grammatical accuracy
- Identify incomplete or fragmented responses
- Determine the complexity of language used by the learner
- Tailor feedback on writing mechanics and language development

Semantic analysis, in contrast, focuses on meaning. It involves interpreting the intended concepts, relationships, and logic conveyed in the learner's input. Techniques such as word sense disambiguation, semantic role labeling, and embedding-based representations (e.g., using models like Word2Vec, BERT) allow the system to grasp the underlying meaning of a sentence, even when different words or structures are used.

Syntax and semantic analysis enhance a cognitive tutor's linguistic comprehension, enabling deeper interaction with the learner. These analyses ensure that the system not only processes what the student is saying but also understands how it is said and what it means. This dual-layered interpretation is fundamental for delivering precise, personalized, and pedagogically effective feedback.

Topic Modeling and Discourse Analysis

Topic modeling and discourse analysis are advanced Natural Language Processing (NLP) techniques that significantly enhance the ability of cognitive tutoring systems to understand the broader context and thematic structure of learner inputs. These techniques allow tutors not only to process isolated sentences but also to grasp overarching ideas, logical flow, and the learning intent embedded within extended student interactions.

Topic modeling is an unsupervised machine learning method designed to uncover hidden thematic structures in large collections of text. It works by identifying clusters of words that frequently appear together, thereby helping infer the main topics present in a document or conversation. Algorithms such as Latent Dirichlet Allocation (LDA) and Non-negative Matrix Factorization (NMF) are commonly used in this process, enabling cognitive tutors to detect the subjects that students are engaging with—even when they use varied expressions or terminology. In educational contexts, topic modeling proves especially useful for identifying key themes in student essays, discussions, or queries. It allows for personalized content delivery based on the learner's areas of interest or difficulty, helps summarize student-generated content for feedback and assessment, and aids in monitoring learning trends across a class or cohort. For example, in a literature-based cognitive tutor, topic modeling can group student reflections around themes like identity, conflict, or transformation, allowing the system to generate targeted prompts or suggest relevant resources.

Discourse analysis complements this by focusing on the structure and coherence of communication over multiple sentences or conversational turns. It analyzes how ideas are introduced, linked, and developed over time, revealing patterns in reasoning, argumentation, and explanation. This enables cognitive tutors to interpret the learner's thought process more accurately, thereby facilitating richer dialogue and more context-aware feedback. Discourse analysis helps evaluate coherence in student writing, track argument progression in essays or debates, and improve tutor-learner interaction by ensuring continuity and relevance. It also aids in detecting shifts in learner focus or signs of confusion that may require instructional intervention.

Topic modeling and discourse analysis empower cognitive tutors to function as intelligent, responsive learning companions. They make it possible to understand not only what the learner is discussing but also how the learner is organizing and expressing their thoughts. These capabilities are crucial for fostering higher-order thinking skills such as synthesis, critical reasoning, and conceptual integration in AI-powered learning environments.

IMPLEMENTATION OF NLP

Natural Language Processing (NLP) is a core enabler of intelligent educational technologies, particularly in cognitive tutoring systems. By allowing machines to interpret and respond to human language in nuanced ways, NLP transforms learning environments from rigid, rule-based systems into adaptive, conversational, and highly personalized experiences. It enables cognitive tutors to address two persistent challenges in education: the ambiguity of student responses and the need for dynamic, individualized feedback.

Traditional tutoring software struggled to process free-form input, often requiring students to select from predefined options. NLP overcomes this limitation by analyzing the structure, semantics, and context of learner-generated language. For example, if a student answers a science question with partial phrasing or uses non-standard terminology, NLP techniques such as syntactic parsing and semantic similarity measures help the system infer the intended meaning. This reduces misunderstandings and ensures that learners receive accurate, context-aware feedback.

The integration of NLP into real-world cognitive tutors illustrates its practical significance. AutoTutor, developed at the University of Memphis, uses natural language dialogue to engage learners in conversational exchanges. By employing techniques such as latent semantic analysis (LSA) and discourse modeling, AutoTutor evaluates student inputs, detects misconceptions, and provides scaffolded hints much like a human tutor. Its success in improving comprehension in subjects like physics and computer literacy demonstrates how NLP can replicate the benefits of Socratic questioning in digital environments.

Similarly, Carnegie Learning's MATHia applies NLP for adaptive problem-solving in mathematics. MATHia interprets the steps students take while solving equations and uses error analysis models to identify misconceptions in real time. By interpreting both structured responses (e.g., equation inputs) and natural language explanations, the system delivers targeted hints and adaptive problem sets. This approach exemplifies how NLP-powered feedback can personalize learning pathways while maintaining alignment with curriculum goals.

Beyond specific systems, NLP contributes to broader educational functions such as automated essay scoring, emotion detection through sentiment analysis, and conversational tutoring for language learning. For instance, sentiment-aware NLP models can detect signs of student frustration, prompting the tutor to simplify explanations or offer motivational feedback. These applications highlight the capacity of NLP not only to process cognitive aspects of learning but also to enhance the socio-emotional dimensions of tutoring.

NLP-DRIVEN PERSONALIZATION IN COGNITIVE TUTORS

Adaptive Feedback Generation

Adaptive feedback generation is a core application of Natural Language Processing (NLP) in cognitive tutoring systems. It involves the real-time creation of personalized, context-sensitive responses based on the learner's input, performance, and emotional state. This capability transforms static digital instruction into a dynamic, interactive experience that mirrors the nuanced support offered by human tutors (Aleven, McLaughlin, Glenn, & Koedinger, 2016)

At the heart of adaptive feedback generation is the ability of the system to understand the learner's intent and the quality of their response using techniques such as syntax and semantic analysis, sentiment detection, and error identification. NLP enables the system to evaluate free-text responses for correctness, completeness, and conceptual clarity. Based on this analysis, the tutor formulates tailored feedback that aligns with the learner's current understanding and learning trajectory.

For example, if a student incorrectly answers a biology question by stating that *"mitochondria help in photosynthesis,"* the system, using semantic analysis and a concept knowledge base, can detect the misconception and respond with: *"Actually, photosynthesis occurs in chloroplasts, not mitochondria. Mitochondria are responsible for producing energy through cellular respiration. Would you like to review the differences?"*

Adaptive feedback can take various forms:

- Corrective feedback to address errors directly
- Elaborative feedback to provide additional context or explanations
- Socratic prompts to guide learners toward self-correction through questioning
- Motivational feedback to encourage persistence and confidence

NLP-driven systems also consider learner profiles, prior interactions, and emotional cues to adapt the tone, depth, and style of feedback. For instance, a student expressing frustration may receive more encouraging, step-by-step guidance, while an advanced learner might be challenged with probing questions to deepen critical thinking.

Moreover, adaptive feedback is not limited to isolated responses. It evolves over the course of the interaction, maintaining continuity and adjusting to the learner's progression. This longitudinal adaptability supports mastery learning and promotes long-term retention.

Adaptive feedback generation powered by NLP enables cognitive tutoring systems to deliver meaningful, personalized guidance that responds to what learners say, how they say it, and how they feel. This intelligent responsiveness is key to enhancing student engagement, correcting misconceptions, and fostering deeper understanding in AI-driven personalized learning environments.

Learner Modeling and Profiling Through NLP

Learner modeling and profiling are essential components of personalized education, enabling cognitive tutoring systems to tailor instruction and feedback based on an individual's unique learning needs, preferences, and progress. Natural Language Processing (NLP) plays a pivotal role in this process by extracting rich, meaningful insights from learners' textual interactions, which serve as dynamic data points to build comprehensive learner profiles (Piech et al., 2015).

Traditionally, learner models relied heavily on structured data such as quiz scores, time spent on tasks, or clickstream patterns. However, much of the nuanced information about a learner's understanding, misconceptions, motivation, and emotional state is embedded in the unstructured text learners generate—through open-ended responses, essays, forum discussions, and conversational exchanges with the tutor. NLP techniques enable cognitive tutoring systems to analyze this text, revealing deeper cognitive and affective dimensions of learning.

By applying methods such as text classification, sentiment analysis, and semantic understanding, the system can identify a learner's current knowledge level, detect misconceptions, and gauge affective states like frustration, confidence, or engagement. For instance, analyzing a student's written explanations can reveal conceptual gaps or mastery, while sentiment analysis of learner messages may indicate motivational challenges. This multidimensional profiling allows the tutor to adapt content difficulty, offer targeted scaffolding, and provide motivational support aligned with the learner's evolving needs.

Additionally, NLP-based learner modeling facilitates the creation of dynamic, continuously updated profiles rather than static snapshots. As learners interact with the system over time, their language use and expressed emotions inform real-time adjustments in instructional strategies. For example, if a learner frequently uses tentative language or expresses confusion, the system might offer more foundational resources or simplified explanations. Conversely, confident and precise language could prompt the tutor to challenge the learner with advanced material or open-ended questions.

Moreover, learner profiles built through NLP can incorporate individual preferences, such as favored learning modalities or communication styles, inferred from the learner's language patterns and interaction history. This further enhances personalization by aligning the tutor's responses with the learner's unique characteristics.

Thus NLP-driven learner modeling and profiling empower cognitive tutoring systems to gain a holistic understanding of learners—cognitively, emotionally, and behaviorally—enabling truly personalized, responsive, and effective learning experiences in AI-powered educational environments.

Context-Aware Response Generation

Context-aware response generation is a sophisticated Natural Language Processing (NLP) capability that enables cognitive tutoring systems to produce meaningful, relevant, and personalized replies by taking into account the learner's prior inputs, current knowledge state, and the ongoing dialogue context. Unlike generic or static responses, context-aware systems dynamically adapt their feedback and prompts based on a nuanced understanding of both the immediate question and the broader learning journey.

In cognitive tutoring, the ability to generate contextually appropriate responses is crucial for maintaining learner engagement, promoting deeper understanding, and fostering a natural, human-like conversational flow. This process relies heavily on tracking the context of interactions, including the semantic content of past learner inputs, discourse structure, and the learner's emotional and cognitive state as inferred from language cues.

For example, if a student previously struggled with a concept such as Newton's laws and now attempts a related question, the tutor's response will reflect this history by providing scaffolding support or revisiting foundational principles rather than simply assessing correctness. Similarly, the system may tailor explanations, hints, or encouragement based on whether the learner has shown confidence or frustration in earlier exchanges.

Technically, context-aware response generation integrates multiple NLP components. Dialogue management frameworks track the state and flow of conversations, while semantic parsing and discourse analysis ensure that the system comprehends the learner's intent and the logical connections across turns. Additionally, knowledge representation modules connect learner inputs to domain-specific content, enabling the tutor to retrieve or generate responses grounded in accurate subject matter.

Moreover, advances in deep learning models, such as transformer-based architectures (e.g., GPT, BERT), have significantly enhanced the quality of context-aware response generation. These models can process and remember extended sequences of dialogue, allowing the tutor to generate coherent, contextually rich replies that reflect previous interactions and anticipated learner needs.

Context-aware response generation is essential not only for delivering instructional content but also for providing affective support. By analyzing linguistic cues indicative of emotions like confusion or motivation, tutors can adjust their tone and style to be more empathetic or encouraging, thus fostering a supportive learning environment.

Context-aware response generation transforms cognitive tutoring systems from static information providers into intelligent, adaptive learning companions. This capability supports personalized, interactive, and emotionally intelligent education, marking a new frontier in AI-powered personalized learning.

Dynamic Adjustment of Instructional Content

Conversational Agents and Intelligent Tutoring Systems

Role of Chatbots and Virtual Tutors. Chatbots and virtual tutors have emerged as transformative components within AI-powered cognitive tutoring systems, fundamentally reshaping how personalized learning is delivered. Powered by advanced Natural Language Processing (NLP) technologies, these intelligent agents simulate human-like conversations and provide learners with on-demand, interactive educational support that is accessible anytime and anywhere (Winkler & Söllner, 2018)

The primary role of chatbots and virtual tutors is to facilitate seamless, natural language communication between learners and the tutoring system. By understanding and interpreting student inputs—whether in the form of questions, explanations, or reflections—these systems generate contextually appropriate responses, guide learners through problem-solving processes, and provide tailored feedback. This conversational approach helps reduce the cognitive load often associated with rigid, text-heavy interfaces and encourages active learner engagement (Xu, Chen, & Chen, 2020).

Unlike traditional computer-based instruction, chatbots offer a more personalized learning experience by adapting dialogue based on the learner's proficiency, learning style, and emotional state. Through continuous analysis of language patterns, sentiment, and discourse context, virtual tutors can detect confusion, frustration, or boredom and respond with encouragement, hints, or alternative explanations. This emotional intelligence fosters a supportive learning environment that motivates learners to persist and explore topics more deeply.

Beyond one-on-one tutoring, chatbots also serve as scalable educational tools that can simultaneously support large numbers of learners. Their availability 24/7 ensures immediate assistance without delays, which is particularly valuable in remote or resource-constrained settings. Additionally, they can facilitate peer-like collaborative learning experiences by moderating discussions or prompting reflection within group contexts.

Technologically, the effectiveness of chatbots and virtual tutors relies on advances in NLP subfields such as intent recognition, dialogue management, sentiment analysis, and knowledge representation. Modern architectures, including transformer-based language models, enable these agents to process complex queries, maintain conversational coherence over multiple turns, and generate human-like, informative responses.

Chatbots and virtual tutors serve as critical enablers of personalized, adaptive learning in cognitive tutoring systems. By harnessing NLP capabilities, they create interactive, responsive, and empathetic educational experiences that enhance learner autonomy, engagement, and achievement, marking a new frontier in AI-driven personalized education.

Dialogue Systems and Natural Language Understanding (NLU)

Dialogue systems and Natural Language Understanding (NLU) form the backbone of effective communication between learners and AI-powered cognitive tutors. These technologies enable tutoring systems to engage in meaningful, interactive conversations by interpreting, processing, and responding to learner inputs expressed in natural language. Together, they create an intelligent conversational interface that mimics human tutoring interactions, thereby enhancing personalized learning experiences.

At its core, a dialogue system is designed to manage the flow of conversation, maintaining context across multiple turns, interpreting learner intents, and generating appropriate responses. This requires the system to handle a range of linguistic phenomena, including ambiguity, ellipsis, and variations in expression. Effective dialogue systems integrate several NLP components such as intent recognition, slot filling, dialogue management, and response generation to facilitate smooth and coherent exchanges.

Natural Language Understanding (NLU) is a critical subfield of NLP that focuses on interpreting the meaning behind learner inputs. It involves parsing the text to identify key entities, intents, relationships, and contextual nuances. For instance, when a learner asks, "Can you explain the difference between mitosis and meiosis?" the NLU module recognizes the intent to seek explanation and extracts the key biological terms. This understanding enables the tutor to fetch accurate, context-relevant instructional content.

In cognitive tutoring, NLU allows the system to move beyond surface-level keyword matching to comprehend the semantic and pragmatic aspects of learner language. This includes identifying misconceptions, detecting uncertainty or confidence, and recognizing follow-up questions. By interpreting these nuances, dialogue systems can provide tailored explanations, hints, or corrective feedback that align with the learner's current knowledge and emotional state.

Dialogue management systems orchestrate the interaction by deciding how to respond based on the learner model, conversation history, and pedagogical goals. Advanced dialogue systems employ machine learning and reinforcement learning techniques to optimize response strategies over time, improving the tutor's adaptability and effectiveness.

Recent advances in transformer-based language models, such as BERT and GPT, have significantly enhanced NLU capabilities. These models allow dialogue systems to understand and generate contextually coherent and human-like responses, even in complex and open-ended educational dialogues.

Dialogue systems powered by robust NLU are essential for creating interactive, responsive, and personalized cognitive tutoring environments. They enable seamless human-AI interaction, fostering deeper engagement, better comprehension, and ultimately more effective learning outcomes.

Maintaining Coherent Multi-Turn Conversations

Maintaining coherent multi-turn conversations is a fundamental challenge and necessity for AI-powered cognitive tutoring systems that engage learners in meaningful, interactive dialogues. Unlike simple question-and-answer exchanges, multi-turn conversations involve extended back-and-forth interactions where context, previous learner inputs, and instructional goals must be tracked and integrated continuously.

Achieving coherence in such dialogues is essential to simulate natural human tutoring and provide personalized, contextually relevant educational support.

In cognitive tutoring, coherence means that each system response logically follows prior learner inputs and maintains thematic consistency throughout the interaction. It also involves understanding implicit references, managing topic shifts, and recognizing when to revisit or summarize earlier points. This level of conversational understanding ensures that learners feel heard and supported, which enhances engagement, motivation, and knowledge retention.

Natural Language Processing (NLP) techniques provide the computational foundation for maintaining conversation coherence. Dialogue management frameworks track the state of the conversation by storing relevant information from prior turns, such as learner questions, answers, expressed emotions, and identified misconceptions. This contextual memory enables the system to interpret ambiguous pronouns, elliptical sentences, or follow-up questions without requiring repetitive clarifications from the learner.

Semantic understanding and discourse analysis further aid coherence by identifying relationships between different parts of the dialogue—such as cause-effect, elaboration, or contrast—and by recognizing the overall discourse structure. For example, if a learner first asks for a definition and then requests an example, the system understands the logical progression and tailors responses accordingly.

Advanced multi-turn dialogue systems often utilize transformer-based language models like GPT or BERT, which excel at processing extended sequences of text and maintaining contextual awareness over multiple conversational turns. These models can generate responses that are contextually appropriate, linguistically fluent, and pedagogically aligned with learner needs.

Moreover, maintaining coherence also involves managing conversational goals. The tutoring system must balance staying on topic with adapting to learner curiosity and needs, deciding when to offer hints, provide explanations, or encourage reflection. Reinforcement learning techniques help optimize these decisions, ensuring that the dialogue remains productive and learner-centered.

Maintaining coherent multi-turn conversations is a cornerstone of effective cognitive tutoring systems. By integrating sophisticated NLP methods and dialogue management strategies, these systems create dynamic, engaging, and personalized learning interactions that mirror human tutoring and support deeper educational outcomes.

NLP FOR STUDENT ASSESSMENT AND EVALUATION

Automated Essay Scoring and Feedback

Automated essay scoring (AES) and feedback represent one of the most impactful applications of Natural Language Processing (NLP) within cognitive tutoring systems, offering scalable, timely, and personalized evaluation of learner writing. By analyzing essays through sophisticated NLP techniques, these systems assess both the content and quality of student work, providing immediate, objective scores and constructive feedback that help learners improve their writing skills and deepen their understanding of subject matter.

The process of AES typically involves multiple NLP tasks, including syntactic parsing, semantic analysis, and discourse evaluation. These components allow the system to evaluate grammar, vocabulary usage, coherence, organization, argument strength, and overall writing style. Machine learning models, often trained on large corpora of human-scored essays, learn to predict scores that closely approximate expert human raters, thereby ensuring reliability and validity.

Beyond mere scoring, automated feedback generation plays a critical pedagogical role. Instead of simply assigning a grade, cognitive tutors equipped with AES capabilities can identify specific areas for improvement—such as unclear thesis statements, weak evidence, repetitive phrasing, or logical fallacies—and deliver targeted, actionable suggestions. This feedback supports iterative learning by encouraging revision, reflection, and self-regulation.

Sentiment and tone analysis further enhance feedback by detecting whether the learner's writing conveys confidence, uncertainty, or emotional nuance. Such insights help tutors address affective dimensions of learning, motivating students and fostering a growth mindset.

The advantages of AES and automated feedback in cognitive tutoring are substantial. They offer rapid assessment turnaround, enabling more frequent writing practice without overburdening human instructors. This immediacy promotes continuous improvement and personalized learning paths. Additionally, automated systems can maintain consistent evaluation standards, reducing subjectivity and bias inherent in manual grading.

However, challenges remain in fully capturing the richness and creativity of human writing. Advanced models now incorporate deep learning techniques, such as transformer architectures, to better understand context, metaphor, and argumentation complexity. Hybrid approaches that combine machine evaluation with human oversight are also emerging to balance efficiency with nuanced judgment.

Automated essay scoring and feedback, powered by NLP, revolutionize writing assessment within cognitive tutoring systems. They provide scalable, personalized, and pedagogically meaningful support that enhances learner writing proficiency and contributes to more effective, learner-centered education.

Real-Time Speech and Text Analysis in Assessments

Real-time speech and text analysis is transforming the landscape of educational assessments by enabling AI-powered cognitive tutoring systems to evaluate learner responses instantly and with high precision. Leveraging advanced Natural Language Processing (NLP) and speech recognition technologies, these systems analyze spoken or written inputs as they occur, offering immediate insights into learner understanding, language proficiency, and cognitive processes.

In formative assessments, real-time analysis allows tutors to monitor learner performance dynamically, identifying misconceptions, knowledge gaps, or skill deficiencies as learners respond. This immediate feedback loop enables adaptive interventions, such as hints, clarifications, or scaffolding, fostering a more personalized and responsive learning experience. For example, a cognitive tutor assessing oral language skills can transcribe and analyze a learner's spoken answer on the fly, evaluating pronunciation, fluency, vocabulary usage, and grammatical accuracy.

The integration of speech-to-text technologies with NLP modules is critical for handling spoken assessments. Automatic Speech Recognition (ASR) converts audio input into text, which is then processed by NLP techniques such as syntactic parsing, semantic analysis, and sentiment detection. This pipeline allows the system to comprehend the content and emotional tone of spoken responses, thereby supporting more nuanced assessments that account for both linguistic correctness and affective states.

In written assessments, real-time text analysis examines learner inputs such as short answers, essays, or chat interactions. Techniques including keyword extraction, topic modeling, and coherence evaluation help determine whether learners have addressed questions accurately and thoroughly. Immediate scoring and feedback facilitate iterative learning, motivating students to refine their answers and deepen comprehension during the assessment process itself.

The benefits of real-time speech and text analysis extend beyond individual learning. Educators gain valuable analytics on class-wide performance trends, enabling data-driven instructional decisions and curriculum adjustments. Additionally, these technologies support accessibility by allowing learners with different needs or language backgrounds to engage in varied assessment formats.

However, challenges such as handling diverse accents, background noise, and informal language in speech inputs, or managing ambiguous or incomplete text responses, require ongoing advances in model robustness and contextual understanding. The emergence of deep learning-based ASR and language models continues to enhance accuracy and adaptability in real-time analysis.

Real-time speech and text analysis empower cognitive tutoring systems to deliver timely, personalized assessments that reflect both learner knowledge and engagement. This capability is instrumental in creating interactive, supportive, and effective learning environments powered by AI.

Detection of Misconceptions and Learning Gaps

One of the most critical functions of AI-powered cognitive tutoring systems is the accurate detection of learner misconceptions and knowledge gaps. Misconceptions—incorrect or incomplete understandings of concepts—can significantly hinder learning progress if left unaddressed. Natural Language Processing (NLP) technologies play a pivotal role in identifying these cognitive barriers by analyzing learners' textual or spoken inputs for signs of misunderstanding, confusion, or partial knowledge, enabling timely and targeted instructional interventions.

NLP techniques enable tutors to move beyond surface-level correctness and delve into the underlying reasoning expressed by learners. For example, when students provide explanations, answers, or reflections in natural language, NLP models analyze the semantic content, logic, and coherence to identify inconsistencies or errors that reveal misconceptions. This analysis can include detecting incorrect use of terminology, faulty causal reasoning, or contradictions within learner responses.

Automated analysis of learner language also helps pinpoint specific learning gaps—areas where a learner lacks prerequisite knowledge or has insufficient mastery. Topic modeling and concept mapping algorithms compare learner inputs with expert domain knowledge to highlight missing or weakly understood concepts. This granular insight allows cognitive tutors to personalize instruction by focusing on foundational content before advancing to more complex topics.

Additionally, NLP-powered systems can track patterns across multiple learner interactions, recognizing persistent errors or recurring confusion that indicate deep-seated misconceptions. Sentiment and discourse analysis further enrich detection by revealing learner uncertainty, frustration, or overconfidence, which are often associated with misunderstanding.

The advantages of automated misconception and gap detection include scalability, immediacy, and personalization. Unlike traditional assessments that may only identify right or wrong answers, NLP-driven systems offer nuanced diagnostics in real time, supporting adaptive feedback and scaffolding tailored to individual learner needs. This responsiveness enhances learner engagement and promotes conceptual change by addressing errors at the moment they occur.

However, challenges persist in capturing the full complexity of human reasoning and avoiding false positives or negatives. Effective systems often combine NLP with domain-specific ontologies, knowledge graphs, and human expert validation to ensure accuracy and pedagogical relevance.

Detection of misconceptions and learning gaps through NLP empowers cognitive tutoring systems to provide precise, personalized support that fosters deeper understanding and accelerates learning. This capability is fundamental to realizing the promise of AI-driven personalized education.

MULTILINGUAL AND INCLUSIVE LEARNING THROUGH NLP

Language Translation and Localization

Language translation and localization are vital components in expanding the reach and effectiveness of AI-powered cognitive tutoring systems, especially in today's increasingly global and multilingual learning environments. Natural Language Processing (NLP) technologies enable these systems to overcome language barriers by translating instructional content, learner inputs, and feedback into multiple languages while adapting culturally and contextually to diverse learner populations.

Machine translation, powered by advanced NLP models such as neural machine translation (NMT), allows cognitive tutors to convert educational materials—texts, prompts, and explanations—accurately and fluently from one language to another. This capability ensures that learners worldwide can access high-quality personalized tutoring regardless of their native language, fostering inclusivity and equity in education.

Localization goes beyond direct translation; it involves culturally adapting the content and interaction style to align with the learner's linguistic norms, values, idioms, and educational context. For instance, examples, metaphors, or references may be modified to be culturally relevant, ensuring better comprehension and engagement. NLP techniques help automate aspects of localization by detecting language-specific nuances and tailoring text generation accordingly.

In cognitive tutoring, effective translation and localization are essential for understanding learner inputs in different languages and dialects. Speech recognition and natural language understanding modules must accommodate linguistic diversity, idiomatic expressions, and syntax variations to accurately interpret learner responses. This adaptability enables the tutor to provide precise, culturally sensitive feedback and support.

Moreover, multilingual cognitive tutors can facilitate cross-lingual learning, helping learners acquire new languages or subjects simultaneously by bridging concepts across languages. They can also support language learners by providing translation aids, bilingual glossaries, and context-aware explanations.

Challenges in language translation and localization include handling low-resource languages with limited training data, preserving the pedagogical intent during translation, and maintaining consistent terminology across languages. Recent advances in transfer learning, zero-shot translation, and domain-adaptive models are addressing these issues, enhancing translation quality and cultural appropriateness.

Thus language translation and localization powered by NLP are transformative for cognitive tutoring systems, enabling global accessibility, personalized learning across linguistic boundaries, and culturally responsive education. These capabilities help democratize knowledge and support diverse learner communities in an interconnected world.

NLP for Students with Disabilities (e.g., Dyslexia, Speech Impairments)

Natural Language Processing (NLP) technologies have opened new horizons for making AI-powered cognitive tutoring systems more inclusive and accessible, especially for students with disabilities such as dyslexia and speech impairments. By leveraging tailored NLP applications, cognitive tutors can better accommodate diverse learning needs, providing personalized support that addresses specific challenges faced by these learners.

For students with dyslexia, who struggle with reading fluency, decoding, and spelling, NLP offers powerful tools to ease text comprehension and expression. Text-to-speech (TTS) systems convert written content into natural-sounding audio, allowing learners to listen to instructional materials, thereby reducing reading load and improving understanding. Conversely, speech-to-text (STT) enables learners to dictate responses or essays, circumventing difficulties with writing or typing. Additionally, NLP-based spell checkers and grammar correction tools are designed to recognize common dyslexic errors and suggest appropriate corrections, helping learners produce clearer, more accurate text.

Beyond basic assistance, NLP can analyze learner writing to detect patterns of errors associated with dyslexia, enabling the tutoring system to tailor exercises targeting specific weaknesses such as phonetic confusions or letter reversals. Adaptive feedback mechanisms can scaffold learning by breaking down complex language tasks into manageable steps, promoting gradual skill development.

For students with speech impairments, NLP-powered speech recognition systems are increasingly sophisticated in handling diverse speech patterns, accents, or atypical pronunciations. Customized acoustic models trained on speech data from individuals with impairments improve recognition accuracy, enabling these learners to interact verbally with cognitive tutors more effectively. Alternative communication methods, such as gesture-based or text-based interfaces integrated with NLP, provide additional access routes for participation.

Moreover, sentiment and emotion analysis tools can detect frustration or anxiety in learner communications, which is particularly valuable for students with disabilities who may experience increased emotional barriers to learning. By recognizing affective states, cognitive tutors can adjust the pace, complexity, or encouragement strategies to better support learner engagement.

Despite advancements, challenges remain in ensuring NLP systems are equitable and effective for all disabilities, requiring ongoing research, diverse data representation, and ethical design. Collaboration with educators and specialists is essential to develop models sensitive to the nuanced needs of learners with disabilities.

DATA COLLECTION AND ETHICAL CONSIDERATIONS

Use of Learner Data for NLP Model Training

The effectiveness of Natural Language Processing (NLP) in AI-powered cognitive tutoring systems depends heavily on the quality, diversity, and representativeness of learner data used for training. Learner-generated inputs—such as essays, spoken responses, chat interactions, and forum discussions—form the backbone of NLP algorithms designed to interpret meaning, identify misconceptions, and deliver adaptive feedback. Unlike generic language corpora, learner data reflects the vocabulary, syntax, and discourse styles specific to educational contexts, making it invaluable for domain-sensitive model development.

Such data supports automated assessments, enabling supervised models to evaluate reasoning, detect common misconceptions, and assess proficiency levels. It also fuels personalization by uncovering patterns in learners' communication that correlate with engagement, motivation, or preferred learning styles. However, the use of educational data raises ethical dilemmas: while it enhances model accuracy, it also risks exposing sensitive personal information and unintentionally embedding inequities into AI-driven systems.

Privacy, Consent, and Data Security

The large-scale collection and analysis of learner data introduce significant ethical obligations around privacy, consent, and security. Because student interactions often reveal more than academic knowledge—touching on beliefs, emotions, and vulnerabilities—there is a heightened risk of misuse or profiling.

Ethical practice requires transparent consent mechanisms, where learners (and guardians, when appropriate) are informed about what data is collected, how it will be used, and who will have access. Opt-out options and data deletion rights should be clearly communicated. Yet, given the complexity of AI systems, presenting this information in a way that is both accurate and understandable remains a challenge.

Data security safeguards are equally vital. Strong encryption, restricted access, and regular security audits are necessary to prevent breaches. Adhering to frameworks like GDPR and FERPA ensures compliance, but ethical responsibility extends beyond regulation. Continuous monitoring and accountability structures are required to protect learners' digital rights.

Fairness, Inclusivity, and Bias Mitigation

A critical ethical concern is how NLP models handle bias and inclusivity. Training data often reflects societal biases—such as gender stereotypes, racial inequities, or socioeconomic disparities—which can become encoded into algorithms. For example, if a corpus underrepresents non-native English speakers, a tutoring system may misinterpret their inputs as errors, leading to unfair assessments. Similarly, biased text generation could reinforce harmful stereotypes in instructional feedback, undermining both trust and learner confidence.

Mitigating these risks requires a multi-layered strategy:

- **Diverse and representative datasets**: Curating balanced corpora that reflect varied dialects, cultural contexts, and learner demographics is crucial for fair performance.
- **Bias-aware modeling techniques**: Tools such as fairness-aware machine learning, adversarial debiasing, or re-weighting methods can detect and reduce discriminatory outputs during training.
- **Human-in-the-loop oversight**: Involving educators in monitoring model outputs allows errors or cultural insensitivities to be corrected in real time.
- **Explainable NLP (XAI)**: Providing transparency into how decisions are made—e.g., showing which linguistic features influenced a feedback decision—helps educators and learners challenge or contextualize outputs.

Ethical Stewardship and Long-Term Responsibility

Fairness and inclusivity extend beyond technical fixes. Developers must ensure that AI-powered tutors empower rather than marginalize learners by avoiding narrow cultural assumptions and ensuring adaptability across contexts. Continuous audits with fairness metrics, collaboration with diverse user communities, and inclusion of ethicists and educators in design cycles are essential.

Technological Infrastructure and Tools

Open-Source NLP Libraries (e.g., spaCy, NLTK, BERT)

Open-source Natural Language Processing (NLP) libraries have become foundational tools in the development of AI-powered cognitive tutoring systems. These libraries provide robust, accessible frameworks that enable educators, researchers, and developers to build sophisticated language understanding and generation capabilities without starting from scratch. Among the most influential are spaCy, NLTK, and BERT, each offering unique features suited to different aspects of cognitive tutoring applications.

The Natural Language Toolkit (NLTK) is one of the earliest and most comprehensive NLP libraries. It offers extensive modules for tokenization, stemming, tagging, parsing, and semantic reasoning. NLTK's educational focus and detailed documentation make it popular for teaching NLP concepts and prototyping text processing pipelines. In cognitive tutoring, NLTK can be employed for foundational tasks such as analyzing student essays, extracting keywords, or performing syntactic analysis to identify errors in writing.

spaCy, in contrast, emphasizes speed and industrial-strength performance, making it well-suited for real-time cognitive tutoring applications. It provides pre-trained models for part-of-speech tagging, named entity recognition, dependency parsing, and text classification optimized for efficiency. SpaCy's modern architecture supports easy integration with deep learning frameworks, allowing developers to customize and extend models for domain-specific educational content. For instance, spaCy can power automated feedback by quickly parsing learner responses and highlighting grammatical issues or concept-related keywords.

BERT (Bidirectional Encoder Representations from Transformers), developed by Google, revolutionized NLP by introducing deep, context-aware language representations. Unlike traditional models that process text sequentially, BERT analyzes the entire context of a sentence simultaneously, improving understanding of nuanced meanings, ambiguity, and inference. This capability is critical in cognitive tutoring systems that must interpret complex learner inputs, such as open-ended questions or multi-turn dialogues. Fine-tuning BERT on educational datasets enables precise tasks like automated essay scoring, misconception detection, and personalized feedback generation.

The open-source nature of these libraries fosters collaboration, continuous improvement, and cost-effective development, enabling cognitive tutors to evolve rapidly with advances in NLP research. Additionally, community-contributed resources, tutorials, and pre-trained models lower the barrier for institutions to adopt AI-powered tutoring technologies.

Integration with Learning Management Systems (LMS)

The integration of Natural Language Processing (NLP)-enabled cognitive tutoring systems with Learning Management Systems (LMS) represents a critical step toward seamless, scalable, and personalized education. LMS platforms such as Moodle, Blackboard, Canvas, and Google Classroom serve as centralized hubs for course content delivery, student management, assessment, and communication. Embedding NLP-powered cognitive tutors within these environments amplifies their potential by bringing intelligent, adaptive learning directly to where educators and learners already engage daily.

Integrating NLP cognitive tutors with LMS offers multiple benefits. Firstly, it enables real-time analysis and feedback on learner submissions within the LMS interface. For example, when students submit essays or open-ended responses, embedded NLP tools can automatically evaluate language quality, detect misconceptions, or provide tailored hints without requiring manual grading. This immediate responsiveness enhances learner engagement and supports formative assessment.

Secondly, the integration facilitates data exchange between the cognitive tutor and the LMS, allowing comprehensive learner profiles to be constructed. These profiles aggregate data from multiple sources, including quiz results, discussion forum posts, assignment drafts, and even peer reviews. NLP algorithms analyze this diverse textual and behavioral data to model learners' knowledge states, preferences, and emotional engagement. This holistic understanding enables the tutor to personalize content recommendations, scaffold instruction, and adapt feedback strategies dynamically.

Furthermore, LMS integration supports scalable deployment of NLP-driven tutoring across institutions and courses. By utilizing standard APIs and interoperability protocols like LTI (Learning Tools Interoperability), cognitive tutoring modules can be embedded as plug-and-play tools accessible within the LMS dashboard. This reduces technical barriers for educators and ensures consistent learner experiences across different subjects and grade levels.

From a technical perspective, integrating NLP systems with LMS also presents challenges, including data privacy, system compatibility, and latency concerns. Ensuring secure handling of sensitive learner data during transmission and storage aligns with legal requirements such as GDPR and FERPA. Additionally, NLP components must be optimized for low latency to maintain smooth user interactions within the LMS environment.

Looking ahead, the convergence of NLP cognitive tutors and LMS platforms paves the way for increasingly intelligent educational ecosystems. As NLP models advance in their understanding of natural language and learner behavior, integration will enable more proactive, context-aware support—transforming LMS from static content repositories into vibrant, interactive learning companions.

Challenges in Implementation and Scalability

The integration of Natural Language Processing (NLP) into cognitive tutoring systems offers enormous potential for advancing personalized learning, but it also introduces a range of complex challenges. These challenges span technical, pedagogical, and ethical domains and must be addressed to ensure that NLP-driven tutors are effective, equitable, and sustainable on a global scale. Zawacki-Richter, Marín, Bond, & Gouverneur, 2019.

A central technical difficulty lies in building NLP models that can reliably interpret the diversity of learner inputs. Human language is inherently ambiguous, context-sensitive, and culturally nuanced. Beyond dealing with variations in dialects and proficiency levels, current models often struggle with non-standard language use, such as slang, informal speech, and spelling or grammatical errors that are common in student responses. While advanced language models have made progress in contextual understanding, they may still misinterpret learner intent or provide irrelevant feedback when faced with creative phrasing or culturally specific expressions. Training models to handle such variation requires vast and representative datasets, which are difficult to obtain due to privacy restrictions, high annotation costs, and the scarcity of domain-specific educational corpora.

Scalability introduces another layer of complexity. NLP models require substantial computational resources to deliver real-time feedback, such as scoring essays, interpreting spoken responses, or analyzing emotional cues. For well-resourced institutions, cloud-based solutions can mitigate infrastructure demands, but for schools in regions with limited connectivity or budgetary constraints, deploying such systems remains a barrier. These challenges are magnified in the case of low-resource languages, where digital data is scarce, linguistic diversity is high, and cultural nuances are often overlooked in mainstream AI development. Without deliberate efforts to support such languages, global implementation risks reinforcing existing educational inequities.

Integration with educational ecosystems also poses hurdles. Learning Management Systems (LMS) vary widely in design and interoperability, making it difficult to seamlessly embed NLP-driven tutors. If these systems remain siloed rather than integrated, their effectiveness as part of a holistic learning environment is diminished.

Pedagogically, reliance on automated feedback raises concerns about reducing human interaction, which is vital for motivation, socio-emotional support, and higher-order learning. Educators need transparency into system operations and the ability to align feedback with instructional objectives. Without this, there is a risk of cognitive tutors drifting away from meaningful pedagogy toward automated but shallow interactions.

Finally, ethical issues must be carefully managed. NLP systems are vulnerable to bias, which can manifest in skewed assessments of learners from underrepresented groups. Protecting learner data is equally critical, requiring compliance with regulations such as GDPR and FERPA, along with robust privacy protocols. Sustaining these systems also demands ongoing adaptation, as languages evolve, curricula shift, and learner demographics diversify.

In summary, while NLP-driven cognitive tutors hold immense promise, realizing their potential requires addressing fundamental limitations in language understanding, scaling across cultural and linguistic contexts, ensuring pedagogical alignment, and safeguarding ethical standards.

FUTURE DIRECTIONS AND RESEARCH OPPORTUNITIES

Future Research Opportunities in NLP for Cognitive Tutoring

Integration with Affective Computing and Emotion-Aware Tutoring

The convergence of Natural Language Processing (NLP) with affective computing represents a pivotal step in advancing cognitive tutoring systems toward greater empathy and responsiveness. Affective computing focuses on recognizing and responding to human emotions, while NLP contributes by analyzing the linguistic markers embedded in learner interactions. Together, these technologies enable emotion-aware tutoring, which adjusts instruction not only to cognitive needs but also to the learner's emotional readiness and engagement.

Emotions such as frustration, boredom, or anxiety significantly influence motivation and retention. NLP techniques like sentiment analysis and emotion classification can detect such states from student language use in essays, chats, or spoken input. When combined with affective computing, these insights allow tutors to intervene dynamically—for example, by offering encouragement when frustration is detected or escalating challenges when engagement is high. This adaptability supports persistence and fosters deeper self-regulation in learners.

Beyond linguistic input, multimodal affective computing incorporates cues from speech tone, facial expressions, and physiological signals. NLP remains central, however, as much of learner interaction is text- or speech-based. By merging affective analytics with language understanding, future tutors can provide a holistic picture of learner progress, supporting both academic achievement and socio-emotional development.

Multimodal NLP and Emerging Frontiers

Future research increasingly points toward multimodal NLP, which integrates text, speech, and gesture analysis to more closely mirror human communication. Traditional NLP often processes written or spoken language in isolation, but learning interactions are inherently multimodal. Combining speech recognition with textual NLP enables tutors to capture nuances such as hesitation, intonation, or emphasis. Adding gestural analysis—such as nodding, gaze, or posture—provides further insight into engagement and comprehension.

For example, a learner responding with uncertain wording, a hesitant tone, and distracted gaze could be identified as struggling far more reliably than through text analysis alone. Such fusion of modalities promises more accurate learner modeling and responsive instructional strategies. Research opportunities lie in overcoming technical challenges such as synchronizing heterogeneous data streams, handling noisy multimodal inputs, and developing robust fusion algorithms capable of real-time adaptation.

Advances in Large Language Models (LLMs) and Generative AI

Recent breakthroughs in Large Language Models (LLMs) such as GPT, PaLM, and LLaMA open unprecedented opportunities for cognitive tutoring. These models can interpret nuanced queries, generate context-specific feedback, and create personalized learning content—ranging from tailored practice questions to adaptive explanations. Their open-domain capabilities also allow tutors to support a broad range of subjects without extensive manual programming.

Future research must address key limitations, including hallucinations (inaccurate outputs), computational inefficiencies, and bias in training data. Investigating ways to adapt LLMs with domain-specific fine-tuning, curriculum alignment, and teacher oversight mechanisms will be essential to ensure educational reliability.

Transparency, Interpretability, and Explainable AI (XAI)

One of the most pressing research areas is improving the transparency and interpretability of NLP-driven tutors. Current systems often operate as "black boxes," making it difficult for educators to understand how conclusions or feedback are generated. In educational contexts, where trust and accountability are paramount, learners and teachers alike need insight into the reasoning processes behind AI-driven feedback.

Developing explainable NLP techniques—for example, by highlighting which words or phrases triggered a particular assessment or recommendation—will help build confidence and facilitate collaboration between human instructors and AI tutors. XAI also plays a vital role in identifying and mitigating bias, ensuring that learners from diverse backgrounds are treated fairly.

Looking Ahead

The future of NLP in cognitive tutoring lies at the intersection of multimodal AI, affective computing, LLMs, and explainable NLP. By combining these elements, next-generation tutors will not only interpret what learners say but also how they say it and how they feel while saying it. Such systems hold the promise of creating empathetic, transparent, and globally scalable learning companions that adapt to both cognitive and emotional needs, ensuring equity and inclusivity in education worldwide.

CONCLUSION

Natural Language Processing (NLP) stands at the forefront of transforming cognitive tutoring systems into more intelligent, adaptive, and human-centered learning environments. By enabling machines to interpret, generate, and respond to human language with increasing sophistication, NLP bridges the gap between traditional computer-based instruction and personalized, context-aware tutoring. This chapter has explored how various NLP techniques—ranging from text classification, sentiment analysis, and named entity recognition to advanced dialogue systems and large language models—contribute to understanding learner inputs, modeling knowledge, and delivering tailored feedback.

The integration of NLP empowers cognitive tutors to move beyond static, one-dimensional teaching methods. Through multimodal inputs including speech and gesture, affective computing, and real-time analysis, these systems gain a deeper awareness of learners' cognitive and emotional states. This awareness facilitates dynamic adjustments in instructional content and feedback, fostering motivation, engagement, and more effective learning outcomes.

Despite the tremendous potential, the implementation of NLP in cognitive tutoring comes with notable challenges. These include addressing data privacy and ethical concerns, mitigating bias inherent in language models, ensuring system scalability, and maintaining the pedagogical alignment of AI-driven feedback. Continuous research and innovation are critical to overcoming these hurdles and maximizing the benefits of NLP-powered tutoring (D'Mello & Graesser, 2012).

Looking forward, advances in Large Language Models (LLMs) and generative AI promise to further enhance the versatility and personalization of cognitive tutors. By combining linguistic intelligence with emotional sensitivity and multimodal communication, future tutoring systems can provide highly contextualized, empathetic support tailored to the unique needs of each learner.

Thus NLP represents a foundational technology in the new frontier of personalized learning. Its ongoing evolution will not only redefine how learners interact with educational technologies but also expand the possibilities for inclusive, engaging, and effective education worldwide.

REFERENCES

Aleven, V., McLaughlin, E. A., Glenn, R. A., & Koedinger, K. R. (2016). Instruction based on adaptive learning technologies. *Handbook of Research on Learning and Instruction*, 522–560. https://doi.org/DOI: 10.4324/9781315680276-38

D'Mello, S. K., & Graesser, A. C. (2012). AutoTutor and affective AutoTutor: Learning by talking with cognitively and emotionally intelligent computers that talk back. [TiiS]. *ACM Transactions on Interactive Intelligent Systems*, *2*(4), 23. DOI: 10.1145/2395123.2395128

Kovanović, V., Joksimović, S., Gašević, D., Siemens, G., & Hatala, M. (2015). What public media reveals about MOOCs: A systematic analysis of news reports. *British Journal of Educational Technology*, *46*(3), 510–527. DOI: 10.1111/bjet.12277

Liu, S., Okonkwo, C., & Xu, F. (2022). Cognitive tutoring systems in intelligent education: A review of natural language processing applications. *Computers and Education: Artificial Intelligence*, *3*, 100067. DOI: 10.1016/j.caeai.2022.100067

Nye, B. D., Graesser, A., & Hu, X. (2014). AutoTutor and family: A review of 17 years of natural language tutoring. *International Journal of Artificial Intelligence in Education*, *24*(4), 427–469. DOI: 10.1007/s40593-014-0029-5

Piech, C., Bassen, J., Huang, J., Ganguli, S., Sahami, M., Guibas, L., & Sohl-Dickstein, J. (2015). Deep knowledge tracing. *Advances in Neural Information Processing Systems (NeurIPS)*, 28. https://doi.org/DOI: 10.48550/arXiv.1506.05908

Winkler, R., & Söllner, M. (2018). Unleashing the potential of chatbots in education: A state-of-the-art analysis. *Academy of Management Annual Meeting Proceedings*, 2018(1), 15903. https://doi.org/DOI: 10.5465/AMBPP.2018.15903abstract

Xu, B., Chen, N. S., & Chen, G. (2020). Effects of teacher role on student engagement in online learning environments: A configurational analysis. *Computers & Education*, *157*, 103963. DOI: 10.1016/j.compedu.2020.103956

Zawacki-Richter, O., Marín, V. I., Bond, M., & Gouverneur, F. (2019). Systematic review of research on artificial intelligence applications in higher education – Where are the educators? *International Journal of Educational Technology in Higher Education*, *16*(1), 39. DOI: 10.1186/s41239-019-0171-0

Zhang, J., & Chen, Z. (2023). Emotion-aware intelligent tutoring systems: Integrating affective computing with NLP for personalized learning. *AI in Education Journal*, *2*(1), 55–72. DOI: 10.1007/s43682-023-00115-4

Chapter 15
STEM for All:
An Equity-Oriented AI Personalization Framework for Inclusive Cognitive Tutoring

Amir Mahmood
https://orcid.org/0000-0002-0215-0278
Zhejiang Normal University, China

Mahnoor Masood Qureshi
Northwestern Polytechnical University, China

Nadia Rehman
https://orcid.org/0000-0002-4172-625X
Fatimah Jinnah Women University, Pakistan

Aiman Batool
https://orcid.org/0009-0001-6539-3461
University of Punjab, Pakistan

Misbah Shafait Abbasi
Zhejiang Normal University, China

Kidega Charles
https://orcid.org/0009-0004-2646-2219
Zhejiang Normal University, China

ABSTRACT

This chapter introduces the Equity-Oriented AI Personalization Framework (EAPF) as a guide for integrating AI-powered cognitive tutors into STEM education through an equity-centered approach. While AI personalization enables individualized learning, it often overlooks sociocultural and structural inequities that shape access and outcomes for marginalized learners. Grounded in Universal Design for Learning, Culturally Relevant Pedagogy, Zone of Proximal Development, and Equity Literacy, the EAPF highlights four dimensions, Access, Representation, Adaptivity, and Agency, supported by Bias Mitigation and Teacher Integration as critical enablers. Through illustrative scenarios, the chapter demonstrates how equity can be embedded in AI tutor design, content, and feedback systems. It offers practical insights for educa-

DOI: 10.4018/979-8-3373-4217-7.ch015

tors, developers, and policymakers, reframing personalization as a justice-driven process that aligns AI tools with the diverse needs of STEM learners, particularly in under-resourced and linguistically diverse contexts.

INTRODUCTION

In recent years, artificial intelligence (AI) has emerged as a transformative force in education, offering new opportunities for personalization, automation, and instructional efficiency(Ng et al., 2025a). Among the most promising innovations are AI-powered cognitive tutors, which simulate human-like one-on-one instruction by dynamically adapting content, pacing, and feedback to individual learners' needs(Seo et al., 2021). These systems, rooted in machine learning and data-driven instructional design, are increasingly being integrated into STEM (science, technology, engineering, and mathematics) education settings, where cognitive load, complex problem-solving, and conceptual scaffolding pose persistent challenges to equitable learning outcomes(Bahroun et al., 2023).

While the advancement of AI in STEM education is often framed in terms of technological novelty and instructional benefit, equity remains an unresolved and often under-theorized dimension of this evolving landscape(Rehman et al., 2025). Many AI-driven personalization systems operate on large-scale datasets that may carry embedded socio-cultural biases, overlook linguistic and identity differences, or privilege high-resource learning contexts. As a result, personalization may unintentionally replicate structural exclusions, reaching some learners more effectively than others, and thereby widening, rather than narrowing, existing educational disparities(Wang et al., 2024).

This chapter addresses a critical tension at the heart of AI-enhanced STEM learning: How can personalization be designed not merely to optimize learning, but to ensure it is inclusive, just, and equitable? Specifically, we explore this question through the development and presentation of a conceptual model, the Equity-Oriented AI Personalization Framework (EAPF), which identifies key design and implementation principles needed to embed equity into the core architecture of cognitive tutoring systems in STEM education.

Drawing on insights from the fields of educational psychology, AI ethics, culturally responsive pedagogy, and universal design for learning, this chapter argues that equity in AI-based learning is not a peripheral concern, but rather a central criterion for responsible innovation. In particular, we propose that four interrelated equity constructs, Access, Representation, Adaptivity, and Agency, must be foundational to any AI system that claims to support personalized STEM learning. We further emphasize two enabling conditions, Bias Mitigation and Teacher Integration, as essential to operationalizing these constructs in real-world classroom environments.

Through the synthesis of these components into a coherent conceptual framework, this chapter seeks to contribute a theoretically grounded, practically relevant model for educators, designers, and policymakers working at the intersection of AI and STEM education. Ultimately, our aim is not just to enhance the technical sophistication of cognitive tutors, but to reorient their development toward a more humanizing and inclusive vision of personalized learning, one that affirms all learners' rights to equitable participation in the STEM disciplines.

PROBLEM SPACE AND RATIONALE

Despite the increasing presence of AI-powered cognitive tutors in educational technology ecosystems, the issue of equity in personalized learning, especially within STEM education, remains insufficiently theorized and operationalized(Ng et al., 2025b). Much of the discourse surrounding AI in education has centered on technological performance, efficiency, and scale, with less attention given to how these tools interact with the sociocultural realities of diverse learners. This imbalance risks reproducing historical patterns of exclusion under the guise of innovation. In STEM education in particular, where deep-seated disparities persist along lines of gender, language, socioeconomic status, disability, and geographic location, the integration of AI without a deliberate equity lens may further entrench these inequities(Dimari et al., 2024).

While AI-powered cognitive tutors offer promise in addressing individual differences in learning pace, prior knowledge, and mastery trajectories, such personalization often operates on narrowly defined learner models(Chiu et al., 2023). These models typically prioritize cognitive variables (e.g., response accuracy, time-on-task, error patterns) while overlooking critical socio-cultural, linguistic, and affective dimensions that shape learning. As a result, personalization becomes a technical function rather than a human-centered pedagogical strategy. For marginalized or underrepresented learners in STEM, such as students from rural schools, those with limited language proficiency, or those with non-dominant cultural backgrounds, this narrow form of personalization risks misalignment, disengagement, and dropout(Pan et al., 2023).

Moreover, most current AI systems rely on data-hungry machine learning architectures, which depend on historical patterns to predict and adapt future instruction. Yet, these historical data patterns often reflect unequal access, biased curricular exposure, and the digital divide. Without mechanisms for bias detection, mitigation, and cultural responsiveness, AI personalization runs the risk of amplifying systemic disparities(Zhai et al., 2021). For instance, learners who fall outside the statistical norm, due to linguistic variation, disability, or underrepresentation in the training dataset, may receive inaccurate recommendations, be over-remediated, or even flagged as at-risk in ways that reflect deficit assumptions rather than genuine learning needs.

This conceptual gap is compounded by the absence of an integrated framework that guides developers, educators, and policymakers in embedding equity into the core design of AI-powered tutors. While there are existing models that emphasize adaptive learning, learning analytics, or user-centered design, few explicitly engage with the equity implications of AI personalization in STEM. Likewise, educational research has yet to fully articulate how constructs such as access, cultural representation, learner agency, and adaptive scaffolding can be translated into AI design features or pedagogical affordances(Selwyn, 2024).

Given this confluence of factors, there is a critical need for a conceptual framework that synthesizes equity theory, AI personalization principles, and STEM pedagogy into a coherent model for guiding inclusive innovation. This chapter addresses this gap by presenting the Equity-Oriented AI Personalization Framework (EAPF), which offers a structured yet flexible tool for centering equity in the design, evaluation, and implementation of AI-based STEM tutors. The EAPF is not intended as a one-size-fits-all solution, but as a set of guiding commitments that align technological capabilities with human-centered values, particularly in contexts where educational inequality is most acute(Ouyang & Jiao, 2021).

In doing so, the chapter builds a bridge between technological design and educational justice, contributing to a broader shift in the field: from data-driven personalization to equity-driven personalization, where all learners, regardless of background, are not only included but meaningfully empowered through AI-enabled STEM learning environments.

THEORETICAL FOUNDATIONS

The Equity-Oriented AI Personalization Framework (EAPF) is anchored in four intersecting bodies of theory that collectively inform its design principles, equity commitments, and practical application: Universal Design for Learning (UDL), Culturally Relevant Pedagogy (CRP), Zone of Proximal Development (ZPD), and Equity Literacy. These frameworks, while diverse in origin, converge on a shared imperative: to position learners as capable, diverse individuals whose learning needs are best served through systems that recognize complexity, value identity, and challenge structural inequities.

Universal Design for Learning (UDL)

UDL offers a foundational lens for understanding how learning environments can be proactively designed to accommodate learner variability. Developed by CAST (Center for Applied Special Technology), UDL proposes three core principles: (1) multiple means of representation, (2) multiple means of action and expression, and (3) multiple means of engagement. These principles are particularly relevant to AI-powered cognitive tutors, which have the technological affordances to deliver multimodal content, support diverse forms of expression, and personalize learning pathways.

In the EAPF, UDL informs the Access dimension, guiding how AI systems can provide equitable entry points for learners who face linguistic, sensory, or cognitive barriers. For example, an AI tutor designed with UDL principles might offer voice-based prompts, translated scientific terms, or scaffolded visual supports for learners in multilingual or low-literacy contexts. By embedding UDL, personalization moves beyond efficiency toward accessibility as a form of equity(Rusconi & Squillaci, 2023).

Culturally Relevant Pedagogy (CRP)

CRP emphasizes the need for instructional practices that affirm students' cultural identities, promote academic success, and develop sociopolitical consciousness. In the context of AI tutors, CRP highlights the importance of Representation: ensuring that learners see themselves, culturally, linguistically, and contextually, reflected in the learning content and interaction patterns(Roman & Ortega, 2019).

AI systems trained on dominant-language corpora or Western-centric curricular standards risk marginalizing learners from underrepresented groups. A culturally relevant AI tutor in a STEM classroom, by contrast, might integrate regional science examples, multilingual dialogue options, or narratives that resonate with local cultural values. The EAPF uses CRP as a guiding ethic to challenge the cultural neutrality often assumed in educational technologies and to promote representation as inclusion(Brown-Jeffy & Cooper, 2011).

Zone of Proximal Development (ZPD)

Vygotsky's (1978) concept of the ZPD, the gap between what a learner can do independently and what they can achieve with guided support, is central to contemporary models of adaptive instruction. AI-powered cognitive tutors are uniquely suited to operationalize ZPD through real-time feedback, just-in-time scaffolding, and intelligent progression algorithms. However, without critical scrutiny, such adaptivity may privilege learners who already demonstrate high performance or alignment with normative learning paths(Silverman, 2011).

In the EAPF, ZPD theory undergirds the dimension of Adaptivity, but with a nuanced interpretation: personalization should not only match cognitive performance but also respond to affective signals, learner confidence, and contextual barriers. Adaptivity is redefined not as automatic differentiation, but as responsive equity, where learners are supported to move toward mastery at their own pace, in ways that reflect their lived realities and prior knowledge(Chaiklin, 2003).

Equity Literacy

Equity Literacy, advanced by Gorski (2015), calls for educators, and by extension, AI systems, to develop the capacity to recognize, respond to, and redress inequities in learning environments. Unlike diversity frameworks that often emphasize awareness or celebration, equity literacy demands structural competence: the ability to locate how policies, practices, and technologies reproduce or challenge inequality, (Gorski, 2015).

This theoretical strand is critical to the Bias Mitigation and Teacher Integration components of the EAPF. AI systems must be audited not only for algorithmic bias but also for epistemic bias, what knowledge is included, whose ways of thinking are prioritized, and whose are erased, (Gorski, 2017). Moreover, educators must be equipped with tools that surface equity-relevant insights from AI systems, enabling human judgment to complement machine precision. In this way, equity literacy becomes the connective tissue that ensures AI personalization is accountable to human values(Posti-Ahokas & Janhonen-Abruquah, 2024).

Synthesis and Theoretical Integration

Together, these theoretical lenses provide a robust scaffold for constructing a personalization framework that resists the technocentric logic of optimization in favor of a human-centered, justice-oriented approach. UDL foregrounds access, CRP demands representation, ZPD enables adaptivity, and equity literacy insists on structural accountability, (Gorski, 2015). These theories are not merely background literature; they actively shape the framework's architecture and its criteria for success.

In situating the Equity-Oriented AI Personalization Framework within these traditions, the chapter advocates for a paradigm shift: from using AI to replicating conventional personalization models to reimagining personalization as a vehicle for educational justice, particularly in STEM fields where access, inclusion, and empowerment are most urgently needed.

Figure 1. Theoretical foundations of the Equity-Oriented AI Personalization Framework (EAPF)

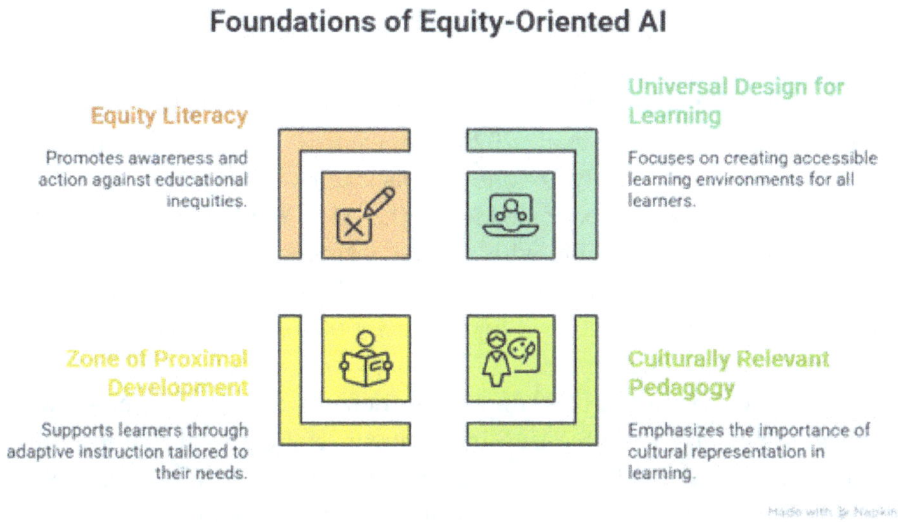

ROLE OF AI-POWERED COGNITIVE TUTORS IN STEM EDUCATION

AI-powered cognitive tutors represent one of the most ambitious applications of artificial intelligence in education, combining computational modeling, real-time feedback, and adaptive instructional strategies to replicate aspects of one-on-one human tutoring. Rooted in intelligent tutoring system (ITS) research and refined through advances in machine learning, these systems promise to personalize instruction at scale, especially in subjects such as mathematics, science, and technology, where students often face abstract content, high cognitive demands, and conceptual stumbling blocks. While these tools have gained momentum in recent years, their integration into STEM education raises both opportunities and tensions, particularly when evaluated through an equity-oriented lens(Glick et al., 2024).

Cognitive tutors typically operate through a cycle of interaction: they present content or problems, capture student input, analyze learner performance in real time, and offer immediate, targeted feedback. Many systems embed domain-specific knowledge models (e.g., algebraic reasoning, physics simulations) alongside student models that track proficiency, errors, and progression. In STEM classrooms, this enables granular differentiation, learners receive problems at an appropriate level of difficulty, struggle productively with concepts, and receive scaffolding that is aligned with their needs(Govea et al., 2023).

From a technical standpoint, this model of adaptive personalization aligns with Vygotsky's Zone of Proximal Development, providing learners with support that is neither too easy nor too difficult. However, when decoupled from the cultural, linguistic, and identity-based experiences of learners, such adaptivity risks becoming narrowly cognitive(Otto et al., 2025). For example, a student in a multilingual context might perform poorly not due to a lack of conceptual understanding, but because of a language barrier embedded in the AI system's interface. Similarly, a learner's hesitation in engaging with a physics simulation may stem from a lack of cultural relevance, not cognitive deficiency. These blind spots expose the limitations of current AI tutors when equity is not treated as a foundational design principle(Leon et al., 2025a).

Furthermore, the training of AI tutors often depends on large datasets drawn from homogeneous or high-resource learning contexts, leading to algorithms that may generalize poorly across diverse populations. In STEM education, where students already face structural barriers, such as underfunded laboratories, gender stereotypes, and curriculum-language mismatches, the replication of biased training data in AI systems can deepen exclusion. AI tutors may over-remediate students from disadvantaged groups, misinterpret cultural expressions of knowledge, or provide feedback that reflects deficit-based assumptions(Létourneau et al., 2025).

A second limitation lies in the assumed neutrality of content and pedagogy. Most cognitive tutors are designed around canonical, often Western-centric curricular frameworks, implicitly assuming a standard learner who aligns with dominant norms of knowledge representation. In doing so, they risk rendering invisible the epistemological diversity that exists across STEM disciplines globally. Students' ways of knowing, problem-solving heuristics, and local scientific practices may be omitted or devalued, leading to a form of curricular erasure masked as personalization(Melo, 2024).

Despite these limitations, cognitive tutors also carry profound potential for advancing equity, if designed with intentionality. Their ability to provide non-judgmental, consistent support, adjust to learner variability, and generate granular data on performance could be harnessed to support marginalized learners in ways that human instructors, constrained by class size and time, cannot always achieve. For instance, AI tutors can serve as low-stakes environments for experimentation, offer multilingual explanations, or surface early indicators of disengagement, provided that such capabilities are integrated through an equity lens(Córdova-Esparza, 2025).

The Equity-Oriented AI Personalization Framework (EAPF) builds on this dual recognition: cognitive tutors are not inherently equitable or inequitable, they reflect the values, assumptions, and design decisions embedded in their architecture. By aligning AI personalization with principles of access, representation, adaptivity, and agency, and by incorporating safeguards such as bias mitigation and teacher integration, cognitive tutors can become tools for not only delivering STEM content, but also affirming the diverse identities and capabilities of all learners(Létourneau et al., 2025).

Thus, this chapter does not reject the promise of AI-powered tutors in STEM education. Rather, it argues for a reorientation of that promise, away from optimization alone and toward inclusion, justice, and human dignity. Only then can AI-powered personalization fulfill its potential, not just as a technological innovation, but as a meaningful intervention in the pursuit of educational equity.

THE EQUITY-ORIENTED AI PERSONALIZATION FRAMEWORK (EAPF)

The Equity-Oriented AI Personalization Framework (EAPF) is a conceptual model developed to guide the design, implementation, and evaluation of AI-powered cognitive tutors in STEM education through an equity-first lens. Synthesizing insights from educational psychology, learning sciences, AI ethics, and culturally responsive pedagogy, the EAPF responds to the growing concern that personalization, without deliberate safeguards, may reinforce exclusion rather than address it(Naggita & Aguma, 2022). The framework identifies four interdependent equity dimensions, Access, Representation, Adaptivity, and Agency, supported by two enabling conditions: Bias Mitigation and Teacher Integration. Together, these components aim to reposition AI tutors from instruments of technical efficiency to tools of transformative inclusion.

The EAPF is visually represented as a four-quadrant circle, with each quadrant corresponding to one of the equity dimensions. The design intentionally moves away from hierarchical or linear representations to signal the co-equal importance of each component(Page et al., 2011). At the center lies the commitment to equity, anchoring the personalization process in a values-based framework rather than a purely data-driven one. Below, each component of the model is described in detail.

Access: Equitable Entry Points to AI-Enhanced STEM Learning

The **Access** quadrant emphasizes the foundational need for learners to engage with AI tutors regardless of linguistic, sensory, geographic, or socioeconomic barriers. This includes multimodal content delivery (e.g., voice, text, visuals), multilingual interfaces, offline functionalities for low-bandwidth environments, and accommodations for learners with disabilities(Leon et al., 2025b).

In many educational contexts, particularly in the Global South, rural schools, or linguistically diverse classrooms, access cannot be assumed. AI tutors that require high-end devices, operate only in English, or lack universal design considerations effectively exclude a large segment of learners. Therefore, the design of access features must be anticipatory rather than reactive, built into the system's architecture from the outset(Voutyrakou & Skordoulis, 2025).

Equity Implication

Access is not merely about availability; it is about designing systems that assume variability and ensure no learner is left behind due to technical or linguistic gatekeeping.

Representation: Cultural and Identity-Affirming Design

The Representation quadrant highlights the importance of embedding students' cultural backgrounds, linguistic repertoires, lived experiences, and epistemological traditions into the AI tutor's content and interaction patterns. This includes inclusive examples, culturally relevant problem scenarios, and identity-affirming feedback mechanisms(Son, 2024).

Current AI tutors often reflect dominant cultural and linguistic norms, unintentionally marginalizing learners who do not see their realities reflected in the curriculum or user interface. When students' identities are omitted or misrepresented, engagement declines and a sense of academic alienation can follow. Representation also involves algorithmic fairness: ensuring that predictive models do not reflect historical biases or treat underrepresented groups as statistical outliers(Lucido et al., 2024).

Equity Implication

Personalization must extend beyond performance data to include cultural relevance and epistemic inclusion, without which personalization becomes assimilation.

Adaptivity: Responsiveness to Learner Growth within Context

Adaptivity is often the hallmark of AI-powered cognitive tutors. In the EAPF, the Adaptivity quadrant is redefined not as reactive tailoring based solely on learner performance, but as proactive, holistic responsiveness. This includes adapting content to the learner's Zone of Proximal Development (ZPD), recognizing affective signals (e.g., frustration or boredom), and adjusting pacing and problem types accordingly(Shi & Liu, 2025).

However, standard adaptive algorithms often over-rely on cognitive metrics while ignoring emotional, cultural, or motivational cues. Moreover, adaptivity may inadvertently accelerate some learners while over-remediating others, particularly when feedback is based on biased training data. The EAPF positions adaptivity as context-aware and equity-attuned, where scaffolding is personalized without being paternalistic or pathologizing(Mejeh & Rehm, 2024).

Equity Implication

Effective adaptivity is about more than matching difficulty, it is about intelligently supporting diverse learner trajectories without normalizing deficit assumptions.

Agency: Supporting Learner Autonomy and Voice

The **Agency** quadrant underscores the importance of giving learners control over their learning path, pace, and AI interaction. Agency includes the ability to choose among learning modalities, revisit explanations, adjust the tutor's feedback frequency, and set personal learning goals within the AI environment(Schaefer et al., 2024).

Traditional instructional technologies often disempower learners by over-structuring tasks or making all instructional decisions through opaque algorithms(Otto et al., 2025). By contrast, AI tutors grounded in agency respect students' metacognitive and self-regulatory capacities. Designing for agency means building user-facing transparency, offering choices, and allowing students to make mistakes, reflect, and recover, hallmarks of authentic learning.

Equity Implication

Without agency, personalization risks becoming surveillance; with agency, it becomes empowerment.

Bias Mitigation: Safeguarding Fairness in AI Systems

Bias Mitigation is a **cross-cutting enabler** that supports all four equity dimensions. This includes auditing datasets for representational fairness, applying algorithmic checks for predictive bias, and involving diverse stakeholders in model development. Bias can enter AI systems through unrepresentative training data, flawed design assumptions, or discriminatory proxy variables. Mitigation must be ongoing, not a one-time audit(González-Sendino et al., 2024).

Equity Implication

Bias is not a bug; it is a design risk. Systems must be built with mechanisms to recognize and redress inequities at every stage.

Teacher Integration: Human-in-the-Loop for Interpretive Equity

While AI tutors can process large volumes of data and personalize instruction in real time, they cannot interpret learner histories, cultural dynamics, or classroom power relations as expertly as a human teacher can. The EAPF includes Teacher Integration as a necessary safeguard, ensuring educators remain central to the personalization process(Al-Zahrani, 2024).

Teacher dashboards, feedback summaries, and student snapshots must be intelligible and actionable, enabling teachers to contextualize AI-generated insights and make informed decisions. Moreover, teachers must be equipped with professional development on equity and AI literacy to use these tools effectively(Ifenthaler et al., 2024).

Equity Implication

AI tutors must enhance, not replace, teacher expertise, especially in matters of equity where judgment and empathy are essential.

Summary of the Framework

The Equity-Oriented AI Personalization Framework provides both a diagnostic tool and a design blueprint. It enables stakeholders to ask critical questions such as:

- Does this system accommodate linguistic and cognitive diversity?
- Whose knowledge is included in the content?
- How are learners' identities affirmed?
- What forms of bias have been detected, and addressed?
- How is the learner's voice reflected in the tutoring experience?
- Are teachers empowered to act on AI-driven insights?

The strength of the EAPF lies in its integrative nature. Each quadrant is essential, but none is sufficient alone. Together, they reframe AI personalization not as a technical solution, but as a pedagogical and ethical commitment to justice-centered innovation in STEM education.

APPLICATION SCENARIOS: EQUITY-CENTERED AI TUTORING IN STEM CLASSROOMS

To bridge the gap between conceptual design and classroom reality, this section presents practical vignettes that illustrate how each dimension of the Equity-Oriented AI Personalization Framework (EAPF) might manifest in real-world STEM teaching and learning environments. These scenarios are not hypothetical abstractions; they reflect the types of challenges and possibilities that educators, learners, and designers commonly encounter, particularly in under-resourced or linguistically diverse classrooms(Schaefer et al., 2024).

Scenario 1: Multimodal Access in a Low-Connectivity Context

Context

A rural middle school in Northern Pakistan integrates an AI-powered science tutor for Grade 8 students studying Earth sciences. Most learners are Urdu-speaking and have limited exposure to English-language technical terms.

Equity Challenge

Traditional versions of the AI tutor only support English instructions and require constant internet access, making it inaccessible for students with limited language proficiency and unstable connectivity.

Framework Application (Access)

An equity-aligned version of the tutor offers:

- **Multilingual content** (Urdu and English side-by-side),
- **Offline sync modes**,
- **Audio-based prompts** for low-literacy learners.

This design ensures that all students, not just those with language fluency and stable broadband, can meaningfully engage with the AI tutor. Access is proactively designed, not retrofitted.

Scenario 2: Cultural Representation in a Chemistry Module

Context

A cognitive tutor is deployed in a Southeast Asian high school chemistry class. The AI system introduces chemical reactions through food preparation analogies, primarily drawn from Western contexts (e.g., baking bread, making cheese).

Equity Challenge

Local students fail to relate to the metaphors, causing confusion and disengagement.

Framework Application (Representation)

An equity-sensitive version of the tutor:

- Integrates region-specific examples (e.g., fermentation in kimchi, rice starch reactions),
- Adapts visuals and narratives to reflect students' cultural references,
- Offers name recognition models inclusive of non-Western naming conventions.

Representation is not decoration; it is a pedagogical strategy for belonging.

Scenario 3: Adaptive Feedback with Human Oversight

Context

A Grade 10 student in an urban math class frequently receives remedial problems from the AI tutor despite being conceptually sound but prone to occasional typos in answers.

Equity Challenge

The AI system flags the student as low-performing, locking them into a repetitive remediation loop that negatively impacts self-efficacy.

Framework Application (Adaptivity + Teacher Integration)

A redesigned tutor:

- Differentiates between conceptual errors and surface-level mistakes,
- Escalates a review prompt to the teacher dashboard after three consecutive flags,
- Enables the student to request "review mode" instead of auto-remediation.

Here, adaptivity becomes flexible and accountable, not deterministic.

Scenario 4: Empowering Student Agency Through Customization

Context

A group of high school girls enrolled in an AI-assisted robotics course request more control over their learning path, including the ability to choose project themes that reflect their interests.

Equity Challenge

The existing AI tutor offers only linear sequences and standardized project templates.

Framework Application (Agency)

An updated version allows:

- Learners to choose between multiple project themes (e.g., environmental sensors, community-based robotics),
- Adjust difficulty level of challenges,
- Track and reflect on personal learning goals through a dashboard journal.

In this design, agency is built into the learner interface, fostering metacognition and self-determination.

Scenario 5: Auditing Predictive Bias in STEM Outcomes

Context

In a high-performing school in the Middle East, the AI tutor consistently recommends science enrichment modules to male students at higher rates than female students, despite equivalent performance metrics.

Equity Challenge

A gender bias is embedded in the recommendation algorithm, subtly reinforcing gender disparities in science confidence and opportunity.

Framework Application (Bias Mitigation)

- A bias audit tool flags the pattern to administrators,
- Adjustments are made to the training data and recommendation engine,
- Students are transparently shown why certain modules are recommended, with override options.

Bias mitigation is ongoing and structural, it is a design commitment, not a patch.

Cross-Scenario Insights

Across these cases, the application of EAPF leads to a reimagining of personalization as a collaborative, inclusive, and culturally situated process. It foregrounds the idea that AI tutors must not only deliver content effectively, but must also understand learners contextually, support them holistically, and empower them meaningfully(Melo, 2024).

These examples demonstrate that equity is not abstract, it is embodied in interface design, data structures, pedagogical choices, and user agency. Without such embedded considerations, even the most advanced cognitive tutors may fail the very learners they claim to serve.

IMPLICATIONS FOR PRACTICE, DESIGN, AND POLICY

The Equity-Oriented AI Personalization Framework (EAPF) offers not only a conceptual guide but also a strategic tool for shaping future directions in STEM education, AI system development, and educational policy. As AI-powered cognitive tutors become increasingly normalized in classrooms globally, the failure to embed equity considerations may not just result in exclusion, it may systematically entrench educational injustice under the guise of technological innovation. This section outlines key implications for three critical stakeholder groups: practitioners (teachers and school leaders), designers (AI developers and EdTech firms), and policymakers (institutional and national actors).

Implications for Educational Practice

Teachers remain the most influential mediators between learners and AI systems. Despite the sophistication of cognitive tutors, human educators hold the interpretive power to contextualize feedback, reframe tasks, and respond to learner affect, functions that AI cannot yet replicate meaningfully.

Practical Implications

- Equity-informed professional development is essential. Teachers must be trained not only in using AI tools but in interpreting AI outputs through a socio-cultural lens.
- Teacher dashboards should be co-designed with educators to ensure usability, actionability, and relevance.
- Instructional planning should incorporate AI insights while also maintaining critical autonomy, not treating AI decisions as final or infallible.

If AI tutors are to support inclusive STEM learning, teachers must be empowered not just as users but as equity-centered agents in the AI-human instructional loop.

Implications for AI System and Interface Design

For AI developers and EdTech firms, the EAPF challenges dominant assumptions that personalization is a purely technical matter. Instead, it demands that equity be treated as a design constraint, not a downstream evaluation metric.

Design Implications

- Equity dimensions such as representation, agency, and linguistic access must be embedded at the level of algorithm design, content generation, and UI/UX decisions.
- Developers should move toward explainable AI (XAI) principles, ensuring that learners and educators can understand how and why recommendations are made.
- Human-centered co-design practices must be prioritized: involving students, educators, and marginalized voices throughout the development lifecycle.

Without intentional inclusion, personalization will reflect the biases of those who build it. With inclusive design, AI tutors can expand, not constrain, possibilities for STEM participation.

Implications for Educational Policy and Governance

At the policy level, national education systems and institutional leaders must recognize that equity in AI-powered learning is not guaranteed by access alone. Merely introducing cognitive tutors into classrooms does not address deeper issues of curriculum design, assessment inequality, or digital infrastructure.

Policy Recommendations

- Governments should adopt equity audit protocols for AI EdTech procurement, ensuring that approved systems meet minimum standards for linguistic inclusion, bias mitigation, and adaptive scaffolding.
- Funding models should prioritize context-sensitive innovation, supporting localized AI solutions rather than importing generic systems ill-suited to diverse educational realities.
- Regulatory frameworks should include data ethics, algorithmic transparency, and inclusion mandates, especially where learner data is collected and used for high-stakes decisions.

Policymakers must not confuse innovation with transformation. Equitable AI integration in STEM education will require infrastructural, curricular, and cultural shifts, not just tool adoption.

Building a Multi-Stakeholder Ecosystem for Equity

Perhaps most critically, the EAPF points to the need for collaborative ecosystems, where equity is not the responsibility of a single actor but a shared priority across sectors.

Key Strategies

- Establish equity-focused research-practice partnerships between universities, schools, and EdTech developers.
- Incentivize open-source AI development models that allow customization for linguistic and cultural relevance.
- Promote youth voice and learner feedback loops in AI system evaluation.

Ultimately, equity in AI-powered personalization is not an endpoint but a continuous commitment, a design ethos, a policy principle, and a pedagogical stance that requires vigilance, humility, and collaboration.

CONCLUSION AND FUTURE DIRECTIONS

This chapter has introduced and elaborated the Equity-Oriented AI Personalization Framework (EAPF) as a response to the growing urgency of embedding equity into the design and deployment of AI-powered cognitive tutors in STEM education. While much of the current discourse on AI in education is preoccupied with scale, automation, and efficiency, this chapter has re-centered the conversation on justice, inclusion, and learner empowerment, arguing that personalization without equity is not only incomplete, but potentially harmful(Otto et al., 2025).

Through the EAPF, we have proposed four central equity dimensions, Access, Representation, Adaptivity, and Agency, each grounded in theoretical foundations and illustrated through practical scenarios. These are further supported by two enabling mechanisms: Bias Mitigation and Teacher Integration, which together ensure that AI systems do not displace human judgment, but rather enhance it in ethically and culturally responsive ways(Al-Zahrani, 2024).

The core contribution of this framework is not technical but conceptual: it redefines personalization as a moral and pedagogical commitment rather than a computational function. In doing so, it invites AI developers, educators, and policymakers to reject reductive assumptions about learning and to instead embrace the complex, situated realities of diverse STEM learners, particularly those at the margins of mainstream systems.

Future Research Directions

While this chapter has outlined the rationale and structure of the EAPF, several directions remain for future empirical and theoretical exploration:

- Validation studies: Future research should empirically test the EAPF in real-world classroom environments using mixed methods, to assess its impact on learning outcomes, engagement, and inclusion.
- Cultural contextualization: Additional work is needed to adapt and localize the framework for different linguistic, national, and epistemic contexts, particularly in the Global South.
- Learner-centered metrics: There is a need to develop new equity-aligned evaluation metrics for AI tutors that go beyond accuracy and efficiency to include voice, dignity, and identity affirmation.
- Ethics and policy analysis: Comparative policy studies could examine how national AI education strategies align, or fail to align, with the equity principles proposed here.

Final Reflections

In a time when AI technologies are reshaping the very architecture of education, we are faced with a choice: to allow personalization to evolve as a neutral, data-driven tool, or to shape it as a human-centered, justice-oriented practice. The Equity-Oriented AI Personalization Framework offers a vision for the latter. It is a call to action not only for more intelligent systems but for more humane systems, ones that see each learner not as a datapoint, but as a full person with histories, identities, and futures worth affirming.

If STEM education is to fulfill its promise as a gateway to opportunity, innovation, and civic participation, it must be reimagined through tools and frameworks that refuse exclusion and build equity by design. AI-powered cognitive tutors, when aligned with these values, can play a transformative role in that reimagining, not as replacements for teachers or panaceas for educational inequality, but as intelligent allies in the pursuit of a more just and inclusive learning future.

REFERENCES

Al-Zahrani, A. M. (2024). Unveiling the shadows: Beyond the hype of AI in education. *Heliyon, 10*(9), e30696. DOI: 10.1016/j.heliyon.2024.e30696

Bahroun, Z., Anane, C., Ahmed, V., & Zacca, A. (2023). Transforming Education: A Comprehensive Review of Generative Artificial Intelligence in Educational Settings through Bibliometric and Content Analysis. *Sustainability (Basel), 15*(17), 12983. DOI: 10.3390/su151712983

Brown-Jeffy, S., & Cooper, J. E. (2011). Toward a Conceptual Framework of Culturally Relevant Pedagogy: An Overview of the Conceptual and Theoretical Literature. *Teacher Education Quarterly, 38*(1), 65–84.

Chaiklin, S. (2003). The zone of proximal development in Vygotsky's analysis of learning and instruction. In *Vygotsky's educational theory in cultural context* (pp. 39–64). Cambridge University Press., DOI: 10.1017/CBO9780511840975.004

Chiu, T. K. F., Xia, Q., Zhou, X., Chai, C. S., & Cheng, M. (2023). Systematic literature review on opportunities, challenges, and future research recommendations of artificial intelligence in education. *Computers and Education: Artificial Intelligence, 4*, 100118. DOI: 10.1016/j.caeai.2022.100118

Córdova-Esparza, D.-M. (2025). AI-Powered Educational Agents: Opportunities, Innovations, and Ethical Challenges. *Information (Basel), 16*(6), 469. DOI: 10.3390/info16060469

Dimari, A., Tyagi, N., Davanageri, M., Kukreti, R., Yadav, R., & Dimari, H. (2024). AI-Based Automated Grading Systems for open book examination system: Implications for Assessment in Higher Education. *2024 International Conference on Knowledge Engineering and Communication Systems (ICKECS), 1*, 1–7. DOI: 10.1109/ICKECS61492.2024.10616490

Glick, D., Miedijensky, S., & Zhang, H. (2024). Examining the effect of AI-powered virtual-human training on STEM majors' self-regulated learning behavior. *Frontiers in Education, 9*, 1465207. Advance online publication. DOI: 10.3389/feduc.2024.1465207

González-Sendino, R., Serrano, E., & Bajo, J. (2024). Mitigating bias in artificial intelligence: Fair data generation via causal models for transparent and explainable decision-making. *Future Generation Computer Systems, 155*, 384–401. DOI: 10.1016/j.future.2024.02.023

Gorski, P. (2015). Equity Literacy for All. *Educational Leadership*. https://www.academia.edu/16837482/Equity_Literacy_for_All

Gorski, P. C. (2017). Reaching and Teaching Students in Poverty: Strategies for Erasing the Opportunity Gap. Second Edition. Multicultural Education Series. In *Teachers College Press*. Teachers College Press.

Govea, J., Ocampo Edye, E., Revelo-Tapia, S., & Villegas-Ch, W. (2023). Optimization and Scalability of Educational Platforms: Integration of Artificial Intelligence and Cloud Computing. *Computers*, *12*(11), 223. DOI: 10.3390/computers12110223

Ifenthaler, D., Majumdar, R., Gorissen, P., Judge, M., Mishra, S., Raffaghelli, J., & Shimada, A. (2024). Artificial Intelligence in Education: Implications for Policymakers, Researchers, and Practitioners. *Technology. Knowledge and Learning*, *29*(4), 1693–1710. DOI: 10.1007/s10758-024-09747-0

Leon, C., Lipuma, J., & Oviedo-Torres, X. (2025). Artificial intelligence in STEM education: A transdisciplinary framework for engagement and innovation. *Frontiers in Education*, *10*, 1619888. Advance online publication. DOI: 10.3389/feduc.2025.1619888

Létourneau, A., Deslandes Martineau, M., Charland, P., Karran, J. A., Boasen, J., & Léger, P. M. (2025). A systematic review of AI-driven intelligent tutoring systems (ITS) in K-12 education. *NPJ Science of Learning*, *10*(1), 29. DOI: 10.1038/s41539-025-00320-7

Lucido, F., Jimenez, D., & Tang, S. (2024). Affirming culture and cultural identity in the bilingual/ESL classrooms. *Frontiers in Education*, *9*, 1338671. Advance online publication. DOI: 10.3389/feduc.2024.1338671

Malik, S. (2025). Analysis of Key Factors Influencing Academic Productivity: Insights From LASSO Regression and AI-Driven Techniques. In *Navigating Barriers to AI Implementation in the Classroom* (pp. 189–234). IGI Global Scientific Publishing. DOI: 10.4018/979-8-3373-1827-1.ch009

Maqbool, S., Maqbool, S., Zafeer, H. M. I., & Qihui, H. (2024). Exploring the Reflection of Teachers to Encourage the Gender Equality for Girls in Punjab Schools: In the Light of Universal Right to an Education. *Asian Women*, *40*(3), 113–138. DOI: 10.14431/aw.2024.9.40.3.113

Maqbool, S., Sarwar, U., Zamir, S., Zafeer, H. M. I., & Wei, Z. (2020). Teaching of Phonics and Fluency in Improving Reading Abilities at Primary Level: Multan Pakistan. European Online Journal of Natural and Social Sciences, 9(4), pp-808

Maqbool, S., Wei, Z., Sarwar, U., Zamir, S., & Zafeer, H. M. I. (2020). An Analysis of Self Concept between Homeless and Common Women in Pakistan. International Transaction Journal of Engineering, Management, & Applied Sciences & Technologies, 11(15), 11A15O https://DOI: 10.14456/ITJEMAST.2020.303

Maqbool, S., Zafeer, H. M. I., Maqbool, S., Zeng, P., Draissi, Z., & Javed, S. (2024). Stance of numerous leadership styles and their effect on teaching to sustain academic performance at the high school level. *Heliyon*, *10*(16), e36438. Advance online publication. DOI: 10.1016/j.heliyon.2024.e36438

Mejeh, M., & Rehm, M. (2024). Taking adaptive learning in educational settings to the next level: Leveraging natural language processing for improved personalization. *Educational Technology Research and Development*, *72*(3), 1597–1621. DOI: 10.1007/s11423-024-10345-1

Melo, D. N. (2024). *The Impact of AI-Powered Tutoring Platforms on Student Achievement in STEM Subjects: The Case of Cameroon* (SSRN Scholarly Paper No. 5249691). Social Science Research Network. DOI: 10.2139/ssrn.5249691

Naggita, K., & Aguma, J. C. (2022). *The Equity Framework: Fairness Beyond Equalized Predictive Outcomes* (No. arXiv:2205.01072). arXiv.

Ng, D. T. K., Chan, E. K. C., & Lo, C. K. (2025). Opportunities, challenges and school strategies for integrating generative AI in education. *Computers and Education: Artificial Intelligence*, *8*, 100373. DOI: 10.1016/j.caeai.2025.100373

Otto, S., Lavi, R., & Brogaard Bertel, L. (2025). Human-GenAI interaction for active learning in STEM education: State-of-the-art and future directions. *Computers & Education*, *239*, 105444. DOI: 10.1016/j.compedu.2025.105444

Ouyang, F., & Jiao, P. (2021). Artificial intelligence in education: The three paradigms. *Computers and Education: Artificial Intelligence*, *2*, 100020. DOI: 10.1016/j.caeai.2021.100020

Page, J. W., Duhamel, P., & Crognale, M. A. (2011). ERP evidence of visualization at early stages of visual processing. *Brain and Cognition*, *75*(2), 141–146. DOI: 10.1016/j.bandc.2010.11.001

Pan, M., Wang, J., & Wang, J. (2023). Application of Artificial Intelligence in Education: Opportunities, Challenges, and Suggestions. *2023 13th International Conference on Information Technology in Medicine and Education (ITME)*, 623–627. DOI: 10.1109/ITME60234.2023.00130

Posti-Ahokas, H., & Janhonen-Abruquah, H. (2024). Towards equity literacy: Exploratory enquiry with Finnish student teachers. *European Journal of Teacher Education*, *47*(1), 5–22. DOI: 10.1080/02619768.2021.1952977

Rehman, N., Huang, X., Mahmood, A., Zafeer, H. M. I., & Mohammad, N. K. (2025). Emerging trends and effective strategies in STEM teacher professional development: A systematic review. *Humanities & Social Sciences Communications*, *12*(1), 32. DOI: 10.1057/s41599-024-04272-y

Roman, J., & Ortega, M. (2019). Culturally Relevant Pedagogy. *John S. Albazi Student Research and Creative Activities Symposium*. https://neiudc.neiu.edu/srcas/2019/schedule/31

Rusconi, L., & Squillaci, M. (2023). Effects of a Universal Design for Learning (UDL) Training Course on the Development Teachers' Competences: A Systematic Review. *Education Sciences*, *13*(5), 466. DOI: 10.3390/educsci13050466

Sarwar, U. (2025). Enhancing Education With AI Tools for Effective Teaching and Better Student Outcomes. In *Navigating Barriers to AI Implementation in the Classroom* (pp. 1–30). IGI Global Scientific Publishing. DOI: 10.4018/979-8-3373-1827-1.ch001

Schaefer, M. B., Pennington, S. E., Divoll, K., & Tang, J. H. (2024). A Systematic Review of Literature on Student Voice and Agency in Middle Grade Contexts. *Education Sciences*, *14*(11), 1158. DOI: 10.3390/educsci14111158

Selwyn, N. (2024). On the limits of artificial intelligence (AI) in education. *Nordisk Tidsskrift for Pedagogikk Og Kritikk*, *10*(1), 3–14. DOI: 10.23865/ntpk.v10.6062

Seo, K., Tang, J., Roll, I., Fels, S., & Yoon, D. (2021). The impact of artificial intelligence on learner–instructor interaction in online learning. *International Journal of Educational Technology in Higher Education*, *18*(1), 54. DOI: 10.1186/s41239-021-00292-9

Shi, P., & Liu, W. (2025). Adaptive learning oriented higher educational classroom teaching strategies. *Scientific Reports*, *15*(1), 15661. DOI: 10.1038/s41598-025-00536-y

Silverman, S. K. (2011). Zone of Proximal Development. In *Encyclopedia of Child Behavior and Development* (pp. 1590–1590). Springer. DOI: 10.1007/978-0-387-79061-9_3131

Son, N. D. (2024). Exploring User Cultural Identity in Shaping Reflective Design Style on Interactive User Interfaces. In *Navigating the World of Multimedia—Innovation and Applications*. IntechOpen. DOI: 10.5772/intechopen.1007184

Voutyrakou, D. A., & Skordoulis, C. (2025). Using AI Tools to Enhance Educational Robotics to Bridge the Gender Gap in STEM. *Education Sciences*, *15*(6), 711. DOI: 10.3390/educsci15060711

Wang, S., Wang, F., Zhu, Z., Wang, J., Tran, T., & Du, Z. (2024). Artificial intelligence in education: A systematic literature review. *Expert Systems with Applications*, *252*, 124167. DOI: 10.1016/j.eswa.2024.124167

Zafeer, H. M. I., Li, Y., & Maqbool, S. (2023). An Approach to Progress Learning Outcomes: International Graduate Students' Engagement in Reflective Practice and Reflective Journal Writing during Pandemic. *Sustainability (Basel)*, *15*(3), 1898. DOI: 10.3390/su15031898

Zafeer, H. M. I., Maqbool, S., Rong, Y., & Maqbool, S. (2024). Mapping the relationship and influence of school internal factors with an eye towards students' science academic outcomes. *Heliyon*, *10*(19), e38696. Advance online publication. DOI: 10.1016/j.heliyon.2024.e38696

Zafeer, H. M. I., Maqbool, S., Rong, Y., & Maqbool, S. (2025). Beyond the Classroom: How Socioeconomic Status, Parental Involvement and Home Environment Impact on Students' Science Academic Performance at Secondary Schools. *European Journal of Education*, *60*(1), e70023. DOI: 10.1111/ejed.70023

Zafeer, H. M. I., Maqbool, S., & Yanping, L. (2022). Psychological and Social Factors and Their Impact on Divorced and Married Women: A Case Study from Punjab Pakistan. *Journal of Divorce & Remarriage*, *63*(5), 352–373. DOI: 10.1080/10502556.2022.2048345

Zafeer, H. M. I., Peng, C., Rehman, S., Wei, Z., & Maqbool, S. (2021). A Study to Investigate the Obstacles of Educational Technology in Curriculum; University Students' Perception. European Online Journal of Natural and Social Sciences, 10(1).

Zafeer, H. M. I., Xue, H., & Maqbool, S. (2020). Delaying Factors Regarding Civil Justice in Pakistan (Lower Courts). Journal of Humanities and Social Sciences Studies, 2(6), 15-22. DOI: 10.32996/jhsss.2020.2.6.2

Zafeer, H. M. I., Yanping, L., & Maqbool, S. (2022) COVID-19 and the Future of Online Learning; Perspective of Pakistani Students from Higher Education Institutions (HEIs). DOI: 10.35629/5252-0410784790

Zhai, X., Chu, X., Chai, C. S., Jong, M. S. Y., Istenic, A., Spector, M., Liu, J.-B., Yuan, J., & Li, Y. (2021). A Review of Artificial Intelligence (AI) in Education from 2010 to 2020. *Complexity*, *2021*(1), 8812542. DOI: 10.1155/2021/8812542

Compilation of References

Aakula, A., Saini, V., & Ahmad, T. (2024). The Impact of AI on Organizational Change in Digital Transformation. *Internet of Things and Edge Computing Journal*, *4*(1), 75–115.

Aarthi, S., Ravikumar, R. N., Khudayberganov, S., Ismailov, A., & Khujaniyozova, O. (2025). Using Intelligent Tutoring Systems to enhance student engagement. In *Advances in Computational Intelligence and Robotics* (pp. 155–188). IGI Global. DOI: 10.4018/979-8-3373-1827-1.ch008

Aarts, P. (1999). The Middle East: A region without regionalism or the end of exceptionalism? *Third World Quarterly*, *20*(5), 911–925. DOI: 10.1080/01436599913406

Aballa Nkechi, A., & Ojo, O. A., & A. Eneh, O. (2024). Impact of artificial intelligence in achieving quality education. In *Artificial Intelligence and Education - Shaping the Future of Learning [Working Title]*. IntechOpen.

Abedi, M., Alshybani, I., Rubayat Bin Shahadat, M., & Murillo, M. S. (2023). *Beyond traditional teaching: the potential of large language models and chatbots in graduate engineering education*. DOI: 10.32388/MD04B0

Abisoye, A. (2024). Creating a Conceptual Framework for AI-Powered STEM Education Analytics to Enhance Student Learning Outcomes. *International Journal of Research and Innovation in Social Science*.

Abrami, , Bernard, R. M., Borokhovski, E., Waddington, D. I., Wade, C. A., & Persson, T. (2015). Strategies for Teaching Students to Think Critically. *Review of Educational Research*, *85*(2), 275–314. DOI: 10.3102/0034654314551063

Abuali, T., & Ahmed, A. A. (2025). Challenges and Opportunities in Implementing E-Learning in Developing Countries. *The Open European Journal of Social Science and Education (OEJSSE)*, 1-12.

Abubakari, M. S. (2025). Overviewing Biases in Generative AI-Powered Models in the Arabic Language: AI Fairness for Sustainable Future. *Achieving Sustainability in Multi-Industry Settings With AI*, 361–390. DOI: 10.4018/979-8-3373-2530-9.ch013

AbuSahyon, A. S. E., Alzyoud, A., Alshorman, O., & Al-Absi, B. (2023). AI-driven technology and chatbots as tools for enhancing English language learning in the context of second language acquisition: A review study. *International Journal of Membrane Science and Technology*, *10*(1), 1209–1223. DOI: 10.15379/ijmst.v10i1.2829

Aderibigbe, A. O., Ohenhen, P. E., Nwaobia, N. K., Gidiagba, J. O., & Ani, E. C.Adebayo Olusegun AderibigbePeter Efosa OhenhenNwabueze Kelvin Nwaobia-Joachim Osheyor GidiagbaEmmanuel Chigozie Ani. (2023). Artificial intelligence in developing countries: Bridging the gap between potential and implementation. *Computer Science & IT Research Journal*, *4*(3), 185–199. DOI: 10.51594/csitrj.v4i3.629

Adeshola, I., & Agoyi, M. (2023). Examining factors influencing e-learning engagement among university students during covid-19 pandemic: A mediating role of "learning persistence". *Interactive Learning Environments*, *31*(10), 6195–6222. https://doi.org/https://doi.org/10.1080/10494820.2022.2029493. DOI: 10.1080/10494820.2022.2029493

Afzal, A., Khan, S., Daud, S., Ahmad, Z., & Butt, A. (2023). Addressing the digital divide: Access and use of technology in education. *Journal of Social Sciences Review*, *3*(2), 883–895. https://doi.org/https://doi.org/10.54183/jssr.v3i2.326. DOI: 10.54183/jssr.v3i2.326

Agbeyangi, A., & Suleman, H. (2024, November). Advances and challenges in low-resource-environment software systems: A Survey. [). MDPI.]. *Informatics (MDPI)*, *11*(4), 90. DOI: 10.3390/informatics11040090

Agrela Rodrigues, F. de A., Moreira da Silveira, F., Moreira de Lima, M. R., & Pinto Uchôa, K. S. (2024). Identificando a Inteligência em Crianças: Traços Físicos e Comportamentais. Ciencia Y Reflexión, 3(2), 21–51.

Ahmad, S., Mohd Noor, A. S., Alwan, A. A., Gulzar, Y., Khan, W. Z., & Reegu, F. A. (2023). eLearning acceptance and adoption challenges in higher education. *Sustainability (Basel)*, *15*(7), 6190. DOI: 10.3390/su15076190

Ahmed, F. (2024). The digital divide and AI in education: Addressing equity and accessibility. *AI EDIFY Journal*, *1*(2), 12–23.

Ahmed, W. M., Azhari, A. A., Alfaraj, A., Alhamadani, A., Zhang, M., & Lu, C. T. (2024). The Quality of AI-Generated Dental Caries Multiple Choice Questions: A Comparative Analysis of ChatGPT and Google Bard Language Models. *Heliyon*, *10*(7), e28198. DOI: 10.1016/j.heliyon.2024.e28198 PMID: 38596020

Aithal, P., & Aithal, S. (2023). How to empower educators through digital pedagogies and faculty development strategies. [IJAEML]. *International Journal of Applied Engineering and Management Letters*, *7*(4), 139–183. https://doi.org/http://dx.doi.org/10.2139/ssrn.4674876. DOI: 10.47992/IJAEML.2581.7000.0198

Akavova, A., Temirkhanova, Z., & Lorsanova, Z. (2023). Adaptive learning and artificial intelligence in the educational space. *E3S Web Conf.*, *451*, 6011.

Akgun, S., & Greenhow, C. (2022). Artificial intelligence in education: Addressing ethical challenges in K-12 settings. *AI and Ethics*, *2*(3), 431–440. DOI: 10.1007/s43681-021-00096-7 PMID: 34790956

Akgün, S., & Krajcik, J. (2024). Artificial intelligence (AI) as the growing actor in education. In *Uses of Artificial Intelligence in STEM Education* (pp. 494–521). Oxford University PressOxford. DOI: 10.1093/oso/9780198882077.003.0022

Akinsemolu, A. A. (2025). Green AI in Education: Can Artificial Intelligence Promote Sustainable Learning? *Journal of Theoretical and Empirical Studies in Education*, *10*(2), 596–629.

Akram, H., Abdelrady, A. H., Al-Adwan, A. S., & Ramzan, M. (2022). Teachers' perceptions of technology integration in teaching-learning practices: A systematic review. *Frontiers in Psychology*, *13*, 920317. DOI: 10.3389/fpsyg.2022.920317 PMID: 35734463

Akram, H., Aslam, S., Saleem, A., & Parveen, K. (2021). The challenges of online teaching in COVID-19 pandemic: A case study of public universities in Karachi, Pakistan. *Journal of Information Technology Education*, *20*, 263–282. https://doi.org/https://doi.org/10.28945/4784. DOI: 10.28945/4784

Aladsani, H. K. (2025). Developing postgraduate students' competencies in generative artificial intelligence for ethical integration into academic practices: A participatory action research. *Interactive Learning Environments*, •••, 1–19. DOI: 10.1080/10494820.2025.2487517

Alahmadi, D. (2025). AI Ethics Principles for AI Developers in Academia: A Critical Assessment and Analysis. *TEM Journal*, 2514–2529. https://doi.org/DOI: 10.18421/TEM143-55

AlAli, R., & Wardat, Y. (2024). Opportunities and challenges of integrating generative artificial intelligence in education. *International Journal of Religion*, *5*(7), 784–793. DOI: 10.61707/8y29gv34

Alam, A., & Mohanty, A. (2023). Educational technology: Exploring the convergence of technology and pedagogy through mobility, interactivity, AI, and learning tools. *Cogent Engineering*, *10*(2), 2283282. DOI: 10.1080/23311916.2023.2283282

Alamäki, A., Nyberg, C., Kimberley, A., & Salonen, A. O. (2024a). Artificial intelligence literacy in sustainable development: A learning experiment in higher education [Original Research]. *Frontiers in Education, Volume 9 - 2024*. https://doi.org/DOI: 10.3389/feduc.2024.1343406

Alamäki, A., Nyberg, C., Kimberley, A., & Salonen, A. O. (2024b). Artificial intelligence literacy in sustainable development: A learning experiment in higher education. Frontiers in Education, Allam, H. M., Gyamfi, B., & AlOmar, B. (2025). Sustainable Innovation: Harnessing AI and Living Intelligence to Transform Higher Education. *Education Sciences*, *15*(4), 398.

Alam, K., & Imran, S. (2015). The digital divide and social inclusion among refugee migrantsA case in regional Australia. *Information Technology & People*, *28*(2), 344–365. DOI: 10.1108/ITP-04-2014-0083

Albannai, N. A. A., & Raziq, M. M. (2025). Navigating ethical, human-centric leadership in AI-driven organizations: A thematic literature review. *Service Industries Journal*, •••, 1–28. DOI: 10.1080/02642069.2025.2534360

Albaroudi, E., Mansouri, T., & Alameer, A. (2024). A comprehensive review of AI techniques for addressing algorithmic bias in job hiring. *ai, 5*(1), 383-404.

Alenezi, A. (2024). *Obstacles to the Use of AI Applications in Blackboard for Faculty Members at Northern Border University*. MIER Journal of Educational Studies Trends and Practices. DOI: 10.52634/mier/2024/v14/i2/2581

Aleven, V., McLaughlin, E. A., Glenn, R. A., & Koedinger, K. R. (2016). Instruction based on adaptive learning technologies. *Handbook of Research on Learning and Instruction*, 522–560. https://doi.org/DOI: 10.4324/9781315680276-38

Al-Gerafi, M. A., Goswami, S. S., Khan, M. A., Naveed, Q. N., Lasisi, A., AlMohimeed, A., & Elaraby, A. (2024). Designing of an effective e-learning website using inter-valued fuzzy hybrid MCDM concept: A pedagogical approach. *Alexandria Engineering Journal*, *97*, 61–87. https://doi.org/https://doi.org/10.1016/j.aej.2024.04.012. DOI: 10.1016/j.aej.2024.04.012

Ali, M., Siddique, A., Aftab, A., Abid, M. K., & Fuzail, M. (2024). AI-Powered customized learning paths: Transforming data administration for students on digital platforms. *Journal of Computing & Biomedical Informatics*, *6*(02), 195–204.

Ali, S., Gulliver, S. R., Uppal, M. A., & Basir, M. (2021). Research investigating individual device preference and e-learning quality perception: Can a one-solution-fits-all e-learning solution work? *Heliyon*, *7*(6), e07343. Advance online publication. DOI: 10.1016/j.heliyon.2021.e07343 PMID: 34195441

Al-Jarf, R. (2021). Investigating digital equity in distance education in Saudi Arabia during the COVID-19 pandemic. Conference proceedings of» eLearning and Software for Education «(eLSE), Aldous, S. M., & Ismail, G. A. (2025). AI for Sustainable Emergency Preparedness and Response in Schools. In *Convergence of AI, Education, and Business for Sustainability* (pp. 51-74). IGI Global Scientific Publishing.

Alkhamees, A. (2024). Evaluation of Artificial Intelligence as a Search Tool for Patients: Can ChatGPT-4 Provide Accurate Evidence-Based Orthodontic-Related Information? *Cureus*. Advance online publication. DOI: 10.7759/cureus.65820 PMID: 39219978

ALMEIDA, M. E. B., & VALENTE, J. A. (2016). Políticas de tecnologia na educação brasileira: histórico, lições aprendidas e recomendações. *Centro de Inovação para a educação brasileira.*

Almeida, S., & Kumalo, S. H. (2018). (De) coloniality through indigeneity: Deconstructing calls to decolonise in the South African and Canadian university contexts. *Education as Change*, *22*(1), 1–24. DOI: 10.25159/1947-9417/3023

Alqahtani, T., Badreldin, H. A., Alrashed, M., Alshaya, A. I., Alghamdi, S. S., bin Saleh, K., Alowais, S. A., Alshaya, O. A., Rahman, I., Al Yami, M. S., & Albekairy, A. M. (2023). The emergent role of artificial intelligence, natural learning processing, and large language models in higher education and research. *Research in Social & Administrative Pharmacy*, *19*(8), 1236–1242. DOI: 10.1016/j.sapharm.2023.05.016 PMID: 37321925

AlSagri, H. S., & Sohail, S. S. (2024). Evaluating the role of Artificial Intelligence in sustainable development goals with an emphasis on "quality education". *Discover Sustainability*, *5*(1), 458. DOI: 10.1007/s43621-024-00682-9

Alsawaier, R. S. (2018). The effect of gamification on motivation and engagement. *The International Journal of Information and Learning Technology*, *35*(1), 56–79. DOI: 10.1108/IJILT-02-2017-0009

AlShaikh, R., Al-Malki, N., & Almasre, M. (2024). The implementation of the cognitive theory of multimedia learning in the design and evaluation of an AI educational video assistant utilizing large language models. *Heliyon, 10*(3), e25361. Advance online publication. DOI: 10.1016/j.heliyon.2024.e25361 PMID: 38352730

Al-Sofi, B. B. M. A. (2024). Artificial intelligence-powered tools and academic writing: To use or not to use ChatGPT. *Saudi Journal of Language Studies*, *4*(3), 145–161. DOI: 10.1108/SJLS-06-2024-0029

Alturki, U., & Aldraiweesh, A. (2021). Application of learning management system (Lms) during the covid-19 pandemic: A sustainable acceptance model of the expansion technology approach. *Sustainability (Basel)*, *13*(19), 10991. https://doi.org/https://doi.org/10.3390/su131910991. DOI: 10.3390/su131910991

Al-Zahrani, A. M. (2024). Harnessing AI for sustainable university practices: Toward a greener campus. *International Journal of Sustainability in Higher Education.* Advance online publication. DOI: 10.1108/IJSHE-08-2024-0566

Al-Zahrani, A. M. (2024). Unveiling the shadows: Beyond the hype of AI in education. *Heliyon, 10*(9), e30696. DOI: 10.1016/j.heliyon.2024.e30696

Ambalavanan, R., Snead, R. S., Marczika, J., Towett, G., Malioukis, A., & Mbogori-Kairichi, M. (2025). Challenges and strategies in building a foundational digital health data integration ecosystem: A systematic review and thematic synthesis. *Frontiers in Health Services*, *5*, 1600689. DOI: 10.3389/frhs.2025.1600689

American Psychiatric Association. (2024). *Privacy and patient security in AI-enhanced psychiatric care*. Retrieved from https://www.psychiatry.org

Amin, M., Davis, C. J., Amjad, A. I., Parveen, S., Ali, S., & Naqvi, A. (2024). Identifying Acoustic Variability Patterns in Spoken English of Fricative Consonants Among Pakistani Native Punjabi Speakers. *Journal of Asian Development Studies*, *13*(3), 1036–1046. DOI: 10.62345/jads.2024.13.3.84

Amjad, A. I., Aslam, S., Abid, N., Tabassum, U., & Shafqat, F. (2025). Bridging the Gap: Overcoming Teachers' Hurdles in Implementing Gamification for Society 5.0 Education. *SAGE Open*, *15*(2), 21582440251340269. Advance online publication. DOI: 10.1177/21582440251340269

Amjad, A. I., Aslam, S., Tabassum, U., Sial, Z. A., & Shafqat, F. (2024). Digital Equity and Accessibility in Higher Education: Reaching the Unreached. *European Journal of Education*, *12795*(4), e12795. Advance online publication. DOI: 10.1111/ejed.12795

Anderson, S. (2023). The Digital Divide and Changing Education in Pandemic Times: A Case Study of Teacher Experiences in a Rural Town.

Anderson, T., & Dron, J. (2020). Emerging technologies in education: An overview. *Educational Technology Research and Development, 68*(2), 463–475.

Anierobi, E. I., Amjad, A. I., Agogbua, V. U., Aslam, S., Fakhrou, A., Alanazi, A. A., Nwogbo, V. N., Eleje, L. I., Alshamsi, H., Khan, S., & Javaid, S. (2025). Artificial intelligence utilization: A determinant of academic self-efficacy, engagement, and satisfaction of university students. *Environment and Social Psychology, 10*(3), 3504. DOI: 10.59429/esp.v10i3.3504

Ariely, M., Nazaretsky, T., & Alexandron, G. (2023). Machine Learning and Hebrew NLP for Automated Assessment of Open-Ended Questions in Biology. *International Journal of Artificial Intelligence in Education, 33*(1), 1–34. DOI: 10.1007/s40593-021-00283-x

Arslan, A., Cooper, C., Khan, Z., Golgeci, I., & Ali, I. (2022). Artificial intelligence and human workers interaction at team level: A conceptual assessment of the challenges and potential HRM strategies. *International Journal of Manpower, 43*(1), 75–88. DOI: 10.1108/IJM-01-2021-0052

Arvin, N., Hoseinabady, M., Bayat, B., & Zahmatkesh, E. (2023). Teacher experiences with ai-based educational tools. *AI and Tech in Behavioral and Social Sciences, 1*(2), 26–32. DOI: 10.61838/kman.aitech.1.2.5

Asad, M. M., Hussain, N., Wadho, M., Khand, Z. H., & Churi, P. P. (2021). Integration of e-learning technologies for interactive teaching and learning process: An empirical study on higher education institutes of Pakistan. *Journal of Applied Research in Higher Education, 13*(3), 649–663. https://doi.org/https://doi.org/10.1108/JARHE-04-2020-0103. DOI: 10.1108/JARHE-04-2020-0103

Asiedu, . (2024). The Case for Globalizing Fairness: A Mixed Methods Study on Colonialism, AI, and Health in Africa. *Proceedings of the 4th ACM Conference on Equity and Access in Algorithms, Mechanisms, and Optimization*, 1–24. DOI: 10.1145/3689904.3694708

Assefa, Y., Fetene, G. T., & Wolle, G. S. (2025). Adaptation and validation of the University Student Engagement Scale (USES) in the Ethiopian higher education context. *Journal of Applied Research in Higher Education.* Advance online publication. DOI: 10.1108/JARHE-05-2024-0215

Athavale, V. A., Selvakumar, P., Poorani, S., Anand, T., & Rathore, D. S. (2025). Designing Chatbots for Educational Leadership. In Musundire, A. (Ed.), *Chatbots in Educational Leadership and Management* (pp. 181–204). IGI Global Scientific Publishing., DOI: 10.4018/979-8-3693-8734-4.ch008

Atkins, D. C., Steyvers, M., Imel, Z. E., & Smyth, P. (2014). Scaling up the evaluation of psychotherapy: Evaluating motivational interviewing fidelity via statistical text classification. *Implementation Science : IS*, *9*(1), 49. DOI: 10.1186/1748-5908-9-49 PMID: 24758152

Attigeri, G., Agrawal, A., & Kolekar, S. V. (2024). Advanced NLP Models for Technical University Information Chatbots: Development and Comparative Analysis. *IEEE Access : Practical Innovations, Open Solutions*, *12*, 29633–29647. DOI: 10.1109/ACCESS.2024.3368382

Avc, G., Owusu-Boateng, O., Vampa, M., & Khalid, A.-M. (2025). Intelligent tutoring systems. In *Deep Science Publishing* (pp. 46–57). Deep Science Publishing. DOI: 10.70593/978-93-49307-53-7_4

Ayanwale, M. A., Sanusi, I. T., Adelana, O. P., Aruleba, K. D., & Oyelere, S. S. (2022). Teachers' readiness and intention to teach artificial intelligence in schools. *Computers and Education: Artificial Intelligence*, *3*, 100099. DOI: 10.1016/j.caeai.2022.100099

Aziz, M. F., Rajesh, J. I., Jahan, F., McMurrray, A., Ahmed, N., Narendran, R., & Harrison, C. (2025). AI-powered leadership: A systematic literature review. *Journal of Managerial Psychology*, *40*(5), 604–630. DOI: 10.1108/JMP-05-2024-0389

Babu, C. S., & Jeneliya, J. S. (2025). Ethical Uses of Generative Artificial Intelligence in Instructional Design: Case Strategies for Responsible Implementation. In *Transformative AI Practices for Personalized Learning Strategies* (pp. 219-268). IGI Global Scientific Publishing.

Badmus, O., Rajput, S., Arogundade, J., & Williams, M. (2024). AI-driven business analytics and decision making. *World Journal of Advanced Research and Reviews*, *24*(1), 616–633. DOI: 10.30574/wjarr.2024.24.1.3093

Badshah, A., Ghani, A., Daud, A., Jalal, A., Bilal, M., & Crowcroft, J. (2023). Towards Smart Education through Internet of Things: A Survey. *ACM Computing Surveys*, *56*(2), 26. Advance online publication. DOI: 10.1145/3610401

Bagde, P., Bobde, A., & Bagde, L. P. (2021). Information and Communication Technology (ICT) enabled Higher Education: Current Trends and Challenges. *Ilkogretim Online*, *20*(1). Advance online publication. DOI: 10.17051/ilkonline.2021.01.286

Baharuddin, M. F., Masrek, M. N., Shuhidan, S. M., Razali, M., & Rahman, M. S. (2021). Evaluating the content validity of digital literacy instrument for school teachers in Malaysia through expert judgement. *International Journal of Emerging Technology and Advanced Engineering*, *11*(07), 71–78. DOI: 10.46338/ijetae0721_09

Bahroun, Z., Anane, C., Ahmed, V., & Zacca, A. (2023). Transforming Education: A Comprehensive Review of Generative Artificial Intelligence in Educational Settings through Bibliometric and Content Analysis. *Sustainability (Basel)*, *15*(17), 12983. DOI: 10.3390/su151712983

Baker, R., & Chen, M. (2025). AI-driven adaptive learning systems: The future of student-centered education. *Journal of Artificial Intelligence in Education*, *31*(1), 1–20.

Baker, T., & Xia, W. (2025). AI-driven curriculum design: Enhancing educational accessibility and inclusivity. *Educational Policy Review*, *19*(3), 78–95.

Balážová, K., Galle, Š., Kandlová, A., & Bendl, T. (2025). *AI IN ENVIRONMENTAL EDUCATION: TOOLS, TRENDS, AND FUTURE DIRECTIONS*. https://doi.org/ DOI: 10.11118/978-80-7701-025-2-0028

Balta, N. (2024). Artificial Intelligence Pedagogical Content Knowledge. *Eur. Educ. Res.*, 1–3.

Balwant, P. T., Birdi, K., Stephan, U., & Topakas, A. (2019). Transformational instructor-leadership and academic performance: A moderated mediation model of student engagement and structural distance. *Journal of Further and Higher Education*, *43*(7), 884–900. DOI: 10.1080/0309877X.2017.1420149

Banihashem, S. K., Kerman, N. T., Noroozi, O., Moon, J., & Drachsler, H. (2024). Feedback sources in essay writing: Peer-generated or AI-generated feedback? *International Journal of Educational Technology in Higher Education*, *21*(1), 1–15. DOI: 10.1186/s41239-024-00455-4

Barbee, A. P., & Martin, M. L. (2013). Skill-based training and transfer of learning. In *Contemporary Issues in Child Welfare Practice*. DOI: 10.1007/978-1-4614-8627-5_8

Barocas, S., Hardt, M., & Narayanan, A. (2020). Fairness and machine learning. *Recommender systems handbook, 1*, 453-459.

Barra, C., Grimaldi, M., Muazzam, A., Troisi, O., & Visvizi, A. (2024). Digital divide, gender gap, and entrepreneurial orientation: How to foster technology adoption among Pakistani higher education students? *Socio-Economic Planning Sciences*, *93*, 101904. https://doi.org/https://doi.org/10.1016/j.seps.2024.101904. DOI: 10.1016/j.seps.2024.101904

Barsha, S., & Munshi, S. A. (2024). Implementing artificial intelligence in library services: A review of current prospects and challenges of developing countries. *Library Hi Tech News*, *41*(1), 7–10. DOI: 10.1108/LHTN-07-2023-0126

Bauer, E., Greisel, M., Kuznetsov, I., Berndt, M., Kollar, I., Dresel, M., Fischer, M. R., & Fischer, F. (2023). Using natural language processing to support peer-feedback in the age of artificial intelligence: A cross-disciplinary framework and a research agenda. *British Journal of Educational Technology*, *54*(5), 1222–1245. DOI: 10.1111/bjet.13336

Baumgart, A., & Madany Mamlouk, A. (2022). A knowledge-model for AI-driven tutoring systems. In *Frontiers in Artificial Intelligence and Applications*. IOS Press.

Bertino, E.. (2021). AI for Security and Security for AI. *Proceedings of the Eleventh ACM Conference on Data and Application Security and Privacy*, 333–334. DOI: 10.1145/3422337.3450357

Bertl, M., Ross, P., & Draheim, D. (2023). Systematic AI support for decision-making in the healthcare sector: Obstacles and success factors. *Health Policy and Technology*, *12*(3), 100748. DOI: 10.1016/j.hlpt.2023.100748

Bettayeb, A. M., Abu Talib, M., Sobhe Altayasinah, A. Z., & Dakalbab, F. (2024). Exploring the impact of ChatGPT: Conversational AI in education. *Frontiers in Education*, *9*, 1379796. DOI: 10.3389/feduc.2024.1379796

Bhatia, A., Bhatia, P., & Sood, D. (2024). Leveraging AI to transform online higher education: Focusing on personalized learning, assessment, and student engagement. *International Journal of Management and Humanities (IJMH) Volume-11 Issue-1.*

Bhola, H. S., & wa Thiong'o, N. (1987). Decolonising the Mind: The Politics of Language in African Literature. *African Studies Review*, *30*(2), 102. DOI: 10.2307/524049

Bhullar, P. S., Joshi, M., & Chugh, R. (2024). ChatGPT in higher education - a synthesis of the literature and a future research agenda. *Education and Information Technologies*, *29*(16), 21501–21522. DOI: 10.1007/s10639-024-12723-x

Bhutoria, A. (2022). Personalized education and artificial intelligence in the United States, China, and India: A systematic review using a human-in-the-loop model. *Computers and Education: Artificial Intelligence*, *3*, 100068. DOI: 10.1016/j.caeai.2022.100068

Biju, P. R., & Gayathri, O. (2025). Indic approach to ethical AI in automated decision making system: Implications for social, cultural, and linguistic diversity in native population. *AI & Society*, •••, 1–26. DOI: 10.1007/s00146-025-02381-z

Binhammad, M. H. Y., Othman, A., Abuljadayel, L., Al Mheiri, H., Alkaabi, M., & Almarri, M. (2024). Investigating how generative AI can create personalized learning materials tailored to individual student needs. *Creative Education*, *15*(7), 1499–1523. DOI: 10.4236/ce.2024.157091

Bird, S. (2020). Decolonising Speech and Language Technology. *Proceedings of the 28th International Conference on Computational Linguistics*, 3504–3519. DOI: 10.18653/v1/2020.coling-main.313

Birhane, A. (2020). Algorithmic Colonization of Africa. *Script-ed*, *17*(2), 389–409. DOI: 10.2966/scrip.170220.389

Black, N. B., George, S., Eguchi, A., Dempsey, J. C., Langran, E., Fraga, L., Brunvand, S., & Howard, N. (2024). A framework for approaching AI education in educator preparation programs. Proceedings of the AAAI Conference on Artificial Intelligence, Borasi, R., Miller, D. E., Vaughan-Brogan, P., DeAngelis, K., Han, Y. J., & Mason, S. (2024). An AI wishlist from school leaders. *Phi Delta Kappan*, *105*(8), 48–51.

Bloch-Atefi, A. (2025). Balancing ethics and opportunities: The role of AI in psychotherapy and counselling. *Psychotherapy and Counselling Journal of Australia*, *8*(2), 15–27. DOI: 10.59158/001c.129884

Bommasani, . (2021). On the Opportunities and Risks of Foundation Models. https://doi.org/doi.org/10.48550/arXiv.2108.07258

Bond, M., Buntins, K., Bedenlier, S., Zawacki-Richter, O., & Kerres, M. (2020). Mapping research in student engagement and educational technology in higher education: A systematic evidence map. *International Journal of Educational Technology in Higher Education*, *17*(1), 2. DOI: 10.1186/s41239-019-0176-8

Booyse, D., & Scheepers, C. B. (2024). Barriers to adopting automated organisational decision-making through the use of artificial intelligence. *Management Research Review*, *47*(1), 64–85. DOI: 10.1108/MRR-09-2021-0701

Borchers, C., Wang, Y., Karumbaiah, S., Ashiq, M., Shaffer, D. W., & Aleven, V. (2024). Revealing networks: Understanding effective teacher practices in AI-supported classrooms using transmodal ordered network analysis. *Proceedings of the 14th Learning Analytics and Knowledge*, 371–381. DOI: 10.1145/3636555.3636892

Botelho, A., Baral, S., Erickson, J. A., Benachamardi, P., & Heffernan, N. T. (2023). Leveraging natural language processing to support automated assessment and feedback for student open responses in mathematics. *Journal of Computer Assisted Learning*, *39*(3), 823–840. DOI: 10.1111/jcal.12793

Brandt, N. D., Lechner, C. M., Tetzner, J., & Rammstedt, B. (2020). Personality, cognitive ability, and academic performance: Differential associations across school subjects and school tracks. *Journal of Personality*, *88*(2), 249–265. DOI: 10.1111/jopy.12482 PMID: 31009081

Braun, V., & Clarke, V. (2006). Using thematic analysis in psychology. *Qualitative Research in Psychology*, *3*(2), 77–101. DOI: 10.1191/1478088706qp063oa

Brock, J. K.-U., & Von Wangenheim, F. (2019). Demystifying AI: What digital transformation leaders can teach you about realistic artificial intelligence. *California Management Review*, *61*(4), 110–134. DOI: 10.1177/1536504219865226

Brown-Jeffy, S., & Cooper, J. E. (2011). Toward a Conceptual Framework of Culturally Relevant Pedagogy: An Overview of the Conceptual and Theoretical Literature. *Teacher Education Quarterly*, *38*(1), 65–84.

Buckland, P., & Purcell, R. (2025). Prompt to Podcast: Reimagining Assessment with Generative AI. *Irish Journal of Technology Enhanced Learning*, *9*(1). Advance online publication. DOI: 10.22554/v3h7jn42

Bulathwela, S., Pérez-Ortiz, M., Holloway, C., Cukurova, M., & Shawe-Taylor, J. (2024). Artificial Intelligence alone will not democratise education: On educational inequality, techno-solutionism and inclusive tools. *Sustainability (Basel)*, *16*(2), 781. DOI: 10.3390/su16020781

Burns, M., Bally, J., Burles, M., Holtslander, L., & Peacock, S. (2022). Constructivist Grounded Theory or Interpretive Phenomenology? Methodological Choices Within Specific Study Contexts. *International Journal of Qualitative Methods*, *21*, 16094069221077758. Advance online publication. DOI: 10.1177/16094069221077758

Cachat-Rosset, G., & Klarsfeld, A. (2023). Diversity, Equity, and Inclusion in Artificial Intelligence: An Evaluation of Guidelines. *Applied Artificial Intelligence*, *37*(1), 2176618. Advance online publication. DOI: 10.1080/08839514.2023.2176618

Cai, J. (2023). Effects of leadership styles and organizational strategy to enhance performance efficiency. *Journal of Enterprise and Business Intelligence, 3*(1), 012-022.

Cai, Q., Lin, Y., & Yu, Z. (2023). Factors Influencing Learner Attitudes Towards ChatGPT-Assisted Language Learning in Higher Education. *International Journal of Human-Computer Interaction*. Advance online publication. DOI: 10.1080/10447318.2023.2261725

Canagarajah, S. (2024). Decolonizing Academic Writing Pedagogies for Multilingual Students. *TESOL Quarterly*, *58*(1), 280–306. DOI: 10.1002/tesq.3231

Casal-Otero, L., Catala, A., Fernández-Morante, C., Taboada, M., Cebreiro, B., & Barro, S. (2023). AI literacy in K-12: A systematic literature review. *International Journal of STEM Education*, *10*(1), 29. DOI: 10.1186/s40594-023-00418-7

Celik, I., Dindar, M., Muukkonen, H., & Järvelä, S. (2022). The promises and challenges of artificial intelligence for teachers: A systematic review of research. *TechTrends*, *66*(4), 616–630. DOI: 10.1007/s11528-022-00715-y

Chaiklin, S. (2003). The zone of proximal development in Vygotsky's analysis of learning and instruction. In *Vygotsky's educational theory in cultural context* (pp. 39–64). Cambridge University Press., DOI: 10.1017/CBO9780511840975.004

Chan, K. S., & Zary, N. (2019). Applications and challenges of implementing artificial intelligence in medical education: Integrative review. *JMIR Medical Education*, *5*(1), e13930. DOI: 10.2196/13930 PMID: 31199295

Charles, K.. (2023). *Exploring Education Access*. Opportunities, and Massification in Higher Education in Uganda.

Charow, R., Jeyakumar, T., Younus, S., Dolatabadi, E., Salhia, M., Al-Mouaswas, D., Anderson, M., Balakumar, S., Clare, M., Dhalla, A., Gillan, C., Haghzare, S., Jackson, E., Lalani, N., Mattson, J., Peteanu, W., Tripp, T., Waldorf, J., Williams, S., & Wiljer, D. (2021). Artificial intelligence education programs for health care professionals: A scoping review. *JMIR Medical Education*, *7*(4), e31043. DOI: 10.2196/31043 PMID: 34898458

Chaudhry, M. A., Cukurova, M., & Luckin, R. (2022). A Transparency Index Framework for AI in Education. In Rodrigo, M. M., Matsuda, N., Cristea, A. I., & Dimitrova, V. (Eds.), *Artificial Intelligence in Education. Posters and Late Breaking Results, Workshops and Tutorials*. Industry and Innovation Tracks, Practitioners' and Doctoral Consortium. DOI: 10.1007/978-3-031-11647-6_33

Chavarría Hidalgo, C. (2024). Calculation of productive capacity: From theory to practice. Ciencia Y Reflexión, 3(2), 194–214.

Chen, F., Zhang, Y., & Chen, G. (2025). Exploring the effects of technology-supported collaborative inquiry and students' ICT competency on scientific literacy and subject knowledge in rural science classrooms. *Education and Information Technologies*, *30*(13), 1–28. DOI: 10.1007/s10639-025-13512-w

Chen, X., Xie, H., Qin, S. J., Wang, F. L., & Hou, Y. (2025). Artificial intelligence-supported student engagement research: Text mining and systematic analysis. *European Journal of Education*, *60*(1), e70008. DOI: 10.1111/ejed.70008

Chen, Y., & Liu, H. (2025a). AI-driven adaptive learning systems: Enhancing personalized education. *Journal of Educational Technology & Society*, *28*(1), 45–62.

Chen, Y., & Liu, H. (2025b). AI-enhanced literacy development: The role of predictive models in student learning. *Journal of Educational Psychology*, *39*(4), 215–232.

Chinta, S. V., Wang, Z., Palikhe, A., Zhang, X., Kashif, A., Smith, M. A., Liu, J., & Zhang, W. (2025). AI-driven healthcare: Fairness in AI healthcare: A survey. *PLOS Digital Health*, *4*(5), e0000864. DOI: 10.1371/journal.pdig.0000864 PMID: 40392801

Chiu, T. K. F., Xia, Q., Zhou, X., Chai, C. S., & Cheng, M. (2023). Systematic literature review on opportunities, challenges, and future research recommendations of artificial intelligence in education. *Computers and Education: Artificial Intelligence*, *4*, 100118. DOI: 10.1016/j.caeai.2022.100118

Chouhan, D., & Shilpi, S.Dr.Neha ChouhanDr. Sonam Shilpi. (2023). A study on artificial intelligence in education. *International Journal of Engineering Technology and Management Sciences*, *7*(1), 449–456. DOI: 10.46647/ijetms.2023.v07i01.063

Ciric, M., & Jovanovic, D. (2016). Student engagement as a multidimensional concept. *Multidimensional Concept. WLC*, 187-194.

Connell, R. (2020). *Southern Theory*. Routledge., DOI: 10.4324/9781003117346

Córdova-Esparza, D.-M. (2025). AI-Powered Educational Agents: Opportunities, Innovations, and Ethical Challenges. *Information (Basel)*, *16*(6), 469. DOI: 10.3390/info16060469

Corrêa, N. K., Galvão, C., Santos, J. W., Del Pino, C., Pinto, E. P., Barbosa, C., Massmann, D., Mambrini, R., Galvão, L., Terem, E., & de Oliveira, N. (2023). Worldwide AI ethics: A review of 200 guidelines and recommendations for AI governance. *Patterns (New York, N.Y.)*, *4*(10), 100857. Advance online publication. DOI: 10.1016/j.patter.2023.100857 PMID: 37876898

CoSn. (2024, 2024-04-09). *CoSN Unveils Groundbreaking CoSN/CGCS K-12 Gen AI Maturity Tool*. Consortium for School Networking (CoSN). https://www.cosn.org/cosn-news/cosn-unveils-groundbreaking-cosn-cgcs-k-12-gen-ai-maturity-tool/

Couldry, N., & Mejias, U. A. (2023). The decolonial turn in data and technology research: What is at stake and where is it heading? *Information Communication and Society*, *26*(4), 786–802. DOI: 10.1080/1369118X.2021.1986102

Coupal, L. V. (2004). Constructivist learning theory and human capital theory: Shifting political and educational frameworks for teachers' ICT professional development. *British Journal of Educational Technology, 35*(5), 587–596. https://doi.org/https://doi.org/10.1111/j.0007-1013.2004.00415.x. DOI: 10.1111/j.0007-1013.2004.00415.x

Currie, A. (2021). Misaligned education. *Journal of the Philosophy of Sport, 48*(3), 332–343. DOI: 10.1080/00948705.2021.1951612

D'Agostino, T. (2023). Examination reform for higher order thinking: A case study of assessment-driven reform in Uganda. *International Journal of Educational Development, 103*, 102918. DOI: 10.1016/j.ijedudev.2023.102918

D'alfonso, S., Santesteban-Echarri, O., Rice, S., Wadley, G., Lederman, R., Miles, C., Gleeson, J., & Alvarez-Jimenez, M. (2017). Artificial intelligence-assisted online social therapy for youth mental health. *Frontiers in Psychology, 8*, 796. DOI: 10.3389/fpsyg.2017.00796 PMID: 28626431

D'Mello, S. K., & Graesser, A. C. (2012). AutoTutor and affective AutoTutor: Learning by talking with cognitively and emotionally intelligent computers that talk back. [TiiS]. *ACM Transactions on Interactive Intelligent Systems, 2*(4), 23. DOI: 10.1145/2395123.2395128

da Costa, M. de C., Olinda, A. L. S., & dos Santos, A. P. (2024, July). Digital technologies in education: Challenges and opportunities for teaching and learning. *VI Seven International Multidisciplinary Congress*. DOI: 10.56238/sevenVImulti2024-019

Da Silva Santos, F., & López Vargas, R. (2020). Efecto del Estrés en la Función Inmune en Pacientes con Enfermedades Autoinmunes: una Revisión de Estudios Latinoamericanos. Revista Científica De Salud Y Desarrollo Humano, 1(1), 46–59.

da Silva, M. C. F., Saraiva, A. C. G. T., Malta, D. P. L. N., da Silva, J. E. C., da Silva, R. L., & dos Santos, S. A. (2024). A INTEGRAÇÃO DE INTELIGÊNCIA ARTIFICIAL NA PERSONALIZAÇÃO DO ENSINO: UM NOVO PARADIGMA PARA A EDUCAÇÃO BÁSICA. *ARACÊ, 6*(3), 5956–5972. DOI: 10.56238/arev6n3-100

Dahri, N. A., Yahaya, N., Al-Rahmi, W. M., Vighio, M. S., Alblehai, F., Soomro, R. B., & Shutaleva, A. (2024). Investigating AI-based academic support acceptance and its impact on students' performance in Malaysian and Pakistani higher education institutions. *Education and Information Technologies, 29*(14), 18695–18744. Advance online publication. DOI: 10.1007/s10639-024-12599-x

Dai, W., Lin, J., Jin, H., Li, T., Tsai, Y.-S., Gašević, D., & Chen, G. (2023, July). Can large language models provide feedback to students? A case study on ChatGPT. *2023 IEEE International Conference on Advanced Learning (ICALT)*. DOI: 10.1109/ICALT58122.2023.00100

Dai, X. (2025). AI-driven assessment tools: Improving learning outcomes through automation. *Assessment & Evaluation in Higher Education*, *50*(1), 33–49.

Dai, Y., Liu, A., Qin, J., Guo, Y., Jong, M. S. Y., Chai, C. S., & Lin, Z. (2023). Collaborative construction of artificial intelligence curriculum in primary schools. *Journal of Engineering Education*, *112*(1), 23–42. DOI: 10.1002/jee.20503

Danial, A., Rafiq, A. H., & Izzuddin, F. (2022). Bridging the Digital Divide: Ensuring Access to Technology in Education for All Children. Proceeding of The International Conference of Inovation, Science, Technology, Education, Children, and Health, Diliberti, M. K., Lake, R. J., & Weiner, S. R. (2025). More Districts Are Training Teachers on Artificial Intelligence: Findings from the American School District Panel.

Darwin, R., Rusdin, D., Mukminatien, N., Suryati, N., Laksmi, E. D., & Marzuki, . (2024). Critical thinking in the AI era: An exploration of EFL students' perceptions, benefits, and limitations. *Cogent Education*, *11*(1), 2290342. DOI: 10.1080/2331186X.2023.2290342

Das, N. K., Sahoo, S., & Pati, L. (2021). Online learning: Challenges for education in rural and remote areas. *suicide, 8*(7). https://doi.org/DOI: 10.17148/IARJSET.2021.8712

Davis, L., & Karmakar, S. (2022). AI in education: Opportunities and challenges for teaching and learning. *Computers & Education*, *179*, 104446.

de Carvalho, W. F., & Zárate, L. E. (2020). A new local causal learning algorithm applied in learning analytics. *Int. J. Inf. Learn. Technol.*, *38*(1), 103–115. DOI: 10.1108/IJILT-04-2020-0046

Debattista, M. (2018). A comprehensive rubric for instructional design in e-learning. *The International Journal of Information and Learning Technology*, *35*(2), 93–104. https://doi.org/https://doi.org/10.1108/IJILT-09-2017-0092. DOI: 10.1108/IJILT-09-2017-0092

Del Sarto, R. A., & Soler i Lecha, E. (2024). Regionalism and alliances in the Middle East, 2011-2021: From a "flash in the Pan" of regional cooperation to liquid alliances. *Geopolitics*, *29*(4), 1447–1473. DOI: 10.1080/14650045.2023.2268542

Dent, A. L., & Koenka, A. C. (2016). The relation between self-regulated learning and academic achievement across childhood and adolescence: A meta-analysis. *Educational Psychology Review*, *28*(3), 425–474. DOI: 10.1007/s10648-015-9320-8

Di Stefano, V., D'Angelo, M., Monaco, F., Vignapiano, A., Martiadis, V., Barone, E., Fornaro, M., Steardo, L., Solmi, M., Manchia, M., & Steardo, L.Jr. (2024). Decoding Schizophrenia: How AI-Enhanced fMRI Unlocks New Pathways for Precision Psychiatry. *Brain Sciences*, *14*(12), 1196. DOI: 10.3390/brainsci14121196 PMID: 39766395

Díaz, B., & Nussbaum, M. (2024). Artificial intelligence for teaching and learning in schools: The need for pedagogical intelligence. *Computers & Education*, *217*, 105071. DOI: 10.1016/j.compedu.2024.105071

Dibley, L., Dickerson, S., Duffy, M., & Vandermause, R. (2020). *Doing Hermeneutic Phenomenological Research: A Practical Guide*. SAGE Publications Ltd., DOI: 10.4135/9781529799583

Dieterle, E., Dede, C., & Walker, M. (2024). The cyclical ethical effects of using artificial intelligence in education. *AI & Society*, *39*(2), 633–643. DOI: 10.1007/s00146-022-01497-w PMID: 36185064

Dignum, V. (2019). *Responsible artificial intelligence: How to develop and use AI in a responsible way*. Springer. DOI: 10.1007/978-3-030-30371-6

Dilmegani, C. (2025). *Bias in AI: Examples and 6 Ways to Fix it in 2025*.

Dimari, A., Tyagi, N., Davanageri, M., Kukreti, R., Yadav, R., & Dimari, H. (2024). AI-Based Automated Grading Systems for open book examination system: Implications for Assessment in Higher Education. *2024 International Conference on Knowledge Engineering and Communication Systems (ICKECS), 1*, 1–7. DOI: 10.1109/ICKECS61492.2024.10616490

Dimitriadou, E., & Lanitis, A. (2023). A critical evaluation, challenges, and future perspectives of using artificial intelligence and emerging technologies in smart classrooms. *Smart Learning Environments*, *10*(1), 12. DOI: 10.1186/s40561-023-00231-3 PMID: 40478141

Dinker, N. (2024). Artificial intelligence and inequality: examining the social divides created by technological advancements. *International Journal of Innovations in Science, Engineering And Management*, 228-236.

Dissanayake, L., & Al-Sharify, A. (2025). AI and Decision Making: How does the integration of AI influence leadership decision making within technology driven companies? In.

Dissanayake, H., & Keppetipola, M. (2024). Artificial Intelligence and Leadership: A Bibliometric Analysis. *Journal of Human Resource Management Perspectives*, *9*(1), 53–68. DOI: 10.4038/jhrmp.v9i1.5

Divayana, D. G. H., Suyasa, P. W. A., & Widiartini, N. K. (2021). An innovative model as evaluation model for information technology-based learning at ICT vocational schools. *Heliyon*, *7*(2), e06347. Advance online publication. DOI: 10.1016/j.heliyon.2021.e06347 PMID: 33718647

Dodick, D. (2024). Localizing AIED: Moving beyond North–South narratives to serve contextual needs. *AI & Society*, •••, 1–11.

Dörner, R., Klimmt, C., & Hille, A. (2020). The effects of virtual reality on player engagement: A systematic review. *Computers in Human Behavior*, *104*, 106157.

Dowell, N., & Kovanović, V. (2022). Modeling educational discourse with natural language processing. In *The Handbook of Learning Analytics* (pp. 105–119). SOLAR. DOI: 10.18608/hla22.011

Dr. Khaled, A. (2024). A Proposed Model For Improving The Quality Of Life Of Persons With Disabilities And Rehabilitating Them Professionally Using Artificial Intelligence Applications. *Educational Administration: Theory and Practice*, *30*(6), 553–558. DOI: 10.53555/kuey.v30i6.5244

Draissi, Z., Rong, Y., Zafeer, H. M. I., Maqbool, S., Malik, S. J., Maqbool, S., & Alemi, S. H. A. (2025). Academic diplomacy and policy borrowing: Media content analysis of Chinese soft power in Morocco. *Humanities & Social Sciences Communications*, *12*(1), 1–11. DOI: 10.1057/s41599-025-04544-1

Drewery, D., Woodside, J., & Eppel, K. (2022). Artificial Intelligence and Résumé Critique Experiences. *Cjcd*, *21*(2), 28–39. DOI: 10.53379/cjcd.2022.338

du Boulay, B. (2023). Artificial intelligence in education and ethics. In *Handbook of open, distance and digital education* (pp. 93–108). Springer Nature Singapore. DOI: 10.1007/978-981-19-2080-6_6

Duan, Y., Edwards, J. S., & Dwivedi, Y. K. (2019). Artificial intelligence for decision making in the era of Big Data–evolution, challenges and research agenda. *International Journal of Information Management*, *48*, 63–71. DOI: 10.1016/j.ijinfomgt.2019.01.021

Dworkin, W. A. Scott Danzis, Christina Kuhn, Olivia. (2023). Framework for the Future of AI: Senator Cassidy Issues White Paper, Seeks Public Feedback. *Covington Digital Health*. https://www.covingtondigitalhealth.com/2023/09/framework-for-the-future-of-ai-senator-cassidy-issues-white-paper-seeks-public-feedback/

Dwyer, D. B., Falkai, P., & Koutsouleris, N. (2018). Machine learning approaches for clinical psychology and psychiatry. *Annual Review of Clinical Psychology, 14*(1), 91–118. DOI: 10.1146/annurev-clinpsy-032816-045037 PMID: 29401044

Edwards, B. A. (2024). *Artificial Intelligence in Mediation: What the Future Holds for Mediators*. Edwards Mediation Academy.

Egger, R., & Gokce, E. (2022). Natural Language Processing (NLP): An Introduction. *Tourism on the Verge*, (Part F1051), 307–334. DOI: 10.1007/978-3-030-88389-8_15

Eguchi, A. (2021). *AI-Robotics and AI Literacy*., DOI: 10.1007/978-3-030-77022-8_7

Eliot, L. (2021). Interoperability Of AI-to-AI Multi-Lawyering. SSRN *Electronic Journal*. DOI: 10.2139/ssrn.3990307

El-Sabagh, H. A. (2021). Adaptive e-learning environment based on learning styles and its impact on development students' engagement. *International Journal of Educational Technology in Higher Education, 18*(1), 53. https://doi.org/https://doi.org/10.1186/s41239-021-00289-4. DOI: 10.1186/s41239-021-00289-4

Farid, S., Ahmad, R., Niaz, I. A., Arif, M., Shamshirband, S., & Khattak, M. D. (2015). Identification and prioritization of critical issues for the promotion of e-learning in Pakistan. *Computers in Human Behavior, 51*, 161–171. https://doi.org/https://doi.org/10.1016/j.chb.2015.04.037. DOI: 10.1016/j.chb.2015.04.037

Fatmawati, F., Fadillah, N., Faizi, A., & Kurnia, H. (2025). Kebijakan Pemerintah Untuk Meningkatkan Akses Pendidikan Bagi Masyarakat Kurang Mampu. *Innovations in Multidisciplinary Education Journal*, 2(1), 1–7. DOI: 10.61476/q1dfs358

Feingold, D. (2020). Working with clients who self-medicate using cannabis: Mind the gap in knowledge.

Felton, L. (2023). *AI in European schools: A European report comparing seven countries*. https://skillsuploadjr.eu/docs/contents/AI_in_European_schools.pdf

Feng, Y., Hang, Y., Wu, W., Song, X., Xiao, X., Dong, F., & Qiao, Z. (2025). Effectiveness of AI-Driven Conversational Agents in Improving Mental Health Among Young People: Systematic Review and Meta-Analysis. *Journal of Medical Internet Research, 27*, e69639. DOI: 10.2196/69639 PMID: 40367506

Fernández, A. (2023). The Social Impact of Independent Audiovisual Production in the Age of social media: A Case Study in Zamora, Ecuador. *Revista Veritas De Difusão Científica*, 4(1), 161–180. DOI: 10.61616/rvdc.v4i1.42

Ferrero, A. M., & Álvarez Sainz, M. (2024). Attitudes of university students towards traditional face-to-face learning systems and learning with ICT. *E-Learning and Digital Media*, *21*(2), 180–200. https://doi.org/https://doi.org/10.1177/20427530231156185. DOI: 10.1177/20427530231156185

Filgueiras, F. (2024). Artificial intelligence and education governance. *Education, Citizenship and Social Justice*, *19*(3), 349–361. DOI: 10.1177/17461979231160674

Filiz, O., Kaya, M. H., & Adiguzel, T. (2025). Teachers and AI: Understanding the factors influencing AI integration in K-12 education. *Education and Information Technologies*, *30*(13), 17931–17967. DOI: 10.1007/s10639-025-13463-2

Finfgeld-Connett, D., & Johnson, E. D. (2013). Literature search strategies for conducting knowledge-building and theory-generating qualitative systematic reviews. *Journal of Advanced Nursing*, *69*(1), 194–204. DOI: 10.1111/j.1365-2648.2012.06037.x

Fischer, M., & Lutz, M. (2020). Virtual reality in education: A review of current applications. *International Journal of Educational Technology in Higher Education*, *17*(1), 1–18.

Fiske, A., Henningsen, P., & Buyx, A. (2019). Your robot therapist will see you now: Ethical implications of embodied artificial intelligence in psychiatry, psychology, and psychotherapy. *Journal of Medical Internet Research*, *21*(5), e13216. DOI: 10.2196/13216 PMID: 31094356

Fitzpatrick, K. K., Darcy, A., & Vierhile, M. (2017). Delivering cognitive behavior therapy to young adults with symptoms of depression and anxiety using a fully automated conversational agent (Woebot): A randomized controlled trial. *JMIR Mental Health*, *4*(2), e19. DOI: 10.2196/mental.7785 PMID: 28588005

Floridi, L., Cowls, J., Beltrametti, M., Chatila, R., Chazerand, P., Dignum, V., Luetge, C., Madelin, R., Pagallo, U., Rossi, F., Schafer, B., Valcke, P., & Vayena, E. (2018). AI4People—An ethical framework for a good AI society: Opportunities, risks, principles, and recommendations. *Minds and Machines*, *28*(4), 689–707. DOI: 10.1007/s11023-018-9482-5 PMID: 30930541

Fošner, A. (2024). University students' attitudes and perceptions towards ai tools: Implications for sustainable educational practices. *Sustainability (Basel)*, *16*(19), 8668. DOI: 10.3390/su16198668

FOUDATION. K. (2015). Four in balance monitor 2015: use and benefits of ICT in education. In: Kennisnet Zoetermeer.

Franklin, G., Stephens, R., Piracha, M., Tiosano, S., Lehouillier, F., Koppel, R., & Elkin, P. L. (2024). The Sociodemographic Biases in Machine Learning Algorithms: A Biomedical Informatics Perspective. *Life (Chicago, Ill.)*, *14*(6), 652. DOI: 10.3390/life14060652 PMID: 38929638

Freire, P. (1970). *Pedagogy of the oppressed, translated by Myra Bergman Ramo.*

Fricker, M. (2007). *Epistemic injustice: Power and the ethics of knowing*. Oxford University Press. DOI: 10.1093/acprof:oso/9780198237907.001.0001

Fulmer, R., Joerin, A., Gentile, B., Lakerink, L., & Rauws, M. (2018). Using psychological artificial intelligence (Tess) to relieve symptoms of depression and anxiety: Randomized controlled trial. *JMIR Mental Health*, *5*(4), e64. DOI: 10.2196/mental.9782 PMID: 30545815

Fu, Y., Weng, Z., & Wang, J. (2024). Examining AI use in educational contexts: A scoping meta-review and bibliometric analysis. *International Journal of Artificial Intelligence in Education*, •••, 1–57.

Gaffney, H., Mansell, W., & Tai, S. (2019). Conversational agents in the treatment of mental health problems: Mixed-method systematic review. *JMIR Mental Health*, *6*(10), e14166. DOI: 10.2196/14166 PMID: 31628789

Gao, L., & Liu, Y. (2023). Blockchain technology in education: A systematic review. *Journal of Educational Computing Research*, *61*(4), 745–766.

Garc\'\ia-Méndez, S., de Arriba-Pérez, F., & Somoza-López, M. del C. (2024). A review on the use of large language models as virtual tutors. *Sci. & Educ.*

Garcia, A., & Adams, J. (2022). Data-Driven decision making: Leveraging analytics and AI for strategic advantage. *Research Studies of Business*, *1*(02), 77–85.

Gautam, N. (2024). *Unraveling the Social Impacts of Artificial Intelligence.*

Gen Digital, I. (2024). *Parents Cautiously Optimistic on AI in Schools: Content Safety and Data Privacy Among Top Worries*. https://www.prnewswire.com/news-releases/parents-cautiously-optimistic-on-ai-in-schools-content-safety-and-data-privacy-302227077.html

George, B., & Wooden, O. (2023). Managing the strategic transformation of higher education through artificial intelligence. *Administrative Sciences*, *13*(9), 196. DOI: 10.3390/admsci13090196

Getenet, S., Cantle, R., Redmond, P., & Albion, P. (2024). Students' digital technology attitude, literacy and self-efficacy and their effect on online learning engagement. *International Journal of Educational Technology in Higher Education*, *21*(1), 3. DOI: 10.1186/s41239-023-00437-y

Giacomazzi, M., Fontana, M., & Trujillo, C. C. (2022). Contextualization of critical thinking in sub-Saharan Africa: A systematic integrative review. *Thinking Skills and Creativity*, *43*, 43. DOI: 10.1016/j.tsc.2021.100978

Gilbert, H., Sandborn, M., Schmidt, D. C., Spencer-Smith, J., & White, J. (2023, November). Semantic compression with large language models. In *2023 Tenth International Conference on Social Networks Analysis, Management and Security (SNAMS)* (pp. 1-8). IEEE.

Gilson, A., Safranek, C. W., Huang, T., Socrates, V., Chi, L., Taylor, R. A., & Chartash, D. (2023). How does ChatGPT perform on the United States Medical Licensing Examination? The implications of large language models for medical education and knowledge assessment. *JMIR Medical Education*, *9*, e45312. DOI: 10.2196/45312 PMID: 36753318

Glais, N. (2023). Challenges of AI in Education: Analysis of UNESCO reports 2019-2021. In *Carnets de Laboratoire RL-2 Bonheurs, 2, 230, ISSN: 2967-3631, 2023.* (Vol. 2, p. 117-129). EDBH. DOI: 10.5281/zenodo.10382844

Glick, D., Miedijensky, S., & Zhang, H. (2024). Examining the effect of AI-powered virtual-human training on STEM majors' self-regulated learning behavior. *Frontiers in Education*, *9*, 1465207. Advance online publication. DOI: 10.3389/feduc.2024.1465207

Glikson, E., & Woolley, A. W. (2020). Human trust in artificial intelligence: Review of empirical research. *The Academy of Management Annals*, *14*(2), 627–660. DOI: 10.5465/annals.2018.0057

Goel, P., & Ghanta, S. (2025). *Assessing large language models for math tutoring effectiveness.* J Emerg Invest. DOI: 10.59720/24-117

Goldberg, N. D. (2025). *Threat Rigidity and the Role of Leadership and Organizational Change in Artificial Intelligence Adoption in Technology Companies.* University of Arizona Global Campus.

Goldberg, S. B., Flemotomos, N., Martinez, V. R., Tanana, M. J., Kuo, P. B., Pace, B. T., Villatte, J. L., Georgiou, P. G., Van Epps, J., Imel, Z. E., Narayanan, S. S., & Atkins, D. C. (2020). Machine learning and natural language processing in psychotherapy research: Alliance as example use case. *Journal of Counseling Psychology*, *67*(4), 438–448. DOI: 10.1037/cou0000382 PMID: 32614225

Gonsalves, C. (2024). Generative AI's Impact on Critical Thinking: Revisiting Bloom's Taxonomy. *Journal of Marketing Education*, 02734753241305980. Advance online publication. DOI: 10.1177/02734753241305980

González-Sendino, R., Serrano, E., & Bajo, J. (2024). Mitigating bias in artificial intelligence: Fair data generation via causal models for transparent and explainable decision-making. *Future Generation Computer Systems*, *155*, 384–401. DOI: 10.1016/j.future.2024.02.023

Gordon, K. W. (2024). *Replacing the traditional classroom with AI augmented Education. Human?* AI Symbolysis.

Gorski, P. (2015). Equity Literacy for All. *Educational Leadership*. https://www.academia.edu/16837482/Equity_Literacy_for_All

Gorski, P. C. (2017). Reaching and Teaching Students in Poverty: Strategies for Erasing the Opportunity Gap. Second Edition. Multicultural Education Series. In *Teachers College Press*. Teachers College Press.

Gouseti, A., James, F., Fallin, L., & Burden, K. (2024). The ethics of using AI in K-12 education: A systematic literature review. *Technology, Pedagogy and Education*, *34*(2), 161–182. DOI: 10.1080/1475939X.2024.2428601

Govea, J., Ocampo Edye, E., Revelo-Tapia, S., & Villegas-Ch, W. (2023). Optimization and Scalability of Educational Platforms: Integration of Artificial Intelligence and Cloud Computing. *Computers*, *12*(11), 223. DOI: 10.3390/computers12110223

Graham, S., Depp, C., Lee, E. E., Nebeker, C., Tu, X., Kim, H.-C., & Jeste, D. V. (2019). Artificial intelligence for mental health and mental illnesses: An overview. *Current Psychiatry Reports*, *21*(11), 116. DOI: 10.1007/s11920-019-1094-0 PMID: 31701320

Granić, A., & Marangunić, N. (2019). Technology acceptance model in educational context: A systematic literature review. *British Journal of Educational Technology*, *50*(5), 2572–2593. https://doi.org/https://doi.org/10.1111/bjet.12864. DOI: 10.1111/bjet.12864

Greene-Santos, A. (2024). *Does AI Have a Bias Problem?* Guàrdia, L., Mancini, F., Jacobetty, P., & Maina, M. (2021). Graduates' employability skills in East Africa. *Journal of Teaching and Learning for Graduate Employability, 12*(2), 169–184.

Green, M., Stangl, L., Denz, F., & Cope, S. (2024). A Qualitative Study and Future Research Agenda for Cultivating Critical Thinking in Culturally Diverse Postgraduate Students. *Journal of Marketing Education*, 02734753241295996. Advance online publication. DOI: 10.1177/02734753241295996

Gul, R., Tahir, T., & Ishfaq, U. (2023). Perspectives of the teachers on challenges and possibilities to online system of education amid COVID-19 outbreak in Balochistan, Pakistan. *SAGE Open, 13*(1), 21582440231155063. https://doi.org/https://doi.org/10.1177/21582440231155063. DOI: 10.1177/21582440231155063 PMID: 36843652

Guo, K., Zhang, E. D., Li, D., & Yu, S. (2025). Using AI-supported peer review to enhance feedback literacy: An investigation of students' revision of feedback on peers' essays. *British Journal of Educational Technology, 56*(4), 1612–1639. DOI: 10.1111/bjet.13540

Hacker, P. (2021). A legal framework for AI training data—From first principles to the Artificial Intelligence Act. *Law, Innovation and Technology, 13*(2), 257–301. DOI: 10.1080/17579961.2021.1977219

Hadžiomerović, N., Hadžiomerović, A. I., Avdić, R., Muminović, A., Tandir, F., Bejdić, P., & Pandžić, A. (2023). Students' performance in teaching neuroanatomy using traditional and technology-based methods. *Anatomia, Histologia, Embryologia, 52*(1), 115–122. Advance online publication. DOI: 10.1111/ahe.12876 PMID: 36259629

Haltaufderheide, J., & Ranisch, R. (2024). The ethics of ChatGPT in medicine and healthcare: A systematic review on Large Language Models (LLMs). *NPJ Digital Medicine, 7*(1), 1–11. DOI: 10.1038/s41746-024-01157-x PMID: 38977771

Hanifah, L., & Ismail, N. M. (2025). HUMAN-CENTERED AI IN LANGUAGE CLASSROOMS. *Proceedings of International Conference on Education, 3*(1), 239–246. DOI: 10.32672/pice.v3i1.3481

Han, X. (2024). Associations between effectiveness of blended learning, student engagement, student learning outcomes, and student academic motivation in higher education. *Education and Information Technologies*, •••, 1–31. https://doi.org/https://doi.org/10.1007/s10639-024-13246-1

Harriden, K. (2023). Decolonising your writing. *A Community Blog and Repository of Resources for Improving Research Impact on Complex Real-World Problems.*

Hashir, M., Sharma, A. K., Faisal, S., & Rawat, G. (2024). Automatic Feedback Generation In NLP: A Systematic Review. *Proceedings - IEEE 2024 1st International Conference on Advances in Computing, Communication and Networking, ICAC2N 2024*, 1492–1497. DOI: 10.1109/ICAC2N63387.2024.10895143

Hatem, R., Simmons, B., & Thornton, J. E. (2023). A Call to Address AI "Hallucinations" and How Healthcare Professionals Can Mitigate Their Risks. *Cureus, 15*(9), e44720. DOI: 10.7759/cureus.44720 PMID: 37809168

Hattie, J., & Timperley, H. (2007). The power of feedback. *Review of Educational Research, 77*(1), 81–112. DOI: 10.3102/003465430298487

Helm, P., Bella, G., Koch, G., & Giunchiglia, F. (2024). Diversity and language technology: How language modeling bias causes epistemic injustice. *Ethics and Information Technology, 26*(1), 1–15. DOI: 10.1007/s10676-023-09742-6

Henriksen, D., Mishra, P., & Stern, R. (2024). Creative learning for sustainability in a world of AI: Action, mindset, values. *Sustainability (Basel), 16*(11), 4451. DOI: 10.3390/su16114451

Herb, A., & Lloyd, C. (2024). The future of feedback. *ASCILITE Publications*, 141–142.

Hoermann, S., McCabe, K. L., Milne, D. N., & Calvo, R. A. (2017). Application of synchronous text-based dialogue systems in mental health interventions: Systematic review. *Journal of Medical Internet Research, 19*(8), e267. DOI: 10.2196/jmir.7023 PMID: 28784594

Holdsworth, J. (2023). *What is AI bias?* Holmes, W., Bialik, M., & Fadel, C. (2023). *ARTIFICIAL INTELLIGENCE IN EDUCATION.*

Hou, C., Zhu, G., & Sudarshan, V. (2025). The role of critical thinking on undergraduates' reliance behaviours on generative <scp>AI</scp> in problem-solving. *British Journal of Educational Technology, 56*(5), 1919–1941. DOI: 10.1111/bjet.13613

Hou, J., Kang, W., Li, Y., Liang, S., & Geng, S. (2024). Does Digital-Intelligence Contribute to Carbon Emission Reduction? New Insights from China. *SAGE Open, 14*(4), 21582440241304462. DOI: 10.1177/21582440241304462

House of Commons. (2025). AI and mental healthcare: Opportunities and delivery considerations. *House of Commons Library POSTnote, 737*, 1–21. https://researchbriefings.files.parliament.uk/documents/POST-PN-737/POST-PN-737.pdf

Hristova, T., Magee, L., & Soldatic, K. (2024). The problem of alignment. *AI & Society, 40*(3), 1439–1453. DOI: 10.1007/s00146-024-02039-2

Huang, X., & Qiao, C. (2024). Enhancing computational thinking skills through artificial intelligence education at a STEAM high school. *Science & Education, 33*(2), 383–403. DOI: 10.1007/s11191-022-00392-6

Huang, Y. M., & Liaw, S. S. (2022). The effects of mobile technology on student learning outcomes: A meta-analysis. *Computers & Education, 176*, 104325.

Hutson, J., & Plate, D. (2023). Enhancing Institutional Assessment and Reporting Through Conversational Technologies: Exploring the Potential of AI-Powered Tools and Natural Language Processing. *Journal of Artificial Intelligence and Robotics, 1*(1), 11–22. https://digitalcommons.lindenwood.edu/faculty-research-papers/483

Ifenthaler, D., Majumdar, R., Gorissen, P., Judge, M., Mishra, S., Raffaghelli, J., & Shimada, A. (2024). Artificial Intelligence in Education: Implications for Policymakers, Researchers, and Practitioners. *Technology. Knowledge and Learning, 29*(4), 1693–1710. DOI: 10.1007/s10758-024-09747-0

Ikevuje, A. H., Kwakye, J. M., Ekechukwu, D. E., & Benjamin, O. (2023). Energy justice: Ensuring equitable access to clean energy in underprivileged communities. *J. Sustainable Energy, 45*(4), 298–314.

Ilyas, S., Umar, M., Riaz, K., & Tariq, Z. (2025). Emotion Recognition in AI-Powered Classrooms Impacts on Student Engagement and Learning Outcomes. *The Critical Review of Social Sciences Studies, 3*(3), 86–103. DOI: 10.59075/x1wkpx78

Imran, M., & Almusharraf, N. (2023). Analyzing the role of ChatGPT as a writing assistant at higher education level: A systematic review of the literature. *Contemporary Educational Technology, 15*(4), ep464. DOI: 10.30935/cedtech/13605

Indumathy, I., & Mujra, P. (2025). *Sustainable Learning. Smart Education and Sustainable Learning Environments in Smart Cities*. IGI Global.

Inkster, B., Sarda, S., & Subramanian, V. (2018). An empathy-driven, conversational artificial intelligence agent (Wysa) for digital mental well-being: Real-world data evaluation. *JMIR mHealth and uHealth, 6*(11), e12106. DOI: 10.2196/12106 PMID: 30470676

Inusah, H. (2025). Rethinking AI ethics through an Akan ontology: Advancing an ethics of becoming for sustainable AI. *Canadian Journal of African Studies / Revue Canadienne Des Études Africaines*, 1–18. DOI: 10.1080/00083968.2025.2524342

Iqbal, J., Hashmi, Z. F., Asghar, M. Z., & Abid, M. N. (2025). Generative AI tool use enhances academic achievement in sustainable education through shared metacognition and cognitive offloading among preservice teachers. *Scientific Reports, 15*(1), 16610. DOI: 10.1038/s41598-025-01676-x PMID: 40360573

Iqbal, S. A., Ashiq, M., Rehman, S. U., Rashid, S., & Tayyab, N. (2022). Students' perceptions and experiences of online education in Pakistani universities and higher education institutes during COVID-19. *Education Sciences*, *12*(3), 166. https://doi.org/https://doi.org/10.3390/educsci12030166. DOI: 10.3390/educsci12030166

Jamil, M., Urooj, T., & Muhammad, N. (2025). Fostering Critical Thinking in Teacher Education Programs: Perceptions, Practices, and Challenges of Teacher Educators. *ProScholar Insights*, *4*(3), 13–22. DOI: 10.55737/psi.2025c-43098

Jamon, B. E. V., Boholano, H. B., Cabanes-Jamon, M. G., & Pardillo, M. F. (2021). Teachers lived experiences in the new normal in Philippine public schools: A phenomenology. *International Journal of Research*, *8*(02), 773–782.

Janjua, J. I., Irfan, M., Abbas, T., Ihsan, A., & Ali, B. (2024). Enhancing Contextual Understanding in Chatbots and NLP. *2024 International Conference on TVET Excellence and Development, ICTeD 2024*, 244–249. DOI: 10.1109/ICTeD62334.2024.10844601

Jantanukul, W. (2024). AI and Human Synergy: Utilizing AI to Enhance Teaching and Learning. *Journal of Education and Learning Reviews*, *1*(4), 1–12. DOI: 10.60027/jelr.2024.749

Jariwala, M. (2024). Incorporating Artificial Intelligence into PMBOK 7th Edition Frameworks: A Domain-Specific Investigation for Optimizing Project Management Performance Domains. *International Journal of Trend in Scientific Research and Development, 8*(3), 63-71.

Javed, S., Rong, Y., & Abbasi, B. N. (2024). Convergence analysis of artificial intelligence research capacity: Are the less developed catching up with the developed ones? *Journal of International Development*, *36*(4), 2172–2192. DOI: 10.1002/jid.3901

Javed, S., Rong, Y., Zafeer, H. M. I., Maqbool, S., & Abbasi, B. N. (2024). Unleashing the potential: A quest to understand and examine the factors enriching research and innovation productivities of South Asian universities. *Humanities & Social Sciences Communications*, *11*(1), 1–15. DOI: 10.1057/s41599-024-03674-2

Javed, T., Mahmoud, A. B., Yang, J., & Zhao, X. (2024). Green branding in fast fashion: Examining the impact of social sustainability claims on Chinese consumer behaviour and brand perception. *Corporate Communications*, *29*(6), 915–934. DOI: 10.1108/CCIJ-12-2023-0169

Javed, T., Yang, J., Gilal, W. G., & Gilal, N. G. (2020). The sustainability claims' impact on the consumer's green perception and behavioral intention: A case study of H&M. *Advances in Management and Applied Economics*, *10*(2), 1–22.

Jeongwan. (2023). A Review of the Legislative Issues of Artificial Intelligence (AI). *Kyunghee Law School, 58*(4), 117-144.

Jiang, J. (2025). Decolonizing critique through non-Western onto-epistemology: Chinese international students' affective engagement with AI-generated artworks. *Teaching in Higher Education, 30*(6), 1573–1590. Advance online publication. DOI: 10.1080/13562517.2025.2465999

Jiang, S., McClure, J., Tatar, C., Bickel, F., Rosé, C. P., & Chao, J. (2024). Towards inclusivity in AI: A comparative study of cognitive engagement between marginalized female students and peers. *British Journal of Educational Technology, 55*(6), 2557–2573. DOI: 10.1111/bjet.13467

Ji, H., Suo, L., & Chen, H. (2024). AI performance assessment in blended learning: Mechanisms and effects on students' continuous learning motivation. *Frontiers in Psychology, 15*, 1447680. DOI: 10.3389/fpsyg.2024.1447680 PMID: 39737232

Jim, J. R., Talukder, M. A. R., Malakar, P., Kabir, M. M., Nur, K., & Mridha, M. F. (2024). Recent advancements and challenges of NLP-based sentiment analysis: A state-of-the-art review. *Natural Language Processing Journal, 6*, 100059. Advance online publication. DOI: 10.1016/j.nlp.2024.100059

Jin, P., Yu, L., Ahmad, K., Shafique, H. M., & Ahmad, A. (2024). Evaluating the factors influencing the adoption of digital culture among university students in developing areas of South Punjab. *Information Development, 02666669241270909*, 02666669241270909. https://doi.org/https://doi.org/10.1177/02666669241270909. DOI: 10.1177/02666669241270909

John, A. O., Adejumo, E. K., & Larbi, S. Y. (2025). AI-Driven Supply Chain Risk Management in the Manufacturing Sector: Tackling Data Bias, Ensuring Algorithmic Transparency, and Enhancing Human-AI Collaboration. [IRE Journal]. *Iconic Research and Engineering Journals, 8*(11), 77–94.

Johnson, W. L., & Lester, J. C. (2016). Face-to-face interaction with pedagogical agents, twenty years later. *International Journal of Artificial Intelligence in Education, 26*(1), 25–36. DOI: 10.1007/s40593-015-0065-9

Jose Gonzalez-Gomez, L., Margarita Hernandez-Munoz, S., Borja, A., Daniel Azofeifa, J., Noguez, J., & Caratozzolo, P. (2024). Analyzing Natural Language Processing Techniques to Extract Meaningful Information on Skills Acquisition from Textual Content. *IEEE Access : Practical Innovations, Open Solutions, 12*, 139742–139757. DOI: 10.1109/ACCESS.2024.3465409

Joseph, A., & Eapen, N. G. (2023). Conversational Agents and Chatbots: Current Trends. *Machine Learning and Deep Learning in Natural Language Processing*, 17–52. /DOI: 10.1201/9781003296126-4

Kalim, U., Irfan, S., Maqbool, S., & Zafeer, H. M. I. (2025). How AI Can Be Successfully Implemented in the Classroom Settings: Challenges and Pathways to Overcome. In *Navigating Barriers to AI Implementation in the Classroom* (pp. 235-266). IGI Global Scientific Publishing.

Kalim, U., Irfan, S., Maqbool, S., & Zafeer, H. M. I. (2025). How AI Can Be Successfully Implemented in the Classroom Settings: Challenges and Pathways to Overcome. In *Navigating Barriers to AI Implementation in the Classroom* (pp. 235–266). IGI Global Scientific Publishing. DOI: 10.4018/979-8-3373-1827-1.ch010

Kamberovic, M., Delic, A., & Krivic, S. (2025). Investigating AI in Programming Education: Self-Reported AI Usage, Individual Traits, and Learning Outcomes. Adjunct Proceedings of the 33rd ACM Conference on User Modeling, Adaptation and Personalization, Kerres, M., & Kalz, M. Generative AI Chatbots for Self-Regulated Learning while Balancing Cognitive Load: Perceptions, Interaction Patterns, and Instructional Designs in K-12 Learning.

Kang, J., Kang, C., Yoon, J., Ji, H., Li, T., Moon, H., Ko, M., & Han, J. (2023). Dancing on the inside: A qualitative study on online dance learning with teacher-AI cooperation. *Education and Information Technologies*, *28*(9), 1–31. DOI: 10.1007/s10639-023-11649-0 PMID: 37361738

Kanwal, F., & Rehman, M. (2017). Factors affecting e-learning adoption in developing countries–empirical evidence from Pakistan's higher education sector. *IEEE Access : Practical Innovations, Open Solutions*, *5*, 10968–10978. DOI: 10.1109/ACCESS.2017.2714379

Karan, B., & Angadi, G. (2023). Potential risks of artificial intelligence integration into school education: A systematic review. *Bulletin of Science, Technology & Society*, *43*(3-4), 67–85. DOI: 10.1177/02704676231224705

Karanikolas, N., Manga, E., Samaridi, N., Tousidou, E., & Vassilakopoulos, M. (2023). Large Language Models versus Natural Language Understanding and Generation. *ACM International Conference Proceeding Series*. DOI: 10.1145/3635059.3635104

Karataş, F., Eriçok, B., & Tanrikulu, L. (2025). Reshaping curriculum adaptation in the age of artificial intelligence: Mapping teachers' AI-driven curriculum adaptation patterns. *British Educational Research Journal*, *51*(1), 154–180. DOI: 10.1002/berj.4068

Karogi, P. M., & Haule, E. L. (2025). School infrastructure for effective implementation of the Tanzania Education and Training Policy 2014 (2023) Edition in secondary schools: A case study of Mpimbwe District Council. *East African Journal of Education Studies*, *8*(2), 923–938. DOI: 10.37284/eajes.8.2.3223

Karpagavalli. (2024). ARTIFICIAL INTELLIGENCE BASED TUTOR. In *Futuristic Trends in Information Technology Volume 3 Book 2* (pp. 290–300). Iterative International Publisher, Selfypage Developers Pvt Ltd.

Kasneci, E., Sessler, K., Küchemann, S., Bannert, M., Dementieva, D., Fischer, F., Gasser, U., Groh, G., Günnemann, S., Hüllermeier, E., Krusche, S., Kutyniok, G., Michaeli, T., Nerdel, C., Pfeffer, J., Poquet, O., Sailer, M., Schmidt, A., Seidel, T., & Kasneci, G.Enkelejda Kasneci a. (2023). ChatGPT for good? On opportunities and challenges of large language models for education. *Learning and Individual Differences*, *103*, 102274. DOI: 10.1016/j.lindif.2023.102274

Kazi, A. M., Ahsan, N., Jamal, S., Khan, A., Mughis, W., Allana, R., Kazi, A. N., Kalimuddin, H., Ali, S. A., McKellin, W., & Collet, J.-P. (2021). Characteristics of mobile phone access and usage among caregivers in Pakistan–A mHealth survey of urban and rural population. *International Journal of Medical Informatics*, *156*, 104600. https://doi.org/https://doi.org/10.1016/j.ijmedinf.2021.104600. DOI: 10.1016/j.ijmedinf.2021.104600 PMID: 34638012

Kenchakkanavar, A. Y., Rathod, A., & Kamble, A. A. (2024). *Artificial Intelligence in Indian Education: Transforming Teaching and Learning for the Digital Age*. International Research Journal of Innovations in Engineering & Technology.

Khalifa, M., & Albadawy, M. (2024). Using artificial intelligence in academic writing and research: An essential productivity tool. *Computer Methods and Programs in Biomedicine Update*, *5*, 100145. DOI: 10.1016/j.cmpbup.2024.100145

Khlaif, Z. N., Alkouk, W. A., Salama, N., & Abu Eideh, B. (2025). Redesigning assessments for AI-enhanced learning: A framework for educators in the generative AI era. *Education Sciences*, *15*(2), 174. DOI: 10.3390/educsci15020174

Kigotho, W. (2018). *Higher education – Caught in a double bind*. University World News. https://www.universityworldnews.com/post.php?story=20180328162530835

Kim, D., & Wu, J. (2024, October). Artificial intelligence in higher education: Examining the AI policy landscape at US institutions. In *Proceedings of the 25th Annual Conference on Information Technology Education* (pp. 68-73). DOI: 10.1145/3686852.3687076

Kim, J. (2024). Leading teachers' perspective on teacher-AI collaboration in education. *Education and Information Technologies*, *29*(7), 8693–8724. DOI: 10.1007/s10639-023-12109-5

Kim, J., & Lee, H. (2020). The role of gamification in education: A systematic review. *Educational Technology Research and Development*, *68*(2), 555–576.

Kim, J., & Wargo, E. (2025). Empowering educational leaders for AI integration in rural STEM education: challenges and strategies. Frontiers in Education, Kim, T. K. (2024). Integrating Learning Analytics, AI, and STEM Education: A Comprehensive Review. *International Journal of Research in STEM Education*, *6*(2), 61–72. DOI: 10.33830/ijrse.v6i2.1745

Kitcharoen, P., Howimanporn, S., & Chookaew, S. (2024). Enhancing Teachers' AI Competencies through Artificial Intelligence of Things Professional Development Training. *International Journal of Interactive Mobile Technologies*, *18*(2), 4–15. DOI: 10.3991/ijim.v18i02.46613

Kleine, A. K.. (2024). AI-enabled clinical decision support tools for mental healthcare. *Journal of Medical Systems*. Advance online publication. DOI: 10.1016/j.artmed.2024.103052 PMID: 39662140

Kodama, N., Sugimoto, H., & Minagi, S. (2021). AI in dentistry and clues for starting AI research. [Journal of Okayama Medical Association]. *Okayama Igakkai Zasshi*, *133*(3), 181–183. DOI: 10.4044/joma.133.181

Koh, J. H. L., & Kan, R. Y. P. (2021). Students' use of learning management systems and desired e-learning experiences: Are they ready for next generation digital learning environments? *Higher Education Research & Development*, *40*(5), 995–1010. DOI: 10.1080/07294360.2020.1799949

Kong, S.-C., & Yang, Y. (2024). A human-centered learning and teaching framework using generative artificial intelligence for self-regulated learning development through domain knowledge learning in K–12 settings. *IEEE Transactions on Learning Technologies*, *17*, 1562–1573. DOI: 10.1109/TLT.2024.3392830

Korhonen, T., Lindqvist, T., Laine, J., & Hakkarainen, K. (2023). Training hard skills in virtual reality: Developing a theoretical framework for AI-based immersive learning. In *AI in Learning: Designing the Future* (pp. 195–213). Springer International Publishing.

Kotsis, K. T. (2025). Integrating Artificial Intelligence into Higher Education Curricula: Challenges and Opportunities for Science-Based Programs.

Kotsis, K. T. (2024). Integration of artificial intelligence in science teaching in primary education: Applications for teachers. *European Journal of Contemporary Education and E-Learning*, *2*(3), 27–43. DOI: 10.59324/ejceel.2024.2(3).04

Kovanović, V., Joksimović, S., Gašević, D., Siemens, G., & Hatala, M. (2015). What public media reveals about MOOCs: A systematic analysis of news reports. *British Journal of Educational Technology*, *46*(3), 510–527. DOI: 10.1111/bjet.12277

Krämer, W. (2014). Kahneman, D. (2011): Thinking, Fast and Slow. *Statistical Papers (Berlin, Germany)*, *55*(3), 915–915. DOI: 10.1007/s00362-013-0533-y

Kukulska-Hulme, A., Giri, R. A., Dawadi, S., Devkota, K. R., & Gaved, M. (2023). Languages and technologies in education at school and outside of school: Perspectives from young people in low-resource countries in Africa and Asia. *Frontiers in Communication*, *8*, 1081155. DOI: 10.3389/fcomm.2023.1081155

Kuleto, V., Ilić, M., Dumangiu, M., Ranković, M., Martins, O. M., Păun, D., & Mihoreanu, L. (2021). Exploring opportunities and challenges of artificial intelligence and machine learning in higher education institutions. *Sustainability (Basel)*, *13*(18), 10424. DOI: 10.3390/su131810424

Kulkov, I., Kulkova, J., Rohrbeck, R., Menvielle, L., Kaartemo, V., & Makkonen, H. (2024). Artificial intelligence-driven sustainable development: Examining organizational, technical, and processing approaches to achieving global goals. *Sustainable Development (Bradford)*, *32*(3), 2253–2267. DOI: 10.1002/sd.2773

Kumar, S., Verma, A. K., & Mirza, A. (2024). Digital revolution, artificial intelligence, and ethical challenges. In *Digital Transformation, Artificial Intelligence and Society: Opportunities and Challenges* (pp. 161-177). Springer. DOI: 10.1007/978-981-97-5656-8_11

Kumar, D., Haque, A., Mishra, K., Islam, F., Kumar Mishra, B., & Ahmad, S. (2023). Exploring the transformative role of artificial intelligence and metaverse in education: A comprehensive review. *Metaverse Basic and Applied Research*, *2*, 55. DOI: 10.56294/mr202355

Kumar, S., & Sharma, P. (2025). AI-powered assessment models: Revolutionizing grading and feedback in education. *Assessment & Learning Technologies*, *14*(2), 33–49.

LaGrotta, V., & Shahbazi, Z. (2024, November). Natural Language Processing applications in mechanical engineering education. *Volume 7: Engineering Education.*

Lakshmikanth, R., Vijai, C., Krishna, S. H., Alla, P. C. R., Lourens, M., & Soni, M. (2024). Utilizing AI to tailor leadership styles and interventions for optimal employee engagement and performance. 2024 International Conference on Trends in Quantum Computing and Emerging Business Technologies, Mabey, C. S. (2023). *Predictive Modeling the Impact of Engineered Products in Dynamic Sociotechnical Systems: An Agent-Based Approach* Brigham Young University].

Larsen, L. (2024). Revolutionizing mental healthcare through AI-enhanced provider–patient relationships. *Patient Safety & Quality Healthcare*. Retrieved from https://www.psqh.com/

Lasekan, O. A., Pachava, V., Godoy Pena, M. T., Golla, S. K., & Raje, M. S. (2024). Investigating factors influencing students' engagement in sustainable online education. *Sustainability (Basel), 16*(2), 689. https://doi.org/https://doi.org/10.3390/su16020689. DOI: 10.3390/su16020689

Lateef, A., Noor, K., & Yousaf, S. (2025). Digital Divide in Education: Barriers to Equitable Access in Punjab, Pakistan. *Journal of Social Signs Review, 3*(2), 434–456.

Lee, . (2025). The Impact of Generative AI on Critical Thinking: Self-Reported Reductions in Cognitive Effort and Confidence Effects from a Survey of Knowledge Workers. *Proceedings of the 2025 CHI Conference on Human Factors in Computing Systems*, 1–22. DOI: 10.1145/3706598.3713778

Lee, E. E., Torous, J., De Choudhury, M., Depp, C. A., Graham, S. A., Kim, H.-C., Paulus, M. P., Krystal, J. H., & Jeste, D. V. (2021). Artificial intelligence for mental health care: Clinical applications, barriers, facilitators, and artificial wisdom. *Biological Psychiatry: Cognitive Neuroscience and Neuroimaging, 6*(9), 856–864. DOI: 10.1016/j.bpsc.2021.02.001 PMID: 33571718

Lee, S. J., & Kwon, K. (2024). A systematic review of AI education in K-12 classrooms from 2018 to 2023: Topics, strategies, and learning outcomes. *Computers and Education: Artificial Intelligence, 6*, 100211. DOI: 10.1016/j.caeai.2024.100211

Leiton Leiton, D. R., Engracia Carvallo, D. E., Tamayo León, J. A., Ramírez González, S. Y., & Ramírez González, E. G. (2024). Estrategia metodológica para el mejoramiento del rendimiento académico en la asignatura de ciencias naturales en los estudiantes de educación básica. Estudios Y Perspectivas Revista Científica Y Académica, 4(2), 273–291.

Lemoine, P., & Mott, B. W. (2021). Adaptive learning technologies: Trends and future directions. *Journal of Educational Technology & Society, 24*(4), 1–14.

Leon, C., Lipuma, J., & Oviedo-Torres, X. (2025). Artificial intelligence in STEM education: A transdisciplinary framework for engagement and innovation. *Frontiers in Education, 10*, 1619888. Advance online publication. DOI: 10.3389/feduc.2025.1619888

Létourneau, A., Deslandes Martineau, M., Charland, P., Karran, J. A., Boasen, J., & Léger, P. M. (2025). A systematic review of AI-driven intelligent tutoring systems (ITS) in K-12 education. *NPJ Science of Learning, 10*(1), 29. DOI: 10.1038/s41539-025-00320-7

Lewis, A. A. Lewis, & Alexus, A. (2025). Unpacking Cultural Bias in AI Language Learning Tools: An Analysis of Impacts and Strategies for Inclusion in Diverse Educational Settings. *International Journal of Research and Innovation in Social Science, 9*(1), 1878–1892. https://EconPapers.repec.org/RePEc:bcp:journl:v:9:y:2025:i:1:p:1878-1892

Liang, M. (2025). Leveraging natural language processing for automated assessment and feedback production in virtual education settings. *Journal of Computational Methods in Sciences and Engineering, 25*(3), 2502–2515. DOI: 10.1177/14727978251314556

Li, H., Fan, X., & Liang, J. (2025). The squirrel AI adaptive learning system accompanying millions of children in their growth. In *Digital transformation of regional education in China* (pp. 51–53). Springer Nature Singapore. DOI: 10.1007/978-981-97-8144-7_7

Lim, C. P., & Chai, C. S. (2021). Technology in education: Past, present, and future. *Journal of Computer Assisted Learning, 37*(5), 1–12.

Lin, C.-C., Huang, A. Y., & Lu, O. H. (2023). Artificial intelligence in intelligent tutoring systems toward sustainable education: a systematic review. *Smart learning environments, 10*(1), 41.

Lin, H.-C. K., & Albahli, S. (2025). Advancing Sustainable Educational Practices Through AI-Driven Prediction of Academic Outcomes. *Sustainability 2025, Vol. 17, Page 1087, 17*(3), 1087. DOI: 10.3390/su17031087

Lindner, P., Miloff, A., Hamilton, W., Reuterskiöld, L., Andersson, G., Powers, M. B., & Carlbring, P. (2017). Creating state of the art, next-generation Virtual Reality exposure therapies for anxiety disorders using consumer hardware platforms: Design considerations and future directions. *Cognitive Behaviour Therapy, 46*(5), 404–420. DOI: 10.1080/16506073.2017.1280843 PMID: 28270059

Lin, M.-H., Chen, H.-C., & Liu, K.-S. (2017). A study of the effects of digital learning on learning motivation and learning outcome. *Eurasia Journal of Mathematics, Science and Technology Education*, *13*(7), 3553–3564. DOI: 10.12973/eurasia.2017.00744a

Liu, J., & Zhang, Y. (2024). Understanding and Facilitating Mental Health Help-Seeking of Young Adults: A Socio-technical Ecosystem Framework. *arXiv preprint arXiv:2401.08994*.

Liu, A., Martin, S., Belousov, M., Fung, C. C., Ben-Ari, R., & May, W. (2023). Impact of AI virtual Standardized Patients (AI-VSP) on performance in a clinical skills examination. In *Research Square*. DOI: 10.21203/rs.3.rs-3516363/v1

Liu, M., & Chang, C. (2023). Digital equity in education: The role of technology in bridging gaps. *Journal of Educational Technology Systems*, *51*(1), 25–45.

Liu, S., Okonkwo, C., & Xu, F. (2022). Cognitive tutoring systems in intelligent education: A review of natural language processing applications. *Computers and Education: Artificial Intelligence*, *3*, 100067. DOI: 10.1016/j.caeai.2022.100067

Lombana Diaz, C. (2025). AI Ethics. *AI and Ethics*, •••, 439–474. DOI: 10.1007/978-3-031-61375-3_5

Lomis, K., Jeffries, P., Palatta, A., Sage, M., Sheikh, J., Sheperis, C., & Whelan, A. (2021). A call to action: Integrating AI in health professions education. *Journal of Health Professions Education*, *12*(3), 127–130. DOI: 10.31478/202109a PMID: 34901780

Losey, R. (2024). *Can AI Replace Human Mediators? Groundbreaking Study Reveals Surprising Results*. Electronic Discovery Reference Model.

Lotfi, F. Z., & Laajan, Y. (2025). When AI enters Moroccan primary schools: what uses, challenges, and prospects for tomorrow's education? *EIKI Journal of Effective Teaching Methods, 3*(1).

Lubbe, A., Marais, E., & Kruger, D. (2025). Cultivating independent thinkers: The triad of artificial intelligence, Bloom's taxonomy and critical thinking in assessment pedagogy. *Education and Information Technologies*, *30*(12), 17589–17622. DOI: 10.1007/s10639-025-13476-x

Lucido, F., Jimenez, D., & Tang, S. (2024). Affirming culture and cultural identity in the bilingual/ESL classrooms. *Frontiers in Education*, *9*, 1338671. Advance online publication. DOI: 10.3389/feduc.2024.1338671

Luckin, R., & Holmes, W. (2016). Intelligence unleashed: An argument for AI in education.

Luckin, R. (2018). *Enhancing Learning and Teaching with Technology: What the Research Says*. ERIC.

Lum, K., & Isaac, W. (2016). To predict and serve? *Significance*, *13*(5), 14–19. DOI: 10.1111/j.1740-9713.2016.00960.x

Lunenburg, F. C. (2011). Critical thinking and constructivism techniques for improving student achievement. National Forum of Teacher Education Journal, Malik, S., Rong, Y., Zafeer, H. M. I., Maqbool, S., Draissi, Z., Rehman, N., & Maqbool, S. (2025). Analysis of Key Factors Influencing Academic Productivity: Insights From LASSO Regression and AI-Driven Techniques. In *Navigating Barriers to AI Implementation in the Classroom* (pp. 189-234). IGI Global Scientific Publishing.

Luo, Q. Z., & Hsiao-Chin, L. Y. (2023). The influence of AI-powered adaptive learning platforms on student performance in Chinese classrooms. *Journal of Education*, *6*(3), 1–12. DOI: 10.53819/81018102t4181

Lu, Z., & Mohamed, H. B. (2025). Teaching Critical Thinking in Civic Education: A Qualitative Study of Novice Teachers' Experiences and Challenges. *International Journal of Research and Innovation in Social Science*, *IX*(V), 6433–6445. DOI: 10.47772/IJRISS.2025.905000496

Macina, J., Daheim, N., Wang, L., Sinha, T., Kapur, M., Gurevych, I., & Sachan, M. (2023). *Opportunities and challenges in neural dialog tutoring*.

Madani, F., & Esfandiari, R. (2022). The influence of social media on student engagement in higher education. *Computers in Human Behavior*, *127*, 107043.

Madden, M., Calvin, A., Hasse, A., & Lenhart, A. (2024). *The dawn of the AI era: Teens, parents, and the adoption of generative AI at home and school*. Common Sense.

Magaña Lara, M. J., Zavala Pérez, I. C., Olea Gutiérrez, C. V., & Valle Solís, M. O. (2024). Programa de Educación para la Salud: Cartografías sociales sobre Lactancia Materna en estudiantes de Enfermería Universidad de Nayarit, México. Emergentes -. *Revista Científica (Maracaibo)*, *4*(1), 142–157.

MAHABUBMD RUSSEL HOSSAINESRAT ZAHAN SNIGDHA. (2025). Data-Driven Decision-Making and Strategic Leadership: AI-Powered business operations for competitive advantage and sustainable growth. *Journal of Computer Science and Technology Studies*, *7*(1), 326–336. DOI: 10.32996/jcsts.2025.7.1.24

Mahmood, A., Huang, X., & Rehman, N. (2025). STEM Education as a Catalyst for Career Aspirations and 21st-Century Competences: Insights From Teachers' Perspectives. *School Science and Mathematics*, ssm.18381. DOI: 10.1111/ssm.18381

Maimela, C., & Mbonde, P. (2025). Artificial intelligence in South African universities: Curriculum transformation and decolonisation—aid or obstacle? *Frontiers in Sociology*, *10*, 1543471. DOI: 10.3389/fsoc.2025.1543471 PMID: 40697567

Ma, L. (2021). An Immersive Context Teaching Method for College English Based on Artificial Intelligence and Machine Learning in Virtual Reality Technology. *Mobile Information Systems*, *2021*(1), 2637439. DOI: 10.1155/2021/2637439

Malik, M. A., & Amjad, A. I. (2025). AI vs AI: How effective are Turnitin, ZeroGPT, GPTZero, and Writer AI in detecting text generated by ChatGPT, Perplexity, and Gemini? *Journal of Applied Learning and Teaching*, *8*(1), 91–101. DOI: 10.37074/jalt.2025.8.1.9

Malik, M. A., Amjad, A. I., Aslam, S., & Fakhrou, A. (2024). Global insights: ChatGPT's influence on academic and research writing, creativity, and plagiarism policies. *Frontiers in Research Metrics and Analytics*, *9*, 1486832. DOI: 10.3389/frma.2024.1486832 PMID: 39583913

Malik, S., Rong, Y., Zafeer, H. M. I., Maqbool, S., Draissi, Z., Rehman, N., & Maqbool, S. (2025). Analysis of Key Factors Influencing Academic Productivity: Insights From LASSO Regression and AI-Driven Techniques. In *Navigating Barriers to AI Implementation in the Classroom* (pp. 189–234). IGI Global Scientific Publishing. DOI: 10.4018/979-8-3373-1827-1.ch009

Mandour, W. S. (2025). AI-Powered Tools for Linguistic and Sentiment Analysis in Language Learning: Applications Using Google Sheets and Large Language Models. In *Using AI Tools in Text Analysis, Simplification, Classification, and Synthesis* (pp. 67–112). IGI Global Scientific Publishing. DOI: 10.4018/979-8-3693-9511-0.ch003

Mansour, N. (2024). Students' and facilitators' experiences with synchronous and asynchronous online dialogic discussions and e-facilitation in understanding the Nature of Science. *Education and Information Technologies*, *29*(12), 15965–15997. https://doi.org/https://doi.org/10.1007/s10639-024-12473-w. DOI: 10.1007/s10639-024-12473-w

Maples-Keller, J. L., Bunnell, B. E., Kim, S.-J., & Rothbaum, B. O. (2017). The use of virtual reality technology in the treatment of anxiety and other psychiatric disorders. *Harvard Review of Psychiatry*, *25*(3), 103–113. DOI: 10.1097/HRP.0000000000000138 PMID: 28475502

Maqbool, S. (2025). Implemented in the Classroom Settings: Challenges and Pathways. *Navigating Barriers to AI Implementation in the Classroom*, 235.

Maqbool, S., Sarwar, U., Zamir, S., Zafeer, H. M. I., & Wei, Z. (2020). Teaching of Phonics and Fluency in Improving Reading Abilities at Primary Level: Multan Pakistan. European Online Journal of Natural and Social Sciences, 9(4), pp-808

Maqbool, S., Zhao, W., Rehman, S., Zafeer, H. M. I., & Maqbool, S. North American Academic Research.

Maqbool, S., Maqbool, S., Zafeer, H. M. I., & Qihui, H. (2024). Exploring the Reflection of Teachers to Encourage the Gender Equality for Girls in Punjab Schools: In the Light of Universal Right to an Education. *Asian Women*, *40*(3), 113–138. DOI: 10.14431/aw.2024.9.40.3.113

Maqbool, S., Sarwar, U., Zamir, S., Zafeer, H. M. I., & Wei, Z. (2020). Teaching of Phonics and fluency in improving reading abilities at primary level: Multan Pakistan. *European Online Journal of Natural and Social Sciences*, *9*(4), 808–819.

Maqbool, S., Sarwar, U., Zamir, S., Zafeer, H. M. I., & Wei, Z. (2020). Teaching of Phonics and Fluency in Improving Reading Abilities at Primary Level: Multan Pakistan. *European Online Journal of Natural and Social Sciences*, *9*(4), 808–819.

Maqbool, S., Wei, Z., Sarwar, U., Zamir, S., & Zafeer, H. M. I. (2020). An analysis of self-concept between homeless and common women in Pakistan. *International Transaction Journal of Engineering, Management, & Applied Sciences & Technologies, 11*(15), 11-19. https://doi.org/DOI: 10.14456/ITJEMAST.2020.303

Maqbool, S., Wei, Z., Sarwar, U., Zamir, S., & Zafeer, H. M. I. (2020). An analysis of self-concept between homeless and common women in Pakistan. *International Transaction Journal of Engineering, Management, &. Applied Sciences & Technologies*, *11*(15), 11–19.

Maqbool, S., Zafeer, H. M. I., & Maqbool, S. (2025). Psychological Impact of Raising a Child With Autism: A Real Life Case Study of Expatriate Family. *Child & Family Social Work*, cfs.70011. DOI: 10.1111/cfs.70011

Maqbool, S., Zafeer, H. M. I., Maqbool, S., Zeng, P., Draissi, Z., & Javed, S. (2024). Stance of numerous leadership styles and their effect on teaching to sustain academic performance at the high school level. *Heliyon*, *10*(16), e36438. DOI: 10.1016/j.heliyon.2024.e36438

Maqbool, S., Zafeer, H. M. I., Yanping, L., & Zhao, W. (2022). Covid-19 and global education: Experiences of Pakistani international students. *International Transaction Journal of Engineering Management and Applied Sciences and Technologies, 13*(3), 1–11.

Maqbool, S., Zafeer, H. M. I., Yanping, L., & Zhao, W. (2022). Covid-19 and global education: Experiences of Pakistani international students. *International Transaction Journal of Engineering Management and Applied Sciences and Technologies, 13*(3). https://doi.org/DOI: 10.14456/ITJEMAST.2022.44

Maqbool, S., Zafeer, H. M. I., Zeng, P., Maqbool, S., Draissi, Z., & Javed, S. (2024). Inventive leadership styles and their impact for achieving sustainable development goals in education at secondary schools: A case study from Multan, Pakistan. *Humanities & Social Sciences Communications, 11*(1), 1–11. DOI: 10.1057/s41599-024-03086-2

Maqbool, S., Zafeer, H. M. I., Zeng, P., Mohammad, T., Khassawneh, O., & Wu, L. (2023). The role of diverse leadership styles in teaching to sustain academic excellence at secondary level. [Maqbool, S., Zhao, W., Rehman, S., Zafeer, H. M. I., & Maqbool, S. North American Academic Research.]. *Frontiers in Psychology, 13*, 1096151. DOI: 10.3389/fpsyg.2022.1096151

Martinez, R. (2024). *HOW AI IS SHAPING SOCIAL STRUCTURES: DIVERSITY, EQUITY, INCLUSION AND BELONGING.*

Martínez, O., Aranda, R., Barreto, E., Fanego, J., Fernández, A., López, J., Medina, J., Meza, M., Muñoz, D., & Urbieta, J. (2024). Los tipos de discriminación laboral en las ciudades de Capiatá y San Lorenzo. [Recuperado a partir de.]. *Arandu UTIC, 11*(1), 77–95.

Marzuki, W., Widiati, U., Rusdin, D., Darwin, , & Indrawati, I. (2023). The impact of AI writing tools on the content and organization of students' writing: EFL teachers' perspective. *Cogent Education, 10*(2), 2236469. Advance online publication. DOI: 10.1080/2331186X.2023.2236469

Masih, M., Suleman, S., Khan, M. H., Sahito, D. Z., & Shahid, D. S. (2025). The Future Classroom: Integrating AI and social media for Adaptive Learning. *Inverge Journal of Social Sciences, 4*(3), 98–111. DOI: 10.63544/ijss.v4i3.150

Massachusetts Department of. E., & Secondary, E. (2024). *Massachusetts Guidance for Artificial Intelligence in K–12 Education.* https://www.doe.mass.edu/edtech/ai/ai-guidance.pdf

Mattar, J. (2018). Constructivism and connectivism in education technology: Active, situated, authentic, experiential, and anchored learning. *RIED-Revista Iberoamericana de Educación a Distancia, 21*(2). https://doi.org/doi.org/10.5944/ried.21.2.20055

Mavlikhanova, K. (2025). Challenges and responses in multicultural teams to AI adoption and usage/Author Kseniia Mavlihanova.

Mbatha, B. (2024). Diffusion of innovations: How adoption of new technology spreads in society. In *Information, Knowledge, and Technology for Teaching and Research in Africa: Human Machine Interaction and User Interfaces* (pp. 1-18). Springer. https://doi.org/https://doi.org/10.1007/978-3-031-60267-2_1

Mbunge, E., & Batani, J. (2023). *Application of deep learning and machine learning models to improve healthcare in sub-Saharan Africa: Emerging opportunities, trends and implications*. Telematics and Informatics Reports.

McArthur, J. (2022). Critical theory in a decolonial age. *Educational Philosophy and Theory, 54*(10), 1681–1692. DOI: 10.1080/00131857.2021.1934670

McCarthy, J., & Wolf, K. (2023). The impact of online learning platforms on student performance: A review. *Education and Information Technologies, 28*(2), 2331–2345.

McDonald, N., Johri, A., Ali, A., & Collier, A. H. (2025). Generative artificial intelligence in higher education: Evidence from an analysis of institutional policies and guidelines. *Computers in Human Behavior: Artificial Humans, 3*, 100121. DOI: 10.1016/j.chbah.2025.100121

McGovern, A., Gagne, D. J., Wirz, C. D., Ebert-Uphoff, I., Bostrom, A., Rao, Y., Schumacher, A., Flora, M., Chase, R., Mamalakis, A., McGraw, M., Lagerquist, R., Redmon, R. J., & Peterson, T. (2023). Trustworthy Artificial Intelligence for Environmental Sciences: An Innovative Approach for Summer School. *Bulletin of the American Meteorological Society, 104*(6), E1222–E1231. https://doi.org/https://doi.org/10.1175/BAMS-D-22-0225.1. DOI: 10.1175/BAMS-D-22-0225.1

Mehta, A. K., Yashoda, L., Selvakumar, P., Mishra, B. R., Das, A., & C. T. C., M. (2025). Teaching Methods: Techniques for Disadvantaged Learners. In S. Hai-Jew (Ed.), Mitigating Learner Disadvantages in Teaching and Learning (pp. 181-206). IGI Global Scientific Publishing

Mejeh, M., & Rehm, M. (2024). Taking adaptive learning in educational settings to the next level: Leveraging natural language processing for improved personalization. *Educational Technology Research and Development, 72*(3), 1597–1621. DOI: 10.1007/s11423-024-10345-1

Melo, D. N. (2024). *The Impact of AI-Powered Tutoring Platforms on Student Achievement in STEM Subjects: The Case of Cameroon* (SSRN Scholarly Paper No. 5249691). Social Science Research Network. DOI: 10.2139/ssrn.5249691

Menberu, A. W. (2024). Technology-mediated financial education in developing countries: A systematic literature review. *Cogent Business & Management*, *11*(1), 2294879. DOI: 10.1080/23311975.2023.2294879

Meng, X., & Yang, Y. (2025). Self-evolving generative AI tutors: Reinforcement learning-augmented ITS for personalized, proactive, and context-aware student engagement. In *Research Square*. DOI: 10.21203/rs.3.rs-6107039/v1

Meskhi, B., Ponomareva, S., & Ugnich, E. (2019). E-learning in higher inclusive education: Needs, opportunities and limitations. *International Journal of Educational Management*, *33*(3), 424–437. https://doi.org/https://doi.org/10.1108/IJEM-09-2018-0282. DOI: 10.1108/IJEM-09-2018-0282

Mesko, Bertalan. (2018). Future Directions of Digital Health. http://dx.doi.org/DOI: 10.1007/978-3-319-61446-5_22

Miao, F., & Shiohira, K. (2024). *AI competency framework for students*. UNESCO Publishing.

Mignolo, W. (2011). *The darker side of western modernity: Global futures, decolonial options*. Duke University Press.

Mikalef, P., Islam, N., Parida, V., Singh, H., & Altwaijry, N. (2023). Artificial intelligence (AI) competencies for organizational performance: A B2B marketing capabilities perspective. *Journal of Business Research*, *164*, 113998. DOI: 10.1016/j.jbusres.2023.113998

Mikropoulos, T. A., & Natsis, A. (2020). Educational virtual environments: A systematic review. *Computers & Education*, *154*, 103891.

Milasan, L. H., & Scott-Purdy, D. (2025). The future of artificial intelligence in mental health nursing practice: An integrative review. *International Journal of Mental Health Nursing*, *34*(1), e70003. Advance online publication. DOI: 10.1111/inm.70003 PMID: 39844734

Miller, A. (2020). The impact of augmented reality on the gaming industry. *Games and Culture*, *15*(3), 288–303.

Miner, A. (2021). Augmenting psychotherapy with artificial intelligence. *Stanford HAI News*. Retrieved from https://hai.stanford.edu

Mintz, S. (2021). Decolonizing the Academy. *Inside Higher Ed's*.

Mishra, P., & Koehler, M. J. (2020). Technology integration for meaningful learning. *Educational Technology Research and Development*, *68*(4), 931–946.

Mishra, T., Sutanto, E., Rossanti, R., Pant, N., Ashraf, A., Raut, A., Uwabareze, G., Oluwatomiwa, A., & Zeeshan, B. (2024). Use of large language models as artificial intelligence tools in academic research and publishing among global clinical researchers. *Scientific Reports*, *14*(1), 1–9. DOI: 10.1038/s41598-024-81370-6 PMID: 39738210

Mitchell, A. J., Vaze, A., & Rao, S. (2009). Clinical diagnosis of depression in primary care: A meta-analysis. *Lancet*, *374*(9690), 609–619. DOI: 10.1016/S0140-6736(09)60879-5 PMID: 19640579

Mohamed, M. S. P. (2024). Exploring Ethical Dimensions of AI-enhanced Language Education: A Literature Perspective. *Technology in Language Teaching and Learning*, *6*(3), 1813. Advance online publication. DOI: 10.29140/tltl.v6n3.1813

Mohammed, I. A., & Madhumithaa, N. (2024). Transforming Decision-Making: The Impact of AI and Machine Learning on Strategic Business Operations. *Library of Progress-Library Science, Information Technology & Computer, 44*(3).

Molloy, E., Boud, D., & Henderson, M. (2020). Developing a learning-centred framework for feedback literacy. *Assessment & Evaluation in Higher Education*, *45*(4), 527–540. DOI: 10.1080/02602938.2019.1667955

Moluayonge, G. E. (2025). Cognitive Offload as a Mediator of AI Usage and Critical Thinking Development in Cameroonian Higher Education Learners. *Asian Journal of Education and Social Studies*, *51*(8), 467–476. DOI: 10.9734/ajess/2025/v51i82253

Mom, A. N., Ndamsa, D. T., Abety, P., & Nguena, C.-L. (2025). The Impact of School Infrastructure on Academic Performance in Cameroon: Empirical Evidence from Cameroon. *Innovation Economics Frontiers*, 31–45. DOI: 10.36923/iefrontiers.v28i1.285

Moon, J. (2021). Effect of Emotional Intelligence and Leadership Styles on Risk Intelligent Decision Making and Risk Management. *Journal of Engineering, Project, and Production Management*, *11*(1), 71.

Morales-Chan, M., Amado-Salvatierra, H. R., Medina, J. A., Barchino, R., Hernández-Rizzardini, R., & Teixeira, A. M. (2024). Personalized feedback in Massive Open Online Courses: Harnessing the power of LangChain and OpenAI API. *Electronics (Basel)*, *13*(10), 1960. DOI: 10.3390/electronics13101960

Morrice, A., Deering, S., Kemsley, A., & Judge, S. (2025). Making use of AI in the Classics classroom. *Journal of Classics Teaching*, 1–9. DOI: 10.1017/S205863102500008X

Mtebe, J. S., & Raisamo, R. (2014). Investigating perceived barriers to the use of open educational resources in higher education in Tanzania. *International Review of Research in Open and Distance Learning*, *15*(2). Advance online publication. DOI: 10.19173/irrodl.v15i2.1803

Müller, S., Bergande, B., & Brune, P. (2018). Robot tutoring. *Proceedings of the 3rd European Conference of Software Education*, 45–49. DOI: 10.1145/3209087.3209093

Naggita, K., & Aguma, J. C. (2022). *The Equity Framework: Fairness Beyond Equalized Predictive Outcomes* (No. arXiv:2205.01072). arXiv.

Naidu, S., & O'Leary, M. (2022). Designing for learning: The role of learning analytics. *International Journal of Educational Technology in Higher Education*, *19*(1), 1–17. PMID: 35013716

Nakatumba-Nabende, J., Suuna, C., & Bainomugisha, E. (2023). *AI Ethics in Higher Education: Research Experiences from Practical Development and Deployment of AI Systems*. Springer International Publishing., DOI: 10.1007/978-3-031-23035-6_4

Nawaz, M. (2024). AI in STEM Education: Enhancing Problem-Solving and Critical Thinking Skills. *Journal of AI Integration in Education*, *1*(4), 38–48. https://researchcorridor.org/index.php/jaiie/article/view/252

Nazaretsky, T., Mejia-Domenzain, P., Swamy Vinitra and Frej, J., & Käser, T. (2024). *AI or human? Evaluating student feedback perceptions in higher education.*

Nazaretsky, T., Ariely, M., Cukurova, M., & Alexandron, G. (2022). Teachers' trust in AI-powered educational technology and a professional development program to improve it. *British Journal of Educational Technology*, *53*(4), 914–931. DOI: 10.1111/bjet.13232

Nazaretsky, T., Cukurova, M., Ariely, M., & Alexandron, G. (2021). Confirmation bias and trust: Human factors that influence teachers' attitudes towards AI-based educational technology. CEUR Workshop Proceedings, Ng, D. T. K., Leung, J. K. L., Su, J., Ng, R. C. W., & Chu, S. K. W. (2023). Teachers' AI digital competencies and twenty-first century skills in the post-pandemic world. *Educational Technology Research and Development*, *71*(1), 137–161. PMID: 33456286

Nedungadi, P., Tang, K.-Y., & Raman, R. (2024). The transformative power of generative artificial intelligence for achieving the sustainable development goal of quality education. *Sustainability (Basel)*, *16*(22), 9779. DOI: 10.3390/su16229779

Németh, R., Tátrai, A., Szabó, M., & Tamási, Á. (2024). Using a RAG-enhanced large language model in a virtual teaching assistant role: Experiences from a pilot project in statistics education. *Hungarian Statistical Review*, *7*(2), 3–27. DOI: 10.35618/hsr2024.02.en003

Ng, D. T. K., Chan, E. K. C., & Lo, C. K. (2025). Opportunities, challenges and school strategies for integrating generative AI in education. *Computers and Education: Artificial Intelligence*, *8*, 100373. DOI: 10.1016/j.caeai.2025.100373

Nguyen, K. V. (2025). The Use of Generative AI Tools in Higher Education: Ethical and Pedagogical Principles. *Journal of Academic Ethics*, *23*(3), 1–21. DOI: 10.1007/s10805-025-09607-1

Ni, A., & Cheung, A. (2023). Understanding secondary students' continuance intention to adopt AI-powered intelligent tutoring system for English learning. *Education and Information Technologies*, *28*(3), 3191–3216. DOI: 10.1007/s10639-022-11305-z PMID: 36119127

Niemi, H. (2025). AI in education: Transforming communication, lifestyle, and learning environments. *Educational Review*, *47*(2), 112–130.

Nijhawan, D. A., Pepa, D. M., & Adam, D. S. (2024). *Decolonising Academic Writing: Enacting a Self in and Through Writing. Part 1*. Decolonial Dialogues.

Noble, S. U. (2018). *Algorithms of oppression: How search engines reinforce racism* (pp. xv, 229). New York University Press.

Nozima, Z., Safarov, B., Namazovna, K. Z., Shaniyazova, Z., Shirinova, F., & Adilovich, N. R. (2026). *Natural Language Processing Methods for Conversation Analysis in Intelligent Tutoring Systems: A Systematic Mapping Study*. 79–90. DOI: 10.1007/978-3-031-95299-9_8

Nsabayezu, E., Habimana, O., Nzabalirwa, W., & Niyonzima, F. N. (2025). Leveraging multimedia-supported flipped classrooms approach to modernize organic chemistry instruction: Exploring students' engagement and motivation. *Education for Chemical Engineers*. Advance online publication. DOI: 10.1016/j.ece.2025.08.001

Nye, B. D., Graesser, A., & Hu, X. (2014). AutoTutor and family: A review of 17 years of natural language tutoring. *International Journal of Artificial Intelligence in Education*, *24*(4), 427–469. DOI: 10.1007/s40593-014-0029-5

O'Neil, C. (2016). *Weapons of math destruction: How big data increases inequality and threatens democracy*. Crown Publishing., DOI: 10.5860/crl.78.3.403

Obioha Val, O. (2024). The Role of Artificial Intelligence (AI) in Enhancing Cybersecurity for Educational Technologies in US Public Schools. *Asian Journal of Research in Computer Science, 17*(11), 10.9734.

Octaberlina, , Muslimin, A. I., Chamidah, D., Surur, M., & Mustikawan, A. (2024). Exploring the impact of AI threats on originality and critical thinking in academic writing. *Edelweiss Applied Science and Technology*, *8*(6), 8805–8814. DOI: 10.55214/25768484.v8i6.3878

Olan, F., Ogiemwonyi Arakpogun, E., Suklan, J., Nakpodia, F., Damij, N., & Jayawickrama, U. (2022). Artificial intelligence and knowledge sharing: Contributing factors to organizational performance. *Journal of Business Research*, *145*, 605–615. DOI: 10.1016/j.jbusres.2022.03.008

Olivier, E., Morin, A. J., Langlois, J., Tardif-Grenier, K., & Archambault, I. (2020). Internalizing and externalizing behavior problems and student engagement in elementary and secondary school students. *Journal of Youth and Adolescence*, *49*(11), 2327–2346. DOI: 10.1007/s10964-020-01295-x PMID: 32710241

Olmos-Gómez, C., Luque Suárez, M., Manuel Cuevas Rincón, J., Zobeida Salas-Pilco, S., Xiao, K., & Oshima, J. (2022). Artificial Intelligence and New Technologies in Inclusive Education for Minority Students: A Systematic Review. *Sustainability (Basel)*, *14*(20), 13572. DOI: 10.3390/su142013572

Omodan, B. I. (2024). The roles of epistemology and decoloniality in addressing power dynamics in university education. *Globalisation, Societies and Education*. Advance online publication. DOI: 10.1080/14767724.2024.2335661;WGROUP:STRING:-PUBLICATION

Orucov, V. (2025). Didactics of artificial intelligence in physics education: New approache. *Scientific Works*, *92*(3), 122–125. DOI: 10.69682/arti.2025.92(3).122-125

Otermans, P. C. J., Baines, S., Livingstone, C., & Aditya, D. (2024). Talking technology tutors: The perceptions of conversational AI in education through the eyes of parents and teachers worldwide. In *Research Square*. DOI: 10.21203/rs.3.rs-4231361/v1

Otto, S., Lavi, R., & Brogaard Bertel, L. (2025). Human-GenAI interaction for active learning in STEM education: State-of-the-art and future directions. *Computers & Education*, *239*, 105444. DOI: 10.1016/j.compedu.2025.105444

Ouaddi, C., Benaddi, L., & Jakimi, A. (2024). Architecture, Tools, and DSLs for Developing Conversational Agents: An Overview. *Procedia Computer Science*, *231*, 293–298. Advance online publication. DOI: 10.1016/j.procs.2023.12.206

Ouyang, F., & Jiao, P. (2021). Artificial intelligence in education: The three paradigms. *Computers and Education: Artificial Intelligence*, *2*, 100020. DOI: 10.1016/j.caeai.2021.100020

Ouyang, J., & Yu, L. (2025). AI-powered intelligent tutoring systems: A new era in education. *Computers & Education*, *190*, 104563.

Owusu-Acheaw, M., & Larson, A. (2020). The role of e-learning in higher education: A review. *International Journal of Educational Management*, *34*(6), 1119–1136.

Ozer, V., ... (2025). *Performance of GPT-4o in the management of toxicological exposures: A comparative analysis with emergency medicine residents—Ozer—2025—Hong Kong Journal of Emergency Medicine—Wiley Online Library.* https://onlinelibrary.wiley.com/doi/full/10.1002/hkj2.70031

Page, J. W., Duhamel, P., & Crognale, M. A. (2011). ERP evidence of visualization at early stages of visual processing. *Brain and Cognition*, *75*(2), 141–146. DOI: 10.1016/j.bandc.2010.11.001

Pan, M., Wang, J., & Wang, J. (2023). Application of Artificial Intelligence in Education: Opportunities, Challenges, and Suggestions. *2023 13th International Conference on Information Technology in Medicine and Education (ITME)*, 623–627. DOI: 10.1109/ITME60234.2023.00130

Panit, M., N. (. (2025). Can critical thinking and AI work together? Observations of science, Mathematics, and language instructors. *Environ. Soc. Psychol.*, *9*(11). Advance online publication. DOI: 10.59429/esp.v9i11.3141

Paranjape, K., Schinkel, M., Nannan Panday, R. A., Car, J., & Nanayakkara, P. (2020). Introducing artificial intelligence training in medical education. *JMIR Medical Education*, *6*(1), e16048. DOI: 10.2196/16048 PMID: 31793895

Pardo, A., Bartimote, K., Buckingham Shum, S., Dawson, S., Gao, J., Gašević, D., Leichtweis, S., Liu, D., Martínez-Maldonado, R., Mirriahi, N., Moskal, A. C. M., Schulte, J., Siemens, G., & Vigentini, L. (2018). OnTask: Delivering data-informed, Personalized Learning Support Actions. *Journal of Learning Analytics*, *5*(3), 235–249. DOI: 10.18608/jla.2018.53.15

Park, W., & Kwon, H. (2024). Implementing artificial intelligence education for middle school technology education in Republic of Korea. *International Journal of Technology and Design Education*, *34*(1), 109–135. DOI: 10.1007/s10798-023-09812-2 PMID: 36844448

Parra-Valencia, J.-A., & Massey, M.-L. (2023). *Leveraging AI Tools for Enhanced Digital Literacy*. Access to Information, and Personalized Learning., DOI: 10.1007/978-3-031-40635-5_9

Paucar-Espinoza, A. F., Erazo-Rondinel, A. A., Arroyo, P., & Salazar, L. A. (2022). Reducing Bias in The Hiring Process Through Choosing By Advantages: A Case Study. Proc. 30th Annual Conference of the International Group for Lean Construction (IGLC30), Priya, M. S., Khan, S., Siddiqui, S., Sharma, M. S., & Verma, S. (2024). The Role of AI in Shaping the Future of Employee Engagement: Insights from Human Resource Management. *Library of Progress-Library Science, Information Technology & Computer, 44*(3). DOI: 10.24928/2022/0217

Pavone, G. (2025). Generative AI in the Learning Process: Threat or Tool? Understanding the Role of Self-Esteem and Academic Anxiety in Shaping Student Motivations. *Journal of Marketing Education*, •••, 02734753251346857. DOI: 10.1177/02734753251346857

Perumal, M. K. K.. (2025). *Artificial intelligence-driven clinical decision support systems in healthcare: Opportunities and challenges*. PMC., DOI: 10.3389/froh.2025.1592428

Peters, A.-K., Capilla, R., Coroamă, V. C., Heldal, R., Lago, P., Leifler, O., Moreira, A., Fernandes, J. P., Penzenstadler, B., Porras, J., & Venters, C. C. (2023). Sustainability in Computing Education: A Systematic Literature Review. arXiv:2305.10369. Retrieved May 01, 2023, from https://ui.adsabs.harvard.edu/abs/2023arXiv230510369P

Pham, C. H. (2025). *University Students' Sense of Belonging in AI-Mediated EFL Classrooms* (pp. 397–422). DOI: 10.4018/979-8-3373-0969-9.ch011

Piech, C., Bassen, J., Huang, J., Ganguli, S., Sahami, M., Guibas, L., & Sohl-Dickstein, J. (2015). Deep knowledge tracing. *Advances in Neural Information Processing Systems (NeurIPS)*, 28. https://doi.org/DOI: 10.48550/arXiv.1506.05908

Pilz, M. (2025). Guest editorial: Not in high regard: an exploration of low reputation of vocational education in the Global South. *Education + Training*, *67*(3), 279–282. DOI: 10.1108/ET-03-2025-569

Pnevmatikos, D. (2025). Creating Critical Thinking Professionals: Challenges for Higher Education. *Higher Education for the Future*, *12*(2), 195–209. DOI: 10.1177/23476311251335374

Polak, S., Schiavo, G., & Zancanaro, M. (2022). Teachers' perspective on artificial intelligence education: An initial investigation. CHI conference on human factors in computing systems extended abstracts, Pucchio, A., Rathagirishnan, R., Caton, N., Gariscsak, P. J., Del Papa, J., Nabhen, J. J., Vo, V., Lee, W., & Moraes, F. Y. (2022). Exploration of exposure to artificial intelligence in undergraduate medical education: a Canadian cross-sectional mixed-methods study. *BMC Medical Education*, *22*(1), 815. PMID: 36443720

Pon, C., & Schendel, R. (2020). Exploring processes of teaching and learning in African university contexts: The case of education for critical thinking in Ghana, Kenya and Botswana. *International Journal of African Higher Education*, *7*(1). Advance online publication. DOI: 10.6017/ijahe.v6i2.11355

Poondej, C., & Lerdpornkulrat, T. (2020). Gamification in e-learning: A Moodle implementation and its effect on student engagement and performance. *Interactive Technology and Smart Education*, *17*(1), 56–66. https://doi.org/https://doi.org/10.1108/ITSE-06-2019-0030. DOI: 10.1108/ITSE-06-2019-0030

Popenici, S. (2023). The critique of AI as a foundation for judicious use in higher education. *Journal of Applied Learning & Teaching*, *6*(2). Advance online publication. DOI: 10.37074/jalt.2023.6.2.4

Popenici, S. A. D., & Kerr, S. (2017). Exploring the impact of artificial intelligence on teaching and learning in higher education. *Research and Practice in Technology Enhanced Learning*, *12*(1), 22. DOI: 10.1186/s41039-017-0062-8 PMID: 30595727

Popenici, S., Rudolph, J., Tan, S., & Tan, S. (2023). A critical perspective on generative AI and learning futures. An interview with Stefan Popenici. *Journal of Applied Learning & Teaching*, *6*(2). Advance online publication. DOI: 10.37074/jalt.2023.6.2.5

Posti-Ahokas, H., & Janhonen-Abruquah, H. (2024). Towards equity literacy: Exploratory enquiry with Finnish student teachers. *European Journal of Teacher Education*, *47*(1), 5–22. DOI: 10.1080/02619768.2021.1952977

Poushneh, A., & Vasquez-Parraga, A. Z. (2020). Augmented reality in retail: A systematic review of the literature. *Journal of Retailing and Consumer Services*, *53*, 102100.

Pradeep, E., Mukherjee, S. K., Selvakumar, P., Koppaka, A. K., Chandel, P. S., & Vats, C. (2025). Empowering Social Media Users With Ethical AI. In Chakraborty, S. (Ed.), *Ethical AI Solutions for Addressing Social Media Influence and Hate Speech* (pp. 91–118). IGI Global Scientific Publishing., DOI: 10.4018/979-8-3693-9904-0.ch005

Prasittichok, P., Jitprapaikulsarn, S., Sriprasertpap, K., & Hwang, G. J. (2024). Technological solutions to fostering students' moral courage: An augmented reality-based contextual gaming approach. *Cogent Education, 11*(1), 2378276. Advance online publication. DOI: 10.1080/2331186X.2024.2378276

Provoost, S., Lau, H. M., Ruwaard, J., & Riper, H. (2017). Embodied conversational agents in clinical psychology: A scoping review. *Journal of Medical Internet Research, 19*(5), e151. DOI: 10.2196/jmir.6553 PMID: 28487267

Purba, N., Pujiati, D., Sihombing, P. S. R., Simanjuntak, H., & Sijabat, D. (2025). The Use of AI in Elementary School Learning: A Systematic Literature Review. *QALAMUNA: Jurnal Pendidikan, Sosial, dan Agama, 17*(1), 83-98.

Putri, N. S. F., Widiharso, P., Utama, A. B. P., Shakti, M. C., & Ghosh, U. (2023). Natural Language Processing in higher education. *Bull.Socinf.The.App*, *6*(1), 90–101. DOI: 10.31763/businta.v6i1.593

Qashou, A. (2022). Obstacles to effective use of e-learning in higher education from the viewpoint of faculty members. *Turkish Online Journal of Distance Education, 23*(1), 144–177.

Qazi, M. A., Sharif, M. A., & Akhlaq, A. (2024). Barriers and facilitators to adoption of e-learning in higher education institutions of Pakistan during COVID-19: Perspectives from an emerging economy. *Journal of Science and Technology Policy Management, 15*(1), 31–52. https://doi.org/https://doi.org/10.1108/JSTPM-01-2022-0002. DOI: 10.1108/JSTPM-01-2022-0002

Rafeeq, K., & Ali, M. Q. (2021). OPPORTUNITIES AND CHALLENGES IN THE USE OF ICT AT TERTIARY LEVEL: TEACHERS' PERCEPTIONS. [BBE]. *Bulletin of Business and Economics, 10*(4), 28–37.

Raghunathan, N., & Saravanakumar, K. (2023). Challenges and Issues in Sentiment Analysis: A Comprehensive Survey. *IEEE Access : Practical Innovations, Open Solutions, 11*, 69626–69642. Advance online publication. DOI: 10.1109/ACCESS.2023.3293041

Rajabalee, Y. B., & Santally, M. I. (2021). Learner satisfaction, engagement and performances in an online module: Implications for institutional e-learning policy. *Education and Information Technologies, 26*(3), 2623–2656. https://doi.org/https://doi.org/10.1007/s10639-020-10375-1. DOI: 10.1007/s10639-020-10375-1 PMID: 33199971

Ramadhani, . (2025). Extensiveness of School Committee Involvement in Maintenance of Classroom Infrastructure: A Guarantee to Adequate Learning Facilities in Primary Schools. *International Journal of Innovative Research and Development.* Advance online publication. DOI: 10.24940/ijird/2025/v14/i5/OJSMAY25001

Ranalli, J. (2021). L2 student engagement with automated feedback on writing: Potential for learning and issues of trust. *Journal of Second Language Writing*, *52*, 100816. Advance online publication. DOI: 10.1016/j.jslw.2021.100816

Rana, V., Verhoeven, B., & Sharma, M. (2025). Generative AI in Design Thinking Pedagogy: Enhancing Creativity, Critical Thinking, and Ethical Reasoning in Higher Education. *Journal of University Teaching & Learning Practice*, *22*(4). Advance online publication. DOI: 10.53761/tjse2f36

Ran, H., Kim, N. J., & Secada, W. G. (2022). A meta-analysis on the effects of technology's functions and roles on students' mathematics achievement in K-12 classrooms. *Journal of Computer Assisted Learning*, *38*(1), 258–284. DOI: 10.1111/jcal.12611

Ranta, A., & Goutte, C. (2021). Linguistic Diversity in Natural Language Processing. *TAL Traitement Automatique Des Langues, 62*(3).

Rathore, A. A., Sultana, N., Zareen, S. J., & Ahmed, A. (2023). Artificial intelligence and curriculum prospects for elementary school. *Pakistan Journal of Humanities and Social Sciences, 11*(4), 4635–4644-4635–4644.

Redican, K., Gonzalez, M., & Zizzamia, B. (2025). Assessing ChatGPT for GIS education and assignment creation. *Journal of Geography in Higher Education*, *49*(1), 113–129. DOI: 10.1080/03098265.2024.2397332

Reed, S. K. (2020). *Cognitive Skills You Need for the 21st Century*. Oxford University Press., DOI: 10.1093/oso/9780197529003.001.0001

Rehman, N., Huang, X., Mahmood, A., Maqbool, S., & Javed, S. (2024b). Research Article Enhancing the Quality of Research Synopsis of International Students Through Peer Feedback: A Case Study.

Rehman, N., Huang, X., Mahmood, A., AlGerafi, M. A., & Javed, S. (2024). Project-based learning as a catalyst for 21st-Century skills and student engagement in the math classroom. *Heliyon*, *10*(23), e39988. DOI: 10.1016/j.heliyon.2024.e39988 PMID: 39660178

Rehman, N., Huang, X., Mahmood, A., Maqbool, S., & Javed, S. (2024). Enhancing the quality of research synopsis of international students through peer feedback: A case study. *New Directions for Child and Adolescent Development, 2024*(1), 1271802. DOI: 10.1155/2024/1271802

Rehman, N., Huang, X., Mahmood, A., Zafeer, H. M. I., & Mohammad, N. K. (2025). Emerging trends and effective strategies in STEM teacher professional development: A systematic review. *Humanities & Social Sciences Communications, 12*(1), 1–23. DOI: 10.1057/s41599-024-04272-y

Rehman, N., Huang, X., Sarwar, U., Fatima, H., & Maqbool, S. (2024). Exploring the impact of family, school and society on the perception and reputation of vocational training in Pakistan: A statistical analysis. *Education + Training*.

Reina-Parrado, M., Román-Graván, P., & Hervás-Gómez, C. (2025). Integration of artificial intelligence and machine learning in education: A systematic review. *International Journal of Educational Methodology, 11*(2), 203–216. DOI: 10.12973/ijem.11.2.203

Rieckmann, M. (2017). *Education for sustainable development goals: Learning objectives*. UNESCO publishing.

Rizzo, A. S., Koenig, S. T., & Daugherty, M. (2020). Virtual reality and immersive technologies in the treatment of anxiety disorders. *Journal of Anxiety Disorders, 73*, 102227.

Roberts, A. B., & Richardson, J. W. (2025). The role of artificial intelligence in schools: A case of policy formation. *Journal of Cases in Educational Leadership, 28*(1), 136–146. DOI: 10.1177/15554589241299320

Rodgers, W., Murray, J. M., Stefanidis, A., Degbey, W. Y., & Tarba, S. Y. (2023). An artificial intelligence algorithmic approach to ethical decision-making in human resource management processes. *Human Resource Management Review, 33*(1), 100925. DOI: 10.1016/j.hrmr.2022.100925

Rodriguez-Ruiz, J., Alvarez-Delgado, A., & Caratozzolo, P. (2021). Use of Natural Language Processing (NLP) Tools to Assess Digital Literacy Skills. *Future of Educational Innovation Workshop Series - Machine Learning-Driven Digital Technologies for Educational Innovation Workshop 2021*. DOI: 10.1109/IEEECONF53024.2021.9733779

Rogers, E. M., Singhal, A., & Quinlan, M. M. (2014). Diffusion of innovations. In *An integrated approach to communication theory and research* (pp. 432–448). Routledge.

Roman, J., & Ortega, M. (2019). Culturally Relevant Pedagogy. *John S. Albazi Student Research and Creative Activities Symposium*. https://neiudc.neiu.edu/srcas/2019/schedule/31

Romele, A. (2025). |*Ethics of AI*| *as a Floating Signifier; or Towards a Politics of AI Ethics* (pp. 157–168). DOI: 10.1007/978-3-031-85478-1_9

Romli, M. H., Wan Yunus, F., Cheema, M. S., Abdul Hamid, H., Mehat, M. Z., Md Hashim, N. F., Foong, C. C., Hong, W. H., & Jaafar, M. H. (2022). A Meta-synthesis on Technology-Based Learning Among Healthcare Students in Southeast Asia. *Medical Science Educator*, *32*(3), 657–677. Advance online publication. DOI: 10.1007/s40670-022-01564-3 PMID: 35573465

Rong, M., Yao, Y., Li, Q., & Chen, X. (2025). Exploring student engagement with artificial intelligence-guided chatbot feedback in EFL writing: Interactions and revisions. *Computer Assisted Language Learning*, •••, 1–30. DOI: 10.1080/09588221.2025.2539979

Roshan, S., Iqbal, S. Z., & Qing, Z. (2024). Teacher training and professional development for implementing AI-based educational tools. *Journal of Asian Development Studies*, *13*(2), 1972–1987. DOI: 10.62345/jads.2024.13.2.154

Rudolph, J., Mohamed Ismail, F. M., & Popenici, S. (2024). Higher Education's Generative Artificial Intelligence Paradox: The Meaning of Chatbot Mania. *Journal of University Teaching & Learning Practice*, *21*(06). Advance online publication. DOI: 10.53761/54fs5e77

Rusconi, L., & Squillaci, M. (2023). Effects of a Universal Design for Learning (UDL) Training Course on the Development Teachers' Competences: A Systematic Review. *Education Sciences*, *13*(5), 466. DOI: 10.3390/educsci13050466

Russell, C., & Bennett, N. (2015). Big data and talent management: Using hard data to make the soft stuff easy. *Business Horizons*, *58*(3), 237–242. DOI: 10.1016/j.bushor.2014.08.001

Sabharwal, D., Kabha, R., & Srivastava, K. (2023). Artificial intelligence (ai)-powered virtual assistants and their effect on human productivity and laziness: Study on students of delhi-ncr (india) & fujairah (uae). *Journal of Content. Community and Communication*, *17*(9), 162–174. DOI: 10.31620/JCCC.06.23/12

Sadman, N., Rahman, A., & Gupta, K. D. (2021a). *Promise of AI in Defi, A Literary Analysis*. DOI: 10.20944/preprints202110.0136.v2

Saeed, L., Khan, R., Durrani, S. A., Mehmood, C. Y., & Hayat, M. A. (2025). HR Beyond the Office: Leveraging AI to Lead Distributed Teams and Cultivate Organizational Culture in the Age of Remote and Hybrid Work. *ACADEMIA International Journal for Social Sciences*, *4*(3), 291–310. DOI: 10.63056/ACAD.004.03.0361

Saidakhror, G. (2024). The impact of artificial intelligence on higher education and the economics of information technology. *International Journal of Law and Policy*, *2*(3), 1–6. DOI: 10.59022/ijlp.125

Salas-Pilco, S. Z., Xiao, K., & Hu, X. (2022). Artificial intelligence and learning analytics in teacher education: A systematic review. *Education Sciences*, *12*(8), 569. DOI: 10.3390/educsci12080569

Saldaña, M., & Martínez, R. (2023). The future of technology in education: Trends and predictions. *Journal of Educational Technology*, *34*(1), 47–58.

Samra Maqbool, M. A., Ijaz, S., Asif, M., & Jahanzeb, M. (2014). An Analysis of Self-esteem between Destitute and Non-destitute women.

Sangeetha, R., Logeshwaran, J., Vats, S., Srivastava, D., & Vishwakarma, P. (2023). Optimization of Natural Language Understanding with Contextual Embeddings. *2023 IEEE International Conference on Research Methodologies in Knowledge Management, Artificial Intelligence and Telecommunication Engineering, RMKMATE 2023*. DOI: 10.1109/RMKMATE59243.2023.10369022

Sanusi, I. T., Martin, F., Ma, R., Gonzales, J. E., Mahipal, V., Oyelere, S. S., Suhonen, J., & Tukiainen, M. (2024). AI MyData: Fostering middle school students' engagement with machine learning through an ethics-infused AI curriculum. *ACM Transactions on Computing Education*, *24*(4), 1–37. DOI: 10.1145/3702242

Sari, H. E., Tumanggor, B., & Efron, D. (2024). Improving educational outcomes through adaptive learning systems using AI. *International Transactions on Artificial Intelligence*, *3*(1), 21–31. DOI: 10.33050/italic.v3i1.647

Sarkar, B., Islam, N., Das, P., Miraj, A., Dakua, M., Debnath, M., & Roy, R. (2023). Digital learning and the lopsidedness of the education in government and private primary schools during the COVID-19 pandemic in West Bengal, India. *E-Learning and Digital Media*, *20*(5), 473–497. DOI: 10.1177/20427530221117327

Sartika, F., Ritonga, M., Lahmi, A., Rasyid, A., & Febriani, S. R. (2021). Online learning in the low Internet area, planning, strategies and problems faced by students during the Covid-19 period. *Artificial intelligence for COVID-19*, 413-421. https://doi.org/https://doi.org/10.1007/978-3-030-69744-0_23

Sarwar, U., et al. (2025). *Navigating Barriers to AI Implementation in the Classroom*. IGI Global. DOI: 10.4018/979-8-3373-1827-1

Sarwar, U., Fazal, K., Zamir, S., Maqbool, S., Hussain, Z., & Qi, Z. Y. (2021). Assessment on Proficiency of Using Information and Communication Technology among Students of University of Lahore (Sargodha Campus), Pakistan. *European Online Journal of Natural and Social Sciences*, *10*(1), 102–115.

Schaefer, M. B., Pennington, S. E., Divoll, K., & Tang, J. H. (2024). A Systematic Review of Literature on Student Voice and Agency in Middle Grade Contexts. *Education Sciences*, *14*(11), 1158. DOI: 10.3390/educsci14111158

Schiff, D. (2022). Education for AI, not AI for Education: The Role of Education and Ethics in National AI Policy Strategies. *International Journal of Artificial Intelligence in Education*, *32*(3), 527–563. DOI: 10.1007/s40593-021-00270-2

Schleiss, J., Laupichler, M. C., Raupach, T., & Stober, S. (2023). AI course design planning framework: Developing domain-specific AI education courses. *Education Sciences*, *13*(9), 954. DOI: 10.3390/educsci13090954

Schmied, A., Ntonia, I., Ng, M. K. J., Zhu, Y., Gibbs, F., & Zou, H. G. (2024). Co-creating with students to promote science of learning in higher education: An international pioneer collaborative effort for asynchronous teaching. *Trends in Neuroscience and Education*, *35*, 100229. DOI: 10.1016/j.tine.2024.100229 PMID: 38879199

Schwartz, S. (2024). Teachers desperately need AI training. How many are getting it? *Education Week*. https://www.edweek.org/technology/teachers-desperately-need-ai-training/2024/03

Schwartz, R., Dodge, J., Smith, N. A., & Etzioni, O. (2020). Green ai. *Communications of the ACM*, *63*(12), 54–63. DOI: 10.1145/3381831

Selim, M. (2020). Skilled based education is the key to sustainable development. *2020 2nd International Sustainability and Resilience Conference: Technology and Innovation in Building Designs*. DOI: 10.1109/IEEECONF51154.2020.9319999

Selvakumar, P., Mishra, B. R., Mohanapriya, T., Shukla, R., & TC, M. (2025). Student Engagement and Motivation in Personalized Learning. In *Integrating Personalized Learning Methods Into STEAM Education* (pp. 123-142). IGI Global Scientific Publishing.

Selvarajan, G. (2021). Leveraging AI-enhanced analytics for industry-specific optimization: A strategic approach to transforming data-driven decision-making. *International Journal of Enhanced Research in Science Technology and Engineering, 10*, 78–84.

Selwyn, N. (2024). On the limits of artificial intelligence (AI) in education. *Nordisk Tidsskrift for Pedagogikk Og Kritikk, 10*(1), 3–14. DOI: 10.23865/ntpk.v10.6062

Sengsouliya, S., Soukhavong, S., Silavong, N., Sengsouliya, S., & Littlepage, F. (2020). An investigation on predictors of student academic engagement. *European Journal of Education Studies.*

Sengul, C., Neykova, R., & Destefanis, G. (2024). Software engineering education in the era of conversational AI: Current trends and future directions. *Frontiers in Artificial Intelligence, 7*, 1436350. DOI: 10.3389/frai.2024.1436350 PMID: 39268193

Seo, K., Tang, J., Roll, I., Fels, S., & Yoon, D. (2021). The impact of artificial intelligence on learner–instructor interaction in online learning. *International Journal of Educational Technology in Higher Education, 18*(1), 54. DOI: 10.1186/s41239-021-00292-9

Sereno, S. I. B. (2025). *AI as Academic Partner: Evaluating ChatGPT's Impact on Learning Outcomes and Perceptions Among Business Administration Students.* DOI: 10.6084/m9.figshare.28876175

Setegn, G. M., & Dejene, B. E. (2025). Improving machine learning models through explainable AI for predicting the level of dietary diversity among Ethiopian preschool children. *Italian Journal of Pediatrics, 5*(1), 91. DOI: 10.1186/s13052-025-01892-1 PMID: 40128875

Shafqat, F., & Amjad, A. I. (2024). Examining Students' Perceptions, Experiences, and Ethical Concerns about Using ChatGPT for Academic Support: A Phenomenological Study. *Pakistan Social Sciences Review, 8*(2), 443–455. DOI: 10.35484/pssr.2024(8-II)36

Shahzad, K., & Khan, S. A. (2024). Role of e-learning for the continuing professional development of university librarians of Pakistan to deliver value-added services: an explanatory study. *Global Knowledge, Memory and Communication.* https://doi.org/https://doi.org/10.1108/GKMC-11-2023-0453

Shaik, T., Tao, X., Li, Y., Dann, C., McDonald, J., Redmond, P., & Galligan, L. (2022). A Review of the Trends and Challenges in Adopting Natural Language Processing Methods for Education Feedback Analysis. *IEEE Access : Practical Innovations, Open Solutions, 10*, 56720–56739. DOI: 10.1109/ACCESS.2022.3177752

Sharma, A. K., & Sharma, R. (2025). Governance in the age of artificial intelligence: A comparative analysis of policy framework in BRICS nations. *AI Magazine*, *46*(2), e70010. DOI: 10.1002/aaai.70010

Shatte, A. B. R., Hutchinson, D. M., & Teague, S. J. (2019). Machine learning in mental health: A scoping review of methods and applications. *Psychological Medicine*, *49*(9), 1426–1448. DOI: 10.1017/S0033291719000151 PMID: 30744717

Shestakofsky, B. (2024). The Social Structures That Shape AI. *The Journal of Applied Behavioral Science,* Nakatumba-Nabende, J., Suuna, C., & Bainomugisha, E. (2023). AI ethics in higher education: Research experiences from practical development and deployment of AI systems. In *AI Ethics in Higher Education: Insights from Africa and Beyond* (pp. 39–55). Springer International Publishing.

Shi, P., & Liu, W. (2025). Adaptive learning oriented higher educational classroom teaching strategies. *Scientific Reports*, *15*(1), 15661. DOI: 10.1038/s41598-025-00536-y

Shortliffe, E. H. (1976). *Computer-Based Medical Consultations: MYCIN*. American Elsevier., DOI: 10.1097/00004669-197610000-00011

Shrivastava, N., Tewari, P., Sujatha, S., Bogireddy, S. R., Varshney, N., & Sharma, V. (2025). Natural Language Processing for Conversational AI: Chatbots and Virtual Assistants. *2025 IEEE International Conference on Interdisciplinary Approaches in Technology and Management for Social Innovation, IATMSI 2025*. DOI: 10.1109/IATMSI64286.2025.10984818

Shtayyat, A., Gawanmeh, A., & Mashaleh, A. (2025). Risk Analysis of AI Integration in Educational Systems: Toward Ethical and Equitable Innovation. In *Examining Cybersecurity Risks Produced by Generative AI* (pp. 401-428). IGI Global Scientific Publishing.

Silverman, S. K. (2011). Zone of Proximal Development. In *Encyclopedia of Child Behavior and Development* (pp. 1590–1590). Springer. DOI: 10.1007/978-0-387-79061-9_3131

Singh, R., & Patel, M. (2025). AI-driven personalized learning: Enhancing student engagement through adaptive systems. *Journal of Educational Technology Research*, *15*(2), 78–95.

Singh, V. V., Kumar, N., Singh, S., Kaul, M., Gupta, A. K., & Kapur, P. (2024). Assessment of artificial intelligence-based digital learning systems in higher education amid the pandemic using analytic hierarchy. *International Journal of System Assurance Engineering and Management*, *15*(8), 4069–4084. DOI: 10.1007/s13198-024-02411-x

Smith, R. D., & Jones, T. M. (2021). AI and personalized learning: An exploratory study. *Journal of Computer Assisted Learning*, *37*(3), 777–790.

Son, N. D. (2024). Exploring User Cultural Identity in Shaping Reflective Design Style on Interactive User Interfaces. In *Navigating the World of Multimedia—Innovation and Applications*. IntechOpen. DOI: 10.5772/intechopen.1007184

Sotirov, M., Petrova, V., & Nikolova-Sotirova, D. (2024). Personalized gamified education: Feedback mechanisms and adaptive learning paths. 2024 8th International Symposium on Innovative Approaches in Smart Technologies (ISAS), Timotheou, S., Miliou, O., Dimitriadis, Y., Sobrino, S. V., Giannoutsou, N., Cachia, R., Monés, A. M., & Ioannou, A. (2023). Impacts of digital technologies on education and factors influencing schools' digital capacity and transformation: A literature review. *Education and Information Technologies*, *28*(6), 6695–6726.

South Eastern European Journal of Public Health. (2024). Ethical considerations in the era of artificial intelligence: Implications for mental health, well-being, and digital health. https://doi.org/DOI: 10.70135/seejph.vi.2893

Srivastav, A. K., & Das, P. (2025). Challenges and Barriers to Adoption. In *Biotechnology and IoT in Agriculture and Food Production: Green Innovation* (pp. 161-168). Springer. DOI: 10.1007/979-8-8688-1469-3_18

Steinert, S., & Dennis, M. J. (2022). Emotions and Digital Well-Being: On Social Media's Emotional Affordances. *Philosophy & Technology*, *35*(2), 36. DOI: 10.1007/s13347-022-00530-6 PMID: 35450167

Stevens-Smith, D. A. (2020). Brain-Based Teaching: Differentiation in Teaching, Learning, and Motor Skills. *Journal of Physical Education, Recreation & Dance*, *91*(7), 34–42. DOI: 10.1080/07303084.2020.1781717

Strielkowski, W., Grebennikova, V., Lisovskiy, A., Rakhimova, G., & Vasileva, T. (2025). AI-driven adaptive learning for sustainable educational transformation. *Sustainable Development (Bradford)*, *33*(2), 1921–1947. DOI: 10.1002/sd.3221

Sudarsan, I., Hoare, K., Sheridan, N., & Roberts, J. (2022). Giving voice to children in research: The power of child-centered constructivist grounded theory methodology. *Research in Nursing & Health, 45*(4), 488–497. DOI: 10.1002/nur.22231 PMID: 35478178

Sugianti, & Rosidah, I. (2024). The use of Artificial Intelligence (AI) in learning results for scientific Indonesian language courses at PGRI Wiranegara University. *International Journal of Applied Research and Sustainable, 2*(1), 1–10.

Sullivan, M., & Kelly, A. (2025) *ChatGPT in higher education: Considerations for academic integrity and student learning*. https://www.researchgate.net/publication/369378950_

Sumana, M., Hegde, S. S., Wadawadagi, S. N., Sujana, D. V., & Narasimhan, V. G. (2022). *Smart Tutoring System for the Specially Challenged Children*. 113–130. DOI: 10.1007/978-981-19-2161-2_7

Sweller, J. (n. d.). (1988). *Cognitive Load During Problem Solving: Effects on Learning*.

Sylvestri, B. (2025). *AI in the classroom: What parents need to know*.

Tama Sánchez, F. A., Vasquez Falconí, J. A., Aguilar Mejía, R. M., Rodríguez Pérez, J. C. A., López Solórzano, A. A., & Paredes Jeréz, K. D. (2024). Xeroderma Pigmentoso Reporte De Caso Y Revisión De La Literatura. Revista Científica De Salud Y Desarrollo Humano, 5(2), 44–55.

Tang, K. H. D. (2024). Implications of artificial Intelligence for teaching and learning. *Acta Pedagogia Asia, 3*(2), 65–79. DOI: 10.53623/apga.v3i2.404

Tao, Y., Viberg, O., Baker, R. S., & Kizilcec, R. F. (2024). Cultural bias and cultural alignment of large language models. *PNAS Nexus, 3*(9), pgae346. Advance online publication. DOI: 10.1093/pnasnexus/pgae346 PMID: 39290441

Tapo, A. A., Traoré, A., Danioko, S., & Tembine, H. (2024). Machine Intelligence in Africa. *Survey (London, England)*.

Tatar, E., & Akçay, H. (2022). Digital storytelling in education: Enhancing student engagement. *Educational Media International, 59*(2), 95–111.

Tavares, S., & Ferrara, E. (2023). Fairness and Bias in Artificial Intelligence: A Brief Survey of Sources, Impacts, and Mitigation Strategies. *Sci, 6*(1), 3. DOI: 10.3390/sci6010003

Tedre, M., Toivonen, T., Kahila, J., Vartiainen, H., Valtonen, T., Jormanainen, I., & Pears, A. (2021). Teaching machine learning in K–12 classroom: Pedagogical and technological trajectories for artificial intelligence education. *IEEE Access : Practical Innovations, Open Solutions, 9*, 110558–110572. DOI: 10.1109/ACCESS.2021.3097962

Tesfaye, A. (2024). Navigating the complexities of decolonizing knowledge production. *A Community Blog and Repository of Resources for Improving Research Impact on Complex Real-World Problems.*

Thakur, A., Ahuja, L., Vashisth, R., & Simon, R. (2023). NLP & AI Speech Recognition: An Analytical Review. *Proceedings of the 17th INDIACom; 2023 10th International Conference on Computing for Sustainable Global Development, INDIACom 2023.*

Thomas, B., Kessler, S., & Karout, S. (2022). EFFICIENT ADAPTER TRANSFER OF SELF-SUPERVISED SPEECH MODELS FOR AUTOMATIC SPEECH RECOGNITION. *ICASSP, IEEE International Conference on Acoustics, Speech and Signal Processing - Proceedings, 2022-May*, 7102–7106. DOI: 10.1109/ICASSP43922.2022.9746223

Thomas, D. R., Gatz, E., Gupta, S., Lin, J., Tipper, C., & Koedinger, K. (2024). Using generative AI to provide feedback to adult tutors in training and assess real-life performance. In *EdArXiv*. DOI: 10.1007/978-3-031-73427-4_21

Tilala, M. H., Chenchala, P. K., Choppadandi, A., Kaur, J., Naguri, S., Saoji, R., & Devaguptapu, B. (2024). Ethical considerations in the use of artificial intelligence and machine learning in healthcare. *Health Care, 11*(3), 588–595. DOI: 10.3390/healthcare11030588

Timotheou, S., Miliou, O., Dimitriadis, Y., Sobrino, S. V., Giannoutsou, N., Cachia, R., Monés, A. M., & Ioannou, A. (2023). Impacts of digital technologies on education and factors influencing schools' digital capacity and transformation: A literature review. *Education and Information Technologies, 28*(6), 6695–6726. https://doi.org/https://doi.org/10.1007/s10639-022-11431-8. DOI: 10.1007/s10639-022-11431-8 PMID: 36465416

Tollon, F. (2025). Reactive agency and technology. *AI and Ethics, 5*(1), 489–496. DOI: 10.1007/s43681-023-00366-6

Torous, J., Larsen, M. E., Depp, C., Cosco, T. D., Barnett, I., Nock, M. K., & Firth, J. (2018). Smartphones, sensors, and machine learning to advance real-time prediction and interventions for suicide prevention: A review of current progress and next steps. *Current Psychiatry Reports*, *20*(7), 51. DOI: 10.1007/s11920-018-0914-y PMID: 29956120

Torous, J., & Roberts, L. W. (2017). The ethical use of mobile health technology in clinical psychiatry. *The Journal of Nervous and Mental Disease*, *205*(1), 4–8. DOI: 10.1097/NMD.0000000000000596 PMID: 28005647

Trang, N. T. Q., & Thu, P. T. (2024). The role of AI in improving student learning outcomes: Evidence in vietnam. *International Journal of Multidisciplinary Research and Analysis*, *7*(06), 2806–2810. DOI: 10.47191/ijmra/v7-i06-48

Treve, M. (2024). Integrating Artificial Intelligence in Education: Impacts on Student Learning and Innovation. *International Journal of Vocational Education and Training Research*, *10*(2), 203–216. DOI: 10.11648/j.ijvetr.20241002.14

Treve, M., & Adiguzel, T. (2025). AI-enhanced classroom dynamics: The impact of intelligent tutoring systems. *Journal of Educational Computing Research*, *42*(4), 89–105.

Troussas, C., Papakostas, C., Krouska, A., Mylonas, P., & Sgouropoulou, C. (2023). Personalized Feedback Enhanced by Natural Language Processing in Intelligent Tutoring Systems. *Lecture Notes in Computer Science (Including Subseries Lecture Notes in Artificial Intelligence and Lecture Notes in Bioinformatics), 13891 LNCS*, 667–677. DOI: 10.1007/978-3-031-32883-1_58

Tsui, E., Dragicevic, N., Fan, I., & Cheng, M. (2024). Co-creating curriculum with students, teachers, and practitioners in a technology-enhanced environment. *Educational Technology Research and Development*, *72*(2), 869–893. DOI: 10.1007/s11423-023-10301-5

Tuhiwai Smith. (2012). *Decolonizing methodologies: Research and indigenous peoples.*

Tulyakul, P., & Meepring, S. (2020). Ethical Issues of Informed Consent: Students as Participants in Faculty Research. *Global Journal of Health Science*, *12*(3), 86. DOI: 10.5539/gjhs.v12n3p86

Tummalapalli, H. K., Rao, A. N., Kamal, G., Kumari, N., & Kumar, J. R. S. (2025). Exploring AI-driven management: Impact on organizational performance, decision making, efficiency, and employee engagement. *Journal of Advanced Research in Applied Sciences and Engineering Technology*, *52*(2), 148–163.

Tupag, R. M., & Ubayubay, R. (2025). Teachers' Practices on Digital Infrastructure towards Schools' Digital Capacity and Transformation. *International Journal on Science and Technology*, *16*(3), 7828. Advance online publication. DOI: 10.71097/IJSAT.v16.i3.7828

Tutsoy, O. (2021). COVID-19 epidemic and opening of the schools: Artificial intelligence-based long-term adaptive policy making to control the pandemic diseases. *IEEE Access : Practical Innovations, Open Solutions*, *9*, 68461–68471. DOI: 10.1109/ACCESS.2021.3078080

Tu, Y., Wang, Q., & Huang, C. (2025). Facilitating students' emotional engagement in synchronous online learning: A systematic literature review. *International Review of Research in Open and Distance Learning*, *26*(1), 261–282. https://doi.org/https://doi.org/10.19173/irrodl.v26i1.7732. DOI: 10.19173/irrodl.v26i1.7732

Tyson, M. M., & Sauers, N. J. (2021). School leaders' adoption and implementation of artificial intelligence. *Journal of Educational Administration*, *59*(3), 271–285. DOI: 10.1108/JEA-10-2020-0221

Ukpe, E. (2023). Information and communication technologies (ICTS) for E-Learning in tertiary education. *Open Journal of Social Sciences*, *11*(12), 666–680. DOI: 10.4236/jss.2023.1112044

Ulyshen, T. Z., Koehler, M. J., & Gao, F. (2015). Understanding the Connection Between Epistemic Beliefs and Internet Searching. *Journal of Educational Computing Research*, *53*(3), 345–383. DOI: 10.1177/0735633115599604

Unesco. (2020). Education for sustainable development: A roadmap. *Transforming Our World: The 2030 Agenda for Sustainable Development A/RES/70/1, available online at.*

UNESCO. (2021). *Recommendation on the ethics of artificial intelligence*. United Nations Educational, Scientific and Cultural Organization.

Usmaan, Mo., & Singh, J. N. (2025). Review of Recent Advancement in Natural Language Processing for Automatic Speech Recognition. *2025 International Conference on Networks and Cryptology (NETCRYPT)*, 795–800. DOI: 10.1109/NETCRYPT65877.2025.11102756

Vaccino-Salvadore, S. (2023). Exploring the Ethical Dimensions of Using ChatGPT in Language Learning and Beyond. In *Languages* (Vol. 8, Issue 3). DOI: 10.3390/languages8030191

Vaidyam, A. N., Wisniewski, H., Halamka, J. D., Kashavan, M. S., & Torous, J. B. (2019). Chatbots and conversational agents in mental health: A review of the psychiatric landscape. *Canadian Journal of Psychiatry, 64*(7), 456–464. DOI: 10.1177/0706743719828977 PMID: 30897957

Vakili, R., Vakili, S., Ajilian Abbasi, M., & Masoudi, S. (2024). Overcrowded Classrooms: Challenges, Consequences, and Collaborative Solutions for Educators: A Literature Review. *Medical Education Bulletin, 5*(2), 961–972.

Valente, J. A., Almeida, M. E. B. d., & Geraldini, A. F. S. (2017). Metodologias ativas: das concepções às práticas em distintos níveis de ensino. *Revista diálogo educacional, 17*(52), 455-478.

Valenzuela, J. M. (2025). Navigating the Future of Education in Critical Thinking and AI in Digital Citizenship. In *Digital Citizenship and the Future of AI Engagement, Ethics, and Privacy* (pp. 377–404). IGI Global. DOI: 10.4018/979-8-3693-9015-3.ch014

Valverde-Berrocoso, J., Acevedo-Borrega, J., & Cerezo-Pizarro, M. (2022). Educational technology and student performance: A systematic review. Frontiers in Education, Xu, Z. (2024). AI in education: Enhancing learning experiences and student outcomes. *Applied and Computational Engineering, 51*(1), 104–111.

Van Brummelen, J., Heng, T., & Tabunshchyk, V. (2021). Teaching tech to talk: K-12 conversational artificial intelligence literacy curriculum and development tools. Proceedings of the AAAI conference on artificial intelligence, Velmurugan, P. R., Swadhi, R., Varshney, K. R., Regins, J. C., & Gayathri, K. (2025). Creating Engaging and Personalized Learning Experiences in Distance Education: AI and Learning Analytics. In *AI and Learning Analytics in Distance Learning* (pp. 103-126). IGI Global Scientific Publishing.

Vaswani, A., Shazeer, N., Parmar, N., Uszkoreit, J., Jones, L., Gomez, A., & Kaiser, L. (2017). *P.* Attention Is All You Need., https://doi.org/doi.org/10.48550/arXiv.1706.03762

Vayadande, K., Bailke, P. A., Khedekar, L. S., Kumar, R., & Dange, V. R. (2024). A Review on Text Analysis Using NLP. *How Machine Learning Is Innovating Today's World: A Concise Technical Guide*, 13–23. DOI: 10.1002/9781394214167.ch2

Vega Alvarez, E., & Huang Chang, Y. (2024). Blended Learning, and Its Impact on English Speaking Skills in Pronunciation in Group 11-4 of Liceo de Santo Domingo, I Quarter 2024. Ciencia Y Reflexi6n, 3(2), 159–173.

Verdecchia, R., Sallou, J., & Cruz, L. (2023). A systematic review of Green AI. *Wiley Interdisciplinary Reviews. Data Mining and Knowledge Discovery*, *13*(4), e1507. DOI: 10.1002/widm.1507

Veselova, I. (2021). Postcolonial theory and its Impact upon modern historical-anthropological research of Latin America. *Исторический Журнал: Научные Исследования*, *4*(4), 61–69. DOI: 10.7256/2454-0609.2021.4.36489

Vieriu, A. M., & Petrea, G. (2025). The Impact of Artificial Intelligence (AI) on Students' Academic Development. *Education Sciences*, *15*(3), 343. DOI: 10.3390/educsci15030343

Vinuesa, R., Azizpour, H., Leite, I., Balaam, M., Dignum, V., Domisch, S., Felländer, A., Langhans, S. D., Tegmark, M., & Fuso Nerini, F. (2020). The role of artificial intelligence in achieving the Sustainable Development Goals. *Nature Communications*, *11*(1), 233. DOI: 10.1038/s41467-019-14108-y PMID: 31932590

Vivek, R. (2023). Enhancing diversity and reducing bias in recruitment through AI: a review of strategies and challenges. *Информатика. Экономика. Управление/ Informatics. Economics. Management,* *2*(4), 0101-0118.

Vongkhamthath, K., & Chiu, S. (2021). The impact of technology on learning outcomes: A longitudinal study. *Journal of Educational Computing Research*, *59*(4), 800–824.

Voutyrakou, D. A., & Skordoulis, C. (2025). Using AI Tools to Enhance Educational Robotics to Bridge the Gender Gap in STEM. *Education Sciences*, *15*(6), 711. DOI: 10.3390/educsci15060711

Vučković, A., & Sikimić, V. (2025). Global justice and the use of AI in education: Ethical and epistemic aspects. *AI & Society*, *40*(4), 3087–3104. DOI: 10.1007/s00146-024-02076-x

Vyortkina, D., & Elsawy, A. (2024). A Systematic Professional Development Framework for Enhancing ICT Skills in the Teacher Education Faculty. EDULEARN24 Proceedings, Wade, B., Dianati, S., Searle, B., & Sankey, M. (2024). Navigating an LMS Review process: Harnessing Next-Generation Digital Learning through evidence-based decision-making. *Journal of University Teaching & Learning Practice*, *24*(7), 63–89.

Wakunuma, K., Ogoh, G., Akintoye, S., & Eke, D. O. (2025). Decoloniality as an Essential Trustworthy AI Requirement. (Eds), *Trustworthy AI: African Perspectives* (pp. 255–276). Springer Nature Switzerland. DOI: 10.1007/978-3-031-75674-0_12

Wakunuma, K., & Eke, D. (2024). Africa, ChatGPT, and Generative AI Systems: Ethical Benefits, Concerns, and the Need for Governance. *Philosophies*, *9*(3), 80. DOI: 10.3390/philosophies9030080

Wang, F., & Hannafin, M. J. (2020). Design-based implementation research: An emerging approach to improve educational practices. *Educational Technology Research and Development*, *68*(4), 1059–1075.

Wang, H., Tlili, A., Huang, R., Cai, Z., Li, M., Cheng, Z., Yang, D., Li, M., Zhu, X., & Fei, C. (2023). Examining the applications of intelligent tutoring systems in real educational contexts: A systematic literature review from the social experiment perspective. *Education and Information Technologies*, *28*(7), 1–36. DOI: 10.1007/s10639-022-11555-x PMID: 36643383

Wang, R., Li, J., Shi, W., & Li, X. (2021). Application of artificial intelligence techniques in operating mode of professors' academic governance in american research universities. *Wireless Communications and Mobile Computing*, *2021*(1), 3415125. DOI: 10.1155/2021/3415125

Wang, S., Wang, F., Zhu, Z., Wang, J., Tran, T., & Du, Z. (2024). Artificial intelligence in education: A systematic literature review. *Expert Systems with Applications*, *252*, 124167. DOI: 10.1016/j.eswa.2024.124167

Wang, X., Gao, Y., Wang, Q., & Zhang, P. (2025). Fostering Engagement in <scp>AI</scp> -Mediate Chinese <scp>EFL</scp> Classrooms: The Role of Classroom Climate, <scp>AI</scp> Literacy, and Resilience. *European Journal of Education*, *60*(1). Advance online publication. DOI: 10.1111/ejed.12874

Wang, Y., Wu, M., & Zhang, X. (2023). The role of augmented reality in surgical training: A systematic review. *Surgical Innovation*, *30*(1), 20–30. PMID: 35582732

Wang, Y., Zhang, C., & Zhou, Y. (2023). Reconstructing self from the illness: A constructivist grounded theory study of posttraumatic growth in patients with Crohn's disease. *BMC Gastroenterology*, *23*(1), 1–14. DOI: 10.1186/s12876-022-02618-x PMID: 36593456

Wankhade, M., Rao, A. C. S., & Kulkarni, C. (2022). A survey on sentiment analysis methods, applications, and challenges. *Artificial Intelligence Review*, *55*(7), 5731–5780. Advance online publication. DOI: 10.1007/s10462-022-10144-1

Warr, M., & Heath, M. K. (2025). Uncovering the Hidden Curriculum in Generative AI: A Reflective Technology Audit for Teacher Educators. *Journal of Teacher Education*, *76*(3), 245–261. DOI: 10.1177/00224871251325073

Wayne, H., Fengchun, M., & UNESCO. (2023). *Guidance for generative AI in education and research*. UNESCO Publishing.

Webb, A., McQuaid, R. W., & Webster, C. W. R. (2021). Moving learning online and the COVID-19 pandemic: A university response. *World Journal of Science. Technology and Sustainable Development*, *18*(1), 1–19.

Wei, S. (2024). Research on the disruptive transformation and future development of American teaching models in the context of intelligent transformation. *Advances in Economics. Management and Political Sciences*, *72*(1), 201–210.

Weizenbaum, J. (1966). ELIZA — A computer program for the study of natural language communication between man and machine. *Communications of the ACM*, *9*(1), 36–45. DOI: 10.1145/365153.365168

Weston, J., Bordes, A., Chopra, S., Rush, A. M., Van Merriënboer, B., Joulin, A., & Mikolov, T. (2015). Towards ai-complete question answering: A set of prerequisite toy tasks. *arXiv preprint arXiv:1502.05698*.

Wills, M. (2024). New APA CEO on uses of artificial intelligence in mental health, the future of psychiatry and more. *AMA Update*. https://www.ama-assn.org/doctor-news/

Winkler, R., & Söllner, M. (2018). Unleashing the potential of chatbots in education: A state-of-the-art analysis. *Academy of Management Annual Meeting Proceedings*, 2018(1), 15903. https://doi.org/DOI: 10.5465/AMBPP.2018.15903abstract

Wong, M. F., Guo, S., Hang, C. N., Ho, S. W., & Tan, C. W. (2023). Natural Language Generation and Understanding of Big Code for AI-Assisted Programming: A Review. *Entropy 2023, Vol. 25, Page 888*, *25*(6), 888. DOI: 10.3390/e25060888

Woodruff, K., Hutson, J., & Arnone, K. (2023). Perceptions and barriers to adopting artificial intelligence in K-12 education: A survey of educators in fifty states.

World Health Organization. (2022). *Global strategy on digital health 2020–2025*. WHO.

World Health Organization. (2024). WHO releases AI ethics and governance guidance for large multi-modal models. Geneva, Switzerland. Retrieved from https://www.who.int/news/

Wu, D., & Zhang, J. (2025). Generative artificial intelligence in secondary education: Applications and effects on students' innovation skills and digital literacy. *PLoS One*, *20*(5), e0323349. DOI: 10.1371/journal.pone.0323349 PMID: 40344078

Wu, P., & Yu, Z. (2025). AI-powered chatbots in education: Enhancing student engagement and support. *Computers in Human Behavior, 134*, 107345.

Wu, Z., Abdul Halim, H., & Mohd Saad, M. R. (2024). Artificial Intelligence (AI) and Gamification in Blended Learning: Enhancing Language and Literacy in Shanxi, China. [MJSSH]. *Malaysian Journal of Social Sciences and Humanities, 9*(12), e003159. DOI: 10.47405/mjssh.v9i12.3159

Xia, L., & Zhang, Y. (2025). AI and creativity in education: Fostering critical thinking through adaptive learning systems. *Educational Technology Research and Development, 73*(2), 98–115.

Xiao, B., Imel, Z. E., Georgiou, P. G., Atkins, D. C., & Narayanan, S. S. (2015). Rate my therapist": Automated detection of empathy in drug and alcohol counseling via speech and language processing. *PLoS One, 10*(12), e0143055. DOI: 10.1371/journal.pone.0143055 PMID: 26630392

Xu, H., & Rangra, N. (2024). Bridging the Digital Divide: The Impact of Public Investment on Urban-Rural Disparities in Pakistan. *Library of Progress-Library Science, Information Technology & Computer, 44*(3).

Xu, B., Chen, N. S., & Chen, G. (2020). Effects of teacher role on student engagement in online learning environments: A configurational analysis. *Computers & Education, 157*, 103963. DOI: 10.1016/j.compedu.2020.103956

Xu, J. (2024). Memorisation is not rote learning: Rethinking memorisation as an embodied practice for Chinese students. *Journal of Multilingual and Multicultural Development, 45*(9), 3963–3979. DOI: 10.1080/01434632.2022.2134878

Xu, Q. (2024). Action research plan: The impact of the use of Artificial Intelligence in education on the cognitive abilities of university students. In *Research Square*. DOI: 10.21203/rs.3.rs-4981281/v1

Yamaguchi, H., Sugihara, G., Shimizu, M., & Yamashita, Y. (2024). Generative artificial intelligence model for simulating structural brain changes in schizophrenia. *Frontiers in Psychiatry, 15*, 1437075. Advance online publication. DOI: 10.3389/fpsyt.2024.1437075 PMID: 39429522

Yang, S. (2025). Intelligent Tutoring System Algorithm: Enhance Personalized Learning Experience. *Lecture Notes in Electrical Engineering, 1355 LNEE*, 431–439. DOI: 10.1007/978-981-96-2794-3_46

Yilma, K. (2025). Ethics of AI in Africa: Interrogating the role of Ubuntu and AI governance initiatives. *Ethics and Information Technology, 27*(2), 24. DOI: 10.1007/s10676-025-09834-5

Yuan, X., Rehman, S., Altalbe, A., Rehman, E., & Shahiman, M. A. (2024). Digital literacy as a catalyst for academic confidence: Exploring the interplay between academic self-efficacy and academic procrastination among medical students. *BMC Medical Education*, *24*(1), 1317. DOI: 10.1186/s12909-024-06329-7 PMID: 39548425

Yu, X., Yang, D., Ding, W., & Gan, W. (2014). Preliminary Research and Development on the Problem-Solving Humanoid Machine for K-12 Education. *2014 International Conference of Educational Innovation through Technology*, 99–104. DOI: 10.1109/EITT.2014.25

Zafeer, H. M. I., & Yanping, L. (2022). The role of gender, socioeconomic factors, and its impact on students' English as a second language (ESL) performance.

Zafeer, H. M. I., Peng, C., Rehman, S., Wei, Z., & Maqbool, S. (2021). A Study to Investigate the Obstacles of Educational Technology in Curriculum; University Students' Perception. European Online Journal of Natural and Social Sciences, 10(1).

Zafeer, H. M. I., Yanping, L., & Maqbool, S. (2022) COVID-19 and the Future of Online Learning; Perspective of Pakistani Students from Higher Education Institutions (HEIs). DOI: 10.35629/5252-0410784790

Zafeer, H. M. I., Yanping, L., & Maqbool, S. (2025). COVID-19 and the Future of Online Learning; Perspective of Pakistani Students from Higher Education Institutions (HEIs).

Zafeer, H. M. I., Yanping, L., & Maqbool, S. COVID-19 and the Future of Online Learning; Perspective of Pakistani Students from Higher Education Institutions (HEIs).

Zafeer, H. M. I., Li, Y., & Maqbool, S. (2023). An approach to progress learning outcomes: International graduate students' engagement in reflective practice and reflective journal writing during pandemic. *Sustainability (Basel)*, *15*(3), 1898. DOI: 10.3390/su15031898

Zafeer, H. M. I., Maqbool, S., Rong, Y., & Maqbool, S. (2024). Mapping the relationship and influence of school internal factors with an eye towards students' science academic outcomes. *Heliyon*, *10*(19), e38696. DOI: 10.1016/j.heliyon.2024.e38696

Zafeer, H. M. I., Maqbool, S., Rong, Y., & Maqbool, S. (2025a). Beyond the Classroom: How Socioeconomic Status, Parental Involvement and Home Environment Impact on Students' Science Academic Performance at Secondary Schools. *European Journal of Education*, *60*(1), e70023. DOI: 10.1111/ejed.70023

Zafeer, H. M. I., Maqbool, S., Rong, Y., & Maqbool, S. (2025b). Culturally Sustaining Cognitive and Behavioral Interventions for Reducing Anxiety in Autistic School-Aged Students: A Systematic Review. *Psychology in the Schools*, pits.70077. DOI: 10.1002/pits.70077

Zafeer, H. M. I., Maqbool, S., Rong, Y., & Maqbool, S. (2025b). Impact of digital learning tools on student's engagement and achievement in middle school science classes. *International Journal of Technology in Education and Science*, *9*(2), 177–196. DOI: 10.46328/ijtes.622

Zafeer, H. M. I., Maqbool, S., & Yanping, L. (2022). Psychological and social factors and their impact on divorced and married women: A case study from Punjab Pakistan. *Journal of Divorce & Remarriage*, *63*(5), 352–373. DOI: 10.1080/10502556.2022.2048345

Zafeer, H. M. I., Peng, C., Rehman, S., Wei, Z., & Maqbool, S. (2021). A Study to Investigate the Obstacles of Educational Technology in Curriculum; University Students' Perception. *European Online Journal of Natural and Social Sciences*, *10*(1), 1–8.

Zafeer, H. M. I., Xue, H., & Maqbool, S. (2020). Delaying Factors Regarding Civil Justice in Pakistan (Lower Courts). *Journal of Humanities and Social Sciences Studies*, *2*(6), 15–22. DOI: 10.32996/jhsss.2020.2.6.2

Zafeer, H. M. I., Yanping, L., & Maqboo, S. (2022). The role of gender, socio-economic factors, and its impact on students' English as a second language (ESL) performance. *North American Academic Research*, *5*(10), 52–59.

Zagouras, C., Egarchou, D., Skiniotis, P., & Fountana, M. (2022). Face to face or blended learning? A case study: Teacher training in the pedagogical use of ICT. *Education and Information Technologies*, *27*(9), 12939–12967. https://doi.org/https://doi.org/10.1007/s10639-022-11144-y. DOI: 10.1007/s10639-022-11144-y PMID: 35729873

Zalat, M. M., Hamed, M. S., & Bolbol, S. A. (2021). The experiences, challenges, and acceptance of e-learning as a tool for teaching during the COVID-19 pandemic among university medical staff. *PLoS One*, *16*(3), e0248758. https://doi.org/https://doi.org/10.1371/journal.pone.0248758. DOI: 10.1371/journal.pone.0248758 PMID: 33770079

Zamir, S., Yang, Z., Sarwar, U., Maqbool, S., Fazal, K., Ihsan, H., & Arif, A. (2021). Teaching methodologies used for learning critical thinking in higher education: Pakistani teachers' perceptions. *Int. Trans. J. Eng. Manag. Appl. Sci. Technol*, *12*, 1–10.

Zawacki-Richter, O., Marín, V. I., Bond, M., & Gouverneur, F. (2019). Systematic review of research on artificial intelligence applications in higher education–where are the educators? *International Journal of Educational Technology in Higher Education, 16*(1), 1–27. DOI: 10.1186/s41239-019-0171-0

Zeshan Haider, S. T. (2024). *AI-Driven Pedagogies: Shaping Critical Thinking Skills in a Data-Rich World*. DOI: 10.13140/RG.2.2.23095.12969

Zhai, X., Chu, X., Chai, C. S., Jong, M. S. Y., Istenic, A., Spector, M., Liu, J.-B., Yuan, J., & Li, Y. (2021). A review of artificial intelligence (AI) in education from 2010 to 2020. *Complexity, 2021*(1), 1–18. DOI: 10.1155/2021/8812542

Zhang, D., Wijaya, T. T., Wang, Y., Su, M., Li, X., & Damayanti, N. W. (2025). Exploring the relationship between AI literacy, AI trust, AI dependency, and 21st century skills in preservice mathematics teachers. *Scientific Reports, 15*(1), 14281. DOI: 10.1038/s41598-025-99127-0 PMID: 40275054

Zhang, J., & Chen, Z. (2023). Emotion-aware intelligent tutoring systems: Integrating affective computing with NLP for personalized learning. *AI in Education Journal, 2*(1), 55–72. DOI: 10.1007/s43682-023-00115-4

Zhang, P., & Tur, G. (2024). A systematic review of ChatGPT use in K-12 education. *European Journal of Education, 59*(2), e12599. DOI: 10.1111/ejed.12599

Zhang, X., & Tahir, S. (2023). LEVERAGING TECHNOLOGY TO ENHANCE ACCESS TO QUALITY LEGAL EDUCATION IN MALAYSIA. *International Journal of Social Science and Business Management, 1*(02). Advance online publication. DOI: 10.59021/ijssbm.v1i02.46

Zhang, Y. (2024). Research on the mechanism of intelligent education enabled by natural language processing technology. In *Advances in Intelligent Systems Research* (pp. 257–267). Atlantis Press International BV.

Zhou, P., Li, J., Chen, F., Zhou, H., Bao, S., & Li, M. (2021). Design of metacognitive scaffolding for k-12 programming education and its effects on students' problem solving ability and metacognition. *2021 Tenth International Conference of Educational Innovation through Technology (EITT)*, 182–186. DOI: 10.1109/EITT53287.2021.00044

Zhumagaliyeva, G., Tleshova, Z., Amanzhol, M., & Smagulova, M. (2025). THE IMPACT OF AI ON ACADEMIC WRITING: ENHANCING SKILLS OR HINDERING CRITICAL THINKING? *National Center for Higher Education Development, 2*(50). Advance online publication. DOI: 10.59787/2413-5488-2025-50-2-122-134

Zimotti, G., Frances, C., & Whitaker, L. (2024). The future of language education: Teachers' perceptions about the surge of AI writing tools. *Technology in Language Teaching & Learning*, *6*(2), 1136–1136. DOI: 10.29140/tltl.v6n1.1136

Zmir, S., Sarwar, U., Maqbool, S., Javed, S., Ishtiaq, M., & Zhang, Y. (2021). Plagiarism practice: Its awareness & dealing and consequences among university students in Punjab province of Pakistan. *International Transaction Journal of Engineering, Management, &. Applied Sciences & Technologies*, *12*(11), 1–11.

Zormanová, L. (2024). Attitudes of Czech Teachers Towards the Use of Artificial Intelligence in Schools. *Horyzonty Wychowania*, *23*(65), 31–41. DOI: 10.35765/hw.2024.2365.05

Zou, D., Xie, H., & Kohnke, L. (2025). Navigating the Future: Establishing a Framework for Educators' Pedagogic Artificial Intelligence Competence. *European Journal of Education*, *60*(2), e70117. DOI: 10.1111/ejed.70117

Жунусов, Е. (2024). РОЛЬ ИСКУССТВЕННОГО ИНТЕЛЛЕКТА В СОВРЕМЕННОМ ОБРАЗОВАНИИ: ПРЕИМУЩЕСТВА, ВЫЗОВЫ И ПУТИ К УСПЕХУ. *Вестник Северо-Казахстанского Университета им. М. Козыбаева*, (2 (62)), 180–188.

About the Contributors

Samra Maqbool is an Assistant Professor at Smart Learning Institute of Beijing Normal University, Beijing, China. Dr. Samra Maqbool is an accomplished scholar and educator with a Ph.D. in Comparative Education from Shaanxi Normal University, Xi'an, China. She is currently serving as an Assistant Professor at the Smart Learning Institute of Beijing Normal University, Beijing, China, where she is actively engaged in research, teaching, and collaborative global initiatives focused on advancing smart learning environments and educational technologies. She has completed her postdoctoral research at the School of Education, Zhejiang Normal University, Jinhua, Zhejiang, China, with a focus on integrating artificial intelligence, augmented reality (AR), and virtual reality (VR) into educational leadership, management, and psychological practices. Dr. Maqbool's research interests span Comparative Education, Educational Leadership and Management, Educational Psychology, Gender and Sociological Theory, and the application of Artificial Intelligence in Education. She is deeply involved in international projects recognized by organizations such as UNESCO, AIED, and ALECSO, including the Global Smart Education Network (GSENet) and the Artificial Intelligence in Higher Education Initiative (AIHEi). Throughout her career, Dr. Maqbool has held multiple academic and professional roles, including Visiting Lecturer at Bahauddin Zakariya University, Pakistan, and Program Associate Officer with the Women Development & Community Organization (WDCO) in Punjab, Pakistan. She also has experience working as a psychologist at Nishter Hospital Multan, Pakistan. Her prolific scholarly contributions include numerous publications in high-impact journals such as Humanities and Social Sciences Communications, British Journal of Educational Technology, Heliyon, European Journal of Education, Frontiers in Psychology, and Asian Women. Her research has explored themes such as cross-cultural educational adaptation, gender equality in education, leadership in teaching, and the psychological impact of technology use on students. In addition to her publishing record, Dr. Maqbool is an active reviewer and editorial board member for several prestigious journals, including Frontiers in Psychology, Sage Open, BMC Medical Education, and Smart Learning Environment. Her academic excellence has been recognized with awards such as the Chinese Government Scholarship (2018–2022) and the Postdoctoral Station Award by Zhejiang Province (2022–2024). She has presented her research at numerous international conferences and symposia, contributing to global discussions on cognitive learning, teacher professionalism, gender, and human rights. Dr. Maqbool is proficient in several statistical and qualitative research tools, including SPSS, AMOS, JASP, and Mplus. She also offers expertise in data analysis, scientific writing, and training facilitation, and she is multilingual, fluent in English and Urdu, with conversational proficiency in Chinese.

Hafiz Muhammad Ihsan Zafeer is a distinguished scholar with a robust interdisciplinary background in education, law, and technology. He holds a Ph.D. in Education from Shaanxi Normal University, Xi'an, China, where he was honored with a prestigious university scholarship. Dr. Zafeer has completed his first Postdoctoral Fellowship at Zhejiang Normal University, China, where his research focused on leadership and management, artificial intelligence in education, educational technology, and STEM education. He is currently pursuing his second Postdoctoral Fellowship at Henan University, Kaifeng, China. In addition to his work in education, Dr. Zafeer has an impressive legal background, holding an LLM (Master of Law) from Beijing Normal University and an LLB (Bachelor of Law) from the University of Punjab, Pakistan. His scholarly contributions span multiple disciplines, showcasing his expertise in education, law, and the integration of technology in these fields. With a prolific research portfolio, Dr. Zafeer has published widely in reputed international journals, including European Journal of Education, Psychology in the School, Child Family & Social Work, Heliyon, Sustainability, Humanities and Social Sciences Communications, and Frontiers in Psychology. His research often explores the intersection of educational leadership, technology adoption in teaching, STEM education reforms, and socio psychological factors influencing academic outcomes. In addition to his publications, Dr. Zafeer has presented at several international conferences, including the International Conference on Social and Educational Sciences in Chicago, USA, and the 14th International Symposium on Teacher Education in East Asia. His contributions to the academic community also include mentoring, data analysis, and leading capacity-building initiatives focused on community development and teacher training. Dr. Zafeer has been recognized for his academic excellence through multiple scholarships, including the Chinese Government Scholarship (CSC) and the Shaanxi Normal University Scholarship. He is proficient in English and Urdu and has working knowledge of Chinese for daily communication.

Ayesha Tariq is currently pursuing an MPhil in Physical Education and Sports Sciences at The Islamia University of Bahawalpur, Pakistan, where she has maintained an excellent academic record with a GPA of 3.80/4.00. She was previously awarded a Gold Medal for securing the first position in her MSc in Physical Education and Sports Sciences from the same university. With a strong research background, Ayesha has published articles in SSCI-indexed journals, including the Journal of Cognitive Psychology and Educational Gerontology (Taylor & Francis Group). Her research focuses on cognitive psychology, financial decision-making, sports management, and the integration of educational technologies in sports sciences. She has a particular interest in innovative teaching methods, traditional exercise regimens, and exploring advancements in sports technology, especially in the context of China. Ayesha has actively contributed to academic and extracurricular activities at The Islamia University of Bahawalpur, organizing and participating in events such as sports galas, athletics training, and national hiking activities. She has presented at various national and international conferences, including the 4th Euro-Pak International Conference on Sports Sciences and Physical Education, and workshops on critical thinking, leadership, and sports management. In addition to her academic pursuits, Ayesha is skilled in quantitative and qualitative research methods, data analysis using SPSS, literature review, and academic writing. She is also an experienced public speaker and team leader with a passion for promoting physical education, sports science innovation, and community engagement.

* * *

Munir Ahmad is a seasoned professional in the realm of Spatial Data Infrastructure (SDI), Geo-Information Productions, Information Systems, and Information Governance, boasting over 25 years of dedicated experience in the field. With a PhD in Computer Science, Dr. Ahmad's expertise spans Spatial Data Production, Management, Processing, Analysis, Visualization, and Quality Control. Throughout his career, Dr. Ahmad has been deeply involved in the development and deployment of SDI systems specially in the context of Pakistan, leveraging his proficiency in Spatial Database Design, Web, Mobile & Desktop GIS, and Geo Web Services Architecture. His contributions to Volunteered Geographic Information (VGI) and Open Source Geoportal & Metadata Portal have significantly enriched the geospatial community. As a trainer and researcher, Dr. Ahmad has authored over 50 publications, advancing the industry's knowledge base and fostering innovation in Geo-Tech, Data Governance, and Information Infrastructure, and Emerging Technologies. His commitment to Research and Development (R&D) is evident in his role as a dedicated educator and mentor in the field.

Amjad Islam Amjad is a PhD and an established international researcher. He earned his PhD (Education) from the University of Lahore, Pakistan, in February 2023. He was a researcher and data analyst at the University of Lahore for three years (2019–2022). He is working as a reviewer and guest editor for several top-ranked (Scopus & Web of Science) international journals. He has taught subjects like Educational Research, Statistics in Education, Policy and Plan Implementation, Educational Philosophy, and Assessment and Evaluation. He has published several articles with leading publishers, such as Wiley, Emerald, Taylor & Francis, and Tech Science Press. His research interests include Positive Psychology, Educational Psychology, AI tools, Neuroscience, Inclusive education, Special education, STEM Education, Gamification, Intergenerational studies, AI-Generative Studies, Social Media, Self-Regulated Learning, Cognitive offloading, Machine Learning, Technology, and Education.

Aiman Batool is a Clinical Psychologist and Researcher based in Pakistan, with a growing body of work focused on the intersection of mental health, technology, and community well-being.

Charles Kidega is a senior education officer in the Department of Geography and Economics. Holds a bachelor's degree in Arts with Education (Economics and Geography) from Kyambogo University, Kampala, Uganda. Graduated with a master's degree in international and comparative education from Zhejiang Normal University, China. Currently enrolled as a Ph.D. student in Comparative Education at Zhejiang Normal University of China. A researcher in the field of education with three years of work experience as a reviewer in more than five journals, and currently working as a reviewer at the International Journal of Education, Culture and Society. Research interests are STEM, TVET, gender studies, and comparative education. Director of the Academic department of the International Students Union (ISU), College of Education, Zhejiang Normal University (2025/2026).

Irene Egbosimba is a dedicated education researcher with a strong passion for cross-cultural learning, equity, and transformative teaching. She holds a Bachelor's degree in International Language, specializing in Teaching Chinese as a Foreign Language, and a Master's degree in Comparative Education from Zhejiang Normal University in China, where she is currently pursuing her PhD. Born in Nigeria, her academic journey has centred on understanding and improving global education systems. Her primary research focus is on curriculum design and teaching methodologies, with specific interests in the integration of comparative education, teacher education, language acquisition, and STEM.

Shabina Fred Rishma F. is an Assistant Professor in the Department of Computer Science and Engineering at Vel Tech Rangarajan Dr. Sagunthala R&D Institute of Science and Technology, Chennai, Tamil Nadu. She holds a Bachelor of Engineering (B.E.) degree from Anna University and a Master of Engineering (M.E.) degree from Sathyabama University, Chennai. Additionally, she has completed a Bachelor of Library Science (B.Lib.Sc.) from Alagappa University. With over three years of experience in the teaching profession, she has been actively involved in guiding and mentoring students in the field of computer science. Her areas of interest include Machine Learning and Artificial Intelligence, where she continues to explore emerging technologies and their applications in solving real-world problems.

S. Ida Evangeline is presently working as an Assistant Professor in the Department of Electrical and Electronics Engineering at the Government College of Engineering, Tirunelveli, Tamilnadu, India. She obtained her Bachelor's in Electrical and Electronics Engineering from Manonmaniam Sundaranar University in 2003, and Master's in Power Systems Engineering from Anna University, Chennai, Tamilnadu, India in 2005. She completed her PhD degree in 2023 at Anna University, Chennai, Tamilnadu, India. She has published six research papers in international journals. Her current research interests include optimal power flow, renewable energy, soft computing, machine learning, and deep learning.

Amir Mahmood is PhD scholar at Zhejiang Normal university China. He earned his Bachelor's degree in Electronic Engineering in Pakistan and later pursued a Master's degree in the same field at Xi'an Jiaotong University, China. His academic and research interests lie at the intersection of technology and education. Currently, he is collaborating on variou research projects focusing on STEM education, artificial intelligence, and digital literacy. He is passionate about integrating emerging technologies into education to enhance learning outcomes and promote innovative teaching practices.

Barno Matchanova is working at Department of National Idea and Philosophy, Urgench State Pedagogical Institute, Uzbekistan

Biswo Ranjan Mishra is an Assistant Professor in the Department of Commerce at Utkal University (Centre for Distance and Online Education), Bhubaneswar, Odisha. He is a dedicated academician with a strong commitment to teaching, research, and student development. Dr. Mishra's academic interests lie in various domains of commerce and management, with a focus on contemporary business practices and economic development. Through his research and teaching, he aims to bridge the gap between theoretical knowledge and practical application, contributing meaningfully to the advancement of commerce education.

|Nida Munawar - Contributing Author|e3069869-5f50-493e-a8a5-75bded5636d4)

Selvakumar P. is currently an Associate Professor in the Department of Science and Humanities at Nehru Institute of Technology, Coimbatore, Tamil Nadu, India. Prior to joining Nehru Institute of Technology, he held positions as an Assistant Professor in the Department of Science and Humanities various engineering colleges in Coimbatore, Tamil Nadu, India, spanning from 2011 to 2023. Dr. P. Selvakumar's academic and research interests lie primarily in the field of phytochemistry. He has made significant contributions to his field, with an impressive record that includes 30 journal publications, 12 patents, and 20 conference papers. Additionally, he has organized 5 seminars and conferences, further demonstrating his commitment to academic and scientific exchange. Throughout his career, Dr. P. Selvakumar has been recognized for his dedication and excellence in teaching, having been honored with several awards, including the Best Teacher Awards. He holds a prominent position in the academic community, contributing actively to research.

Ravikumar R. N. is an experienced academician with over 12+ years of teaching and research expertise across institutions in India, the UAE, and the Maldives. He currently serves as an Assistant Professor at Marwadi University, Rajkot, specializing in Machine Learning, Recommender Systems, and AI-driven applications in healthcare and security. He holds a Ph.D. in Machine Learning and Recommender Systems from Amity University, Jaipur, a Master of Engineering in CSE from VMRF University, Salem, and a Bachelor of Engineering in CSE from Anna University. He also has a MiniMBA from the Swiss eLearning Institute. Dr. Ravikumar has authored more than 8+ multiple SCIE/Scopus-indexed journal articles, 25+ IEEE/Springer conference papers, and co-authored a book on Artificial Intelligence. He has also published 9 patents and contributed 10+ book chapters in emerging domains such as Federated Learning, Blockchain, and Digital Twins for IGI Global, Wiley and Springer publisher. He actively mentors students through initiatives like the Research Activities Club (RAC) and Student Research Internship Training (SRIT), promoting innovation and research culture.

Mariam Rajabu Ibrahim a senior education officer in Geography department,with master degree in international and comparative education from Zhejiang Normal university, China.As a PhD student in Zhejiang Normal university, my research is in education field with two years of work experience as a review in two journals.My research interests are TCPT,TVET,,Higher education, and comparative education

Swati Raturi is a faculty member and researcher in the Department of Education at ICFAI University, Dehradun. Her research interests include educational technology adoption, e-learning, teachers' attitudes towards technology, technophobia, and digital pedagogy in higher education. She has contributed to academic discourse through research papers, literature reviews, and conference presentations focusing on technology integration in teaching and learning. Her academic journey reflects a strong focus on combining quantitative and qualitative methodologies to explore challenges and opportunities in educational innovation.

Aarthi S. is a dedicated Assistant Professor in Computer Science with over six years of teaching experience. She is currently pursuing her Ph.D. at Marwadi University, Gujarat, and holds an M.Phil. and MCA from Bharathiar University, Tamil Nadu. Throughout her academic career, Aarthi has specialized in programming languages such as C++, Java, and C, and contributed to research in recommender systems and AI-related data privacy. She has published journal articles, contributed to book chapters, and actively participated in technical workshops. Known for her student mentorship and engagement in academic events, Aarthi remains committed to fostering innovation and excellence in computer science education.

Rayhon Sapaeva is a scholar in the Department of Roman–Germanic Philology at Urgench State University, Urgench, Uzbekistan. Her academic interests include English and German linguistics, translation studies, and comparative literature. She is active in university teaching, curriculum development, and research projects that bridge language theory with classroom practice, and she presents her work at regional and international conferences.

Jaya Saxena is an Assistant Professor at the School of Business, Indira University, Pune. With a strong academic background and a passion for teaching, she specializes in areas such as management, marketing, and business strategy. Dr. Saxena is dedicated to fostering critical thinking and innovation among her students, preparing them to excel in the dynamic business environment. Her research interests include organizational behavior, consumer psychology, and strategic management, and she has contributed to several academic journals and conferences. Through her commitment to academic excellence and holistic development, Dr. Saxena continues to inspire the next generation of business leaders.

Rajeswari V. is Professor, Department of Information Technology, Karpagam College of Engineering, Coimbatore. She has 27 years of teaching and 10 years of research experience. Her areas of expertise and interest are AI and Machine Learning, IoT Technologies, Industry 4.0, J2EE, Database Management Systems, Big Data, Ontology, Computer Networks and Pedagogical Research.

Index

A

Index

A

C

D

E

G

H

V